On Odd Karsten Tveit's books:

Krig og diplomati (War and Diplomacy), 20

"A veritable political thriller" John Harbo, *Aftenposten*

"Tveit's sources and his solid knowledge make the book a milestone" Carsten Thomassen, *Dagbladet*

"Warmly recommended" Sten Inge Jørgensen, *Morgenbladet*

Libanon farvel (Goodbye Lebanon), 2010

Norwegian Edition:

"Goodbye Lebanon is a rare epic of an enormous book, an impressive and imposing work both in its content, its form and its execution, driven by knowledge, insight and respect, moral empathy, indignation and revulsion" Jan Askelund, *Stavanger Aftenblad*

"Of this season's weighty Middle East books, Norwegian journalist Odd Karsten Tveit's rises above all others with humor and a myriad of detail in a fascinating representation of a tragic conflict…Karsten Tveit's coup is that his book is populated by real people in flesh and blood in a scenario which (referring to the present) covers the 22 year period from 1978 to 2000, when Israel intervened in Lebanon" Lasse Ellegaard, *Informationen* (Denmark)

English Edition:

"I would say, as a journalist who covered Lebanon during its darkest hours, that *Goodbye Lebanon* is a powerful addition to the narrative of that unfortunate country- especially so, because it doesn't always conform to the version to which many Americans have been exposed" H.D.S Greenway, a syndicated US journalist who has read the manuscript

"…the book…is wonderful and important… with the unfolding drama of the Arab Spring, it is more vital than ever to understand the complex domestic relationships within Middle Eastern nations. Perhaps of them all, Lebanon's web of antagonistic parties needs clarifying. *Goodbye Lebanon* does just that through a riveting story of Israel's invasions, first 1978, then 1982, which inflamed the country, hardened positions and has left a very disturbing legacy" Jane Fletcher Geniesse, author of *Passionate Nomad*

GOODBYE LEBANON

Israel's First Defeat

ODD KARSTEN TVEIT

Translated by

PETER SCOTT-HANSEN

 RIMAL PUBLICATIONS

Odd Karsten Tveit © 2010

English language translation © Peter Scott-Hansen 2011

The right of Odd Karsten Tveit to be identified as the author of this work has been asserted by him in accordance with the Copyright, Designs and Patents Act 1988.

Original published 2010 by H. Aschehoug & Co. (W. Nygaard), Oslo, as *Libanon Farvel, Israels Første Nederlag*

First English edition 2013
Rimal Publications
Nicosia, Cyprus
www.rimalbooks.com

ISBN 978-9963-715-03-9
This Translation has been published with the financial support of NORLA.
Maps: Børre Ludvigsen
Cover photo: Falak Shawwa
Cover design: Ali Shawwa
Back cover photo: Marwan Wakim taken outside the American Embassy in Beirut 18 April 1983
Odd Karsten Tveit portrait: Berit Mortensen

In memory of two extraordinary women

Ane-Karine Arvesen and Ana Maria Acevedo Borge Tveit

1. Map of Beirut-map-detail

2. Map of Beirut-map-overview

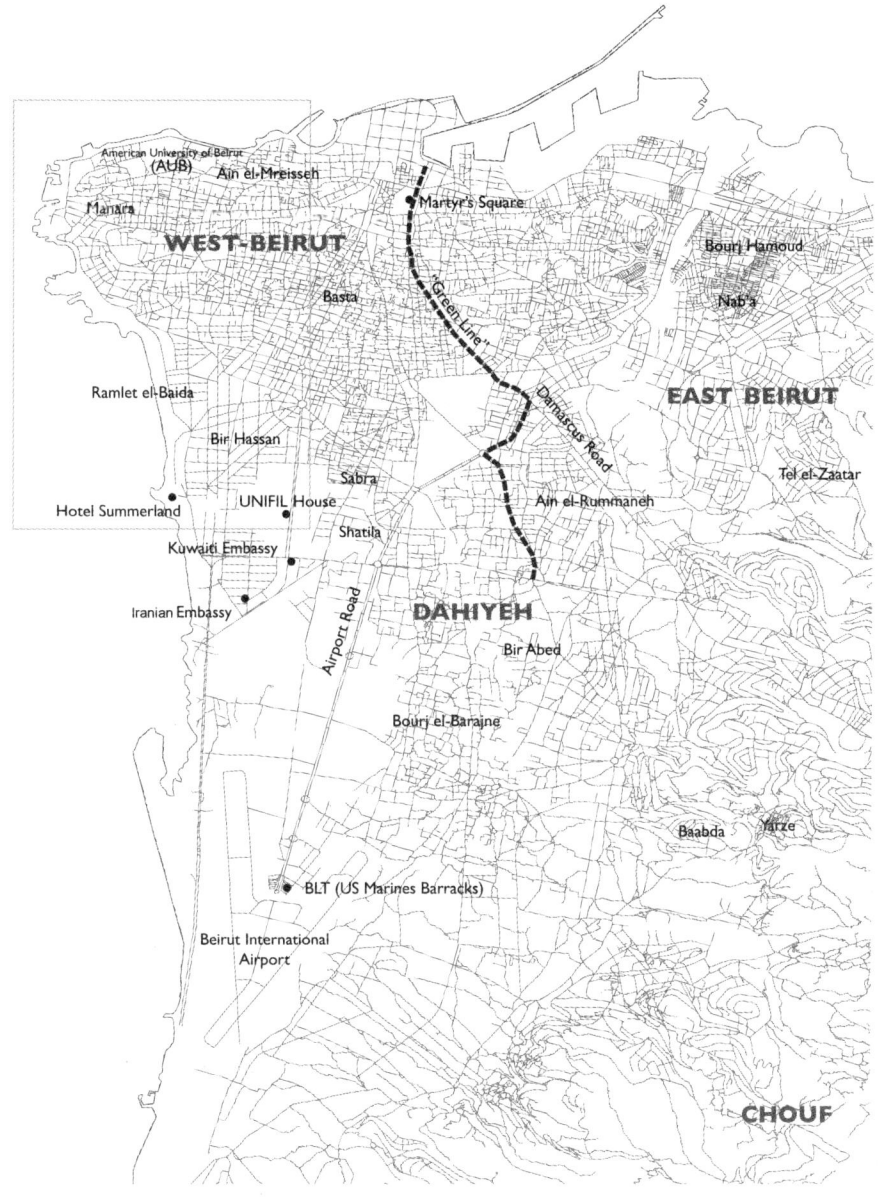

3. Map of Lebanon-overview

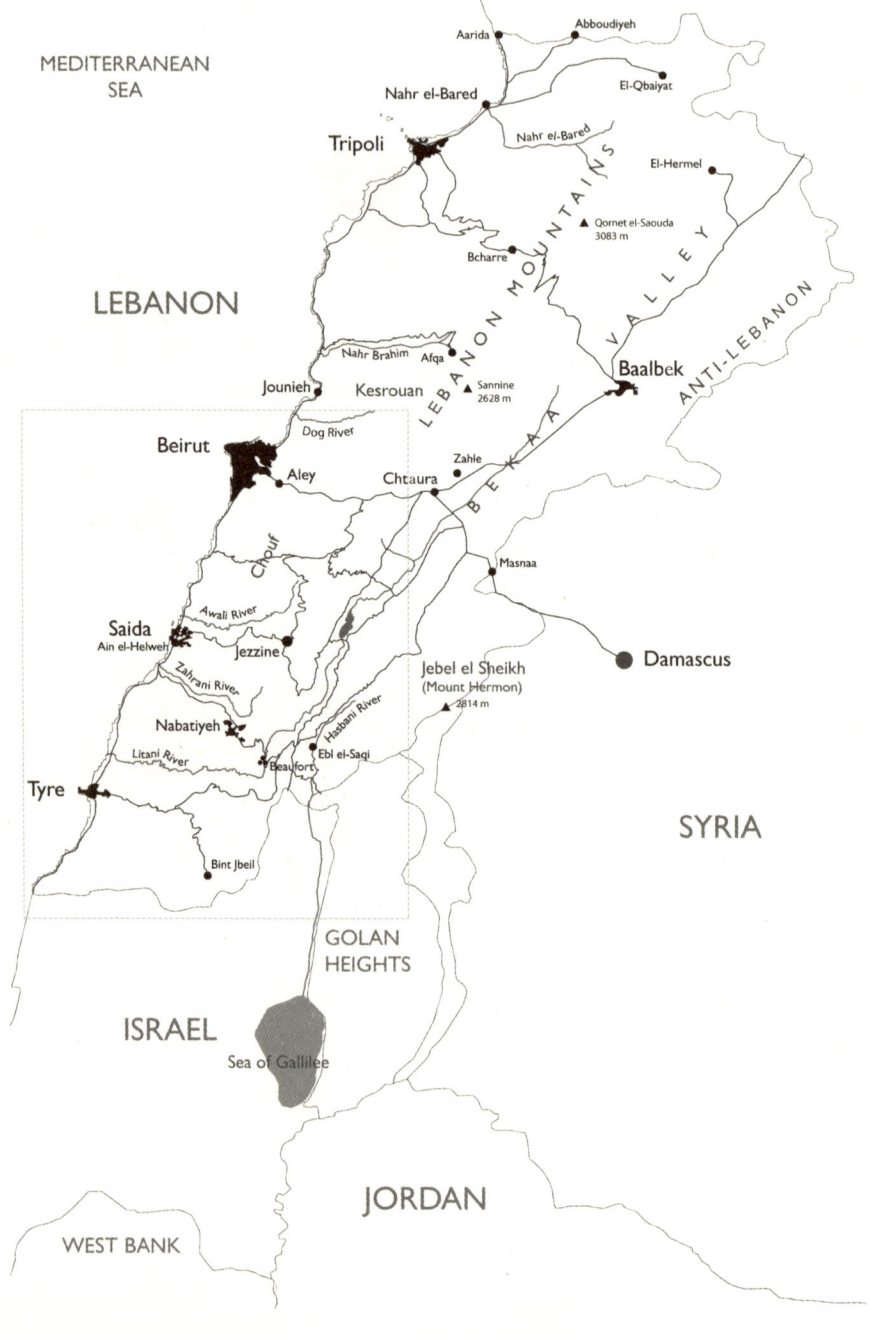

4. Map of South lebanon

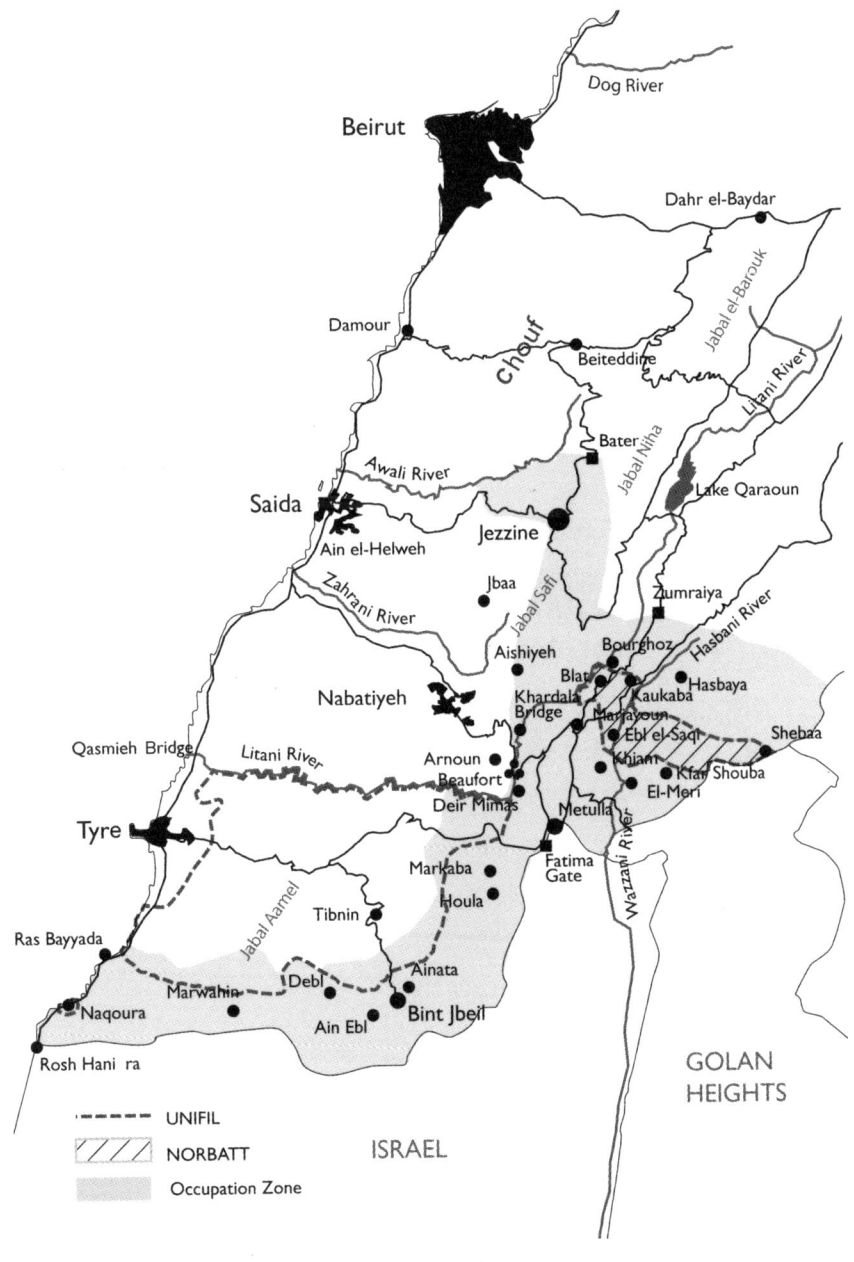

Dog River

Beirut

Dahr el-Baydar

Jabal el-Barouk

Damour

Chouf

Beiteddine

Litani River

Bater

Jabal Niha

Awali River

Saida

Lake Qaraoun

Jezzine

Ain el-Helweh

Jbaa

Jabal Safi

Zahrani River

Zumraiya

Aishiyeh

Bourghoz

Hasbani River

Nabatiyeh

Blat

Khardala
Bridge

Kaukaba

Hasbaya

Qasmieh Bridge

Litani River

Marjayoun

Ebl el-Saqi

Shebaa

Khiam

Arnoun

Kfar Shouba

Beaufort

El-Meri

Deir Mimas

Metulla

Tyre

Jabal Aamel

Fatima
Gate

Markaba

Wazzani River

Ras Bayyada

Tibnin

Houla

Marwahin

Debl

Ainata

GOLAN
HEIGHTS

Naqoura

Ain Ebl

Bint Jbeil

Rosh Hani ra

- - - - UNIFIL

///// NORBATT

ISRAEL

Occupation Zone

There is nothing new in the world except the history you do not know.

Harry S. Truman

Contents

FOREWORD

Goodbye, Lebanon, is a reporter's account of Israel's longest war and first defeat, as well as the story of the Hizbullah militia and other resistance groups that fought the Jewish state's occupying forces in Lebanon.

The book contains my personal experiences and those of journalist colleagues, aid workers and others who were kidnapped by Lebanese and Palestinian groups, as well as the kidnappings and torture of the Lebanese by Israelis, and how hostages were used as bargaining chips in a larger political game. It covers my time as Middle East correspondent for the Norwegian Broadcasting Corporation (*NRK*) and as a Major in the UN Peacekeeping forces (UNIFIL), who came to South Lebanon to foster peace, yet became targets of attacks. It is a history of Israel's conduct of war against UNIFIL, and how peacekeeping soldiers reacted to the Israeli occupation and its abuses.

By examining the components of the Lebanese civil war, I recount the brutal side of Syria's policies toward Lebanon; Iran's plan to transform Lebanon into an Islamic republic; and the American soldiers who came to West Beirut to protect the civilian population but took sides and left in humiliation.

Lebanon's more recent history is quite complicated. The country is like a stage play portraying the entire Middle East, where acting on this stage affects development in the region. What happens throughout the Middle East in general also has its consequences for the Lebanese.

To me, Lebanon was like a well-used oriental carpet, where the pattern and threads are worn and sullied with filth and blood. In an effort to discern the pattern more clearly, I have sought out politicians, officers, academics, journalists, guerrilla soldiers, intelligence agents, former hostages and prisoners. I have traveled throughout Israel, Lebanon, Syria, the United States and Europe to obtain firsthand reports. I have had access to a series of private and public archives, studied hundreds of books and an even greater number of articles about the events which have dominated the news scene for many years. All this has led me to believe that he who understands a little about Lebanon will understand more about the Middle East.

This Mediterranean country encompasses an area one-third the size of Belgium. When the Arabs arrived around the year 600 CE, the region was Jabal Lubnan—The Lebanon Mountains—an insignificant Byzantine province. When the Crusaders and Salahuddin al-Ayoubi's Arab, Turkish and Kurdish soldiers fought for power in 1187–1188, the area was divided into small fiefdoms. Later, the Lebanon Mountains became the spoils of war for the Mamluks, Ottomans and the French. Everyone came with weapons in hand, and with their own ideas how the Middle Strip, the mountains in the East and the fruitful Bekaa Valley were to be governed.

Early in the 1970s, the leadership of the Palestine Liberation Organization (PLO) came to Beirut from Jordan, and in 1975 a civil war broke out in Lebanon. Syrian troops moved into the country in 1976, and the Israelis took South Lebanon in 1978. Neither the Palestinian, Syrian nor the Israeli leaders had learned from the experiences of others: Lebanon was easy to swallow but hard to digest.

When Israel swept north to Beirut in 1982, and then forced the PLO leadership and its guerrillas out of all of South Lebanon and then Beirut, the stage was set for a new chapter in Lebanon's history. And when, after 22 years of occupation, the Israeli army pulled its soldiers out of the country, it was a bitter, though not final goodbye.

Beirut/Jerusalem/Oslo, February 2012.
Odd Karsten Tveit

LEBANON — A CONDENSED TIMELINE

According to the Bible, Christianity is introduced to Lebanon in the time of Jesus, but the new religion does not take root until the 4th century CE. At that time, St. Maron establishes a religious community which took its name after the saint (the Maronites). During the Arab invasion in the 600s, Islam comes to the area.

The 1500s: When the Ottomans take control of the Lebanese Mountains, Syria and Palestine, they eventually give the local population control of its separate enclaves without any day-to-day intrusion. The occupiers support a system which provides the foundation for a strong religious sense of belonging among the peoples of the area.

1860: Conflicts arise between the Christian Maronite group and the Druze, a religion whose origins are from Shia Islam, that leads to a civil war where around 10,000 Maronites are massacred. French forces are sent to the area to protect the Maronites.

1861: The Lebanon Mountains are given the status of an autonomous province in the Ottoman Empire.

1918: France occupies the Lebanon Mountains.

1920: The League of Nations—the predecessor of the United Nations—gives France a mandate to govern the Lebanon Mountains as well as Syria. France establishes Greater Lebanon as one of the several ethnic enclaves within Syria.

1926: Lebanon is declared a republic and receives a constitution.

1940: At the beginning of the Second World War, Lebanon comes under the control of France's Vichy government, which is allied with Nazi Germany.

1941: Lebanon is occupied by the "Free French Forces" and troops from the British Empire.

1943: Lebanon becomes an independent state and receives an unwritten National Pact. This pact states that Lebanon would be an independent Arab country with a Christian President from the Maronites, a Prime Minister from the Sunni Muslims and a Head of Parliament from the Shia Muslims.

1948: The state of Israel is formed. Around 100,000 expelled Palestinians flee to Lebanon.

1958: Civil war erupts in Lebanon. American troops enter Beirut at the request of President Camille Chamoun.

1964: The Palestine Liberation Organization (PLO) is formed. In following years the guerrillas use bases in South Lebanon to attack Israel.

1969: Lebanon's Chief of the General Staff and the PLO leader sign an agreement where the PLO is given formal right to have guerrilla bases in the southern part of Lebanon. Through the so-called Cairo Agreement, the Palestinians are accorded a form of self-rule in the 16 refugee camps in Lebanon.

1971: The PLO leadership has to leave Jordan and sets up its headquarters in Beirut.

1975: New civil war breaks out in Lebanon.

1976: Following a request from Lebanon's president to the Arab League, Syrian troops enter the country to protect the Christian militias in East Beirut from the PLO and its allies.

1978: Israel invades South Lebanon up to the Litani River. The UN Security Council passes Resolution 425, requiring immediate Israeli withdrawal from Lebanese territory. An international peace force from the UN—UNIFIL—is to confirm Israel's withdrawal and assist the Lebanese government with reclaiming control of the area. Norway participates with a substantial force.

1982: Israel invades Lebanon. During the Israeli attack, the Lebanese parliament elects a new president, Bachir Gemayel, from the Kataeb Party, better known in the West as the Phalange Party. The new president is murdered before taking office. In the days that follow, Christian militia forces massacre over 1,300 Palestinians and others in the refugee camps of Sabra and Shatila in West Beirut with help from the Israeli army. Bachir's elder brother, Amine Gemayel, is then elected president. An American, French, Italian and British multinational force arrives in West Beirut to protect the civilian population.

1983: The US Embassy in West Beirut is blown up by a suicide bomber. Israel and Lebanon sign an agreement on May 17th for Israeli withdrawal and an end to the war between the two countries. The American and French forces headquartered in West Beirut are attacked by suicide bombers driving trucks filled with explosives. 241 American Marines and 56 French parachutists are killed.

1984: The multinational peace force, led by the US and France, withdraws from Lebanon.

1985: The Shia Muslim party, Hizbullah, announces its first official program. Israeli occupation forces withdraw to the south and established a new front line.

1986: Syrian soldiers enter West Beirut to end the chaos and the battles between the various Muslim militias.

1987: Lebanon cancels the May 17th agreement with Israel.

1988: President Amine Gemayel's presidential term ends without a new president being elected. Gemayel names the Christian Brigadier General Michel Aoun as leader of a military government. A rival government is led by a Sunni Muslim, Salim el-Hoss.

1989: Lebanon's parliament meets in Taif, Saudi Arabia. An agreement is reached to reduce the power of the president and transfer power to a prime minister and government. The parliament is to contain equal numbers of Christian and Muslim members. René Muawwad is elected president but assassinated 17 days later. Elias Hraouis elected as the new president.

1990: Battles begin in the Christian areas in and around East Beirut, between parts of the army which are loyal to Michel Aoun and the militia (Lebanese Forces) led by Samir Geagea. Syrian troops take up the fight against Aoun, who finally seeks asylum in the French Embassy. Lebanon's 15-year-long civil war ends. Over 100,000 people have been killed.

1991: The parliament decides that all militias in Lebanon, with the exception of the Hizbullah guerrillas fighting against the Israeli occupation forces, are to be dissolved.

1992: Elections for a new parliament are held for the first time in 20 years. The Sunni Muslim businessman Rafic Hariri becomes prime minister.

1993: Israel launches a full-scale attack on civilian targets north of the occupied zone in South Lebanon.

1994: Mustafa Dirani, the leader of a breakout faction of Amal, is kidnapped by Israeli commandoes. A Maronite church near Beirut is bombed and 10 people are killed. The leader of the Christian militia, (Lebanese Forces) Samir Geagea, is arrested and condemned to life in prison for the killing of Christian Lebanese.

1995: Lebanon's constitution is changed to allow a sitting president to extend his term of office for three years.

1996: Israeli planes, artillery and gunships attack large areas of Lebanon. In Qana, over 100 Lebanese civilians are killed. They had sought refuge in UNIFIL's encampment in the town.

1997: Two Israeli troop transport helicopters collide on their way to Lebanon. All 73 onboard lose their lives. This leads to increased opposition in Israel to the occupation of Lebanon.

1998: Lebanon's Chief of the General Staff, Lieutenant General Emile Lahoud, is elected as the new president. Rafic Hariri is replaced as prime minister by Salim el-Hoss. Norway's UN forces are withdrawn after 20 years in South Lebanon.

1999: New elections are held in Israel. The Labour Party's candidate for prime minister, Ehud Barak, promises to withdraw all Israeli forces from Lebanon within a year. He wins the election.

2000: Israeli forces withdraw from South Lebanon.

INFORMATIONAL FACTS ABOUT LEBANON

Area: 10,452 square kilometers. Length of borders 454 km. Coastline 225 km.
Climate: Mild and rainy winters, warm and dry summers.
Population: ca. 4,017,000 (2009).
Largest cities: Beirut (ca. 2.2 million), Tripoli (ca. 500,000), Sidon (ca. 200,000), Tyre (ca. 120,000), Nabatiyeh (ca. 35,000).
Population groups: Arabs—95%, Armenians—4%, others—1%.
Religious affiliations: 60% Muslim (Shias, Sunnis, Druze, Ismailites and Alawites), 39% Christian (Maronites, Greek Orthodox, Armenian Catholics, Armenian Orthodox, Copts, Chaldeans, Eastern Assyrian Church, Syrian Catholics, Syrian Orthodox and Protestants), 1% Other (among them Jews).
Languages: Arabic is the official language; many speak English and French. Armenians also use Armenian.
Life Expectancy: Males 71 years, Females 75.5 years.
Government: Republic.

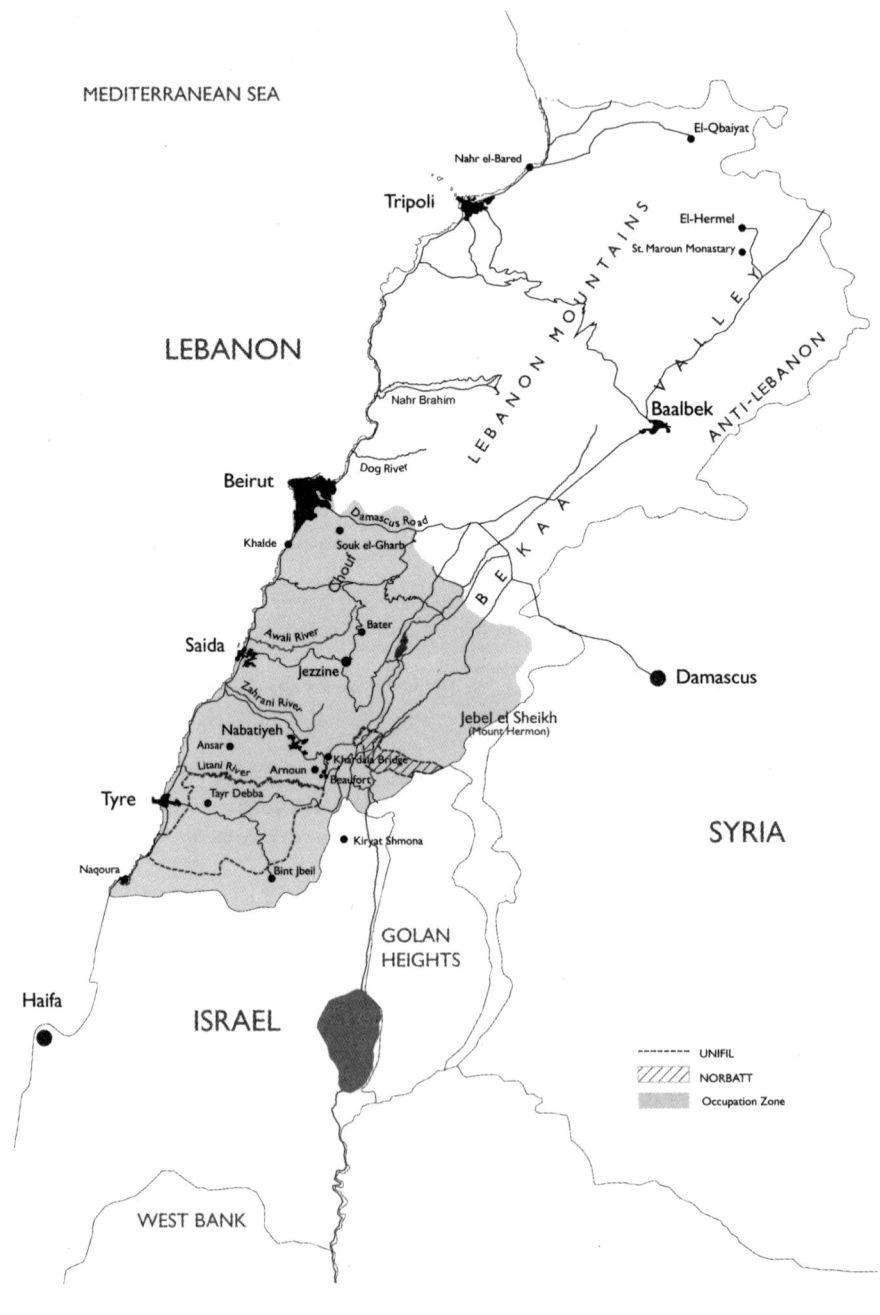

PART ONE

Secret Alliances

1982-1983

Following Israel's invasion of Lebanon in the summer of 1982, the scene had been set for Lebanese resistance, but these forces were poorly organized and had little effect. Forces from the United States and France, among others, come to Lebanon to protect the civilian population in West Beirut following a massacre of Palestinian refugees in Sabra and Shatila. Iranian Revolutionary Guards arrive in the Bekaa Valley in East Lebanon to help radical Lebanese Shias fight against the Israelis and the Americans. The US is seen as an extension of Israel. The alliance between Iran and the Lebanese Shias became a danger for American diplomats, for the soldiers in the multinational force and for many civilian Americans and Europeans in West Beirut.

MAIN CHARACTERS

Ane-Karine Arvesen — Attaché at the Norwegian Embassy in Beirut
Hafez al-Assad — President of Syria
William Buckley — CIA's Station Chief in Beirut
Timothy Geraghty — Colonel and Chief of the US Peacekeeping Force in West Beirut
Walid Jumblatt — Druze Leader
Ayatollah Ruhollah Khomeini — Iran's Supreme Leader
Robert McFarlane — President Ronald Reagan's Special Envoy to Lebanon
Imad Mughniyeh — radical Shia activist, later Hizbullah's Chief of Staff
Moussa Sadr — Founder of Amal (The Shia's First Political Party in Lebanon)

CHAPTER ONE

The Letter at Beaufort Castle

When Israeli forces invaded Lebanon in June 1982, Prime Minister Menachem Begin said on the first day of the invasion, "This is a limited operation. It will last 24 hours."[1]

Defense Minister Ariel Sharon interjected: "48 hours."

Prime Minister Begin continued: "We have learned the lessons of the war in 1967. A war should not be extended beyond its original objective."

The official goal was to force the Palestinian guerrillas 40 kilometers north of the Israeli border so missiles could not be fired into Israel.

The defense minister said nothing of *his* plans. Sharon wanted to create a new Lebanon, led by a president who could be remote-controlled from Jerusalem and Tel Aviv, and the excuse used for the invasion was an assassination attempt against the Israeli ambassador in London. The Israeli government ignored the fact that the Palestinian assassin was not operating on orders from the Palestinian Liberation Organization (PLO), but from Iraq's secret services.

"Operation Peace for Galilee" was launched despite the fact there was already peace in Galilee, as the Israelis totally ignored the fact that the PLO had upheld the ceasefire reached the year before.

When more than 100,000 Israeli soldiers swept northward toward Beirut in the summer of 1982, with planes bombing civilian targets in the Muslim-dominated part of the capital, I was the Norwegian Broadcasting Corporation (*NRK*) correspondent for the Middle East. Twenty-six years later, as I drove southward from Beirut on a gorgeous spring day, there *was* peace in Lebanon. I stopped at a Crusader fortress in the central part of South Lebanon which dated in its current form from 1139, when it had been conquered from the Arabs by the Christian invasion army. The Crusaders rebuilt the fort to make it bigger and stronger. They called it Beaufort, the beautiful castle.

From atop the ramparts, I could see the Litani River wending its way several hundred meters below through a ravine, which made the fortress nearly unconquerable. In the east, a magnificent mountain stretched toward the heavens. The Israelis called it Hermon, The Holy Mountain. To the Arabs it was Jebel el-Sheikh, The Mountain of the Sheikh, also called the Snow Mountain. In the south, I could see golden hills rolling towards a Galilee clad in green. In the west, low ridges stretched toward the Mediterranean Sea, and around me everywhere lay Lebanon's former killing fields.

In my jacket pocket I had a copy of a letter written by an Israeli father whose son was killed at Beaufort on the first day of the invasion. Standing atop the castle, I read the words of the father, who had also died by now: "I have not stopped crying since that day and my hand trembles as I hold my pen."[2]

I looked down along the road northeast of the fortress where the young Israeli had been killed. He had been shot while he and hundreds of other soldiers stormed Beaufort, which at the time was a guerrilla base for 15 young Palestinians. It took the superior Israeli forces six hours to kill them all. Seven Israeli soldiers lost their lives.[3]

The following day the flag flying over the castle bore the Star of David. Prime Minister Menachem Begin and Defense Minister Ariel Sharon flew to Beaufort by helicopter to pose for Israeli photographers. Neither Begin nor Sharon wanted to talk about the attack. Neither one even asked whether the victory at Beaufort had cost Israeli lives.

In his letter, the father of the slain soldier, Yaron Zamir, wrote: "On the evening of Monday, June 7th, 1982, I was deeply hurt when you and Sharon appeared on the Beaufort, all smiles, and with the blood of our fallen sons not yet dry, you turned to him and remarked, 'How fresh the mountain air is atop this fortress.'" He continued: "You cannot bring back my son, Yaron. But do not add further bereavement, pain and suffering. Let the bombing of civilian-populated areas cease. Do not use the bodies of our sons as spears to try to dictate who shall rule in Lebanon."

When I stood at Beaufort with the letter in my hand, Israel's blue-and-white flag no longer flew over the castle. Instead there was the yellow and green flag of Hizbullah, although there were no guerrilla soldiers to be seen. I was alone with my thoughts of war, and what I had experienced in Lebanon.

I first arrived in Beirut during the summer of 1978, when the country was in the midst of a civil war. It was not easy for a newcomer to grasp the complex political and religious landscape. Just to get an overview of 17 different religious communities in Lebanon was a challenge. Here there were Shia Muslims, Sunni Muslims, Alawites, Ismailites, Druze, Jews and 11 different Christian communities.[4] A number of these groups had their own militias. At times, it was belief in Jesus, Mohammed or Moses that determined who lived or died. The Lebanese identity card, listing the religion of its owner, became a deadly document. This was the only country in the Arab world where the religious groups and their militias were so strong that they had effectively eliminated the power of the state.

Prior to the civil war, when the Lebanese lived in nearly mythical harmony, there had also been a kind of competition between the Christians and the Muslims. On Sundays, the church bells had their ropes pulled as vigorously as the ringers had ever learned, while on Fridays the Muslims turned up their loudspeakers as far as possible so the call-to-prayer or speeches would be heard by as many as possible. Beirut's cinemas were also an arena for demonstrations. A cross or a crescent moon which might flash momentarily across the screen could create an uproar. And it was a land of humor. In the Muslims' repertoire was the story of an old believer who lay on his deathbed and asked for a priest. When the priest came, the dying man said he wished to convert. His family, gathered round the deathbed, was shocked and asked, why? With a mischievous smile the old man answered, "It is better that one of them dies, than one of us."

The humor did not disappear with the civil war. It only became more grotesque.

For the newcomer in Beirut, the myth remained that Lebanon was the Switzerland of the Middle East, or the Paris of the Levant – the geographic and cultural term referring to the region of the eastern Mediterranean – where the Levantines lived in two or more worlds at the same time, without belonging to any.

The heart of the city featured more nightclubs, luxury automobiles, swimming pools and gigantic apartments per square meter than most places in the rich world. But not far from Rue Hamra—Beirut's prestigious shopping street—were hundreds of small, dirty back alleys that wound their way through the belt of poverty surrounding the city. Palestinian refugees inhabited theses slums in filth and deprivation, and the lower class of Shias lived in small, shabby houses made of light cement or corrugated metal. The even poorer Kurds, Egyptians and other migrants from Asia and Africa lived wherever they could, in cellars and shacks. They were all separated from each other, plunged into various cultural identities, and divided into groups which fought for their clan leaders' interests and competed for their alms. Few believed the war would last long when it began in 1975. Creative Lebanese businessmen tried to make money out of the situation. One publishing house produced *The Bullet Dodger's Guide to Beirut*. Another put out a book which told you what to buy in Beirut's many exclusive shops: Christian Dior combat boots; an automatic weapon of the Kalashnikov type, inlaid with mother of pearl; or an Alexander Calder barricade. The Lebanese interested in culture knew Calder was the American artist who brought movement into the world of sculpture. Those who bought the book quickly discovered that everything in it was pure fantasy.[5] I was given advice on what should be said and done at the various militia checkpoints. The Muslim and secular militias were considered Leftist, the Christians Right wing. Not everyone appreciated the labels. The Phalangists, for example, did not like to be called right wing; they wanted to be recognized as social democrats. But the labels stuck. We journalists would put our press cards from the militias in West Beirut into our left back pockets, the cards from those in East Beirut in our right pockets, and the government's useless press pass into our breast pockets. A colleague told me how the American ambassador and his counsellor had been killed when they crossed the front line between East and West Beirut. Their corpses were dumped onto a garbage heap. I was also shown live footage of a man who was lying on the ground, wounded by one of the snipers. A friend threw him a rope to pull him to safety. The sniper could easily have killed the wounded man with a new single shot. Instead he chose to cut the rope with a bullet, so the victim would bleed to death.

The civil war and Israel's invasion had given many of us correspondents and photographers a golden opportunity to prove to ourselves and others that we had what it takes. Beirut life became a virtual narcotic which we could not resist, even if we were surrounded by kidnappers and torturers, or former neighbors and school chums who might now shoot at each other to kill. A few months later these combatants might sit together again, not as friends, but as allies against common enemies in the constantly shifting patterns of war.

Beirut made fatalists out of many of us. We would cross the front line at the most dangerous point simply to avoid sitting a bit longer in a line of cars at a safer crossing. We ate at exclusive restaurants close to the fighting. We stayed at our window tables until the shells were detonating within 100 meters of us, and could not understand why some of our colleagues chose to observe the whole thing from Larnaka or Limassol in Cyprus.

I eventually felt at home among Beirut's blend of Arabic roots and the western refinement. I found it easy to live side by side with Muslims, Christians, Jews and Druze, and listen to how they all spoke with two tongues, saying one thing to their own and something else to others. At times, I reflected on what the wars in the Middle East had done to me, an economic sociologist who chose journalism over petroleum research. Did Lebanon make one cold and callous? Had I become a war junkie? Was it possible not to become involved in all the injustice I witnessed? In the back of my mind swirled Dante's threat: "The hottest places in hell are reserved for those who, in times of great moral crisis, maintain their neutrality."[6]

In Lebanon's civil war there was only one person with whom all the Lebanese had a stable relationship. This was Fairuz, a songstress with a silky soft, yet fiery voice. A Christian, Fairuz refused to take sides and also would not perform in Lebanon so long as the war raged. She would not give a concert while admirers could not cross the front lines to hear her, and was afraid the militia leaders would take advantage of her popularity if she performed in their domains. Many prominent Lebanese had fled the country simply because it was deadly to live there, but Fairuz refused to do so and would not stop singing. When the artillery shells fell in the various parts of the city, and people hid themselves in cellars and bomb shelters to save their lives, the militia radio stations would play her songs. And when the bombardments were at their worst, people tried to calm their nerves by listening to Fairuz sing praises to the war-torn city:

Li Beirut

To Beirut—peace to Beirut with all my heart.
kisses to the sea and the houses,
to a rock resembling the face of an old fisherman.
From the soul of the people she is wine,
from their sweat she is bread and jasmine.
How can it be that the city now tastes of smoke and fire?

The Israeli invasion of Lebanon did not bring an end to the taste of smoke and fire. There would likewise be no peace for the international forces, led by the United States, which had come to West Beirut in September 1982 to protect the civilian population after a Christian militia, well-aided and observed by the Israeli army, had massacred Palestinian men, women and children in the refugee camps of Sabra and Shatila.[7]

CHAPTER TWO

Attack on the United States

The beautiful voice of Fairuz flowed from the radio around noon on Monday, April 18, 1983, as I was driving a borrowed, old, orange and dented Volkswagen Passat to the *Associated Press* news bureau in West Beirut. After checking on the latest news, I thought it would be a quiet and peaceful day, so I drove back toward the Ain el-Mreisseh district where I was living.

I eventually turned into a narrow, crooked, steep street which ended near the American Embassy all the way down by the beach promenade. The embassy was a nine-story Y-shaped building. The rather unattractive, salmon red colossus had not been designed by an architect, but by a Lebanese engineer. The embassy had also not been built to house US diplomats, but as a residence block in the mid-1950s. A few years later intelligence agents from the Central Intelligence Agency (CIA) moved in. Later the State Department took over the building.[8]

I drove past the embassy and saw two Lebanese soldiers in olive green uniforms talking in the horseshoe-shaped entrance area. The soldiers watched cars and people going in and out. In the lobby, behind a bulletproof door, was an armed US Marine with a white cap, standing at strict attention. A civilian guard was taking care of the security corridor. On the walls were marks of gunfire, one of which was hidden behind a portrait of President Ronald Reagan. There were also hidden containers of teargas, ready to be sprayed. The focus of the security staff was mainly to protect the building against mobs. They definitely wanted to avoid what had happened in Tehran in 1979, when the embassy was occupied and the diplomats held hostage for 444 days.

At the intersection in front of the embassy, I turned to the right and drove into Avenue de Paris—the wide street, lined with palm trees was called "the Corniche" in local slang—which wound along past rough rocky outcrops and on southward toward a hotel quarter which had been severely damaged. It had become a dangerous front line. I stopped in front of a five–storey building three hundred meters east of the embassy, parked and went inside. On the ground floor was a restaurant, the Spaghetteria Italia, and on the fourth floor was my apartment.

From a room towards the south, I could look down on a narrow one-way street, Rue Dar el-Mreisseh, but I could not see the cars go by under the window. I could therefore not see the old green Mercedes which was driving toward the mosque. It did not particularly stand out among the many old, worn out cars. The driver turned to the left and stopped behind the monument to Egypt's late president, Gamal Abdel Nasser, and flashed his headlights. This was the agreed-upon signal.[9]

At this point, I was sending a report for the radio edition of the *Norwegian Daily News Hour* in Oslo, about the Israeli actions in occupied South Lebanon. From Oslo, I was informed that my report might not make the first broadcast. The shift manager said there was an annual meeting going on of the Christian People's Party, and the government had come with a new wage proposal in the national labor negotiations. There had also been some promising results from the oil drilling going on in the North Sea.

I crossed into the living room, where I had a view of the Avenue de Paris, the Mediterranean, and the snow-covered mountains to the east and north. To the southwest, I could make out the

American Embassy, but I did not notice the young man, dressed in a black leather jacket, who was sitting behind the wheel of a delivery truck a few hundred meters away, not far from the burned-out St. George's Hotel, a grotesque structure from 1975 when the Christian Militia was forced out of Beirut's fashionable hotel district during the first year of the civil war. Its engine idled as he watched the traffic. He waited until the green Mercedes flashed for the third time, then put the vehicle into first gear and swung out into the traffic lane. He barely missed being hit from behind by a garbage truck. I had listened to the local newscast and went outside to where my car was parked near the building entrance on the seaside. The lunch traffic was heavy. My eyes caught a slender, beautiful woman in a red dress as she drifted by. It was as if she were walking on air; as if she were dancing, past a few sidewalk vendors serving hungry and thirsty souls from their rebuilt Volkswagen buses. It was a magnificent spring day with the smell of fresh sea air, Turkish coffee, and fresh *ka'ak*, small circular breads spiced with thyme.

The delivery truck moved at a snail's pace toward the embassy. At the corner in front of it, the man in the black leather jacket stopped the vehicle. Behind him other drivers honked impatiently. Oncoming traffic showed no signs of letting him move the heavily loaded vehicle into the intersection. Only when there was a small opening was he able to move forward, barely missing a woman driving her children home from school. Then he floored the gas pedal and steered toward the embassy entrance. Before the guards could shoot, he surged toward the lobby and consular section, where a long line of Lebanese were seeking visas to escape Lebanon's hell. Then everyone was dead.

I was just about to get into my car when I saw the powerful flash of light. Then came the boom and crash of the shock wave. I threw myself to the ground. When I got up, I could see flames and black smoke 300 meters away. The stillness which followed gave me the shivers. Was it a bomb? A missile? Would there be more?

After waiting a few seconds longer, I ran upstairs into my apartment to report the American Embassy had been attacked and was on fire. The telephone line was dead. This was before the time of mobile phones. I ran down again and sprinted toward the burning embassy. On the street, cars were in flames. Screaming people wandered aimlessly. The woman in the red dress was sitting on her haunches beside an elderly woman covered in blood. I ran between burning wrecks to get closer. French soldiers, who were stationed a few hundred meters away on the other side of the embassy, came racing to give first aid.

I ran back to my apartment again to try to call the *NRK*. The phone line was still dead. After five or six minutes I went back to find that fire engines, ambulances and crews from the Red Cross had arrived. The firemen tried to put out the flames and fought their way through the black smoke. The sidewalk was wet with water and blood. Crews loaded casualties on stretchers into ambulances. Blankets covered the dead, with remnants of crushed arms and legs hanging out. One of the Lebanese soldiers cried uncontrollably.

My colleagues Terry Anderson from the *Associated Press*, and Robert Fisk from *The Times* also showed up. We spoke with a man who claimed it was a bomb inside the embassy that had exploded. Another man said the bomb had been placed in a parked police car by the entrance. A third spoke about a suicide bomber.

From the back of the embassy, survivors came streaming out. One diplomat said he had not heard the explosion, but only saw the powerful, white flash. At the same moment he was thrown over by an incredible force. It was as if he were in a centrifuge which threw him and the others in the room against the closest wall, while glass, dust and cement flew through the air like in a slow-motion film.

Once the firemen got control over the fire and the smoke disappeared, they were able to enter the embassy itself. Six of the seven floors above the lobby were flattened: the building had fallen like a house of cards. A balding man, dressed in a suit, lay half hanging in the air with dangling arms, crushed between two floors. The rescue team went about with megaphones calling into the ruins: "Is anyone there? If you can hear me, answer, please."

There was no response from the embassy's visa section. Every man and woman there had been incinerated. One man in work clothes came out of the first-floor cafeteria carrying a plastic bag full of hands. Others swept smaller body parts into a bucket. After a while a large crane arrived and carefully lifted the flat concrete slabs of the entrance roof, moving them as far away as possible, while bulldozers scraped through the ruins. When the big shovel hit a teargas canister, everyone without a gas mask had to disperse. At times, calls came again from the ruins, "If you can hear me, please call for help."

Ten minutes after the explosion, a man called the French *AFP* news bureau in Beirut. He spoke Arabic with a Lebanese accent. Calmly and in full control, he said the operation was part of the Iranian Revolution's campaign against the imperialists the world over: "The operation is part of the Iranian revolution's campaign against the imperialist presence throughout the world. We will continue to strike against the imperialist presence in Lebanon including the multi-national force."[10]

After a brief silence, he hung up. Sometime later another man called to take credit for the attack. He said he represented the group, "Avengers of the Martyrs in Sabra and Shatila."[11]

We journalists asked ourselves if it could be the Palestinians who were out for revenge against the US. It was known that Washington had given Israel the green light for the invasion the year before.

In the course of the evening, I sat on the balcony of Ane-Karine Arvesen, a Norwegian diplomat who lived one floor below me. I had gotten to know Ane-Karine when I came to the Lebanese capital five years before. The friendship had grown to something more. Behind her green eyes and curly blonde hair the 42-year-old attaché had a sharp mind. She had a slender and elegant body which had survived several hundred parachute jumps. That was a rather difficult hobby to pursue in Lebanon; instead, she occasionally enjoyed sitting behind the stick of a small Cessna, when the warlords were taking a break.

From the balcony, we could see and hear the bulldozers dig into the ruins under gigantic floodlights. It was as if we were present at the production of an apocalyptic catastrophe film, while surrounded by lovely ceramic pots, blood-red hibiscus and fragrant jasmine plants. It was surreal.

Over a table of Lebanese wine, cheese and fruit, we discussed the attack with clinical sobriety. We did not dwell much on the 60 people who had been killed. (The last survivor had been found by the rescue team at 5 pm.) We also did not talk about the families in the US and Lebanon who now had lost their loved ones, or about the 100 people who were maimed for life. We were concerned with what had happened beyond what we had seen, the hows and whys.

At that point, none of us knew about the vehicle loaded with explosives which had been driven into the embassy. We asked each other: Had a bomb been smuggled into the building? Was it the police car in the entry area that had blown up? Could it have been a suicide bomber? Should the telephone calls be taken seriously?

A number of foreign correspondents, diplomats and Lebanese came to Ane-Karine's balcony that evening. Some thought it had to have been one of the radical Palestinian groups behind the attack. A Lebanese radio station reported that the Soviet secret police were involved. The militia leader in Ain el-Mreisseh, Saleh Deek, gave fresh fodder to new speculations when he said Mossad's station chief had been seen driving past the American Embassy several times a few days before the attack. Deek, had close contact with the American Embassy's security people and knew what the Mossad station chief in Beirut looked like. He also knew that relations between the Israeli and the American secret services had chilled because the Israelis constantly misled their counterparts. "What do we need enemies for when we have Mossad as friend?" one of the Americans had said to the militia leader.[12] Ane-Karine had a good relationship with the Druze militia leader, who lived in the area. He made certain no foreigners living there were robbed or kidnapped. But he demanded protection money from certain international organizations with offices nearby. This was in the form of contributions to the quarter's soccer team. I had earned credits to see the team train or play. The Arabic expression, *hamiah haramiah*—he who protects you steals from you—fit like hand-in-glove.

Ane-Karine brushed off the militia leader's speculation that the Israelis were guilty. She was not the kind of diplomat who thought twice before saying anything. She often stretched the language farther than the grammar allowed. She went over to the well-stocked bookcase and took out a piece of paper, reading, "It was Sunday, March 19, 1950, when the Israeli agents placed a bomb which exploded at the American Cultural Center in Baghdad. Saturday evening, April 8, at 9:15 pm, they threw grenades toward the city's El-Dar El Bida Café while Iraqi Jews were celebrating their Passover." The piece of paper was in a book titled *Ropes of Sand, America's Failure in the Middle East*. The book was written by former CIA agent, Wilbur Crane Eveland. Ane-Karine read on: "In attempts to portray the Iraqis as anti-American and to terrorize the Jews, the Zionists planted bombs in the US Information Service library and in synagogues. Soon leaflets began to appear urging Jews to flee to Israel." There had also been an assassination attempt against the US ambassador to Lebanon with weapons that were traced back to Israel. Ambassador John Gunther Dean was riding in a car with his wife on August 27, 1980, when the car was attacked from a hill on the right side of the Damascus Road. The firepower was from two light anti-tank weapons—LAWS—and from automatic guns.[13] The attack did not penetrate the armored doors of the car, nor smash the plexiglass windows. Since the tires were automatically inflatable, the driver managed to speed away, while the ambassador's bodyguards, a car behind, sprayed the hill with bullets. Tracing weapons and ammunition left at the scene provided precise confirmation: the name of the boat that shipped the guns from America, the date it sailed to Israel, and the numbers of the light anti-tank weapons, which included the two missiles used against the American ambassador's car.

"I know as surely as I know anything that Mossad, the Israeli intelligence agency, was somehow involved in the attack. Undoubtedly using a proxy, our ally Israel had tried to kill me," Ambassador Dean wrote later.[14] Scurrilous attacks on Dean in the Knesset and in the Israeli press just prior to the assassination attempt indicated the displeasure with the activist role Ambassador Dean played in Lebanon, defending Lebanese sovereignty and maintaining an active relationship with the PLO.

Yet here on her balcony, Ane-Karine maintained that even if Israel previously had undertaken terrorist acts, even against their own, she did not think the attack against the American Embassy was the work of Mossad. This time the attackers were angry, revolutionary Shia Muslims, tied to Iran. We all knew that in Beirut, in the Bekaa Valley and in the South, Shias were the largest religious group, but nevertheless were lowest on the Lebanese totem pole. Many had been radicalized following the Iranian revolution and the Israeli invasion. Now they wanted the US and Israel out of Lebanon. To them the US was 'The Great Satan', and Israel 'The Small One'.

After a while, it was clear the attack against the embassy was a carbon copy of a suicide action against the Israelis in South Lebanon six months earlier. On that occasion, the target was the Israeli intelligence headquarters in Tyre. A few weeks before the attack on the embassy, another Lebanese had blown himself up, taking with him an Israeli soldier. The bomber had first written to the Shias' supreme spiritual leader, Ayatollah Khomeini, to ask permission. According to Islam, it is forbidden to commit suicide, but it is allowed to die in battle against the enemy. The young Shia was given the go-ahead by the Ayatollah's representative in Beirut.

It did not take long for news to get out that nearly the entire CIA staff in Beirut had been killed in the embassy explosion. The CIA's top Middle East expert, Robert Ames, also lost his life. He had come to Beirut to repair the damage following the loss of the important Lebanese figure, Bachir Gemayel. Ames had recruited the young Christian, who cooperated with Israel. Gemayel was elected Lebanon's president in 1982, but was killed before his inauguration.

About six months later, the CIA's Middle East staff in Beirut was down to bare bones. Not since the Vietnam War had the CIA lost as many agents in a single attack. Just three of the CIA's eight intelligence agents in Beirut survived the embassy attack. One agent, Susan Morgan, was spared because she had driven to a meeting in Sidon, known as *Saida*. Another escaped because he had dropped out of the staff meeting so he could haggle down the price of a carpet he was in the process of buying. A third survived because he was on a mission so secret he had not reported it to the American Embassy.[15]

This vicious attack on the CIA, of course, created new speculation and conspiracy theories. This had to have been an operation planned by people with inside information.

CHAPTER THREE

Hotel Commodore and The

Smuggler's Inn

Over the following evenings, correspondents and diplomats gathered at the bar of West Beirut's most important news center. The Hotel Commodore had been built with seven stories, right in the heart of the city's commercial district. It fit into a row of rather trim hotels in the modernistic style of the 1960s, the type which the British often describe as "a smart hotel." The Commodore became the base for most journalists after the nicer Hotel St. George, built in the functionalistic Levantine style, was destroyed during the first years of the civil war. Not only journalists frequented the Commodore. Diplomats, businessmen, narcotics dealers, emergency workers, murderers, prostitutes and spies also came by. Hotel guests who journeyed to Beirut without visas received their necessary papers delivered at the airport by the hotel's omnipresent fixer. He was dressed in a pilot captain's uniform and was known as Captain Midnight. In the reception of the hotel, new arrivals were often asked, "Grenade or car-bomb side?" This was meant as a joke, but in it contained a truth: several car bombs had gone off in the district's small streets and the hotel's seventh floor had been hit by artillery shells where it faced to the east.

In a large cage near the circular bar sat an African Grey parrot that its previous owner, *BBC* correspondent in the Middle East, donated to the Commodore. Coco chirped its own welcomes such as "Hello boy, Hello girl," and could imitate the whistling sound of a mortar or artillery shell—a sound that, at times, caused newcomers to the bar to throw themselves to the floor. The parrot could also sing the opening notes of La Marseillaise, and Beethoven's Fifth Symphony.

On the fourth evening after the attack, I was at the bar with Ane-Karine, a couple of other journalists and a Brit who had previously worked for the intelligence organization MI6. The Englishman, David Cornwell, had been exposed by a double agent, became an author instead, and was now in Beirut to introduce his newly written spy novel about the Israeli-Palestinian conflict. Over gin & tonic, he told us how he had received help from Mossad and the PLO secret services while writing it.

Those of us unfamiliar with David Cornwell had long before heard of his pseudonym: John Le Carré. Those of us who were sitting around the bar at the Commodore really wanted to hear what the former intelligence agent thought of the attack on the American Embassy.

"If you find out what the Israelis, the Syrians, the Iranians, and all the militia groups are doing, you will have your answer," the charming Englishman said with a sly smile. He had been recounting how he thought about writing a new George Smiley book that pitted the hero against the KGB's Karla in Lebanon, but that he was unable to find an intrigue sufficiently Gordian or manipulative. Now he added, "The only thing certain is that I will never write a new novel about the Middle East. Here the conspiracies are more Machiavellian than I can make up."

I was not sure if it was Cornwell or Le Carré who was speaking.

Cornwell left the bar for a dinner engagement at the Commodore's Chinese restaurant, while the rest of us joined a group going to the Smuggler's Inn, a favorite place for Lebanese artists, academics, diplomats and journalists, despite Beirut's lawlessness in the evenings. Over juicy entrecôtes and Lebanese red wine, we continued our conversation about the recent dramatic events and what might happen now. The man, who had taken the blame for the attack on behalf of the organization, Islamic Jihad, had said to the *AFP* news bureau the next target would be the US-led multinational force in Beirut. The American soldiers had their headquarters near the international airport in the slum district in the southern part of the city. None of us around the table was familiar with the organization which wanted to wage "Islamic holy war" against the Americans.

Some of the people around the table made fun of the Shias in Lebanon, and agreed that they were the poorest and least educated group in the country, and would never be able to take on the world's greatest military might.

Ane-Karine was not so sure. "The truth has many facets," she said. "First it is laughed at. Then it is fought against, and then it will be accepted as obvious. The truth about what revolutionary Shias are doing in Lebanon, we do not know. But we do know the politics of the United States."

This was not the first time the Americans had become involved in the political game over Lebanon. Back in 1958, the US had put in forces to stop the so-called civil war. The battle between the government and the opposition had cost in excess of 2,500 lives.

President Camille Chamoun's forces were on the defensive and only had control over the "old Lebanon" of the Ottoman times, plus the Christian parts of Beirut. The rest was in the hands of the opposition. It appeared as if the Greater Lebanon that the French had created was about to disappear. The Americans thought Lebanon was in danger from intrigue on the part of Egypt and Syria, who recently had joined in a union called the United Arab Republic, supported by the Soviet Union. The opposition in Lebanon for its part suspected the pro-western president, Camille Chamoun, of wanting to tie Lebanon to the Baghdad Pact, an alliance among Great Britain, Iraq, Iran, Turkey and Pakistan. The intention was to form a buffer of strong states that could stand against the Soviet Union. The opposition in Lebanon was also strongly critical that Lebanon had not broken diplomatic relations with France and England when, together with Israel, they attacked Egypt in 1956.

Officially, the Americans went into Beirut to rescue President Chamoun, who was also under strong pressure because he wanted to extend his presidential term beyond its legal limit, in breach of the constitution. In order to do this Chamoun, assured himself of a large majority during the 1957 election for a new National Assembly by bribing candidates and voters with huge sums of money. The funds had been given to Chamoun personally by the CIA, delivered in suitcases by the American agent Wilbur Crane Eveland.[16]

American soldiers waded onto Beirut's beaches under the broiling July sun in 1958, among bathing nymphs, gold-laden Lebanese men and ice cream vendors. They would have been unlikely to come to save the Christian president had there not just been a coup d'etat in Baghdad. Iraqi nationalists had killed the pro-British king of Iraq, Faisal, and his entire family. Faisal's Iraq had been the most important pillar of the Baghdad Pact, and it was important for the US to convince its remaining friends in the alliance that it would use its power to defend their interests. The easiest demonstration was to flex its muscle in Lebanon.

The day after the landing, soldiers marched through the center of Beirut behind three columns of Lebanese policemen on motorcycles. President Chamoun's most prominent opponent, Prime Minister Saeb Salam, had gone underground. The American force grew to 14,000 men and remained in Lebanon for three and a half months. The force lost three men; one was the victim of a sniper, and two drowned while swimming off Beirut's beaches.

Seen through American eyes, the intervention was a success, and American politicians got a picture of Lebanon and the Lebanese as easy to control. When the Americans withdrew, the US had made an agreement with Egypt to replace President Chamoun with the head of the army, Major General Fouad Chehab. For many, this was confirmation that Lebanon could not solve its own crises through its political system, but only with the help of outside forces.[17]

Around the table at the Smuggler's Inn that April evening in 1983, the talk was not about Lebanon's history and the day's political situation. The conversation wandered to an infamous book,

The Perfumed Garden, that a male diplomat had recently gotten hold of. The original was written in Arabic around the year 1400 and was unknown in Europe until it was translated by a French officer some 400 years later. With great enthusiasm, the diplomat read some lines from what amounted to a medieval sex guide: in order for a woman to be relished by men, she must have a perfect waist, and must be plump and lusty. Her hair will be black, her forehead wide. She will have eyebrows of Ethiopian blackness and large black eyes, with the whites very limpid. With cheeks of perfect oval, she will have an elegant nose and a graceful mouth. Her lips and tongue will be vermilion; her neck, long and slender; her breath of pleasant odor.

There was great interest in the book at the table, and the discussion gradually slid over to today's Lebanese women, of the many myths surrounding the women in Beirut, and how easy it was for foreigners to misunderstand the way they communicated. There was one such woman at the table, who laughed to a man pursuing her, "Don't get your hopes up. The only thing I will open for you this evening are my ears." She added, "The Israelis should also not get their hopes up with regard to Lebanon. They look at Lebanon as a woman they can easily conquer. Just wait until they discover she has poisoned them."

Those who also reported from Israel were well aware that most of the young soldiers who fought in Lebanon had an arrogant attitude toward Arabs in general. These soldiers did not question why they were in Lebanon. The young draftees had been brainwashed since their first year in school: It was right to kill for the Jewish state, no matter whether the situation was different from 1967 or 1973. During those times, the Israelis were fighting against Jordanian, Egyptian and Syrian soldiers in uniform. In Lebanon, the fighting was against an enemy dressed in jeans. And if a soldier still dared to ask the question whether it was right to bombard densely populated areas, the answer he got was: They are all terrorists! Kill them!

A few days after the dinner at the Smuggler's Inn, I drove to South Lebanon to check out if it was true that the Israelis had begun building what were referred to as permanent military positions and large supply bases. It seemed almost as if they were going to be there forever: well-fortified positions were erected from one height to the other, but nowhere was the view more fantastic than from Beaufort Castle. Before the invasion, the Israelis had only seen the Crusader fortress, 717 feet over the sea, from Galilee and from the occupied Golan Heights. Only in 1983, serving their military obligation in Lebanon, could the soldiers see the fortress from the inside.

One such soldier was David Hyman, who told me he was there to escort men and supplies to Beaufort and other Israeli bases in Lebanon.[18] Sergeant Hyman's column comprised of three trucks with soldiers, two water trucks, a few trucks with supplies and a tank truck with diesel and gasoline. One jeep drove ahead, with another at the rear for protection. From the road, the soldiers could see the fortress looming. Three kilometers north of the Khardala Bridge over the Litani, the column swung westward and then in an arc south toward the Shia village of Arnoun, on their way to Beaufort where the Israeli camp had been built of cement blocks in a messy formation below the castle. The sergeant felt privileged. For most Israelis, the name Beaufort evoked the same exotic sound as Petra or Damascus. He climbed up to the top, even though there were warning signs written in Hebrew about possible mines and unexploded ammunition. After a few hours the escort left the camp. It was exciting to be at the fort those first few weeks, although eventually everything became routine.

Seventeen years later, Beaufort would become a name Israelis connected with death and horror. By that time, Hizbullah had become the Middle East's most professional guerrilla group, and attacked the fortress with mortars and grenades. The Israeli soldiers were so frightened that they dared not venture to the toilets, even if they were only a few tens of meters away from their bunkers. Instead, the soldiers urinated into plastic bottles, which were stacked up along the walls. The garbage began to pile up. The soldiers slept with their shoes on. Beaufort, which in 1982 marked the beginning of Israel's successful invasion of Lebanon, would in 2000 become a poster for the occupation's fiasco.[19]

CHAPTER FOUR
Little Tehran

In the weeks following the embassy attack, dozens of American investigators arrived in Beirut. At first, the criminal pathologist experts found no trace of the suicide bomber. They did not even find parts of the explosive device or the kind of explosive material that had been used. Finally, the technicians discovered a piece of the undercarriage of the vehicle, which could be traced to Texas, where the vehicle had been sold and sent to the Persian Gulf. Then the trail grew cold. Who had owned the vehicle, or how it had come to Beirut, they never discovered.[20]

The Americans eventually came to the conclusion that it had been radical Shias, tied to the Iranian Revolutionary Guards in the Bekaa Valley, who were behind the attack. The Iranians had come to Lebanon on orders from the radical Lebanese Shia clerics when Israel invaded the country in 1982. According to the Americans, the Syrians were also involved, since they controlled that part of the Bekaa Valley. In any case, the Syrians must at least have looked the other way. The Iranians, who numbered some 1,500 men, belonged to an elite brigade named after the Prophet Mohammed. They were placed in a military encampment not far from the border with Syria, with a view of Mount Lebanon in the west and Mount Anti-Lebanon in the East. Between the mountain ranges was a green fertile valley, 120 kilometers in length, running north-south. From their base the Iranian Revolutionary Guards could see Mount Lebanon. It was as if the mountains quietly kept watch over the Bekaa Valley, which lay there green in winter and spring, and golden-brown in summer and fall. Seen from the Mediterranean, Lebanon was even more picturesque than from the Bekaa. The western side of the mountains presented dramatic ravines and irregular ridges. Deep beneath the ground were grottoes of calcite, and the sources of Nahr Brahim, Abraham's river, or Adonis as the Phoenicians called it. According to Greek mythology, Adonis was a god famous for his beauty and beloved by Aphrodite, the goddess of love and fertility. The river is said to run out to the sea at the spot where Adonis died in Aphrodite's arms. While she sprinkled nectar over his dead body, every single droplet became an anemone, and the river which ran past turned blood-red. Men of science, however, do not consider the river's color to be red. The water is rust-colored because veins of iron in the mountain wash away when the snow melts. But for hundreds of poets, it is the legend of Adonis—the god of life, death and rebirth—which provides the nectar for poetry and stories. When Nahr Brahim ran red in the spring of 1983, it was not Adonis the Lebanese mourned, but Lebanon itself. The civil war had lasted for eight years. The Israelis occupied half the country. Syria controlled the rest. It was as if one war overlapped into another.

The Iranian Revolutionary Guards, in the Bekaa Valley, were there with the full agreement of Syria. Some of this goodwill could be traced to a trade agreement with Iran ensuring cheap oil to Syria. But President Hafez al-Assad refused to let the Iranians fight against the Israelis, fearing that an Israeli invasion further north in Lebanon, would be viewed positively by the West. But perhaps more importantly, Syria did not want Iran, through a battle against Israel, to have increased influence in Lebanon.[21]

There was little the Iranian forces could do in their camp, far from both people and the front, except to train beneath pictures of Ayatollah Khomeini and the Iranian flag. The war against Saddam

Hussein required reinforcements and the leadership of the Revolutionary Guards soon wanted to use these experienced soldiers in that effort. Khomeini agreed and decided the Iranian forces should be pulled back. Only 300 Iranians remained for training and indoctrination of revolutionary Lebanese Shia Muslims.

In Iran, it was these Revolutionary Guards who had been victorious in the inner struggle for power after the fall of the Shah. When I had been in Tehran three years earlier to follow the revolution at close hand, it was obvious the Islamic revolution was too complex to be described simply by the one word "Islamic." The adjective did not explain why millions of diverse Iranians went on strike, marched and distributed leaflets in opposition to the Shah. The 2,000-year-old monarchy came to a rather bloodless end because the revolution ideologically combined the Left, feminists, nationalists and others from all social classes. In 1977, it had been the liberals and the Left who followed up on President Jimmy Carter's criticism of the Shah's human rights policies. Simultaneously, businessmen complained about the Shah's strict anti-profit measures. Industrial workers and those in the civil service supported the students' protest actions, while the Shah wavered between hitting hard at the demonstrators and granting concessions.

By now the nearly 80-year-old Ayatollah Khomeini had become the symbolic leader of the revolutionary opposition. In 1964, he had been forced into exile, first to Turkey, then to Iraq, and finally to France, where he recorded messages of anti-imperialism and equality, distributed secretly inside Iran via tape. His ideas resonated with the people, but not initially with Iranian clerics. Certain ayatollahs even resisted Khomeini's theory that Iran must have an Islamic leadership, with all power concentrated in the top cleric. When the Shah fled Iran and Khomeini returned, the unity of the revolution began to crumble. Khomeini's supporters were the best organized and had the most money. Secular groups and the more liberal Islamists lost ground. When the radical Islamists occupied the American Embassy with Khomeini's blessing and held the diplomats hostage, I traveled to Tehran to experience how the Iranian opposition had been gagged. There were reports of political killings and torture in the prisons, and I met many who were planning to flee to avoid arrest. There was no doubt Iraq's attack on Iran in the fall of 1980 made it easier for Khomeini's supporters to suppress their political opponents and to monopolize power.

When Ane-Karine Arvesen and I left West Beirut on a Sunday in May, 1983, and drove over the mountains and into the Bekaa Valley, it was to discover more about the "winners" of the Iranian revolution. We drove first to Baalbek, named for the Canaanite's god, Baal, and which in local parlance now was referred to as "Little Tehran." A certain amount of excitement came with the trip because the Shias in the Bekaa Valley were known to be wilder and more dangerous than those in South Lebanon. This perhaps had something to do with the large-scale production and smuggling of *hashish*. Outsiders were regarded with suspicion. For that reason, we chose the simplest excuse for our visit: we wanted to look at the impressive ruins of the Roman temple there.

The Lebanese did not speak of ruins or temples, because for them this was an Arab fortress, "Al Qala'at." Salahuddin al-Ayoubi, the leader of the armies that captured Jerusalem from the Crusaders, had gone to school there. Likewise, it was from this fortress that Arab forces attacked those Crusaders who had not chosen the coastal route along the Mediterranean for their march to the Holy Land.

Ane-Karine and I entered the historic town over the same stones the Roman laborers had placed, and looked up at the six remaining pillars of the Temple of Jupiter. We went into Bacchus' temple nearby, where the walls were crowned with massive stone sills, greater than in the Parthenon in Athens. We stopped by the Palmyra Hotel just across the street from the ruins, where drawings by the multi-talented French artist, Jean Cocteau, hung in the foyer alongside photos of world-famous stars. We were told that an old guest book locked in the safe contained the signatures of Ella Fitzgerald, Louis Armstrong, Cole Porter and Ginger Rogers. They had all performed on the steps of the Bacchus Temple. Lebanon's own diva, Fairuz, had also performed there, as had the greatest of all the Middle East's songstresses, Egypt's Umm Kulthum.

We had made an appointment with a knowledgeable local man. He was a bit nervous to talk about the Iranians, but since there was no one else in the hotel garden, he agreed to speak. Over cups of black tea, he told us that the radical Shia Muslims in the Bekaa Valley had formed a nine-member committee to lay the foundation for a new political organization. Their goal was to create a revolution in Lebanon, following the Iranian pattern.

Later, we would learn that the committee had met Ayatollah Khomeini and asked him to name a judge who could decide the internal conflicts between the Shias in Lebanon. Iran's highest defense council worked out a plan after a while, to form a council to build up the new organization in Lebanon. Most of the members were from the Bekaa, where Shias traditionally had been less involved in politics than in South Lebanon. Khomeini took the initiative of sending a representative to Bekaa. The council worked in secrecy without any single leader. The leadership was collective. Gradually, an organization was formed with an ideological identity. Pictures of Khomeini were displayed throughout the village, and the Iranian flag waved from the rooftops. Some Shia Muslim women covered themselves in the Iranian fashion with black *abayas*. This was the traditional form of the *hijab*, draped from head to foot. A woman would hold the edge of the material pressed between her lips and adopt a strict stare.

Foreigners who had lived in Lebanon during the 1950s could remember that many women used the *hijab* and covered their faces. They could have been the mothers or grandmothers of the women we saw in Baalbek in 1983. It had been customary for women of all religious groups to use the *hijab* until late into the 19th century. Under western influence, the *hijab* was eventually considered reactionary. In many places, initially Christian and then Muslim women removed their veils to show they were modern. That the *hijab* was again coming into use among radical Lebanese Shias was in turn a reaction to the imperialism of western culture.[22]

For those Shias seeking an Islamic revolution in Lebanon built on Khomeini's sovereign leadership, the use of the *hijab* was just one element. The Iranian Revolutionary Guards knew they had to win the support of the people by various means. They helped the farmers with their planting and harvests; they helped with education and did social work. Yet the Iranians in Lebanon did not want to follow the old saying: "Kiss the hand you cannot bite, and pray to God the hand may break." They wanted to crush the hands and feet of Israel and other western powers that had influence in Lebanon. At the top of their target list was the United States of America.

CHAPTER FIVE

Escape from Ansar

On Tuesday, May 17th, 1983, I reported from Beirut that Israeli and Lebanese negotiators had signed an agreement to end the state of war between Israel and Lebanon, which had been in effect since 1948. The Israelis thought the agreement assured them a close and beneficial relationship with Lebanon. The opposition to President Amine Gemayel and his government believed this meant that Lebanon would become an "Israeli protectorate."[23] The agreement was signed at a second-class hotel in Khalde, just south of Beirut, and later it was countersigned at the cultural center in the northern Israeli town of Kiryat Shmona. Lebanon's chief negotiator, Antoine Fattal, applauded politely when his Israeli counterpart, the former Mossad agent David Kimche, finished his speech praising the agreement between the two countries.[24] Correspondents and diplomats did not know about the secret annex that had been negotiated between the US and Israel, without the knowledge of the Lebanese. It stipulated in black and white that Israeli soldiers would not be withdrawn until Syrian forces and the remaining PLO fighters were out of the country. There were nearly 40,000 Israeli soldiers south of Beirut, and 50,000 Syrians in the northern and eastern parts of Lebanon, including the PLO guerrilla camps. The secret agreement also gave Israel the right to retaliate against any attacks on the Jewish state originating in Lebanon. The Syrians expressed their dissatisfaction with the May 17th agreement by blocking the main road between Beirut and Damascus, and the one between Beirut and Tripoli, and by cutting off telephone and telex connections between Lebanon and Syria. When the CIA learned about the agreement (interestingly, not until it was publicly released), one of its analysts who covered the Middle East said, "Anyone who thinks Assad will buy the agreement must be high on marijuana."[25] A few weeks earlier, a new contingent of CIA agents arrived in Beirut to replace those who had been killed in the attack on the embassy in April. The CIA's new station chief was William Buckley, a colonel who had received the Silver Star for bravery in Korea, and had intelligence experience from posts in Vietnam, Damascus and Cairo. Buckley came to Beirut directly from a job at the CIA's Langley, VA headquarters. He had been part of a group which approved the killing of those the organization labeled "terrorists."[26] The American forces stationed at the Beirut Airport also got a new chief, Colonel Timothy Geraghty. It was not long before Buckley showed up at Geraghty's office to discuss the formidable tasks ahead of them – keeping peace in Lebanon. A few days later, Buckley called and said he wanted the colonel to meet a knowledgeable source. The CIA station chief promised to pick him up and said, "Wear civilian clothes."[27] It was dark when Buckley picked up Geraghty at his barracks by the airport. He drove the car himself and brought the colonel up to date on the way toward East Beirut, where they were to meet the chief of Lebanon's army intelligence service, Colonel Simon Qassis, for dinner. Outside a tall building they were met by stern-faced young men in civilian clothes carrying automatic weapons. These were the chief's bodyguards. They led the Americans up to a top-floor restaurant with a wonderful view over Beirut, where Colonel Qassis waited at a table. Geraghty was surprised that there were no other guests in the beautiful restaurant. During dinner, Colonel Geraghty learned that the multinational force's task was no simple peace mission. The colonel knew from before that the US was looked at as Israel's top supporter, now he heard that the CIA station chief was building up a new intelligence apparatus in Lebanon in close association with the Lebanese intelligence service, which was a part in the internal conflict. He thought this could be dangerous for the American troops in Beirut.

The CIA station chief moved into an apartment near Manara—the black and white lighthouse which stood high over the city's western most point. As time went on, I occasionally noticed a tall American diplomat with dark hair and bushy eyebrows as he walked along the beach front of the Avenue de Paris, or ate a meal in the Spaghetteria Italia restaurant, speaking in a loud voice. I did not know then that the American Embassy's "political advisor" was the CIA station chief. But there were many who did know. Buckley had been identified as a spy in the American magazine *Counter Spy*. He was also discussed in *Who's Who in the CIA*, a book published in 1968.[28]

One day in May, 1983, while the new CIA staff at the American Embassy established themselves, Ane-Karine and I drove out of Beirut once again. This time we headed south toward a large prison camp the Israelis had erected on a plain in the central part of South Lebanon. The camp lay close to the Shia village of Ansar, and had been set up when the Israelis invaded in June, 1982.

During the course of their advance toward Beirut, the Israelis took thousands of prisoners. Some were driven to Israel, while others were placed in the camp at Ansar. Some of the prisoners were guerrilla soldiers, others were not. Among them were also Palestinians, Lebanese, Syrians, Jordanians, Iraqis, Turks and others from third-world countries who more or less happened to be in the area when the Israelis rolled through. A year later, there were still prisoners there who had never fought against the Israelis. These included people employed by various UN organizations, such as doctors and nurses, communications workers, businessmen, teachers, students and others the Israelis and their allies saw fit to grab and place in the tent encampment behind large earthen berms and barbed wire. At the high point, there had been about 9,000 prisoners in all.

We knew the prisoners were routinely beaten and made to sit blindfolded for hours—sometimes even days—without food or water. Israel's Supreme Court had established the previous May that the prisoners were enemy foreigners who were held because they belonged to forces from terrorist organizations, or because of their connections or closeness to terrorist organizations. They were not, therefore, considered "war prisoners" with all the according rights. The Israelis maintained, however, they were following "humanitarian guidelines" in line with the Fourth Geneva Convention on the treatment of civilians. This was not true.

In Ane-Karine's old and dented Volkswagen Passat with diplomatic plates, we drove so close to Ansar that we could see the earthen ramparts surrounding the tent encampment, but not close enough to smell the stench of 5,000 sweating men and their excrement, which lay in open pits. The camp was divided into sections and around each section ran a four-meter high fence with barbed wire on top. Every hundred meters, there was a tall metal tower. Soldiers patrolled the perimeter in jeeps equipped with machine guns.

Each morning, there was a prisoner count, during which the incarcerated had to sit on the ground with their hands over their heads. Israeli soldiers would beat them with wooden batons to get them to sit in straight lines. There were daily interrogations. Collaborators with hoods over their heads would enter the tent areas and point out prisoners with ties to different political or military organizations. Those who were taken away often returned with broken fingers or other signs of having been tortured.

The guards were forbidden to speak with the prisoners, although some broke the ban. Certain Israeli soldiers could not manage to hide their own despair over the living conditions in the camp. Others seemed to thrive on the brutality. Sympathetic guards alerted Israeli journalists to the state of the camps, and so many ugly things were written about the conditions in Ansar that the commander of the camp was replaced in the fall of 1982.

The new commander arranged for warmer tents, kerosene heaters and better clothes for the prisoners. They were allowed to form committees that could negotiate with the prison leadership, which led to a list of 20 demands. Many prisoners were released. Among other reforms for those remaining were sufficient water supplies, better food, radios and newspapers. Prisoners were also provided with pens and paper so that they could write to their families and friends. The most important improvement was that the Red Cross was given access to the camp.

The prisoners organized. They created a local newspaper which was distributed by wrapping each edition around stones that were thrown from section to section. On Monday, November 22, 1982, the prisoners celebrated Lebanon's independence day, first by raising a Lebanese flag, then a Palestinian flag. The "flags" were made of underwear, colored with crayons from the Red Cross. Speeches were made and the prisoners sang the Lebanese and Palestinian national anthems. This celebration ended in a demonstration where slogans were hurled at the Israelis:"No to occupation! Yes to a free Lebanon! Yes to the PLO! No to the new fascism!"

The winter that followed was cold and awful, and in February 1983 the prisoners went on a hunger strike because there was insufficient heat in their tents. The Israelis called the hunger strike a "mutiny" and shot with live ammunition toward the activists. Several were killed. In March, Israeli Radio reported that most of the tents had slogans written on them comparing Israel's army to the Nazi SS troops. As time went on, the prisoners became more courageous in their resistance. They refused to raise their hands above their heads during the morning line up. They said nothing during their interrogations. They threw stones at the Israeli guards and swore at them. It began to look like a true revolt. The Israelis responded by dissolving the prisoner committees. The prisoners then began to burn their tents in section 25. Guards shot teargas grenades toward them, and they answered by throwing stones and encouraging others to ignite their tents as well. But most of the prisoners remained passive until June, the first anniversary of the invasion. Then a few prisoners, at first, began to shout anti-Israeli slogans, throw stones and burn tents. The Israeli guards did not dare to go into the camp itself. They were afraid of being attacked. Over loudspeakers, they asked the prisoners to calm down and announced in Arabic that "A prisoner exchange is nearly ready." This did not help.

Eventually the Israelis agreed to release old or sick prisoners, and living conditions improved for those who remained. Now the prisoners had more opportunity to concentrate on what most had been dreaming of: Escape. Their attempts involved a lot of hard work and great imagination. One prisoner rolled himself in a carpet bound for the garbage heap. He was collected along with the other trash and dumped in a landfill outside the camp. But his freedom did not last long. He did not stay hidden long enough, and was spotted by the garbage truck's driver in his rearview mirror. The driver turned the truck around and brought the man back. Other prisoners managed to hook themselves underneath outgoing trucks, but the practice ended when the soldiers began checking the undercarriages. Some tried going straight over the fences and earthen berms, but these attempts did not succeed. Still others dug tunnels that were discovered and sealed off with cement.

Ane-Karine and I were unable to drive all the way into the camp before we were stopped by an Israeli roadblock. Though we had not found anything particularly new to report, we did get a good impression of daily life in Lebanese villages under Israeli occupation.

It was only several months later, during a visit to the Palestinian refugee camp Nahr el-Bared (The Cold River) near Tripoli in North Lebanon, that I got firsthand knowledge of the conditions in the stinking concentration camp. A tall, slender Palestinian, Raouf, had escaped from Ansar and told me what life was like there. He had been taken prisoner by the Israelis during the summer of 1982 and was placed in section 31, which had about 50 tents, each three by three meters in size. Raouf's tent lay close to the camp's outermost high fence. Israelis patrolled outside, and at night the guard towers' searchlights swept the area.[29]

From his very first day in the camp, Raouf had thought about escape. He was not alone: others in section 31 discussed various plans, and eventually they all agreed on a plan under the leadership of Atef Danaf, a Lebanese militia leader. Danaf belonged to the Syrian Social National Party (SSNP) which was a secular party seeking a single state encompassing Syria, Lebanon, Palestine and

Cyprus. They began to dig a tunnel at the start of June, fashioning spades out of tent stakes. These were heated over kerosene burners until they glowed, then were hammered out, welded together, and hardened in cold water. The hammer they used had been lent to them by the Israelis to put up their tents, and when the soldiers came back to collect it, the prisoners said coldly and calmly, "You have already collected the hammer." The Israeli soldier believed him.

The escape planners had calculated they would have to dig 25 meters beyond the tent closest to the fence and earthen ramparts. This distance was measured by throwing a stone attached to a string toward the fence. The digging was done by two groups, each comprising five to seven men. One group worked at night, the other during the day. The tunnel opening was concealed by a mattress, though there was seldom any danger since the Israelis had become lazier with their inspections. The guards avoided getting involved in the prisoners' daily activities so long as there was calm. Soldiers did not come back into the camp after the morning line up, so Raouf and the others were able to dig in peace. They used the tent poles to support the walls and prevent collapse.

At first they encountered a lot of stone, but after just two meters they ran into red soil with fewer rocks and the digging went much easier. After two and a half meters they began in earnest to dig in the direction of the fence. They had only a 10 centimeter long ruler to measure their way, stolen from the medical tent. The red earth was carted in plastic cans with a rope attached at both ends, so they could drag it back and forth in the tunnel. Another rope went from the digger to the man sitting in the tent. Each time a can was filled, the digger pulled on the rope and it was withdrawn. The earth was emptied into a large trash can and carried out. They first filled the holes that were used for latrines, then had to find another way to get rid of the dirt. The solution was to build a kitchen garden. They had received seeds from the Red Cross and the garden, which grew larger and larger, was watered carefully and often so the guard would not discover that it was constantly receiving new soil.

Based on the previous, unsuccessful attempts at escape, the planners knew they had to solve problems of light and air availability in the tunnel. Since the weather had now become warm, they no longer had a need for their kerosene heaters. Plastic tubes running from the heater to the tank outside the tent made suitable air hoses. They coupled several such tubes together using the Bic ballpoint pens they had received from the Red Cross, removing the blue stoppers, writing heads and ink tubes—voila, they had a plastic tube for coupling. They sealed the joints with Band-Aid they got from the clinic. A jerrycan acted as an air pump. One end of the tube was passed through a small hole in the screw cap on the can. Asphalt from the Israelis' newly paved road inside the camp was used as a sealer. They made a 15-centimeter-wide hole on the broad side of the can, and using the palm of a hand over it, the man in the tent could pump air into the tunnel. Every now and then a weak voice was heard calling, "*Kbeis yalla!* (Start pumping!)" Then they pumped like mad.

At first Raouf and the others dug in a straight line toward their goal, but after a while they had to shift a little to the right when they hit soil that was less dense. After about 23 meters, they began digging slowly upward. They had passed the barrier. They were nearly there. Raouf was on shift when water began to leak from the roof of the tunnel. The tunnel passed by the camp chief's room, and the soil was so loose that water had begun to ooze through. Raouf still thought they were a good enough distance from the surface, even though strange sounds were coming from the stones above them. But then the bottom of the tunnel began to get wet as well, and when he stuck his finger into the roof above him, the water started running like a faucet. He crept back and told a fellow digger, Turki, "Get some clothes and help me seal up the hole."

But it did not help. "Get me a mattress." The fear the tunnel would be discovered suddenly became serious when earth started falling from the roof. The mattress they stuffed into the hole was soon also soaked and started to fall. They found another mattress, covered the surface with earth, and pushed it up into the hole that had formed. Luckily, dawn had not yet arrived: the mattress had been pushed all the way to the surface and would be visible when daylight came. They couldn't risk that, so they agreed to make their escape that same evening, Monday, August 8, 1983. They had been digging for 45 days, 24 hours a day.

But one important thing remained: at the exit from the tunnel there was a barrier of barbed wire rolled into a spiral, layer upon layer. Beyond that lay an earthen berm, two and a half meters high. Finally, five meters from the exit of the tunnel was a cement pipe which was in the berm. This was a runoff pipe about 60 centimeters in diameter, fronted by an iron grate. Turki thought he could cut his way through the grate and crawl through. This would be better than trying to crawl over the earthen berm. First, he made hooks in the shape of an "S". With these he could hold back the barbed wire. He planned to make a five meter long tunnel through it and then make his way over the cement pipe.

The planners also thought up a system of signals. Turki was to crawl through the tunnel with string tied to the back of his belt. Once through the barbed wire, he would tie this string to the cement pipe and pull on it so the next man, who would be holding the string at start of the tunnel, could begin to creep through. The plan called for the prisoners in other sections to sing and make noise to divert any attention from the escape attempt. One of the Palestinians who spoke Hebrew would stay near the guards to listen to what they were doing.

Just before Turki was to crawl through, a fight broke out among the tunnel diggers. One of the men from the other digging shift came into the tent and wanted to go first. The other shift was afraid that Turki's team of Raouf, Abu Awad and Abu Jassin, would trick them. The fight was narrowly avoided when Raouf grabbed one of them by the shirt and snarled, "I will kill anyone who stops Turki from doing his job. He has guerrilla training, which none of you has."

Turki proceeded, followed by Abu Awad. Turki fixed the opening with his hooks, and slithered through the spiral of barbed wire as planned, then crept toward the cement pipe. The time was just a little past 8 PM. Behind him he could hear the singing and games from his fellow prisoners. He saw the guards in the watchtowers, but they were not sweeping the area with their searchlights. Then at the cement pipe, everything came to a halt: it was impossible to remove the iron grating. He saw no other possibility than to crawl over the earthen berms, but before he went on he tugged on the string as a signal to Abu Awad.

A few minutes later Abu Jassin was ready with the string in hand. The minutes passed. No signal. He decided to crawl back, and learned that one of the prisoners had seen Turki crawl over the berm, but none of the Israelis had discovered him.

"Maybe Abu Awad forgot to tug," said Raouf. "If you want, I will go first." Abu Jassin nodded and Raouf took off. He managed to cut his way through the barbed wire using a pair of scissors he had with him. He did not dare take a chance to look for the hole Turki had made, but he also managed to get away unseen over the earthen rampart. He could not see Turki or Abu Awad.

Suddenly he stiffened. A lone Israeli soldier came ambling along. He was less than a hundred meters off. Raouf got ready to fight, although he would have to do it silently. His weapon was ready: all the escapees had fashioned iron gloves from barbed wire, formed into a point at the hand. But the soldier disappeared and he did not have to use it. Raouf quickly made his way toward a huge rock formation several kilometers away that had been chosen for their meeting place. No one else was there. After 10 minutes, he began to worry. He was from Jerusalem and did not know South Lebanon. He saw lights from several villages, but had no idea in which direction he should go. Ten more minutes passed. No one came. He decided to go off alone: if the escape was discovered, he would not be far enough away.

Tears came, but he got up and started off toward the farthest village. He had never felt so alone before. Raouf walked for some two hours. It was past 11 PM when he arrived at a village and heard the sound of helicopters. He noticed the area around Ansar was lit up: the Israelis had fired illumination grenades. In the village he saw two men sitting on a balcony playing cards. Raouf called up to them, "I have escaped from Ansar. Would you hide me or give me some clothes?"

"We would gladly, but we don't trust our neighbors. If they find anything out, we'll end up in Ansar," was the answer he got.

"Maybe you can show me the direction to the Bekaa Valley?"

The card player pointed, then tossed Raouf a pack of cigarettes and a lighter. "Be careful," the one said.

That helped. Raouf immediately felt better and said to himself, "I will make it."

He continued on in the dark. After some 30 meters, two young men came toward him. He readied his "fighting glove," but he chose to trust his intuition, which said they were not dangerous.

"I have escaped from Ansar. Can you help me get further?"

"Yes," was the answer, "but you have to wait until the situation has calmed down."

Raouf stayed in a shed for several days and then received help getting to the north and freedom. He later found out that several of the others had also escaped. For the prisoners left behind in Ansar, security was tightened.

CHAPTER SIX
Squeeze Out the Past

My contracted term as correspondent ended in August 1983, but I did not want to go back to Oslo, and instead took leave from the *NRK* to work on a book about Israel's war against Lebanon. No longer bound by a correspondent's short deadlines, I now wanted to explore the depths of this subject with an open mind.

I was given lots of good advice. A Lebanese friend put it this way:"If you want to write a book about Lebanon, then write about your impressions from your first weeks in the country. The longer you stay here, the less you understand." Another said,"In order to understand the Middle East, you must first understand Lebanon. But when you think you understand Lebanon, it just means you have been poorly briefed."

For me and others, many Lebanese came across as vain navel contemplators who used metaphors to whitewash discussion of their fractured society, full of corruption and disloyalty. They cultivated their differences, loved to push responsibilities over onto others and showed an impressive ingenuity crafting romantic stories and remarks, which, in all cases, I fell for.

One of my Lebanese friends wished me luck with the words,"Squeeze out the past like a sponge, smell the present like a rose, and send a kiss to the future."

I began squeezing out the past by going through old books about Lebanon—Jabal Lubnan, Mount Lebanon—which for 400 years was a province of the Ottoman Empire. It was pretty heavy stuff, but if I was to understand the Lebanon of today, I had to know the history. The modern period began following the First World War, when the Ottoman epoch ended. The war's victors, Great Britain and France, had divided the Middle East among them. The region referred to as Greater Syria, including Lebanon, came under French rule. Palestine, Transjordan and Iraq went to the British.

The United Nations' predecessor, The League of Nations, gave France the task of separating Lebanon from Greater Syria, and developing it into an independent state. The Maronites rejoiced when General d'Armée, Henri Gouraud, established Greater Lebanon on Tuesday, August 31, 1920. It was right in line with what the Maronites had wished for. The new Lebanon was given territory which previously had been part of Muslim Syria. Most Sunni Muslims were opposed to the new, artificial state that lacked defined borders. But some Christian groups, particularly the Greek Orthodox, also wanted to remain under Syrian rule. So did the Druze, who resided in the Chouf Mountains east of Beirut and further south toward the border with Palestine. The Shias were virtually invisible since Shia Islam had not been an official religion under the Ottomans' Sunni rule.

When Lebanon became independent in 1943, the groups comprising the Lebanese population entered into a National Pact. The pact was never put on paper, but it stipulated that the president would always be from the Maronites, the largest of the country's twelve Christian sects. Further, the prime minister would always be a Sunni. The Shias had to be satisfied with the presidency of the National Assembly.

As far as the Maronites were concerned, it was completely natural for them to have the presidency. They considered the country theirs and they wanted to have a Lebanon separate from

Syria, with their own leaders at the top. They did not even consider themselves Arabs, but as descendants of the Phoenicians. The Maronites wanted to be a Mediterranean people with Rome as their spiritual Mecca, and Paris as their cultural Mecca. For them the sea was their connection to Europe, while the mountains and the desert provided separation from the Arab world. The Arab nationalists in Lebanon saw things quite differently, and wanted to be a part of Greater Arabia.[30]

In the National Pact of 1943, it was also decided that the lawmaking body would have a Christian majority, with six Christians for every five Muslims. This same ratio would apply to all ministries and to the rest of the government apparatus. Here again the Shias were the losing party in the division of power, even though they made up the largest religious group, according to the census of 1932.

In order to understand what ambitions Israel had in Lebanon, I would of course have to read about the plans of the Zionists, which built in large measure on their interpretation of the Hebrew Bible. Many had been taught from childhood that two Jewish tribes had lived in South Lebanon, with the Asher tribe ruling the region around Tyre, and the Naphtali tribe occupying land north of the Sea of Galilee and into the valley between the two Lebanese mountains. This was one of the reasons that at the end of the 1800s a Jewish organization in Russia—a forerunner of political Zionism—wanted to establish Jewish colonies in South Lebanon. Members of the organization believed there was no salvation for the Jews unless they established colonies in *Eretz Israel*, Israel's Land.[31] They set up clubs, parties and associations to prepare for emigration. The organization and others like it had a number of different names, but collectively, they were best known as "the lovers of Zion." In 1908, there was talk of buying a large farm between Sidon and Nabatiyeh from a Christian Lebanese. This area would become the first in a chain of colonies in Lebanon that stretched southward toward Palestine.

When the British took Palestine, they promised the land would become a homeland for the Jews. Two years later, the British Zionist leader, Chaim Weizmann, urged the government to take control over South Lebanon. The Litani River would, in his view, be a natural border for Palestine, the future Jewish homeland. In a letter to Prime Minister Lloyd George, Weizmann maintained the economic future of Jewish Palestine would be at risk if the Litani were not included in its territory. With but the stroke of a pen, the Zionist leader had swept away Lebanon's own need for the water in the river.

Weizmann had traveled around in Lebanon to see what potential the area might have. He suggested the purchase of industrial companies in the Sidon area, among them a soap factory, a lemon juice producer and firms that made olive oil. The thought was that the Zionists should form a monopoly and control the entire Lebanese olive industry. In the Zionists' opinion, the southern part of Lebanon would become the northwestern portion of Israel's Land.[32]

Fast-forwarding to 1956, Prime Minister David Ben-Gurion put forth a plan for how the future Middle East would evolve. He thought Jordan should be divided, with the West Bank of the Jordan River going to Israel. The Arabs who lived there could move to the area east of the Jordan, and the East Bank and the desert should then become part of Iraq. In Lebanon, a solid Christian state should be established.[33] Ben-Gurion believed, however, this would be difficult because the Christian Lebanese lacked the necessary courage. He disregarded completely the idea that the Christians might not want their own state.[34]

Israel's Chief of the General Staff, Lieutenant General Moshe Dayan, was of the opinion that the only thing Israel needed in order to acquire South Lebanon was a Christian Lebanese officer—"Even a major would do." The Israelis could either buy the major, or appeal to his emotions to get him to declare himself to be the savior of the Christian Lebanese. Then the Israeli army would takeover the necessary areas, and later a Christian regime could be established in Beirut, to be allied with Israel.

During the Lebanon civil war in the 1970s, Israel did indeed get its Christian Lebanese major—along with an excuse for an invasion. A Palestinian guerrilla group had entered Israel from Lebanon by sea in March 1978. There they killed a woman, hijacked two buses, and drove towards

Tel Aviv. They planned to trade the passengers for Palestinians jailed in Israel. The bus was attacked en route. In the exchange of fire, 35 Israelis were killed, most by Israeli bullets. This was the deadliest Palestinian attack in Israel's history, and enough to ignite plans to invade South Lebanon.

While the soldiers awaited their marching orders, some of the rabbis sang:"You shall expand, you shall expand, west, east, north and south."[35]

The Israelis conquered South Lebanon north to the Litani River, but the UN Security Council demanded an immediate retreat. The Council also established a peacekeeping force, UNIFIL—United Nations Interim Force in Lebanon.[36]

The Peace Force, comprising about 6,000 men, was to observe that the Israelis withdrew from Lebanon and to assist the Lebanese government in regaining control over the area. But instead of retreating, the Israelis turned over the southern border strip to a Lebanese militia, the so-called South Lebanon Army (SLA). The militia was equipped, trained, paid, and commanded by Israelis—and led by a Christian Lebanese major, Saad Haddad, as predicted by Moshe Dayan.

When the Israelis expanded their occupation north to Beirut four years later, the extreme Zionist group, Gush Emunim, Block [of the] Faithful, put in motion plans to establish Jewish colonies in Lebanon. Gush Emunim was formed after Israel occupied East Jerusalem, the West Bank, Gaza, Sinai and the Golan Heights in 1967, and the organization used the *Fifth Book of Moses* as the basis of their demands for all the land described as belonging to the Jews in the Hebrew Bible.

The extremist Zionists were not alone in their demands. The Chief Rabbi in the Israeli Defense Force (IDF) thought South Lebanon should become part of Israel. He was supported by Rabbi Shlomo Eliahu, who said: "Some say Israel's border in the north should be the Litani River, and some say the border should go to Turkey. I choose the restrictive interpretation. South Lebanon belongs to us."[37] Those who warned that Lebanon would become Israel's Vietnam were not listened to.

CHAPTER SEVEN

The Frog and the Scorpion

As the *NRK* correspondent, I was often driven about the country by a young Shia taxi driver. His name was Mohammed Maatouk and he had moved from South Lebanon to Beirut during the civil war. It was the 22-year-old Maatouk who first told me how important it was to read about the history of the Shia Muslims in order to understand Lebanon. "It is perhaps difficult for you to believe that something which occurred several hundred years ago is important to understand our battle against Israel. But just wait, and you will see. The Israelis will not be able to hold on to Lebanon," said Maatouk, who also told me about the Shias' foremost advocate in modern Lebanon. He was just a young boy when Moussa Sadr laid the foundation in the 1970s for the Shias' growing influence in the country.

The Shias in Lebanon had not had a good spokesman to deal with the authorities. Where they lived, they lacked schools, hospitals, roads, water pipes and power. Compared with the Sunnis and the Christians, many Shias lived as if they were in the Middle Ages. Their few clan leaders were mostly interested in their own power; they were feudal landowners who gave little hope to the poor tobacco farmers and agricultural laborers under their rule.

Maatouk had personally heard Moussa Sadr speak. The cleric was nearly two meters tall and could virtually hypnotize listeners with his intense eyes that radiated beneath his raven black turban. However, he could do more than just give fiery speeches. He established Lebanon's Higher Shia Council, and then a popular organization that he called the Movement of the Disinherited. When the civil war began in 1975, a Shia militia was gradually built up. At first, Sadr was against setting up such a militia, but he eventually acceded. The name of the militia became *Afwaj al-Muqawama al-Lubnaniya*, The Lebanese Resistance Batallion, known by the acronym Amal. It means "hope" in Arabic.[38]

Born in the holy Iranian city of Qom, Sadr had good contacts with Ayatollah Khomeini while the latter lived exiled in Iraq. But Sadr also had connections with the Shah's secret police, SAVAK, and was supported financially by official Iran.[39] In 1975, Sadr broke with the Shah's secret services, and Amal found financial support from Libya, where Colonel Muammar al-Ghaddafi hoped to fulfill Egyptian President Gamal Abdel Nasser's dream of creating a united Arab world.

Sadr also strove to establish good relations with Syria's President Hafez al-Assad, who belonged to the Alawite minority group, which had its origins in Shia Islam. Most Muslims did not recognize the Alawites as true believers. Sadr, however, issued a *fatwa*—a religious decree—accepting Alawites as Shias. His connection to the Syrian president grew closer.[40]

At the end of August, 1978, Moussa Sadr went to Libya together with an assistant and a journalist to meet Ghaddafi. Following the meeting, Sadr and his associates disappeared. Their baggage arrived in Rome on Alitalia flight 881 on the evening of August 31, and the suitcases were checked in at the Holiday Inn by two Libyans.

There is no lack of speculation surrounding Sadr's disappearance. A finger pointed to Libya's leader: it was said he and Sadr had argued. Another pointed toward Yasser Arafat; it was well-known he regarded Sadr as a threat to the Palestinians' hegemony in South Lebanon. A third finger pointed at Iran's secret services.[41]

I was in Jerusalem the last Sunday in August, 1983, when some Shia youth from Amal were pasting posters of Moussa Sadr in West Beirut to commemorate the fifth anniversary of his mysterious disappearance. All of a sudden a passing car opened fire, killing and wounded some of them. Both Shias and American soldiers from the multinational force on duty nearby suspected it was Christian militia soldiers who had attacked the youths. Amal's people took up the hunt, and furious Shia Muslims targeted the Lebanese government army. Eventually, a number of other Muslim militia groups joined with Amal. Some hid their faces behind pillow cases with the eyes, nose and mouth cut out. Others wore carnival masks. In the course of 24 hours, 40 percent of the government army—about 13,000 soldiers—had become involved in the battles. An order for a ceasefire was ignored. Shias, Sunnis and Druze loaded down with weapons had tasted blood.

In an attempt to calm tensions, President Amine Gemayel invited all eleven opposition leaders to meet with a number of Christian officials. The most prominent Druze, Walid Jumblatt, travelled to Damascus to get advice. Jumblatt had taken over the leadership role among the Druze from his father, Kamal Jumblatt, who had been assassinated in March 1977. Most thought the Syrians were behind the killing, and the young Druze leader knew he might suffer the same fate if he did not play his cards right. When Walid Jumblatt sat before the Syrian president, he did not bring up his father's death, but Assad mentioned how Kamal Jumblatt had sat in the same chair during the last visit before he was killed.[42] Following the meeting, Jumblatt announced that there would be no dialogue with Amine Gemayel since the government army had attacked Muslim-dominated West Beirut. The well-informed Norwegian major, Egil Hagen, who led the work of the Norwegian Peoples Aid program in Lebanon, told me that Walid Jumblatt had plans to take control of mountain villages held by the army.

The Lebanese Chief of the General Staff, Lieutenant General Ibrahim Tannous, was particularly fearful the Druze militia would occupy the strategic Souk el-Gharb city, where both Christians and Druze lived. A few days earlier, Tannous had brought the American Brigadier General Carl Stiner with him to that part of the front. Stiner was the contact link between the US Special Envoy, Robert McFarlane, and the Lebanese defense leadership. The two generals were received by the brigade chief, Colonel Michel Aoun, who would later have a central role in the civil war.[43]

Aoun was desperate on the evening of Saturday, September 10, when he reported that the Druze, supported by other militia groups, had attacked his forward positions in Souk el-Gharb. The Druze were also shooting with artillery against the government positions near the American Embassy residence, not far from the Presidential Palace. The colonel reported that seven of his men had been killed, and many more were wounded or missing. A company chief had been hacked to death with an ax. Around three in the morning, Lieutenant General Tannous called Elie Salem, the vice-prime minister and foreign minister, and told him that the front was on the verge of collapse. If this portion of the front fell apart, the road would be open to the Presidential Palace in Baabda, and to Beirut, with areas near the airport exposed.

"You must evacuate the Palace—if not, you will be killed," the general said.[44]

"Hold your position at any cost. We have no intention of evacuating," Salem responded. The collapse of Souk el-Gharb had a larger implication than a local conflict, he added.

McFarlane was scared to death and sent off an emergency message to the White House. He wrote that there was a serious danger of a military defeat for the Lebanese army within the next 24 hours. McFarlane wanted American forces to enter the battle on the side of the government army. "Last night's battle was waged within five kilometers of the Presidential Palace. For those at the State Department, this would correlate to the enemy attacking from Capitol Hill. This is an action message," he wrote, and added that they expected a new attack against the government army that same evening. "Ammunition and morale are low... In short, tonight we can be in enemy lines," wrote McFarlane.[45]

In Washington, D.C., President Reagan, Secretary of State George Shultz, CIA-Chief William Casey and Chief of Staff James Baker met to discuss the telegram. Reagan decided to follow McFarlane's advice. He gave the green light for American warships to be put in on behalf of the government army. The president fully realized that the American soldiers on the ground in Beirut were about to lose the one thing they had of value, their neutrality.

The chief of the American forces at the airport, Colonel Geraghty, was opposed to shooting at the militia. This led to a heated argument with Brigadier General Stiner, who had taken McFarlane's side. In an outburst, the colonel shouted:"General, don't you realize we'll pay the price down here? We'll get slaughtered! We're totally vulnerable!"[46]

Colonel Geraghty did not understand the logic behind McFarlane and Stiner's argument to support the government army against the opposition. The multinational force was there to protect the civilian population, not the president. But the colonel also did not understand much about Lebanese logic. Nor was that easy. Even experienced observers had difficulty understanding the Lebanese thought process. The story of the scorpion who could not swim shows how difficult it was to navigate this particular labyrinth:

One day a scorpion wanted to cross the Litani River, but since he could not swim, he had to hitch a ride. All the animals he asked answered no. All knew the scorpion was both poisonous and unreliable, and none wanted such a dangerous creature on his back.

It was only when a frog came by that the scorpion got a hearing for his argument:"You can feel safe. If I kill you, then I will also drown, for I cannot swim."

The frog finally agreed and let the scorpion crawl onto his back. In the middle of the Litani River, he felt a paralyzing sting in his back. In the throes of death, he screamed,"You are killing me, but then you will also die! Where is the logic?""Stupid frog! Don't ask about logic in Lebanon. There is none," answered the scorpion just before they both sank to the bottom of the river.

Colonel Geraghty had thought he could learn to understand Lebanon when he came to Beirut nearly four months earlier. Now he understood less and less. The head of the force's intelligence officers did not understand either. But they all saw eventually that the table was set for a bloodbath in the Chouf Mountains east of Beirut.

Ane-Karine Arvesen learned from the Druze militia leader in Ain el-Mreisseh that the militia would fight in Chouf if no agreement were reached before the Israelis pulled out from their positions in the mountains to the south. It was known the Israelis wanted to set up a new front line further south, and the Lebanese feared this line would become permanent. If the Christian militia that had sided with the Israelis did not leave the area, the Druze would attack them. Ane-Karine knew from a different source that Lebanon's Chief of the General Staff was trying to negotiate an agreement with the Druze and the Christian militia, known as the Lebanese Forces, but he needed time.

On Saturday, September 3, 1983, Lieutenant General Ibrahim Tannous invited his Israeli colleague, Lieutenant General Moshe Levy, and the chief of Aman, the military intelligence service, Major General Ehud Barak, to dinner. The Lebanese general was in for a big surprise: the Israelis told him the retreat from the mountains would start the next day. According to Levy, the decision was made at the highest political level in Jerusalem. It was to be put in motion without delay. The Lebanese Chief of the General Staff said he needed time for the government forces to fill the vacuum left by the Israelis. Lieutenant General Levy answered that this was impossible. Israel had its own interests to take care of. For Tannous it was obvious the Israelis wanted to create chaos.[47]

The next morning in Tel Aviv, Israeli Defense Minister Moshe Arens met with Richard Fairbanks, deputy to Robert McFarlane. The Americans asked for a postponement to the plan, but received a clear no. Later in the day the US National Security Council met at the White House to discuss the situation. From Beirut, McFarlane reported there was some hope for a peaceful development, but the Israelis first had to be convinced to wait with their retreat from the Chouf Mountains. President Reagan tried to telephone Prime Minister Begin, but the Israeli leader would not talk to him and transferred the call to Defense Minister Arens.

"It was too late—the Israelis are already on the move," Reagan wrote in his diary that same evening.[48]

On Monday, September 5, 1983, the Israelis shot up illumination grenades while their tanks, armored personnel carriers and jeeps rolled down from the mountain roads toward the coast. From the airport, the Americans watched 100 Israeli tanks disappear to the south. It was the previous year's Israeli invasion that had drawn the Americans to Lebanon. Now it was the Americans' job, along with the other Western powers, to make certain Beirut did not become a slaughterhouse once more.

The Israelis' hasty retreat from the mountains created a race between the government army and the militias. A ceasefire order was again ignored, and merciless fighting took place from street to street all of Monday, Tuesday, and Wednesday. Civilians hid in basements or wherever else they could find refuge. On Tuesday, Druze and Syrian fighters in the Chouf Mountains had fired upon the Americans at the airport with rockets and artillery. The Americans responded with artillery from the USS Bowen, which destroyed the Druze firing positions. This was the first time American ships had fired in the Mediterranean since the Second World War. Colonel Geraghty was quick to realize his soldiers were now about to change from a peace force to a defense force.

Colonel Geraghty received orders on Wednesday to support the government army with ammunition. The Lebanese army could then bombard militia positions, and civilian targets as well, at the rate of 1,200 shells per hour.[49] Rockets, mortars, and artillery were fired at the Americans at the airport and French forces a few kilometers away. Two Americans and five Frenchmen were killed. The Americans sent helicopters to destroy the militia positions utilized in the attacks, while the Lebanese Forces and the Lebanese army bombarded residential areas in the poor sections of South Beirut. The aircraft carrier USS Dwight D. Eisenhower, from the Sixth Fleet, came closer to shore in a show of muscle aimed at the various opposition groups, which included the Druze militia, Amal, the Communists and other so-called Leftist groups.

The Americans reported that the Lebanese army northeast of Beirut was firing toward the east, south and west. The Druze militia in West Beirut fired toward the east. Their militia in the Chouf Mountains, supported by Palestinian forces controlled by Syria, fired northwards. Kataeb's militia—from the Phalange Party—in the northeastern mountains controlled by Syria, were shooting toward the south. There were mortar attacks in all directions, while fire of automatic weapons rained all over the city. The Americans' command center in Beirut reported to Washington. The chaos was best described by the American ambassador. It was unclear who did what toward whom and why.[50]

For Prime Minister Menachem Begin, Lebanon had become a nightmare. The investigative commission following the massacres in Sabra and Shatila had destroyed the myth that the IDF was a defensive force for the protection of Israel. To many, it had been revealed as an attack machine. Begin must have recognized that the occupation had not gone as planned. Evening after evening, Israeli TV showed burials of soldiers killed in Lebanon.

When Begin's wife, Aliza, died, he lost his strength: the 70-year-old prime minister announced he would retire. Foreign Minister Yitzhak Shamir would take over. The former Israeli underground leader had served with Mossad for many years. In Israel's first years, it was he who had given the order to kill the UN peace mediator, the Swedish Count Folke Bernadotte; Shamir regarded the UN as Israel's enemy.[51] After his service with Mossad, Shamir went into politics. He was elected to the Knesset and later became its leader.

As prime minister, Shamir believed Israel should have been able to keep control over Lebanon without much trouble. His belief was that the Lebanese government army would not fight. Most of the Christians in Lebanon were Israel's allies, and many Shias were happy to be rid of the Palestinian guerrillas. The various Lebanese militias that chose to fight against the occupation, were badly organized, lacking both money and weapons.

Israeli generals cared little about advice from observers that they should befriend the Shias and not just focus on the Christians. Officers distrusted academics. Israeli leaders had an historic and emotional reaction toward the Arabs, which became a mental blindfold for them. They did not hide their racism either. Prime Minister Begin called the Palestinians "two-legged beasts"; to Knesset leader, Yitzhak Shamir, they were "grasshoppers," and to Lieutenant General Rafael Eitan, they were "drugged cockroaches, worms, snakes and scorpions."[52]

CHAPTER EIGHT

Fateful Day

The Israeli arrogance toward the Shias was so apparent that officers did not even bother to investigate when Shias time and again said: "Don't join forces with those who murdered Hussein ibn Ali—Hussein, son of Ali. You will make an enemy with a power no Israeli government can manage to tame." The least knowledgeable Israeli officers did not even realize that the Hussein the Lebanese were taking about was the son of Prophet Mohammed's daughter, the first Imam of Shia Islam.

At the Israeli military encampments in South Lebanon during the fall of 1983, there was no one who was particularly bothered that the Shias were gathering for their annual holiday in memory of Hussein, the martyred first Imam of Shia Islam. During the first nine days of the holiday, known as Ashura, the Shias processions were ceremonially themed black and white. Men wore robes, or carried large shawls about their shoulders. Women wore long dresses with scarves on their heads. The tenth day culminated with hundreds of men walking through the streets of Nabatiyeh and flagellating themselves bloody to remind themselves of what had happened 1,303 years earlier along the banks of the Tigris.

From Lebanon to India, I have seen many drawings of Imam Ali. Unlike the Sunnis, Shias had no prohibitions against portraying holy figures. Ali was always shown as a handsome man in his 40s, with a well-trimmed beard and striking dark eyes. The portraits remind me somewhat of pictures of Jesus, except that Ali seems much stronger.

After his assassination, his sons, Hassan and Hussein, washed their father's body and anointed it with myrrh and other fragrant spices. Covered in three burial cloths, Ali was placed upon his favorite camel, which was let to roam freely in search of a resting place. Forty years earlier, Mohammed's camel had similarly determined the Prophet's place of burial, where a new mosque was built. Ali's camel wandered for half a day before it rested at the top of a bare sand hill—a *najaf*, in Arabic—about 10 kilometers from the place where he had been killed.

Hassan and Hussein laid their father into the ground. But no monument was placed over the grave, lest Imam Ali's enemies find his burial place and desecrate it. Ali's followers continued the fight against those responsible for the rebellion against him and his murder. These followers were called Shiat Ali, later known as Shias or Shia Muslims.[53]

On a reporting trip to Najaf in Iraq, I was told the story of how a later caliph discovered Imam Ali's grave. Harun al-Rashid—Aaron the Righteous—the famous caliph from One Thousand and One Nights, was hunting one day when he came upon a gazelle. He rode wildly in pursuit of the lightening-fast animal and had nearly managed to trap it when it jumped up onto a mound of earth. There the gazelle stood quietly with no sign of fear. The caliph dismounted and was about to aim an arrow, when he found to his surprise that he could not pull the bowstring. He tried three times, and each time his arm and fingers became paralyzed.

The caliph began to tremble, and when he noticed an old man nearby, he asked:"What sort of place is this?"

The old man answered:"Commander of the faithful, if I told you, it would bring me bad luck."

The caliph swore by the Prophet Mohammed that he would bring no harm to the man, and ordered him to speak the truth.

"This is the resting place of Imam Ali," the old man said. "But because many feared his remains would be destroyed, the location of the grave was kept secret. The gazelle you were hunting knows that this is holy ground and that no person can hurt it here. Just dig and you shall see that I have spoken the truth."

Three meters down, the caliph found the alabaster stone beneath which lay the remains of Ali. He gave a solemn promise that the place would not be desecrated. Initially, a mosque was built over the grave, and later the city of Najaf grew up around it. The city became an important center of learning for Shia Muslims, not least for those who later would become the leaders of Lebanon's Hizbullah.

The 1983 celebration in Nabatiyeh, South Lebanon was not in commemoration of Ali's assassination, but the story of his son Hussein and the final battle fought. Thousands of Shias from throughout the land had come for the annual commemoration. Among them was a 19-year-old named Soheil Hammoura from a village in the far south of Lebanon. Hammoura was not one of those who flagellated himself bloody. It was a mixture of tradition and curiosity which lured the teenager there. Besides, his brother was a doctor at the local hospital.

Local amateur actors had practiced for weeks to show how Hussein ibn Ali had fought for his father's honor at Karbala. Together with 72 armed men and their women and children, Hussein had been pursued for days by Caliph Yazid's soldiers. Finally, they were surrounded a few meters from the River Tigris, which ran through the Karbala plain.[54] Around dawn on the ninth day of the Muslim month of Muharram, the caliph's soldiers began to advance toward their small tent encampment near a grove of trees on the plain. The orders from the caliph in Damascus had been clear: Hussein was to be killed, and the women and children taken as prisoners. Hussein sent his half-brother out as an emissary; he accepted word of the death sentence with noble calm, but asked for one night's postponement so that the camp could prepare themselves. The caliph's commandant agreed, since he too had respect for the grandson of the Prophet.

As night fell over Karbala, Hussein gathered his followers and gave his final speech to them. He began by praising God, who had given him the privilege of bearing the Prophet's mantle and had given him his faith. Then released his followers from all ties of loyalty: "I ask you, let me be alone. Get yourselves away. I release you from whatever responsibility you might have toward me."

Most remained, but Hussein knew well that he would not get out of Karbala alive. He had decided to fight for the honor of his family and for his faith. By sacrificing his life he would give his followers the strength to defend the teachings of the Prophet.

Hussein and his sworn supporters spent the night preparing for the final battle. The tents were placed one against the other and tied with rope. On three sides of the grove they dug deep trenches and filled them with branches and tree stumps. They spent what remained of their night in prayer. When the sun rose, they put fire to the wood. The flames protected them from behind and at their flanks. Hussein had donned the Prophet's mantle, and with the Koran in one hand, he rode several times out onto the plain in front of the tents and shouted, "Search your hearts! Understand that what you are doing is sacrilege."

Each time he was met with words of ridicule and scorn. The only thing the soldiers wanted to hear was that Hussein promised to be subservient to the caliph in Damascus. For Hussein this was a blasphemous thought. He was no slave, he was the son of Ali, he was the son of the Prophet's daughter. The Caliph's men asked for the impossible.

When the attack came, Hussein's followers defended him bravely, but the enemy's force was too great. Later that afternoon, the only warriors left alive were Hussein and his half-brother Abbas. Abbas was the flag bearer for the flock of Shias, widely known not just for being an unusually handsome man, but for his enormous strength and courage. Now the time had come for Abbas and Hussein to give their lives in the battle for their faith. Abbas threw himself toward the enemy swords, and managed to reach deeply into their ranks before he fell. Hussein withdrew wounded to his tent camp to comfort the despairing women and children. The soldiers came closer. But they hesitated to attack the grandchild of the Prophet. It was Hussein who brought the battle to an end, rushing the enemy and slashing right and left with his sword. Finally he fell to the ground, impaled by many swords. It was now the tenth day of the month of Muharram.

Year after year on this day of Ashura, the Shias in South Lebanon relive the massacre of Karbala and the martyrdom of Hussein through their dramatic processions. An amateur photographer was using a camcorder to document the hundreds of men who walked the streets, beating themselves bloody on a small part of their scalps, which they had shaved and cut in advance. Others used their fists to beat their breasts and whipped their shoulders with chains, staining their white robes with blood. Many carried swords made of wood or metal. And they came by the thousands toward the large square in the center of Nabatiyeh, shouting, "Haidar! Haidar!" This was the warrior name of Imam Ali, Hussein's father. Gradually, the religious intensity passed into ecstasy. The air vibrated with the sounds, and the streets smelled of blood.

This year, an Israeli soldier happened to be driving his truck into the heart of the city, and made the decision to go down the main street and right into the middle of the seething masses. It was no intentional provocation, simply an example of inconsiderate arrogance. One of the many Lebanese who had come to Nabatiyeh that day was a 19-year-old student, Salma Salame, from the Shia village of Blat. Standing with her 11-year-old little brother Kamal, she noticed one of the youths, dressed in white with blood streaming from his head, ripping open the door of the Israeli truck and dragging the driver out into the street. The truck's passenger jumped out after them, and a fist fight ensued between the Israelis and the youths.[55]

Salma grabbed her brother and ran away. Many others followed suit when they saw an Israeli jeep arrive carrying more soldiers. The soldiers jumped out, firing into the air. The two from the truck managed to get away from the angry youths, but their truck was set on fire. At first, the Israeli reinforcements from the jeep kept their distance. Then many of the teenagers who arrived for a religious procession suddenly became demonstrators. They threw rocks, screamed curses, and swung the ceremonial swords they carried. The soldiers lined up with their backs against a low wall under some trees. One knelt with his finger ready at the trigger.

Another volley of rocks broke the jeep's windscreen. The Israelis responded with more shots, and a roar went up immediately from the crowd. The soldiers moved away from the jeep and some youths quickly set it on fire. Black smoke blanketed the square. The soldiers fired again, and this time Soheil Hammoura, the visitor from South Lebanon, was struck. He had been trying to run for safety, and while he managed to reach the hospital where his brother worked on his own, he only had time to say, "I am wounded," before falling dead. Six other wounded youths were driven to the hospital, but survived.

In Beirut, the leader of the Shias' spiritual institution, Mohammad Mehdi Shamseddine, issued a *fatwa* which gave everyone permission to join the resistance movement against Israel. The religious decree said that Shias should engage in civil disobedience. They should "rise up and make sacrifices" in order to end the occupation. All of a sudden, it was more difficult for many Shias to remain lukewarm regarding the occupation forces. Collaborators became free game for reprisal. Lists of those who worked with the Israelis were publicly posted on walls in the larger towns in South Lebanon during the night hours. Israelis' ignorance became the object of Lebanese ridicule. All over Lebanon the story spread about the Israeli intelligence officer who, on the day of the Ashura conflict, wanted to know where he could find this "Haidar" whose name everyone had called during the procession.[56]

Later these events in October 1983 were seen to mark a turning point in the Shias' relationship with Israel. The Israelis had made a fatal mistake. What had happened in Nabatiyeh sounded the religious starting gun for resistance, and from then on the Shias in Lebanon associated the State of Israel with Caliph Yazid, the man who killed the son of the Prophet's daughter.

CHAPTER NINE

October Surprise

There was one particular Lebanese both the Americans and the Israelis wanted to learn more about. His name was Imad Mughniyeh. He was born in the village of Tayr Debba, not far from Tyre, on Friday, December 7, 1962. Imad was the oldest of three brothers; the other two were named Fuad and Jihad. All of them had fled to Beirut in their teens; there they had been hired by the Palestinians as bodyguards for the PLO leadership. When the PLO guerrillas were evacuated from Beirut in August 1982, the three brothers looked for new jobs as bodyguards, this time for the Shia Muslim leaders.[57]

Early in the fall of 1983, neither the CIA, Mossad nor the Lebanese intelligence service realized that Imad Mughniyeh, together with other radical Shias, had created a databank with information about foreigners in Beirut. The idea had come from Tehran, and the Iranians had provided the funds. The foremost intent was to find out as much as possible about Americans and others who could be kidnapped. The Lebanese group responsible for the kidnappings would use the name Islamic Jihad. The Iranian backers made clear there should be no tracks leading back to them.[58]

Several hundred Lebanese Shias were asked to find names, addresses and other information about the work locations of targeted foreigners. Only a few recruits knew that the databank would become the foundation for future kidnappings. CIA station chief William Buckley was at the top of the list. Terry Anderson, chief of the *Associated Press* in Beirut, was also on it. He was wrongly identified as the CIA's second in command for the city.[59]

Kidnapping Americans was nothing new. Only a month before the Israeli invasion, the acting president of the American University of Beirut (AUB), David Dodge, was taken hostage. This happened on July 19, 1982, on orders from the Iranian Revolutionary Guards. The Iranians wanted to exchange Dodge for four Iranians who had been captured by the Phalange militia a few weeks earlier. Led by the Revolutionary Guards' Baalbek office brigade chief, the four Iranians were on their way to the Iranian Embassy in West Beirut when they were stopped at a control post north of the city. The Iranians, who all had diplomatic passports, were fearful the Israelis would get into their embassy and steal secret documents. In addition to the brigade chief, the team included the Iranian chargé d'affaires, a driver, and a photographer from Iran's official news bureau, IRNA .

Dodge was taken to Baalbek, then secretly moved to Tehran. There he was interrogated and placed in the Evin Prison. The Iranians never asked the US to pressure the Phalangists to exchange the Iranian hostages for Dodge.[60] After a while, President Hafez al-Assad learned that the American had been moved to Iran via Syria. Assad was furious that the Iranians would use Syria as a transit country, and demanded Dodge be released to the American Embassy in the city. The Iranians complied.

They would not make the same mistake again, but would give their Shia allies free rein in order to avoid future diplomatic entanglements. Nevertheless, US surveillance eventually made the connection to Iran by intercepting a transmission in which Tehran gave orders to the Iranian Embassy in Damascus to take Americans in Lebanon as hostages. American intelligence services also discovered that the Revolutionary Guards' intelligence chief in Baalbek had contact with Imad Mughniyeh, who had attracted Mossad's notice as well.[61]

At the beginning of October, 1983, Ane-Karine heard that the US intelligence organizations had also picked up a coded message from Tehran to the Iranian Embassy in Damascus. The Guards' leaders had given instructions to attack the multinational force in West Beirut. The Norwegian diplomat did not put any particular weight on this information. There were so many rumors flying around in Beirut.[62]

But this time it was no rumor. The American electronic listening service had also learned that $25,000 had been transferred to the Iranian Embassy in Damascus in order to prepare for a special operation. Later they picked up a telephone conversation from the Revolutionary Guards in Baalbek, in which it was said that the attack would be "spectacular, and that the earth would shake beneath the foreign forces."[63] The Americans were stationed at the International Airport in West Beirut. The French, Italians and British units were spread around in the city. The Lebanese intelligence officer believed the attacks would come via one of the many underground caverns that snaked their way beneath Beirut from seaside entrances. Some of the caves were large enough for small boats to enter.

Following a meeting between the Lebanese Chief of the General Staff and higher-level officers from the multinational force, it was decided to check the caves that stretched under the coalition's bases of operation. The effort employed seismic equipment brought in from the US and Europe, as well as Lebanese drilling rigs. Nothing suspicious was discovered.

At the time, I was in Israel to learn more about the Israeli plans for South Lebanon, and had not been thinking about the multinational force when I received a dramatic phone call from Ane-Karine on Sunday morning, October 23, 1983. She told me the American military encampment at the airport had been blown up. The gray, four-story cement colossus had a V-shape and was located between two runways. It was called the BLT, an acronym for the "battalion's landing team."[64]

Somewhat later, I learned more details. The sun had come up over the Chouf Mountains in the east and just past 6:20 am, Sergeant Stephen Russell heard unusual sounds, "a sort of popping or crackling" near the parking area to the right of the BLT building. He was stationed at his small guard post, protected by sandbags and plywood that ran all the way into the lobby of the building on the south side. The sound was not strong, and Russell did not even turn around. Had he done so, he would have seen a yellow Mercedes truck drive through the barbed wire barrier toward the public parking area of the airport. A few seconds later the sound turned into the roar of a diesel engine, and Russell did turn, catching sight of the yellow truck as it crashed through the chains at the gate. He was not afraid, just curious.[65]

From post number 7, just east of the gate leading to the main entrance from the parking area, a corporal on duty noticed the yellow truck as it drove toward the chained gate. An hour earlier, he had seen it circle the parking area once at high speed. The truck was the type which often picked up goods from the freight terminal at the airport. A few more seconds passed before Corporal Eddie DiFranco reacted. He saw a man with a black beard behind the wheel in the high driver's cab, and also noticed that the driver had a dark green or blue shirt. DiFranco raised his automatic weapon and put the stock against his shoulder. The ammunition was in place, but standing orders were that the M-16 was to be kept on safety. He made the weapon ready to fire, and turned the muzzle in the direction of the yellow vehicle, which rolled on at high speed. It was through the gate and out of view before he could fire.

DiFranco lowered his weapon and ran toward the bunker to call Sergeant Russell. The sergeant had to have seen the vehicle, he thought, and put the handset down and waited. Another corporal on duty at post number 6, just to the right of number 7, had not yet seen the truck since it was behind him. As it came into view, he instinctively ducked behind the corner of the bunker. A third corporal at post number 5 also heard the noise at the gate and turned just in time to see the yellow truck drive past the two large mess tents in the open area. He too readied his M-16, but the vehicle passed before he was able to position or fire.

Sergeant Russell remained at his post and saw that the vehicle was coming straight at him. Without thinking, he ran toward the front hall of the building. He shouted to a passing jogger, "Get the fuck outta here!" and raced through the lobby toward the back door. His mind focused. "Get down on the floor!" he shouted. The whining noise of the truck engine had come closer. "Get down on the floor," he repeated a few more times. He reached the back exit, saw another soldier and again shouted, "Get down!" The soldier threw himself behind a low cement wall while Russell ran toward the open parking area between the battalion building and a trash dump to the north. When he turned around, he saw the truck had smashed through the sergeant's guard post just in front of the building, effectively throwing it into the lobby. It looked as if a tidal wave had filled the entire entrance area. Russell continued running then turned to see that the vehicle itself was now inside the lobby. There was no movement to be seen in the driver's cab, but Russell noticed that the front windshield had been smashed and the roof on the driver's side had been damaged by the collision with the guard post. The driver must be injured, he thought.

At that same moment, Colonel Geraghty, the chief of the American forces at the compound, was shaving before the mirror in his combined office and living quarters on the second floor of the airport's low, flat-roofed fire station. Geraghty had been up for an hour and had already checked the schedule in the operations center—something he did each morning. It had been a peaceful night. The colonel had taken off his camouflage uniform with its silver eagles on the collar before he began shaving.[66]

At the other end of the fire station, the American press officer, Major Robert Jordan, was lying in his bunk wondering if he should get up. It was Sunday, and he could sleep an hour longer than on weekdays. Normally he would have been on his way to the mess hall in the BLT building to eat an omelette with toast, drink several large cups of coffee and talk with his fellow officers. But this morning, he decided to skip breakfast; he had been invited to a champagne brunch at the French headquarters to celebrate the anniversary of the French Foreign Legion. He closed his eyes and listened to birds chirping outside his window.

A few hundred meters away, Sergeant Russell was still running. The time was 06:22:18, to be precise, when he saw a bright yellow flash from the grill of the Mercedes in the lobby. Then he was thrown some tens of meters by a powerful concussion accompanying a deafening explosion. The driver of the Mercedes had set off his cargo—five and a half tons of TNT, the most powerful conventional explosion ever ignited. It gained extra from gas containers that constituted the core of the bomb.

The roof of the four-story building lifted and then fell, crushing every floor below from top to bottom. The explosion blew out the windows of Colonel Geraghty's quarters, tore the doors off their hinges, and threw him to the floor. He thought it must have been an artillery or rocket attack, managed to get to his feet and ran out, only to encounter a thick grey haze. The colonel continued running around the corner of the fire station and for a second became totally disoriented. He was looking toward the BLT building, but he could not see it. Instead he saw the control tower at the airport, which should have been hidden by the tall building that contained around 250 of his men. And then he understood: the BLT was gone, disappeared!

At the fire station the steel door had been blown in. It barely missed the force's rabbi and its Catholic priest, each of whom had their field beds not far from the entrance. The press officer managed to put on his field uniform and run to the operations center, which was also in the station. Wires hung in the air like spaghetti. On the other side of the room he grabbed two of the gray telephones which had a direct line into the Pentagon. There was no dial tone. Running outside, Jordan noticed all the leaves had been blown off the hedges. The cars parked in the lot had been thrown helter-skelter, and refuse had been flung up into the large trees. He saw something which looked like roots. It was the upper torso of a soldier whose legs had been blown away.

When Sergeant Russell was found, he lay on his stomach with a broken left thighbone and pelvis. His leg was cut open from the knee down to a crushed ankle. His left hand was likewise a gaping wound. Yet Russell, who survived later to tell what he had seen, asked to be helped up on his elbows so he could see the building.[67]

At the French military headquarters in Ramlet el-Baida a few kilometers away, a number of soldiers ran out onto their balconies to look at the black smoke that was suddenly rising from the airport. At that same moment, a second truck bomb drove into the building, collapsed it too like a house of cards. Colonel Geraghty fully realized the Americans and the French had been attacked because they had taken sides in the Lebanese civil war. The US had bombarded the opposition in the mountains east of Beirut, and France had dropped bombs onto Shia targets in the Bekaa Valley.[68]

Just a few minutes after the attacks, American intelligence picked up a message:"We succeeded to undertake a spectacular action which caused the earth to shake."[69]

This claim was not entirely true. Brigadier General Carl Stiner and the CIA Station Chief William Buckley were still alive. But the suicide bombers took 56 French and 241 American soldiers with them to their deaths. For the US, this was the largest military loss in one day since D-Day on Iwo Jima in 1945.

Once again, the mysterious Islamic Jihad claimed responsibility for both attacks. But when the Americans declined to retaliate for the attack, it was Israel that struck the Iranian Revolutionary Guards' training camp for Lebanese Shias near Janta village in the Bekaa. They did so on November 16, 1983, the first time Israel had staged an air raid against its new enemy. The jets dropped bombs for 30 minutes, killing nearly three dozen Hizbullah recruits and Iranian instructors. It would be nearly a quarter of a century before Sheikh Sobhi Tufayli, who had been Hizbullah's first secretary-general but had since left the party he helped to found, admitted that people from the then unknown Hizbullah were responsible for bombing the US marine barracks.[70]

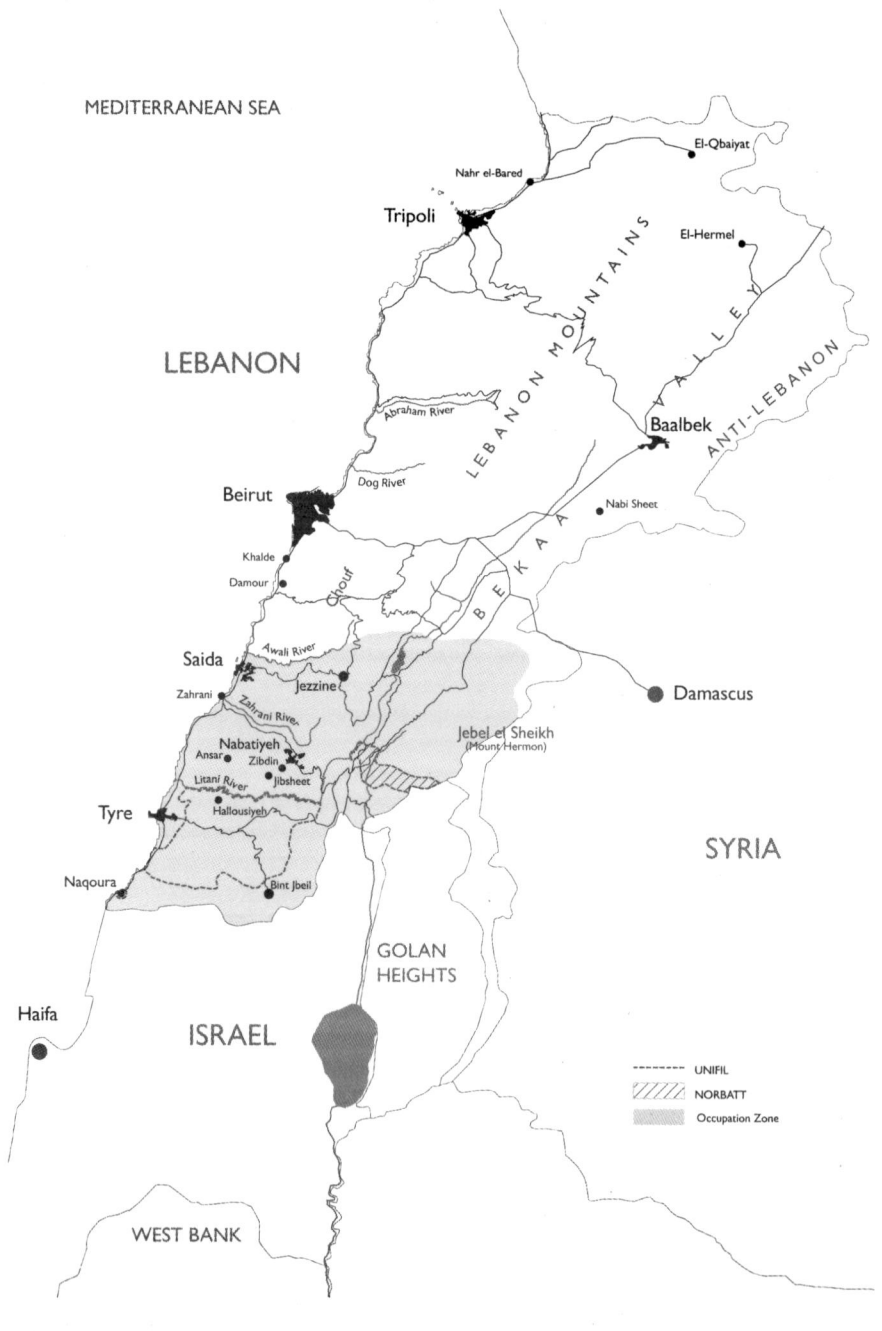

PART TWO

The Militias Take West Beirut

1983-1984

Guerrilla soldiers from the Muslim and secular parties of the Left in Lebanon are the most active in the battle against the Israelis and their Lebanese allies in South Lebanon. But the most spectacular attacks are carried out by young, religious Shias via car bombs.

Israel and the PLO exchange war prisoners with the help of the Red Cross, but the Israelis deceive the aid organization by transferring prisoners to Israel, in violation of the Geneva Conventions. Israel argues that the prisoners would threaten the country's security if they were set free.

In West Beirut, allied militia groups attack the Lebanese government army. The US brings in the world's largest warship against the militias. Following huge losses, the multinational force, led by the US and France, has to withdraw from Lebanon.

MAIN CHARACTERS

Hussein Abbas, Lebanese Shia, Secret Agent for Israel
Ane-Karine Arvesen, Attaché at the Norwegian Embassy in Beirut
Yussef Bazzi, Lebanese Militia Soldier
Nabih Berri, Leader of the Shia Party, Amal
William Buckley, CIA's Station Chief in Beirut
Mohammed Hussein Fadlallah, Shia Cleric
Amine Gemayel, Lebanon's President
Ragheb Harb, Radical Religious Shia Leader in South Lebanon
Jerry Levin, CNN-Correspondent in Beirut
Hussein Moussawi, Second-in-Command of Amal, and Founder of Islamic Amal
Imad Mughniyeh, Radical Lebanese Shia

CHAPTER TEN

Cadmus and the Serpent

Prior to his work with the aid organization Norwegian Peoples Aid, Major Egil Hagen had been the company chief in UNIFIL. He lived next door to the American officers at the Cadmus Hotel in Ain el-Mreisseh, a few hundred meters from Ane-Karine Arvesen's apartment. At the hotel, he met Brigadier General Carl Stiner and the American instructors assisting the Lebanese army. Hagen knew Lebanon better than many of the Americans and had a talent for eliciting stories from his fellow officers.

One evening Hagen and I were eating dinner on Ane-Karine's balcony along with several diplomats when we heard about the plans the Americans were working on. One of the guests called the Americans the Cadmus serpents who had come to Lebanon to serve Israeli interests, not to make Lebanon more democratic. Ane-Karine countered with a reference to the source of the name Cadmus: in Greek mythology, Cadmus was a Phoenician prince who had been transformed into a serpent. His sister, Princess Europa, had been kidnapped by Zeus, the king of the gods. The king ordered all his sons to search for his beloved daughter, and threatened them with exile if she were not found. Prince Cadmus sailed to Greece and sought out the oracle of Delphi, who warned him that the search for Europa was useless. She has become Zeus' wife and did not want to be rescued. The oracle told Cadmus to stay in Greece and build a city that would forever be famous.

Cadmus did as he was asked, and set out to found the city known as Thebes. First he had an altar built to Athena, and then he sent his men out to fetch water for a ritual to procure the goddess' blessing. But the nearby spring belonged to a serpent, a descendent of Ares, the god of violence and war. The serpent would not allow any water to be taken from the spring, and killed all of Cadmus' men. When they failed to return, the prince himself searched for them until he met the giant serpent at the spring. There was a battle, which Cadmus won.

When Ares discovered what had happened, he furiously demanded that Cadmus be transformed into a serpent to take over the guardianship of the spring. However, the goddess Athena protected him. She said to Cadmus, who stood over the dead serpent, "Do not put your eyes upon the creature, or you yourself will become a serpent one day. You should instead plant its teeth in the fields near the city, so Thebes can become mighty in war."

When the teeth were planted, and warriors grew from the soil bearing swords and lances, ready for battle. Athena gave Cadmus a stone. "Am I to fight an entire army with this?" he asked. Athena nodded, and Cadmus realized he could trick the warriors by throwing the stone into their midst. It hit one, and in the ensuing confusion of the warriors fought each other until the ground was soaked with blood. Finally, only five of the strongest remained. Cadmus asked them to put their swords down and join him. Together they would build a new city populated by Phoenicians and the native sons of the Earth.

Ares was embarrassed by how easily Cadmus had slain his warriors, but he saw that they had been neither intelligent nor disciplined. So he made peace with the prince on the condition that he provide eight years of service as a punishment for killing the serpent. Cadmus agreed and became king of Thebes, though his story had a tragic end. After a series of misfortunes, he was ultimately transformed into a serpent, just as the war god had originally demanded.

Ane-Karine ended the story by noting that little had changed so far as the discipline of warriors was concerned. She believed the militia and soldiers operating in Lebanon, whether they were Lebanese, Syrians or Israelis, deserved the bad reputation they had gained for themselves. As far as the Americans were concerned, she thought the soldiers on the ground did as well as they could; it was the leaders in Washington, D.C. who lacked an understanding of what was happening in Lebanon.

Following other stories, wine, coffee and calvados, Egil Hagen returned to his well-guarded hotel. The following morning, he noticed Brigadier General Carl Stiner being driven away. The general was now using the British Embassy in West Beirut as his base, where American diplomats and military advisors also had offices following the destruction of the US Embassy. At the office, Stiner read the daily intelligence reports from the CIA in Beirut, and noticed that Buckley had now reactivated parts of the network destroyed when the CIA agents had been killed in the earlier attack on the embassy. Stiner also realized that he and Buckley were on the Iranian hit list. When he brought the matter up with Buckley, the CIA station chief did not seem concerned. "I have a good intelligence network," he said. "I think I am safe."[1]

There were many working for him, and through their efforts he had managed to map the activities of some of the Iranian Revolutionary Guards and their Lebanese allies in the Bekaa Valley. Correspondents in Beirut and visiting journalists also tried to learn more about groups friendly with the Iranians, who were suspected of being behind the attacks against the Americans and the French.

One of the most experienced was R.W. Apple from *The New York Times*, known as Johnny by his colleagues. I knew him from the time we both reported on the oil spill at the Ekofisk field in the North Sea in April 1977. Together with his colleagues, Apple drove to Bekaa to meet Iran's best-known spearhead in Lebanon, Hussein Moussawi. He had heard rumors that Moussawi had obtained the explosives used in the three big car-bombing attacks in Beirut, and that his cousin, Haidar Moussawi, had gotten a hold of the vehicles that were used. These were rumors, not facts.[2]

Hussein Moussawi had previously been second-in-command of Amal under Nabih Berri. Berri, like Moussawi, was a believing Muslim, but he respected middle class society more than the lower class within the Shia community. While Berri sought political changes to the Lebanese system, mostly for his own interests, Moussawi was influenced by the Islamic revolution in Iran. When Berri had agreed in the summer of 1982 to take part in the so-called National Rescue Committee, which included participants from all the larger religious groups in Lebanon, Moussawi resisted. He did not want Amal to cooperate with the "enemy" Bachir Gemayel, who led the Christian Phalangist militia, the Lebanese Forces.

Moussawi regarded the arrangement as a clever plan put into play by the United States, and his position was supported: from London, Iran's ambassador approached the media and asked Berri to withdraw from the "American Committee." Amal's representative in Iran also opposed Berri, and when Moussawi, who headed the Amal militia in the Bekaa Valley, accused Berri of betraying Imam Moussa Sadr's legacy, the dispute was put before the Iranian ambassador in Damascus.

The Iranians took Moussawi's side. This was understandable for a number of reasons. The Moussawi clan from Nabi Sheet in the Bekaa Valley had a close relationship with the power elite in Tehran. Young men from the village had gone to Iran for their education for generations, while Iranians who were being persecuted by the Shah's secret police, SAVAK, were allowed to hide in the village.

After the Islamic revolution in Iran, the Moussawi clan used these connections to increase its own influence in Lebanon. The clan was not alone in having contacts in Iran. For several hundred years there had been close connections between Shias in Iran and Lebanon. But not all Shias could travel to Tehran and meet prominent Iranian leaders. As a reward for the loyalty they had shown, the Moussawis were given economic support by the Iranians, and with it much prestige.

But Berri refused to bend. It was at that point Moussawi broke with the party. He took several hundred supporters with him and formed a new militia which he called Islamic Amal. Later, it became one of the building blocks for the new Shia party, Hizbullah, which was then developing.

Moussawi had his headquarters in a villa in Baalbek, a few hundred meters from the famous Roman ruins. The Islamic Republic's emblem hung in the entrance area of the villa, and when Moussawi emerged, he smiled broadly at the little group of unannounced journalists led by Johnny Apple from *The New York Times.*

Bodyguards dressed in a hodgepodge of military uniforms stood along the walls, in the entry area and the driveway leading to the secluded villa. A group of Iranian Revolutionary Guards stood nearby. Moussawi sat down in a large chair and fingered his prayer beads. He mumbled *"Bismillah ir-Rahman ir-Rahim"*—in God's name, the most gracious, the most merciful—moving his forefinger and thumb from pearl to pearl along the chain, where each represented one of Allah's ninety nine names.

Though Moussawi came across as calm and balanced, his message was hard and irreconcilable:"The multinational force in Beirut is the army of oppression. The French and American soldiers will not be accepted by Lebanon's Muslim population. We are the ones who make up the majority in the country. There are only a few leaders, with no contact with the people, who wish the forces of the evil powers welcome."

When Moussawi was asked about the car bombings, he replied:"I do not know who drove the vehicles with explosives into the American and French military quarters, but I am certain they were Muslims, perhaps members of a group, perhaps not. It was not just revenge, but a blow on behalf of Lebanon's honor and independence. I bow to the souls of the martyrs who carried out the operations."

The Lebanese militia leader sat with legs crossed and said the Lebanese had prepared themselves for many years to fight against the Israelis and Americans:"We have obtained weapons, and we have obtained burial cloths. We are willing to defend our honor and our country and will be killed in God's name," he said and stroked his black beard. "It is right to fight against evil. Every faithful Lebanese Muslim will be willing to take part in an operation against foreign oppressors. There will be new operations, and I will gladly participate."

When Apple asked whether Moussawi feared retaliation, which President Ronald Reagan had promised, Moussawi just shrugged his shoulders and laughed. Then he added:"If the Americans lay the blame on Islamic Amal, they do me an injustice. Threats such as these are not civilized language."

When asked what several hundred Iranians were doing in Baalbek, he answered that they were here to help the local population to "defend themselves and live a free life." But Moussawi refused to say how many there were. Just before the bombings in Beirut, Moussawi had described the relationship between Iran and Lebanon's Shias as that between a mother and her sons: "We are her children. We are seeking to formulate an Islamic society which in the final analysis will produce an Islamic state… The Islamic revolution will march to liberate Palestine and Jerusalem, and the Islamic state will then spread its authority over the region of which Lebanon is only a part."[3]

CHAPTER ELEVEN
From Flowers to Bombs

I had no difficulty traveling back and forth between Israel and Lebanon that fall of 1983. Things went smoothly with Israeli press credentials and a Norwegian passport, though I had to wait at the Israeli front lines along the Awali River, north of Sidon, together with hundreds of Lebanese. An opening had been made in the front near the village of Bater, just north of Jezzine. A sort of official "border post" had been created where Lebanese had to ask permission of the Israelis to be able to pass within their own land.

The Israeli soldiers at the crossing seemed scared. One day I saw a Lebanese driver walk about 100 meters to report that his car had broken down, and that he had to fetch a mechanic. The soldiers waved him away. Then a soldier shot at the car's fuel tank. The car caught fire. Everyone around fled in panic.

"It could have been a car bomb," the Israeli said coldly.

In the city of Sidon, large intersections bore Israeli signs in Hebrew. All the streets were vigilantly patrolled by Israeli soldiers with their weapons at the ready. One day I was asked by an Israeli officer what I was doing in Sidon. I said I was a journalist, and asked him the same question in return.

"We are here just temporarily in order to protect northern Israel," the officer said, and continued: "This is not any military occupation. We have no military administration here. We have the power, yes, but we do not control the local authorities."

"That does not prevent many Lebanese from calling South Lebanon the North Bank," I answered, and compared the occupation with the conditions on the West Bank, Gaza Strip, Golan Heights, and East Jerusalem. I added that many Lebanese who lived south of the Israeli front lines were eager to know what their new life under permanent occupation would be like. Many were afraid to be completely cut off from Beirut.

There were not only Israelis patrolling Sidon. I saw many men in uniform, but without weapons. They belonged to the Lebanese police. There were also men who lacked uniforms but had weapons. They belonged to the so-called National Guard, a militia controlled by the Israelis. The militia received weapons from the IDF, but no pay. They made their money by extorting funds and goods from the local economy, like the mafia does in other countries, and they did dirty work for hire. In a final configuration, there were uniformed Lebanese with weapons. They belonged to the South Lebanon Army (SLA), under the leadership of Major Saad Haddad. The major had his headquarters in Marjayoun, which in Arabic means "the meadow of springs." Everyone in the SLA was trained, equipped, paid and led by Israelis. Young and grown men from the militia manned the control posts at the intersections in and around Sidon.

During the day, city life seemed normal. The stores in Sidon's main street were full of shoes and clothing from European fashion houses, French cheeses, Danish butter, Swiss chocolate and the latest electronic items from Japan. Israeli soldiers could buy everything much more cheaply than in Israel, and they bought like mad! But when evening came, the streets, stores, restaurants and movie theaters were nearly empty. Few wanted to be seen near an Israeli patrol. The Israelis would shoot wildly if they felt threatened.

Religious Israelis I met spoke of the cities of Sidon and Tyre as a part of Eretz Israel, Israel's Land. I was told Tyre was mentioned 37 times in the Old Testament, the first being in the *Book of Joshua*, where it says that the "fortress town Tyre was a part of the land which God gave to the tribe of the sons of Asher."

The Greek historian Herodotus maintained Tyre was founded at the beginning of the Phoenician age, 2,750 years before Christ, and that the town's tradesmen were "the world's most honorable." The Phoenicians, who did not have any ambition to conquer other lands, made alliances and were long able to protect the city from foreign invasion. They became voluntary allies instead of vassals, and could thereby conduct their trading in peace. This did not mean they allowed themselves to be cowed, as they proved when Alexander the Great tried to take the town, which at the time lay on an island. Only after seven months of siege did Alexander manage to take Tyre by building a causeway from the mainland to the island. When the city had been conquered, half of it was destroyed. The king and his family were spared, while 30,000 of the inhabitants were sold as slaves.[4]

When Israel conquered Tyre some 2,300 years later, it was easy work for the soldiers. The Lebanese did not use their weapons. Only when the Israelis established themselves in the city did attitudes change. The Israelis understood after a while that the majority of Lebanese no longer wanted them in the country. They could see and feel the hate. The flowers and rice they had been greeted with by many, became hand grenades and homemade bombs.

At first, it was the Communists who were best organized to run the resistance fight. Their attacks were not large or spectacular: often a lone man took shots with a pistol or rifle, threw a hand grenade from a housetop or placed a mine or bomb by the roadside. It was the religious Shias who were responsible for the most serious attacks, such as the one that occurred in Tyre on November 11, 1982.

This attack was against an eight-story apartment block, a seemingly innocuous building that lay just north of the intersection of the main street and the coast road which connected the harbor. It was here that the Israeli occupation forces maintained an operations center; quarters for soldiers; improvised cells for Palestinian and Lebanese prisoners and an interrogation center run by the Israeli intelligence and security service, Shin Bet, which operated in parallel with Mossad and the IDF's military intelligence service, Aman.[5] It was a young Shia with thick, dark hair, emotional eyes and a thin, adolescent mustache, Ahmad Qassir, who crashed a white Peugeot fully loaded with explosives into the building. He took 75 Israeli soldiers with him to death, as well as 15 Lebanese and Palestinian prisoners. Qassir's final request was that his identity remain secret until the withdrawal of the Israelis so his family in Deir Qanoun al-Nahr, near Tyre, would not face reprisals.[6]

The 17-year-old Qassir was a childhood friend of Imad Mughniyeh, who would later become very famous as the Chief of Staff for Hizbullah. Mughniyeh had planned the attack carefully and personally reconnoitered the military headquarters in Tyre. The timing was to coincide with the return of eight Israeli night patrols, before the morning patrols departed. In addition, the building was fuller than usual that November day, because Israeli troops had relocated their headquarters when heavy rains damaged their tents in a nearby encampment.

The attack was so shocking that the Israeli High Command would not admit that so many Israelis had been killed in a single attack. A committee was formed to investigate what had happened, and the report concluded the explosion had been an accident. The report, which was long, included a detailed description of household gas containers, leaks and sloppy handling and storage practices. Israeli commentators wrote that it was criminal of the Lebanese to build houses that could collapse simply from a gas explosion in a kitchen.[7]

Since the attack had been filmed, few Lebanese were convinced by the report. Once again Islamic Jihad was credited with the attack—the same organization which planned and carried out the attacks against the American Embassy and the two encampments of the multinational force in Beirut. Islamic Jihad was just one of many names used for a constellation of groups that were all in one way or other tied to the Iranian Revolutionary Guards in Baalbek, and led by Imad Mughniyeh. To Syria's intelligence chief of many years in Lebanon, General Ghazi Kanaan, Mughniyeh was nothing more than "the Iranians' hunting dog."

At 11:05 AM on November 4, 1983, roughly one year after the first attack in Tyre, another Shia drove toward an Israeli roadblock in front of a two-story building in the same city. This building was used by the infamous security service, Shin Bet. The guards shot at the driver, but he managed to keep going for another 20 meters until the vehicle exploded. This time 29 Israelis were killed, most of them members of Shin Bet. In addition, 32 Lebanese lost their lives. They had been held captive in the cellar of the building. Islamic Jihad, once more took responsibility for the operation in an announcement.

The Israeli and American intelligence services were convinced the Lebanese Shias had Iran behind them, directed by the ambassador to Damascus, Ali Akbar Mohtashemi. Since the bombing of the American Embassy in Beirut in April, 1983, he had been wiretapped, and it was noted he had been evacuated just before the attacks against the multinational force in Beirut. Despite their advanced electronic listening equipment, the US had not been able to prevent the attack because they could not infiltrate the most extreme Shia organizations with their own agents.

The CIA later made a few attempts at revenge against the Iranian ambassador. A few months after the attacks on the Americans and the French, Mohtashemi received a book in the mail. It was a bomb masquerading as a beautiful Koran. When the ambassador opened the package it exploded but failed to kill him. He lost sight in one eye and a few fingers on his right hand.

The Phalangist intelligence service had also been able to point to another participant in the car bombings against the multinational force. Colonel Simon Qassis advised that a Lebanese Shia cleric, Sayyed Mohammed Hussein Fadlallah, had blessed the drivers in advance of the attacks. Fadlallah denied this, but did not condemn their actions. The cleric said Muslims are allowed to go into battle and be killed; there was no difference between someone who died with a rifle in hand, and one who attacks an enemy with a car filled with explosives.[8]

Once more, Ane-Karine Arvesen was among the best informed of the western observers in West Beirut. She was able to tell that Fadlallah's father had been an ayatollah, a title which derives from *Ayat Allah*—God's sign—and that the family came from Ainata near Bint Jbeil in South Lebanon. The family had moved to Najaf in Iraq, but remained in constant contact with the Shias in Lebanon.

When Mohammed Fadlallah moved to Lebanon, he first settled in a district in East Beirut near the area called Bourj Hamoud, where both Shias and Armenians lived. Here, in the Nab'a district, Fadlallah wrote poetry and books about religion, and also founded a children's home. But in the summer of 1976, the Shias were driven from the Nab'a by the Phalangists, to the advantage of Christian refugees. These had in turn been driven from their homes in Damour, south of Beirut, which now had been taken over by Palestinian forces. After this, Fadlallah changed from a quiet cleric to a radical activist. In his next books he argued that the weak were within their rights to use all available means to defend themselves. Fadlallah denied this was terrorism; it was justifiable self-defense. Ane-Karine quoted one of his statements:"Power allows people to make a choice from free will. Power helps to determine fate. Only the strong can live a just and god-fearing life."

After a year in South Lebanon, Fadlallah moved to the Shia-dominated part of the city called Bir Abed in the southern portion of West Beirut. He gathered around him young men who were part of the Muslim Students' Association. Among those were several who would play important roles in the growth of Lebanon's Hizbullah.

CHAPTER TWELVE

Growing Shia Activism

During the late summer of 1983, Yasser Arafat and his closest supporters were back in Lebanon, but only in the north of the country. They had been smuggled in through Syrian control posts less than a year after their evacuation from Beirut.

There were battles going on between Arafat's men and Palestinian factions under Syrian control as I drove to the Palestinian refugee camp Nahr el-Bared—Cold River—near Tripoli, in October 1983. But I had not gone there to report on the battles. Together with the French photographer Françoise Demulder from *Time Magazine*, I had come to the camp to meet six Israeli prisoners of war. The Israeli soldiers had been held in a private house along with their guards—the same Palestinian soldiers who had taken them captive in the first place. It had been the PLO leader's second-in-command, Khalil al-Wazir, better known as Abu Jihad, who had given us permission to meet the Israeli soldiers.

With a tape recorder and a small notebook, I spoke to each man in turn, away from where the Palestinian guards could hear us. Eliyahu Abutbul, Dani Gilboa, Rafi Hazan, Reuven Cohen, Avraham Motevaliski and Avraham Kornfeld had all been taken on the same day, September 4, 1982, near the front lines in the Bekaa Valley. They has been fooled by a Hebrew-speaking Palestinian while they were on guard duty.[9] All six were of course homesick, but they said they had been treated well. They ate the same food as their guards, who spoke to them in Hebrew. After I had interviewed each of them, they were all allowed to send a greeting to their families in Israel. I promised to bring the greetings on my next visit to Jerusalem. But when I contacted the Israeli authorities to obtain the families' addresses, I got no help.

The conditions of the Palestinian prisoners in Ansar were different. There, the prisoners were treated so brutally that the chief of the International Red Cross Committee (ICRC) in Lebanon, Michel Amiguet, threatened to boycott the camp in protest. The day the Shin Bet headquarters in Tyre had been blown up was particularly bad. With dead Israelis being dug from the ruins, the guards in Ansar took their anger out on the prisoners.

During the evening count, five prisoners were found missing, and things got even worse. The Israelis spotted the underground tunnel where they were hiding. Two came out on their own after the Israelis opened fire and injured one of them. The others were killed when two bulldozers drove back and forth over the tunnel, collapsing it and crushing the helpless men. The Red Cross protested to Israel, but since the organization was bound by a pledge of silence, the killings did not become publicly known.[10]

In the Palestinian refugee camp near Tripoli, the PLO's second-in-command said the Red Cross was in the final stages of negotiations with Israel on a prisoner exchange. The negotiations had been going on for nearly two months. Initially, Arafat had demanded the release of between 2,000 and 3,000 Palestinians from Israeli prisons, in addition to the nearly 5,000 prisoners in the Ansar camp. The Israelis refused to release any prisoners from Israeli prisons, but agreed to release everyone in Ansar. After a while Arafat reduced one of his demands: He would be satisfied if 100 Palestinian prisoners in Israel were freed. Among those were 36 high-level PLO officers whom the Israelis had captured from a passenger ship sailing between Cyprus and Lebanon.

When the agreement was reached, the Israelis turned over 4,500 prisoners from Ansar to the Red Cross. Of these 1,100 were driven to Israel in buses and then flown to Algeria. The rest were let out of the camp gates and helped further by the Red Cross.

The six Israelis in Nahr el-Bared were driven by the Red Cross to the harbor in Tripoli, just a few kilometers from the villa where they had been held. From there a small boat took them to a French ship, which then transferred them to an Israeli naval vessel on November 23, 1983. In the meantime, the Israelis had deceived the Red Cross. In secrecy, they had driven nearly 200 Palestinian prisoners to Israel in the weeks prior to the exchange. They also rearrested one of the released prisoners while he was supposed to be under the protection of the Red Cross, just before his flight from Tel Aviv to Algeria. When the Red Cross protested to Israel's prime minister and defense minister about this breach of promise, the response was that they had acted because of "national security concerns."[11]

By January 1984, the Israelis were once again filling up the concentration camp at Ansar. Many of the 200 prisoners had been behind the barbed wire and earthen berms before, but the majority were there for the first time. The conditions in the camp were better than before and the prisoners were no longer mistreated, according to what a representative of the Red Cross told Ane-Karine. This was only a half-truth. This time the prisoners were mistreated and tortured by the Israelis and their Lebanese allies at other locations. Some young Shias were interrogated and tortured for up to 30 days before they were sent to Ansar and were able to tell the Red Cross what they had undergone.

The aid organization also reported on Israeli abuse of religious leaders in South Lebanon. In the Shia village of Hallousiyeh, the Israeli forces ransacked the local Imam's house and threw all his books out the window before taking him into custody. Later he was forced to tell them who belonged to the resistance movement. Five young men from the village were arrested and carried off. The Israeli soldiers ended the operation by destroying the Iman's house with a bulldozer. Then they brought the Imam along to Israel. The Red Cross also told of children who were taken for interrogation. After an eight-year-old had been thoroughly interrogated, he was released in the dark of night many kilometers away from his village.

The Norwegian diplomats in Beirut were in the meantime most preoccupied reporting on the political developments in Lebanon, among other things on how Shia activism was growing. While Amal's leader Nabih Berri seemed open to the Norwegian diplomats, the radical Shias were less willing to talk about their strategies. The diplomats had to piece together bits of information like a jigsaw puzzle.

From her office at the embassy in Rue Bliss, Ane-Karine could look down on the American University of Beirut. The campus consisted of a group of yellow-brown buildings with red roof tiles, a clock tower and pine trees, with the blue Mediterranean as a backdrop. The university, which in Beirut was simply referred to as the AUB, , had become a symbol of the United States along with the embassy and The American University Hospital. For over a century it had been the gateway to knowledge for many Arab youths.

On January 18, 1984, two men in their 30s entered the university grounds. They were seen taking the elevator to the third floor where the university president, Malcolm Kerr, had his office. The 52-year-old American arrived after them, and when he stepped outside the elevator, there waited the two Lebanese. They shot him with a pistol equipped with a silencer, and left before anyone could react.

Diana Mahfouz, a full-time student, was on the fourth floor when the shots were fired. She had not heard anything, but several minutes later was told about a man lying on the floor. Diana ran down and saw the university president lying lifeless between the elevator and the stairs, his glasses at his side. Her first thought was that the Israelis had to have been behind the attack. Two years earlier when the Israelis invaded West Beirut, Kerr had stood in the entrance to the university and single-handedly stopped soldiers who wanted to arrest Palestinians inside. "This is American property," Kerr had said, something which made him quite popular among the students and employees.[12]

Diana Mahfouz was wrong: it had not been Israelis who killed Kerr. A few hours later the *Associated Press* office received a phone call from a man who said he represented Islamic Jihad. Once more the voice spoke with a Lebanese accent. The speaker explained that this murder, along with the kidnapping of David Dodge the previous year, were revenge for the kidnapping of four Iranian diplomats taken by the Phalangists in 1982. Then the man hung up.

Despite this explanation, Malcolm Kerr was killed primarily because he was a symbol of the West. The murder was well-planned. A young female student had smuggled in the pistols and buried them by a tree near College Hall, where they remained until a *fatwa* was issued condemning the American to death.[13] Not only was the murder cold-blooded, it was also a warning that no American in Lebanon should feel safe.

The diplomats at the Norwegian Embassy did not feel threatened, though an American had been killed just a few hundred meters away. There were many killings in Beirut, and it could have been anyone who was behind this latest one, even if Islamic Jihad took responsibility. The Hizbullah Party had still not established itself in the Lebanese conscience as a new political movement. Only the best informed diplomats, academics and journalists mentioned this new phenomenon, which took its name from a verse in the Koran that promised victory for those who joined Hizbullah—God's Party. During a number of intense and informal, long and at times alarming dinners, I got to hear about the new, loosely connected umbrella organization. It was the product of a series of historical events, not just the Israeli invasion.

The seeds for what would become Hizbullah were found in the 1979 Islamic revolution in Iran. In the new Iran, a religious cleric—in this case, Ayatollah Khomeini—was to have the supreme power. No one could go against his authority, either in spiritual or political questions. Ideologically, the eventual founders of God's Party in Lebanon were inspired by an ayatollah from Iraq, where Khomeini had also been active. Muhammed Baqir al-Sadr was leader of the Dawa Party, which was pushing for an Islamic state in Iraq. The goal was also to spread the Islamic *dawa*, or awakening, to the rest of the Islamic world. After a while Islamic Amal, Islamic Jihad and groups that called themselves God's Army, Hussein's Death Squadron and The Revolutionary Justice Organization all fused together to become Hizbullah. Other members came from the business world, from various trade guilds and from the working class. The common goal was to destroy the existing Lebanese state and create an Islamic Republic following the Iranian model, with Ayatollah Khomeini as the supreme authority.

These radical Shias viewed the election of President Amine Gemayel as a consequence of the Israeli invasion. Gemayel represented Kataeb—The Phalange Party—which officially was called Lebanese Social Democratic Party and was dominated by Maronites. But for the Shias, the Gemayel regime was less of a threat than Israel and the US. The "serpent's head" was Israel, and its "back" was the United States; the Lebanese government was merely the tail of the snake. The tail would be incapacitated once the head and back were truncated, stated the founder of Islamic Amal.[14]

CHAPTER THIRTEEN

The Fight for West Beirut

At the end of January 1984, Ane-Karine Arvesen reported to the Norwegian Foreign Office that President Amine Gemayel was the biggest roadblock to reconciliation among Lebanon's many factions. According to the diplomat, the president was "even according to Lebanese standards, too rough, too corrupt and too egotistical." If Gemayel remained, he would have to change the style and content of his politics. But he was unwilling to do this. In cooperation with the Americans, the president instead was planning an offensive.

From his base at the Cadmus Hotel, Egil Hagen kept Ane-Karine informed of what he heard from the American instructors. One day she learned the Lebanese army was getting ready to attack the Druze and Shia militias. Hagen told her the army would first attack the Druze in the Chouf Mountains, and that the attack would come in the next 10 days. The American advisors thought the army was not strong enough to hit the Druze and Shia militias at the same time.

Hagen thought the Druze would win the fight for the Chouf Mountains, where the Christians and Druze lived together in the same villages, much like Christians and Muslims lived together in other places in Lebanon. Many of the Christians in Chouf, according to Hagen's view, would be driven out. He thought the Israelis wanted chaos, and that a new flood of refugees to the Christian villages near the Israeli border would suit them well. Young vengeful Christians could join the SLA and make the militia stronger.

Ane-Karine checked her story. She learned that the Druze and the Shias were going to get a jump on the army through a political move. The leader of the Druze, Walid Jumblatt, and Amal's leader, Nabih Berri, challenged the Sunni prime minister, Shafik al-Wazzan, to withdraw from the government. He acceded, and President Gemayel was therefore left isolated. The government's plan to send the army into the Chouf Mountains was put aside.

In an attempt to form a new government, the president tried to negotiate with the part of the opposition that wanted political reform. All issues were on the table: legislation, exercise of power, the legal system and the composition of the government. Too late, answered the opposition, those suggestions should have come months ago.

Then Gemayel tried to get the opposition allied with him by refusing to ratify the agreement with Israel that had been signed the previous May. On February 5, 1984, he announced, "This agreement has not led to any withdrawal. Instead it has led us to the breaking point." This move did not help. The opposition wanted the government army out of West Beirut.

Berri and Jumblatt gathered new supporters, among them members of the Syrian Social National Party (SSNP) and also the radical Shias supported by Iran. The Shias threw in their lot with the opposition because a victory over the government army might enable them to become more active in West Beirut. Many of the young Shias who were getting ready to fight there had little sense of their radical co-religionists. One of these was Yussef Bazzi. His father came from a well-known family in Bint Jbeil. His mother was Christian. He himself was not particularly concerned with religion. Three years earlier he had joined the SSNP militia—but he had been paid to participate.

When the Israelis advanced into West Beirut in September 1982, Yussef was ready to fight. But when the soldiers drew nearer, he and several friends were overcome with panic. Yussef took off his uniform and ran home to his mother in only his underwear.[15]

Two years later Yussef had become a bit braver, and when the signal came around midday he did not run home, but to a house near the Bristol Hotel where there was an ammunition stash. Together with seven others he drove on toward the central business district. Traffic was light. People in the shops and on the sidewalks did not know what was about to happen. Suddenly, like lightning from a clear blue sky, the militia group struck. Yussef and his gang took over the whole quarter surrounding a shopping center near Rue Hamra.

The government declared martial law and said anyone out of doors would be shot on the spot. Those who did not want to fight went home. Everyone else tried to find shelter from the bullets as the horns of the cars honked. Thunder from artillery, rockets and automatic weapons could be heard over vast areas of West Beirut.

"Let's go to the prison and free our friends," Yussef suggested. But they arrived too late: others had been there first. They tried the radio station next, but found a similar situation. Militia from Amal had taken over the station without firing a shot. Yussef and his gang were told to go to one of the bombed-out hotels near the front.

Throughout the civil war in the 1970s there had been whorehouses in the area; some lay right up against the front lines. One of these bordellos was particularly infamous among the militia in West Beirut. Here the clients might experience death right after their orgasms. Two of the prostitutes cooperated with the Christian militia on the other side of the front, and when preselected Muslim militia clients had "finished", they were taken out through a secret door on the wrong side of the front line. There they fell right into the hands of a Christian militia group that awaited them with sharp knives. When the Muslim militia leader in the Ain el-Mreisseh district finally discovered why some of his men were disappearing without a trace, he made short shrift of the two women. One was killed, dismembered and placed in two barrels, which were filled with concrete and dropped into the Mediterranean right in front of where I had been living for four years.

On this February 6, 1984, Yussef and his friends had been given orders to drive the government army out of West Beirut. But when they arrived at the hotel district, they found only two lost, uniformed men who said they were Muslims. Yussef and his gang took the soldiers' American M-16 rifles and ordered them to take off their uniforms, which two of the youths put on as camouflage in exchange for their civilian clothes. They got little use out of them, however, because the fight for the central part of West Beirut—that is, the business district—was already over before the government army had time to organize itself. Instead, Yussef and his friends robbed a warehouse full of Toyotas, Jeeps and Land Rovers. The youths, who had curly hair, tight jeans and Marlboro cigarette boxes rolled into their sleeves, were in their element.

Diplomats at the Norwegian Embassy were not gun-shy, but when cannon fire increased and the grenades impacted closer, they decided it was best to stay at home. Embassy Counsellor Gunnar Flakstad managed to get a telex message through to the Foreign Office: "There are now fierce battles and explosions all over West Beirut, and absolute martial law. The embassy employees are in their apartments and do not know whether they will be able to get to the embassy tomorrow... I must cut the connection now because there are explosions right outside the house, and I am sitting by an open window..."[16]

Even if the government army was caught with its pants down in West Beirut, it continued to fight in the southern part of the city, firing artillery on large, densely populated areas from positions in East Beirut. Desperate refugees poured from the quarters nearest the front line. In some streets it was impossible to drive because of all the junk that had fallen from the buildings or because the streets were full of bomb craters. Shots were exchanged as some refugees tried to enter abandoned apartments. Others went into cellars to wait until the fighting was over.

Ane-Karine eventually made contact with two observers from the UN ceasefire organization, the United Nations Truce Supervision Organization (UNTSO), which was positioned in the hills east of Beirut, not far from the defense ministry in Yarze.[17] Two Irish observers with binoculars were watching the irresponsible bombardment of the Shia parts of the city. They concluded that the government army was trying to destroy as much as possible. The bombardments were not directed at military targets. At one point the observers counted 24 tanks that rolled into that part of the city and fired away at apartment buildings where there was no militia.

In West Beirut, Nabih Berri called a press conference. "I can understand that the army wants to try to get control over areas we have taken," he said. "But why must it bombard Shia residential areas? Why must the army destroy schools, hospitals and children's homes?"

While Berri spoke, bomb detonations could be heard. Again he challenged every "Lebanese and patriotic soldier" to refuse to take part in the attacks against the civilian population. "I don't ask you to desert," Ane-Karine heard him say on the radio. "But if you get orders to fight, leave your posts."

Yussef Bazzi and his militia gang went to the party headquarters where their leader, Abu Rashid, was furious that they had been looting. "Get into the car!" he screamed.

"Where are we going?"

"Damned assholes! To Dahiyeh!" This was the name of the southern part of Beirut which was mostly occupied by Shias from South Lebanon.

Beirut had once more become the Chicago of the Levant. Everyone could hear the intense firing in the region of the front. The air was thick with the smoke of artillery fire and dust, and houses were burning everywhere. Yussef could see that artillery had been set up in the middle of the streets, shells streaking from their muzzles at regular intervals. More fell constantly all around him, on all sides. Balconies collapsed in front of his eyes, just a few meters away.

Yussef's militia group joined the fight and were given new supplies of ammunition. He took a shoulder weapon to use against tanks. His friend, Ali, dragged a case of ammunition along. The group advanced under the command of a third man who knew the area. To their left they saw militia from what was to become Hizbullah, advancing toward a church near the no man's land between East and West Beirut. To their right were the militia from Amal moving against another quarter.

As the militia groups' offensives began, friendly positions in the mountains to the east and in Beirut ceased their artillery fire. This was to prevent Yussef and the others who were near the army positions from being killed by friendly fire. The army continued its bombardment. Yussef ran ahead to enter a building but encountered a barricade at the entrance. He emptied his automatic weapon and reloaded while the group split in two. One part would cover the other while it advanced, and then they would switch.

The group leader went first, running and then throwing himself onto the ground. Yussef followed. A grenade exploded just a few meters away. He froze and checked to see he was in one piece. He had not been hit, but his companion was holding his stomach as blood gushed out. He did not scream, but suffered in silence while Yussef and the others fired at the enemy. Their weapons were glowing hot. But their volley was not answered. Perhaps the soldiers behind the barricade had fled? There was another minute of silence. Several of the militia members came running and threw hand grenades against the barricade. Still no return fire. They advanced into the building. It was empty. But out in the back courtyard they were fired at by a sniper and barely managed to take cover behind a wall of cinder blocks.

Yussef decided to wait until dark. An allied militia group took over a nearby house, and from the top floor they could see where the sniper was hiding. They peppered him with bullets, and then gave Yussef a signal that he could take the chance to run ahead. He did so but the sniper was not dead. Bullets hit just centimeters from Yussef's head.

It was as if the angel of death was toying with him. His eyes wide open, Yussef was blinded by a trick of the mind, like an inexplicable fog lay before him. Just the same he fired like a wild man, ran and fired again, until his magazine was empty. He had then come into the lee of a building which seemed abandoned. Three others were standing out of breath nearby; a fourth hid just in front of them. It was impossible to count the number of cannons thundering, and these young men were in the middle of it all.

One of the more daring fighters entered the building and the others followed. Yussef lay down by the entrance that opened onto a residential area to the right. His heart was pounding and his throat was dry as sandpaper. It was then that a mother and her several daughters carefully stuck their heads up from the cellar steps. More militia gradually arrived at the building and silence took over for a brief while—at least long enough for them to spread out. They found abandoned tanks and a bunch of ammunition boxes. Then they were given sandwiches, cigarettes, water and reinforcements.

A few hours later, Yussef could relax. It was evening and he had not slept for a long time. Three corpses were carried in—three Lebanese soldiers. Yussef could not remember who pulled out their gold teeth, but the gold was worth four grams of cocaine. Eventually the woman and her daughters went to sleep in the cellar. Eighteen-year-old Fatima, the oldest, came up to the resting soldiers with a candle. She whispered to Yussef, asking him to come in and play cards with her. They went off into a corner near the bathroom, where the young militia soldier was rewarded with half an hour's love.

Beirut and the surrounding area was in chaos, of a sort described in Thomas Hobbes' *Leviathan*. He wrote that in a state without an absolute government, everyone would be warring against everyone else. Even if it was more realistic to speak of a "strong" government than an absolute one in 1984, contemporary Lebanon did not put Hobbes' prediction to shame.

The militia that Yussef had joined was only one of roughly 150 armed groups in Lebanon, including the government's own army, which, to be sure, was not the strongest. There were 10 mini-states, or cantons, where people lived based on one religious belief, or several of them together. Along the 200 kilometer long coastline were approximately 18 illegal ports. The various militias collected income by demanding taxes or tolls on goods, and in exchange they protected "their own" against "others."[18]

CHAPTER FOURTEEN
Defeat

On February 14, 1984, I wrote in my little black notebook:"Yesterday, the Druze forced out the Phalangists and the government army from the villages in the Chouf Mountains. Amal forced the army out of Khalde and Damour. All of West Beirut is in the hands of the militia."

That same morning, Ane-Karine had driven around West Beirut to observe. She was so hungry for knowledge that she wanted to check the situation before the embassy even opened for the day. She knew the news in the morning press would already be old. Her daily report to the Foreign Office would be fresh blood.

At lunch time, she went to the Commodore Hotel where she had an appointment with William Claiborne from *The Washington Post*. The two had barely sat down when a group of bearded young men came into the hotel reception. The youths were loaded down with weapons and ammunition. Some were dressed in army uniforms. Ane-Karine wondered if the uniforms were spoils of war, or if the soldiers had deserted. One of the men approached the bar. The bartender, who was a Shia, had expected a visit from the militia and had replaced his shelves of liquor bottles with Coca Cola, tonic, soda and mineral water. But the intruders were not fooled. Under the circular bar counter they found the whiskey, gin, and cognac bottles. They smashed the bottles, one after the other, and left the hotel.[19]

The lunch guests were not distracted. Within the course of the next hour, Ane-Karine learned more about what had happened over the last two days. More than 300 people had been killed in Beirut, and the numbers at the American Embassy had been reduced to a skeleton staff. Around 40 diplomats and their families had been evacuated by military helicopter. President Reagan had given orders to use air attacks and cannon from the American warships off the coast in order to protect the soldiers on land. Ane-Karine said she had been in the Chouf and had seen how the American artillery shells toppled the ruins of the abandoned villages. The bombardments were apparently a demonstration of force toward the Muslims, to show what power supported the Phalangists.

During the meal, powerful new explosions could be heard, caused by the USS New Jersey, the world's largest battleship, which had taken up a position just off the coast. Built during the Second World War, the ship had not taken part in any military actions since 1945, but it was known that its cannon could fire shells weighing around 1.2 tons each against targets 38 kilometers away. From the southern parts of Beirut people could see the silhouette of the battleship and the long tongues of flame from its gun barrels. The city shook. The horrendous explosions caused many to head for the shelters.

With the initial strike, Ane-Karine had checked her watch. It was 1:25 pm. The battleship could spit out shells as heavy as a Volkswagen, and over the next nine hours it fired around 700 shots, 250 of which were the largest caliber. The bombardment by the world's largest battleship did not help President Amine Gemayel. West Beirut had been lost. The Shias dominated the map. Water bearers and woodcutters from South Lebanon and the Bekaa Valley, who had come to Beirut to improve their living conditions, had just taken a large step up the power ladder in Lebanon.

Right before the New Jersey began bombarding the mountains, the large British contingent of 115 men had left Beirut, picked up by helicopter and flown to a transport vessel. Their positions were taken over by the Lebanese army. Later, the Italians and the French also pulled out of the city.

At the airport, 1,470 American soldiers awaited new orders from the Pentagon. President Reagan had decided they should be withdrawn in phases. Everyone knew this was capitulation. The American soldiers' arrogant tone had been noticeably reduced. Reagan had previously said that the American presence in Lebanon was necessary so the government in Beirut could survive. His administration had stood firm against Congress on the matter. As late as February 3, 1984, the president had said, "As long as there is a chance for peace, the mission remains the same. If we get out, that means the end of Lebanon."[20] The US Commander-in-Chief had also believed that if "Lebanon lands under the heels of forces which represent enemies of the West, not only our strategic position in the Middle East will be threatened, but the stability of the entire region."[21]

The American government's spokesman tried to give the impression that the retreat was in accordance with previous policy. Secretary of Defense Caspar Weinberger maintained that the US forces would not be removed, just repositioned to a place where they could be more effective. Few believed him. The US defeat in Lebanon was a fact, and the Americans had recognized they could no longer play a determining role in the country. There was no longer any peace to preserve, no national government to defend. These lay in ruins, just like the city of Beirut. The army had crumbled. Fewer than half of the soldiers followed the orders of the Chief of the General Staff. The rest had joined various Muslim militias. With every single American shell fired, the situation became more dangerous for President Gemayel and for the more than 2,500 American citizens living in Beirut. The next kidnapping victim was a 50-year-old American professor at AUB. Frank Regier had grown up in the Lebanese capital as the son of a missionary. He was abducted on February 10, 1984, as he left the university campus. Once more, Islamic Jihad announced it was responsible.

Few foreigners in Beirut connected the kidnapping with a trial that would begin a few days later in Kuwait. Seventeen men were accused of bombing six targets in the capital two months before, on December 12, 1983. The attacks resembled those perpetrated against the American Embassy and the multinational force in West Beirut. First, a truck bomb rammed the annex to the American Embassy building in Kuwait City. Its cargo was 45 gas cylinders bound with wire to an igniter. The L-shaped building collapsed, although the embassy building itself remained standing.

An hour later a car exploded where it had been parked outside the French Embassy in the Gulf State. In that case, only the wall surrounding the embassy was destroyed. Yet another car bomb detonated by the airport control tower, a fourth at the control center for the power station, and a fifth in a residential quarter that housed American employees of Raytheon Company, which was installing new defense missiles in Kuwait. The sixth bomb was set to go off at Kuwait's largest oil refinery. A large yellow truck with no license plates drove 200 gas cylinders into the complex. The vehicle exploded but did not ignite the oil installation.

The men behind the attacks would probably not have been caught if the driver at the American Embassy had not left a clue behind—his own thumb, with its fingerprint in tact. With this information about the bomber, the police were able to trace his co-conspirators, 21 men in all. Four managed to flee Kuwait, but 17 were arrested.

The trial began February 11, 1984, in what was once a school. Military forces were on guard around the building. Inside there were twice as many soldiers as permitted. The accused were locked in a large cage, each dressed in the dark blue sweat shirts and baggy canvas pants that were standard dress for prisoners in Kuwait. Only a few diplomats and selected government representatives were given access to the courtroom because the trial was to be conducted in secrecy.[22]

Six weeks and 46 witnesses later, the decision came. Six of the defendants were condemned to death. All belonged to the forbidden Dawa Party, which supported an Islamic revolution throughout the entire Middle East and Gulf. Two were Lebanese Shias. One of them, Mustafa Badruddin, was the brother-in-law of Imad Mughniyeh, who was the architect behind the kidnapping of Professor Regier. Mughniyeh decided he would get the 17 accused in Kuwait set free.

In Beirut, the Americans' humiliating evacuation was nearing an end. Midday on February 26, 1984, when the last American soldiers left the war-torn city, Ane-Karine was standing with an American journalist on the beach to the south of the airport. To see his own people go off like this seemed degrading to the journalist. From an evacuated American watchtower nearby, they could hear the jubilation of Shia militiamen celebrating their victory over a superpower.

Just before, there had been a short ceremony at the airport, where the Americans turned the area over to the Lebanese army. When the American flag had been lowered and folded, a Lebanese officer approached with a Lebanese flag, which he gave to the Americans and said, "You may as well take this one with you also." Then the officer asked if the Americans could take him to the defense ministry in Yarze by helicopter. He was a Christian and feared for his life if he had to pass through the Muslim roadblocks in West Beirut. The American officer agreed and dropped the Lebanese off on the way to the 20 American warships that waited off the coast.

The airport in Beirut was now in the hands of Amal, who turned it over to the Lebanese army's sixth brigade, which was under the command of a Shia colonel and likewise manned by Shias. They had all refused to fight against Amal in the battle for West Beirut. The military positions along the front line between East and West Beirut, which the French soldiers previously had manned, were taken over by Amal's militia and the Druze on the west side, and by the Phalangists on the east side. Gradually these positions were taken over by Lebanese police forces and reserves called up from the army. The front, which early in the civil war was called "the red line," stretched from Beirut harbor southward along the old Damascus Road. As the years went on, trees and bushes grew in this no-man's-land, and the front got its name changed to "the green line."[23]

From Tehran, Ayatollah Khomeini congratulated the Shias in Lebanon. He said it was his own martyrs who had thrown the Americans out of Lebanon, and he challenged Hussein Moussawi and other radical Shia leaders in Lebanon to intensify their fight against the United States.

In the US, President Reagan's new national security advisor, Robert McFarlane, blamed President Amine Gemayel for not having undertaken internal political reforms. McFarlane, who had been appointed the previous October, also blamed Secretary of Defense Caspar Weinberger and Ambassador Philip Habib. They should have been better negotiators, he thought. Further, the State Department and George Shultz came under criticism for not having foreseen the mess Israel and Syria had created. On the other hand, Caspar Weinberger accused McFarlane and Secretary of State George Shultz of not realizing what adventures they had launched. The Lebanese government, for their part, blamed the United States for having run off with its tails between its legs, and Syria and Israel for having divided Lebanon between them.

Meanwhile in Kuwait, Imad Mughniyeh's brother-in-law and the other Shias condemned to death sat hoping their friends in Beirut would get them freed. Professor Regier's kidnapping had not led to anything. Mughniyeh thought the pressure against the US had to be increased. As he saw it, the use of force was the only language the Americans understood.

CHAPTER FIFTEEN
A Drop of Honey

When the multinational force left Lebanon, the situation for President Amine Gemayel became increasingly difficult. The pressure from the opposing militias and from Syria eventually became so strong that he had to turn his back on Israel. On March 5, 1984, he officially cancelled the May 17th Agreement with the Jewish state. In practice, the agreement had been dead ever since news leaked of the Israelis' secret agreement with the US that the withdrawal of the IDF was conditioned upon Syria retreating from Lebanon.

With the May 17th Agreement officially out of the picture, President Assad could once again demonstrate that he was the foremost player behind the scenes in Lebanon. Assad had used cunning and power to prevent Israel from harvesting a political or economic gain from the invasion. It was "a victory for the Lebanese and Syrian people as well as for the entire Arab nation," according to an announcement from Syria, when the agreement was filed away in the archives and Israel's offices in East Beirut were shut. In the streets of Damascus there was a mixture of elation from victory and fear for what might happen.

When I spoke with the Lebanese about what role foreign powers had played in Lebanon's history in the 19th and 20th centuries, it often led to long discussions. Some thought all of Lebanon's bad luck could be blamed on foreign intervention. Others thought deep internal division was itself the reason various factions sought help from outside groups.

Ane-Karine was well acquainted with Lebanese history and gave me a thorough introduction to the developments following the outbreak of civil war in 1860, when the Maronite farmers revolted against other Christian overlords in North Lebanon. The revolt spread southward and changed character. The Druze went after the Maronites. France had long supported the Maronites; Great Britain was on the side of the Druze.

The shots that started the civil war were fired by a group of Maronites against several dozen Druze in the outskirts of Beirut on Friday, May 18, 1860. After only a few days, more than 60 villages were partially destroyed. The battles spread to Damascus, where the Ottomans and the army shut their eyes while tens of thousands of Christians were massacred by the Druze and other Muslims.

The Druze belong to a tight-knit religious community with origins in Shia Islam. "The Sons of Mercy" were loyal to each other to the extreme. The community grew following the battle for leadership within Islam during the 8th century. Shias had already separated from the Sunnis, but then the Shias split up as well, during an internal conflict over who was the rightful successor to the sixth Shia Imam. The splinter group became the Druze.

The 1860 massacres were kept alive through historical retellings. But there were various versions, and when the Lebanese discussed the different civil wars in the country's history, the atmosphere could become quite tense even at the nicest dinner parties. In such cases, it was often good to refer to the story of the drop of honey, which goes like this: There once was a man who went hunting with his dog in the Lebanese mountains. It was a warm day, so warm in fact that all the animals hid in whatever shade they could find. The hunter walked and walked but saw nothing he could shoot. Only when he had arrived outside a well-known hunting area did he see something of interest: a bee!

If there are bees, there must also be honey, the hunter reasoned. He followed the bee with his eyes until it flew into a cave not far away. The hunter followed and found the beehive with its honey. He packed the honey carefully in his headscarf, or *kuffiyeh*, and decided to return home. But the weather was so hot that the hunter feared the honey would melt before he got there. Catching sight of a closer village down in the valley below, he decided to go there to sell the sought-after honey. The hunter's faithful hound followed along.

In the village there was a small shop, and the owner was sitting outside in the shade of a tree. The hunter offered him the honey and opened the scarf to show what he had. That same second, a drop of the honey fell to the ground. The sweet smell attracted a fly, which landed on the droplet. A small bird flew by and immediately dove down and swallowed the insect. The shopkeeper's cat, which had been asleep at his side, leapt forward, caught the bird and killed it. The hunter's dog threw his powerful paw out and killed the cat with a single blow. When the shopkeeper saw his beloved cat lying lifeless on the ground, he became furious and beat the hunter's dog to death.

Now it was the hunter's turn to react. He shot the shopkeeper and left the village in haste. When the villagers discovered what had happened, they armed themselves and followed his trail. When they arrived at the hunter's village, they attacked and killed the hunter and his family. The rest of the village then sought revenge, and thus began the civil war in Lebanon, according to the story.

Regardless of political position, everyone knew that it was not a drop of honey that had led to civil war in 1975. At this point agreement ended, however, even if certain historical facts were not in dispute. On April 13, 1975, several hundred Maronites had gathered outside to inaugurate a new church in the poor and densely populated Christian quarter in Ain el-Rummaneh in East Beirut. The leader of the Phalangists, Pierre Gemayel, was also present. In the middle of the ceremonies a car drove up to the church and peppered the gathering with bullets. Four men, among them one of Sheikh Pierre's bodyguards, lay dead as the gunmen disappeared. Kataeb's militia, led by Pierre's youngest son Bashir, took up weapons to avenge the killings.

That same morning, Palestinian refugees from the Tel el-Zaatar camp in East Beirut took part in a ceremony in West Beirut. The route back was led straight past Phalangist gunmen waiting in Ain el-Rummaneh. The bus carrying the Palestinian refugees was riddled with bullets, killing 27, many of them women and children. No one knew at that moment that Ain el-Rummaneh would become Lebanon's Sarajevo. And only later did prominent historians recognize the shooting in the greater context of the Arab-Israeli conflict. The shots fired in April 1975 as US Secretary of State Henry Kissinger was negotiating the Israeli withdrawal from the part of Sinai that lay closest to the Suez Canal.[24] Leaders in Syria and in the PLO did not regard this as a positive step: they feared Kissinger would go no further toward a comprehensive peace settlement in the Middle East. They looked at the Israeli retreat from Sinai as the first step toward a separate peace agreement between Israel and Egypt, and feared that the Golan Heights, the West Bank, East Jerusalem and the Gaza Strip would remain in Israeli hands.[25]

In an effort to change the balance of power in the Middle East, Lebanon was set on fire. On the one side, the PLO fought in alliance with the militias from the Druze, Sunnis, Shias, Communists and others which were supported by Syria, the Soviet Union and some East Bloc countries. On the other, the Christian militias were discreetly supported by Israel, the Shah's Iran, Saudi Arabia and the United States. At first the battles in Beirut were sporadic. The clashes moved from one part of the city to another, each with greater frequency and growing intensity. Some lasted a few hours, others a few days or weeks, before ending in either formal or informal ceasefires.

The cold war's conventional alliances did not last very long. After a year of fighting, President Hafez al-Assad was concerned the PLO and its allies would win, and that this would provoke Israel to invade Lebanon. With this in mind, Syria turned back to its previous allies.[26] Initially, Assad gave orders to stop attacks against the Christian forces; he had authority over some Palestinian forces and over militias allied with Syria. When this did not have the desired effect, Syrian troops entered Lebanon in July 1976 to rebalance the scale and rescue the Christian side from being overrun.

The US also played a role in this process, regarding the development in Lebanon as a golden opportunity to get Syria, one of the Soviet Union's client states, over to its side. Again, Henry Kissinger took the lead and made certain the Israelis did not get involved in negotiations. At the same time he assured Assad that neither Israel nor the US would act if Syrian soldiers intervened in Lebanon on behalf of the Christian side. The one condition, imposed by Israeli Prime Minister Yitzhak Rabin, was that the Syrians would not advance south of Sidon, the "new red line" in the Levant.

The Soviet Union saw through Kissinger's plan, but Moscow could not prevent Syria from acting in its own interest and did not stop the Syrian incursion into Lebanon. Moscow also did not provide any particular weapons support to the PLO, the Lebanese Communists or the Druze. The so-called Left and the Palestinian guerrillas, who had nearly won the war, were now under siege, in and around West Beirut and south to Sidon. When the Palestinian guerrillas were thrown out of West Beirut in 1982, the civil war gained a new dimension. Two years later it was the occupation of South Lebanon which drew the greatest international interest.

CHAPTER SIXTEEN

Assassination in Jibsheet

There was relative calm in Beirut in early 1984 as my regular driver from Lebanon Taxi, Mohammed Maatouk took us to the village of Jibsheet, where a radical Shia imam had become famous throughout the country for his brave attitude toward the Israeli occupation forces. Sheikh Harb—*harb* means "war" in Arabic—challenged the Lebanese not to fight the Israelis with weapons, but instead to use civil disobedience. That was dangerous enough. Little did we know that the 32-year-old sheikh was secretly among those who had sown the seeds of the future Hizbullah Party. He had been in Iran and met Ayatollah Khomeini when the Israelis invaded Lebanon. Khomeini asked Harb and other future leaders of God's Party to mobilize the Shias and convert their mosques to bases for *jihad*, or holy war, against the Israelis.[27]

Sheikh Harb became known all over Lebanon for having refused to shake hands with an Israeli officer. The young sheikh told the officer, who stood there with his hand outstretched, "You are occupiers. I will not give my hand to an occupier." He added: "A position is a weapon and a handshake is an acknowledgement."[28] In March 1983, the Israelis arrested the sheikh and took him to an Israeli military camp. Within hours, Shias over large parts of occupied South Lebanon were in revolt. The protests soon increased in force, and after having held the sheikh for 17 days, the Israelis realized it was smarter to set him free. But the Jibsheet religious leader refused to give up and he continued with his fiery sermons. It was just such a sermon that I wanted to hear. I had learned ahead of time that Harb had been educated in Najaf in Iraq and had been a supporter of the forbidden Dawa Party. Like many other Shia students from Lebanon, he became blacklisted and had to leave Iraq.

Following a wait at an Israeli control post, we were given access. Again, my Norwegian passport and Israeli press credentials helped a lot. We drove through Nabatiyeh and a couple of smaller villages before we arrived in Jibsheet. There we went to a blue mosque with a black flag hanging limply from the top of the minaret. When we asked for the sheikh, we were told he was not there nor at his home nearby. We decided to wait.

We were invited to tea by a man who called himself the sheikh's advisor. The taxi driver, Maatouk, was good at talking for me. After waiting an hour, I understood that Sheikh Harb was not going to show up. The advisor's excuses were many and not believable. To let him know that we were not fooled, I told an old story with Maatouk as my interpreter:

There once was a sheikh whose advisor always gave excuses when he had made a mistake. The sheikh finally tired of all the excuses and said, "Can you give me an example of how an excuse is worse than the mistake itself?"

The advisor squirmed and said, "I will have to think about it."

That same evening the sheikh took an evening walk alone in the garden surrounding his house. The advisor followed silently behind. At a dark spot, the advisor approached the sheikh and embraced him.

"What are you doing?" the Sheikh shouted as he shoved the advisor away.

The advisor excused himself and said he did not know it was the sheikh he had embraced.

"Who did you think it was?" asked the Sheikh.

"Your wife."

"What? You dare to touch my wife!"

"No, my friend, but you asked me to give you an example of an excuse that was worse than the mistake. Now you have one."

Sheikh Harb's advisor smiled, and when we left the village, he promised I would get to meet the radical sheikh the next time I came to Jibsheet.

On the way back to Sidon, we saw two Israeli trucks loaded with blindfolded Lebanese prisoners. The prisoners were going to the Israeli concentration camp at Ansar. By now the camp was referred to as Ansar II, since it had been moved some distance away from the first one. Following several successful mass escapes, the Israelis built prefabricated houses instead of tents. They asphalted the roads and open areas to prevent prisoners from digging tunnels.

Some prisoners still tried to get to freedom. One of these was Hussein Abbas. As a 16-year-old he had fought against the Israeli occupation. At first he had handed out pamphlets, then he participated in blowing up a vegetable store which sold Israeli products and finally he had attacked an Israeli patrol along with four other Shias. The operation failed, and they were all taken prisoner and sent to Ansar.

While in captivity, Hussein Abbas and others were interrogated by officers from the intelligence and security service, Shin Bet. He was asked about his family on both his mother's and father's sides. His mother was from the Shia town of Khiam near the border with Israel, and his father was from Jibsheet. One day Hussein was taken from the camp and driven to an Israeli military installation in the village of Zibdin near Nabatiyeh. There he was interrogated by a new Israeli officer, who belonged to Shin Bet and was called Ghazi.[29] In perfect Arabic the Israeli told him he knew much about Hussein and his family on his mother's side, the Abdallah family. This was one of the powerful families in Khiam who, Hussein was told, had cooperated with the Israelis for many years. Ghazi gave him a proposition: freedom, money and a shiny new 7mm pistol in exchange for secretly becoming the Israelis' eyes and ears in Jibsheet.

Hussein was reluctant and was sent back to captivity—not to Ansar, but to a Lebanese prison the Israelis had taken over. A few days later the youth was picked up again and sent to a meeting with the Shin Bet officer, who was both friendly and understanding. Tempted by a new pistol, freedom and a good life with money in his pocket, the 17-year-old said yes this time.

A few days later he was back home with his parents in Jibsheet. His father was a retired police officer, and highly respected in the village. No one questioned why Hussein had been set free. Each week the Israelis' new agent went the few kilometers from Jibsheet to Nabatiyeh where he was picked up by a Peugeot 304. He snuck into the car, which had darkened windows, and lay flat on the back seat. Then he was driven to the Israeli encampment outside the city where Ghazi, his Shin Bet handler, was waiting. But the Israelis did not completely trust Hussein—he had to remove the ammunition clip from his pistol each time he was driven into the camp.

The Israelis also had collaborators who did not hide their activity. Some of these were part of the so-called Home Guard, and their task was to keep an eye on the villages on Israel's behalf. In Jibsheet, the Israeli-controlled group was led by Abbas Badr el-Din, a man who almost never was seen without a glowing cigarette hanging from the left corner of his mouth.

Eventually it became known among Israeli collaborators that Hussein had been recruited as Shin Bet's informer. At a meeting with the Israelis in early February 1984, he became well acquainted with Badr el-Din and two others from Jibsheet who had also entered Israel's service. One of these was Fouad Fahs, a tall, powerful and dangerous man in his 30s, known and feared for having shot another player during a poker game. The other, Nabil Haidar, was missing two fingers on one hand as a result of an assassination attempt.

Hussein and the other three collaborators had been called in because Sheikh Ragheb Harb was creating big problems for the Israelis. Ghazi indicated that the sheikh with the white turban and black beard was a cancerous tumor that had to be removed. With two other Israelis at his side, he said neither he nor any other Israeli could be involved in the operation. After a bit of discussion back and forth it was decided the sheikh should be killed in his village by Hussein, Abbas Badr el-Din and Fuad Fahs. Nabil Haidar was to block the small roads out of the sheikh's neighborhood with stones. In case the sheikh did not die immediately, this would delay transport to the hospital in Nabatiyeh. Nabil's wife Fatima, who had grown up in the sheikh's neighborhood, was to follow his movements and report by radio to her husband.

On the evening of February 16, 1984, Harb went to the mosque in Jibsheet to pray a special prayer named after Kumayl ibn Ziyad. It was said Kumayl had learned the prayer from a holy man who said, "Kumayl, take this prayer with you and recite it every evening. If you cannot say it every evening, then say it once a week. If you cannot say it once a week, then say it once a year. And, Kumayl! If you cannot do that, say it at least once in your life."

When Sheikh Harb had said his Kumayl, he recited so many more prayers that his neighbor Hajj Mahmoud Younes got the feeling that the sheikh knew his life was nearing its end, and that he was "ready to meet his God." Following the hour of prayer, Hajj Mahmoud invited Harb to his home to watch the television news from Iran, adding, "This will please our hearts."[30]

Around 9:30 PM, Fatima radioed that the sheikh had gone over to his neighbor's. The three assassins drove to the house, sought cover behind a stone wall and waited. After half an hour, Harb emerged and walked home. Hussein and the two others let him pass, then jumped out and shot him. Sheikh Harb stumbled and called out "*Allahu Akbar*," (God is Great), before he fell to the ground. The three shooters ran to the BMW they had parked a short distance away and drove off.

When neighbors heard the volley of shots, several ran out and found Harb lying on the ground. Hajj Mahmoud lifted the sheikh and could feel through his robe that his insides were hanging out one side. He carried the bloody Harb to a car and began driving to the hospital at high speed—but he had to stop because of Nabil's roadblocks. Turning around, he found a gravel road which brought him out again on the main road to the al-Hikma Hospital in Nabatiyeh.

The sheikh was dead on arrival. A few minutes after his admission, Israeli forces surrounded the hospital. When they got confirmation Sheikh Harb was dead, they left. The three murderers were already safe in the Israeli base at Zibdin. When I heard about Harb's assassination, I became irritated at myself for not renewing my attempts to interview the man who was now one of Shia Islam's greatest martyrs in Lebanon.

A few weeks later Hussein Abbas went to the United States, having obtained a visa through his father Ali. In America he lived at the home of two well-known academics, both half-brothers of his father. One of them was Professor Fouad Ajami, who later became an advisor to the American government when the US went to war with Iraq in 2003. Ali accompanied him to the US, but went back to Lebanon after a while. By then Hussein's participation in Harb's murder was known in the village. Soon after returning, Ali was shot and killed on the balcony of his home. The murderer had to have been a man Ali knew, with whom he had been sitting just before the shots were fired.

When Hussein came back to South Lebanon some months later, he wanted to avenge his father. Once more he went into service for Shin Bet, but this time as a clearly visible agent with his own Mercedes and an American M16 automatic rifle. Hussein would come to play an important role in an Israeli action against Harb's successor, a new imam in Jibsheet named Abdel Karim Obeid.

CHAPTER SEVENTEEN
The Journalist and the Spy

In Beirut the American, British and French embassies warned their citizens: Be extremely careful. There is a great danger of being kidnapped. Do not walk to work. When you drive, change your route each day.

As a Norwegian I felt safe. When I was in Beirut, I would walk a lot rather than waiting stuck in the heavy traffic of the city center. Most of my journalist colleagues, whether American, French or British, also wanted to live the way they were used to.[31]

CNN's chief in Beirut, Jerry Levin, was no exception. On March 7, 1984, around 8 a.m., Levin walked in typical fashion to his office near the Commodore Hotel, just 15 minutes away. As Levin approached the Saudi Arabian Embassy in Rue Bliss, he felt a light tap on his shoulder and heard a male voice say, "Excuse me."[32]

Levin turned and felt the barrel of a pistol being pressed against his stomach. The man said:"Come with me." A small car rolled to a stop next to them. The man with the gun pushed Levin into the back seat, saying, "Close your eyes. If you look, I will kill you!"

A few hours later Levin was lying on a bed blindfolded.

The accusations came fast: You are a CIA spy.

"No, I am a TV journalist."[33]

"Then you're an Israeli spy," other voices cried.

"Why are you holding me?"

"Stand up!"

He was told to kneel. For several long seconds, he thought he was going to be executed. But then he was gagged and wrapped in tape from shoulder to ankle. The tape was so tight that Levin could feel his toes and fingers stiffen. Strong hands lifted him, and then he was shoved into something that reminded him of a tomb. But then he heard an engine start and understood he had been put into a delivery truck.

Levin tried to make note of every sound in hopes of figuring out where he was being driven. If the trip took two and a half hours, he would be in the Bekaa Valley and the kidnappers would probably be from Islamic Jihad. If the trip were longer, he was afraid he would end up in Iran. An hour or so later he could no longer hear the noises of Beirut. They drove up several long hills, apparently toward the mountains. Then the landscape leveled out and Levin thought: I am in Bekaa. Somewhat later he was brought upstairs in a house. There he was placed on a cargo pallet. The tape was removed, but not the blindfold. He felt a chain being wrapped tightly around his ankle and locked to something near the floor. There was not much more for him to do than lie still.

If the kidnapping created an uproar in the US or among journalists in Beirut, it had little impact on my own work researching a book about Israel's war in Lebanon. Much of my time went to interviewing people. At the same time I was looking for stories that could give insight into the Lebanese and Israeli ways of thinking and behaving.

Three days after the kidnapping, a coded message came to the IDF. The message was from one of Israel's Shia agents in Lebanon, under the code name "Hypnosis." Fearful that the agent would be discovered, the IDF had not provided him with a radio or other advanced communications gear. Hypnosis kept contact with another agent in Lebanon who walked past a certain house each day. If there was a new pot of flowers outside, it meant that Hypnosis wanted to meet with his Israeli handler.[34]

The Lebanese agent had been recruited by Unit 504, a special group within Aman. Besides military intelligence, Aman operated seven additional intelligence organizations tied into Israel's occupation of Lebanon. These were Mossad, Shin Bet, the Military Police Intelligence Service, the Israeli Border Police Intelligence Service, the Army Liaison Unit and the Intelligence Organization. There was no coordination among these secret services, and rivalries were at times bitter. It was said that the network was like a drunken octopus.

On March 9, 1984, a flower pot indicated Hypnosis wanted to meet with his handler, Major David Bakai, as soon as possible. In his youth, the major had been a commando soldier. Later he became an instructor and officer in the Air Force rescue unit, before earning a master's degree in Middle East studies from the Sorbonne. In addition, he held a black belt in Judo.

Major Bakai waited at the prearranged time and place, and after Hypnosis had been to the toilet, Bakai entered to retrieve a paper note. On several occasions, Hypnosis had received handwritten notes with orders from Islamic Jihad's leader. But Hypnosis did not dare keep the documents on his person; each time, he stuffed the notes into a condom, which he then swallowed. When the agent arrived at the meeting place, he would do what was necessary to produce the document.

This time Hypnosis had brought along an order to a group that had been training for months to kidnap an unnamed American. The group was told to be ready to take action within a few days. The paper was signed Hajj Imad—in other words, Imad Mughniyeh. The Israeli intelligence officer knew Mughniyeh was the spearhead for Iran in Lebanon, and they already had a thick file on him.

Major Bakai thanked Hypnosis and drove back to his base in northern Israel. From there he sent an encrypted message to the intelligence service headquarters in Tel Aviv. The officer on duty asked who is going to inform the Americans, and it was decided that Mossad would warn the CIA. Within the Mossad, however, the information was disregarded since it came from a competing intelligence unit. The Americans never learned anything.

Six days later on March 15, CIA station chief William Buckley received a coded message he had been expecting. It said that American military specialists land in Beirut via an Israeli naval vessel. The ship would wait over the horizon, and Mossad's agents ashore would place car bombs outside the homes of several Shia leaders. Panic following the explosions would make it possible for the American special forces to kidnap selected leaders. Buckley had been involved in similar actions in Vietnam. That time the Americans had kidnapped a known Vietcong leader.

Early the next morning, as Buckley awoke in his apartment, he first turned on a cassette of classical music. The player was on his night table. He brought the beautiful music with him into the bathroom where he showered and shaved. People who knew Buckley knew his routines.

That morning, he chose a short-sleeved shirt and a lightweight, gray summer suit, size 38. Buckley's friends also knew that for the past thirty years he had bought his suits at Brooks Brothers in New York, four each year, two lightweight, and two in worsted wool.[35]

After he was finished in the bathroom, he brought his cassette player along to the kitchen. He ate his breakfast mix, drank his apple juice, fixed his toast and had a cup of black coffee. This routine had been with him as long as his friends could remember. They also know he often listened to Dean Martin sing "Return to Me" while he fixed his sandwich pack for lunch. Buckley, who would be 56 in a few months, did not like the lunch offered at the embassy canteen.

He put his lunch in his briefcase, known in the CIA as a "burn bag" since an imbedded ring of gas would burn up the contents if the key was turned in a normal fashion. His lunch was packed alongside documents marked Top Secret, Secret or Confidential. He locked the briefcase by turning the key to the left and attaching it to his wrist with a lockable chain.

Buckley got onto the elevator at 8 AM. When the elevator stopped on the floor below, a young, well-dressed man carrying a briefcase got on, as well as another female tenant. Buckley greeted the woman. The man, whom he did not know, said nothing. The woman got off at the ground floor, wishing Buckley to "have a nice day."[36]

The two men rode down to the basement, where Buckley had his car parked in the common garage. Usually he was picked up by the embassy driver, but this morning he had decided to drive himself. This was a breach of security rules: it was forbidden for American diplomats to drive alone in Beirut.

On the way to the car, the unknown man hit Buckley over the head with his briefcase, which contained several heavy stones. He fell to the ground. A white Renault came up, and Buckley, half in a daze, was shoved in. The driver exited the garage without closing the one back door properly. The woman who had taken the elevator with Buckley was now standing outside and thought she saw the American in the car with two men lying on top of him.

Several hours passed before the embassy learned about the kidnapping. It was already night time in Washington, D.C., and the CIA chief was only informed of the news at 3 AM. His face ashen gray, William Casey drove to the office to read the message that his top man in the Middle East had been kidnapped. For three decades Buckley had served the CIA loyally and without any complaints. He was the man who could do the job, wherever he was.

"So how the hell had this happened?" Casey asked. Without waiting for an answer he continued: "Find him! I want him found. I don't care what it takes. I want him found."[37]

Buckley's kidnapping was right out of a spy novel. Buckley's fate was sealed by a female Shia agent whom he had recruited. She went by the name Zeynoub and was the sister of a woman involved in the killing of AUB President Malcolm Kerr a few months earlier. Zeynoub was a double agent. She was so charming and beautiful that Buckley fell in love with her, and an intimate relationship developed between the two. Buckley eventually grew suspicious, but before he could take action, she had disappeared. By then it was too late.[38]

In Baalbek, the kidnapped CNN correspondent, Jerry Levin, sat alone in a small room chained to a radiator. The chain was so short that Levin could only lie down or sit, and constantly had painful cramps. The room was bare and had one window, which had been painted over. Levin counted 28 marks on the wall; he tried to keep track of the number of days he was in captivity.

When the guards came in, he had to cover his eyes, but he noticed nonetheless that they were young. Levin could see their hands and feet through a small opening in the blindfold. One of the guards regularly put a pistol to his forehead and pulled the trigger. Click. The chamber was empty. Then he heard him say: "Blindfold okay, you okay. You see out, we kill!"[39]

The room Levin was held in lay near a bathroom. After a while the guards left him alone while he used the toilet. In the bathroom, Levin removed his blindfold and went over to the little window, which had also been painted over. He scraped away a little bit of the paint with his nail to make a hole he might see through. A few minutes later he put the blindfold back on and knocked on the door. The guard returned him to his little prison.

One day Levin heard someone being led down the corridor to the bathroom. He was no longer alone. He heard the guards say: "Come." He was speaking English.[40]

More Americans, Levin thought in his helpless state. But who?

CHAPTER EIGHTEEN

"I Want You!"

Every CIA station in the Middle East got orders to hunt for Buckley as a top priority. If he were tortured long enough, he could reveal uncomfortable amounts about the CIA's work and agents, including outside of Lebanon. The CIA's professionals worked together with investigators from the FBI and specialists in ground communications from the US National Security Agency (NSA). The Americans also asked the Israelis for help. The IDF had a listening post on the top of Barouk Mountain, the highest point in southern Lebanon, but the Israelis, who did not like the US military involvement in Beirut, refused to provide any assistance.[41]

The Americans turned to Lebanese intelligence and reached an unofficial agreement to build a sophisticated signal intelligence site near the summit of Mount Sannine northeast of Beirut, the third highest mountain in Lebanon, rising 2,600 meters over the Mediterranean. The listening post, run by the Signal Service of Lebanese Military Intelligence, was staffed with experts fluent in English, Farsi, French and Hebrew. It could intercept radio communications throughout the Middle East as far east as Iran and to southern Europe in the west. The surveillance focused on Baalbek, a few dozen kilometers to the east, and all information gathered was shared with the CIA.

In Beirut's southern sections, the Amal militia mounted searches for kidnapped Americans. It offered significant rewards to anyone with useful information. Amal's leader, Nabih Berri, wanted to show the outside world that extremist Shias were not the ones running Lebanon. He hoped for increased visibility in the US and wanted at the same time to teach Islamic Jihad a lesson.

In the middle of April, Amal got a lead. A pair of young boys playing on a rooftop in the southern section of West Beirut had noticed two men sitting chained to a wall in a room. Amal's men rushed in and the kidnappers gave up without a fight. The seeming triumph brought a disappointment: neither hostage was Buckley, but rather the American professor, Frank Regier, and a Frenchman who had not yet been reported missing. The guards did not know anything about either Buckley or Levin. But it did not take long for Islamic Jihad to issue an announcement threatening Amal with revenge.

CIA analysts wrote a long series of secret memos about the wave of kidnappings in Lebanon. One referred to an envelope that the Algerian military attaché had found in the crack of a door. It contained a note and another sealed envelope. The note had instructions in English that the second envelope should not be opened, but delivered personally to the US ambassador in Algiers. When the ambassador received the letter a few days later and opened it, he found Polaroid pictures of, among others, Buckley, Levin and Saudi Arabia's consul in Beirut. Enclosed with the pictures was a note with the words "Islamic Jihad" on it.[42]

On May 7, 1984, the Americans received a videocassette at the embassy in Athens. The cassette was a cheap East German brand sold all over the Middle East. It had been packed in the same type of paper the Lebanese use for packing vegetables. The handwriting on the package indicated it had been written by someone not highly educated. When the American ambassador had studied the contents, the cassette was immediately sent to CIA headquarters in the US. There William Casey watched the video, which contained footage of Buckley. There was no sound, but the images depicted a naked, beaten man. In front of his genitalia he held a document marked "Most Secret."

Only then did the CIA leader get confirmation the burn bag had been opened without destroying the contents.[43]

CIA technicians enlarged each scene of the video in an effort to find out where Buckley was being held. The brick walls in the background suggested a Beirut cellar. Buckley's eyes were dull and his lips drooped. He blinked and clearly had difficulty seeing. The experts thought he must have been living with a hood over his head for an extended period. Abrasions on his wrists and neck indicated he had been tied with rope or chain, and there were several small needle marks on his skin.

The day after the video was delivered to the American Embassy in Athens, Reverend Benjamin Weir was kidnapped just after he and his wife had left their Beirut home. The Presbyterian minister thought he was safe, having lived in the city since 1958 and worked for several Muslim aid organizations. But that did not help him.

"What do you want?" Weir asked, when a car stopped next to him and a man emerged to say a few words.[44]

"I want you!" the man answered, grabbing the reverend by the arm and pulling him toward the car. Weir understood right away that this was a kidnapping attempt and cried out for help. He also tried to resist, but the men were young and strong. One of them grabbed his tie and pulled him toward the car. Weir tried to hold on to the door frame, but could not overcome the pressure from behind. Then one of the kidnappers jumped into the front seat and pointed a pistol at Weir's head. Another pushed the reverend in and held his head to the floor, placing a sack over him.

Weir felt just as helpless as the hundreds of Lebanese who had been dragged away in the same manner through the years. He had read about kidnappings and had spoken with the desperate relatives of the victims. "Now it is happening to me," he said to himself. "This is no small notice in the newspaper. Now I know how it is to be kidnapped." [45]

Once again, Islamic Jihad announced they were behind the kidnapping. In a telephone call to the *AFP* news bureau, a voice said the group also was holding Jerry Levin and William Buckley captive.

"There will not be a single American left on Lebanese soil," said the man, who did not give his name before he hung up.[46]

Weir had read about the bombings in Kuwait and about the trial against those accused "17 from Dawa." The reverend did not believe these were connected to his kidnapping, until one day the guards gave him pen and paper and asked him to write the following: "To His Highness, Prince of Kuwait…" He had to explain that his fate was inextricably bound to what happened to those jailed in Kuwait. If they were executed, the same would happen to him. If they were set free, he would be set free as well.

The guards led Weir into a room to read his message in front of a video camera. When the reverend was brought back to his chains, he could hear that others in the adjacent room were also reading a message. He thought it had to be the same one.[47]

The CIA concluded that the kidnappings were part of a coordinated campaign to put an end to American influence in Lebanon. The bombing of the American Embassy in April 1983, those of the American and French military installations in October of that same year, the murder of university President Malcolm Kerr in 1984 and the kidnappings of Levin, Buckley and Regier, along with the most recent victim, the Presbyterian reverend, had to be seen in the same context.[48]

Many wondered why the Americans bothered so much with Lebanon, a small country with no oil of its own. One reason was that Lebanon was deeply involved in the West's expanding big business of oil transport and finance. In 1958, Secretary of State John Foster Dulles had said the United States "must regard Arab nationalism as a flood which is running strongly. We cannot successfully oppose it, but we could put sandbags around positions we must protect – the first group being Israel and Lebanon and the second being the oil positions around the Persian Gulf."[49] A quarter of a century later the US still had ambitions to protect Lebanon against anti-Western powers, even if Washington no longer wanted to sacrifice the lives of American soldiers.

On May 30, 1984—Buckley's 56th birthday—the US Embassy in Rome received another videocassette containing horrible images of the kidnapped Beirut station chief. This time there was sound on the cassette, and Buckley spoke into the camera. His voice was unclear and his gaze suggested he had lost interest in what was happening around him. His hands trembled and his feet drummed the floor while he mumbled an appeal that the US must give up all presence in Lebanon and convince Israel to do the same.[50]

Can he survive this, wondered the experts at the CIA. His last medical exam in freedom had shown Buckley to be in excellent health, but now they were uncertain whether his defense mechanisms were still intact. The medications he had been given had no doubt had a strong effect on the man, but it was not certain they would do lasting damage. This hope led to a plan hatched by the CIA, the Pentagon, the State Department and the White House.

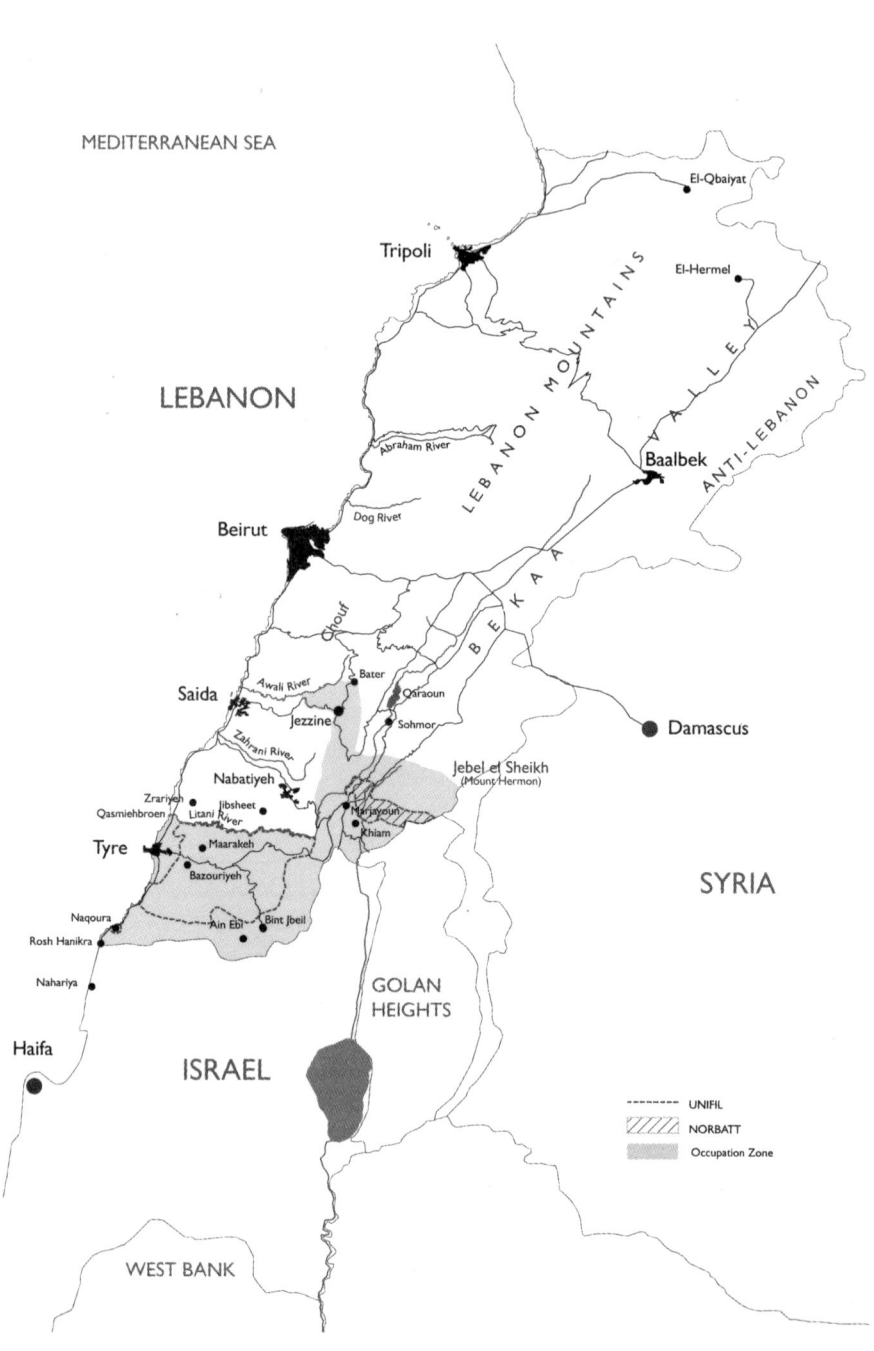

PART THREE

Three-Sided Hazard

1984-1985

The spring of 1985 draws the Israeli occupiers south to a new front line by the Litani River—but this is not the result of pressure from the Shias. Hizbullah's guerrillas are not yet strong enough to budge the Israeli military power.

Hizbullah officially releases its party platform. The most important objectives are the fight against Israel's occupation and the establishment of an Islamic republic in Lebanon.

Radical Shias continue kidnapping Americans and Europeans, while the CIA has proxies assassinate the foremost Shia cleric in Lebanon. The fight against the United States escalates when radical Shias hijack a TWA passenger plane.

In cooperation with Israel, the Americans begin secret negotiations with Iran about the release of American hostages in Lebanon.

MAIN CHARACTERS

Terry Anderson, Bureau Chief, *Associated Press*, Beirut
William Buckley, CIA's Station Chief in Beirut
Mohammed Hussein Fadlallah, Shia Cleric
Antoine Lahd, General, Chief of the South Lebanon Army (SLA)
Robert McFarlane, National Security Advisor to the US President
Imad Mughniyeh, Radical Lebanese Shia
Oliver North, Lieutenant Colonel in the Staff of the National Security Advisor
Shimon Peres, Israeli Foreign Minister, later Prime Minister
Terry Waite, Envoy of the Archbishop of Canterbury

CHAPTER NINETEEN
From Correspondent to Officer

In order to get closer to the Israeli occupation and the fight against it, I applied for a position with the UN peacekeeping force in South Lebanon (UNIFIL) during the winter of 1984. As a correspondent, I had made many TV and radio reports from UNIFIL. Norway had been strongly represented from the beginning in 1978, with a helicopter flight wing, a field hospital, a repair company and an infantry battalion. Six years later only the battalion and the repair company remained. But Norway had filled several key positions at UNIFIL's headquarters, where I was hired with the long title of Assistant Chief Military Information Officer.

My main responsibility was to issue the UN Force's monthly magazine, *Litani,* which was edited and printed in Beirut. This way I could maintain my contacts in the city. I also drove about to all eight national battalions in South Lebanon. At headquarters, I had access to data from UNIFIL's operations and information staffs.

The UNIFIL headquarters were built around an old Lebanese toll station, six kilometers north of the border with Israel. The station had been in use until the British left Palestine in 1948 and the State of Israel was created. Just below the bright white buildings and along the beach lay an old cemetery and a small fort from the time of the Crusaders. To the north were remains of a rail spur. The rail line had been built by South African engineers during the Second World War, but train traffic ceased in 1948 when Jewish forces blew up the tunnel running through the cliff side that marked the border between Israel and Lebanon. The Lebanese called the cliff, Ras en-Naqoura, and the Israelis, Rosh Hanikra.[1]

On a ridge east of the UNIFIL headquarters lay the village of Naqoura. From the outside it seemed unthreatening and peaceful where it towered above the rugged mountain cliffs. The village had a view of the Mediterranean and of the UN headquarters containing the force's field hospital and helicopter wing.

Five times a day I could hear the muezzin,person who calls to prayer, cry out *"Allahu Akbar"* from the mosque's minaret. Each time the beautiful voice called, I listened. He would hold the second "a" in *"Allahu"* for nearly 20 seconds, his voice fluctuated from a high pitch to a low one in rhythm, until *"Akbar"* came like the crack of a whip. Certain mornings the call and the song were also signals for me: it was time to get up and write for the book about Israel's war in Lebanon, before the daily work at UNIFIL began.

Many of Naqoura's inhabitants got work in the UN camp or in the many stores and restaurants that grew up along the main street outside its fences. Some of the village's Shias joined the SLA, but far more joined the opposition movement. The SLA militia was equipped, paid for and controlled by Israel. It recruited from all religious groups—Sunnis, Shias, Druze and Christians. Some of those who chose the SLA did so for the pay, others because they were pressured by the Israelis.

When I put on my uniform and flat, blue UN beret, it was easier to get around in South Lebanon. The Israelis generally refrained from shooting at the white vehicles with "UN" on their roofs and doors, although it sometimes happened that they did.

From Naqoura I could drive northward, pass through an SLA checkpoint with its gray Sherman tank and go on toward the first UNIFIL post, manned by soldiers from Fiji. A few kilometers further north along the coast road, I swung to the right and eastward, into the areas of the various battalions where the Israelis were now masters.

Before joining UNIFIL, I had interviewed a number of young Lebanese who fought against the Israelis. Among them was one of four youths from West Beirut who in mid-January 1984 had snuck past Israeli lines a few kilometers from the control post near Bater, north of Jezzine. All four were Shias, representing a cross section of the Lebanese opposition movement in development. Each had made his own decision to undertake an operation against the Israelis; no one had ordered them to do it. The oldest, Abed R., was 20 and belonged to the Syrian Social National Party (SSNP). Abed was actually a Communist, but had joined the SSNP because they paid the best. Mohammed H. was about the same age and belonged to the Socialist Baath Party. The youngest, Mohammed T., was 16 and a supporter of Khomeini. He carried a picture of the ayatollah around his neck. The fourth, 18-year-old Hassan M., did not belong to any party. He had learned to shoot from the Palestinian guerrillas. Hassan was disappointed that the Palestinians, who called themselves *fedayeen*, freedom fighters, had disappeared like morning dew in the sun when the Israelis advanced into South Lebanon in 1978, and further north in 1982. "Something inside me says a soldier in the *fedayeen* must fight till death. He cannot leave the battlefield," said Hassan.[2]

The four youths had agreed to buy weapons and explosives from a local man in Nabatiyeh. The weapons dealer was Mohammed Saleh, a Shia who had joined the SLA because he needed the money. As member of the militia, Saleh received $300 per month. On the morning of the attack, the four resistance fighters met Saleh in Nabatiyeh. They depended on him, and fearing they might be betrayed, asked him to come along with them to the site of the intended attack. Saleh had no choice but to follow.

The four placed a bomb along a stretch of roadside where there were no houses, and lay in wait behind some boulders. At 4:50 PM an Israeli column came along. The bomb, which was a simple design, blew up. The youths followed up by turning their guns on the Israelis, who ran for cover and began to return the fire. At this point the four boys fled, thinking they had killed several Israeli soldiers. Saleh was left behind with a bullet wound in his foot. The four had at first thought to kill him, but allowed him to live when he promised to stay silent. The news reports that day said much about how disorganized the various resistance groups were at this point: there had been several actions against the Israelis that same day, but it was unclear if anyone had been killed.

The day before, the leader of the SLA, Major Saad Haddad, died of cancer at his home in Marjayoun. The news media in Lebanon spoke only briefly of his death. The Israeli media, on the other hand, wrote a lot about it, and the government in Jerusalem honored the major with a minute of silence. It had been Israel that created Haddad's official profile: a tough officer who had defended his part of the country against the PLO and Muslim forces during the civil war. But later it was Israel's needs and political goals that determined Haddad's actions. Without Israeli officers surrounding him, Haddad would have been unlikely to live to be 48 years old.

Even before his death, the Israelis had begun the search for a new commanding officer for the SLA. They wanted a Lebanese general as their figurehead. Former President Camille Chamoun's son Dany, whom the Israelis knew well, thought Major General Antoine Lahd would be a good fit. The Christian general had recently retired. Major General Meir Dagan and Mossad's station chief in Beirut, Eliezer Tsafrir, were given the task of convincing him.

When Lahd was asked to takeover, he initially said no. He viewed himself as a true Lebanese patriot, and did not want to be in the service of Israel. But after the Israelis promised him full command of the militia, and gave him a clear understanding that the position would be lucrative, he was nearly convinced. Before he gave his final answer, he wanted to speak privately with former President Chamoun.

"Will the Israelis betray me?" Lahd asked when the two met.[3]

"No," answered Chamoun. Then he added,"But remember that the Israelis are not thinking about Lebanon's interests, only of their own."

Afterwards, Lahd asked his elderly father, who in his time had traded with the Jews in Palestine, "Will the Israelis betray me?"

"Perhaps they won't betray you," answered his father, "but be ready for the day you go together with two Jews on a dangerous road and suddenly discover they have disappeared."

The thought of being betrayed was distant when General Lahd got new and convincing assurances that Israel had no intention of withdrawing its forces from South Lebanon. He agreed to take the job as commander-in-chief of the SLA. "It was to be able to help the Christians in South Lebanon to live a good life," he told me later.

A few days before Lahd officially took command Israeli tanks soldiers, together with Israel's Lebanese mercenaries, invaded the Shia village of Jibsheet. Israeli helicopters circled the town, shooting at anything that moved except their own. The soldiers stopped at the market square in the town center and took to the rooftops. Outside Jibsheet's religious community house, or *husseinieh*, they ordered via loudspeaker for all males between 12 and 60 to come out. I made note of the day: April 4, 1984.

When the Israelis began to spray-paint the walls with Hebrew slogans, some of the Lebanese responded by throwing rocks. Women also took part. The Israelis responded with bullets; six men and one woman were killed, along with two wounded. Nearly 2,000 of the town's Shias were crowded into the school yard. After interrogation, several hundred were driven away in buses.

Jibsheet's new imam, Abdel Karim Obeid, appealed to all Muslims in South Lebanon to support the popular uprising against the occupiers. Everyone had to be ready to be arrested, even to die for the cause. The Israeli army now had truly brought Hussein ibn Ali back to life. The occupation had nourished the creation of several figurative Karbalas—the site commemorated on Ashura, where Hussein had fought for Ali's honor—in South Lebanon. People came as pilgrims to the villages fighting the Zionists in order to congratulate them on the latest attack and their newest martyr.

On April 12, 1984, a young Shia named Ali Safieddine drove an explosive-laden car between two Israeli armored personnel carriers near Deir Qanoun, killing six soldiers and himself. Safieddine was Hizbullah's first official martyr bomber, and his immolation was revenge for Sheikh Harb's assassination. The bomber who had struck the Israeli headquarters in Tyre in November 1982 had not yet been identified as Ahmad Qassir.

As a major in UNIFIL, I was not allowed to go to any of the villages outside the peace force's operations area while in uniform. But since I was acquainted with South Lebanon from before, I left the camp in civilian clothes when I was off duty. Now and then I went with a Lebanese to the villages where young and old had gathered in churches or mosques, or in Shia assembly houses. I got a clear impression of how strongly the people in South Lebanon felt about their countryside, their villages and their families. Occasionally I met youths who openly admitted they had joined Amal, or the Lebanese Communists or other parties that wanted the Israelis out. The Palestinians' sorry history since 1948 reminded them of what could happen if they did not fight against the occupation.

Resistance groups got weapons from West Beirut and the Bekaa Valley. The weapons were hidden in secret compartments on trucks, in cement bags or in washing machines. They were hidden in potato cellars or goat barns, or buried in the midst of age-old vineyards and groves of trees.

One of the villages I visited in the UNIFIL zone was Maarakeh, which spread over a ridge east of Tyre. During the first seven months of the occupation, no one among the 13,000 inhabitants took to arms, despite the fact Maarakeh in Arabic means "fight" or "battle." At the end of the 1970s the village had become known for its fight against the Palestinians, who at that time were behaving like the lords of South Lebanon. When the Israelis took over the town in 1982, women had thrown flowers and rose water at them in thanks. But gradually, the Israelis became worse than the Palestinians had been.

For every Israeli raid against villages in South Lebanon, the Shia resistance grew ever more visible. Pictures of Ayatollah Khomeini and Imam Moussa Sadr showed up on outer walls, in stores and in mosques. Earlier pictures like these hung only on the inside walls of private homes. Now we could also read slogans on whitewashed walls and on fences. "Islam has given us strength for martyrdom," was one of many.

Before the prayer caller in Maarakeh had taken his place on the morning of June 28, 1984, the inhabitants of the town were awakened. The sheep and the goats reacted first, then the dogs. By the time the noise aroused the sleeping village, the Israeli foot patrols had already taken up positions on the walking paths into and out of the village. Armored personnel carriers blocked the roads. Soldiers had been given orders to shoot to kill anything that moved outdoors. A jeep drove the streets, its loudspeakers ordering everyone to gather in the schoolyard immediately.

Snipers had already taken up positions on the rooftops. Before many had time to dress, the Israelis were already at their doors to undertake house inspections. Everyone was sent to the school yard, where the Israelis had established their local headquarters. Whoever might resemble a "terrorist" was tied with hands behind his back, and blindfolded or hooded. Everyone was commanded to line up facing a wall. Then the interrogations began. Throughout the rest of the day, each was questioned, one after the other. The prisoners were shown photographs of men and asked to identify them. Israeli security officers from Shin Bet and their Lebanese quislings asked the questions. All the youths and adults were "terrorists" until they could prove otherwise.

The Israelis marked up the prisoners with felt pens. They were divided into three groups: The dangerous, the less dangerous and a third category—those whom the Israelis would simply take with them. At the same time, other soldiers went from house to house. Every house was inspected, then marks were sprayed on the doors or walls. Houses where weapons or ammunition were found got an extra marking in green, indicating that the house would be bulldozed to the ground or blown up.

Eventually the Israelis released some of the youngest and the oldest, and they prepared to withdraw. New armored vehicles came to pick up the prisoners, who were shoved in with their arms tied behind their backs and their eyes blindfolded. The Lebanese prisoners were not allowed to carry either food or drink. The women began to protest and became so excited they were nearly hysterical. The Israeli soldiers seemed nervous and warned them that whoever approached, man or woman, would be shot. A helicopter circled over the village as Israeli soldiers pulled out of the town. They were afraid of being attacked.

In all, 119 men between the ages of 13 and 60 were hauled away. An even older man stepped forward and asked why they were taking someone only 13 years old. An Israeli officer told the man to put out his hands, and he too was bound and arrested. Here was another village where young boys swore they would join the guerrillas and kill Israelis when they were given the chance.

CHAPTER TWENTY

Brother Against Brother

On a wall in my room in the prefabricated barracks at the UNIFIL camp, I had a large map of Lebanon. Sometimes, when I got home late, I would be too tired to read, but not tired enough to sleep. I'd stretch out on the bed and look at the map. Now and then a few words from Michael Herr's book, *Vietnam Dispatches*, would come to mind—words which were good to remember when writing about Lebanon:"We knew that the uses of most information were flexible, different pieces of ground told different stories to different people. We also knew that for years now there had been no country here but war."[4]

The civil war and invasion had turned life upside down for most people, both in Beirut and in other towns. Even before the Israelis came, many children and young people had not ventured outside their villages for several years. They were scared to death of the so-called "flying roadblocks" erected by youths who were ready to kidnap or kill anyone of a different religion than their own. No one knew exactly how many Lebanese or Palestinians had been kidnapped and never found since the civil war began in 1975. Numbers between 10,000 and 20,000 had been estimated.[5]

As a correspondent I had crossed the front lines of the civil war without any particular fear of being kidnapped. As a UN major, I could also travel about, with or without my uniform, looking for stories, both for the UNIFIL *Litani* magazine and for the book I was working on. Several officers in UNIFIL thought it strange that this former correspondent was so eager to search for sayings and stories, and would ask everywhere if someone knew a *hakawati*, the Arabic word for a mix of poet, actor, historian and storyteller. In Damascus, there was still a professional *hakawati* who appeared at the Café al-Nafoura, just behind the Umayyad Mosque. But in South Lebanon, there were no longer any who told stories for pay. Nevertheless, I met a number of people who knew stories and liked to tell them apropos of a current event, or of something which was being talked about.

Late one afternoon I left my uniform at home and got a ride in a private car to the village of Ain Ebl in the Israeli occupation zone. The village, which in English meant "The spring of irrigation," had been populated by Christians—Maronites, Greek Catholics and Armenians. The houses lay in clusters on either side of a winding road. The oldest had been built in a yellowish stone, the newer ones in cement painted white. Cypress and almond trees grew in the small garden plots. In the evenings the lights from the Israeli *kibbutzim* to the south were brighter than the lights from Ain Ebl's neighboring Muslim villages.

I had been invited for dinner by a family I knew from before. Among the guests were two brothers, each of whom had chosen different sides at the beginning of the civil war. The older had joined the Phalangists, the younger the PLO. Along with seven other boys from the Christian village, the younger brother attended secondary school in neighboring Bint Jbeil, a Muslim market town.[6] Like his friends, the young 14-year-old Christian boy was attracted to his young female teacher. She was beautiful and Leftist, and spoke warmly of Palestinian heroes and their fight to return to their homes. It was not a big step to meet the guerrilla fighters themselves.

In secret meetings in the woods between Ain Ebl and Bint Jbeil, the young boys got to hear about Arab nationalism, about the battle against the Zionists and about the Palestinian cause. They also got to hear that the worst enemy of the PLO in South Lebanon were the Phalangists. Few Palestinians even mentioned that the Phalangists represented the Christian people of Lebanon. The youths of Ain Ebl themselves were Christians, and so were also many Palestinians, for that matter. The conflict was not about religion, but about politics. These secret meetings continued until the beginning of the civil war. By then the youths were convinced supporters of the Palestinians and the Leftist alliance in Lebanon, but they represented a tiny minority within the Christian villages along the border with Israel.

When the civil war began, the older brother, who had been studying in Beirut, found his way back to Ain Ebl and into the Kataeb, the Phalange Party. If there were going to be battles in his village, he wanted to defend it against Muslims and Palestinians. He was quite disappointed at his younger brother's political choice, but like his father, he thought that the young pup would eventually come to his senses. During the summer of 1975, it became increasingly difficult to be both a Christian and a PLO sympathizer in South Lebanon. In Ain Ebl, people no longer talked about politics like they used to: now they talked about religion—Christians against Muslims.

The PLO, for its part, depended on the local population's more-or-less silent support to maintain their bases in the villages. When it became more difficult to reach Beirut because of fighting there, the PLO guerrillas took on the responsibility of organizing food supplies. In Ain Ebl, families were given sugar, salt, flour and gasoline. The people in the village had only one place to turn to, and that was the PLO. The Palestinians largest political faction, Fatah, had an office in the neighboring village of Bint Jbeil. From there the Palestinian guerrillas would often visit Ain Ebl to assure the Christian population that they were under PLO protection.

When the Lebanese army split along religious lines in the spring of 1976, the Muslim soldiers took over the barracks in South Lebanon. The PLO's allies, the Leftist and the rebellious Muslim factions from the army, took on more and more control in the village committees. With the PLO behind them, they often got what they wanted.

To move among villages became more difficult. The war was always hiding nearby: a Muslim killed yesterday, a Christian tomorrow. It was no longer possible for everyone in Ain Ebl to go to the market in Bint Jbeil. The Palestinians began to pass out weapons to those who wanted them. The younger of the two brothers at first said no, but changed his mind and took a Kalashnikov (AK-47). He did not want anyone in his family to know about the weapon, so he hid it in an empty space over the cabinet in the kitchen.

At the same time, the Israelis began secretly handing out weapons to the Phalangists in the Christian villages along the border. The first deliveries were modest: sympathizers in Ain Ebl got 25 rifles with 100 bullets each. The older brother also got a rifle. He, too, did not want his family to know. Balancing on a kitchen chair, he was surprised to find his hiding place was already in use: there lay his younger brother's weapon.

With their secrets out in the open, the two brothers agreed that their weapons were just as safe in their bedroom. Anyway, their mother had already discovered their "secret," and laughed at her two sons and their rifles—one from the PLO, the other from Israel.

The Israelis did not just supply weapons: they also opened their border to Lebanese Christians who needed medical help or supplies. After a few months, they began to provide military training in Israel. When the older brother was offered special training, he accepted enthusiastically. Together with some 40 other youths from Ain Ebl, he was brought under the cover of night to a training camp near the Sea of Galilee. The instructors were generally Israeli Druze, together with the odd Jew who spoke Arabic. After the training, the Phalangists received more weapons and ammunition. They also got uniforms and field equipment of the same type the Israelis used.

It became more dangerous for the younger brother to be a sympathizer for the Palestinians and Muslims of the Left. When Fatah guerrillas and the Phalangists from Ain Ebl clashed at a road crossing outside the village, he decided to leave. It was with a heavy heart that his parents saw the family split and their younger son depart. At the same time they were relieved to avoid a battle of brother against brother.

An old farmer in Ain Ebl smuggled out the young brother and a few others, via an old escape route through the forest. In his pockets the teenager had 1,000 Lebanese Pounds (about $250 at that time), which he had received from his parents to buy a plane ticket to Abu Dhabi. There, relatives were ready to help him find a job.

The older son remained in Ain Ebl to fight. He was not only happy to be cooperating with the Israelis, but most Christians along the border thought this choice was the lesser of two evils. It was clear the neighbors to the south were mainly thinking of themselves, and he was afraid Israel might take over control of South Lebanon. The worst option would be to come under Palestinian and Muslim control.

Ten years later, I sat with the family at a table covered with delicious dishes, keen to learn as much as I could about the civil war. The younger boy was back in the village, now running a restaurant close to the UNIFIL headquarters in Naqoura—together with his brother.

During dinner, which lasted for many hours, I was served small glasses of Lebanese *arak*, a colorless alcohol distilled from grapes, unsweetened and flavored with anise seeds. Combined with water, it turned milky white, similar to Greek *ouzo* or Turkish *raki*. "It warms in the winter, and cools you off in the summer," my host said, making sure my glass was always replenished. There was a certain protocol to serving the *arak*. A small glass was filled one-third full, then bits of ice and water were added. A new glass was provided for each round. Around the table, the talk was of the "olden days," about archeological excavations with discoveries from Biblical times, about the Christian inhabitants of Ain Ebl who helped the Crusaders and about the massacre of Christians in 1920. The stories had been written down and placed in an empty bottle, which was cemented into a monument in the village so as never to be forgotten.

Over the course of the evening one of guests touched on a militia leader in South Lebanon who was tough and brutal with his men, but was a pussycat at home. The story of the tough leader who was afraid of his wife led to yet another story. This did not come from the Israeli occupied area, but from A Thousand and One Night's Baghdad. It began when one of the adult guests mentioned the famous Caliph Harun al-Rashid, who lived in a palace on the banks of the Tigris River, surrounded by women, musicians, and learned men. The palace was surrounded by beautiful gardens; one was called the Garden of Delight.

We ate and listened and did not expect the storyteller would get to the point of his story quickly. New dishes arrived at the table while he worked himself up to a hot state talking about the caliph's harem. He had 200 women, but only had children from 20 of them. Among the caliph's wives, Zubaidah was the most prominent. She was her husband's cousin, and it had been their common grandfather who had given her the nickname Zubaidah—little pat of butter.

That the caliph was also busy with other women, caused the jealous Zubaidah many sleepless nights. She made a song in which was said: "They can tear out my heart, but I will never let him go."

Early in the summer, Harun al-Rashid announced he wanted to spend the warmest months in the mountains north of Baghdad together with his closest advisors. He wanted to sit in the shade of the large oak trees and feel the cool moisture from the rivers and small waterfalls.

His court got orders to bring along tents, equipment, food and servants, according to their needs. But no one dared ask if they could also bring with them their families, since Harun al-Rashid had decided that just Zubaidah should come along. After having discussed the matter amongst themselves, the caliph's advisor decided they should bring with them only male cooks and servants.

A large tent was set up for the caliph and Zubaidah. The tent was divided in the middle by a beautiful woven carpet. Behind the carpet which divided the tent, the caliph and his wife had their private quarters.

When the domineering Zubaidah, who was no less jealous than usual, discovered she was the only woman in the camp, she was not particularly happy. She could according to custom not mix with the male guests, and said to her husband: "Paradise without people is not worth coming to. Here I am alone with no one to talk to."

He answered: "I will sit with my back to the dividing carpet. You can sit hidden on the other side. There you will be able to hear everything—conversations, discussions, and all the entertaining stories. That is much more interesting for you than female gossip."

One evening when the caliph and his staff had gathered in the royal tent, Abu Nuwas, the foremost poet in the land, was also present. He told stories which got everyone to laugh. When the evening was nearing its end, Harun al-Rashid was so satisfied he ordered the famous poet to be rewarded with a gold Dinar.

"God forbids me from taking payment from the caliph," answered Abu Nuwas.

Harun al-Rashid thought the entertainer was not satisfied with the price and ordered the payment to be increased to two gold Dinars. This then went to three, four, and five, while Abu Nuwas constantly protested: "Over my dead body, I can not take anything from my Lord."

Finally, Harun asked him: "What is it you wish?"

"That my Lord should give me a *firman*—an official edict—which gives me the right to condemn any man, who is afraid of his wife or her anger, to pay a fine. The fine will be one donkey."

Harun thought this was an amusing idea and gave orders to his scribe to create a document which he could stamp with his signet ring.

The following evening, Harun wanted to hear more stories from Abu Nuwas and sent for him. But the poet was nowhere to be found. One afternoon a few days later, while the caliph was resting in front of a large tent, did Abu Nuwas return.

The caliph had noticed a large dust cloud in the valley below. He called out to his guards and asked them to ride out and stop what he thought were bedouins on their way to a *ghazu*—a raid. When the cavalry returned, the leader said they had only found one man riding in front of three hundred donkeys. "That has to be Abu Nuwas," said the caliph. "Bring him over!"

Abu Nuwas tried to excuse himself because he was so dirty, and that he first had to take a bath and change clothes before he could present himself. But it was no use, he had to come as he was and go straight to the tent of the caliph.

"Now," Harun al-Rashid asked, "how many donkeys did you get for yourself?"

"Around three hundred."

"Impossible," answered the caliph. "In a land where I rule, there cannot be so many unmanly pussycats."

"Count the donkeys, my Lord, and you will find the number is right," replied Abu Nuwas.

"Tell me then something interesting which you experienced on your little journey."

"I did not hear or see anything worth telling."

"That can't be true! Tell me what you remember. Come on. Out with it!"

"I saw a caravan on its way to Baghdad. On the back of the lead camel was a wonderful saddle, and in it sat a virgin, as beautiful as only God can create."

"Tell me more," said Harun.

"She was as tall as a cypress tree, smooth as a palm, with eyes like a wild deer. Her neck was like a pillar of ivory, her hair as black as a raven's feathers, her cheeks like red apples and her lips like purple tulips, but what a shame..."

"What," interrupted the caliph, "was she lacking something or had some flaw?"

"No," answered Abu Nuwas, "she was perfect as God had created her. The only thing which was sad or unfortunate, is that she did not belong to my Lord."

"Hush," whispered Harun and put his finger to his lips. "Zubaidah is behind the carpet and can hear you."

"Two donkeys, my Lord!" Abu Nuwas thought in this case it was appropriate to double the fine.

When I was driven back to Naqoura the following morning, I heard on the car radio that a new attack against Israeli forces had occurred near Sidon. According to the news, the attack was the 1,000th of its kind since 1982.

My driver smiled at the news as he said, "It makes no sense to fight against the Israelis as we do amongst us Lebanese: if Israel is to be forced out, we must be willing to sacrifice our own to take Israeli lives. Only when enough Israelis bleed will opinion shift against her leaders, and they will understand that they have made a big mistake. The Israelis have to realize we are not Palestinians."

My thoughts went back to the dinner table the night before, to the two brothers who now were reconciled, and to the thought-provoking story told during dinner. Once again I was happy and thankful that many old legends live, even if lives were lost in war.

CHAPTER TWENTY ONE
"A Game They Cannot Master"

On September 6, 1984, many at UNIFIL headquarters shook their heads when the US vetoed a resolution in the Security Council demanding that Israel "immediately lift all restrictions and hindrances" which had been placed on the civilian population in Israeli-occupied South Lebanon. The American UN ambassador called the resolution "unbalanced."

Five days later, I noted in my little black book,"The IDF killed a Shia near Tyre 'because he had behaved suspiciously.' I notice great sympathy for the poor Shias among the well-informed officers in UNIFIL's various battalions. The Israelis will undoubtedly bleed more when the Shias have seriously woken up."

In the meantime, few among my colleagues paid much attention to the Shias who were holding hostages in West Beirut and the Bekaa Valley. Among those hostages was Jerry Levin, who was still kept locked in a house above Baalbek. Levin no longer had shoes or eyeglasses. The guards had taken them from him several weeks earlier. Without glasses, he could only see what was up close, but he tried to keep his mood up by remembering faces—any faces. Time and again he had gone over the operas and football games he had seen, and had re-imagined wonderful moments with his wife, Sis.[7]

Levin had lost weight. His hands and arms were like sticks. His daily meal consisted of something in a tin can and a small, triangular piece of soft cheese, packed in foil. When one of the guards left behind a box with his ration of cheese, it was like a gift from God. On the box was a beautiful picture of a farmer in the French countryside. With him were two red-and-white cows grazing on a rich, green meadow surrounded by shady trees. Levin held the box close up to his eyes so he could see every detail.

One day he heard a sudden knocking at the door. He put on his blindfold, and the guard came in to place something on the floor. Alone again, Levin discovered it was a well used copy of *Romeo and Juliet*, full of notes. The exhausted prisoner nearly laughed as he held the book up to his eyes and began to read.

Later—he did not know the date—Levin was once again ordered to remove his blindfold and record a message. He was handed a piece of paper and told,"Stare directly into the camera lens and read what is written there!"

Levin read:"I am Jerry Levin. My life and my freedom depend on the life and freedom of the prisoners in Kuwait."[8]

Only then did he understand how important the prisoners in Kuwait were for the kidnappers. He did not know that CIA Director William Casey had already contacted the Kuwaiti Emir to get the 17 freed. The answer Casey got was no. Apparently both the US ambassador in Kuwait and the CIA station chief there supported the Kuwaitis' uncompromising position. The Kuwaitis promised, however, that those condemned to death would not in fact be executed.

For leaders in Washington, the hunt for Levin did not have the same priority as the one for William Buckley. The CIA's man was more than just a station chief in Beirut; he possessed secret information from other countries as well. The US did not have an embassy in Iran or Iraq, so important parts of the CIA operations for those countries were controlled from Lebanon, where the organization had greater freedom than in Damascus, Cairo or Amman.[9]

Much of the money the CIA paid informants claiming to know something about Buckley was wasted. Only in June 1984 did a credible message arrive—and it was free. The American ambassador to Algeria, Michael Newlin, received information that Buckley, Levin and Weir were being held by an organization that called itself Hizbullah. According to the informant, who was Algeria's military attaché in Beirut, Hizbullah was willing to release the hostages in exchange for the prisoners in Kuwait. Rumors had previously circulated about a prisoner exchange but this was the first time the Americans were presented with a direct request.[10]

The Israelis did not know where William Buckley was being held any more than the Americans did, but Mossad's people spoke condescendingly of the CIA. They thought the American agents were playing "a game they could not master," and therefore Mossad only shared information with them when it suited their own interests.[11] William Casey feared at times that the Israelis were misleading the CIA. For that reason, the CIA's reports to the American administration sometimes ignored information they had received from the Israelis.[12]

The hostages, of course, got no information whatsoever, either about the request to the US or what was happening in the Middle East in general.

On September 14, 1984, I was listening to the radio when Israel got a national coalition government with Shimon Peres from the Labor Party as prime minister. According to an agreement with the coalition partners, the right-wing Likud Party, Peres would be prime minister for two years, while Likud leader Yitzhak Shamir would be foreign minister. After that they would change places. Yitzhak Rabin became defense minister.

Shimon Peres was a master at presenting himself as a peace activist and a person of little ambition. Many foreigners actually believed Peres when he sometimes said: Basically, people go into politics to hunt for drama, to strike, to win. I am not sure if my temperament or my conscience is made for this. The Israelis generally did not fall for such talk. They knew Peres was no peace activist, but a warrior dressed as a do-gooder. It was said that he could strangle a woman while he gave her a manicure. Likewise, few Israelis believed Peres when, a few days into his term, he said that the army would be out of Lebanon within nine months.

In Lebanon, the main conduit between the chaotic north and the occupied south went through Bater, just north of the Christian city of Jezzine. The stretch of road before the control point was like an anthill with all the people waiting to pass. Israeli guards split women from men, inspected purses and suitcases and checked travel passes. Those traveling in either direction had to obtain permission from an Israeli office in South Lebanon before they could cross.

People from West Beirut wishing to visit relatives in the south had to make arrangements with friends or relatives in East Beirut to help with travel documents. The trip between Sidon and Beirut, previously about a 40-minute drive along the coast road, now required passing through the mountains, which could take hours or days. The regulations for Christians and Muslims were different: Christians could also take a ferry to East Beirut. They then avoided the long lines at the control posts, where the Israelis tried to defend themselves as well as they could behind sandbags and concrete. The Israeli army put increasing trust in their security services to warn them, through a network of informants, of possible enemy operations. The Israelis also hoped that General Lahd's militia would become professional enough to do the daily work for them. In theory, Lahd had command over 2,100 men, but he felt the SLA needed at least 5,000 men to control South Lebanon in an effective manner.

In Tel Aviv, Defense Minister Rabin threatened that the Israeli army would strike back forcefully if attacks against Israeli soldiers continued in South Lebanon. His government referred to the Lebanese Shias as fanatics, and Rabin figured Ayatollah Khomeini's bad reputation in the West would give Israel free rein in Lebanon.

Israeli operations against the villages in South Lebanon, like the one UNIFIL had seen in Maarakeh, became routine. But what happened on September 20 in the Shia village of Sohmor was no daily event, not even for the hardened Israeli veterans. The village lay at an altitude of 1,050 meters, south of Lebanon's largest lake, Qaraoun. The inhabitants were primarily farmers, but the village was also known for its capable glass-blowers.

At first, the SLA and Israeli soldiers surrounded Sohmor. The SLA soldiers were Druze, and most were frothing for revenge after four of their comrades had been killed the day before. They believed the attackers were Shias from Sohmor.

The Druze comprised only a small part of the Israeli-controlled militia, which was dominated by Christian officers, but they were known to be extra brutal. When Sohmor's inhabitants had been gathered in the market square, the invaders shot wildly at the crowd. Only after an Israeli officer gave the order to stop did the Druze lower their weapons. Thirteen dead lay on the ground, while over 60 had suffered nonfatal wounds. That same day a young Lebanese Shia was willing to sacrifice his life to kill as many Americans as possible. Behind the wheel of a van filled with explosives and bearing diplomatic plates, he headed toward his target, followed by an orange BMW with two men in the front seat. On the way the young van driver swerved into an Opel station wagon. When the driver of the Opel tried to talk to him, he got no response. It seemed as if the man behind the wheel was paralyzed. But one of the two men in the BMW got out and offered the owner of the Opel compensation. The amount, around $300, was far more than what the repairs would cost. The man said yes to the offer and drove away.[13]

At 11:40 am guards at the temporary US Embassy in East Beirut, known as the Embassy Annex, noticed a van with diplomatic plates working its way around the concrete barriers toward the entrance area. One tried to shoot at it, but his weapon locked. However, the British ambassador's bodyguard, who was escorting his boss to a meeting with the American ambassador, shot and hit the van five times. The van rolled toward a car parked 10 meters from the embassy's entrance, where it exploded. The young attacker took two Americans and 21 Lebanese with him.

Once more the CIA accused Sayyed Mohammed Hussein Fadlallah, insisting that the cleric was Hizbullah's spiritual leader, and that he had blessed the driver of the van before the attack. Once more there came a suggestion that Fadlallah should be killed. In Washington, Director Casey agreed, but he thought the time was not right. The US presidential election was approaching, and it would be unwise for the CIA to do anything that could cast the organization in a bad light. The director said, however, that he was willing to increase the aid to the Lebanese intelligence service by two million dollars per year. The money was to be used in the hunt for the kidnappers and their hostages, together with preparations for an assassination attempt against "Hizbullah's spiritual leader."

With this bombing, Hizbullah had emerged from the shadows. But God's Party had not yet presented any political platform. Nor was the Islamic resistance movement strong enough to mount resistance at full-scale. It was the other resistance groups, with the Communists in the lead, who were the most active in South Lebanon. But these groups themselves did not present any particular threat against the Israeli army.

CHAPTER TWENTY TWO
"Merry Christmas"

When I arrived at the office of the UNIFIL headquarters on November 8, 1984, barbed wire had been placed around the conference barracks inside the camp. None of the UN's civilian employees were allowed near the building. Only officers with a reason to be there were permitted to enter the pale yellow barracks where the scene had been set for direct negotiations between Israel and Lebanon. Lebanese officials had agreed to meet the Israelis once the new government was in place in Jerusalem and it had dropped Syrian withdrawal as a condition for an Israeli retreat.

The Israelis I spoke with admitted it was a bittersweet victory to get the Lebanese back to the negotiating table. It was bitter because it reminded them of how dramatically Israel's position had been weakened since the invasion, and sweet because some thought the negotiations in Naqoura actually could come to serve Israel's interests. The Israelis hoped at least that various opposition groups would stay quiet while negotiations took place.

Some of the most radical Shias in West Beirut were still obsessed with freeing "the 17 from Dawa," and when a Kuwait Airlines passenger plane took off from Kuwait on December 3, 1984, destined for Karachi, there were four Lebanese hijackers among the passengers. They forced the captain to land in Tehran and demanded the release of the 17, Kuwait refused.[14]

At the airport in Tehran, the hijackers showed their negotiating skills. Two American passengers were killed and thrown onto the tarmac. Women, children and Muslim passengers were set free. After six days of nervous negotiations, Iranian soldiers stormed the plane and freed the remaining passengers. The authorities arrested the four hijackers and promised they would be tried, but they were secretly released.[15] In Baalbek, 1,170 meters above sea level, the winter cold was beginning to bite. Jerry Levin tucked his knees tightly against his body as he lay on a cargo pallet and tried to keep warm. Levin had folded his sheet four times and tried not to think about the approaching winter.[16]

He had been moved to a room with no heat, and the chain around his ankle was now attached to the ceiling. He was even more uncomfortable than he had been before. The wash basin was a modified toilet bowl, and a hole in the floor was his toilet. He would rinse himself off with water from a rubber hose attached to a faucet in the wall.

The unseen guards spoke a simple English. They told him they hated the US because it had supported the Israeli invasion and occupation of Lebanon. They also told him that American warships had bombarded their homes and killed family members. Levin got no information about when this had happened. He also did not ask, but simply listened to what the guards said as he tried to imagine what they looked like.

After a while his treatment improved. Nearly every day he received a warm midday meal, although the portions were small. Two new blankets also helped; he folded them together to make several layers. He also got new socks, long underwear, two t-shirts and a pair of gloves. But it was cold and getting colder. Levin was afraid his health would not hold and that he would die in captivity. When Christmas approached, he thought it might be his last.

The guards made sure to make noise when they approached so Levin would have time to put on his blindfold before they undid the lock on his ankle and led him to the bathroom. One day Levin returned from this routine to a surprise: from the edge of his blindfold he could make out a bowl of oranges, grapes and some chocolate. He touched the oranges and could scarcely believe what he saw.

Then he heard one of the guards say, "We want to give you a Christmas present. What would you like?"

"A Bible."

For a religious Shia guard this did not seem an unreasonable request. To him, the Jews and the Christians were all "people of the book." Two evenings later Levin got his gift with the words "Merry Christmas." When the guard was out of the room, he saw there was a book, *The New Testament*, bound in red. For the first time in his life, Levin began to read "the Holy Scripture."[17]

In South Lebanon, the peacekeeping force celebrated its seventh Christmas. Sixty Christmas trees arrived from Norway, along with 850 hunting knives in leather sheaths and a greeting from Defense Minister Anders C. Sjaastad. Prime Minister Kåre Willoch sent his greetings through the battalion's own radio station, Radio NORBATT.

Willoch said the next year could be decisive for developments in Lebanon. He also warned that, without progress in the peace negotiations between Israel and Lebanon, Norway might withdraw from the UN force.[18] There were few of us in UNIFIL who believed there would be any progress in the negotiations, but few thought Norway would withdraw, either.

At the beginning of January 1985, we learned Yitzhak Rabin wanted to pull his army farther south, away from the front line which then lay at the Awali River and stretched eastwards to Jezzine. Each time I heard the name Jezzine, my thoughts would drift to the beautiful mountain town with its houses built from yellow and white limestone and red, earthen roof tiles from Marseilles. The inhabitants were Maronites, famous for their knives, the bone shafts of which decorated with inlaid patterns. I had read in Colin Thubron's book, *The Hills of Adonis*, how powerful families in Lebanon could be traced back to this town, and how its family chieftains had come to power through acts of courage and intrigue. While the Ottomans ruled Lebanon, leaders in Jezzine were more or less independent of their overlords, at least for a short while.

When there was talk of an Israeli withdrawal from Jezzine in 1985, many Maronites feared the Muslims' revenge. Those who had served the Israelis calmed the others down, saying that the town would not be abandoned. The new front would be at the Litani River, but in Central South Lebanon there would be an Israeli-controlled corridor northwards to Jezzine. The crossing at Bater would continue to be one of the main arteries between the two parts of Lebanon, but it would also still be possible to enter or exit the occupied zone elsewhere.

To the outside world, the Israelis gave the impression they eventually would pull their forces completely out of Lebanon. Only a few Israeli officers would remain as advisors to the SLA. However, there were few Lebanese who believed the promises of a full Israeli retreat. There was also skepticism among the diplomats. Ane-Karine Arvesen put it this way: "Don't listen to what the Israelis say, but see what they are doing." She was no longer stationed at the embassy in Beirut, but had taken leave and moved in with me in Israel. We rented an apartment in Weizmanns Street in Nahariya, a few kilometers south of the Lebanese border.

I travelled back and forth between Nahariya in Israel and Naqoura in Lebanon while Ane-Karine helped me work on my book about Israel's war in Lebanon and followed the political developments in Israel and Lebanon carefully.

Israel's Lebanon policy had reached a crossroad. The invasion had radicalized the Shias in Lebanon, and Israel's allies in the country were in decline. The strategic alliance between Persian

Iran and Arabic Syria had been cemented. The big question was: When would the Israelis themselves recognize the occupation of South Lebanon was a lost cause?

On January 14th, Defense Minister Rabin presented a plan for the withdrawal. It would not be a full one: the southern portion of the country would stay in Israeli hands, with General Antoine Lahd as the figurehead, and his militia as Israel's puppets. The occupation zone would be called a "security zone." This had a better ring to the outside world, as opposed to terms like "full occupation" or "partial withdrawal."

Ane-Karine learned from an intelligence source that the Israelis had begun to pass out weapons in the towns of South Lebanon, to Shias, Sunnis, Druze and Christians. This was a recipe for new tension among the religious groups in that part of the country, and it reminded her of what had happened in the Chouf Mountains east of Beirut in the fall of 1983, when the Israelis armed the Christians and the Druze. The following battles and massacres were some of the worst in the history of the civil war. The Druze and Phalange militias bombarded each other while gangs from both sides raped and killed.

For the nearly 400,000 Lebanese in the Chouf, the worst nightmares from the civil war returned. Some of the most gruesome stories found their way to the mass media. One story involved Phalangists who had stopped cars and ordered 15 Druze men out, while their wives and children remained in their vehicles. The men were marched onto an old bridge, knifed and tossed into the ravine below. One survived his wound and landed softly because he fell onto his dead counterparts. It was he who later told the story to the world. The Druze had been just as merciless. We heard stories of how they poured boiling water over naked men. An eyewitness also told of a baby who was thrown over a cliff. In January 1985, it seemed as if the Israelis were planning a withdrawal that would precipitate a new wave of violence. Some wondered if the Israelis wanted South Lebanon to be split into cantons.

In Sidon, political and religious leaders met to discuss what should be done to avert civil war in the town when the Israelis pulled out. A respected Sunni politician named Mustafa Saad would play a key role in the work of reconciling former enemies. But not everyone wanted peace. On January 21, in the middle of the reconciliation meeting, a 100-kg bomb exploded just outside Saad's house. He was severely injured, and his daughter and three others were killed.

UNIFIL's headquarters was contacted to transport the wounded to Beirut by helicopter, but at first the Israelis would not allow it. Only half an hour later was a UN helicopter able to set a course for the American University Hospital. Saad's life was saved, but he lost his sight.

The head of the Israeli-controlled National Guard in Sidon, Mohammed Gharamti, better known as Abu Arida, was suspected of having been behind the bombing. A Sunni Muslim from the Sidon area, he had been hired by the PLO guerrillas prior to the Israeli invasion. When the Israelis captured him, he promised to work for them and was then released from the prison camp at Ansar.

The negotiations between Israel and Lebanon at UNIFIL did not last long. Israel had hoped the Lebanese opposition groups would stay calm while negotiations were taking place, but they had perpetrated over 40 attacks in the course of a month. At the same time it became known that the intelligence chiefs from Iran, Syria, and Libya had discussed how they might support the Lebanese in their fight against the occupation. Iran would still continue to support the Shias with expertise, training, and cash. Libya promised to pay for new Soviet weapons for Syria. The Syrians gave the Iranians easier access to Lebanon on roads reserved for the Syrian military.[19]

In my little black notebook, I wrote, "Monday, January 14, an Israeli captain and a regular soldier were killed. Six others wounded. Thursday, January 17, four Israeli soldiers were wounded. Monday, January 28, a seven-year-old girl was killed when the Israelis fired on a car at a control post. Wednesday, January 30, the secretary-general at the Israeli foreign office, David Kimche, called in foreign ambassadors. He predicted new massacres in South Lebanon if Israeli forces are withdrawn."

CHAPTER TWENTY THREE

"I Am Buckley"

In West Beirut, 1985 began with new kidnappings off the open streets. The first victim was a Swiss diplomat, but he was released so quickly that the newspapers never got his name. A few days later, on Tuesday, January 8, a 50-year-old American priest, Lawrence Martin Jenco, was snatched just a few meters from a police station. Jenco was on his way to his monthly blood pressure check-up when he was dragged out of his blue Pontiac on Rue Sadat. The policemen who witnessed the abduction closed their eyes and ears as the priest was forced into another car that drove off. Jenco was the eighth American to be kidnapped in ten months.

I was in Beirut to prepare a new edition of *Litani* when Jenco was taken, and it was only by chance that I was not at the Smuggler's Inn two days later. The restaurant on Rue Makhoul was still a popular place for journalists, authors, artists and others who dared to be out during the evening hours in West Beirut. George Zeini, one of two Greek Orthodox brothers who owned the restaurant, had invited me to an exhibit at his gallery on Rue Bliss, the same street as the Norwegian Embassy. I had promised to go, but did not—otherwise I would have been at the Smuggler's Inn on January 10th.

There were many others at the restaurant, however, despite the fact that guests had been robbed six times over the previous three months. Each time, men with pistols arrived and demanded money, rings and jewelry before they disappeared. This evening in January, things got a lot worse than that: four of the guests were killed and 12 wounded when a bomb, hidden in a briefcase, exploded close to the red leather sofa by the bar.

Fifteen minutes later a reporter from *The Daily Star* arrived. Those most severely injured were driven to the American University Hospital just a few hundred meters away. Others sat or lay in small groups on the bloodstained floor. Zeini who was bleeding from one arm, sobbed, "I have built this place with my life, my entire life. Now it is destroyed."[20]

From the shambles of the bombed-out restaurant, the reporter and a photographer went to the hospital. There they were met by young, bearded men from Amal, which had control over the emergency room. One of the armed youths pressed the barrel of his Kalashnikov into the reporter's stomach and shouted, "Get lost!"

"Why was the Smuggler's Inn bombed?" the reporter later asked Zeini. He said that he had refused to pay protection money to a local leader of the Amal militia. But there was more to the story, I later found out. The militia leader, Abu Fadi, was religious and did not like the free flow of wine and spirits in the neighborhood. Since he was not a bomb expert, the bomb came out too powerful. According to Abu Fadi there was never any intention of killing guests, only to injure and scare them.[21]

Amal's men were not as active against the occupiers in South Lebanon as they were against the civilian population in West Beirut. Those who fought the Israelis in South Lebanon were for the most part youths from the secular parties and the militant Shias from Hizbullah. Some women participated as well, on equal footing with the men. In January 1985, 17-year-old Sana'a Mehaidli became the first woman to blow herself up, killing two Israeli soldiers. Sana'a was a member of the SSNP. She drove a white Peugeot filled with explosives into an Israeli patrol near Jezzine.

At CIA headquarters in Washington, the leadership was not particularly interested in the Lebanese battle against the Israelis in South Lebanon. The Americans wanted revenge against the perpetrators of the bombings of the embassy in West Beirut, the multinational force and the embassy annex in East Beirut. The Israelis, Phalangists and the Saudi Arabian intelligence services corroborated the American belief that Sayyed Mohammed Hussein Fadlallah was the brains behind all the evil deeds.

Saudi Arabia's secret services had their own interests in Lebanon. The Sunni Muslim kingdom did not want Iran and the Shias in Lebanon to get power at the expense of the Sunnis. Their own candidate to take over as prime minister in Lebanon was Rafic Hariri, a billionaire from Sidon who also had Saudi Arabian citizenship. Leaders in Saudi Arabia feared their kingdom's own Shia population might become radicalized. If Iran succeeded with its plans to create an Islamic republic in Lebanon, the revolution might spread.

There was no proof that Fadlallah was Hizbullah's spiritual leader or that he had blessed those who had chosen to sacrifice their lives in the fight against the occupiers. The CIA based its belief on the facts that he was known for his "fiery sermons on social fairness and national independence" and for his verbal assaults against Americans, and that he had asked for help from the Iranian Revolutionary Guards when Israel invaded Lebanon.

One of the foremost American experts on Lebanon, Professor Augustus Richard Norton, maintained on the other hand that Fadlallah was not Hizbullah's spiritual leader. According to Norton, the cleric certainly gave advice to Hizbullah's leaders, but it was not always followed. Hizbullah's hard core listened first to Ayatollah Khomeini,[22] and Fadlallah was absolutely not in favor of the Iranians dictating what Lebanon's Shias should or should not do. The cleric had rejected pressure from Tehran several times. He also disagreed with the Iranians' plan to create an Islamic revolution in religiously diverse Lebanon. He had insisted so strongly that certain Iranians suspected him of being sympathetic toward the United States.

Plans to assassinate Fadlallah could not be executed immediately. The CIA did not have good enough agents in Beirut's southern section, so CIA Director William Casey chose to postpone the operation. He asked the Saudis to take the lead and to hide any tracks leading back to the US. The king of Saudi Arabia agreed and ordered his ambassador in the US, Prince Bandar bin Sultan, to cooperate with the CIA.

The prince had a military career as a jet pilot. Later he had become the military attaché in Washington, and now ambassador. His mother, a dark-skinned Saudi commoner, had given birth to Bandar out of wedlock when she was 16 years old. His father was the Saudi defense minister, Prince Sultan bin Abdulaziz al-Saud, but Bandar had thousands of other princes to compete with regarding his career. Nevertheless, he had one great advantage: his father and King Fahd were among the so-called "Sudayri Seven," i.e., seven sons of King Saud whose mothers were from the Sudayri tribe, one of the oldest tribes in the country. The seven comprised the topmost elite in Saudi Arabia.

One day in early 1985, Director Casey was invited to lunch at the Saudi Embassy. Prince Bandar had received word that the kingdom's fee for killing Fadlallah would be three million dollars. After lunch, the prince and the CIA director went out into the garden of the embassy residence. There Casey pulled a small card from his suit pocket; on it was written the number of a Swiss bank account The three million was to go there. "As soon as I have transferred the money Switzerland," Bandar said:"I will close the account and burn the papers." Bandar would make sure there were no tracks on the Saudi end.[23]

Both Casey and Bandar knew how it was to have conversations that never took place. Yet again it was the end justifying the means. It was time to crush the symbol of Hizbullah. Neither Saudi Arabia nor the United States wished for the radical Lebanese to grow stronger.

In the US, certain officers wanted to send soldiers to Beirut to retrieve the American hostages by force. The defense leadership thought such an operation would be pure madness. No one even knew where they should search. One CIA agent reported that Buckley had been transferred to the

Bekaa Valley; another rumor had him sent to Tehran for deep interrogation. After a while, all the rumors faded. Not even the newspapers in Beirut, which had revisited the stories from different angles time and again, devoted any column space to the kidnapped Americans. But William Casey would not give up. He thought the hostages, particularly Buckley, were like "stock certificates" for the kidnappers: regardless of who they were, they were worth more alive than dead.

In Baalbek, Jerry Levin was once again moved to a new house. He heard voices there indicating other western hostages. During his first trip to the bathroom, he climbed up onto the toilet and looked out the window. What he saw gave him palpitations: Farther down in the valley was a town, and in the west he saw the easily recognizable, snow-clad Mount Lebanon. He also noticed the main road that passed through Baalbek. If he could only get out of the house, it would be possible to flee.

On the evening of February 13th, 1985, Levin realized that the guard had been sloppy and had not tightened his chain. Around midnight, Levin got loose. He tiptoed quietly out of his room and opened the bathroom window. There was a balcony outside, on the second floor.[24] Levin tied two sheets together to make a rope, remembering the old tricks from his time as a scout. He tied one end to the balcony's iron grating, worked his way down and ran toward the road. He heard dogs bark, and was afraid he would be discovered, but he continued running barefoot.

Eventually he heard voices. He hid under a parked car and was frightened by a warning shot. Levin saw the beam from a flashlight and could hear someone calling in Arabic that he should show himself. He crawled out from his hiding place and said in French, "*Aidez-moi*,"—help me. A soldier with a red beret came toward him smiling. He was a Syrian. He wanted to show the soldier the house where the other hostages were being held, but without his glasses, he could not find it. They drove to Damascus, where the following morning he was turned over to the American Embassy.

That same day, a man called the *AFP* news bureau in Beirut and said he represented Islamic Jihad: "We let Levin go after many requests from brotherly countries. Our intelligence research had by then already established that he was not involved in espionage or the undermining of Islamic forces." It was Damascus that had applied the pressure to get Levin released. Since the kidnappers could not let one hostage free without getting something in return, they and their Iranian backers preferred to let Levin "escape." When the Americans later briefed journalists, a spokesman at the State Department said, "We are grateful for the role the Syrian government played in this matter."[25]

The other American hostages were moved again, driven away one after the other. Finally they were collected in a large, bare room where the windows and walls were covered with paper. Guards stood stationed at the entrance. The next day they began to build small cubicles out of plywood. The hostages could hear children playing outside the house. They were given the following message: Not even to cough or clear their throats, and not to peek through the cracks in the crude partitions.[26]

Later in the afternoon, Reverend Weir tried to contact his fellow captive in the adjacent cubicle. "My name is Ben Weir, a Protestant reverend. Who are you?" he whispered.

"Lawrence Martin Jenco, a Catholic priest," came the whisper from the cubicle next to him.

The two priests began to pray for each other and for the other hostages whom they knew were in the same room. The next day, from a cubicle a bit further away, Jenco and Weir could hear a voice whisper: "I am Buckley... William Buckley. Who are you?"

Somewhat later, when Jenco was able to move his blindfold slightly, he discovered a yellow, waxy, cone-shaped object connected to some wires. One of the guards later said the building was full of explosives; if the Syrians or Americans made a rescue attempt, he and his comrades would blow it up.

"We are not afraid of death," said the guard.

CHAPTER TWENTY FOUR
Retreat and Rejoicing

I was in Beirut on February 16, 1985, when the Israelis began a new phase of their withdrawal southward. We knew the new front was to run eastward from the mouth of the Litani River to the southern part of the Bekaa Valley. As planned, Israelis would also control a corridor north towards Jezzine.

The chief of the Northern Command, Major General Ori Orr, spoke of a new Lebanese civil war. "I do not know what will happen in Sidon," he said, "but I want this problem to be Amine Gemayel's. I will not even suggest we involve ourselves even if massacres should occur in these areas."[27]

The last Israeli column, with 300 soldiers and two dogs—their mascots, Vodka and Ester—rolled out of Sidon at 11 AM. There were few smiles to be seen. The Israeli soldiers seemed tense and scared. Perhaps it was the weather, the cold, gray February day which put a damper on the mood. Perhaps it was the fear of snipers, or was it the thought that they had not achieved much in Lebanon? Many of the locals who had cooperated with the Israelis also left Sidon.

Immediately after the last Israelis had left town, the streets filled with rejoicing crowds. To avoid civil war and massacres, Lebanese government soldiers quickly entered the town. They were welcomed and many present were overcome with joy.

Four reporters from Beirut had arrived before the Israeli departure. They were now sitting in a café when they suddenly heard the clatter of automatic weapons just outside. People threw themselves to the floor. More fire shattered the window of the store across the street and covered the sidewalk with shards of glass.

The reporter from Beirut's *The Daily Star* grabbed his camera and crawled to the door. He did not see anything. Suddenly, a new salvo came from inside the store across the street. A young man in blue jeans raced from the store, his white sweater stained with blood. Two men followed him and fired again. He fell to the sidewalk. The reporter went over to the gunmen and asked what had happened. He was told the man they had killed was an informant for the Israelis.[28]

Then suddenly two Israeli Skyhawk jets swooped low over Sidon, dropping swarms of leaflets in the center of town. They read, "Israel's fundamental interests in Lebanon are to give the land back in its original, independent and stable character. But foreign powers once more are at the door with deadly means, firmly determined to come back to sow the wind and reap the harvest." The Israeli leaflets made no impression on the Lebanese, who threw them away.

At the Israelis' new front line, a mobile telephone was set up where soldiers could call home and say they were out of Sidon, the city of fear. And when they crossed the border into Israel, they lit red smoke bombs, happy to be safe.

The same day as the Israelis left Sidon, Hizbullah in Beirut issued an open letter to "the oppressed in Lebanon and the world." It was the first time the party had made its goals and ideology public. The date, February 16th, was chosen with purpose—it was exactly two years since Sheikh Ragheb Harb had been killed in Jibsheet. Harb was now hailed as one of Hizbullah's founders.

In the open letter, Hizbullah wrote that its first priority was the battle against Israeli occupation and against the presence of the US and France in Lebanon. The attack on the American Embassy in

1983 was the "first punishment." Further, it said the occupation of Muslim lands and the oppression of the population made it necessary to use violence.

For Hizbullah, Holy War—*jihad*—was far more than just a military fight in self defense. The fight against the occupiers was to be waged ideologically, politically and economically, and it was a religious duty of all faithful Muslims to fight. The letter also made clear to everyone that Hizbullah's objective was to create an Islamic republic in Lebanon, based on Ayatollah Khomeini's vision. But force should not be used to establish a government with the supreme religious cleric as the highest authority; persuasive dialogue should be the revolution's weapon in that regard.

Two days after the Israeli retreat from Sidon, 200–300 cars and minibuses filled with young Hizbullah supporters drove into town from Beirut. The drivers honked their horns while the passengers shouted *"Allahu Akbar."* Dressed in jeans and uniforms, the youths swung their automatic weapons in rhythm and took control of the town. They marched through the streets in columns of five-to-ten men and waved placards bearing pictures of Ayatollah Khomeini and Lebanese martyrs. "We want an Islamic republic!" was one of the slogans. The Sunnis, who had been dominant in Sidon, absolutely did not like what they saw and heard.

The Shias set fire to stores that sold alcohol. Pictures of Amine Gemayel were torn down, and instead, banners were put up characterizing the president as "the Shah of Lebanon." Lebanese flags were burned while some of the demonstrators waved the Iranian flag. Hizbullah's show of force did not last long. A few hours later the activists had left town, but "they destroyed the joy of having the Israelis out, and gave little hope for the future," said one young man I spoke with on the way to South Lebanon. Hizbullah had little support in Sidon, even among the Shias. Of those, most supported Amal.

Large portions of the Lebanese population did not welcome Hizbullah's open letter and show of force in Sunni-dominated Sidon. Amal distanced itself from the disorders. Negative reactions came from Syria as well. These were directed towards the Iranians, whom Damascus thought were about to breed fanatics in Lebanon. President Assad wanted Amal to bring the Islamic radicals under control.

On February 25, 1985, Nabih Berri gave orders to Amal to close down Hizbullah's offices in Beirut's southern sections. Hizbullah's men did not resist this time, but later they would return even stronger.

CHAPTER TWENTY FIVE
Israel's Revenge

At the beginning of February, 1985, the first Israeli colonel was killed, then a major, both while driving through Shia villages. Colonel Avraham Hildo, who was the advisor to General Lahd, died not far from Nabatiyeh, and Major Shaul Zehavi outside of Bazouriyeh. Up to now the Israelis had lost 600 men in uniform. On a per capita basis, the losses were larger than America's in Vietnam over a decade.[29]

Israel's revenge, as usual, was a collective one. First they sent forces from the IDF into Bazouriyeh, and then into 16 other villages. Men were shot in the street and left to bleed to death because none of the neighbors were allowed to come outdoors. In response to questions from UNIFIL, the Israelis maintained that during operations that day, they shot "seven fleeing terrorists."

In order to make things difficult for journalists from Beirut to travel to the occupation zone, the Israeli army sent out telexes to the news bureaus in the capital. These stated that anyone wishing to report from South Lebanon had to apply for permission from the IDF. Journalists and photographers would be escorted by the Israelis. Anyone without an escort would be arrested. In Beirut there were a few who allowed themselves to be intimidated. Some managed to get smuggled through the porous front line; others applied for permits and drove south by way of the "border crossing" at Bater.

"Go back!" shouted the Israeli soldier in Hebrew and threatened to use his automatic weapon. "Go back! The road is closed today."[30]

The Lebanese understood. So did the American reporter who had made sure to get a permit, but who would get no further that day in February 1985. The Lebanese, who were lined up along the chained-off road, had been through the same thing many times before. Most lived in Jezzine or nearby villages, on the southern bank of the Awali River.

"I have to go through this at least once a week," one woman told me. "They open and close the road without any reason. If I cannot get through, I will have to spend the night here in Bater."

"We live in Jezzine!" shouted an elderly man to the soldiers who were posted behind sandbags, high above the road. "Here are our permits!" He waved his white piece of paper.

"Not today, the road is closed," answered the soldier in Arabic.

"You are Druze as we are! How can you do this to us?" asked the old man in despair.

The Israeli soldier did not answer. When Palestine, Syria and Lebanon were divided between France and Great Britain after the First World War, the Druze found themselves living in three separate entities. All the Druze in Palestine became Israelis.

The road remained closed that day, and those who did not want to make the long return journey went to a small inn nearby. It was in a low brick building with just two rooms, one for women and one for men. Both rooms had small wood stoves, so the people could at least stay warm during their wait.

It was Walid Jumblatt's Progressive Socialist Party (PSP) that ran the inn. The PSP was a member of the Socialist International, something which made Jumblatt and his men part of the so-called Lebanese Left. In reality, the Druze leader was among the most conservative in the country, despite the fact he looked modern and progressive, preferring to dress in jeans and short, black leather jackets.

From Israel, Defense Minister Rabin announced a curfew from dusk to dawn in all Shia villages in South Lebanon. Whoever broke the curfew would be shot. It was forbidden to drive a car alone; the same went for all motorcycling. Cars parked along roads would be destroyed. "We must protect ourselves from suicide bombers and car bombers," an Israeli officer I spoke with explained.

UN observers who had been in Maarakeh said Hizbullah's men were not afraid of the new Israeli actions. At the same time, one of the guerrilla leaders made a point that, as a Shia Muslim, he did not have anything against the Israelis as a people or the Jewish religion. "We will fight the Israelis because they are occupying our country. We are not fighting because they are Jews or because we are Muslim," said 25-year-old Khalil Jaradi.

Jaradi, a slender man with a scraggly beard and an ascetic face, said Maarakeh was a confrontation village in the Israeli occupation zone, and added: "We are proud that so many resistance fighters are coming here. We challenge the Israelis who will try to force their way into the villages around us. Of course, they can do that. They have thousands of soldiers, tanks and helicopters. But they do not dare to come here in small groups."

Jaradi was standing next to another young man from Maarakeh, Mohammed Saad. He believed the Israelis were not as strong as people thought. "We attack in groups of three. First we observe our targets for a period of time, then we attack. Now we expect the Israelis will attack us. It could happen at any time."

When dawn arrived in Maarakeh on March 2, 1985, such an attack occurred. Around 800 Israeli soldiers arrived in 150 armored vehicles, 30 jeeps and trucks, along with five tanks and two bulldozers, pulling in from three sides. They gathered approximately 350 men from the village for interrogation. The two resistance leaders, Jaradi and Saad, managed to get away. The soldiers went from house to house, bulldozing any where weapons were found. In shops and homes, the Israelis damaged various stores of grain and mixed heating oil with cooking oil, rendering these supplies unusable. They also looked through the village mosque and *husseinieh*, the Shia religious community house. In the mosque, soldiers ripped up the Koran and threw the remains onto the floor.

When they were finished, the officers gave the impression they were satisfied and the soldiers left Maarakeh. The following day, the village welfare committee convened to discuss the supply situation. Along with the other villages east of Tyre, they had been isolated for many days. But now that the siege was lifted, they could discuss how to obtain new provisions and help those most in need.

They met in a small back office on the first floor of the *husseinieh*. The building had been searched for explosives after the raid, but nothing turned up. Unknown to the resistance commanders, however, their arrival had been noted by a collaborator who had been keeping watch from the balcony of his nearby home. When he saw Saad and Jaradi walking into the *husseinieh* he informed the Israelis with a walkie-talkie.

Jaradi spoke to the group, sitting on the edge of the desk, while Saad leaned against the open doorway and listened. Suddenly, he interrupted his friend, exclaiming,"Something is wrong! We should leave immediately!" [31]

But he was told that the building had been searched and was safe.

"No, no," Saad insisted, "We need to leave right now!"

Just then, the 12-kilogram bomb hidden beneath the desk where Saad sat exploded, destroying the office and most of the second floor.

Over the communications network at UNIFIL headquarters, we learned that UN soldiers had arrived on the scene. They worked to dig the dead and wounded from the rubble. The death count reached 12, with 25 survivors. One of those killed was Khalil Jaradi. Helicopters came to fetch the most seriously injured, among them Mohammed Saad.

"Don't send him to the hospital in Tyre," shouted some from the crowd, "The Israelis will certainly carry out a raid!"

Saad was flown to the UNIFIL field hospital, while many of the others were sent to Jabal Amel Hospital in Tyre, where vehicles drove through the streets, asking people to give blood over loudspeakers. Eventually nearly 70 donors, men and women, assembled under the partially covered entrance to the hospital.

Captain Bernard Pascal from France and Major Tor Planting from Finland came to the hospital as well. They belonged to the UN observer corp. (United Nations Trust Supervision Organization; UNTSO). Then the Israelis arrived. First one group of six foot soldiers, led by a young and aggressive lieutenant. At first the unarmed French UN observer tried to stop the Israelis before they attempted to force their way through the crowd and into the hospital.[32]

"Don't you think we will manage to get in?" asked the Israeli lieutenant scornfully.

"Yes: you have weapons," answered Pascal. The two UN observers placed themselves between the Israelis and the Lebanese who had come to give blood. "*Allahu Akbar*," shouted some of the women. The UNTSO officers briefly succeeded in calming the crowd.

A few of the Israeli soldiers tried to get in through the back entrance. Major Planting placed himself in the doorway. The Israelis called for reinforcements over the radio, and 12 more soldiers showed up. The temperament of the crowd, which up to that point had been nervous, now became heated.

Several women renewed the shouts of, "*Allahu Akbar, Allahu Akbar!*" The phrase served as a slogan against the occupation, and it was widely called from the minarets whenever Israeli forces approached. The crowd began to move. The UNTSO officers again tried to calm them down. The Israelis became nervous, and the lieutenant fired live ammunition over the heads of the unarmed UN observers. The shots drew more Lebanese civilians to the entrance of the hospital. A new crowd formed on the other side of the parking lot, behind the Israeli soldiers.

"Israel is a devil, and will always be a devil," someone shouted. The soldiers began to fire at the ground in front of the crowd. Two Lebanese were injured by the ricochets.

New Israeli reinforcements arrived: four armored personnel carriers full of soldiers. A major showed up together with men from Shin Bet in civilian clothes. The crowd by the parking lot kept shouting slogans at the Israelis, the curses coming like hail.

Suddenly, the soldiers got the signal to storm the hospital. They threw shock grenades, which gave off an ear-shattering bang, and used the confusion to rush forward through the crowd, knocking people to the floor with the butts of rifles. They ran through the corridors, firing into the ceilings and walls. The chief doctor at the hospital, Ahmed Mroueh, tried to stop them from forcing their way into an operating room. The doctor, dressed in a white coat, got a rifle butt to the head. Another Lebanese, Hassan Hawila, who was in the process of donating blood, was also hit. Several male nurses were thrown to the floor. There they lay helpless while the Israeli soldiers beat and kicked them.

Captain Pascal offered first aid to a man who had been hit by a shock grenade. Major Planting tried to fetch water for another Lebanese who lay in shock. He was stopped by an Israeli soldier, who stuck his rifle's muzzle in Planting's face, screaming, "Are you a Palestinian?"

"Not yet, but soon I will be," answered the Finnish major coldly. He pushed the rifle to one side and went into the hospital to get water. Several of the Israeli soldiers seemed to be amusing themselves. They pointed their rifles at Lebanese faces and did the same to Captain Pascal. Then they fired into the air instead.

After 20 minutes the entire hospital was under Israeli control. Armed soldiers stood on the roof and balconies with their fingers on their triggers. Finally, an Israeli colonel who called himself "Gaby" arrived with several agents from Shin Bet. They brought along computer printouts and began a systematic interrogation of the patients. Sometime later the French UNIFIL Colonel Max

Rabeyrolles arrived. He was chief of the UN force's assistance group for civilian Lebanese. He told the Israeli colonel, "I have to help those who are lying outside bleeding."

"My men can do that," answered the Israeli.

"The men you are looking for are dead," Colonel Rabeyrolles advised. "I have just come from Maarakeh."

The Israeli colonel did not do as he had promised and they were still lying bloody on the ground when the Israelis left with 20 injured men from the hospital. They tagged the prisoners on their foreheads or backs with red or black markers, and bound them with plastic bands. They were then shoved into armored vehicles or, if there was no room, tied to the outside.

Standing outside the hospital, a 12-year-old boy shouted after the soldiers in halting English, "We will attack a town in Galilee as revenge for Maarakeh. Tomorrow, or the day after, and every day we will make car bombs."

The Israelis denied they were behind the bomb explosion in Maarakeh. But there were a few who believed them. Well-informed Israeli journalists told me later that the army had used "unorthodox methods" to get the better of the "terrorists" in the north. The collaborator who alerted the Israelis to Saad and Jaradi's arrival at the *husseinieh* was subsequently arrested by Amal and executed. His family was expelled from Maarakeh.

CHAPTER TWENTY SIX
A Gruesome Month

March 8, 1985, was the day Sayyed Mohammed Hussein Fadlallah was to be assassinated. A car full of explosives was driven from East Beirut to the suburb of Bir Abed in the southern part of West Beirut. The car bomb was placed at a corner just outside the apartment building where the Shias' top cleric lived with his family.

The 51-year-old Fadlallah was at the mosque to deliver the Friday sermon. As the popular cleric preached from the pulpit, the CIA's new station chief in Beirut, Bruce Jackman, received a call from the chief of Lebanese army intelligence, Colonel Simon Qassis.

"Can you come to the defense ministry? There is something I want to show you," said Qassis. Jackman, who was in his office at the American Embassy in East Beirut, answered, "I will come this afternoon."

"No, come now! Immediately! This is important." Jackman jumped into his car and drove to the defense ministry in Yarze.

When Fadlallah had finished his sermon, he was scheduled to go to his home nearby. But a woman stopped him before he left the mosque. She said she had an important question. Fadlallah asked her to come back another day. The woman insisted, so Fadlallah yielded and listened to her. After he had answered her, he led the woman and some others in prayer.[33]

That was when the car with 200 kilograms of TNT exploded, while the CIA station chief and Colonel Qassis watched from the roof of the defense ministry. Both saw the flames, heard the explosion and observed the smoke which came billowing up from the Bir Abed quarter.

"This is revenge for the attack on the quarters at the airport. This equals 50 American soldiers," Qassis said.[34]

The delay at the mosque saved Fadlallah's life. But 81 other Lebanese were killed, among them the cleric's bodyguard, Jihad Mughniyeh—a younger brother of Imad, the man responsible for most kidnappings of western hostages from West Beirut.

There was a crater in the middle of the street of destroyed shops and residences, three meters deep and five meters in diameter. Journalists who arrived later found a large banner hanging from the ruins, written in English: "Made in America."[35]

Bruce Jackman had previously sent a message to headquarters in Langley in which he warned that America's Lebanese partners were difficult to control. He was not alone: the vice-director of the CIA, John McMahon, had also advised against supporting the Lebanese intelligence service with money and equipment. He thought the Christian officers were on a vendetta against the Shias. The warnings fell on deaf ears; the CIA director did not care what methods the Lebanese used to kill Fadlallah.[36]

Later, President Reagan's national security advisor Robert McFarlane refused to admit the CIA was behind the mass killing. He thought it had to have been "villains" who were operating without American approval. CIA people, however, briefed the Israelis and said they had hired three Christian Lebanese from Tripoli to do the job. They had received $100,000 in payment.[37]

Hizbullah's security service eventually discovered that the assassination attempt was planned by Major Adonis Nehme, under the command of Colonel Qassis. During the hunt for other participants, Hizbullah's men captured a number of Lebanese. They were all executed.[38]

Two days after the car-bomb attack in Bir Abed, I went to Tel Aviv and Jerusalem to find out what well-informed Israeli contacts could relate about developments in South Lebanon. I noticed an open arrogance toward the Shias, and a lack of understanding about them. Neither leading Israeli politicians nor their supporters understood what power the Shias represented. Hardly anyone had absorbed the importance of the October 1983 Ashura incident in bolstering religious Shias' will to resist and fight.[39] The Israelis only talked about Shia terrorism, about messianic Shia fanaticism, about the Shias' ultimate goal: to take Jerusalem. Few placed any blame on the Israeli occupation of South Lebanon in these matters.

When I arrived back in Nabatiyeh that evening of March 10th, 1985, Ane-Karine told me what had happened in South Lebanon that afternoon. Around 2 pm an Israeli column drove into Lebanon near the Israeli border town of Metulla and continued northward between the Shia town of Khiam and the Christian villages of Qleia and Marjayoun, not far from the area assigned to the Norwegian UN battalion.

There was a large fireball, then a black cloud of smoke rose toward the sky. Both Lebanese and Israelis had seen similar things before, and it did not take long for radio stations and news bureaus to report that a Mercedes had driven into a truck and exploded. This time 12 Israeli soldiers were killed, while 20 were seriously injured and sent to various hospitals in northern Israel.

Around 4 pm one of Beirut's radio stations received an anonymous phone call claiming that a martyr from the national resistance movement had avenged the attempted murder of Fadlallah in Beirut. Later that evening another caller told a western news bureaus in Beirut, "Tell our enemy Shimon Peres that his iron glove against our people will be answered by Hussein's victorious and faithful fist." Once more the Islamic resistance emphasized that the Prophet Mohammed's grandson, Hussein, was the great inspiration for the fight against Israel.

Israeli investigators thought the vehicle used in the attack came from the Shia village of Zrariyeh. The village lay in a strategic position north of the Litani River, between the coastal city of Tyre and Nabatiyeh. That same afternoon, one of the Amal militia operations chiefs, Riad al-Assad, was sitting on a hill outside Zrariyeh, looking up at the sky. The tall, slender 27-year-old Lebanese engineer, who had been educated in the United States, thought the Israelis would attack within a day. His concern grew when he saw an Israeli plane flying in circles over the village.[40]

Riad gave orders to place bombs along the roadside just outside the village, and around 4 am on March 11th, he saw the lights of a vehicle column approaching Zrariyeh from the north, through the so-called Devil's Valley. Riad had placed his car outside the village to escape being hemmed in. As Amal's chief of operations in the district, he was not expected to fight on the front lines, and he got away when there still was time. But before he could leave, he noticed to his concern that the bombs along the roadside had apparently been disarmed by the Israelis.

The Lebanese government soldier Mohammed Mouazen was among several stationed in Zrariyeh. He kept watch on a small encampment outside the village. When the first Israelis showed up, Mouazen put down his rifle and raised his hands to show he would not fight. An Israeli officer went over to the unarmed soldier and shot him in the temple.

Closer to the village, the Israelis faced militia soldiers willing to die in battle. But the Israelis were a superior force and showed no mercy. They killed everyone with a rifle, and many others who were weaponless.

Over loudspeakers, the Israelis ordered all men between 15 and 60 to meet at the village square. No one came. The inhabitants of Zrariyeh remembered the invasion of 1982, when the Israelis had given a similar order. On that occasion, the men complied and were arrested. Now the Israelis went house to house and brought the men to the square by force. There waited an Israeli intelligence officer, called Abu Zaid—apparently a pseudonym.

The officer sat at a table with a list of names in front of him. Beside him was a man in civilian clothing with a hood over his head. One after the other, each man was called forward and asked to give his name. The officer checked against the list and asked the hooded man to confirm if the identity was correct. Those marked for arrest were driven away in buses.

"You will die here, and in Beirut sits Nabih Berri and he knows that you will die," the officer told the crowd in Arabic, while Israeli soldiers stood about eating their field rations.

All of a sudden, he ordered a Lebanese prisoner to take his clothes off. Then four Israelis dragged the man around the village to scorn and derision. The officer then had his soldiers remove a Lebanese captain's shoes and socks, then strip him of his officer medals and force him to parade in front of the village's inhabitants.

"Poor you!" called Abu Zaid to the Lebanese officer. "While President Amine Gemayel lives in his luxury palace, Lebanese soldiers are sent out into the field without enough weapons to defend themselves."[41]

Abu Zaid said he knew the car bomb had been rigged in Zrariyeh. Then he added, "If there are more operations like this, then we will gather you all on this square and drive tanks over you. And each time one Israeli soldier is killed, we will come back and kill ten of you with our own hands."

Soon after, the Israeli turned to the man who had confirmed the identities of everyone scheduled for arrest. He tore off the hood from his face, revealing Ahmed Zurot, a 25-year-old local who had previously fought the Israelis.

When the Israeli soldiers left, 11 houses lay in ruins and 150 men had been taken prisoner. The last thing the Israeli intelligence officer said was, "Tell everyone it will cost 100 Lebanese lives for every drop of Israeli blood spilled."[42]

At UNIFIL headquarters I saw pictures of the destruction in Zrariyeh. One showed a crushed Volvo with tank tracks across the roof. In the back seat lay a dead man. Only shoes were visible.

Six corpses were in such bad condition that no one could identify them. The relatives of Na'ami Hashem found only his legs. His ankles had been bound and he had apparently been dragged behind an Israeli jeep. A tank had then driven over him, by which point he must already have been dead or dying.

The dead were driven to a hospital near the village of Sarafand, where Amal was on guard. The hospital registered 34 bodies, which were sent back to be buried later that week.[43]

Zrariyeh was now a village of mourning men and women. One older man told journalists that the Israeli intelligence officer had threatened to return and flatten the village, killing everyone, "if one word, photo or TV image from Zrariyeh came out."

"They cannot be proud of what they have done," he added.

But the Lebanese in the village refused to be intimidated. They freely admitted that some of the dead had puncture wounds from knives or bayonets; some had been blown up inside their homes; some immolated in their cars.[44] One widow said the Israelis had stolen her savings, equal to about $1,500. This was a lot of money for a widow without work. One woman, standing beside her burned-out house, described how the Israelis had set her home on fire because they found a Lebanese army uniform in a closet. She had said the uniform belonged to her son, who was doing his military service in Sidon. But that did not help: the Israeli officer just looked at her coldly and told the soldiers, "Burn the house."

When a journalist asked what would happen to the collaborator Ahmed Zurot, one woman said, "If I ever see him again, I will kill him." Four of her brothers had been taken captive because of the informant.

When a four-year-old boy was asked why he had a rifle made out of wood, his mother responded, "To kill Israelis. One day it will not be made of wood." Another woman added, "When we breast-feed our infants, the milk will contain a strong desire to destroy Israel."

When Riad al-Assad returned to the village, he read a greeting from an Israeli soldier that had been written on a wall: "We come here to avenge every drop of blood." On a wall near the village square was spray-painted,"This is how the IDF avenges itself."[45]

One mother from Zrariyeh said it just as plainly:"Every time they destroy a house or kill one of us, another will be ready to kill them."

She did not have to wait long. The following day a station wagon was on its way to the Qasmieh Bridge over the Litani out near the coast. The driver stopped just before an Israeli control post, turned his car around and parked by the edge of the road. When Israeli patrolmen approached, men from the back seat shot and killed two of them.

That same day, March 12, 1985, Defense Minister Rabin came to Tyre. Dressed in an olive-green uniform jacket, Rabin spoke Hebrew to the reporters outside the army headquarters. A salvo of shots could be heard in the distance. Rabin said: "The raid on Zrariyeh was carried out to disabuse terrorists of the idea that they could plan actions near the Israeli front line without being punished. The Shia leaders had a choice "Either allow calm to reign on both sides of the border, or attack and destroy everyday life to such a degree that they would eventually beg to be allowed to live peacefully alongside Israel."[46]

CHAPTER TWENTY SEVEN

"Don't Take it Personally"

When the United States vetoed a Security Council resolution condemning Israel's occupation of South Lebanon on March 12, 1985, it was bad news for the foreigners who lived in the country. The Americans who worked for the UN were allowed to leave; several diplomats did the same.

With regards to my own work, American support for the occupation meant little. I travelled back and forth between Naqoura and Beirut as usual to edit the UNIFIL monthly magazine. I typically went by UN helicopter and stayed overnight at the so-called UNIFIL House, not far from the refugee camps of Sabra and Shatila.

In Beirut, I drove around in Ane-Karine's old, slightly rusty, dented Passat. The car no longer had diplomatic plates; I had gotten new ones for myself in the Lebanese style, acquiring both the plates and registration card through a "fixer."

I continued to feel secure in West Beirut. The Shias did not seem to be out after officers from UNIFIL. But as the work at the magazine took place in a Shia-dominated area, I chose not to walk around locally in the evening. Instead, I drove to the Commodore Hotel to meet friends. In the bar, Coco chattered as usual, "Hello boy, Hello girl!" before shifting to Beethoven's well-known notes or whistling the sound of mortar grenades.

At times I would meet Terry Anderson of the *Associated Press* and Robert Fisk from *The Times* there at the bar. Anderson thought there was a greater danger of being robbed in Beirut than of being kidnapped. He wrote so in a telex to his boss in New York, who was concerned for his staff in the lawless city.

After a while *AP*'s Beirut chief began to feel he was being watched, but not by car thieves. Privately, he told Gerry LaBelle, the bureau's news editor, that he had possibly been subjected to a kidnapping attempt. Anderson said four men in a Mercedes had tried to stop his car a few hundred meters from his apartment, but he had made a sharp turn to the left and gotten away. He thought they must have been a gang of free-lancers who wanted to scare him. This was two days after the US veto in the Security Council.[47]

Earlier that same day, Terry Anderson had interviewed Fadlallah at his office in the Shia-dominated part of South Beirut. What thoughts did the foremost Shia Muslim thinker and cleric have about the kidnapping of Americans? Fadlallah had been friendly, but immovable: If the Americans insisted on remaining in Lebanon, they made targets of themselves. If all Americans left Lebanon, there would be no more kidnappings. Fadlallah's warnings did not scare Anderson. He interpreted the Shia leader's warnings as being directed at Americans officials, not journalists.

Early the next morning, Anderson had his usual tennis appointment with *AP* photographer Don Mell. While they hit balls over the net, the photographer's sharp eyes noticed a green Mercedes with three bearded men drive by the court twice.

After practice, Anderson drove to Ain el-Mreisseh to drop Mell off at his apartment. Mell stepped out, but remained outside the car for a moment. While he spoke to Anderson through the window, the same green Mercedes he had seen earlier approached. It stopped in front of Anderson's car, blocking the way. The three men jumped out bearing weapons and advanced slowly toward the two Americans.

"I don't like this. Terry, get out of the car," said Mell.[48]

The first of the young men aimed a 9mm pistol at the photographer's forehead and forced him up against the nearest house wall. The other two headed for Anderson's car. One pulled the big, powerful journalist out and held him in a bear hug. Mell was paralyzed. He wanted so much to help his friend but could not. He just stood there and stared at the black pistol. Not a word was said, but Anderson's eyes pleaded, "Do something!" Mell's eyes answered, "I can't."

The three men shoved Anderson into the green Mercedes and drove down a small street toward the front line separating West from East Beirut. Mell remained where he was, stiff with fright and shock.

"Don't take it personally. This is political," one of the kidnappers had said in English as a foot pressed Anderson's head toward the floor. The journalist thought of the other Americans who had been kidnapped for political reasons: William Buckley had been taken 12 months earlier, Reverend Benjamin Weir 10 months earlier and Father Lawrence Martin Jenco two months earlier.

Anderson could feel the barrel of a pistol pressed into his back. It was difficult to breathe where he lay with a blanket over him. He could tell the car had gone onto a main road and then turned onto a side street and into a garage. Inside, the blanket was replaced by a dirty rag over his face, held up with tape that they wrapped around his head. His shoes were taken away, along with his watch, a gold bracelet and gold chain he had around his neck. Anderson got more tape around his wrists, arms, ankles, knees and thighs. Then he was pushed across the floor into a room and set down onto a chair.

"What is your name?" asked a voice with a thick Lebanese accent.

"Terry Anderson, I am a journalist."

"You are a spy."

"No, I am a journalist," answered Anderson and explained what he did at the news bureau.

His colleagues in Beirut "moved heaven and earth" searching for him. We who knew Terry knew that he was a respected journalist, even within Lebanon's militant and anti-western environment. He was accepted as a decent and serious man. Several with whom I spoke thought it was unfair that he was the one to be abducted.

"I hope the kidnappers are freelance, and that they at least do not belong to Islamic Jihad," said Eileen Alt Powell, one of the journalists at the *AP*. I was sitting with Eileen and Gerry LaBelle, her husband and colleague, in the bar at the Commodore. We did not know then that Anderson had been taken to a house where there were already hostages. Father Jenco was there, chained to the wall in a closet that was 60 centimeters deep by 180 centimeters wide. Through a crack in the door, he saw the new hostage chained to a bed. Anderson, traumatized, had no idea as of yet that there were other captives nearby.

After a few days an English-speaking guard arrived with pen and paper. He ordered Anderson to write a short letter, which the man dictated. Once again, the message was that Anderson's fate would mirror that of the 17 imprisoned in Kuwait. The letter ended with the words, "Please do your best to put an end to my imprisonment, because I cannot stand this any longer."

Anderson now understood why he had been kidnapped, and that Shias were responsible. As a reporter, he had time and again heard that many Shias considered the Americans to be the extended arm of Israel in Lebanon. The country had been bombed by planes made in the USA, its houses destroyed by artillery made in the USA. Raiding villages in South Lebanon, many Israelis fired American ammunition from American automatic weapons.

A number of the soldiers had dual American and Israeli citizenship, and it was also not unusual to run into Israelis who spoke English with an American accent. For many of them, any Lebanese who did not belong to the SLA was a possible "terrorist." Several of the young Israeli Americans I spoke with had not thought about the fact Israel was an occupying power in Lebanon.

Among these was James Ron, a 19-year-old with dual citizenship. Ron belonged to one of the IDF's paratrooper corps.[49] One of the first days he was in Lebanon, his company was sent to a village, the name of which he did not even know. The Israeli soldiers had the job of breaking down the door in a dwelling, then locking the mother and her child in a room while they took the middle-aged father outside. They blindfolded him and bound his hands behind his back, then brought him to an out-of-the-way road. There they forced him to his knees, put a pistol to his head and threatened to shoot him if he did not talk. When a UN observer suddenly showed up, the Israelis let the man, whom they had nearly scared to death, go back home.

The following day the paratroopers carried out a mock execution. The victim was a 10-year-old boy. The soldiers first forced his family into their kitchen, and then pulled him into a fruit orchard nearby. The Israeli lieutenant leading the group pushed the boy's face down into the dirt while Ron placed an automatic weapon against his skull. The officer threatened to blow his head off if he wouldn't speak, but the 10-year-old refused to answer anything that was asked of him. Even when the lieutenant threatened to throw him off the roof of a three-story house, the youth did not say a single word.

Private Ron was transferred to another unit. There his soldier colleagues were more used to handling Lebanese. The newcomer learned how he should breakdown doors, empty flour onto a dirty floor, mess up larders, break kitchen equipment and look through drawers and closets.

The Israelis might stay in the villages for days at a time while they hunted for members of the resistance. The elderly, women and children were ordered to stay indoors 24 hours at a stretch. But the men were assembled in the center of the village, had blindfolds put over their eyes and were led away for interrogation.

For two years, Ron went in and out of South Lebanon. At times he was there to protect Israeli agents who paid the South Lebanese militia's salaries. Other times he was sent to defend SLA positions that were under attack. The SLA had mostly Christian officers, but there were also Druze and Shias that rose in the ranks.

Ron and another soldier in the company began to oppose the methods being used against the civilian population, but they were simply laughed at by the other soldiers. Ron was surprised that many of the other young Israelis did not give a thought to the brutal treatment they inflicted on innocent people.

Some of the soldiers had grown up in kibbutzim, others came from middle class families, still others from the upper levels of the social hierarchy. One of the most brutal soldiers Ron fought beside was called Omri. He was the son of an officer in the Israeli intelligence service. Omri liked to shoot anyone who peeked out from a door or window. Another soldier of a similar mind was Rafi, the son of a Liberal member of Parliament. One day he kicked a cup of tea into an old man's face. Ron was most disgusted by his own chief, a lieutenant who was religious but did not have the least consideration for civilians.

After his service ended, James Ron left Israel. He did not want to live in a brutal Zionist state. When I spoke with him later by telephone, he seemed truly sorry for what he had been part of in Lebanon.[50]

CHAPTER TWENTY EIGHT
Buckley's Last Day

When the Israelis established their new front at the Litani River, the prison camp near the village of Ansar was closed. Seven hundred and fifty-two prisoners were set free. Roughly 200 others were blindfolded and driven to Israel. Neither generals nor politicians cared whether this accorded with international law. Israeli leaders of course knew that Israel had ratified the Geneva Conventions, which stated that persons could only be held captive in occupied areas, and could not be moved to the occupiers' own territory for any reason. The Israelis maintained the conventions were not valid for Lebanon since Israel had not declared South Lebanon to be an occupied territory. Additionally, they employed their well-worn argument: Israel had a right to move prisoners for security reasons and to prevent them from being retrained as guerrilla soldiers.

Most of the prisoners set free from Ansar were Shias from South Lebanon. Not all of them were allowed to go home. Many were from villages in the Israeli-occupied zone, and the Israelis did not want more questionable Shias there. They were forced northwards toward Beirut.

The Israelis' insistence that all Shias were "terrorists" was shamelessly worked into the mass media: We are face to face with fanatical Shia terrorists on Israel's northern border. This terrorism is being carried out by a small minority of extremists. They receive no sympathy from the rest of the population in Lebanon.

A noticeable shift had taken place within Israel as to who were viewed as terrorists. Previously, it had been primarily Palestinians whom they fought against in Lebanon. The Shias were then seen as friendly. But as the occupation drew out, the Shias had increasingly realized Israel's intentions with the invasion. Then they too became "terrorists."

This propaganda had an effect on the young Israeli soldiers. One day in April 1985, a Finnish UN major told me he was upset over the Israeli behavior in South Lebanon. Major Martii Makkonen had, together with his French superior, Colonel Jean-Claude Verité, driven the coast road from Tyre toward Naqoura. When they passed an Israeli foot patrol, they saw a little girl of six or seven among the soldiers. The little girl was a living shield against attack: the Israelis assumed no Arab would set off a bomb or attack the soldiers if it also risked the life of a Lebanese child.

The French colonel was upset. "I am a professional soldier," he said, "I know about dirty warfare from Algeria, but this exceeds everything and gives me goose bumps. And if that were not enough, when relayed what I had seen to well-educated adult Israelis, they were neither shocked nor surprised. They thought human shields were defensible and understandable. It was a question of saving their own lives."

When the state-controlled Israeli television channel showed six paratroopers on patrol in South Lebanon, the entire nation learned what the occupation did to their young soldiers. The camera ran as a small van emerged from a side street 200 meters ahead of the patrol. The soldiers threw themselves to the ground, shouted and waved the vehicle away from the road as they fired into the air. The van stopped and an elderly woman stepped out. With great dignity, and without looking at the soldiers, she went into a barn nearby. Everything was filmed. And when the reporter later asked one of the paratroopers what tasks he was carrying out in Lebanon, he replied:"I am not fighting. I am only bothering people. I am afraid of every 12-year-old."[51]

On May 17, 1985, the militia in East and West Beirut were bombarding each other. The Palestinian soldiers who had been evacuated from West Beirut in 1982 were back in the refugee camps of Sabra, Shatila and Bourj el-Barajne. Yasser Arafat wanted bases as close to Israel as possible. The PLO headquarters were in Tunis, and the guerrilla soldiers were otherwise spread to the winds. But neither Syria nor their Lebanese Shia allies in Amal wanted the PLO to become a factor of power in Lebanon again. The militia decided, therefore, to attack the camps.

Three days later I stood on a balcony at UNIFIL House looking toward Shatila, where three years ago I had gone about counting corpses. Amal's militia and the Shia Muslim Sixth brigade from the army were moving ahead toward the camp. The following day other soldiers moved toward Bourj el-Barajne near the airport. Once more, tens of thousands of civilian Palestinians were fleeing their homes.

It was difficult for journalists to get into the besieged Palestinian refugee camps, but stories of new massacres began to leak out. The Amal militia threw grenades into the temporary hospital. The wounded were dragged from the operating table and shot. Some reports were factual, others fiction.

In Shatila the Palestinians hid in tunnels and underground bunkers and continued fighting. Nabih Berri accused Yasser Arafat of mixing the Palestinian cause with Lebanon's internal problems.

Thanks to help from Hizbullah, the Palestinians managed to resist the Amal attacks, albeit with large losses. Hizbullah's militia was still not strong enough to confront Amal. Asked to comment on Amal's attacks, Arafat compared the killings of the Palestinians in Beirut to the massacre in Karbala when the Prophet Mohammed's grandson Hussein and his flock were killed by Caliph Yazid. The caliph, had been situated in Damascus, like Amal's supporter, President Hafez al-Assad.[52]

The Amal militia hunted for Palestinians all over West Beirut. The militia killed and tortured, acts which led Palestinian factions allied with Syria to switch sides and fight together with Arafat's forces against Amal. From Druze territory in the Chouf Mountains, the Palestinians bombarded Shia areas in southern Beirut, where Amal was more or less in control.

In Beirut, the number of western hostages increased. The French journalist Jean-Paul Kauffmann and a French sociologist, Michel Seurat, were abducted on May 22, 1985. Five days later a British teacher at AUB, Dennis Hill, was kidnapped. Two days later, Hill was found with a bullet in his head. "Killed while trying to escape, it is said," I noted in my little black book. The director of American University Hospital in Beirut, David Jacobsen, was abducted too, at gunpoint, on his way to the office. Guards at the entrance a few tens of meters away looked the other way.

At first, Jacobsen was interrogated and accused of being in the CIA. Then the conversation took a sinister turn: "You are Jewish; You have a Jewish name."[53]

"No, I'm not Jewish. It's a Jewish-sounding name, but I am a Christian. I was raised a Lutheran. My parents came to America from Denmark in 1917, and the name had an 'e' at the end. I can prove my background. I can say something in Danish," Jacobsen assured them.

He was happy they did not ask him for a demonstration, because all he could say was "*Glade jul,*"Merry Christmas, which he doubted would have passed muster.

Wooden partitions running from floor to ceiling divided the room where he was kept into three cells. Jacobsen had the cell in the middle. To one side was Terry Anderson, two months into his imprisonment. In the third cell, William Buckley lay suffering.

The other prisoners were elsewhere in the building. Father Jenco's little cell, a clothes closet, was out in the hallway which led to the toilet and bath. Jenco slept on a mat which had been placed partly in the closet and partly in the hall. He grunted each time the other hostages kicked his pillow on their way to the toilet.

Buckley was sick. Jacobsen heard him say to the one of the guards,"I don't know what is happening to my body. Thirty days ago, I was strong."[54]

A few days later, Buckley coughed and babbled deliriously. The guards did nothing to help. Father Jenco could hear Buckley hallucinating. "I'll have my hot cakes with blueberry syrup now," he said.

Around 6 PM on Jacobsen's fourth day of captivity, June 3, 1985, one of guards asked him, in a weak effort to disguise what was going on, "I have a friend who is sick. What can I do for him?" He described Buckley's symptoms.

"I understand. He is one of us," answered Jacobsen. The guard said nothing. He had not ever admitted there were other prisoners in the room. Jacobsen assumed he had been asked because the guard knew he worked at a hospital. But he was, of course, no doctor and had no training in treating the sick. He just said, "On the basis of what I hear, you better get him to a hospital or a doctor, or else he is going to die."

"That's not possible," answered the guard. "You must help. Tell us what we can do here."

Jacobsen tried to recall everything he had learned in first aid courses or heard when physicians discussed cases at medical staff meetings. He suggested the guard should first give the sick man something to reduce the fever and then settle his stomach. The guard said he would go to the pharmacy for medicine, but he did not. He just remained sitting, watching the TV.

The other prisoners heard Buckley's constant muttering. At one point, he managed to raise himself half-way up, squatting. He fantasized about food: soft-boiled egg on toast and pancakes.

Around 10 PM the babbling turned to gurgling. Jacobsen and Anderson understood these were the sounds of a dying man. Then all was still. A few minutes later the two of them heard Buckley being dragged out with the chains still on his legs.

As Buckley was carried past Jenco, the priest asked where they were going. One of the guards said they were going to the hospital. Jenco asked why the patient was so quiet, and the guard admitted he was dead. A few hours later Jacobsen was told that the deceased "now was in a wonderful place where the sun is shining and the birds are chirping." This was how Paradise was described in the Koran. It seemed unbelievable to the others that the guard would envision the CIA station chief for Beirut there and not in Hell.

CHAPTER TWENTY NINE
Hijacking in Athens

On June 6, 1985, the third anniversary of Israel's invasion, its chief of the Northern Command, Major General Ori Orr, announced the army had completed the third phase of its retreat from Lebanon. Orr said that the 2,500 men of the SLA, led by General Antoine Lahd, would now have the primary responsibility for South Lebanon. Around 1,000 Israeli soldiers would remain in the "security zone."

While Hizbullah wanted to lead the fight against the Israelis in South Lebanon under Islam's banner, Amal wanted an umbrella organization, the National Lebanese Resistance Movement, to take the lead. Amal wanted cooperation between all groups and factions in order to keep Iran from a dominant role in the resistance fight. It was no secret that Syria and Iran were competing to fill the vacuum left by the Israelis.

When the president of Iran's national assembly, Mehdi Karroubi, arrived for a visit in the middle of June 1985, Amal's leadership decided to show its muscle. Politely but firmly, they stopped Karroubi and his entourage at a control post in South Lebanon, a bit north of the occupation zone. The Iranians were escorted back under strong protest. They initially directed their anger at the Syrians: it was obvious that Damascus had a part in the decision to deny them access to areas recently abandoned by the Israelis.[55]

In Beirut the chaos increased. The Sunni militia, Mourabitoun, began to fight against Amal and the army's Shia Muslim Sixth Brigade. The Mourabitoun received funding from Libya and carried out its attacks to ease pressure on the Palestinian camps. Earlier the Druze had quietly supported the Palestinians by giving them free passage and making certain weapons came in to the camps. These weapons were also bought and paid for by Libya. After a while, Walid Jumblatt's Druze militia were directly involved in the fight against Amal.

To get an even better position in the Lebanese power struggle, and to increase pressure on the US, the most radical Shias in Hizbullah decided to do something that would gain visibility throughout the world. On June 13, 1985, three Lebanese Shias in their 20s flew from Beirut to Athens, where they bought tickets for Rome with Trans World Airlines (TWA), an American company. TWA flight 847 was overbooked, however, and only two of the well-dressed Lebanese were able to board when the time came.

The two men made a big fuss as they went through security. One of them, dressed in a so-called Palm Beach outfit—navy blue blazer; oxford-cloth, slate-colored shirt; gray pants and brown loafers—pushed his way through the crowd and put his shoulder bag onto the conveyor belt in between hand baggage belonging to an American couple. The second Lebanese set off the alarm when he went through the metal detector. He took a pen and lighter from his pockets, then went through again and triggered a second alarm. Only after the third try did he get the green light. Then he pushed his way through the crowd to be the first onto the bus shuttling passengers out to the aircraft. At 10 AM local time the plane taxied for take-off.

Twenty minutes later, the two Lebanese rose from their seats waving pistols and grenades. They soon had control of the aircraft, which carried 153 passengers. One of the hijackers seemed calm and spoke in a low voice, while the other shouted and threatened. They ordered Captain John Testrake to fly to Beirut.

When the air controllers in Beirut heard that the hijacked American plane was coming, they received orders to block the runways with empty buses and vehicles. But the captain said over the radio, "We have to be allowed to land in Beirut. He is ready to blow the plane up. I repeat: We have to be allowed to land in Beirut!"

Following discussions in the control tower and some initial reluctance, leadership at the Beirut airport gave in. On the ground the plane was supplied with fuel as the hijackers had demanded. They also insisted to be allowed to speak with the head of Amal, but were refused. After putting forth demands that Lebanese prisoners in Israel, Algeria and Cyprus be set free, they released 19 women and children.

The plane then took off for Algiers, a trip calculated to take four hours flying over Cyprus and Crete. En route, one of the hijackers suddenly assaulted a number of passengers. He tore off an armrest and severely beat Kurt Carlson, a major in the US Army Reserves, leaving him slumped on the floor in the cockpit door.[56]

As the plane neared Algeria, the pilot learned the authorities would not give him permission to land. "Then we will blow up the plane," responded the hijackers. Only after President Reagan had called Algeria's president was the plane allowed to land.

Meanwhile, the third hijacker who could not get onboard was arrested and identified. A Mossad officer in Athens named Haim Nativ had come to the airport to find out if any Israelis were onboard. With some bribery, he obtained a copy of the passenger list and the retained halves of the boarding passes. In this way he traced where the passengers with Arabic names had purchased their tickets, and discovered that one of the three hijackers' tickets, issued to a Mr. Ali Atwa, had not been used. Figuring that Atwa must still be at the airport, he got the police to call his name over the public address system. Ali Atwa fell right into the trap and was arrested. But the arrest was kept secret.[57]

In Algiers, the hijackers released 21 more passengers and then gave orders to return to Lebanon. The plane refueled and took off, landing in Beirut after midnight. The crew in the control tower had done its best to deny permission to land, but Captain Testrake said the plane was nearly empty of fuel and the hijackers were threatening to kill him.

Once more the hijackers asked to speak with representatives from Amal, but no one showed up. They responded by shooting a marine named Robert Stethem. The captain screamed into the microphone, "He just killed a passenger! He just killed a passenger!" Then the controllers in the tower heard the voice of one of the hijackers: "Do you understand? Do you believe us now? The same will happen again in five minutes."

The Lebanese in the control tower answered, "Is it not shameful to kill an innocent passenger?"

"Have you forgotten the massacre in Bir Abed?" the hijacker shouted back. He was referring to the car bombing which had targeted Sayyed Mohammed Hussein Fadlallah, but instead killed 81 others.

Just minutes later an Amal militia leader, accompanied by his bodyguard, boarded the plane. Soon the hijackers demanded all lights at the airport be shut off. The press, who were following the drama minute by minute, thought this was because they feared an Israeli commando raid. But they actually wanted to hide the fact that a dozen armed men from Amal had joined the hijackers. In addition, they took seven passengers with Jewish-sounding names from the plane and had them driven to the Shia-dominated part of Beirut.

After the body of Robert Stethem, which had been thrown onto the tarmac, had been lying there for two hours, one of the hijackers said over the radio, "The Red Cross can pick up the corpse." Then came a new order:"I want 200 sandwiches, 150 apples and 40 kilos of bananas. But first fuel. Quickly!"While the food was being delivered and the tanks refueled, the pilot requested a clear runway. Asked for the destination, he answered, "I don't know."

News leaked that Ali Atwa had been arrested in Athens. The hijackers were also informed and they demanded that the Greek authorities release him immediately and send him to Algiers, or else they would kill all eight Greek passengers onboard. The Greeks did not hesitate for long before complying.

The hijackers forced the pilots on TWA Flight 847 fly there as well, and after landing two high-level representatives came onboard to negotiate. This resulted in 60 additional passengers being set free. Before the passengers were allowed to leave, however, the hijackers took all of their money and valuables.

That same evening, June 15, the hijackers announced that since their demand to free Lebanese in Israeli jails had been ignored, the plane would fly on to another destination, then the plane would be destroyed and with the remaining passengers onboard. The next morning they flew for a third time to Beirut. Before they landed, 200 soldiers from the Lebanese army were ordered to disperse. The entire airport was now in Amal hands. Fearing a possible American commando action, most of the passengers were divided into groups and sent to various places in Beirut's southern sector. The airport was mined, to make it more difficult for the Americans or Israelis to free the hostages.

From the plane, the hijackers demanded newspapers, food and videocassettes. They asked the International Red Cross Committee to work on freeing 50 Shias in Israel. And they also asked for a meeting with Nabih Berri, a representative from the UN, another from the Red Cross Committee and the ambassadors from France, Spain and Great Britain.

One of the pilots, Christian Zimmermann, who also had studied to be a reverend, struck up a conversation with the hijackers. He got the impression that the young Lebanese from Hizbullah were not fanatics, and that they were uncertain in which direction Lebanon should go. Should the country become like Iran, or remain like the Lebanon they knew from the past?[58] The hijackers told Zimmermann that they heard one thing from Ayatollah Khomeini and another thing from Sayyed Mohammed Hussein Fadlallah. The Iranian leader said the world was on its way to becoming an Islamic state, and when that happened there would no longer be borders between nations, and there would be peace. The first goal was a united Lebanon, free from civil war. Then the fight should be directed against Zionist Israel, which would be overturned.

The American pilot sensed the hijackers from Hizbullah thought this approach was problematic. A united Lebanon would require pluralism, coexistence between people of fundamentally different views, between Shias and Sunnis, Druze and Christians. Even the arch-enemy, the Maronites, would have to be included. How could those who belonged to Hizbullah—the party of God—make compromises and at the same time follow God's will, as Khomeini interpreted it? They were fighting against Israel and Israel's allies, but they were also fighting against other Muslims in Beirut. And what would become of this world peace if the Muslims could not find peace with each other?

CHAPTER THIRTY
Triangular Game

In the middle of that dramatic month of June 1985, Nabih Berri took on the task of negotiating with the hijackers to free the hostages. By then Hizbullah had already removed seven Americans from the plane, all with Jewish-sounding names, and taken them to various places in the southern part of Beirut. Imad Mughniyeh, the chief architect of most of the earlier kidnappings, had control over them.

The 46-year-old Berri, who was minister of justice, of water and electricity supplies and of South Lebanon, demanded the US ask Israel to release 700 Shias prisoners. He also demanded that American warships leave Lebanese waters. But the United States refused to be "dictated to by demands of terrorists." The Americans would not recommend that Israel release Shia prisoners, but said a prisoner exchange might be possible. The Israelis refused to "negotiate with terrorists," but would consider releasing prisoners if the US asked for it.

The Norwegian Embassy counselor in Beirut, Odd Wibe, wanted to know what had been happening behind the scenes. He arranged a meeting with Lebanon's military intelligence chief, Colonel Simon Qassis. The Christian colonel was full of praise for Nabih Berri.

"There is no longer talk of a hijacking, but of a hostage situation which resembles the one the US was dealing with in Tehran six years earlier," said Qassis, continuing "It will be impossible to free hostages by military operations. Berri has mobilized Amal's forces in West Beirut and along the coast to Sidon. Under serious threat he can arrange for 10,000 Shia Muslims to sit at the airport and prevent any attack."[59]

Qassis saw only one way out of the mess: the Israelis had to release a large number of Lebanese prisoners. This could possibly be done under the cover of what had been planned for a long time. "Nabih Berri would nevertheless be a great hero," Qassis thought.

Later in the evening of June 20, a message came to journalists waiting at the Commodore Hotel. There would be a press conference at the airport. In all haste, members of the media jumped into taxis and proceeded in a cortege to the airport in pitch blackness. In the transit hall was a long table covered with a white tablecloth, water bottles, and small cakes. Amal's leader had figured maybe 50–60 journalists would come along with photographers. Twice that many showed up.

Armed Amal men led out five of the passengers and placed them at the head of the table. The journalists and photographers pushed in around them, and the situation grew chaotic as those in the back tried to get closer. Shoving devolved into fist fights. People swore, and some of the photographers jumped onto the table. They terrified the five passengers as they came tramping toward them down the white tablecloth, stepping between the glasses and the cakes. After being held in captivity for six days, they had hoped they could finally tell their story to the world and assure their loved ones they were okay. Now they were virtually assaulted by an undisciplined, uncontrollable and rowdy gang from the press.

Amal's coordinators realized they had lost control. The guards quickly led the hostages out through a door. After loud media protests, they announced there would be another opportunity if everyone behaved properly. A few minutes later the hostages returned. Their spokesman, Allyn

Conwell, spoke. Calmly and carefully, he explained that he had been in contact with all the hostages. They were spread in various places around Beirut, and everyone was fine: they were provided with decent housing, food and drink and, if needed, medical assistance. In a statement on behalf of all the captives, he said: "We understand that Israel is holding as hostage a number of Lebanese people who undoubtedly have as equal a right and as strong a desire to go home as we do…We sincerely ask and pray that this task be expeditiously completed, especially now that the Israeli forces are (in the) south of Lebanon or almost out of this country."[60]

Before the press conference, the president of Iran's national assembly, Ali Akbar Hashemi Rafsanjani, had sent a message to the US National Security Council promising to do what he could to resolve the TWA crisis. When Rafsanjani stopped in Damascus after a visit to Tunisia, he quickly gave instructions to the Iranian ambassador in Syria: "Pressure Hizbullah to release the hostages."[61] Ambassador Ali Akbar Mohtashemi had not only been a driver for the establishment of Hizbullah, he had also run parts of the organization and had a close working relationship with Imad Mughniyeh.

It was clear to many that the Iranian National Assembly leader wanted a better relationship with the United States. The Iranians sorely needed weapons, ammunition and parts for their war with Iraq. During the Shah's time, Iran had received weapons from the US, but that was now over. The Americans had broken off all contacts following the 1979 embassy occupation in Tehran, and had banned any weapons or ammunition sales to Khomeini's Iran. Washington had additionally chosen Iraq's side in the war, and the CIA station chief in Amman, Thomas Twetten, traveled to Baghdad personally to deliver satellite reconnaissance and other intelligence material—secretly, of course.

Following discussions between Syrian President Hafez al-Assad and Nabih Berri, and after consultations with Hizbullah's leadership, the decision came to release the hostages. They would be driven to Damascus and turned over to the western ambassadors there. Imad Mughniyeh, the head man behind the hijacking, had been under strong pressure from Syria—but he also understood that a protracted crisis would not be to Hizbullah's advantage.

The following day, Israel announced they were freeing 79 Shia prisoners, without admitting any connection with the hijacking. The promise from Israel was enough for the hijackers to free the last 39 passengers from the TWA plane. They flew back via an American military base in West Germany on June 30. One month later, 70 Lebanese prisoners in Israel were allowed to go home. The Israelis maintained their release had nothing to do with the hijacking. There were of course few who believed that.

For my part, the summer of 1985 was spent finishing *Nederlag. Israels krig i Libanon*, or *A Pattern for Defeat: Israel's War in Lebanon*. I delivered the manuscript to my publisher, Cappelen Damm, who had announced a competition for the year's best documentary book. In the final chapter, I wrote that Defense Minister Rabin's hard line policy in Lebanon was beginning to resemble the policy the Israelis had initially had toward the Palestinians in the West Bank and Gaza Strip during 1970–1972. At that time the generals thought that, if only they had free reign, they would be able to defeat their enemy. It was the same argument the American generals had used in Vietnam.

Influential Israeli politicians were also paying attention beyond their neighboring countries. Even though Iran was Israel's enemy in Lebanon, it was not in Israel's interest that Iran lose its war with Iraq. The intelligence services followed events there closely. As seen through Israeli eyes, Saddam Hussein was a more threatening enemy than Ayatollah Khomeini. Therefore, the Israelis offered to help Iran, through a middleman, to get ammunition and parts from America for weapons which had been purchased during the Shah's regime. The Iranians for their part could promise,"If we win this war, we will not forget to thank those who helped us... You will be witness to a dramatic change in Tehran's position toward Israel."[62]

The Reagan administration also sought better contacts with the Iranians, not least because of the many Americans who had been kidnapped in Lebanon. National Security Advisor Robert McFarlane wanted to gain influence with revolutionary Tehran before the Soviet Union did.

McFarlane, who had a background in the State Department, believed Israel had good contacts in Iran despite the severe criticism of the Zionist state from leaders in Tehran. He got in contact with Michael Ledeen, who was not only his friend, but also a true American Zionist. Would Ledeen secretly go to Israel to check the situation? The professor agreed and had no problem getting an appointment with Prime Minister Shimon Peres without the Pentagon, CIA or State Department knowing anything about it. Face to face with the Israeli prime minister on May 6, 1985, McFarlane's envoy asked straight out, could Israel help the US with contacts in Tehran?[63]

The wily Peres first said that Israel's intelligence service was not particularly good, and that it was important for Israel to cooperate with the US in order to gain entry into Khomeini's Iran. Fortunately, he added, Israel did have one good Iranian contact, who had previously worked for the Shah's secret service, SAVAK. He was living in exile now, but nevertheless maintained good connections with the leaders in the new Iranian regime.

When Professor Ledeen returned and gave his report, McFarlane wrote a memo to Secretary of State George Shultz and Secretary of Defense Caspar Weinberger. Shultz' closest military colleague, Major General Colin Powell, was the first to see the top secret memo with the title "US Policy Towards Iran." Powell, who would later become Chief of the General Staff and Secretary of State, understood quickly that McFarlane's desire for a dialogue with Iran would also involve the sale of weapons. Powell reacted strongly; he could hardly believe that the national security advisor was in favor of delivering weapons to a country which had held 52 American diplomats hostage for over a year, and whom the US formally characterized as a terrorist state. Besides, Reagan had officially promised to have nothing to do with Iran. The president had even asked US allies to boycott the Islamic Republic. When Defense Secretary Weinberger read McFarlane's memo two days later, he wrote, "This is nearly too absurd to comment on... Here [in the Pentagon] it is assumed Iran is about to collapse, and that we can deal with the country in a rational manner."[64]

McFarlane went to the Pentagon to explain. The US had an opportunity to get Iran's moderate politicians over on its side before the Soviet Union filled the vacuum left by the Shah's exile. In addition, the initiative could lead to the release of American hostages in Lebanon. Weinberger was not convinced. "The only moderates in Iran... are in the cemetery," he said. George Shultz was just as negative regarding the sale of weapons to Iran. The agreement between the two Secretaries did not help; McFarlane continued his own efforts in secret.

CHAPTER THIRTY ONE
Missiles for Hostages

In Israel, Prime Minister Shimon Peres briefed Foreign Minister Yitzhak Shamir and Defense Minister Yitzhak Rabin. All three agreed to help the US to get a link into Iran. On instructions from the foreign minister, the general director of the foreign ministry, former Mossad agent David Kimche, went to Washington, D.C.[65]

It was warm and humid in the city on July 3, 1985, when the slender Israeli with the big horn-rimmed glasses and toupé came to the White House. After a general discussion, where diplomats from the Israeli Embassy and some from McFarlane's staff were present, Kimche asked to continue the conversation on a man to man basis with McFarlane.

The Israeli said that, a year prior, his former colleagues in the intelligence service had begun secret discussions with Iranians who were dissatisfied with the confusion in Tehran. Many in the Iranian capital were willing and able to establish a new government in Iran if they had help from outside, Kimche said, adding, "And they believe this support can only come from a country large enough to deal with Iran, which is the United States, and with the ability to deter any Soviet involvement, which is the United States."[66]

Kimche further said that Israel's contact could put pressure on Hizbullah to release the American hostages, but this required something in return: weapons. Kimche told him the information came from the former SAVAK agent, Manucher Ghorbanifar. "Ghorba." as he was called, had given the Israelis a list of 1,000 Iranian officers and servicemen who sought closer cooperation with the US.[67]

Ghorbanifar was known to the CIA. The day after William Buckley had been kidnapped in Beirut, Ghorba told American agents in Paris of his contacts in Iran. He thought he could use them to get the kidnapped American freed. The CIA's people did not believe the promises; the Iranian had sold them false information before. Ghorba was challenged when he had to undergo the CIA lie detector test. After that, the CIA operations staff sent out a so-called "burn notice" on the man. Everyone was warned about having anything to do with Manucher Ghorbanifar.[68]

For David Kimche, Ghorba's lies meant little. Israel had its own agenda. Kimche had himself lived with lies during his 30 years in Mossad, and he thought he knew that Ghorba had contacts "high up" in Tehran. He had personally confirmed so much when he had watched Ghorba call someone whom he maintained was the vice-prime minister in the new Iranian regime. The call had taken place from a hotel room in Hamburg. At a more recent meeting, this time in London, Ghorba briefed Kimche specially on the "moderate forces" in the Khomeini regime that wanted contact with the US.[69]

When Kimche left the White House, McFarlane contacted the leadership in the CIA to have them evaluate the Israeli's proposal. Director William Casey said he personally trusted Ghorba's information. He did this without checking with his staff. Casey did not care that the CIA had long forbidden contact with Ghorba; he was desperate to get the hostages out, particularly his own man, William Buckley. Casey of course did not know that Buckley had already been dead for a month.

When McFarlane met Reagan and proposed cooperating with the Iranian opposition in the hopes they could help free the American hostages, Reagan said, "Gosh, that's great news. How would they do it, and how soon?"[70] He asked McFarlane to tell the Israelis that he wanted certainty that the opposition in Tehran had real power. The hostages in Lebanon would have to be freed before it was realistic to make closer contact. One week later the message came back from Israel: The Iranians wanted proof of America's good intentions before they could influence Hizbullah to release the hostages.

In Lebanon, Anderson, Jacobsen and Weir had been moved at odd intervals. Sometimes they were in Shia villages south of Beirut, other times in the Bekaa Valley or in West Beirut. Their treatment improved over time.

One day a guard said to David Jacobsen, "Here is a friend of yours."

"Who is that?" asked Jacobsen, as he sat with a blindfold over his eyes.

"Take a look, then you will see."

Jacobsen lifted his blindfold and saw a man he knew from the agricultural faculty at AUB. It was Thomas Sutherland.

For the hostages, this was almost like Christmas, even though it was only July. They were served beef, vegetables and fruit. They were examined by a doctor—a Lebanese Jew who had been kidnapped—and they were allowed to have religious services once a week, in the "Church of the Locked Doors" as Reverend Weir said.

Each morning they put their mattresses along the walls and did exercises. Their chains were long enough so they could "march in place." They did this for 30–40 minutes and repeated their march in the afternoons.

The hostages were allowed to remove their blindfolds when the guards were out of the room. Terry Anderson made chess pieces out of aluminum foil, but when he asked for a piece of paper to make a board, the guards did not respond for several days, until all of a sudden they confiscated the pieces, claiming chess was a sinful game. Later, Anderson made a deck of cards from empty cheese cartons, which the guards also confiscated. But Anderson did not give up: he made a new deck, which he hid from the guards.

Anderson and Jacobsen were at opposite ends of the political spectrum, a liberal and a conservative, respectively. They argued constantly, sometimes heatedly, and when one of them was on the toilet, the other would talk behind his back. But when evening came, they gave each other what Jenco called "the kiss of peace."[71]

The guards gave the hostages Arabic newspapers, which Weir would translate. Anderson tried to teach himself the language. He used cheese cartons to make flashcards—Arabic on one side and English on the other. When the guards disagreed with Weir's translations, they took over. Sutherland knew French, and when Lebanese newspapers occasionally came in that language, he would translate for the others.

The hostages also created fantasy trips. One evening Jacobsen took his four fellow prisoners along to his apartment and made dinner for them. Jenco took them to Rome. Sutherland led an expedition to Scotland, where he was born, and Anderson brought them to Japan, where he had served as a soldier before he became a journalist.

One day one of the guards said to them, "The US government does not want to talk with us. How can the situation be solved when the government won't talk with us? We are not thieves. You were taken as hostages so that we could get our friends in Kuwait free. I am sorry for the conditions here, but we have no alternatives."

Anderson and Jacobsen suggested then that they could release them, "and we would gladly put forth your demands."

"We will think about that," was the answer they got.

In Washington, McFarlane received a new message from Tehran via Israel and Professor Ledeen: According to Kimche, delivery of 100 American Tube-launched, Optically tracked, Wire-guided (TOW) missiles anti-tank missiles would show the US had good intentions. There was still no word that the rockets might lead to a release of the hostages anytime soon.[72] TOW missiles could penetrate the heavy armor of tanks and concrete walls up to a meter thick. They could be fired from shoulder-mounted tubes, or from vehicles. The TOW calculated its own distance to its target, and the rocket was steered by two copper wires, which unwound behind it.

When George Shultz got wind that Professor Ledeen had been on a secret mission in Israel without informing the State Department, he asked McFarlane for an explanation. "The professor is working on his own," McFarlane said, promising to stop the operation. He lied without blinking.[73]

When President Reagan was recuperating from colon cancer in July 1985, McFarlane went to the hospital to give him a briefing on foreign affairs. Hearing that the Iranians wanted anti-tank missiles, the president became obviously disappointed. "We can't do it," he said. The sale of US weapons was subject to strict laws. But McFarlane nevertheless was given full permission to work further on the matter.[74]

When the Israelis learned Reagan had reacted negatively to trading missiles for hostages, David Kimche went to the United States. On August 2, 1985, he again sat with McFarlane at the White House.

"Are you sure about this?" He wanted to hear it directly from McFarlane.[75]

"Yes, that's the President's position."

"Well," Kimche said, " what if we ship these weapons?"

"David," McFarlane answered, "that's a distinction without difference. The issue is whether or not these people are of sufficient power and inclination to get results."

"All right. You say you're not going to do it. But if we do it, can we buy new weapons from you?" Kimche pressed on.

"Israel will be able to buy weapons from the US forever," McFarlane said. " You know that. So that's not the issue."

"I am under instruction to determine whether, if we go ahead with this, we will be able to replace the weapons from the United States."

"I'll get an official response for you,"McFarlane promised.

Three days later, McFarlane spoke with Reagan about the suggestion. The president was enthusiastic. The next day Reagan gave the Israelis a formal yes, despite the fact both Shultz and Weinberger were opposed.[76] McFarlane got in contact with Kimche and advised him that the US agreed to the proposal of sending 100 missiles from Israel to Iran, which the US would later replace with new ones. The Iranians, for their part, learned the arrangement was necessary to keep Congress from giving the administration problems, since there was a ban on trade with Iran.

When the 100 missiles were delivered August 30, 1985, the Iranians promised that an additional 400 missiles would secure the release of one hostage. The new missiles were shipped from Israel via Cyprus and Turkey on September 14. During the count, there were actually 408. Now everything would be cleared for the release of the one hostage.[77]

In Lebanon, Anderson, Sutherland, Weir, Jenco and Jacobsen continued to share the same room. They learned from a guard that one of them would be released. He added,"You may yourselves choose which."

Reverend Weir and Father Jenco were both reluctant to choose. Sutherland was too much of a gentleman to suggest himself, but Jacobsen did. During the discussions, which went on long into the night, Anderson nearly attacked the egotistical hospital director. Finally, a vote was taken. Anderson won.

When the guards heard the result, their chief said,"Terry Anderson will not be the first to be set free. He may be the last."

He did not explain why.

A few days later, a man called Hajj arrived. In reality, he was Imad Mughniyeh. The hostages learned that Reverend Weir would be released that same evening. Hajj traveled with a guard, whom he ordered to trim the reverend's beard, and to get him a shower. Sometime later Weir was led out to a car. Hajj sat in the front seat next to the driver. While they drove, Hajj said,"You are to do two things. First, tell the American government that they are to put pressure on Kuwait for the release of the men being held there. Second, say that you have been released as a sign of our good intentions of solving this situation, and to do it quickly without publicity."[78]

"You mean on behalf of the other hostages?" Weir asked.

"Yes, all five of you."

In Cyprus, Brigadier General Carl Stiner and his group of well-trained soldiers were ready to receive the hostage. The force was prepared for a rescue operation if something went wrong. They expected the hostage would be released near AUB. When Weir got out of the car around midnight, however, and removed the knitted ski mask he was wearing, the road was empty. There was no one to meet him—but Weir recognized where he was. He was indeed near the university.

The reverend waited a few minutes, then walked to the home of a friend who lived close by. From there he called the American Embassy. The person on duty was surprised: no one had expected to get a freed hostage out so quickly, even if they knew it was going to happen.

The next day, a helicopter brought Weir to the USS Nimitz. On-board the ship, the reverend was given a warm meal in the admiral's mess. Then he was examined by a doctor. Weir proved to be in good shape even after 16 months in captivity. When Washington learned who had been set free, many at the CIA were disappointed that it was not Buckley.[79]

Later, Weir was flown to Sicily and then to the US. There he learned President Reagan wanted to talk with him. The president was on-board Air Force One, and Weir was told not to use the president's name or title over the telephone.

"You can just refer to him as 'Rawhide,'" said the telephone operator.

Weir could hardly believe what he heard. Reagan came on the line and told Weir he had prayed for the hostages. He continued speaking without pause, and Weir understood he would have to interrupt to pass his message to the president. When he finally got a chance, Weir said, "I have a message I want you to hear. First: Those who took me captive expect you will put pressure on Kuwait so the 17 who are in prison there will be set free. Then: They asked me to say my release is a sign of goodwill that they wish to have a solution to the matter."[80]

The president did not respond, but continued with what Weir thought must have been a prepared text. Then Reagan hung up. But Imad Mughniyeh had succeeded in bringing his message directly to the American president.

When Weir later was debriefed by the American intelligence people, he did not say very much about the other hostages or where they were being hidden. He was afraid the military would try to free them by force. He was able to confirm that Iranian Revolutionary Guards in full uniform had occasionally given him food, and therefore that Iran was directly involved in the kidnappings.[81]

CHAPTER THIRTY TWO

Advanced Carpet Trade

Since my time at UNIFIL was over and my manuscript had been delivered to the publisher, I returned to the foreign news section of *NRK*. Ane-Karine had also moved to Norway to work in the Middle East section of the Foreign Office. In Oslo, I was still able to draw on her analytical skills and broad range of contacts.

I tried to follow developments in Lebanon through the news cables that arrived. I interviewed UN officers who returned home, and kept track of certain key words in my growing number of notebooks. On September 4, 1985, I wrote "Israeli jets bombed PLO bases in Lebanon. Shia militia from Amal fought against Palestinians in Bourj el-Barajne in southern Beirut in some of the worst battles since June, when the Syrians were able to arrange a ceasefire in three of Beirut's refugee camps." On September 13, I noted that the US once more had vetoed a resolution in the Security Council. This time it was one condemning "the oppressive actions which were begun since August 4th, against the Palestinian civilian population in Israeli-occupied areas."

On September 25th, three Israelis were killed in a sailboat docked at Larnaka in Cyprus. Two Palestinians and one Englishman were behind the attack. When they were arrested by the Cypriot police and interrogated, the Englishman maintained he had volunteered his service after having seen a video of the massacres in Sabra and Shatila. The Israelis identified the three victims as tourists. The PLO insisted they were Mossad agents who had been responsible two weeks earlier for the kidnapping of the second in command of Arafat's security guard and twelve other Palestinians on their way from Cyprus to Lebanon by boat.

With these killings the Israeli government was handed the excuse it needed to act on an existing plan and kill Yasser Arafat. Early in the morning on October 1st, jet bombers took off from a base in Israel and set course for the PLO headquarters outside of Tunis. When the planes reached the hotel complex where Arafat and his staff were housed, the PLO leader was walking in a park nearby. He had decided to take the stroll because of a delayed meeting, which ended up saving his life.

When the dust had settled and the flames were extinguished, the rescue crews counted 74 dead. Most were Tunisian civilians who worked at the hotel that the PLO had leased. The building was reduced to a pile of rubble.

The following day, spokesmen for Islamic Jihad announced they had executed William Buckley. Accompanying the announcement were a photo of the corpse and a copy of a secret document from Buckley's burn bag. Americans knew that the story of the execution was not true. Four months earlier, they had wiretapped the chief of the Iranian Revolutionary Guards, Ali Shamkhani, and heard him swear at one of his subordinates for not taking better care of Buckley. The conversation included orders for the Revolutionary Guards in Baalbek to fetch a doctor immediately if any of the other hostages became ill. Thus the US intelligence service established that Buckley died because the guards could not be bothered with preserving his health.[82]

The remaining hostages in Lebanon gave President Reagan more than a headache. Every morning he asked his briefing staff for any news, and every day they assured him that they were working intensively to get the hostages freed. A young lieutenant colonel named Oliver North promised that all the hostages would be home by Christmas. North had been working in the National Security Council since 1981, and was supposed to be an expert on terrorism. Sarcastic colleagues said he had only been hired to do routine office work—in any case he was not supposed to have anything to do with secret operations. North's political position was so extremely conservative that people joked he would stand at attention whenever he was outside the US and saw an American flag or a neon Coca Cola ad.

But his views, combined with hard work, bore fruit. By November 1985, he and his superior, Vice-Admiral John Poindexter, had the longest service of all the president's ad-hoc advisors.[83] Little by little, North had gotten control over the work to free the hostages, even if he had little experience or understanding of diplomacy and international relations. In practice, this meant North had control over parts of US policy toward Iran.[84]

In West Beirut, the hostages felt forgotten. One evening they heard Henry Kissinger, the former Secretary of State, say in a TV interview that the hostages had to use their own resources to get free. Sitting in his underwear, on a thin mattress, in a room without windows, David Jacobsen said,"Dear God Henry, what resources do you think I have?"

Jacobsen, Anderson, Sutherland and Jenco were moved to a new location near the Kuwaiti Embassy, since Imad Mughniyeh feared Weir might reveal where they had been. When Weir was set free, the others lost their interpreter. But they felt better with a stack of old copies of the International Herald Tribune. The papers told the story of the TWA hijacking, but the hostages did not find many lines about them. There was also nothing there about the freed Reverend Weir.

The Norwegian Embassy in Beirut had little to report about the western hostages. The diplomats spent most of their time following Lebanon's domestic politics, and the developments in occupied South Lebanon. The embassy was headed by Odd Wibe, a knowledgeable and sociable bachelor. He travelled regularly to the UNIFIL headquarters, to NORBATT and to the repair company which was located in Tibnin.

Through contacts in the International Red Cross Committee and socially engaged UN officers, Wibe received credible information that torture was taking place at the newly established prison center in the Shia village of Khiam. Wibe had previously reported on the conditions at the Ansar camp, and in NORBATT he was introduced to a man who recently had been released from Khiam. Wibe could see the marks left by torture with his own eyes.

He reported what he had seen and heard to the Foreign Office in Oslo. The return message regarding the report was not particularly positive. The leadership in the Foreign Office had difficulty believing the Israelis could be behind systematic torture of prisoners. In addition, claims of such practices were rejected in reports from the Norwegian Embassy in Tel Aviv. The Foreign Office chose not to put a spotlight on the reports from Beirut about prisoners who did not receive visits from the Red Cross, human rights organizations or UN observers.[85]

The prison complex at Khiam, just north of the Israeli border, had originally been a French military facility. It had been built in 1933, and the walls still had bullet holes from the Australian participation in the liberation of Lebanon from the Vichy French regime in 1941. Later the camp was used by the Lebanese army, but it was abandoned when the army fell apart during the civil war. Now Mossad and Shin Bet had control. Old horse stalls were converted to cells; new ones were also constructed, some of light concrete.

Even if torture happened, usually the perpetrators were not Israelis from Mossad or Shin Bet. It was their Lebanese underlings who did it, under Israeli supervision. The western hostages in Beirut had been mistreated, but not as brutally as the prisoners in Khiam.

In November, 1985, the hostage takers realized that the US would not cooperate with their demand to get "the 17 from Dawa" out of Kuwait. It was decided the hostages themselves should appeal for help in open letters to President Reagan and the Archbishop of Canterbury. This led to an invitation to Lebanon for one of the Archbishop's colleagues, Reverend Terry Waite, who previously had succeeded in solving difficult conflicts.

On November 13, Waite flew first class to Beirut with Middle East Airlines. The reverend was not just the envoy of the Archbishop of Canterbury: secretly, he was in league with Lieutenant Colonel Oliver North. Just before his departure from London Heathrow, North showed up and handed him a photograph of lead kidnapper Imad Mughniyeh. North wanted as much information as could be had about the man.

When Waite landed in Beirut, he immediately became the central figure in a classic Lebanese military conflict. Both Amal and the Druze had sent armed guards to the airport for his protection. They began to quarrel as Waite was collecting his baggage, and it was only respect for the Archbishop's envoy that prevented a firefight. Finally, they agreed that Amal would have responsibility for the Englishman's security. The area around the Commodore Hotel, where Waite was to stay, was controlled by the Amal militia.

The international press followed Waite through Beirut with eagle eyes. He had previously mediated with success in Tehran and Libya, and he knew many of the journalists who had come with him on the plane. As soon as he arrived, he was also besieged by Lebanese journalists and photographers. He now told them his plans and asked sincerely not be followed anywhere.

Eventually, Waite found a hiding place in Terry Anderson's rented apartment, not far from the ruins of the American Embassy. The apartment, in contrast to the Commodore, was in a quarter of West Beirut that the Druze controlled. In the same building lived Robert Fisk of *The Times*, Juan Carlos Gumicio from the *AP* and Agneta Ramberg of Swedish Radio. Waite had nothing against socializing with correspondents while he waited to be contacted by the kidnappers' middlemen.

One evening Waite and the journalists were sitting together drinking wine. Ramberg thought the situation seemed absurd: Here sat "the hostage rescuer in the hostage's apartment drinking the hostage's wine." Suddenly, the phone rang. The man on the line presented himself as Ali and spoke English with an American accent. After Waite was convinced Ali truly had direct contact with Anderson, they arranged a meeting. Waite brushed his teeth and managed to down some black coffee.

A bit later he was sitting in a car with a blindfold over his eyes, scared to death of what might happen. He calmed down when he met a masked man who spoke in a quiet and businesslike manner about the hostages, avoiding slogans or political phrases.

Just before midnight, Waite was back in Anderson's apartment. He had polaroid pictures of all the hostages holding up copies of the *London Times* that he had autographed in advance. The kidnappers had also given him a message for Washington. The condition for freeing the western hostages was the same as before: the 17 from the Dawa Party in Kuwait had to be allowed to go home. The kidnappers demanded that Waite visit the prisoners in Kuwait as well.

Waite flew to the US via London. Oliver North was waiting for him in Washington, and took him to Vice President George Bush. Following their meeting, Waite was convinced he had received a green light from Bush to visit the 17 from the Dawa Party in Kuwait, and that they would be allowed to exchange letters with their families.

On November 18th, Waite was back in Beirut. He clearly saw his task as being on the same level as a three-day summit meeting in Geneva which would begin the following day, and where President Reagan would meet the new Soviet leader, Mikhail S. Gorbachev, for the first time. Waite declared that "the eyes of the world are on two places, Geneva and Beirut."

This time Waite was escorted from the airport to Terry Anderson's apartment by Walid Jumblatt's militia. When he received a message and again met the kidnappers, he learned they were surprised that he had not fulfilled their previous demands. Why had he not visited the prisoners in Kuwait? He was meant to speak with the Kuwaitis, not the Americans. The spokesman went on to say that time was running out. This was a matter of life and death, and it would be best for all if Waite concentrated on the demands put forth at the first meeting. Waite did not yet understand that he was to be used in a trade of hostages for weapons. The kidnappers pretended the objective was to get the 17 prisoners in Kuwait released; in actuality the hostages were being sold. When and if they were released, the kidnappers would maintain it happened out of humanitarian concern.

In Geneva the following day, McFarlane told the American leadership details about the plan to sell new missiles to Iran through the Israelis. This time Homing All the Way Killer (HAWK) anti-aircraft missiles were involved. The Shah had bought such missiles in his time, but many were unusable because they lacked spare parts. McFarlane sat together with President Reagan, his chief of staff, Donald Regan, and Secretary of State Shultz in a bedroom on the second floor in the Villa Palmetta. It was a modest room, normally used by one of the teenaged daughters of the family which owned the villa. President Reagan sat in a chair against a wall and George Shultz on another chair, while McFarlane and Donald Regan sat on the edge of the bed.[86]

The Israelis were to deliver 80 HAWK missiles from their own inventory to a secret location in Portugal. There they were to be loaded onto three transport planes and brought to Tabriz in Iran. As soon as the first plane was in the air, the message would be given to the Iranians, who would ask the kidnappers in Lebanon to release the four Americans still in captivity. The planes would not land, and no missiles would be delivered, until the hostages had been turned over to the American Embassy in Beirut. If customs authorities became involved in one way or other, the cover story was that the planes were loaded with oil drilling equipment.

The briefing at Villa Palmetta lasted about twenty minutes. The president did not ask many questions, and had only looked at McFarlane and occasionally glanced over at Shultz and Regan. This was the first time the president heard about the plan in its entirety, but he did not seem particularly interested in the details.

Everything went wrong with McFarlane's operation. In Portugal, the planes from Israel were initially refused permission to land, but with the help of the CIA, the Americans were still able to deliver 18 of the promised 80 missiles. The Iranians were furious when they discovered that the boxes were marked in Hebrew. In addition, the delivered missiles were an older model that the Israelis wanted to get rid of and replace. Further still, one of them proved defective upon testing. When it was fired at an Iraqi plane over Kharg Island in the Persian Gulf, it exploded on the launch ramp.

The Iranians sent back the remaining 17 missiles, while the Americans returned most of the $24 million fee. But the Iranians could not just turn their backs on the US: They had no other way to get missiles, something they absolutely needed to withstand attacks from Iraq. Tehran, therefore, continued to negotiate with the Americans for new missiles and promised once more to secure freedom for the hostages in Lebanon.

Eventually, it dawned on McFarlane that he had been drawn into a game that he did not understand. The experienced CIA agent Miles Copeland went further and commented on McFarlane's role, "You can hardly win a game if you don't even know you're in it."[87] The situation became so complicated that McFarlane asked the president to accept his resignation. He also had big problems working with Donald Regan who also played a role in his decision.[88]

Before McFarlane resigned, he was able to convince Reagan to choose Vice Admiral John Poindexter as his successor. When Poindexter took the job, he continued in McFarlane's footsteps. He also decided that the secret profits from the sale of American weapons to Iran should be used to support the Contras in Nicaragua. "Contra" was the common name for various militia groups that fought against the leftist Sandinistas who had overthrown President Anastasio Somoza Debayle in 1979. The decision to use the profits this way was a serious breach of a rule of thumb for secret services worldwide: never mix two secret operations together!

This would have to go wrong.

CHAPTER THIRTY THREE

Free Tickets to Disneyland

In October 1985, the book I had been working on was released. To my surprise, it took first place in Cappelen's documentary book competition. The convicted spy, Arne Treholt, came in second place with his book *Alene*, or *Alone*.

It was painfully clear to me there was much more to tell about what had already happened and was happening now in South Lebanon, and about the respective roles played by Israel, Iran and Syria. It became a calling for me to discover more. Now I would follow developments in the Middle East from the foreign news section of the *NRK* in Oslo, and also travel to Lebanon, Israel, Iran and Iraq for short periods. But none of these trips gave me any inkling of what was happening in secret between the Americans and the Iranians.

In the United States, neither Secretary of State Shultz nor Defense Secretary Weinberger changed their opposition to any missile sales to Iran. The second in command at the CIA, John McMahon, was also skeptical of North and Poindexter's belief that the missiles would strengthen "moderates" in the Islamic Republic. "In Iran, a moderate is a Mullah who was running low on ammunition," he added.[89]

"Are there any pragmatists in Iran?" the CIA's Clair George once asked rhetorically. "Does anybody play piano in the Fiji Islands? Yes, somewhere."

But their stance made little difference. On December 7, 1985, President Reagan approved the sale of more missiles in order to free the hostages. He had recognized they could not be freed by force. A few months earlier, there had been a real alternative when one of the US intelligence services located some of the hostages in the southern section of West Beirut. The Americans got drawings of the building where they were held, and the US commandoes began to train for a rescue mission. But two weeks before the operation was to begin, Hizbullah's counter-espionage service uncovered one of the American's Lebanese agents. He gave in the names of his co-conspirators, and all were executed.

Christmas Eve, 1985, the hostages in Beirut heard on the *BBC* that Terry Waite had gone back to London. Anderson felt crushed. Father Jenco tried to sing Christmas carols, but was unable. Jacobsen drew a Christmas tree on a piece of paper and hung it on the wall.

On Christmas Day, the police found the body of a Lebanese Jew with three bullets in his head. The man had been held hostage by the so-called Organization for the World's Oppressed. An announcement revealed that he had been executed in revenge for Israel's bombardment of Shia villages in South Lebanon three days earlier. The organization said it had an additional three Lebanese Jews as hostages, and warned Israel against further bombing.

In the area where the hostages were being held, the two Shia Parties, Amal and Hizbullah, continued fighting for power. But even if they and certain other militias were constantly fighting each other, they shared a hostility toward the traditional political elite in Lebanon. They defended their own "black economies," infiltrated what was left of the official bureaucracy and cooperated financially. The drug trade in the Bekaa Valley, for example, led to cooperation among Syria, Hizbullah, the Christians in Bekaa, various pro-Syrian militias and the Christian militias in East Beirut.

In Israel, Prime Minister Shimon Peres had hired a so-called anti-terrorist expert who was to represent him in the operation exchanging American weapons for hostages. The "anti-terrorist expert," Amiram Nir, had earlier been a military correspondent for the State TV network. Now his job was to ensure the prime minister's office gained control over the hostage trade at the expense of the Israeli Foreign Office's David Kimche.

In a memo, Nir wrote:"It is in Israel's interest to make sure the Americans reach their goal: to build a strategic bridge to Iran and get the hostages in Lebanon free. This must be viewed in the light of the total relationship Israel has toward the United States. If it is also possible to achieve something through the Iranian channel to get kidnapped Jews being held by extremist Shia organizations in Lebanon released, then it should be done."[90]

The kidnapping of Lebanese Jews in West Beirut had received little attention in the western media. Those holding the western hostages also had little interest in adding more captives to the trade. The Israelis therefore did little to rescue these Lebanese Jews.

Eventually, Nir told the Americans that Israel had received a promise from Iran to release four American hostages in exchange for 4,000 TOW missiles. He brought the news with him to the White House in the beginning of January 1986. Nir said also that the hostages would be set free when Iran had received 500 of the missiles. To sweeten the deal further for the Iranians, he suggested Israel should release between 20 and 40 men from Hizbullah who were being held as prisoners in Khiam.

Poindexter and North liked the Israeli's plan. North wrote a draft memo to authorize selling the weapons to "moderate elements in and outside the government in Iran." President Reagan was shown the draft and put his signature on it. The memo was kept secret from the Pentagon and the CIA.

Having secured the president's signature, North called Nir in Israel and said,"Joshua has approved proceeding as we have hoped...If these conditions are acceptable to the Banana, then Oranges are ready to proceed." Reagan was Joshua, Israel was Banana and the US was Oranges.[91]

Four days later, the Iranian who had opened the door to the "moderate forces in Iran" came to the CIA so they could again strap him into the lie detector. Like before, the test indicated he was lying. As far as the CIA was concerned, Manucher Ghorbanifar was useless, even if Professor Ledeen and Lieutenant Colonel North vouched for him. Six days later, the chief of the CIA's operations issued another "burn notice" on Ghorba, the second in the course of the 18 months. But this had no effect on the operation. It was not the CIA running the sale of missiles to Iran; the organization was only a henchman for the White House.

On January 17, President Reagan signed North's top secret "Finding of Necessity," a document authorizing the sale of American weapons to Iran. The scheme was still daring, but now it was arguably legal. The following day a request went to Caspar Weinberger to execute the decision. He asked Colin Powell to transfer 4,000 TOW missiles to the CIA, which would send them on to Iran.[92]

It was pure serendipity which led me inside this case, when I stumbled over Thomas Twetten, an American with roots in the Norwegian district of Tveiten in Telemark.[93] He had been appointed the second in command of the CIA staff, which ran some of the secret operations the US was undertaking in the Middle East, as of January 1, 1986. Before that Twetten had a long career behind him in the Middle East and Africa. Twetten was quite accommodating when I visited him in the US, but he was not willing to be interviewed "on the record" about everything he had been involved in.

After only 20 days at his new job, Twetten drove to the White House with his boss, Clair George, who was number three in the CIA hierarchy. They were there to meet Admiral Poindexter and Lieutenant Colonel North. In the security advisor's conference room they were able to read the president's memo authorizing the sale of missiles to Iran. It was full of writing errors, suggesting it had been written in haste.

Neither George nor Twetten was able to get a copy. Twetten smelled a "rotten fish," and was afraid he was about to be drawn into a fateful game. When he came home, he said to his wife, Kay, that he was worried:"This is the end of my career." But he had no other choice than to do as he was told.

The plan was for the CIA to oversee the delivery of TOW missiles from the defense department. To carry out the trade, they would set up a secret bank account in Switzerland and provide Oliver North with false intelligence about Iraqi positions that he could offer to Iran.[94] North also wanted to have sound and video equipment he could use to record his next meeting with Manucher Ghorbanifar.

North wrote a new document detailing how the deliveries should take place, but there was nothing in it about being able to demand a higher price for the weapons than the one the defense department had set. There was also nothing saying North could use the profits to purchase weapons for the Contras, something which was illegal since Congress had banned actions supporting those who fought against the democratically elected government in Nicaragua.

On February 5, 1986, North flew to Europe to meet Ghorbanifar, Nir and some Iranian bureaucrats. They agreed that the US would deliver 1,000 missiles to Iran via Israel. But first Ghorbanifar had to arrange payment to an Israeli bank account, from which the Israelis would transfer the money to the CIA's secret account in Switzerland. When the missiles were delivered from the defense department to the CIA, North wrote to Poindexter that "Operation Rescue" was underway. He figured the American hostages would be released 18 days later.

The missiles were unloaded from a cargo plane in the Iranian city of Bandar Abbas. According to the agreement, Ghorbanifar's contact at the Iranian prime minister's office would now meet the Americans in Europe. After that, all the hostages would be set free. That meeting made clear, however, that Ghorbanifar had lied to both sides.

Twetten realized that Ghorbanifar had promised the Iranians far more than just TOW missiles. He had misrepresented the weapons, a more advanced type of air-to-air missile, called PHOENIX, and had also promised them artillery. He had told the Americans that the hostages would be freed after they had delivered two shipments of missiles, and that they would get to meet the president of the National Assembly, Ali Akbar Hashemi Rafsanjani, along with President Ali Khamenei, within two months. He also suggested that Ayatollah Khomeini would retire by April 1986 and give up all power. Everything was "extraordinary nonsense," according to Twetten.[95]

North was still optimistic, and bragged that he had fooled the Iranians:"I promised them they would get free tickets to Disneyland and a trip on the space shuttle when we got the hostages home."

The shipments of various types of missiles continued. At the end of February, the Iranians had received another 1,000 TOW anti-tank missiles as well as the falsified intelligence material about Iraqi forces along their border. The Americans got nothing in return, except for arguments with unimportant Iranians. These were, according to Twetten, people who were "at the bottom of the intelligence scale."

Vice Admiral Poindexter had promised CIA leadership to cancel the weapons sale if the hostages were not freed after the first 1,000 missiles were delivered. But the deliveries continued. Following another frustrating meeting in Paris with Ghorbanifar, Twetten said:"We had delivered the missiles. The ball was in their court, but they behaved as if it was in ours." Twetten realized that North could keep the whole thing going because President Reagan was determined to free the American hostages. The pressure from their families was enormous, and the media was full of stories of the "forgotten hostages." The administration also had President Carter's unsuccessful handling of the hostage crisis in Tehran fresh in their minds. The White House was so desperate that they secretly planned to send a joint American-Israeli delegation to Iran.

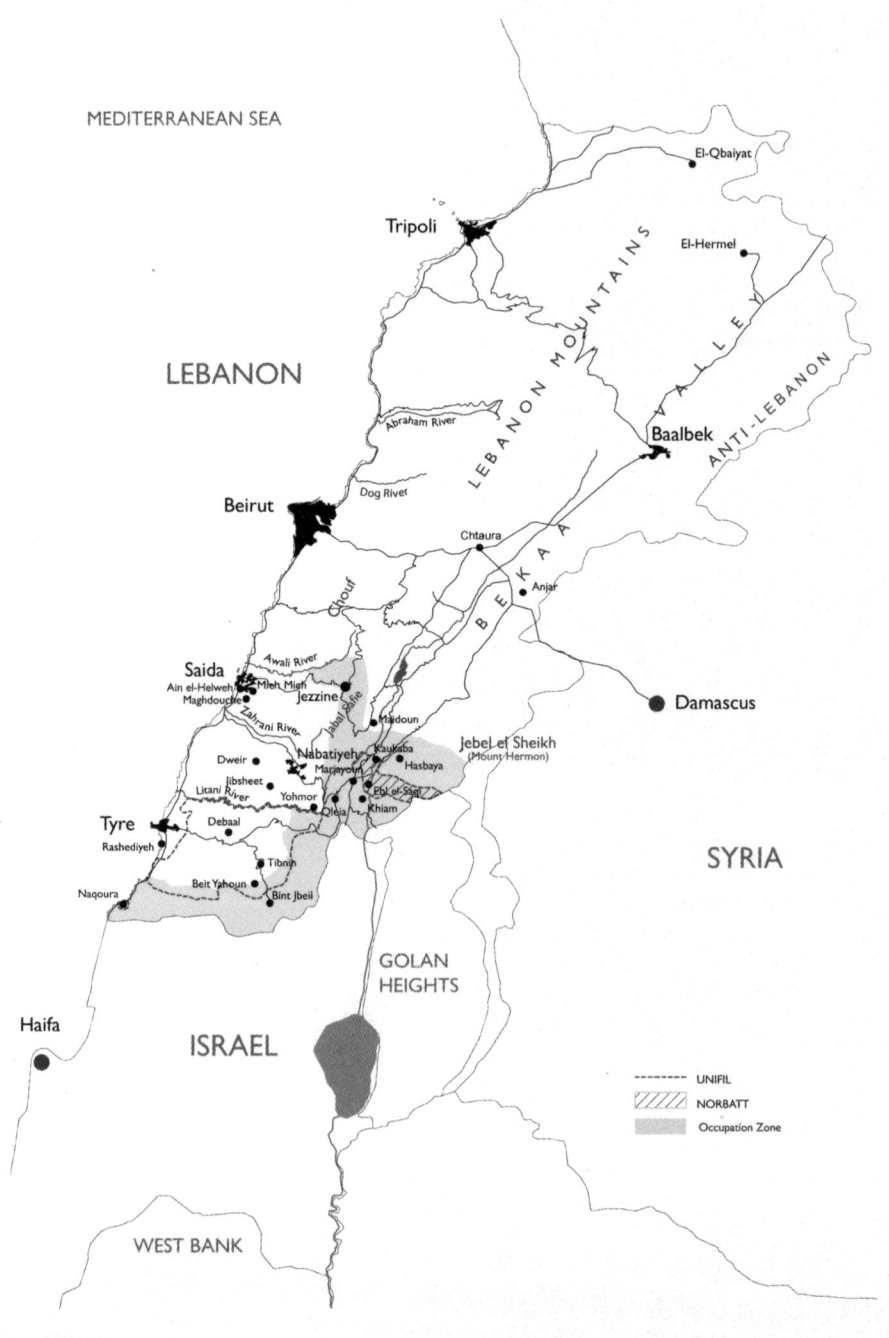

MEDITERRANEAN SEA

El-Qbaiyat

Tripoli

El-Hermel

LEBANON

Abraham River

Baalbek

Dog River

Beirut

Chtaura

Anjar

Damascus

Saida

Awali River

Ain el-Helweh
Maghdouche

Mieh Mieh

Jezzine

Zahrani River

Haidoun

Dweir

Nabatiyeh

Kaukaba

Jebel el Sheikh
(Mount Hermon)

Jibsheet

Marjayoun

Hasbaya

Litani River

Yohmor

Ebl el-Saqi

Tyre

Debaal

Ofeia

Khiam

SYRIA

Rashediyeh

Naqoura

Tibnin

Beit Yahoun

Bint Jbeil

GOLAN
HEIGHTS

Haifa

ISRAEL

WEST BANK

- - - - - UNIFIL

NORBATT

Occupation Zone

PART FOUR

Hostages in a Larger Game

1986-1988

In Israel there is no noteworthy political opposition to the country's brutal occupation of South Lebanon. The Lebanese fighting the Israeli army also present no serious threat to the occupiers, since neither Hizbullah nor the militias on the Lebanese Left have many resources available.

In West Beirut and in South Lebanon various groups take new western hostages. The kidnappings gain great international attention. The Israelis regularly take new prisoners and hostages as well, but for the most part they are forgotten by the world.

Syrian troops march in anew to West Beirut to get control over that part of the city.

Norway and Sweden are drawn into a hostage drama where the government in Sweden eventually goes behind the back of the Norwegians.

MAIN CHARACTERS

William Higgins, Lieutenant Colonel, Chief of the UNTSO corps in Lebanon
Ghazi Kanaan, General, Syria's Chief of Intelligence in Lebanon
William Jørgensen, Employee of the UN aid organization, UNRWA
Imad Mughniyeh, Radical Lebanese Shia Muslim
Tor Planting, Lieutenant Colonel, and UNIFIL's Liaison officer to Amal and Hizbullah
Jan Stening, Employee of the UN aid organization, UNRWA
Ali Akbar Hashemi Rafsanjani, President of Iran's National Assembly

CHAPTER THIRTY FOUR
A Horrible Prison Camp

In my black notebooks, I often wrote keywords which usually did not get into the *NRK* broadcasts. On January 17, 1986, when the US again issued a veto in the UN Security Council, I noted that the Americans stopped a resolution condemning Israel's merciless treatment of civilian Lebanese in the occupation zone.

A short month later, I noted that the Lebanese police had found a dead and badly mutilated Lebanese Jew in West Beirut. The Organization for the World's Oppressed announced the man had been executed for spying for Israel. The Shia groups had taken steadily more Jewish Lebanese as hostages. Now they were being executed one after the other. "This is Lebanon at its worst," I wrote in my little book.

In South Lebanon, Hizbullah was the primary attacker of Israeli soldiers. The leaders of God's Party also gave orders to take in prisoners. Having living Israeli soldiers in enemy hands always served to shock the Israeli grassroots.

On February 17, a group of uniformed Shias lay in hiding when two civilian vehicles drove northward from the village of Beit Yahoun. The first contained militia soldiers from the SLA, the other Israeli civilian agents from Shin Bet. The first vehicle drove over a mine the guerrillas had planted, and two of the militia soldiers were killed in the explosion. The guerrillas opened fire at the second vehicle and severely injured two Israeli intelligence agents, whom they forced into a waiting Mercedes.

Shortly after, the alarm went off in Israeli military headquarters. More than 600 soldiers were committed to the hunt for the attackers and their prisoners. The Israelis blocked roads and marched into 18 Shia villages, where all men between 15 and 60 were interrogated. But there was no sign of the two Shin Bet agents.

The Islamic resistance movement then announced that the two prisoners would be killed if the Israelis did not begin withdrawing their forces from Lebanon within 24 hours. Lebanese TV showed pictures of an injured Israeli as proof the prisoners were still alive.

Israel first accused Syrian intelligence of the kidnapping. The operation was so professionally done that Israeli analysts thought the Shias from South Lebanon could not have been the ones behind it. According to them, it had to be a Syrian revenge operation for the Israeli Air Force having downed a Libyan passenger plane with Syrian officers on-board. Yet again the army leadership demonstrated arrogance regarding the Shias' professionalism.

The Israelis soon understood that Syria had nothing to do with the matter, however, and the IDF's experts had to accept that the kidnapping was undertaken to procure a prisoner exchange for Lebanese captives. One of 80 Lebanese arrested in the ensuing hunt was Hassan Nassar. Hassan's captors tied him up, covered his head with a black hood, beat him and threw him into the trunk of a Mercedes. He later found himself in a dark little cell without windows. Had he been able to see the journey, he would have recognized that he was being held captive in the old French base at Khiam.

From the ramparts in the five-sided fortification were views westward of two Christian villages, Marjayoun and Qleia, and northward of Ebl el-Saqi, the village where the Norwegian UN battalion had its headquarters. The prisoners in Khiam—or rather hostages, as the aid organizations called them—came from 70 Lebanese villages and towns, most in the occupation zone. There were also Palestinians and other Arab hostages behind the walls. There was also a section for women, with interrogation rooms, a kitchen, showers and toilets, as well as a room for the guards.

In all there were 90 small and dirty cells in Khiam, as well as 16 so-called "chicken cages." Eight of the cages were two-by-two meters, the other eight were smaller—only 0.9 by 0.9 meters. In these smallest cages, prisoners had to hunch over. Held there in isolation, prisoners were not even allowed to go out to the courtyard, or the "sun yard" as the inmates called the five-by-six-meter open area surrounded by walls and barbed wire.

A Christian Lebanese from Qleia, named John Homse but called Abu Nabil, was the boss. He was a large man in his mid-forties with graying hair, a moustache and an alert and searching gaze, which caused some of the prisoners to say he was a wolf. Abu Nabil was known to have a terrible temper.

When Hassan Nassar arrived in February 1986, he entered 30 days of hell. They hoisted him up on an utility pole, as had happened to so many others before. The tips of his toes barely reached the ground. They beat him with an iron rod, and threw alternating buckets of cold and hot water in his face. Later he was led into a room where the Lebanese interrogator attached electric wires to his ears, tongue and testicles. They turned on the electricity, low at first, then stronger. Between shocks they questioned him. If the interrogators were not satisfied with his answers, they began a new round. On occasion Israeli agents were present. The Israelis usually did not torture the prisoners themselves, but guided the Lebanese torturers. Hassan caught glimpses of some under his blindfold, and he heard his answers being translated into Hebrew.[1] During this period, Hassan Nassar was held in one of the chicken cages. The food he received consisted of a bowl of carrots and some bread, olives, occasionally a hardboiled egg and a potato in the evening. Later they moved him to an ordinary cell.

Nassar had been lucky compared to Suleiman Ramadan. The previous year on September 17, the Israelis captured Suleiman near the village of Hebarieh in NORBATT's zone. Along with two other youths from the Lebanese Communist Party, he had fired a primitive rocket at a house occupied by Israelis in the village of Hasbaya, just outside the UN zone. They attacked at dawn, but were spotted and tracked when the sun came up. One of them managed to hide, but Suleiman and the other youth were drawn into a firefight. Suleiman received a wound to his right leg, as well as shrapnel in his neck and stomach. His friend was also hit and was able barely to whisper, "Rabi', don't say anything," before he died. (Rabi' was Suleiman's alias.)[2] Suleiman was bandaged and brought to the hospital in Marjayoun. He remained there for three days without any medical treatment, but Israeli officers came to question him at times. One grabbed his injured foot and twisted it so hard that Suleiman heard the bone crack.

On the fourth day he was transferred to a hospital in Haifa. There they gave him anesthesia, and when he awoke, the doctors told him that they had performed an operation. He did not know what they had done until he lifted the sheet covering him, to find his right leg had been amputated midway. He was told they had done it because of the risk of gangrene. They transferred him back to the hospital in Marjayoun for more interrogation and torture.

Suleiman tried to play dumb, but another Lebanese eventually revealed that he had been the leader of a resistance cell in the Communist Party. Nonetheless, Suleiman stuck to his story, even though the interrogators beat him, tore at his hair and put out burning cigarettes on his chest.

One day an officer told him, "Suleiman, now we are going to put a mark on your body so you will always remember us. We are going to burn a Star of David on your chest."

Suleiman did not answer, but sat chained to a wheelchair during an increasingly brutal interrogation. After a few hours, the Israeli made good on his threat. Using a lit cigarette, he burned a small ring on the left side of Suleiman's chest, and then the six points of the star.

After several further interrogations, the Israelis gave up. They were not getting anything from Suleiman, so they sent him to Khiam, where he was put on a stretcher in one of the corridors between cells. Suleiman was not alone in the corridor. He saw several oblong bundles on the floor. At first, he thought they were corpses, but then realized that they were moving. He realized they were prisoners when, in the half-dark, he saw they had chains attached to their feet, along with handcuffs and hoods. A guard chained his foot, handcuffed him and placed a hood over his head, too. The stump of his amputated leg grew wet with blood because the guards stepped on or kicked it whenever they walked by.

Even though the weather got colder, he did not get any more clothing. He remained lying in underpants and a t-shirt. Now and then the guards removed his hood and gave him water from a can with a narrow spout. Occasionally he got a hardboiled egg yolk or egg whites before they pulled the hood back over his head. One day a guard came with a fried egg in a plastic bag full of oil. Suleiman was so hungry he both ate the egg and drank the oil. Then his stomach let loose, but he was not allowed to go to the toilet. So he lay on a stretcher full of excrement, which eventually dried on his body. It was several days before they allowed him to shower.

Suleiman was left in the corridor for 72 days before the guards moved him to a cell, where he still had to wear handcuffs. When Abu Nabil finally decided to remove them, the lock was too rusty to open. The guards had to use a hammer to free his hands. Despite the danger of being killed or tortured, many young Lebanese women and men were willing to sacrifice themselves in the fight against the occupiers. One of them was a 16-year-old Lebanese from the Syrian Social National Party (SSNP) who on April 8, 1986, drove a Mercedes filled with explosives into an SLA control post near Kaukaba. In a video before the operation, the youth had said he wanted to praise Syria's President Hafez al-Assad. That same evening, the testimonial was shown on Syrian and Lebanese television.

One who had seen the news clip in Beirut, was Brian Keenan. The 35-year-old Irishman had come to Lebanon to teach English at AUB. Keenan, who also had a British passport, rented a small house on Rue d'Amerique, just a 10-minute walk from the university. On April 11, 1986 , he went out into his little garden in front of the pretty, old villa, the morning sun had burned away the clouds, and he enjoyed the sight of butterflies playing in the wild bougainvillea near the gate. Today, he had planned to lecture on one of his favorite authors, T.S. Eliot. But he could not know the prescience that Eliot's famous line, "April is the cruelest month..." [3] would have for him that day.

Keenan did not have the poem in his head as he locked the iron gate. Walking down the sidewalk, he noticed an old green Mercedes with its roof painted another color. It was a hundred meters away, uphill and to the right. He went to the left, but had not gone far when the green car pulled in front of him and stopped. The driver opened the door and blocked the sidewalk. Two men jumped from the car and aimed pistols at him. A few minutes later Keenan lay on the back seat with the barrel of a pistol against his head. At the same time he felt the gunman carefully patting his hair. The whole thing seemed completely bizarre.

I made news pieces on the kidnapping at the *NRK*, and the video material I used came from *WTN* (World Television News). I did not know the Englishman, John McCarthy, who was their acting news bureau chief in Beirut; he had not been in the city very long. Five days later, McCarthy himself was kidnapped on his way to the airport for a flight to London. Kidnappers pulled the *WTN* journalist from his car, and half an hour later he was lying on a mattress, chained to the wall and covered by a dirty sheet. [4]

At the Norwegian Embassy in Beirut, the diplomats began to worry. The wave of kidnappings was becoming dangerously close. Were Norwegians in Lebanon safe? First Secretary Arne Gjermundsen went to see Amal's leader, Nabih Berri. There he learned that Hizbullah was under orders from Tehran to kidnap Frenchmen, Englishmen and Americans. Norwegians were not a target. [5] Nabih Berri was otherwise mostly interested in discussing Amal's policies.

Gjermundsen knew Berri as Syria's tool in Lebanon; to Berri, Syria was an insurance policy. Berri had many opponents, among them Palestinian guerrilla soldiers who had snuck back to the refugee camps in West Beirut, Sidon and Tyre. These were Fatah guerrillas under Yasser Arafat's command. Most guerrilla soldiers stayed at the largest Palestinian camp, Ain el-Helweh, or the Sweet Spring, outside of Sidon. Arafat's men put up their command center there, and it was from there that they snuck out to establish small bases in areas where they had to share power with other Palestinian factions. Together they threatened Amal's lines of communication from West Beirut to South Lebanon. An armed confrontation was in the offing.

The Druze had assured themselves control from the Chouf Mountains down to the Mediterranean south of Beirut. The PLO and Walid Jumblatt had agreed the Druze could support the Syrians and Amal if there were military actions against Arafat supporters among the Palestinians. In exchange, the Palestinians in West Beirut would help Jumblatt takeover the part of the city that was presently a no man's land where militia groups and armed gangs ran various streets. Because Amal's militia was badly organized, the Druze eventually got control over the middle-class districts in the heart of West Beirut.

Amal appealed to the Syrians for help. The Sunni Muslim politicians in West Beirut did the same, since they no longer had a militia to support them. But President Assad said no. He did not want to use Syrian forces as a police in West Beirut. Not just yet.

CHAPTER THIRTY FIVE
With Cake to Tehran

On May 25, 1986, efforts to free the western hostages in Lebanon took a new direction when an American-Israeli delegation secretly landed in the Iranian capital. I was in Turkey to develop a report.

It was former American National Security Council advisor Robert McFarlane who led the delegation. With him he had Lieutenant Colonel Oliver North, the Israeli anti-terrorism expert Amiram Nir and technical experts. Prime Minister Shimon Peres had insisted Nir go along, "masquerading" as an American. Everyone was travelling on Irish passports that had "disappeared" from the Irish Embassy in Athens some time earlier.[6]

When the unmarked American aircraft landed at 9 am Iranian time, the plane was immediately surrounded by armed Revolutionary Guards, who escorted the visitors to a VIP room. The delegation had brought along a chocolate cake formed into the shape of a key, a symbol of a new opening toward Iran. North and Nir had come up with the gimmick and brought the cake from Tel Aviv. The Americans also brought along eight Colt Revolvers to give to select Mullahs, and their plane carried a pallet of spare parts for the HAWK missiles. The Americans thought the gifts and the weapons would be enough to get all the hostages in Lebanon released.

The delegation had to wait nearly two hours before Manucher Ghorbanifar showed up with two cars. They went to the former Royal Hilton, now called the Independence Hotel. The chocolate cake did not come with them, as the Revolutionary Guards at the airport had already finished it.[7] McFarlane's delegation was given the entire top floor of the hotel. Lunch was served—rice and grilled lamb, prepared under the able supervision of Ghorbanifar's mother in her own home.

The president of the Iranian National Assembly, Ali Akbar Hashemi Rafsanjani, was disappointed when he learned what the Americans had to offer. Ghorbanifar had given the impression the delegation would bring 1,000 TOW missiles with them. Rafsanjani brought the bad news to Khomeini.

Later in the afternoon, a functionary from the Foreign Office came to the hotel. He lectured McFarlane on earlier American sins toward Iran. In the 1950s, the Americans had supported a coup against the democratically elected government in Iran. Through this coup, the Shah came to power. McFarlane said this was now history.

Through further conversations, McFarlane realized that the Iranians had not expected President Reagan's former security advisor to lead the delegation. He also understood that North and Ghorbanifar had promised more than they could deliver with regards to a meeting with Rafsanjani. But the Americans continued to hope the spare parts would lead to the release of the hostages.

Apparently no one had informed Khomeini who was in the delegation. The ayatollah had been told Americans were coming with rockets and that they had sent along some "technicians" to discuss the details of new deliveries.

When Iran's Supreme Leader had approved the visit, he had said: "Listen to what the Americans have to say, and then let them go in peace." The phrase alluded to a similar visit that had taken place hundreds of years before, when the warrior–emperor of the Byzantine Empire, Heraklios, had sent a delegation to the Prophet Mohammed. The envoys brought weapons as gifts, but their goal was to split the Muslims and recruit spies.[8]

Discussions took place over endless cups of tea. They ate watermelon during the day and big dinners after sunset, followed by sweets, according to the tradition during the Muslim's fasting month of Ramadan. McFarlane, for his part, got the impression that Khomeini's advisors were willing to solve the hostage conflict. He was told the Iranians had sent a delegation to Beirut to discuss the matter with Hizbullah. The following day, however, McFarlane realized nothing would happen. The hostage takers were still stubbornly maintaining their condition that the 17 condemned prisoners from the Dawa Party would have to be released.[9]

By the evening of May 27, McFarlane had enough, and delivered an ultimatum: "If the hostages are out within the next 12 hours, I guarantee new spare parts will be flown to Tehran. If not, we leave." It took McFarlane two days to grasp that negotiating with the Iranians was like bargaining down the price of Persian carpets. Finally, he realized this was a "mission impossible."

At 2 am, North woke McFarlane and told him that the main Iranian negotiator was back from Beirut. He was a short man in his early sixties who spoke good English. McFarlane told him that he had asked his staff to get ready to leave. If the Iranians could produce a firm time for the release of the hostages, however, Mcfarlane could get a plane full of weapons to them two hours before the hostages were handed over to the American ambassador in Beirut. The Iranian left but said he would be back before 6 am.[10]

McFarlane's ultimatum reached Khomeini at 5 am, one hour before the American deadline. Khomeini agreed to arrange freedom for two hostages—Jenco and Jacobsen—but only after further agreement with Iran's envoy in Beirut. McFarlane would not budge. He wanted to have the promise that all the hostages would be freed. Not even the promise of a meeting with Rafsanjani would get the Americans to postpone their departure. The delegation insisted on being driven to the airport. The Iranian negotiator came along in the car and said, "Please, don't leave; we are quite close to a solution."[11]

But McFarlane thought he had to leave to protect President Reagan's prestige. The Iranian was very surprised: he had expected McFarlane to accept the release of two hostages. Amiram Nir, had indicated to the Iranians the Americans might accept that proposal.[12]

On June 6, with McFarlane and the delegation safely out of Iran, President Reagan said in a security briefing that the hostages should be freed by force. The CIA was told to intensify its plans for an armed operation. A few days later agents in Beirut reported they had reached a breakthrough: They were informed two of the hostages were being held in the cellar of an old jail in the Basta quarter of West Beirut. They made a model of the jail, and the CIA checked whether the Syrians could confirm that the hostages were there. The Syrians promised to help. "Nice words, but no action," Thomas Twetten said later.[13] In West Beirut, Terry Anderson, David Jacobsen, Martin Jenco and Thomas Sutherland were sitting in their underwear on dirty mattresses with blindfolds over their eyes and chains around their ankles. All four had been kidnapped between January and June, 1985. The hostages ate cheese, bread, and drank water for breakfast, got rice and beans for lunch, bread and jam for dinner. Some of the guards were mean, others friendly. Sutherland suffered from hemorrhoids and high blood pressure. Jenco had a toothache, and got help from a dentist to get the rotten tooth pulled.

The hostages after a while were allowed to read newspapers and watch TV. When they received new shoes, shirts and pants, they thought perhaps they were about be turned over to the Red Cross. Jacobsen was led out first, but not into a bus, only to another room. Anderson and Sutherland followed after five-minute intervals. They then understood that only Jenco would be set free.

Jenco was not sure what would happen when they put him into the trunk of a car. The kidnappers gave back the cross they had taken from him at the beginning of his imprisonment, and drove him over the mountain to the Bekaa Valley. When the car stopped, they told Jenco to get out and gave him two Lebanese pounds and a message: "Father, take a taxi and go home." They also handed him a videotape with information about the other hostages, warning him, "Do not give the tape to the Syrians: we hate them. If you do that, we will kill the others. If the Syrians take the cassette from you, then say so at the press conference." Then they left.

A policeman discovered Jenco a bit later and turned him over to the Syrians, who drove him to the American Embassy in Damascus. From there he would go to Wiesbaden in West Germany. Robert Baer, an Arabist and CIA agent who had previously been stationed in Damascus and was now part of the Counterterrorism Center, received orders to fly there and meet him. Baer knew a lot about the American priest from reading the archives. Jenco had been kidnapped January 8, 1985, but there was no trace of him after that. Baer also read that Benjamin Weir, who had been released earlier, had not revealed very much about his time in captivity. Now Baer hoped Jenco could fill in the gaps.

But he was disappointed. Jenco had a good memory, but had been chained to a wall and blindfolded most of the time. He was able to relate that the guards had reacted with a mixture of surprise, anger and panic when CNN's Jerry Levin disappeared. He also recounted how he had seen uniformed men from a small window in the toilet. Only then was Baer convinced the hostages must have been held by Iranian Revolutionary Guards in the Sheikh Abdullah barracks in Baalbek.[14]

Oliver North also went to West Germany to talk with Jenco, and when the priest later received an audience with the Pope, North made sure Terry Waite went along. In a memo to President Reagan, North wrote that the release of Jenco was the result of McFarlane's visit to Tehran, and further, that "Our Israeli contacts and the Iranian intermediary in Europe advise that the Iranian government now expects some reciprocal move on our part—though exactly what, we are uncertain."[15]

North recommended to President Reagan to give a clear signal with the delivery of two HAWK radar units, and more spare parts for the HAWK missiles. He wrote that his Iranian contacts were awaiting the rest of the spares, and that it would be a huge personal defeat for them if the parts did not come. North was afraid the situation could deteriorate, particularly because the hostage takers in Hizbullah were not particularly happy with Jenco's release. Reagan did not hesitate. On August 3, 1986, 12 pallets of spare parts were delivered to the Iranians.

To make the Israelis happy, the Attorney General's office in Washington withdrew the Customs Bureau's subpoena against eight Israelis in connection with an investigation into the export of cluster bomb technology to Israel. Israeli authorities had requested this. The Reagan administration approved it as a "reward for the promises from the Israeli government to cooperate."[16]

CHAPTER THIRTY SIX
Screams from Khiam

At the prison center in Khiam, neither the guards nor the prisoners realized they were pawns in a game between Israel, the US and Iran. Nor were the correspondents reporting from the Middle East aware of what was happening behind the scenes.

I tried a number of times to get into the Khiam prison. In Tel Aviv, I visited Israel's Lebanon coordinator, Uri Lubrani. He had his office in the defense ministry, where he sat behind a desk up on a podium with pictures of his grandchildren prominently displayed. At the foot of the podium was a rectangular conference table which had space for eight people. The walls were covered with maps of Lebanon and neighboring countries.

Uri Lubrani had been ambassador to Iran when Israel invaded Lebanon in 1978. He knew well the concern the Iranians had for their Shia brethren's welfare. Lubrani also knew that contacts between Iran and South Lebanon had existed for centuries. By now it was clear to him that the Iranians were working to export their Islamic revolution to Lebanon. In an interview, Lubrani said:"Iran is a nation of carpet weavers, and it takes one year to weave a carpet. They are chess players who look three moves ahead. They are not impatient Jews or Arabs who want instant gratification."[17]

He told me with a straight face that Israel did not have control over the prisoners in Khiam. He said he understood that the SLA would not give the press or the Red Cross access so long as the western hostages in Lebanon were not allowed visits. I also sought out the SLA leadership in Marjayoun. But the Lebanese echoed Lubrani's point: no outsiders were allowed into Khiam while their own captive soldiers did not receive visits from the Red Cross or from journalists.

The closest I got to Khiam was the road that passed a few hundred meters below its walls. The prison was close enough to the UNTSO observation post OP Khiam, that, I was told, observers often could hear screams from the prisoners under torture. But such reports never produced Norwegian protests against Israel.

The only way to learn about conditions in the infamous torture center was to interview former prisoners. I visited a number of those who had been set free. Some dared to be interviewed in front of a television camera. Others only wanted to speak anonymously. Some had been released without any explanation, while others were set free because of illness, and others because a constant influx of prisoners meant there was not enough room for everyone. In other words, there was no clear pattern for who got freedom and who remained.

A woman who had been in Khiam for over a year told me the daily rhythm hardly ever changed. Everyone was woken up at dawn. They were given a simple breakfast, they cleaned their cells and they were allowed out one after the other to dump the buckets containing their excrement. Then each was allotted five minutes to wash in a small room, where they also could fill their cans of water. A guard kept time with a stopwatch, and delays were severely punished. At midday, the guards came with a modest lunch, and later in the afternoon there was a bit more food. During the rest of the day, quiet was to be observed. If anyone raised their voice, there would be extra punishments. Prisoners could talk with their cellmates, but contact with prisoners in other cells was forbidden.[18]

The male prisoners had worse conditions than the women, mainly because the cells were overfilled and the prisoners were beaten and kicked. The men were also not allowed to empty their toilet buckets more than once a week.

New prisoners could keep nothing but their clothes and the shoes. These were washed and patched over and over again, until after a few years nothing remained but rags. Clothes were also loaned or traded away. Families of prisoners from occupied South Lebanon could now and then smuggle in new clothing by bribing the guards. Later the male prisoners were given uniforms, sewn from a dark blue material—the same material as the hoods guards used on them from time to time.

Everyone who was released had something to tell of their time there. Kamel Issa, a corporal in the Lebanese army, was wearing his uniform when he was captured in the village of Yohmor on November 7, 1984. Issa said the guards had left him lying out in the exercise yard for 10 days, bound with his feet chained together. Occasionally, they would put a box on his head with two electric wires running through it to his ears. They put a third wire into his mouth, and stuffed in a rag so he could not spit out the wire when the power was turned on. Issa fainted from the torture, and his tormenters alternately threw cold or hot water on him to wake him up. When he came to, he noticed blood was coming from his mouth. In 1995, after 11 years in Khiam, Issa was freed in a prisoner exchange and could tell his story.

Not everyone the Israelis captured ended up in Khiam. A young Shia, Bilal Dakrub, told how he had been taken by a group of Israeli soldiers on February 16, 1986, while he was hiding in a cave near the city of Tibnin in central South Lebanon. Bilal had been accused of belonging to an enemy organization by one of the Lebanese who worked for Shin Bet. For 10 days he was held captive in a military camp near Bint Jbeil. Occasionally, he was tied to the bumper of an Israeli military vehicle to serve as a human shield. Dakrub was interrogated by the Israelis and kicked and beaten by their Lebanese helpers. He was tortured and suffered electric shocks on orders from the Israeli interrogators.

A court condemned him to two and a half years in jail. When the sentence had been served, Dakrub was still not set freed. He was kept in prison to be used for bargaining, if necessary. Nine years later Bilal Dakrub still remained a hostage in Israel.[19]

The western hostages in West Beirut and Baalbek were also treated badly, but they did not face systematic torture like the prisoners in Khiam. Furthermore, the western hostages received great international attention. The Israelis' hostages were nearly forgotten, and when the Israelis took new ones, the mass media did not, as a rule, report it. When the Shias took new westerners hostage, it became big headlines.

On September 8, 1986, one of the American diplomats in East Beirut called Joseph Cicippio, an American auditor at AUB, and asked him to check out a rumor that the director of the Lebanese International School in West Beirut, Frank Reed, had been kidnapped. This proved to be true. When Cicippio and his wife were sitting in front of their television that evening, the screen was covered with photographs of the foreign hostages who had been taken in the past two years. In the middle of the screen was an empty space—who would be next?

Cicippio recognized the risk he took living in West Beirut. But he lived in an apartment on the university grounds, surrounded by security guards. Besides, he had converted to Islam, and his wife was a Lebanese Muslim. In addition to working at the AUB, Cicippio did welfare work. He felt safe.[20]

But he was not. The next day his life turned upside down when he became the man to fill that empty space on the TV screen. Like the other hostages, he was snatched on an open street, forced into a car and driven to the southern part of Beirut. There he was led into a house and chained to the wall in an unfinished kitchen. When his captors finally fed him, he noticed the plate and the utensils were marked TWA. He remembered the hijacking of the TWA plane the year before, and understood that Islamic Jihad was holding him.

A few days later, September 15, Amnesty International issued a report on torture at Khiam. The human rights organization simultaneously presented a similar report on the Israeli torture of

Palestinians from the West Bank. Amnesty announced the reports were being made public because Israel would not respond to the organization's appeal for an international investigation.

Eight days later, I noticed that Defense Minister Yitzhak Rabin visited several of the SLA locations in South Lebanon. The past week, Hizbullah had killed 16 militia soldiers from the SLA. Rabin promised to crush those who attacked Israel's allies.

On September 29, fighting broke out outside the occupation zone. Soldiers from Amal's militia attacked the Palestinian refugee camp Rashidiya south of Tyre. The local fighting spread to Sidon, where Palestinian forces took over the Christian village of Maghdouche, above the Palestinian refugee camps Ain el-Helweh and Mieh Mieh.[21]

Maghdouche had previously been under Amal control, and Amal wanted help from the Syrians to take the village back. Israeli planes took to the air and bombed Palestinian positions outside the village.

CHAPTER THIRTY SEVEN

Exposé

In the United States, the Reagan administration's hostage negotiator was beginning to doubt the Israeli approach to get the hostages freed. Ghorbanifar and Nir should be replaced, he thought. Oliver North had found other Iranian contacts. On October 5, 1986, North met Iranians from "the other channel" in Frankfurt. He had brought a Bible with a dedication by Ronald Reagan as a gift to the Iranians.

North had a lively imagination, and he told the Iranians: "We inside our government had an enormous debate, a very angry debate over whether or not my president should authorize me to say, 'We accept the Islamic revolution of Iran as a fact...' He [the president] went off one whole weekend and prayed about what the answer should be and he came back almost a year ago with the passage that he wrote in the Bible I gave you. And he said to me, 'This is a promise God gave to Abraham. Who am I to say that we should not do this.' "[22]

After the meeting in Frankfurt, North went on to Hamburg together with a former CIA agent and two assistants. They were to meet another Iranian contact. This contact, who was supposedly close to Rafsanjani, promised to help get another American hostage freed if the Americans would deliver 500 new TOW missiles. Iran would pay for the missiles in advance.

In order to ensure new shipments of weapons, the Iranians decided to grab another American hostage in Lebanon. The victim this time was the writer Edward Tracy. On October 21, a group calling itself the Organization for Revolutionary Fairness abducted him. The number of American hostages had now reached six, exactly the same as when Israel sent the first 100 missiles to Iran 13 months earlier.

In the middle of the missile shipments, Iran's foreign minister, Ali Akbar Velayati, came to Damascus. Assad had long been pressuring Iran to put an end to the hostage crisis. The hostages diverted attention away from Syria's objective: to get the US to force Israel to accept a comprehensive peace solution for the Middle East, including Israel's withdrawal from all occupied areas.

In a meeting on October 31, Velayati advised President Assad that another release was imminent.[23] This time it was David Jacobsen's turn. In West Beirut, his captors had him read to a video camera from a prepared text. Jacobsen occasionally looked up into the camera lens as he read. The message was that Terry Anderson, Thomas Sutherland and he himself would only be released if the American authorities met the kidnappers' demands. Jacobsen read that he did not know what the demands were. (Martin Jenco had received instructions to tell the Americans what they were). Furthermore the message said that William Buckley had been executed because of Washington's unwillingness to negotiate.

On November 1, Imad Mughniyeh came in to Jacobsen. The hostage did not know the Iranians had received their latest delivery of TOW missiles the day before. Again, Mughniyeh asked if Jacobsen was a Jew. He repeated that his name was Danish, that the ending "sen" had an "e," and that if it had been written with an "o," it would have been the Swedish version.[24]

Mughniyeh, referred to as Hajj Imad, spoke English, but he still asked a guard to translate the message he instructed Jacobsen to pass onto President Reagan. Additionally, he asked Jacobsen to go to Kuwait and make a personal effort to free the 17 Dawa prisoners.

Through the interpreter, Hajj Imad told Jacobsen the procedure for his release: "When you are given orders to get out of the car, you must remove your blindfold, but keep your eyes closed. Then, you are to wait for one minute, look straight ahead and walk toward the wall which is in front of you. Then, you shall pretend you are urinating, and after a few minutes go to the left and on to the American Embassy."

"Do you mean the place in East Beirut?" So far as Jacobsen knew, this was the only embassy in operation. The old one in West Beirut had been bombed more than three years earlier.

"No, no, in West Beirut. There are still security forces on duty there."

Because of the lack of housing, people fleeing bombed out areas used "war damaged" buildings to get a roof over their heads. For this reason, the Americans had put guards outside the old embassy.

"Above all, you must not go into the Hotel Riviera, because the Syrians are there," warned Mughniyeh. "We do not want the Syrians to take the credit for your release." Then he threatened, "If you make this mistake and they do claim to have saved you, we will harm your friends. Do you understand?"

He smoked as he spoke, and concluded, "Forget my instructions about Kuwait. Go home, see your family, have a good vacation, and come back to work as director of the American University Hospital in Beirut. We need you, and you will be safe and protected from all further harm." Then Mughniyeh left.

At 6 am on November 2, 1986, with blindfold securely in place, Jacobsen was escorted up a spiral staircase and run out into the faint rays of the early morning sun. Mughniyeh greeted him with the words, "Do you remember your instructions?"

"Yes," Jacobsen answered. It was not the moment to ask for clarifications or recapitulation.

"Good bye. Good luck. Have a safe trip," Mughniyeh said, and left.

Jacobsen was released close to the Hotel Riviera, a few hundred meters from the burned-out ruins of the American Embassy. A militia soldier from the Druze Party, PSP, noticed him, and he was soon on his way over the Green Line to the new American Embassy in the hills east of the city.

The Syrians got no credit for having delivered a new hostage to the Americans. This infuriated the leaders in Damascus. But Imad Mughniyeh and the Iranians got their small revenge for the extra strong pressure President Hafez al-Assad had exerted to get Jacobsen freed.[25]

West Beirut was on the brink of war. That part of the city was in the hands of the Druze and Shias, while Maronites controlled East Beirut. In the southern part of the city, the Amal militia once more attacked the Palestinian refugee camp Bourj el-Barajne. The fighting spread to Sabra and Shatila. In the Palestinian camps near Sidon and Tyre, there were battles among various Palestinian factions.

The mini-war between the Druze militia and Amal in West Beirut began when Walid Jumblatt gave orders to remove the Lebanese flag from that part of the city. He wanted to fly the Druze flag, with each of its five colors commemorating one of their five prophets. "The War of the Two Flags" raged in the heart of West Beirut. Wounded militia soldiers were hastily brought to the American University Hospital. There, throughout the entire conflict, each of the various groups had its own health representative who knew all the routines and practices at the hospital, how to get their wounded in as quickly as possible to the operating table, which doctors were the best and where they could get needed medicines and equipment.

The militia representatives threatened doctors and nurses with weapons to ensure their comrades were first on the list to get care. On one occasion, a doctor attempted to revive a patient in shock by slapping him. The patient's friend became furious and shot his automatic pistol into the ceiling. The poor doctor was so scared he ran off.

One of the American nurses told of a day when several groups stormed in to the hospital reception area. They fired into the air, shouted and ran from one department to another, apparently hunting for a particular man. Suddenly, they began to fight each other. Patients, doctors, nurses and visitors looked for places to hide. One of the patients had a heart attack and died on the spot. A militia soldier began waving a hand grenade about and forced a doctor to surrender his white coat. The soldier put it on to impersonate a doctor and resumed his search for the man. When he found him, he took out his pistol and killed him. No one knew why. But the story was told over and over to show what a workday was like at Beirut's hospital.[26]

From the bar at the Commodore Hotel, and from its windows and balconies, daring journalists could watch militia soldiers run through the streets shooting at their former allies. The bullets flew through parked and moving vehicles. When one car was hit, a photographer ran from the hotel lobby to take pictures of the driver as he tried to pull a bloody passenger to safety.

"What are you doing? Why don't you help?" The angry driver shouted at the photographer.

He got no help and the passenger died, senselessly joining the many victims in one of Beirut's many small wars.

Right in the middle of the fighting, a small group of Iranians visited the editor of the Lebanese weekly *Ash-Shiraa*. The editor, Hassan Sabra, tried to wriggle out of the visit. He asked his secretary to tell the Iranians, who were waiting in the reception area, that he was not in the office. To the editor, Iranians meant trouble. But the Iranians insisted on waiting that Monday, October 27, 1986.

The editor gave up and discovered that he knew some of the guests. They belonged to Khomeini's inner circle from the time the ayatollah was living in exile in Paris. Sabra started the conversation by asking about the radical religious leader Mehdi Hashemi, who recently had been arrested on orders of the National Assembly President Rafsanjani.

Hashemi led an organization which was working to export the Islamic revolution. He accused Rafsanjani of destroying the revolution by courting the West. He was closely tied to the kidnappers in Lebanon. The Iranians visiting Sabra said that Hashemi's arrest was the reason for their visit. They continued that what they had to say would not be particularly advantageous for the current Iranian regime and National Assembly president.

The story was long and involved. The Iranians spoke of the secret American visit to Tehran in May. Then recounted how the delegation was led by McFarlane, dressed as a pilot, and how they arrived in an Israeli Boeing 707 loaded with important spare parts for the war against Iraq. Also that the Americans had travelled on fake Irish passports, had brought a Bible with President Reagan's signature and—most important of all—that it was Rafsanjani who had personally invited them to Iran, but the visit was unsuccessful because Ayatollah Khomeini had stepped in. The Iranians explained to the magazine's editor that they were there in Beirut to expose Rafsanjani's deceit and his attempt to negotiate with The Great Satan.[27]

Sabra listened, but did not believe what he was hearing. He knew his guests were friends of Hashemi, who was now in prison accused of treason. He understood why the Iranians had come to him, namely to discredit Rafsanjani, who was in the process of building himself up to be Iran's new strong man. The guests thought Rafsanjani would be overthrown if the story went public, and that this would mean freedom for the jailed Hashemi. They said that they had personally come to Sabra in Beirut to avoid revealing their source.

Sabra knew a brutal power struggle was taking place in Iran between Rafsanjani's pragmatists and the radicals. This was the angle that interested him the most, so he wrote a long, detailed article about it. He did not care much about the American involvement, and even doubted that the Americans had come with a cake and a Bible from Reagan. President Reagan had of course said there was no possibility of negotiating for the hostages' release.

When the magazine exposé hit the streets of Beirut on November 3, 1986, it created a greater uproar in the US than in Iran. Robert McFarlane heard the news on the radio, but felt relieved that the story was full of mistakes. He had not brought a Bible signed by President Reagan; that was Oliver North, and it happened much later. McFarlane also had not come dressed as a member of the flight crew. Because of these errors, McFarlane tried to dismiss the report in the Lebanese magazine as "fantasy."

The State Department was furious over what had happened. Oliver North thought Israel and Shimon Peres should take the blame, as Peres should have informed George Shultz of developments. The then-Israeli prime minister had talked with Shultz many times, but never mentioned the Iranian contacts. He later explained,"My admiration for the United States was such that I was naturally convinced that they could always rely on the most thorough and coordinated staff work in reaching policy decisions."[28]

When it came out that profits from the missile sales went to the Contras in Nicaragua, the United States's reputation suffered further damage in the Middle East. US-friendly Arab states felt betrayed. First, the Americans had begged them to confront Iran and take the lead for an international weapons boycott. Then the Americans undertook a secret cooperation with the revolutionary Iranians themselves. This was certainly proof of America's duplicity.

The entire world was witness to Washington's elite being caught with their pants down. Getting into bed with Iran had not helped much either, as only three hostages had been set free. Then the Lebanese, with Iran's blessing, had taken three new ones. The main things the US had succeeded in doing were to arm Iran with several thousand TOW missiles, to give them vital spare parts for their inventory of HAWKs and to transfer illegal funds to the Contras. That transfer sealed the issue, taking it from a painful affair to a scandal.[29]

CHAPTER THIRTY EIGHT

Damascus in Beirut

Reverend Terry Waite did not give up his work to free the hostages. On January 12, 1987, he went back to Beirut surrounded by journalists, not realizing Hizbullah had discovered he was secretly working with Oliver North. The Englishman was no longer viewed as a religious envoy, but as an American spy.

Hizbullah's security service knew Waite had flown with an American helicopter from Cyprus to Beirut, and that North had given him a tiny electronic device by which an American satellite could track him.[30] At first Hizbullah made no effort to kidnap Waite; he was simply ignored. He was, however, able to meet the cleric Fadlallah, and was invited to dine at the home of Walid Jumblatt whose men were his bodyguards. During the dinner, Waite repeated to the point of boredom that he was there on "a purely humanitarian mission." Jumblatt knew nothing about Waite's connections with Oliver North, but he was not particularly impressed by the British church envoy, who on top of it all got himself drunk during the meal.[31]

After seven days and nights of waiting, he decided to go back to London. He packed and got ready to leave his room at the run-down Riviera Hotel, not far from Terry Anderson's apartment on Avenue de Paris. The Druze guards sat in the corridor waiting for him. Suddenly, he got a telephone call that the kidnappers were ready to talk, and he agreed to a meeting. The contact person was Adnan Mroueh, the Lebanese doctor from Jabal Amel hospital in Tyre. He had his office and apartment in Ain el-Mreisseh, a few hundred meters from my former residence.

The Druze guards drove Waite to a gasoline station just outside the Spaghetteria Italia Restaurant. From there the reverend walked down a few alleys to a yellow-brown building where Dr. Mroueh's white office plaque hung on the wall. A few minutes after the doctor let Waite in, the phone rang. Mroueh took the call, said something in Arabic and hung up, telling Waite, "I am so sorry, but I have to leave."[32]

"Why?"

"A patient is in labor. I am needed urgently."

"Can't you wait a little longer?"

"That is not possible—I am sorry."

They shook hands, and the doctor said: "I'll leave the door on the latch. When you leave, please lock it behind you."

Waite remained and waited. After a while he heard the elevator moving, and seconds later the doorbell rang. A small, thick-set man dressed in a single-breasted suit was standing outside. Waite had met the man before. He was the direct link to the kidnappers.

"Are you alone?"

"Yes."

The man came in. "Are you armed?"

"No."

"Please, I shall have to search you."

His hands glided over Waites clothing, and he said, "We must leave right now."

It was raining when they entered the narrow, empty street. Just after they did so, a large car stopped beside them.

"You sit in the back," said the little man in the suit. "If we are stopped, you must say I am responsible for driving you around Beirut."

Then they drove off. Suddenly the driver stopped, the two passengers transferred to another car and Waite was blindfolded. A few minutes later, the car stopped again. Waite was led up to the second floor in what he thought was an apartment building. He could see little through his blindfold.

"Mr. Waite, I must ask you to change your clothes," said a voice.

Waite was handed a robe and a pair of sandals with the message that he would be staying overnight. He was not allowed to talk, but he could sleep if he wanted. The whole time someone would be nearby.

Waite slept through the night, and remained blindfolded the next day as well. Because journalists who were covering the matter figured Waite would stay in hiding for a few days, the outside world did not know he was again a hostage.

Imad Mughniyeh had carried out a clever plan: he had long ago decided to kidnap Waite, but did not want to do it by force. The reverend was a big and powerful man who could create problems if he was nabbed in the open street. For that reason, Mughniyeh wanted to lure him into a trap. And now he was in it.

At first Waite's captors treated him with a certain respect. Later, however, he was chained to a radiator, then beaten and exposed to mock executions. When enough time passed, it was obvious to the whole world that the Shias had taken the archbishop's envoy as a hostage.

Dr. Mroueh did not know that Waite had been kidnapped. Only after a few days did the Druze responsible for Waite, came asking where he was. It was clear something must have happened. The two went to see Sayyed Mohammed Hussein Fadlallah, whom the doctor knew. There he got the bad news: "Doctor, I am afraid no one can free him now except the Iranian intelligence. The only person in Beirut who is capable of doing something about this is the chargé d'affaires of the Iranian Embassy. Do not waste your time with anyone else."[33]

I flew off to Tehran and, on January 28, 1987, attended a press conference where the National Assembly President Ali Akbar Hashemi Rafsanjani was to be present. A few years before, I had interviewed him under the alias, "The Shark." I was surprised when one of his colleagues came over to me and said,"Ask Rafsanjani about the Bible with President Reagan's signature."

I was in a line of questioners along with Robert Fisk, who had changed jobs—he was now working as Middle East correspondent for *The Independent*. Fisk pointed out that Rafsanjani was looking at a pile of photocopied documents including passport photos of Robert McFarlane.

Before I got to ask my question, an American reporter asked what proof the Iranians had that McFarlane had come to Tehran under a false Irish passport. Rafsanjani took the pile of photocopies and waved for them to be passed around. They clearly showed the American's picture on an Irish passport.

"They falsified the passports," Rafsanjani's interpreter said in translation.

A bit later, Rafsanjani showed the Bible. We were able to see the signature, "Ronald Reagan, October 3, 1986," in the president's neat handwriting. Rafsanjani wanted to demonstrate that the Americans had lied before the whole world when they said they had broken all contact with Iran. Just one month before, in December 1986, an American weapons dealer had met Iranian colleagues in order to get in contact with the leadership in Tehran. The press conference, however, did not provide any answers as to what Rafsanjani thought about the hostage situation.

After reporting from the war front between Iran and Iraq, I went back to Oslo. On February 9, another report came from West Beirut that four new hostages had been taken. I wrote a report for the *Daily News Hour*. In all there were now five Americans, four Frenchmen, Two British, an Italian, an Irishman, a South Korean and a Saudi Arabian chained to walls or radiators in that part of the city. Some of the hostages were allowed to watch Lebanese TV and saw the announcement that, if Israel did not release 254 Palestinian prisoners from Israeli jails, many of them would be killed. Hostage Joseph Cicippio did not doubt the threat was real. And when the auditor saw pictures of a smiling, waving Israeli prime minister on the screen, he felt animosity toward the Israeli government for the first time. It obviously did not care the least about the Americans.

The kidnappers moved Cicippio, and in his new prison he could hear a man being beaten in the adjacent room. "You're killing me, you're killing me, Oh God help me! Save me," shrieked the man.[34] One of the guards came in to Cicippio and told him not to worry. "The man is a German thug. He refuses to obey and deserves no pity." Cicippio could hear the man was American, not German.[35]

The torture continued for several weeks, and Cicippio covered his ears to avoid listening to his fellow prisoner's treatment. Finally, they brought the man into Cicippio's cell. He was Edward Tracy, a writer who had been kidnapped as he was drinking coffee at his favorite café in West Beirut. What the kidnappers did not know was that Tracy was a poor, tragic soul with serious mental problems. The torture did not stop until the guards figured out that he was mentally ill.

On February 16, Tracy and Cicippio were moved to the same place as three French hostages: 35-year-old *Antenne 2* reporter Jean-Louis Normandin, 31-year-old photojournalist Roger Auque and another unidentified sound technician. All three were kidnapped after they had covered Terry Waite's meeting with Fadlallah.

In the streets of West Beirut, the fighting continued. Amal fought against the Druze militia, which had the support of other Muslim and secular militia groups including the Palestinian militia soldiers. In the course of a few days, the Druze and their allies had taken over three-fourths of that part of the city. The warriors were merciless. None took prisoners or bothered with appeals for a ceasefire.

The Syrian military intelligence chief in Lebanon, Brigadier General Ghazi Kanaan, warned that he would send troops into West Beirut, but he was met with deaf ears. Previously, Syrian forces had evacuated the area together with the PLO in August 1982. Now they came back with 500 soldiers. Several thousand more waited in North and Eastern Lebanon, ready for action.

In a new attempt to arrange a ceasefire, General Kanaan drove from his headquarters in the Bekaa Valley to West Beirut. When he arrived there was a short pause in the fighting, but the bloodbath resumed the next morning. The Druze militia, supported by artillery, went on the offensive toward a number of Amal positions. Amal responded by bombarding Druze parts of the city and their villages in the mountains. The Druze shot at the State television station, *Tele Liban*, in West Beirut, which was in Amal hands.

All telephones in West Beirut died when an artillery shell hit the post office and telecenter. Most newspapers could not be printed because few employees remained on the job. The Red Cross appealed for a pause in the fighting to collect the dead lying in the streets.

A young Palestinian fighting with the Druze against Amal was positioned atop a building at the western end of Rue Hamra. He belonged to a group that had smuggled weapons and food into Sabra and Shatila. Now the young man was surrounded by enemy soldiers from Amal. Fearing for his life, he managed to contact his Druze allies via walkie-talkie and began pointing out targets for them. It did not take long for the Druze to take control of Rue Hamra and the quarters nearby. Finally, Amal controlled only one short section of street in the district, north of the main shopping street.[36]

The fighting brought an end to the famous Commodore Hotel. After a seven-hour battle, the Druze militia took the hotel. The employees had fled, and the kitchen, bar and stores had all been plundered for food and drink, utensils, pots and pans, plates, towels and bedding. Television sets were taken from the rooms. Coco the parrot disappeared, as did Tommy, the fat cat who usually lay between the telex machines for *Reuters* and the *AP*. The following day gunmen came with a large truck and carted away the hotel's grand piano.

Walid Jumblatt had gone to Damascus the day before together with the secretary-general of the Lebanese Communist Party, George Hawi. There they were to meet Nabih Berri, who was in the government with Jumblatt. The militia used any excuse to continue fighting, however, and there was no ceasefire agreement. Berri ordered his militia to continue, ignoring the Syrian warning that anyone appearing on West Beirut's streets with a weapon would be treated as an outlaw. General Kanaan had broadcast the threat on several of Beirut's private radio stations. The militia did not care. They strengthened their positions and got ready for a new round.

The Syrians finally decided that enough was enough. On February 22, 8,000 Syrian soldiers advanced into West Beirut. The initial 500 had been there as a sort of police force, and were clearly insufficient to stop the fighting.

It was Lebanon's Sunni prime minister, Rashid Karami, who formally requested Syria to halt the brutal warfare between Amal and the Druze militia. President Amine Gemayel was not consulted. His power barely reached beyond Christian East Beirut.

Israel did not particularly care about the massive Syrian buildup. And the US government, which had its own political misadventure fresh in mind, thought it would be a positive move if the Syrians could create peace in West Beirut. Only the Iranians seemed concerned, fearing that the Syrians would try to tame Hizbullah.

Many civilians breathed a sigh of relief. "*Ahlan! Ahlan!*" Welcome! Welcome! cried women from the roadside, throwing kisses to the Syrians who arrived in trucks, tanks and armored vehicles. In my old quarter of Ain el-Mreisseh, the Syrians used heavy guns to get the militia to surrender. On Rue Hamra, they rounded up 60 armed young men into trucks.

For people who dared to go out, it was like walking on ice: crunch, crunch, crunch was the sound over the broken glass that had fallen from windows. Syrian soldiers were there to hand them pictures of Hafez al-Assad. In the Basta quarter, where Hizbullah was strong, the Syrians showed no mercy. Their commanding officer had previously been mistreated by the Shias in the area. Soldiers went into buildings where the Shias were saying their prayers. They lined up 23 men and four women against a wall and mowed them down. Those who did not die of gunshot wounds were bayoneted. This was a clear message: You are now dealing with General Ghazi Kanaan. He will not be stepped upon. The corpses were dumped onto a trash heap in West Beirut. There was only one survivor, who would later be able to tell what had happened.

The following day, 50,000 people took part in the burial of the massacre's victims. Sayyed Mohammed Hussein Fadlallah spoke. Then the militant Shias marched to the shouts from the streets: "Death to the murderers of the martyrs! Death to Syria! Death to Kanaan! Death to America! Death to Israel!"

In Iran cries echoed, "The murders are the 20th century's Karbala."[37]

The Shias in West Beirut mobilized and wanted to fight, but Khomeini said no. He issued a *fatwa* to Fadlallah: It is forbidden to fire at the Syrian force. It will lead to a full-scale war with Syria, something which will spell the end of the Hizbullah militia. Instead, Hizbullah's secretary-general, Sheikh Sobhi Tufayli, suggested escalating the fight against the Israelis in South Lebanon.

To show who was ruling West Beirut, the Syrian soldiers tore down portraits of Ayatollah Khomeini and put up pictures of Hafez al-Assad. They closed 75 militia offices in all, and banned young men from growing beards since these were a trademark for warriors. Soon there were long lines outside barber shops: everyone knew the Syrians were not joking.

After 24 hours it seemed that General Kanaan had reached his short-term goal to bring calm to the city. But the Syrian forces did not enter South Beirut's Dahiyeh suburb where around 800,000 Shias lived. Amal was permitted to dominate this area, even if Hizbullah was increasing in strength with each passing month.

The Syrians supported the Iranians in the war with Iraq, and as thanks received Iranian oil at a bargain price. But Damascus did not want a militant, Islamic Lebanon on the Iranian model. President Hafez al-Assad had personally crushed the Sunni Muslim Islamists at the beginning of the 1980s. For the Syrians, it was important to have a strong Amal, but not stronger than they could control from Damascus. Nor should Hizbullah become too dominant, as that would involve Iran getting power and influence at the expense of Syria.

There would not be any long-lasting Pax Syriana in Lebanon. The Lebanese had a peculiar way of conquering their conquerors, and Lebanon became like a Rubik's Cube for Assad: however hard the Syrian president tried, he could never get the last piece in place.

CHAPTER THIRTY NINE
A Furious Norwegian

In April 1987, Ane-Karine Arvesen was stationed at the Norwegian Embassy in Tehran. For me the war between Iran and Iraq, which had dragged on for nearly seven years, was taking a lot of my time. I reported from both sides of the front, from Baghdad and Tehran. Even though my focus was not on Lebanon, I also followed what was happening in the south.

On January 2, 1987, Hizbullah attacked the SLA outpost overlooking the village of Bra'sleet. This was the first concerted attempt to storm and overrun a militia position. The assault was headed by a shy young man who had earned his reputation by executing collaborators in the Sidon area. Now he was a well-respected combatant and commander in a part of the western sector of the occupation zone.[38] It was the dark of night when 12 men of the attack unit walked up the hill toward the SLA outpost and then split into two columns. Another unit was held in reserve, and a fire support group was ready with mortars at the rear.

The attackers cut a path through barbed wires and reached the wall of the compound, close enough to see a guard's glowing cigarette on the fortified position above. Seconds later, the SLA machine gun nests were knocked out by RPG fire.

The Hizbullah fighters scrambled over the parapet and down into the center of the compound. The surviving defenders ducked into concrete bunkers and bolted the steel doors from the inside, while the Hizbullah men blew up an old Sherman tank and drove an armored personnel carrier from the compound and out of the occupation zone. They had no intentions of holding on to the captured post; their strategy was to terrorize and exhaust the SLA.

Four months later, in April 1987, I noted in my little black book that a third of a Hizbullah unit of 60 fighters were killed attacking another outpost in the occupation zone. This time the Israelis were also involved in the fighting. Four Israeli soldiers were wounded, while 18 men from Hizbullah lost their lives. The guerrillas had apparently not had enough training to fight against a regular army.

On May 1, I noted further that Israeli planes bombed the Palestinian refugee camp Mieh Mieh near Sidon. Nineteen people were killed and 37 wounded. Not since 1982 were so many Palestinians killed in a single attack. On May 7, Israeli forces killed two Palestinian guerrilla soldiers and took three captive when they tried to sneak through the occupation zone and carry out an attack. The Lebanese resistance movement did not make attempts like this. For Hizbullah and the others, the targets were Israeli soldiers in Lebanon, and there was no lack of volunteers.

One of the many Shias who offered to fight was a 22-year-old father of three, Ali Fawaz, from the village of Debaal in South Lebanon. Fawaz had some experience in the Lebanese army, and got some additional training when he reported for duty. The last day of May, 1987, two days after the end of Ramadan, he prepared himself for a mission.[39] Its code name was "*Badr al-Kubra*,"—the Big Badr Operation—in memory of a battle the Prophet Mohammed fought at Badr in Hijaz, Saudi Arabia during Ramadan in the year 624. The battle was decisive in the fight against his opponents.

Hizbullah's plan was to attack one of the SLA outposts on Jebel Safi, a mountain where a Lebanese radar station had been placed. But things went wrong from the start for Fawaz and his group.

They were discovered before firing a single shot, and Fawaz was wounded by a grenade from an Israeli tank. He was bleeding from his leg and arm, but did not want help.

"You all fight! I will manage," he shouted to the others in the group.

Later Fawaz was given first aid, but then shrapnel from another explosion killed several of the soldiers around him. Helpless and bleeding on the ground, Fawaz could hear their dying cries. He felt thirsty, but happy. He did not want water as he thought that his bleeding would get worse if he drank.

Suddenly, Fawaz heard a friendly voice:"Take it easy. This will be fine." Then another grenade came, and the voice was gone. He thought God had spoken to him.

Still later he heard quite different voices. They came from SLA militia soldiers who were shooting at the wounded and dying as they approached. Fawaz said a quiet prayer, and he thought it would be his last.

Then he heard a voice say, "Here is another dead man." He felt bullets hit the ground around him, felt their heat, and was nearly blinded by the flashes. There was a sensation like the bullets had burnt off his hair.

When all was quiet, he was surprised to still be alive. He heard steps and another voice saying,"There is a live one here."

"Bring him here," a third voice said. "What is your name? Get up!"

Fawaz saw a man with a helmet standing over him. It must have been one of Lahd's men.

"I can't, I am wounded in the hip and my leg below the knee is destroyed," he answered.

He felt a hand around his foot. It was terribly painful. He screamed, and the soldier dropped the foot to the ground. Then someone kicked him before two men put him on a stretcher and brought him to the post he was supposed to have attacked. They dumped him on top of some sandbags and one of the militia soldiers kicked him again.

Fawaz saw a bottle of water close by, but did not touch it. A voice said, "Ali does not want water," and then he felt the water being poured over his face. Another militia soldier came over to him and said,"You are just a rag who can be used to polish boots." The soldier rubbed one of his boots on Fawaz's clothes. After being moved several times and continually mistreated, he heard the rumble of a helicopter, and then he was in the air on the way to Israel.

When he came to, he was lying in a hospital bed. He did not know how long he had been there. Shortly afterward, an Israeli came in to question him. Fawaz wanted to know what day it was.

"June 7."

It had been seven days since he had been wounded. Fawaz noticed that his hand and foot were chained to the bed. A nurse came and changed his bandage. Then medical students arrived to practice on his wounds. This was pure torture because he got no painkillers. But he was given food, at least: olives, yoghurt, bread, a cup of tea, now and then eggs or tomatoes.

Every day, after he saw a doctor and then a nurse, men came to interrogate. One of them spoke Arabic, albeit poorly. He was so impolite that Fawaz said one morning, "Didn't you have any upbringing? Can't you even say, 'good morning'?"

"No, not to terrorists"

"I am from South Lebanon and I am fighting to liberate my country."

"You kill children in South Lebanon."

"If you send children as soldiers, then we kill children."

"We have an army, and we have tanks," said the Israeli. "What do you have?"

"We have God."

The Israeli pulled out his pistol and put it against Ali's head. But he did not shoot.

While Ali Fawaz was in Israeli captivity, Norwegian Defense Minister Johan Jørgen Holst was sitting in a meeting with Syrian Foreign Minister Abdul Halim Khaddam in Damascus. Holst, who was nearly 50 years old, would have preferred to be foreign minister, but that job went to Thorvald Stoltenberg. As defense minister, Holst could still travel to the Middle East without stepping on

Stoltenberg's turf: Norway was part of UNIFIL, and that was reason enough for Holst to come to Syria, Lebanon and Israel in June.

Khaddam suggested that throughout history there had never been extreme Muslim parties in Lebanon. There had been the extreme Christian movement that had crossed the line, however, and Hizbullah was the result of the Christian's extreme positions.

"While in Muslim-dominated West Beirut there are tens of thousands of Christians, there is hardly a single Muslim living in the areas with a Christian majority. They have either been killed or forced to move. Extreme actions produce extreme reactions," Khaddam said.[40]

Holst agreed, and continued, "The extremists exert enormous pressure on the cohesiveness of Lebanese politics. I am worried that what has happened in Beirut might spread to South Lebanon, even if the situation there is different. The main pressure in South Lebanon is caused by the presence of the Israelis. This creates frustration, which makes it possible for Hizbullah to advance, and forces the moderates to become more extreme to be able to 'steal the thunder from the true extremists.'"

Holst made quotation marks in the air with both hands when he said, "steal the thunder from the true extremists," without naming who they were. He added that Amal needed to confront an uncomfortable face: "A polarizing process can lead to dissolution."

"I quite agree," answered the Syrian vice president. "If the Israelis withdraw, extremism will diminish. The continuous presence of Israel in South Lebanon kindles extreme actions. Occupation in any country leads to opposition."

When Holst sat with a smiling Shimon Peres three days later, he wanted to talk about the prisoners the Israelis were holding in Khiam. He had come directly from South Lebanon, and he was furious. The anger came from the stories he had heard from the Norwegian battlion chief, in Ebl el-Saqi. At NORBATT, Holst had received a full briefing on how the Norwegians' interpreter in the village of Shebaa had just been released from Khiam with burns on the soles of her feet. The Norwegian officers could see that she had been tortured. Fosland told him that he had brought up the subject of torture with the Israeli officers, but they denied Israel had anything to do with the prison center.

Both Fosland and Holst knew the Israelis were lying. Holst had been brought well up to date on how prisoners in Khiam had live wires attached to their bodies during interrogation, how they hung naked for hours by their wrists from a utility pole out in the yard. He knew that as of 1987, the Israelis no longer interrogated prisoners in Khiam themselves, but ordered the Lebanese guards to interrogate and torture their countrymen.[41]

As Holst sat in front of Peres, he said, "I would like to bring up a controversial question which has become the object of much attention in Norway, namely, the situation in Khiam. This question has raised particular attention within the Labour Movement, something which ties in with the Left's traditional strong engagement with human rights."[42]

Foreign Minister Peres' face stiffened, but he did not say anything, and Holst continued, "Norwegian UN soldiers are following what Israeli soldiers are doing when they operate inside of our area of responsibility. They are witnesses to arrests of the local population. Our soldiers, as with Norwegian popular opinion, are concerned with the fate of those arrested. Just the fact that Norwegian soldiers are present during the arrests causes us, from the Norwegian standpoint, not to be indifferent to the reports of torture and abuse. The civilian population looks at UNIFIL as its protector."

It was unusual to see or hear the Norwegian defense minister so upset. "I hope Israel can use its influence and control over the SLA to allow the Red Cross to gain access to the prison center," Holst said to Peres, who had not shown any visible sign of reaction. Despite his apparent calm, those who knew the Israeli politician well would have known he was seething with fury.

Only when Peres began to speak did his anger come out: "I will not accept any criticism from a Norwegian foreign minister in this matter. The Red Cross will get access to the prison center in Khiam when the Red Cross gets access to the SLA people who are sitting in Lebanese prison holes. I cannot put pressure on the SLA to forget their prisoners of war."[43]

Holst replied, "This matter is a question of human rights. We are talking about absolute values tied to the sanctity of human beings. This cannot be considered as a question of reciprocity."

"I agree prisoners should be treated with fairness, but Israel cannot instruct the SLA," Peres answered.

Everyone around the table knew this was not true. The Norwegian defense minister did not give in. "We have indications that abuse is being committed against the prisoners. This is a breach of values that both Norway and Israel subscribe to, and it is a breach which none of us can accept," said Holst, looking Peres firmly in the eyes the entire time. Ali Fawaz from Hizbullah still lay in a military hospital in Israel. A few weeks later he was moved to a dark brown prison cell in Haifa. He had to urinate into a bottle and empty his bowels into a hole. At times the guards threw him in new bandages, and Fawaz would out the old ones as they began to smell. The interrogations did not end, nor the torture. One day Fawaz pulled off an old bandage and found maggots in his sores. He asked a guard, "Could you call a nurse? I've got worms in my sores."[44]

"That is not dangerous. Just drink water," the guard said and got him a bottle.

The sore smelled bad—so bad that the guards would no longer come into his room with food. They put the tray down by the door and pushed it in with their feet. It was useless for him to complain.

"You Know, you are getting dog food," said the Israeli lieutenant who now and then talked with the prisoner. "We only give you food because we want to keep you alive."

The infection worsened, but Fawaz did not receive medical attention. He also did not get a visit from the Red Cross. The aid organization did not even know about him. During the interrogations, he learned that no one else knew he was alive: "Even your family thinks you are dead."

Only when he was finally brought to a hospital was he registered with the Red Cross. But his treatment did not improve.

At the end of November 1987, Fawaz was moved from the military hospital to a prison in Ramle, a city between Tel Aviv and Jerusalem. The prison had previously been a British police station, and had also been used as a horse stable. It was so crowded there that many of the prisoners could not sleep in beds. They were given a few square meters of space for themselves and slept on mattresses on the floor. On the second story of the prison was a section for the mentally ill. Fawaz could hear their screams throughout the day and night. On the third story was the hospital section.

Before Fawaz was captured, he weighed 75 kilograms. When he was put on the scale in the prison at Ramle, it showed 48 kilos. The other prisoners joked about how bony his sides were. Fawaz braced himself, reading a Koran he was able to borrow from a Palestinian. Otherwise he could do nothing but wait for a prisoner exchange. He knew it would come sooner or later.

CHAPTER FORTY

The Art of Diplomacy

In Beirut, Tyre and many of the villages outside Israeli control, more and more Shias began turning their backs on Hizbullah. They were tired of the group's dictates, and the talk of an Islamic republic in Lebanon. For the most part, people did not like bans on the sale of alcohol in restaurants or prohibition on parties and loud music.

In South Lebanon, Hizbullah closed down cafés where older men played cards or backgammon. Strict new regulations were introduced regarding how people could dress. In Tyre, women were forbidden to wear bathing suits. The beaches were divided, with separate areas for men and women. It did not take long for restaurants that had once been full of guests to sit empty and ghostly. The same was true for popular bathing places along the coast.

People welcomed the Iranians who came with money and equipment to pave the lousy roads, but not their missionary activities. The combination of roadwork and preaching made it clear to UNIFIL officers that the Iranians were intent on influencing the Lebanese both through concrete assistance and revolutionary Islamic ideology.[45]

Hizbullah's leaders began taking their signals from the majority of Shias in Lebanon: they no longer wanted a regime modeled on Iran's Islamic Republic. Slowly but surely the pendulum was swinging back. In Tyre, Christians could continue to sell alcohol without fear their stores and restaurants would be set afire or bombed.

In the Lebanese capital, the civil war continued. Various intelligence services operated both in East and West Beirut, but CIA agents were not allowed in the Muslim-dominated part of the city. Even in Christian East Beirut, agents took all sorts of precautions. Security regulations were even stricter for bonafide American diplomats who were not attached to the intelligence services. The State Department decided no one should stay outside the embassy, unless they already owned their homes. They were driven back and forth in armored cars, escorted by a dozen armed men.

Robert Baer continued to work at the CIA's Counterterrorism Center in the US. The center had been established to coordinate the resources of the various departments and break down walls which had been built inside the organization. Baer had taken an intensive course in combatting terrorism. He also had access to all the CIA archives and databases on the subject and felt like "a kid in a candy shop."

I had not met Robert Baer while he was in Beirut, but I had experience with several CIA agents from the bar at the Commodore Hotel. Some of them were caricatures straight out of films and comic strips. I was introduced to Baer later, after he had left the CIA. He told me about his youth in Aspen, Colorado, where he had pictured a future as a professional slalom skier. Instead, he did his military service and got his education at Georgetown University's School of Foreign Service. This led to the CIA, and after a year's training he was sent to India. Later he took a two-year course in Arabic in Tunis.

Baer had gone through the file on the bombing of the American Embassy in 1983. Stored in a thin, worn, green folder, it clearly showed the case had reached a dead end. The newest information was two years old. There were two reasons for that: The bombing decimated the CIA staff, and when replacements arrived at the new embassy in East Beirut, many of the Muslim CIA sources would not show themselves there. They were afraid of being kidnapped or killed by the Phalange militia if they crossed the Green Line dividing the city.[46]

The first person Baer studied closely was Imad Mughniyeh. The file indicated that, according to Algeria's military attaché in Beirut, Mughniyeh was operating on his own. The archive also had information from a "well-placed agent" suggesting that Mughniyeh was the brains behind the hijacking of TWA Flight 847.

To Baer, Mughniyeh was a mystery. After reading through more reports, he became convinced the Algerian attaché had been mistaken: Mughniyeh did not operate as a freelancer. He was a part of Hizbullah. And he was the one who had control over the western hostages.

It was decided that Robert Baer would be sent to Beirut. Before he left, he talked with his immediate superior, Duane Clarridge. Baer wanted to know what restrictions he had in his hunt for Mughniyeh and the other hostage takers. "No restrictions," answered Clarridge. "You can do whatever you want."

"We have to try to hit Mughniyeh where he is most vulnerable, namely in his own family," Baer said, explaining that Mughniyeh had close ties to his family. Perhaps one might try to take one of his family members hostage, and then propose a trade?

When Baer began to look more closely into the bombing of the embassy, he realized that trying to solve it was like piecing together an ancient Roman mosaic that had been destroyed in an earthquake. He discovered as well that the CIA was no longer interested in looking for the perpetrators. His bosses were only concerned with the hostages.

In East Beirut, Baer had a number of apartments at his disposal. He would spend alternate nights in them and tried to be as invisible as possible. He used multiple cars, often old rust buckets. He was forbidden to drive in West Beirut, and remained mindful that the Christian part of the city could also be life threatening, considering that the French military attaché had been shot just outside his office in East Beirut.

While the CIA was trying to get information about the American hostages, Ane-Karine Arvesen reported from Tehran. She related intense speculation that Iraq was trying to get the Syrians over to their side. Further, she wrote, Saudi Arabia supported this by tempting the Syrians with cheap oil, as Iran had done for many years.

When Syrian Foreign Minister Farouk al-Sharaa was in Tehran in July 1987 to bring a message from President Assad to President Khamenei, Ane-Karine reported that Syria had put limits on the activities of the Revolutionary Guards in Lebanon. In order to get better control, Syria had denied the Iranians the use of the military roads to Lebanon.[47]

In August 1987, I travelled again to Iran. At the front facing Iraq, photographer Sindre Løkstad and I met an officer in the Revolutionary Guard who previously had been in Lebanon. The officer thought it had been humiliating to go back to Iran without having fought the Israelis. In response to my questions, he said he knew nothing about an Israeli prisoner of war named Ron Arad. Arad was a plane navigator who had been taken captive by the Amal militia on October 15, 1986. He was said to have been held in a Lebanese village not far from the Guards' camp in the Bekaa Valley.

Together with the pilot, Yishai Aviram, Ron Arad had taken off from Ramat David airbase in North Israel to bomb the nearby village of Maghdouche, southeast of Sidon. But when the plane neared its target, one of the 360-kg Marc-55 bombs under the wing exploded. The plane shook so hard that it broke Arad's arm, and a piece of shrapnel entered the cockpit, cutting Aviram's ear.[48]

Both pilot and navigator managed to eject before the plane fell into the sea. Aviram landed on a hillside full of stones and scrub. With the small radio in his survival kit he was able to contact a Cobra helicopter, which picked him up. But Israel's Rescue Unit 669 did not manage to find Arad before he was taken captive by the Amal militia.

Amal's security chief, Mustafa Dirani, took control over the Israeli. He wanted to use Arad to trade against Lebanese in Israeli captivity. Negotiations began less than two weeks later. Contact with the Lebanese was arranged by a Russian Jew, Shabtai Kalmanovich, who was a diamond trader in West Africa; many of his colleagues there were Shias from South Lebanon. The Russian had offered his assistance to Mossad as "a sign of goodwill." This gesture would later prove to be on orders from the KGB. Soviet intelligence hoped to gain valuable information about the Israeli secret services through the negotiations, which would give them access to the highest military and political circles in the country.

The Russian, whom Mossad code-named "the Tourist," got in contact with Uri Lubrani. Through his Shia contacts in West Africa—one was a relative of Nabih Berri—he conveyed three letters from Arad, along with two photographs. The letters were checked by the best Israeli handwriting experts, photo experts and experts in criminal technology. Everyone agreed the letters and pictures were authentic. But they gave no clue where Arad was being held.

Kalmanovich negotiated an agreement with the Lebanese. They wanted a large sum of money and unhindered allowance for Amal to import weapons on the coast of Lebanon, as well as for Israel to release many Lebanese and other Arab prisoners. But Defense Minister Rabin put his foot down. He thought the price was too high. Rabin wanted to avoid the same criticism he had faced in 1983 when 1,150 Arab prisoners were exchanged for the six Israeli soldiers I had met in Tripoli before they were released.

To prove Arad was still alive, Dirani's people allowed him to write to his family in Israel. Written in September, the letter was delivered sometime in late October, after Israeli experts had checked it for possible secret messages. Finally, Arad's family could read the following:

Hello Everyone,

Today is Sunday (I think for us it's Rosh Hashanah), September 27, 1987. Let me first tell you how much I long to see all of you (so much time has passed— I think it's been about a year, right?). I do dream about you at times, but I try not to think too much during the day to avoid getting too demoralized. In general, I'm in good health, and feeling all right. They treat me well. My hand is slowly getting better, but it will be totally better when I return to my normal routine. (G-d and the leaders willing). Every day, I spend hours praying for this [to return home], and hope that you do too. I know it's difficult, but please try to do everything you can for me.

I don't know how, but please send a message to the powers that be, to our leaders, to the government, to anyone who is able to do something to get me out of here. Please do your best, because Lebanon is no place to be, and I really want to see you all—for one shouldn't have to be held in captivity when there are other alternatives. With hope and good intentions, anything can be accomplished. Just please, don't "play with time"; act as if we've run out of time! You have to speak [to the leaders, the public, the terrorists] as much as you can, and compromise whenever possible. Our lives (the hostages on both sides) are in your hands, and we are counting on you. I've heard very little about how you are doing, however one day, everything will be different.

Tammy, I want to tell you, I now fully understand the subject that we've often spoken of, your wanting to help prisoners (not necessarily prisoners of war). You can try to do something for the prisoners of this organization, to help the time pass, and help them live a better life (a little food, a prayer book, anything you do is significant). You can't imagine how important such small things are to a lonely man who is far away.

I have written the most important things that I wanted to tell you. On the whole, I'm all right, and usually feel OK They are treating me well (I hope you do the same). Please build our (new) house, get advice from your father. Please put your all into raising our daughter (which you do wonderfully). Please guide her with the right values, she is our hope for the future! I hope to see you very soon. Just look back at the year that has passed, and you will realize that not much has been done. Please try to do more, for all our sakes. I know that it's hard, but please, convey the message that it is up to us to overcome the obstacles of hate, fear and suspicion through compassion, love and mercy... And then everything would change.

I pray that with G-d's help, we will be able to see each other soon, in this new year. Yom Kippur is approaching, and I will be praying together with you that G-d blesses all of us. Let's hope that He will help the leaders make the right choices. You also can help, please try! I hope that you are taking care of yourselves, and the others as well. Don't lose hope, there will be other, better, days. With all my might, I'm trying not to give up. I'm holding my breath and crossing my fingers.

Love Always, Ron [49]

There was strong pressure from Ron Arad's family and friends to place his fate high on the Israeli agenda. In Washington, leaders were more involved with the American hostages. Norwegian diplomats in Tel Aviv, Beirut and Damascus were not particulary interested in any of this. They tried their best to follow what was happening on the political front, otherwise fulfilling their duties for their own country.

In Damascus, it was difficult to find out what was happening behind the scenes, something diplomatic and journalistic reports confirmed. These contained references to stories other diplomats had heard, or what the state-controlled media in Syria had written or announced. And when journalists and diplomats learned about Syria's involvement in Lebanon, the stories were filled mainly with rumors or reports from third-hand sources.

When the men and women of the Foreign Office in Oslo took time to read chargé d'affaires Peter Ræder's reports, they quite often broke into smiles. The Norwegian envoy in Damascus had a sharp wit. Early in January 1988, he reported an episode that had occurred at the airport in Damascus the week before. The story was meant to illustrate conditions such as they were among the different public services in Syria.[50]

The daughter of Syria's agricultural minister, Mohammed Ghabbash, was flying out of the country around Christmas. Ghabbash had previously been the interior minister and therefore had good connections at the airport. He called the immigration services and requested VIP treatment for his daughter. The immigration officer who took the call answered that he would arrange it. But when Ghabbash's daughter showed up at the airport, the air force's security service demanded she follow normal procedures. She did do without any hesitation.

The immigration officers felt they had lost face toward the minister, and when three security service officers landed at the airport a few hours later, they decided to take their revenge. The three officers were picked up by their colleagues and brought to the VIP room, while their passports were delivered to the immigration authorities with the request to have them stamped.

The immigration officers refused and insisted the three officers had to follow protocols for normal passengers since they had arrived by civilian aircraft. The security officer who received the unstamped passports pulled out his pistol in rage, put it against the head of the immigration officer who had the passports and demanded they be stamped. But the security officer had miscalculated the situation: there were far more immigration officers than air force security officers present. The security officer was disarmed and beaten up. His three colleagues who had arrived by plane were also beaten up before they were all thrown out of the airport.

At the next shift change, three times as many security men as usual showed up. They carried rifles in addition to their pistols. The security officers ran through the airport, beating up every immigration officer they could find. The immigration officers called for reinforcements. Before the night was over, there were tanks surrounding the airport terminal. Over a megaphone, the security officers got a clear message: "Come out or you will be shot!"

All the officers chose to live. They came out and were thrown in jail.

The Norwegian envoy in Damascus ended his report by saying that Syria had established a commission to investigate the matter.

About the same time, in January 1988, those interested in the Middle East conflict could read that the US had vetoed a resolution condemning Israel's treatment of civilian Lebanese in occupied South Lebanon. Thus the Israelis were able to continue their practices without interference from the international community.

CHAPTER FORTY ONE
The Secrets of the Rose

In South Lebanon the meadows were filled with anemones when I was driven to Naqoura at the beginning of February, 1988. The blood-red flowers reminded me of the drops of blood from the dead Adonis, god of beauty according to Greek mythology.

Just before we arrived at UNIFIL headquarters, I noticed one lone flowering almond tree. The tree also had its place in the Greek lessons of the gods. The connection was this: According to legend, Agdistis, a newborn demon, had both male and female genitalia. The Greek gods feared hermaphrodites and cut off Agdistis' male organ, which was thrown onto the ground. But there it took root and grew into an almond tree. When a virgin later sat beneath the tree, an almond fell into her lap. This made the virgin pregnant, and nine months later she gave birth to a son.

When we arrived in Naqoura, I made a note in my little black book: "The flowering almond tree stood there as an expectant young bridegroom, not a bride, for the tree is actually a man."

I stopped abruptly trying to be poetic when an American lieutenant colonel showed up and introduced himself as William Higgins. He was head of the UN Observer Group Lebanon, OGL for short. The observers were part of the United Nations Truce Supervision Organization (UNTSO), which had its headquarters in Jerusalem. In Lebanon it was subordinated to UNIFIL's operational command.

When Higgins heard I had been a major in UNIFIL, and had lived in one of the yellow prefabricated barracks a few meters from his office, he proudly told me about the important position he had in the Pentagon. Seven months earlier, he had been a military advisor to Caspar Weinberger, the secretary of defense. "Not a single secret landed on the secretary's desk until it had passed mine," the 43-year-old officer bragged. I thought it strange that an American with such a background was sent to Lebanon, where his countrymen had become fair game.

Higgins began right away to ask me about Hizbullah. That was not so surprising but I thought, nonetheless, there was something odd about him. First of all, he had camouflaged the flag sewn onto the upper arm of his uniform sweater. He had colored the red, white and blue Stars and Stripes dark green. I also thought he seemed overly vain. He wore thin white leather gloves which did not fit with his field uniform.

Together with photographer Odd Iversen from the *NRK*, I had arrived on February 5, in South Lebanon to make a TV reportage about the Israeli occupied part of the country. We requested to accompany a regular observer patrol around the area to witness the situation up close.

The unarmed observers were stationed along the border with Israel and had six permanent posts. The one farthest to the east was called OP Khiam and was only 300 meters from the infamous prison center. The post farthest to the west, OP Lab, had been built a few kilometers from the UNIFIL headquarters. From these permanent positions the observers would patrol the border area by car.

We were surprised when Lieutenant Colonel Higgins said he would drive us himself—alone. The rules were UNTSO observers should patrol in pairs in the war zone, but he did not bother with that. When we got into the car, he warned: "We may drive onto mines, be shot at, attacked or kidnapped. This is part of our everyday life. If you'll take the chance, we'll go."

We knew a UNIFIL soldier from Nepal had been shot and killed by Israel's Lebanese allies three months earlier. We also knew an Australian UNTSO officer had just lost his life in a mine explosion, and the same day we arrived in South Lebanon, Palestinian guerrillas had gone into Israel. Two Israeli soldiers had been killed.

Iversen had also served in UNIFIL, and we knew, of course, that South Lebanon could be dangerous. But the danger that something would happen to us that day, we figured was small, so with Higgins behind the wheel, we drove east along the border.

We had not driven far before Higgins continued to ask us about Hizbullah, about the resistance movement's strategy and tactics and about Iran's activities in Beirut, the Bekaa Valley, and South Lebanon. Higgins was not particularly interested in telling us what the UN observers had seen with regard to Israeli abuse in the occupied zone. What happened in Israel's torture center in Khiam, he knew little about—or so he said.

What neither Iversen nor I knew was that Higgins was doing intelligence work, and with the full knowledge of the American officer, Colonel Ty Tisdale, in UNTSO's headquarters in Jerusalem. It was no secret Colonel Tisdale was an intelligence officer. To his UN colleagues he at times proudly would show them the small rose which was attached to his uniform next to his medals. The so-called Tudor rose originated in the Rose Wars in the last half of the 15th century in England.[51] At that time there were many manor houses in the Yorkshire district which were decorated with carved roses in the ceiling panels and beams. Secrets discussed "beneath the roses" were carefully talked about and could not be repeated under pain of death. The expression "sub rosa" early in the 20th century was used as a reference to secrets and is still being used in professional intelligence organizations, including Norway.

At UNTSO's headquarters in Jerusalem, it was known Colonel Tisdale and Lieutenant Colonel Higgins secretly worked to free the American hostages in Lebanon. Higgins thought that through his contacts in South Lebanon, he could get far.[52]

After we had visited one of the observation posts, we drove along a narrow road on the ridge of a hill. In a curve on the other side stood an old Mercedes with three men standing beside it. It was as if they were waiting for someone. The American officer suddenly said: "It is too dangerous to drive further." He stopped, turned the car around and drove back.

In my mind I thought kidnappers would not line up along the road in that way. But it was okay by us, because just a few minutes later we got a message over the radio that two foreigners had been kidnapped in South Lebanon. Both were from the UN aid organization, UNRWA, which helped Palestinians. They had been taken from the car they were driving just south of Sidon a bit before 10 in the morning. This was news we had to follow-up on.

Higgins also became enthusiastic. He suggested to drive us north "to see what he could do." We said no thanks; we did not want to have an American officer with us outside of the UN operational zone.

When we got back to UNIFIL headquarters, we heard that a Norwegian, William Jørgensen, and a Swede, Jan Stening, had been kidnapped. They had been taken on the main road near Sidon while they were on their way from Tyre to Beirut. The white UN-marked Renault was now abandoned by the side of the road along the coast near the Palestinian refugee camp Ain el-Helweh, with its doors wide open and windshield smashed.

We had thanked Higgins for the trip and promised to return, without speculating further on what the American was actually doing, and without knowing that was the last time we would see him alive. For Iversen and me, it was simply a question of how we would get to the place where the kidnapping had occurred. What had happened and why?

First we went to Tyre, where the two UN employees had been stationed. With the help of a Norwegian UNIFIL officer, Major Ola Kaldager, we were driven to the house where they lived. We spoke with people to find a motive for the kidnapping, and we filmed the area. Later we made a news report for the *Daily News Hour*. When we finished, we headed towards Sidon with Major

Kaldager and his driver and interpreter, Geir Furuseth. By the time we arrived it was late in the evening and pitch dark.

A few kilometers south of Sidon, we encountered a group of armed men, bodyguards for the leading Sunni politician in Sidon, Mustafa Saad. One of Major Kaldager's contacts had organized an escort. Iversen and I jumped into a militia jeep and drove on with Kaldager and Furuseth following in the UN vehicle.

As we drove past an orange grove not far from the Palestinian refugee camp, where the two UN employees had been taken earlier, Iversen noticed the militia soldiers in the jeep getting ready for a possible ambush. But we drove on peacefully into Sidon to the UNWRA office there. Per Olof Hallqvist, who was heading the aid organization in Lebanon, was there. I knew Hallqvist from before, but did not get the hearty welcome I had hoped for. We were standing between armed militia soldiers and a bunch of Lebanese journalists and photographers, when I heard Hallqvist say: "What the Hell are you doing here, Karsten? It is dangerous to be here when people are being kidnapped all over Lebanon."

He calmed down after a while, and held an *ad hoc* press conference without saying very much. We slept overnight on a floor, and the next day we learned that UNRWA's people thought the kidnapping was a private matter tied to an internal investigation into swindle and theft within the organization. In a secret report to headquarters in Vienna, Hallqvist wrote that the two UN employees were being held prisoner in a house near a park not far from Ain el-Helweh, and that the PLO's local leader was just waiting for Yasser Arafat's orders to storm the house.[53]

The next day, Hallqvist together with Sweden's former Lebanon ambassador, Ingemar Stjernberg, and Agneta Ramberg, the heavily pregnant Middle East correspondent for *Swedish Radio*, went to the chief of Arafat's Force 17 in Ain el-Helweh. As they waited for radio contact with Arafat in Tunis, they were served a large Lebanese meal with arak. When Arafat finally was available on the radiophone, he said: "Now we will storm the house and set your boys free."[54]

Hallqvist quickly asked to speak with Arafat. The Swede, whose background included being an officer in the military, was crystal clear: The house must not be stormed. If this happened, the prisoners might be killed.

Of course, then, the house was not stormed. Later in the evening, the Norwegian chargé d'affaires, Peter Ræder, who had arrived to Beirut from Damascus, reported that negotiations were under way. It was Sidon's most powerful man, Mustafa Saad, and the PLO coordinator in Lebanon, Salah Salah, who were negotiating with the kidnappers through a middleman. The Palestinian belonged to the Popular Front for the Liberation of Palestine (PFLP). He was known as a tough negotiator and bridge-builder between various Palestinian factions.

At the Foreign Office in Oslo, the leadership realized the kidnapping drama might last awhile. Ane-Karine Arvesen, who had come back from the embassy in Tehran, was asked to go to Beirut to help the embassy. Another experienced Middle East diplomat, Counsellor Odd Wibe, went to the PLO headquarters in Tunis.

When Wibe met Arafat, the PLO leader said: "I have promised the kidnappers safe passage if they deliver the hostages to us, but I am worried they might smuggle them out."[55]

Arafat thought the kidnapping was a set up to draw attention away from the rioting—the Intifada—in the Gaza Strip and the West Bank. He said Palestinians were not behind this, but Shias from the Amal militia who wanted to take control over the Palestinian refugee camps. Arafat indicated further that the kidnappers had to have had Syrian connections since Amal and Syria were allies.

CHAPTER FORTY TWO
Hidden Truths

In Sidon, I asked many people what they thought was the reason for the kidnappings. Was it about money or politics? Could it have been personal? It was hard to learn anything from the answers I got. They varied from person to person, and some individuals gave different answers just hours apart.

As usual, while I sought news in the Middle East, I also looked for stories and legends. When I heard that a Palestinian who knew lots of stories frequented the Café Sharkh, I went there. In the café the guests played *tawleh* (backgammon) or cards. Some smoked water pipes, others drank tea or Turkish coffee. Among the guests was Abu Ahmad, a Palestinian over 80 years old with ice-blue eyes, a black-and-white headscarf and a nice smile that exposed his few teeth.

"This kidnapping is not what it seems to be," said Abu Ahmad. "Nothing of what happens in the Middle East is. There is something else behind the actions than what is given in the official explanation," he continued in rather good English.

"This kidnapping was done to frighten. I don't know whom. But there are disloyal servants in UNRWA. So perhaps it is the leaders who are to be frightened. But perhaps there is something else behind it. And I don't know anything about that. I don't think I can be of any help to you," he said. He then paused and drew on his water pipe and said: "But perhaps you can learn something from the story of Tambal?"

"Tambal?"

"*Tambal* means a lazybones," Abu Ahmad said, and then told me the story.

Long ago in a small village, there lived a man called Tambal. He was in his prime, but did all he could to avoid a day's work. One day his wife had enough. "If you cannot manage to provide for your family, I don't want you here any longer," she said.

Tambal complained that the village was too small for him to find a good job, but if she was willing to move to the capital, he would certainly find something to do there. "You will have one last chance," his wife said, and began to pack the few things they had. Then they left for the capital, the city of the sultan.

When they arrived, his wife said, "Tambal, now you have to find yourself work!"

"How much money do you have?" the husband asked.

"Two bishlik," his wife said, showing him the two small coins she had hidden away.

"Go to the bazaar and buy a large jute sack and a piece of rope for one bishlik. With the other you should hire a laborer," said Tambal.

His wife went to the bazaar and came back with what her husband had asked for. Tambal crawled into the empty sack, asked his wife to tie it closed, and told the laborer to put the sack on his back. Then he said, "Go into the bazaar and call out, 'Here's something wonderful and different for 100 dinars.'"

The wife did not get far before hordes of curious youths began to follow her and the man with the sack on his back. Finally, they reached the square in front of the palace. The young sultan also became curious and sent one of his servants out to investigate. The woman and the laborer were hurried into the forecourt of the palace. When the sultan asked what the woman had to sell, she only said, "Something wonderful and different for 100 dinars."

The sultan felt the sack. He could tell there was something alive in it, and could also hear a bear-like growling. This made him so curious that he ordered his advisor to pay the 100 dinars. The woman accepted the money and left. When the laborer put down the sack and they opened it, Tambal got out. All of a sudden he was face to face with the sultan, who asked, "Who are you?"

"I am Tambal."

"What is your profession?"

"I am Tambal."

"So your name is Tambal, and you are a *tambal*. I am going to teach you a thing or two," answered the sultan and called for his stablemaster. "This lazybones will sweep the stable floor and take care of not just one horse, but two. And do not give him anything to eat. Give him bread and water," the sultan said, repeating, "Just bread and water!"

Tambal was taken to the stables. His first orders were to wash and groom a new mare, a gift from a Bedouin sheikh who was coming for a visit that evening. And when the sultan came to check the mare, Tambal was in full swing. He had washed her legs and mane and prepared her hooves.

"What do you think of this mare, Tambal?" asked the sultan.

"She is beautiful, clearly the most beautiful of your Arabians, but..."

"But what?" asked the sultan.

"She is like a cow."

"A cow?" wondered the sultan.

When the Bedouin sheikh arrived at the palace a few hours later, he and his retinue were seated at the table. As they sat around the fragrant dishes, the sultan thanked the sheikh for his gift and asked about the mare's genealogy. The sheikh named the mother, a famous mare.

"But that mare is long since dead," commented the sultan.

"That is true," the Sheikh responded. "She died the day after this mare was born. To keep the foal alive, we taught her to suck milk from a cow."

The next morning, the sultan went to the stables, where he found Tambal busy grooming the new mare.

"What caused you to say that this beautiful Arabian is a cow?" asked the sultan.

"Because she licks her mouth like a cow," answered Tambal.

"I see you have a keen ability to observe, even if you are a *tambal*," the sultan mumbled. "Now I am going to give you a task," he continued, "Tonight I am going for a walk with my sultana. You are to hide yourself in the trunk of the old, hollow olive tree in the middle of the park. Later, you will tell me what you see in her."

"For goodness' sake, don't make me do this. The sultan will find a mistake I might make, and will punish me," Tambal begged.

"Just tell me everything you see, don't hide anything, and nothing will happen to you," the sultan assured him.

Tambal hid in the tree that evening, and when the sultan and his wife walked in the park he followed them with his gaze. Later, when the sultan came to the stables, Tambal quickly told him, "Your wife is in truth beautiful."

"Anyone can see that," the sultan sneered. "I give you the peace of God, but tell me what you are thinking."

Tambal hesitated, before he said with a quavering voice, "She is a gypsy woman."

"A gypsy! Gypsy!" the sultan repeated to himself and went off.

Later that evening, he went to see his father-in-law, who was also his top advisor, and said, "Tell me where you got your daughter from?"

"Why do you ask?" The father-in-law seemed nervous.

"Tell me the whole truth! I know enough that you cannot hide it from me," said the sultan.

"I will tell you the whole story in all honesty. When I was the grand vizier for your father, he sent me with his warriors to a Bedouin tribe that was plundering the caravans. When we arrived, the Bedouins had abandoned the camp. No men, women, children or animals were to be seen, not a sound to be heard. But in the outskirts of the camp, where a gypsy family had lived, I heard the crying of a child from a tent. The parents, while hurrying, must have forgotten the little girl. I decided to take the orphaned girl home with me. The thought was that one of the servant girls could take care of her. But when I got home to my wife, who had no children, it did not take long for her to be so taken by the infant. Because no one knew the story, people began to talk of the little one as if she were our own daughter.

The girl grew up beautiful and wise. When she was grown, the sultan, wanted her to be his sultana. Why should I stand in the way of God's Will?" said the father-in-law with a sigh.

The sultan did not say a word.

The next morning he went to the stables, took Tambal aside and asked, "How could you know the sultana was a gypsy woman?"

Tambal began to walk in front of the sultan, exaggerating the movement of his hips, raising one shoulder and then the other. With every step he took, he pushed his chest out to show femininity. Then Tambal said, "Your wife walks like a gypsy woman."

The sultan, who immediately recognized that Tambal was right, turned to leave, but then stopped. He turned back and asked, "Tambal, tell me, who am I?"

"The sultan is the son of a long line of sultans. May the sultan live long."

"Yes, well, but what does your gut say?"

Tambal went to his knees and begged for mercy.

"God's peace shall be with you. I give you my word, just tell me what your gut says," the sultan said. Tambal raised his arms to the sky and continued begging not to have to speak, but the sultan insisted so strongly that he finally said, "You are the son of a cook."

The sultan returned to the palace wondering. He went to his old mother and said: "Mother, this evening we are going to have dinner together, just you and I." And when they were alone, he asked, "Who is my father?"

"What a question! You are the sultan, son and grandson of a long line of sultans."

The sultan said he knew better. His mother sighed and answered, "Your father and I had been married for a long time without having any children. It occurred to me the sultan might remain childless even if he married another woman, and I decided to save the throne. We had a young, good-looking and strong cook. Now you know the story. But you also know that I, as an honorable woman, did not have any more children. The cook was sent away."

The next morning the sultan again took Tambal aside and asked, "Tambal, how did you know I am the son of a cook?"

"Your majesty, everyone knows that the sultan's cook makes the tastiest and most wonderful dishes. After he spends hours making these things, he does not want the servants to eat the same food as the sultan. Therefore, he throws the remains away rather than let others taste the food. From the very first day, you have given me only bread and water. I have not tasted anything which the cook has made. When I understood that you did not want to give me the food you were eating, I concluded that you had to be the son of a cook."

The sultan took a handful of gold coins from his pocket and gave the money to Tambal, saying: "Leave the capital, never come back and never tell these secrets to anyone. You have enough gold to be a *tambal* for the rest of your life."

The storyteller at the café in Sidon finished his tale with the words "The truth behind the kidnapping of the Swede and the Norwegian will come to light one day. But nothing is as it seems to be. To find the answer you must search many places. But be careful. It can be dangerous."

CHAPTER FORTY THREE
An Arrogant UN Colonel

While I was running after the story behind the story, Jan Stening and William Jørgensen lay tied up in a house, not knowing where they were or why they had been kidnapped, but remembering in detail what had happened. First, four masked men with weapons had forced them to stop their car. One of the gunmen smashed the windshield with the butt of his rifle and ordered them out. Stening was pushed into the front seat of a yellow Mercedes between the driver and one of the kidnappers, while Jørgensen was shoved into the back seat between the other two men.[56]

They drove for ten minutes, then forced the hostages into the trunk of a large American car. The car wound through small and crooked streets for another ten minutes, then stopped, and the men led them into a shed, lined them up against a wall and robbed them of their ID cards, money and watches. Several hours later they again found themselves in the trunk of the big car. The kidnappers had unscrewed the backlight so they would get enough air.

The next morning, the men ordered them into a Volkswagen van and covered them with boxes and plastic bags. While the van drove south on the main road, Stening managed to loosen his ropes. He struggled to get up and saw out the rear window that they were in Sidon. He tried to open the side door of the van, but could not. However, he was able to stick one arm out of the window to try the door from the outside. As he was about to roll out of the door, the van swerved into a small courtyard, and the Swede fell out onto the ground. The men surrounded him, beating him on the kidneys before throwing him back into the van again. Once more, the two were covered with boxes and bags so that only their heads stuck out. One of the kidnappers had punched Stening in the face, and he could feel two teeth break.

The van drove south past stores both captives recognized. Half an hour later they turned off the road and drove toward the coast, stopping before an unfinished house. There they were brought in to a room without windows, but with a hole in the wall. They placed them in chairs with their faces toward the wall and told them not to speak or turn their heads. The wind was blowing and it was cold in Lebanon that February day.

Suddenly, one of the guards asked, "Arafat good?"

Carefully the prisoners answered, "Yes, Arafat good."

"No! No! Abu Nidal good!" they heard behind them.[57]

The prisoners knew Abu Nidal was the nom de guerre of Sabri al-Banna, a Palestinian who was accused of murder-for-hire and kidnapping. He lived in Baghdad and had been condemned to death in absentia by Arafat.[58]

"Yes, yes, Abu Nidal number one, yes."

The guards were satisfied with the answer. A bit later the hostages received something to eat. When evening came, several more men arrived. They brought with them blank pieces of paper, which the captives had to fingerprint and sign. Then they allowed Stening and Jørgensen to lie down on a straw mat for a few hours before driving them to a new house with concrete floors. The captors chained their ankles and provided them with a thin mattress and a cup of tea.

They had a lot of time to think about why they had been abducted. Jan Stening had for some months been leading an investigation to uncover whether there was corruption within the aid organization's transport unit. He had come up with a series of recommendations for improvements as far as UNRWA's inventory and repair facilities were concerned. This made the Swede rather unpopular among the locally employed Palestinians. But was that the only reason? They asked themselves over and over again.

Over the next few days, the prisoners received better food, better treatment and even an apology. One man came into the room, sat down behind them and said in English, "I am very sorry that you are here, but I think the matter will be settled soon, and I hope you will be treated well. I will come back on Sunday to give you your instructions."[59] The man had a mask on, and Jørgensen had the impression he was with Arafat. Both felt better right away.

When a week had gone by, one of the guards came in to their room and looked at the bottle of pills Jørgensen had been given for his heart a few days earlier. The guard then gestured that he had to take his medicine. Strange types, thought Jørgensen: one moment they were brutal without compunction, then caring the next.[60]

Norwegian and Swedish diplomats worked around the clock to get the two released. In Tunis, Counsellor Wibe and the Swedish ambassador met Yasser Arafat. The PLO leader felt that the pressure from Norway and Sweden to avoid armed force had given advantage to the kidnappers. He suspected that Stening and Jørgensen had been smuggled out of the area, and went on to say that there was a number of Syrian intelligence officers in the Sidon area, and that the most important Sunni politician and strongest militia leader in the city, Mustafa Saad, was under Syrian command. "He had a four-hour-long meeting with the Syrian intelligence service today," Arafat said, suggesting once more that the Syrians were involved in the kidnapping.[61]

In Lebanon, Arafat's men put out rumors that Amal's militia was behind the kidnapping. Amal had battled the Palestinians for several years, both in Beirut and in South Lebanon. It was said that the two Scandinavians had been kidnapped to put the Palestinians in a bad light.

When the Norwegian ambassador to Cairo, Knut Mørkved, went to see the Syrian vice president, Abdul Halim Khaddam, the latter said, "It is out of the question to think that the Syrians had anything to do with the kidnapping." The key lay with the Palestinians in Lebanon, he maintained.

The PLO coordinator in Lebanon, Salah Salah, was charged with helping the UN free the hostages. Like Yasser Arafat, Salah tried to deflect responsibility away from the Palestinians. He said that Lebanese kidnappers must have mistaken the two Scandinavians for Germans, because Germans made good bargaining chips.[62] He mentioned the Shia Mohammed Hamadi, who was being held in jail in Germany for having taken part in the TWA hijacking in 1985. He had been arrested when he arrived in Frankfurt from Beirut two years after the incident. Salah further said he had been contacted by a man who represented the kidnappers. To prove the Scandinavian hostages were still alive, Salah showed their ID cards.

I had gone back to Oslo. The new Middle East correspondent for the NRK, Torgeir Kvalvaag, had arrived in Lebanon. He would now document the drama from Beirut.

Further to the south, Lieutenant Colonel William Higgins continued to drive alone in his white car. At UNIFIL headquarters, many noticed how Higgins ignored safety regulations and the UN's rules for neutral observers. He often bragged that he was a special envoy of the US government.

There was no reaction to Higgins' behavior until the Finnish Lieutenant Colonel Tor Planting learned Higgins had planned to meet Amal's leader in Tyre on February 17, 1988. Higgins had said he wished to meet him in order to talk about peace between the US and the Shias in Lebanon.[63] Planting, who four years earlier had been a UNTSO officer, knew the Amal leader in Tyre very well. He was a man named Abdul Majid Saleh. Planting was now UNIFIL's liaison officer and represented the Force Commander of the peace force, Major General Gustav Hägglund, for Hizbullah and Amal. Neither Planting nor Hägglund wanted Higgins to play solo, and particularly not on behalf of the US.

General Hägglund therefore decided Higgins could meet Saleh, but only accompanied by UNIFIL's liaison officer. UNTSO's team in Lebanon was operationally subordinated to the peacekeeping force, and Lieutenant Colonel Planting suggested to Higgins they could drive together to Tyre. They could meet at 10 AM the next day at UNIFIL headquarters.

But when Planting showed up the next day at Higgins' office, it was empty. He had left headquarters two hours earlier. "Goddamned Higgins," Planting swore. He was furious that the American had driven alone to Tyre with his decorations on his chest, in strict contravention of the general's orders. Planting drove immediately to Saleh's office in Tyre and waited outside until Higgins showed up.

"Why did you break our agreement?" Planting asked.[64]

"I have my own business to take care of," Higgins answered curtly.

"We had agreed to drive together in our car, and we are armed, unlike you," argued Planting. He had his Finnish driver and Arab interpreter, Captain Paavilainen, found with him.

"Everything is under control," answered Higgins arrogantly.

Planting was certainly not convinced everything was as it should be. He had made note of several men observing Saleh's house. As far as Planting could tell, they belonged to Hizbullah and not Amal.

During the meeting, Planting said little. Higgins said that he was a "peace dove" sent from Washington, whose goal was to establish good relations with the Shia Muslims in Lebanon. Abdul Saleh seemed surprised that the UN officer spoke on behalf of the United States.

When the meeting ended and the three UN officers went out onto the street, Planting noticed that the Amal leader's house was still being watched.

"Come along in my car. I have an armed escort," said Planting to Higgins.

"No, everything is under control," the American repeated and added in an arrogant tone: "You are a colonel in the Finnish army. I am in the American army, and I have experience from Vietnam!"

"Drive with us!" Planting insisted. Higgins replied tersely that he had other things to do. He wanted to drive alone. The Finn did not want to get into a long discussion of what General Hägglund had said about operating alone, and asked his driver to drive to Naqoura. Just south of Tyre, they both noticed a reddish brown Volvo with three bearded men in it. It seemed they were waiting for someone. Planting said to Captain Paavilainen, "Those three are from Hizbullah."

A few minutes later Major Ola Kaldager and Captain Joe McDonagh came driving into Tyre to meet the UNTSO liaison team there. They also met with Higgins while they were in the city. Without knowing of the dispute between Planting and Higgins, Kaldager suggested that Higgins should drive behind their car to Naqoura since he was alone. Again the American said no and drove off alone.

CHAPTER FORTY FOUR

Into the Trap

A few hours later, I received a phone call in Oslo from a contact in UNIFIL, who told me that Lieutenant Colonel William Higgins had been kidnapped on the road between Tyre and Naqoura. By chance another UNIFIL vehicle was also on the road, but it was several hundred meters in front of him. Because it was raining and visibility was poor, the driver of the UNIFIL vehicle had not seen Higgins stop at a curve in the road, where three men forced him into a brown Volvo. A few minutes earlier, the kidnappers had blocked the radio frequency that UNIFIL headquarters used, and managed to get a bare-bones Motorola radio that covered the UN's entire frequency spectrum, and put their unit on "send." This occupied the network so that no one else could come on. The search operation was delayed and Higgins was long gone before French soldiers were able to erect barriers on the roads. Hizbullah had bribed a local Amal security officer to ensure safe passage for the kidnappers through the territory that the movement controlled.[65]

With Higgins in the trunk, the Volvo drove inland on one of the narrow, rain-soaked roads. When the car got stuck in mud, the driver had to get help from a bulldozer to free it. Then the muffler broke, and the kidnappers moved Higgins to a white Peugeot. The second car collided with a truck full of oranges, and Higgins had to be moved again. This time he was transferred to a red Mercedes, which brought him to the first hiding place, the *husseinieh* in Siddiqine, around 8 kilometers east of the coast road.[66]

When the alarm sounded that Higgins had been kidnapped, Planting was sitting in the sauna at the UN headquarters in Naqoura. A few minutes later he was on his way to see Abdul Saleh and ask him for help in the search. The Amal leader immediately began his own search effort; among other things he had Hizbullah's cultural center in Tyre ransacked. In all, 45 members of Hizbullah were arrested. But Higgins was not found.

In Oslo, I was able to find photographer Odd Iversen's tape of Higgins wearing his blue UN beret and green sweater with its camouflaged American flag on the shoulder. From *NRK*'s Eurovision office, we distributed worldwide the only photograph of Higgins in a UN uniform.

When the US woke up a few hours later, I got a call from *ABC News*. Could I be available for a live interview for the first newscast? The Americans wanted to hear about my meeting with Higgins 12 days earlier. Was the officer irresponsible for driving around alone in war-ravaged South Lebanon? Was he a cowboy? In the interview , I did not use the expression "cowboy." I also did not say anything about my suspicions that Higgins was carrying out intelligence activity alongside his job in the UN observer corps. However, I did manage to convey that Higgins was operating alone in South Lebanon, against regulations.

I knew that Higgins had put the pressure on for an assignment in South Lebanon in order to create a career for himself. He handed out visiting cards that included mention of his position as advisor to the secretary of defense. Besides, he had bragged openly to his colleagues that he would return to a brilliant career in the US.[67]

While Nabih Berri was intent on getting hold of Higgins and his kidnappers, Amal's security chief, Mustafa Dirani, was opposed to the idea. Dirani had learned Higgins was collecting information about Hizbullah and supplying it to the American Embassy in Tel Aviv. From there the information went on to the Israelis.[68]

The day after the kidnapping, the group responsible issued an announcement accusing Higgins of being a CIA agent.[69] In Beirut, CIA agent Robert Baer knew the kidnappers were wrong: Higgins did not in fact belong to the CIA. Baer did not even know there was an American in South Lebanon named William Higgins. Eventually he realized Higgins was running his own "cowboy intelligence."[70]

In Higgins' apartment in Nahariya, the CIA found his diary. He wrote that he felt he was being watched, and that he had avoided previous kidnapping attempts. When Baer told me this, I wondered whether Higgins had exaggerated his story that day Iversen and I drove with him in South Lebanon.

Two days after the kidnapping a news bureau in Beirut received his ID card, and four days after that the bureau received a grainy amateur video of Higgins reading an announcement from his kidnappers. Dressed in a t-shirt, and with a sweater around his neck, the balding Higgins seemed calm and self-assured as he peered into the camera and read the kidnappers' demands: "First: withdrawal of all Israeli forces from the occupied South Lebanon. Second: release of all Lebanese and Palestinians from Khiam and from all the prisons under the Zionist regime in occupied Palestine. Third: Cease US intervention in Lebanon. Finally: Do not send delegations to the Middle East that destroy what the Islamic revolution has achieved in occupied Palestine!"

For all those who saw the video and knew something about the Palestinian Intifada that began in December 1987, it was clear that the Palestinians involved had not been inspired by the Islamic revolution in Iran. It was also clear that the kidnappers' demands would not be fulfilled.

The CIA learned from informants in Amal that the party had significant internal problems in South Lebanon. This was part of the reason that Amal did not use all of its resources to find Higgins. The CIA staff also realized that Hizbullah was trying to compromise Nabih Berri in various ways. He chose to kick out two key members of the party who had disagreed with the decision to arrest a number of men from Hizbullah. Mustafa Dirani was removed as security chief, and Sheikh Adib Haidar as the party's chief of culture.[71]

The conflict between Amal and Hizbullah led to a skirmish in the village of Dweir in the outskirts of Nabatiyeh. The fighting took place around a control post that Amal had set up. Machine guns were used, as well as antitank rockets. Six Amal members and one from Hizbullah were wounded in the exchange, which lasted for about an hour.

A few days later a CIA analyst wrote, "The chances that Lieutenant Colonel William Higgins will be rescued diminish as time passes." The writer believed both Hizbullah and Iran realized the UN observer had been an advisor for Secretary of Defense Weinberger and that he probably had detailed knowledge of US programs and plans in Lebanon and the Middle East. Furthermore, the CIA thought Hizbullah was hiding behind other organizations. One calling itself "The Islamic Revolutionary Guard" that had sent out the first communiqué claiming possession of Higgins. The next one came from the Organization for the World's Oppressed, which was also able to show Higgins' ID card.[72] Once again confusion reigned about who actually was behind the kidnapping. UNIFIL leadership believed the two groups were cover organizations for Hizbullah.[73]

CHAPTER FORTY FIVE

Spy Alarm in the Foreign Office

On February 18, the evening after William Higgins had been kidnapped, Ane-Karine Arvesen received some disturbing information—not about Higgins, but about the two Scandinavians from the UN. She wrote a secret, coded message to the Foreign Office, in which she emphasized that the information must not be passed around the Office. She had said nothing else to anyone.[74]

In her report she wrote: "Jørgensen is said to have been forced to sign a piece of paper that he had been engaged in intelligence activity for Israel. The 'spying' was to have taken place once a week, when Jørgensen would bring information to a UNIFIL officer in Naqoura. The Norwegian officer was to have sent everything south to Israel." Ane-Karine's source went on to say that "there would be no release until Stening signed. This could happen in the course of the weekend." Both Jørgensen and Stening seem to "have been exposed to firm methods of persuasion."[75]

From the Foreign Office in Oslo, a secret message was immediately sent to the Norwegian Embassy in Tel Aviv. Ambassador Torleiv Anda was told to get in immediate contact with the Norwegian battalion chief at the UNIFIL headquarters in Naqoura, Colonel Wegger Strømmen, and to ask him to come to Israel. The background for the request could not be given on the telephone.[76]

In Tel Aviv, Anda instructed Colonel Strømmen to speak immediately with Major Ola Kaldager, who was the so-called "information officer," about his contacts with Jørgensen. The major was in reality one of UNIFIL's intelligence officers, who were supposed to keep in contact with various groups to discover what was going on in South Lebanon; since the UN did not have enemies, they were called information officers. Strømmen was instructed that his conversation with Kaldager had to take place one-on-one. No foreign or other Norwegian officers in UNIFIL could be involved or informed. The mission had to "be carried out with the utmost discretion." Once Kaldager had explained himself, Strømmen was to return to Israel immediately to give his report to the embassy. The report would then be sent on to the Foreign Office as quickly as possible, stamped secret. Strømmen was also asked to judge which security measures should be put in place with regard to the Norwegian battalion generally, and Kaldager specifically, in light of the accusations that Norwegians in UNIFIL were spying for Israel.[77]

When Strømmen contacted Kaldager, he learned that the major had only met Jørgensen three times. The first time was by chance in November 1987, when Jørgensen was on a visit to Naqoura. The second time in December that same year in Tyre. Kaldager had then visited the UNRWA office and received a briefing about Jørgensen and his work. The final meeting was February 3, 1988, in Naqoura. Jørgensen and Stening had both visited the UNIFIL headquarters. "No information of any sensitive nature was given," Kaldager explained.[78]

The First Secretary at the Norwegian Embassy in Tel Aviv had been given the task of writing the final report to the Foreign Office. In it he mentioned that Jørgensen normally went to Naqoura every Friday to pick up or send mail, and that he was in contact with the lieutenant who was the secretary of the Norwegian battalion chief's office. Jørgensen had, according to the report, no particular contact with other Norwegian officers.

No threats or other actions had been noted which could put the security of the Norwegians in UNIFIL in danger: "For the moment the situation in the area is more affected by the search for the kidnapped American lieutenant colonel, something which had led to a general tightening of security and limited the traffic in sensitive areas."

On the night of February 20, Kaldager, who was then in Israel, was called by Ambassador Anda. The ambassador asked him to come to his residence in Herzliya, north of Tel Aviv. When he arrived, the ambassador put on a record of classical piano music at high volume to counter any possible listening devices. Anda was convinced that the Israelis had installed secret microphones in his residence. Major Kaldager advised that he had been in contact several times with Jørgensen's bodyguard in Tyre, a Shia who belonged to Amal's security service. He only knew the guard's first name, Hassan, and that he spoke good German, having lived in Germany for 10 years. Hassan had good contacts both in the PLO and in other militias.[79] He added that Hassan had arranged a meeting with a PLO officer who informed him of the spying accusations directed at Stening and Jørgensen. The Palestinian said Jørgensen had confessed after brutal interrogation, and that the two would be set free after signing the declaration that they had "weekly meetings with a Norwegian captain who passed information to Israel." Following the conversation, Ambassador Anda was convinced that the spying rumors were put forth by the Palestinians to obscure the true reason for the kidnapping.

In the political section of the Swedish foreign ministry, Mathias Mossberg of the Middle East department wrote a secret report establishing that "the kidnappers were Palestinians who have fallen out with Arafat, and who were interested in a political rebellion against him. In the meantime political aspects have come to take over and dominate the matter completely."[80] The report went on: "...the dimensions of the affair have grown steadily, and has now begun to develop into a question of Arafat's continued influence in South Lebanon. It has previously been assumed that Arafat has about 80 percent influence over the Palestinians in the Sidon area. The developments in this matter are thought to prove that Arafat has in no way such a dominant position. Instead, there seems to be a balance of power between those faithful to Arafat on the one hand, and on the other, more radical forces who in many ways are under Syrian influence."

Seen from the Swedish point of view, it was not unreasonable that Arafat would try to deflect blame onto others in this situation. By accusing Hizbullah or Amal, he could get off the hook if something went wrong. He could also take the credit if there was a happy conclusion to the kidnapping.

Stening and Jørgensen had now been held hostage for three weeks. They were chained to the wall and slept on mattresses on the floor. On the night of February 25 they were moved again to a house where they had been kept earlier, the one without windows or doors.[81] There their captors gave them shots to knock them out, and then loaded them onto a truck. They were bound and covered with containers of fruit and vegetables. The injections did not work as expected, however, and they were able to observe that the vehicle drove northward along the coast road, through many control posts.

After an hour and a half, they noticed streetlights and a large house; they had to be in Beirut. The truck stopped and they were transferred to a passenger car, which took them to an apartment building with an elevator. The kidnappers led them into a well-furnished apartment that seemed unoccupied, and into a children's room with teddy bears and toys. For the first time they were able to take a shower and were not kept in chains. Now there were other guards who spoke English were accommodating, and wore no masks.

On February 26, Stening and Jørgensen were questioned for the first time by a well-spoken man. He wore glasses over a mask made with a green and brown camouflage pattern. Stening and Jørgensen called him "the philosopher" because he tended to lecture at length about the Palestinian cause, and how the Palestinians had been weakened and were trying to advance their interests and rights.

"Was the situation not the same for you Norwegians under the German occupation?" asked the philosopher.[82]

William Jørgensen answered yes. The man nodded and said, "You see, now you understand this."

The questioning went on for several sessions. Now and then the philosopher whispered and peered over his glasses through the eyeholes in his homemade mask. He was interested in knowing whether the Scandinavians knew particular Frenchmen, British or Americans in Naqoura. He showed them a picture of Lieutenant Colonel Higgins. But neither had seen him nor knew the names of the French officers in UNIFIL who were mentioned.

Two other masked men presented a letter written in Arabic, and told Stening and Jørgensen to sign it and put their fingerprints on the paper. They then told the prisoners to write a letter in English confirming that they were fine.

CHAPTER FORTY SIX

Swedish Ransom

Late one night the UNRWA chief in Lebanon, Per Olof Hallqvist, shared a bottle of whiskey with the former Swedish ambassador to the country, Ingemar Stjernberg. Hallqvist talked of his suspicion that there were two key Palestinians in Sidon who were the prime architects of the kidnapping.[83] He thought the kidnapping had originally been planned by the transport chief in UNRWA. The idea had been to hold Stening and Jørgensen for a few days and then let them go, with a goal of intimidating the reformer Stening. The matter took a different turn when two local PLO leaders got word of the plan. Arafat had recently put them out into the cold, and they decided to takeover the kidnapping and use it to pressure him to take them back.

One of the two had previously been associated with Arafat's bodyguard in the Ain el-Hilweh camp. Arafat discharged him on the suspicion that he was behind the 1987 murder of the force's leader, Lieutenant Colonel Rasem al-Ghul. The corpse was discovered on the outskirts of the camp, full of bullet holes. The assassin was a criminal who had murdered dozens of men before.[84] The other kidnapper, according to Hallqvist, was the head of the Palestinian Labor Union. He was known because he had been on an official visit to Norway.

Hallqvist also said the two main culprits had allied themselves with a gang of criminal Palestinians who went by the name "The Seven Dwarfs." Some were tied to Fatah, others had worked for UNRWA. In the gang there were also men tied to Abu Nidal's group. Hallqvist thought Arafat knew all of this, but had knowingly misled outsiders. He maintained as well that the UN organization's top leader in Vienna had been informed of Arafat's double-crossing but did not want to confront the PLO leader about it.

What neither Hallqvist nor Stjernberg knew was that Sweden's ambassador to Damascus, Rolf Gauffin, had already been in contact with a middleman for the kidnappers. He had approached Gauffin and told him that the hostages would be killed if the Swedes did not pay $500,000 in ransom. There was no question of negotiation, and the Swedes had to act quickly.[85]

Ambassador Gauffin immediately called Cabinet Secretary Pierre Schori at the Swedish foreign ministry. He told him what had happened, and said that the money had to be found quickly. Schori made contact with Foreign Minister Sten Andersson, who said that the ministry had no secret funds which could be used to pay for the hostages' release. Only when Defense Minister Roine Carlsson was asked, did Schori discover that in fact there was such a fund. The Swedish government met on February 25 and decided to allocate five million Swedish Kronor in the form of securities from Sweden's National Bank. The securities were put into a briefcase and entrusted to a Swedish diplomat.[86] Norwegian Prime Minister Gro Harlem Brundtland and Foreign Minister Thorvald Stoltenberg were not advised that the Swedish government was about to pay ransom for the hostages. Nor was the leadership in the Norwegian Foreign Office's political department in Oslo.[87]

Meanwhile, Stening and Jørgensen sat under close guard and waited for something to happen. Late in the day on February 28, two men showed up wearing masks. They presented a form in English and had the prisoners write out information about their names, families, military service, which countries they had visited and why they had been there, and whether they knew particular American and French officers in Naqoura.

Jørgensen wrote that he had visited the United States, figuring he would be interrogated about it. The only item the masked men asked about, however, was what *Heimevernet* (The National Guard) was, since Jørgensen had listed it. Otherwise, they were more interested in digging into Stening's history. He had been a UNTSO observer twice and also an instructor on an observer course in Finland. The interrogators suspected Stening of being German.

On February 29, Hallqvist was called to the UNRWA headquarters in Vienna. He was not very happy to leave Lebanon, but had no choice. Ane-Karine Arvesen drove over to the UNRWA office in East Beirut to check if Hallqvist's deputy, John Fennessy or security chief, John Carolan, had anything new to report. The security chief was cautiously optimistic. UNRWA had threatened to stop all aid supplies to the Palestinian refugees in Lebanon if Stening and Jørgensen were not set free. He said the deadline UNRWA had set was about to run out. Carolan said he would drive to Sidon the next day to get into contact again with Mustafa Saad, the key Lebanese politician and militia leader in the city.

While UN Under Secretary-General Marrack Goulding was having breakfast with Norwegian Foreign Minister Johan Jørgen Holst in Oslo on March 1, he said, "It will take several weeks for Stening and Jørgensen to be set free."[88] Goulding was certain Arafat's insistence that Hizbullah was behind the kidnapping was not true. Palestinians were responsible, and Arafat had known that the whole time: "The theory that Hizbullah was behind this, is a diversionary manoeuvre."

Later in the afternoon, Ambassador Rolf Gauffin met Ane-Karine Arvesen, Peter Ræder and Ingemar Stjernberg at the Summerland Hotel in West Beirut. Gauffin told Stjernberg that he had been in the Lebanese town of Chtaura to negotiate that very day. There was a rather poor choice of imported goods in Syria, and what was there was expensive. The diplomats in Damascus therefore would often drive across the border to buy cheap food and drink. Gauffin went on to say he had been stopped along the road by a car. At first he was afraid of being kidnapped, but the men wanted to talk about a solution for Stening and Jørgensen. The ambassador did not say any more to his Swedish colleague, but he later told Ane-Karine that he had been contacted by the kidnappers or their representative at his office in Damascus.[89]

That same evening around 6 PM, the Swedish ambassador's driver, Geryies Haddad, drove to West Beirut's southern section. In the car with him was Rolf Gauffin. The ambassador handed over a black briefcase to a masked man who was waiting for them. The Lebanese driver had no idea who the man was or what was in the briefcase.[90]

Stening and Jørgensen waited impatiently to be set free. Around 7 PM, when both were about to lose hope, the "philosopher" returned, saying, "Hurry up. In one hour you are going to be handed over near the Summerland. The Swedish ambassador to Damascus is coming in a Volvo with a Swedish flag. You have to shave."[91]

It was not easy to get rid of a four week's growth of beard in one go. Each man shaved one side of his face while two of the guards took care of the other. Then they got their passports back, but not their watches, clothing or money.[92]

They were instructed to say: "It was not Palestinians who held you. But there is a relationship between them and us. You must not say how you were transported from Sidon to Beirut. Say you were unconscious and do not know. Say also that you were well treated. You must not say you were beaten." The whole thing seemed absurd. But neither Stening nor Jørgensen protested.

Since the power had gone out where they were being held, they had to walk down the stairs from the apartment. In the courtyard they got into the back seat of a car, but without blindfolds this time. It took nearly half an hour to reach the Summerland Hotel, since the driver took back streets to avoid the Syrian control posts. A few hundred meters south of the hotel, Stening and Jørgensen were let out with the orders, "Walk slowly up toward the hotel. Do not speak to anyone. Do not look back." The time was 8 PM.

Ambassador Gauffin had not told Ingemar Stjernberg or his Norwegian colleagues about the black briefcase he had handed over to a masked man. Gauffin had only repeated the kidnappers instructions to him: that the embassy car was to stop some 300–400 meters south of the hotel and wait there. Gauffin's colleague, Stjernberg, had misgivings about the plan. The staging area was right between two Syrian control posts and it was dark because there were no streetlights. From that street an unguarded alley led right into the Hizbullah-controlled part of the city. This could be dangerous.[93]

At that moment, Ane-Karine interrupted and said, "I am coming along in the car. That will be more natural. Besides, women are not being kidnapped in Beirut."[94]

Together they drove south from the hotel parking lot and parked outside a closed garage. Around 20 meters further on was a jeep with a half dozen men beside it. They appeared to be doing something with the back door. Both Gauffin and Ane-Karine felt the suspense: had they driven into a trap?

About that time, Stening and Jørgensen were walking slowly toward the hotel, but they did not see a car with a Swedish flag. They were confused. The minutes crept by. In the dark, Ane-Karine and Gauffin could not see them either. It was nerve-wracking to sit in the car and wait. Suddenly, Stening and Jørgensen saw the car and ran toward it. When they got there, they banged on the trunk and shouted, "Here we are!"

Ane-Karine got out and received a big hug from Jørgensen. Then they jumped into the back seat, and Gauffin drove back to the Summerland, where Ambassador Stjernberg was waiting together with Gauffin's driver. Ane-Karine went to her room to report to the Foreign Office that the hostages were free, while the others hurried toward the Green Line. The diplomatic car was waved through the control post; then Stening and Jørgensen went to Hallqvist's apartment in East Beirut.

The following day, Yasser Arafat received Counsellor Odd Wibe and the Swedish ambassador to Tunis. He was in a good mood, and had no scruples about misleading the diplomats. He did not say a word about having forgiven the kidnappers. He implied that Hizbullah had nothing to do with the matter, but firmly maintained that Lebanese fundamentalists were behind it, working together with Abu Nidal's men. Since the PLO leader had not had to pay a ransom, he would give a gift to a social institution in Lebanon. But it would have to be "secret" which institution would get the gift, he said. Later his secretary said in confidence that Arafat would give the money to a Shia fundamentalist institution. There was no end to his smokescreens.[95]

UNRWA's local chief, Per Olof Hallqvist, wrote to his highest superior, Commissioner General Giorgio Giacomelli, "We now know, almost in detail, what happened, why, and who planned and carried out the action. We were badly misled by Chairman Arafat the first four days, when everyone tried to blame everyone else, and most ended up blaming UNRWA. From the beginning on, at least at an early stage, Arafat knew the kidnapping was a conspiracy linked to a feud between him and one of his ex-colleagues." He continued, "When Mustafa Saad also realized he had been misled, and the truth began to leak out in Sidon, we understood the kidnapping was put into motion as a part of an internal Palestinian dispute. The timing was not carefully chosen. Certain members of the UNRWA staff, particularly in the transport unit, were fooled into using some of their criminal contacts and people in Abu Nidal's group. One or two in UNRWA's staff helped with the operation. Others in UNRWA were informed of what was happening, but chose to be loyal to the shady groups they apparently belonged to."[96]

In Damascus, the Syrians were furious they had not been given the credit for the release of the two hostages held in a Syrian-controlled area, and when the PLO coordinator in South Lebanon, Salah Salah, drove across the border from Lebanon to Syria on March 7, he was arrested.[97] During his 10 months in a Syrian prison, no one asked Salah about the ransom the Swedes had paid. Later he learned that the Syrians thought that it amounted to five million dollars, and that he had stashed it away.[98]

CHAPTER FORTY SEVEN
Shia Against Shia

In April 1988, UNIFIL's Lieutenant Colonel Tor Planting arranged a meeting in South Lebanon with one of Hizbullah's local leaders, Khalil Harb. Planting had been told he was behind the kidnapping of William Higgins. Harb was distantly related to Imam Ragheb Harb from Jibsheet, one of Hizbullah's founders, who had been killed four years earlier.

He drove to Tibnin together with his Finnish interpreter. They met Harb's men, who brought them further by private car. Both had to wear blindfolds, and these were not removed until they were sitting in a potato cellar, face to face with Khalil Harb. Harb was a small, thin man in his 30s with brown hair and a well-trimmed beard and mustache. He had been educated in Iran.

"Why did you have to take Higgins?" asked Planting.[99]

"Colonel Planting, if we had not taken Higgins, God would have punished us. We had to take him," answered Harb.

"I understand what you say," Planting responded. The Finn did not want to condemn or defend the kidnapping. Personally, he thought Higgins had acted provocatively.

Harb said there was no question of negotiating for his release: "Higgins is a spy. He is in a different category than the other western hostages in Lebanon. They will be freed eventually."

Harb was generally right about the western hostages. About one month later on May 4, three French hostages were released from their prison hole. When the freed hostages—Marcel Fontaine, Jean-Paul Kauffmann, and Marcel Carton—arrived at a French military base southwest of Paris, Fontaine said to the gathered journalists there, "We survived, but we did not live."

Retiring Prime Minister Jacques Chirac was there. He said the way was now open for normal diplomatic relations between Iran and France, after a break of 10 months. What Chirac did not say was that the French government had promised to cancel Iran's debt to France. The spokesman for the new government did not discuss any details of the agreement with Iran, either. The incoming Socialist prime minister, Michel Rocard, just said, "France had given its word, and it will be honored."[100]

The day after the Frenchmen were set free, Terry Anderson's guards moved him before sunup. They were afraid Fontaine would give the American intelligence service dangerous clues as to his whereabouts. The guards bound and blindfolded Anderson, hid the blindfold with sunglasses and then dressed him in a black chador of the type which covered the entire body from head to toe. They loaded him into the back seat of a Mercedes; he thought it was the same car which had been used to kidnap him 38 months earlier. This time Anderson was allowed to sit instead of lying down.

The guard beside him did not notice that the blindfold had fallen off behind the sunglasses. Anderson could then see they were driving through small streets in the south of Beirut. The car bumped into garbage as it veered around burned-out car wrecks and potholes in the pavement. Finally, it backed into a driveway and up against a big truck. The guards removed the chador and wrapped Anderson with tape like a mummy, before shoving him into a hidden space under the floor of the vehicle. One of the guards lay down beside him.

The drive was a long one, and it was unusually warm. The vehicle left Beirut and went up into the mountains on lousy roads. After a while they started down into what Anderson thought must have been the Bekaa Valley. The exhaust made him nauseous and scared. He had to concentrate to keep his stomach under control: with the tape over his mouth, he could choke on his own vomit.

Finally the truck stopped. Anderson was lifted out and the tape removed. He was outside a large villa. One of the guards doused his face with water and gave him something to drink. Then they led him through several rooms in the villa and down into a secret cellar. Guards chained his legs and left.

All was quiet. Anderson thought he was alone. Carefully, in case there was a guard there, he lifted the blindfold and looked around. There were two other men in the room. One proved to be Thomas Sutherland, who had been kidnapped in June 1985. The other was Frank Reed, a hostage since September 1986.

Sutherland spoke first: "I thought you'd gone home, but the Frenchmen were sure you hadn't."[101] Reed had been kept isolated since Anderson saw him last. Sutherland had been together with two of the Frenchmen, Kauffmann and Carton, for six months, while Anderson was being held with the third Frenchman, Michel Fontaine.

In July 1988, Washington learned that Imad Mughniyeh had been in Iran during the negotiations over the three French hostages. A CIA report noted that Mughniyeh might also be willing to release more hostages for a ransom. Since Islamic Jihad had tied any release to the fate of the 17 prisoners from the Dawa Party, however, the CIA analysts thought this might be difficult. The report concluded that the Iranians would not be able to just order a release, since the hostage takers did not take orders from them directly.[102]

Hizbullah's guerrillas increased their readiness from month to month, but Israeli politicians did not listen to warnings from the officer corps that the fight for South Lebanon was moving into a new phase. Fresh Israeli soldiers went in unprepared for Shias who failed to run away from their advancing forces. (Previously they had done so regardless of which side had greater numbers.)

In May 1988 when Lieutenant Aharon Khaliba led a group toward the village of Maidoun in the western part of the Bekaa Valley, he was prepared for a "walkover." He later said, "We fired and we were in the clouds. But when Hizbullah counterattacked, we were surprised and scared."[103] Khaliba was leading a troop to support an Israeli company, both part of Israel's 202nd Paratrooper Battalion. The plan was to advance into several villages north of the occupation zone. The Israelis met little resistance until they arrived at the outskirts of Maidoun, where Hizbullah's guerrillas decided to fight.

The leader of the operation, Colonel Yitzhak Gershon, was just as surprised as his men by Hizbullah's willingness to resist. For eight hours the Lebanese fought against the superior Israeli force. When the battle was over 40 guerrillas lay dead, but the Israelis had also lost several men.[104] When Colonel Gershon returned to Israel, he told his colleagues this was something new. The Shias were not like the Palestinians: "They are really difficult to fight. This also became costly for us."

Defense Minister Yitzhak Rabin did not care about such feedback. In a radio interview he said, "In order to assure peace in Galilee, we have to fight unceasingly. We have not gotten control over terrorism in Lebanon. It exists, and it is active. Even if we, for the most part, are running a defensive battle, we must now and then go on the offensive to prevent terrorism from attacking us."[105]

Israel's full-scale attack in South Lebanon was taken up in the Security Council of the UN. On May 5, 1988, the United States once again vetoed a resolution that condemned the Israelis' brutality and called for an Israeli withdrawal from Lebanon. As before, the US stood alone against all the other members of the Council.

That spring Hizbullah had to withdraw forces in order to fight against Amal north of the occupation zone. The conflict was primarily over who would run the villages. The fighting spread to Beirut. The Lebanese government army was weak and political groups that did not have their own militias were helpless. But no single militia was strong enough to govern alone. Therefore new alliances were continuously forming, breaking and forming again.

Foreign participants increased the polarization. When the Shias fought each other, Syria's intelligence chief in Lebanon, Brigadier General Ghazi Kanaan, again tried to create calm. He feared that Hizbullah would defeat Amal and threaten Syria's domination over West Beirut and Bekaa.

The Syrians had 7,500 soldiers stationed in West Beirut, but President Assad hesitated to send this force into Beirut's southern sections where Amal and Hizbullah were fighting. In Assad's view, it was not in Syria's interest to go to full war against Hizbullah in order to support Amal; he wanted first and foremost to reach a political compromise with Iran. The two countries remained strategic allies in Iran's war against Iraq, which was in its eighth year.

After three weeks of fighting, Hizbullah had taken control over almost all of the southern part of the city. But it was Syria's president who won the political prize: during negotiations at his villa in Latakia on the Mediterranean coast, Amal and Hizbullah struck a ceasefire agreement. It said that both parties could have political offices in the city's southern sections, but that the militias could not show themselves there. One day later, 900 Syrian infantry soldiers advanced into the buffer zone along the city's front line with the Lebanese police at their heels. Syria's security network thereby spread into Beirut's southern sections, and President Assad demonstrated that he was still Lebanon's real leader.

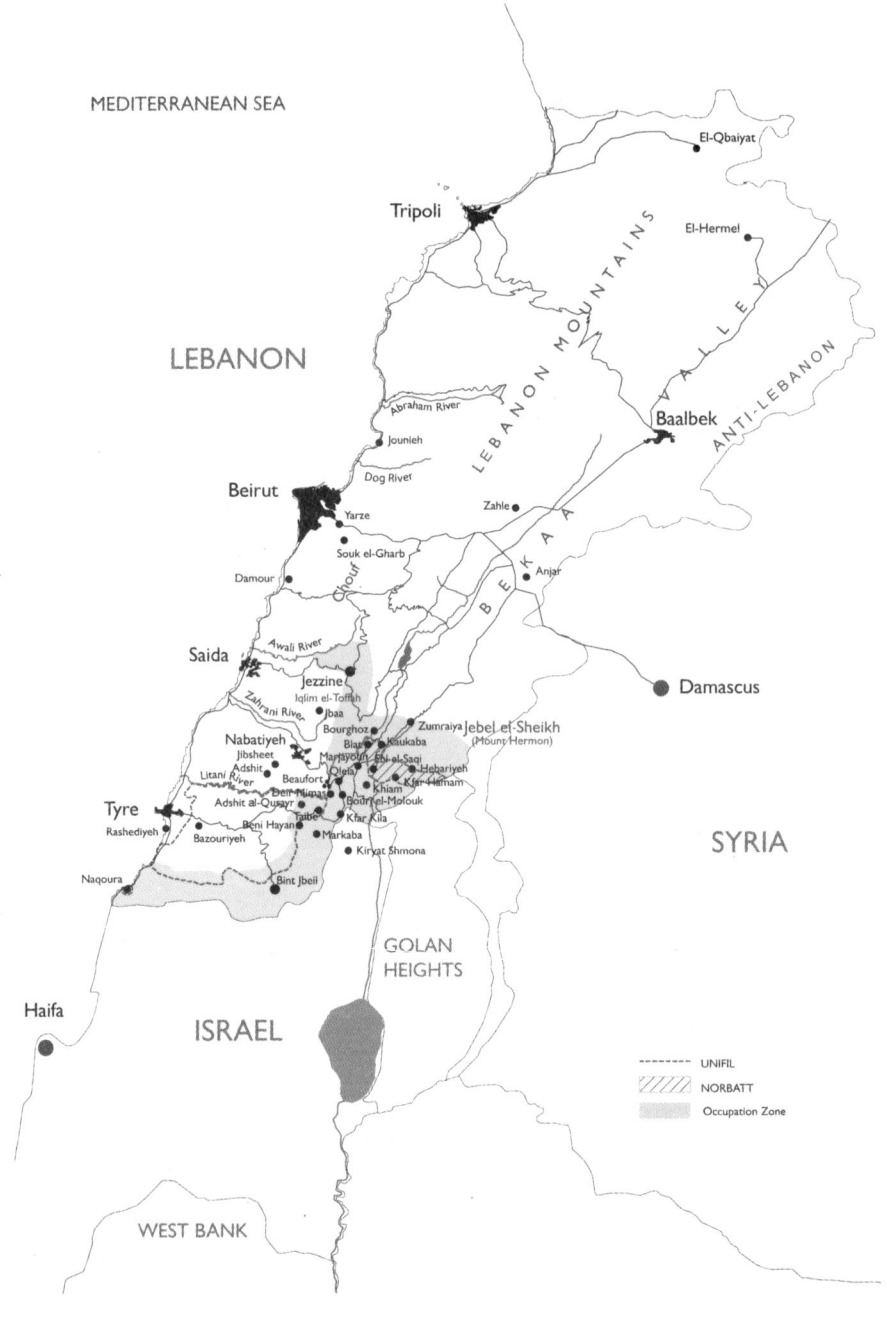

MEDITERRANEAN SEA

El-Qbaiyat

Tripoli

El-Hermel

LEBANON

Abraham River

Jounieh

Baalbek

Dog River

Beirut

Yarze

Zahle

Souk el-Gharb

Anjar

Damour

Saida

Awali River

Damascus

Jezzine

Zahrani River

Iqlim el-Toffah

Jbaa

Bourghoz

Zumraiya Jebel el-Sheikh
(Mount Hermon)

Nabatiyeh

Kaukaba

Biare

Marjayoun Ebl el-Saqi

Jibsheet

Litani River

Adshit

Olela

Hebariyeh

Beaufort

Kfar Hamam

Ben Mujana

Khiam

Tyre

Adshit al-Qusayr

Bourj el-Molouk

Taibe

Rashediyeh

Beni Hayan

Kfar Kila

SYRIA

Bazouriyeh

Markaba

Kiryat Shmona

Naqoura

Bint Jbeil

GOLAN
HEIGHTS

Haifa

ISRAEL

- - - - - UNIFIL

/////// NORBATT

Occupation Zone

WEST BANK

PART FIVE

The Civil War is Over

1988-1991

After long negotiations and pressure from outside, the 15-year Lebanese civil war came to an end. At the same time Syria solidified its control over the part of Lebanon not occupied by Israeli forces.

In South Lebanon, attacks continued against the Israeli occupation forces and against UNIFIL. The Israelis still took Lebanese as hostages. Some were set free as a part of an exchange with American hostages. The last American to get his freedom was *Associated Press* journalist Terry Anderson. He had been in captivity for nearly seven years.

In Israel, a human rights lawyer revealed that the country was secretly holding a number of Lebanese prisoner in order to use them for a future exchanges.

MAIN CHARACTERS

Hussein Abbas, Shia Agent of Shin Bet
Michel Aoun, Lebanese Brigadier General
Soha Bechara, Female Lebanese Resistance Member
Johan Jørgen Holst, Norwegian Defense Minister
Jan Erik Karlsen, Colonel, Norwegian Battalion Commander in UNIFIL
Imad Mughniyeh, military leader in Hizbullah
Hassan Nasrallah, Hizbullah's Secretary General
Abdel Karim Obeid, Shia Cleric
Giandomenico Picco, UN's Negotiator for Freeing the Hostages
Zvi Rish, Israeli Lawyer

CHAPTER FORTY EIGHT

Lebanon's "Protector"

The Swedish ransom payment for Stening and Jørgensen's gave criminal Palestinians a taste of blood. Among Abu Nidal's group in the Sidon area, some began to look around for new victims from Europe, preferably Scandinavia.

In the refugee camp Rashidiya, south of Tyre, the Norwegian Aid Committee (NORWAC) had a medical team at work. One of the doctors was 32-year-old Jan Cools. He was from Belgium, not Norway, but this did not matter to Abu Nidal. On May 21, 1988, Cools was kidnapped as he left his apartment in the refugee camp. The kidnappers accused him of spying for Israel. The leaders in NORWAC took immediate steps to get him free, while the Belgian authorities refused to negotiate with "terrorists." As a result, Cools remained in captivity for more than a year, and was only released upon a request from Libya's Muammar al-Ghaddafi. Actually, Libya had secretly "bought" his freedom in return for Belgium's promise to lift the trade boycott against them. In Lebanon, the sale of this hostage was taken as further proof that crime does pay.

One month later, 21-year-old Soha Bechara moved from Beirut to her home village of Deir Mimas in South Lebanon. Three years had passed since Soha had secretly joined the Communist Party to have a role in the resistance. Now she wanted to carry out a military attack, even if this cost her her life.

Bechara decided to look for a job in the occupation zone. This would make matters simpler. She first thought she would get a job as a telephone operator, and asked a cousin for help, but he refused. Telephone operators had a bad reputation among ordinary people; they were closely tied to the SLA security service. Next she went to the Sports and Culture Center in Marjayoun and told the man in charge, "I could teach young people to play ping pong and gymnastics."[1]

"Excellent," he answered, and added: "General Lahd's wife is looking for an aerobics instructor." Bechara was thrilled. Perhaps she could manage to kill the chief of the SLA himself.

While Soha Bechara was getting prepared, historic events were taking place in other areas in the Middle East. After eight years, Tehran and Baghdad signed a ceasefire on August 20, 1988. The war between Iran and Iraq had in many ways resembled the First World War, with trench warfare and tens of thousands of soldiers storming over a mine-laden no man's land toward enemy positions. The war concluded without either party having gained or lost any land. It had cost the lives of between 500,000 to 700,000 soldiers.

On the same day as the ceasefire, I made a notation in my little black book: "Former President Jimmy Carter met the PLO leader in Cairo. He, like six other former leaders, was there to repair the injustice which he had done as president by not recognizing the PLO." I also wrote down the result of an opinion poll which had been taken by the *Jerusalem Post*. It showed that about 50 percent of Israeli Jews thought the Arabs should leave Israel so the Jewish state could retain its democratic character. I asked myself, will any Israeli government dare to deport hundreds of thousands of Palestinians as they did in 1948?

In Oslo, Defense Minister Johan Jørgen Holst was concerned with Israel's conduct of the war, not least because Norwegian soldiers in South Lebanon were at times exposed to Israeli fire. In the second half of October, Holst was again on his way to the Middle East. On the flight to Damascus he read reports from specialists in the Foreign Office and Defense Department.

Ane-Karine Arvesen, who once again was working for the Middle East section, had written a background note on Lebanon. In it, Holst read that focus in the Middle East would most likely now shift to Lebanon. With the war between Iran and Iraq over, presidents Saddam Hussein and Hafez al-Assad would perhaps use war-torn Lebanon to finish their fight. There were certainly enough Lebanese proxies to choose from.

The two presidents were still enemies, even if both belonged to the Socialist Baath Party. Ten years earlier they had signed a union treaty to establish a strategic balance in the Middle East after Egypt's President Anwar Sadat had gone to Jerusalem in 1978 to make peace with Israel. The union treaty lasted only a year because the presidents suspected each other of planning coups. Their mutual hatred grew even stronger when Syria took Iran's side after Iraq attacked it in 1980. Ane-Karine believed that Saddam was determined to make the situation difficult for Assad in Lebanon.

In her note, Ane-Karine also wrote that Lebanon was without a president for the first time in its history. Amine Gemayel had completed his term of office on September 22, 1988, and because of the civil war, no new president had been elected. Before Gemayel retired, however, he named a fellow Maronite, Brigadier General Michel Aoun, as acting prime minister. He did so despite the fact Lebanon already had a prime minister, the Sunni economist Salim el-Hoss. As a result, Lebanon now had two governments: a Christian one with its seat in East Beirut, and a Muslim one in the caretaker government in West Beirut.

It was no secret Saddam Hussein supported Michel Aoun, even though the latter had contacts with the Israelis. For Saddam, Aoun's relationship with Israel meant nothing. Once more there were echoes of the old saying: my enemy's enemy is my friend.

When Defense Minister Holst sat across the table from Syrian Vice President Abdul Halim Khaddam on October 18, he learned that the situation in Lebanon had worsened since they had last spoken. Holst did not bring up the danger of an indirect Syrian-Iraqi confrontation in Lebanon. And Khaddam, who was used to European ministers ignorant of Lebanon's history, spent some time telling him that the greatest problems in the country derived from the nature of its political system.

"The system is unique, there is no other like it in the world. The citizens belong to themselves rather than the country," said the vice president, who in practice ran North Lebanon, the area of the country which was not occupied by Israel or governed by Brigadier General Michel Aoun.

Khaddam went on to say that French colonialism had created the system: "The French gave the power to the religious minority—the Maronites. The conflict today takes place between this minority, which wants to retain power, and the majority, which wants democracy."[2]

"Is Lebanon on the way to being divided up further?" Holst wanted to know.

"No. All over Lebanon, the religious groups are mixed in with each other geographically. The majority in the country rejects a split, and Syria is definitely against every attempt to divide Lebanon."

"Is Syria then Lebanon's protector?"

"Syria cannot just passively observe what is going on there. Lebanon is an Arab country. We do not want to risk a new Israel." Khaddam was firmly determined that Syria would use its power to prevent Lebanon from becoming a client state of the US and Israel.

"Norway agrees Lebanon should not be split up," Holst replied and pointed to the many foreign interests that were interfering in the country. "No one has difficulty in finding supporters," Holst said, without naming Israel, Iraq, Iran or Syria by name.

"Israel is the problem in two ways," Khaddam interjected. "First of all, the Israelis are in South Lebanon. Second, they have influence over the Christians in East Beirut. Iran's influence on Hizbullah is marginal, and Iraq does not have any great influence."

"Yes, it is Israel and Syria who are the main actors," said Holst.

"Syria cannot be compared with Israel," answered Khaddam and pointed to the old and close connections between the Lebanese and Syrians: "Before the French divided the area, Syria and Lebanon were more or less considered one land."

"What about the fighting between Amal and Hizbullah?"

"This is a fight for control, a part of the Lebanese crisis," answered Khaddam.

Later in the day, Holst met his Syrian colleague, Defense Minister Mustafa Tlass. Like his friend President Assad, Tlass was a general; both had been educated at the Homs Military Academy. While Assad chose the air force, Tlass went to a tank battalion. The two rose quickly in the ranks, and when General Assad carried out his bloody coup in 1970, he was supported by Tlass. Defense Minister Tlass and Vice President Khaddam were both Sunni Muslims, something that came up frequently to contradict accusations that the Syrian government was strictly led by Alawites like Assad.

The Syrian defense minister was a charming man. He spoke quite openly of what Holst already knew: Syria had 40,000 soldiers in Lebanon, divided into three divisions. The force controlled 80 percent of the country, while the Israelis controlled the remaining 20 percent.

"Does Syria have problems with the armed militias in West Beirut?" asked Holst .

"Syria has full control. When the orders were given to go into the southern sections of West Beirut, the soldiers waited one week in order to avoid fights. Then they took over that section of the city without problems. President Assad is opposed to violence," Tlass added, "but he can be tough if necessary."

Holst's face did not give any indication he knew all about Assad's use of violence, both against his political opponents in Syria, and in Lebanon. He just asked: "How is the relationship with the militia in East Beirut?"

"The Lebanese Forces (as they are called) consist of 10,000–20,000 men, and can be controlled. Assad wants to avoid bloodletting and expects the militia will give in. Sooner or later it will. The Lebanese Forces are surrounded by Syrians and they know it," said Tlass.

That evening there was an official dinner, and Johan Jørgen Holst's live-in partner, Marianne Heiberg, a researcher at The Norwegian Institute for International Affairs ,, was not looking forward to it. She knew she would be matched with the 56-year-old defense minister, who often touched his female dinner partners underneath the table.

The Syrian minister had never hidden his like for women. He often bragged about his flirtation with Henry Kissinger's wife during the US Secretary of State's shuttle diplomacy in the Middle East. Tlass said Nancy Kissinger liked it when he recited poetry, and how jealous her husband was. Once when the couple had come to Damascus, Kissinger sent his wife to shop at the bazaar instead of meeting Tlass at lunch.[3]

Marianne Heiberg told me that most likely Kissinger's wife preferred to shop instead of being pestered with bad poetry by a pushy Syrian minister. Heiberg, for her part, was able to avoid both the poetry and any awkward moments during the dinner.[4]

Holst arrived in South Lebanon two days later, and was given a full briefing by the Norwegian UN officers. After many previous visits as undersecretary, first in the defense department and later in the Foreign Office, he knew that part of the country quite well. He knew for example that the village of Kfar Hamam in the Norwegian battalion's area was 500 years old. After 1975, many of the Christian inhabitants had emigrated to Canada or Brazil as the civil war emptied the village. Some families had returned in 1978, when the Norwegians arrived with their blue helmets. Now some 300 people lived in Kfar Hamam, side by side with the Norwegian troops.

Some Lebanese felt a certain security having the Norwegians nearby, but that did not help everyone. Young men in the occupation zone, both Shias and Sunnis, Christians and Druze, were confronted with difficult choices: either they had to serve the Israelis in the SLA militia or Shin Bet, or they could risk being thrown into the infamous prison holes at Khiam.

In January 1988, the brothers Jamal and Ahmed Shahrour decided to leave Kfar Hamam. For several months the two young men had been approached to join the SLA. When they left, their mother Youmna, and their youngest brother of 13 were arrested and brought to Khiam. Their father was allowed to remain in the house in order to care for his three small girls.

For 15 days, Youmna was interrogated and tortured. The pattern was the same each time: First she was blindfolded and a small hood was placed over her head, then she was kicked and sprayed with alternating jets of cold and hot water. The torturers put electric wires to her fingernails and nipples. Suddenly, the torture would stop and silence would fill the room. Then came more kicking and beating. She heard voices say: "We will set you free if your sons come back."[5]

"I cannot ask them to do that," the mother answered.

After three months in Khiam, Youmna and her son were set free. But the cell did not remain empty: a Palestinian teenager, Kifah Afifi, took her place. One day in December, 1988, one of the guards came into Afifi's cell and said: "Put on your clothes. There is an Israeli journalist who wants to talk with you."[6] The 17-year-old began to cry. "Don't hang me, I want to go home," Afifi managed to say amidst her sobs; she was afraid of being hung by the wrists from one of the utility poles in the camp so that her toes could barely reach the ground.

The guard calmed her; she was only going to be interviewed. Blindfolded and dressed in a brown sweater and blue pants, Afifi was driven to the Israeli headquarters in Marjayoun. There she met the Israeli journalist and began to tell her story: "I grew up in the Shatila camp in West Beirut and was among the lucky who escaped when the Israelis' Lebanese allies massacred several thousand civilians in the neighborhood in September 1982. Two of my older brothers were killed in the fighting near Shatila."

Afifi went on to say that her father, who was born in Haifa, was lame. Her mother was also sick, and Afifi was therefore happy when a guerrilla leader from Fatah named Munir Makdah asked her: "Kifah, do you want a new home for your family?" Afifi thought about her sick parents and said yes. In return, she had to join a group of six others, all men, who would sneak through the occupation zone and on into Israel. There they would hijack a bus and demand freedom for the Palestinians in Israeli jails.

The operation would mimic one conducted in March 1978, when another woman from Shatila, Dalal Mughrabi, led a group of 13 Palestinians in hijacking a bus full of Israelis. In his conversation with Afifi, the Fatah leader did not mention that the earlier operation was a failure, and that 11 of the Palestinians had been killed, including Mughrabi. He thought they had learned from their previous mistakes and that this time would be a success.

Over the following three weeks, Afifi and the six young men received training in how to shoot, run and climb. Then they were driven to Sidon, where a guide from the Amal militia agreed to lead them to the border for 500 dollars. The group crossed the Litani River and continued south without any problems. After two days the youths came to the Shia village of Kfar Kila, near the border with Israel. Their guide got his 500 dollars and said farewell. They broke through a barbed wire fence, and threw themselves down to kiss the ground, thinking they were in Palestine. However, they quickly realized the border fence itself lay further south. They were still in Lebanon.

Dawn was approaching so the group decided to wait until it was dark again, and chose in the meantime to take refuge in the closest house. They woke the sleeping family there. They had come to a Shia village, and when the father of the house heard there were two Shias among the guerrillas, he promised them food and rest.

After a few hours, the father said he had to go to work in an olive grove nearby. The Palestinians believed he was sympathetic toward their cause and let him leave. Instead he went to contact the Israelis. When Israeli soldiers showed up, Afifi and the others surrendered without resistance. All were taken to Israel and interrogated; then Afifi was sent to Khiam.

When the interview was over, the journalist returned to Israel and Afifi was driven back to prison. She was not aware then that press coverage of the interview would help her. When the story became known, the leading human rights lawyer in Israel decided to look into her case. For many years, Lea Tsemel had spent her time and effort helping Palestinians who were jailed without ever appearing before a court.

CHAPTER FORTY NINE
Israel Versus NORBATT

In Marjayoun, Soha Bechara had spent many weeks waiting for the right moment to kill the leader of the SLA. During the training sessions with Lahd's wife, Minerva, the two women had gotten to know each other quite well. It was not unnatural, therefore, that Soha went to the general's home on the evening of November 7, 1988. She felt the time had come because someone apparently was becoming suspicious. The day before, SLA security service members had come to her home and rummaged around her bedroom, but did not find the 5.5mm, Soviet-made revolver, she had hidden.

Minerva, who was much younger than her husband, sat in the garden with a Spanish female friend. They welcomed Soha, and when the Spanish woman's husband arrived, all four went into the house. Lahd eventually joined them and sat down on a sofa by the telephone, with Soha to his right.

When the Spanish woman's husband got up and stepped outside, Soha mumbled that it was getting late and she should go. But General Lahd insisted she should stay. The SLA chief was sitting watching television. A report came on about the Palestinian Intifada, where youths throwing rocks at the Israelis were met with live fire. Lahd looked at the TV report as if in thought. Then he changed to another channel.

All of a sudden the phone rang and the general answered. His face darkened. It must have been bad news, Soha thought, and looked at the clock in the living room. As he spoke on the phone, Lahd intermittently glanced over at her where she sat close by on the sofa. She calmly reached into her purse while saying to Lahd's wife: "I brought the video you asked about."

She grasped the revolver and pulled it from her purse as if it were the most natural thing in the world. Supporting her right hand with her left, she aimed at the general's heart and fired. She thought she could see the bullet go through his shirt.

A shocked Lahd stood up and shouted, "*Sharmouta!*" meaning "You whore!"

Soha fired a second time. The general crumpled.

It was as if the whole room froze for a second. Minerva then threw herself to the floor screaming. Her Spanish friend sat completely still, ashen-faced. Soha went into an adjacent bedroom and threw the pistol on the bed. She knew there were only seconds before the bodyguards would come storming in. A few meters away her victim lay still on the floor. The Spanish woman's husband came running back into the room, grabbed Soha by the shoulders and asked in French "Why did you kill him?"

"It is he who is killing us."

"Who sent you?"

"I belong to the Communist Party."

Minerva lunged for Soha, but was held back by her friend's husband. One of the general's guards came in. He tore Soha up from her chair and pulled her toward the door. At the doorway, he stopped and shouted "Don't shoot! It is me."

Soha was taken to the guardroom and put in handcuffs. A little later several men came in. One of them pointed a pistol at her temple and screamed, "Talk or I will kill you!"

"I have already said everything."

The questioner pulled out a whip. He hit her over and over. Soha screamed in pain. Two more men arrived, put a hood over her head and led her to a car. They drover her to Israel, where her hood was removed and interrogations began in earnest. One Israeli who called himself Tommy questioned her at length. In the meantime, the unconscious General Lahd was flown to Israel to be operated upon.

After several periods of interrogation, Soha was sent back to Lebanon. In Khiam she was turned over to John Homse, the chief torturer with wolf-like eyes who went by the name Abu Nabil. Her cell contained a thin rubber mattress, a stinking old toilet bucket and a drinking mug.

In Kfar Hamam, in the Norwegian UN battalion's area, Youmna Shahrour was again picked up by the SLA security service a few months later. The mother of the two sons who had fled to Beirut, was now going to be punished in a new manner. They ordered her into a car and drove her north to a roadblock near Zumriya. Here was a crossing from the occupation zone to the "Free Lebanon". Youmna was let out and given a clear message: "Don't come back without your two sons."

It was raining. Youmna sat down on the wet ground. She could do nothing but wait. She had a sister in Bekaa, but it was too far to walk. Finally, a car came and gave her a lift.

The leaders of the SLA security service in the area were not satisfied. A few weeks later Youmna's husband and the three small girls were picked up during the night. Lebanese working for Shin Bet arrived at their house with Israeli soldiers. The soldiers went through the house but found nothing of interest. Then one of the Lebanese soldiers cut open the living room sofa with a knife and tied pieces of the material around the father's eyes. Only the children could see the soldiers carrying off their TV set, and taking whatever money and jewelry they found. Then all four were driven to the "border crossing" at Zumriya, like Youmna, and were left in their nightclothes.

After a while so many were deported from the Norwegian UNIFIL area that the leader, Colonel Jan Erik Karlsen, sent out a press release. In all, 65 Lebanese had been deported during January 1989. Most of these were women and children, among whom several were mentally handicapped. All had been forced out of the Israeli occupation zone in whatever clothes they were wearing at the time.

The 42-year-old Norwegian colonel, who had been in Lebanon for nearly eight months, was furious with the Israelis'. He did not believe their excuses that 11 of those deported had actively supported the Lebanese "terrorists". Karlsen himself used the expression "resistance movement."

The Norwegian battalion was surrounded by the Israelis. There had been several verbal agreements that whenever the SLA militia operated in the NORBATT area alone, the UN soldiers were allowed to stop arrests of the civilian population. As soon as the SLA teams were accompanied by Israeli officers, however, international law required the UN force to yield to the occupying power. This meant the Norwegian soldiers had few opportunities to intervene.

Therefore they were powerless to stop Israelis in the village of Shebaa, to the far east of the area of Norwegian responsibility, when they noticed that 37 inhabitants were being expelled, mostly women and children. The deportation followed another failed attempt to pressure village youth into joining the SLA. The mayor and the elected officials had refused to let the Israelis open a recruiting office there. Israel's answer was to deport citizens and close the roads to the isolated village, which literally clung to the mountainside 1,200 meters over the sea. Shebaa's 10,000 inhabitants were completely dependent on open roads for the transport of goods in and out.

When the expelled Lebanese arrived in West Beirut, journalists were told that UNIFIL had done its utmost to prevent the deportations. The Norwegians had tried to close the road with their white UN-marked vehicles but the Israelis destroyed them, according to the expelled rector of the village school, Yahya Ali.

Colonel Karlsen had personally driven to Shebaa to protest before the SLA men in the village. Later he drove to Israel, where he met Israeli officers in Kiryat Shmona. He declared that Israel had to take responsibility for the deportations. An Israeli lieutenant colonel replied that the IDF had nothing to do with the deportations, and asked the Norwegian to take the matter up with the leaders of the SLA.[7]

"I have heard similar arguments before," answered Karlsen. He referred to Nazi-Germany-occupied Norway, where German officers maintained that their Norwegian collaborators operated on their own. "Germany did not want to take responsibility for what the collaborators did, either. But in the trials after the war, it was made clear that the abuse that occurred were the responsibility of the occupying power," Karlsen continued, "Israel is an occupying power and must take responsibility for what happens inside the area held by the IDF. I am disappointed that you permit clear breaches of the Geneva Conventions by allowing deportations. I suggest you get those expelled back into their homes."

Colonel Karlsen looked carefully at the Israeli officers as he spoke. A few of them blushed; others looked down at the table, or out into the distance. The Norwegian ended by repeating he was disappointed that Israel permitted clear breaches of international law, and reminded them of the many Norwegians who had lost their lives during the Second World War while attempting to prevent Jews from being exposed to abuses that contradicted international law.

There was a short pause after he had delivered his criticism, then the Israeli lieutenant colonel ended the meeting. Karlsen returned to South Lebanon with the belief that those present had been affected by his remarks. But not many hours passed before the Israelis turned their focus away from breaches in international law and toward Karlsen's analogy. The following day, Israeli newspapers and news bureaus wrote that the UNIFIL colonel had compared the Israelis to the Nazis. With that the deportations were forgotten and Karlsen became the news. Demands were made for the Norwegian colonel to be sent home. At UN headquarters in New York, Israel's ambassador was able to get a quick apology from the world organization.[8]

Colonel Karlsen wrote a report to UNIFIL chief Lieutenant General Lars-Eric Wahlgren, in which he maintained he was not surprised at the IDF protest, and summed up his earlier criticism of the Israelis as well as his own complaints against them. Karlsen also wrote, "The Israelis have accused me of being difficult and for being behind a conspiracy against them. This most recent occurrence therefore added to a series of Israeli efforts to pin something on me. I feel I am on firm ground because I have tied my comments to deportations, which, in fact, have occurred."

He wanted the Swedish UNIFIL chief to send out a press release and put emphasis on the deportation of civilians and the contradiction of international law. "I hope there will be notice taken of the abuses which have occurred, in particular, that there are many mentally retarded women and children among those deported. It would not hurt to point out that the population in Finnmark was exposed to this same type of abuse during the Second World War," concluded Karlsen.

But instead of sending out a strong press release, the Force Commander chose to call Karlsen in. When the NORBATT chief reported to Naqoura, he was given a military "reprimand" and told that wording of the reprimand would be made public in the *Jerusalem Post* and in Beirut newspapers.[9]

Karlsen said little. A verbal reprimand struck him as an easy solution. When his subordinates in NORBATT learned of the matter, however they spoke openly of their Swedish boss in Naqoura as a coward. The Beirut newspapers referred quite positively to Karlsen as a brave man who dared to confront his superior.

In Oslo, the head of the Mosaic Faith Community, Rabbi Michael Melchior, wanted to focus on Norwegian anti-semitism instead of on Israel's deportation of civilians. In the *NRK* radio newscast on the evening of February 5, the rabbi said that Colonel Karlsen's remarks were an expression of increasing anti-Jewish sentiment in Norway. He told the newspaper *Arbeiderbladet* that the colonel "fits well with the line of official Norwegian representatives who utter comments which are hostile to the Jews."[10]

In the newspaper *Aftenposten*, on the other hand, Colonel Karlsen was praised for his criticism of the Israelis. A commentary read in part: "It seems, mildly speaking, pathetic when Rabbi Michael Melchior at the Mosaic Faith Community attacks the head of the Norwegian UNIFIL battalion and accuses him of having demonstrated 'anti-Jewish' sentiments. Colonel Jan Erik Karlsen in NORBATT deserves all honor and full credit for having put the Israelis' inhuman advances in the occupied areas in perspective."[11]

The matter also came up in the Norwegian Parliament, where Kåre Kristiansen from the Christian People's Party asked Defense Minister Johan Jørgen Holst the following question: "The head of our UNIFIL forces has publicly put forth accusations against Israel for Nazi-like methods in South Lebanon. Does this coincide with the view of the government, and if not, will the defense minister make sure the colonel in question will be removed from his position as head of UNIFIL?"[12]

Holst responded: "The UN force has both the right and the duty to react and protest against breaches in international law which occur in UNIFIL's area. The deportations have also been reported to the UN, which from its side has taken the matter up with the Israeli government. Norway has also done this, and has asked that actions be undertaken so that the deported persons can return to their homes." Holst would not hear of calling Karlsen home. This would "weaken the authority of the forces and the UN," and the Norwegian authorities did not want this.

Karlsen was happy that his criticism of the Israelis had reached such a level of awareness in Norway. It gave him an opportunity to put the spotlight on the civilian population in the Norwegian UN area.[13]

In Israel, Brigadier General Zeev Zaharin decided to show Colonel Karlsen who was the boss in South Lebanon. He maintained the Norwegian battalion was a springboard for infiltration and attacks, and wanted to teach the Norwegians a lesson. At 1 PM on March 7, several civilian vehicles and a jeep from the Israeli army drove to one of the control posts between the occupation zone and the Norwegian battalion. The Israelis said they wanted to go to Ebl el-Saqi to visit "friends." According to the verbal agreement between UNIFIL and the occupying power, the Israelis could drive to the village, but only in civilian vehicles. The Norwegian UN soldiers at the post therefore refused to let the military jeep through, and blocked the road. After several hours of quarreling, Israeli armored vehicles showed up along with a Centurion tank. Eight UN vehicles were shoved aside, and then the entire column of Israeli military and civilian vehicles entered Ebl el-Saqi. An Israeli brigadier general sat in one of the civilian vehicles, smiling.

The next day, the IDF blocked all UN traffic around the Norwegian battalion. Around midday, after word of the conflict had reached the highest levels, the Israeli Northern Command promised to open the roads in the UN's own operating area. At the same time, the Israeli brigadier general threatened to make things more difficult for all of UNIFIL.

Both the battalion chief and the Defense Minister Johan Jørgen Holst rejected the accusations that NORBATT was a springboard for infiltration. It was an unreasonable claim since the battalion lay entirely within the Israeli occupied area. Holst's Israeli colleague, Yitzhak Rabin, responded that since Norway was not satisfied with the Israeli position, they should get out of UNIFIL. Rabin said the incident at the battalion headquarters was caused by a lack of understanding on the Norwegian side. According to Rabin, the Norwegians should now have learned a lesson that they could not interfere with the Israeli army's every movement.

The UNIFIL Force Commander, Lieutenant General Lars-Eric Wahlgren, and the chief of the Israeli Northern Command, Major General Yossi Peled, got together five days after the confrontation. They agreed to replace the verbal arrangements with written rules, which stated that "Israeli forces may only have access to Ebl el-Saqi in civilian vehicles and only with light weapons— rifles and pistols." There were few in the NORBATT leadership who believed the Israelis would have any greater respect for written rules than verbal ones.

CHAPTER FIFTY
Salma's Fate

A few days later Foreign Minister Thorvald Stoltenberg went to Israel. During his talk with Prime Minister Yitzhak Shamir on April 3, there was no discussion about the harassment of the Norwegian UN soldiers or the Israeli deportations of civilian Lebanese. Stoltenberg did not share Holst's need to lecture the Israelis about breaches of international law, or to point out Israeli abuses. He was more interested in listening. Shamir's colleagues were not surprised Stoltenberg avoided these controversial subjects. In the Foreign Office, Stoltenberg was known to shy away from conflicts.

Shamir did not bring up the subject of the occupation of Lebanon either. He chose to talk about the Palestinians. "If Europe's dream of a Palestinian state becomes a reality, the whole region will be transformed into a new Lebanon," he commented.

Stoltenberg neither agreed nor disagreed, but said that Norway's contacts with the PLO did not imply they were distancing themselves from Israel. When he met with Shimon Peres the next day, he similarly refrained from bringing up questions of the occupation or torture at Khiam, as Holst had done.

The Norwegian foreign minister had previously visited South Lebanon and was well acquainted with what the Israelis were doing there. He knew the Shia village of Blat, which lay at the outskirts of the Norwegian UNIFIL area, was being kept under particularly close surveillance by the Israelis. No one in Blat had joined the SLA; if anyone felt the recruiting pressure, they would simply leave. The village was therefore emptied of young men over time. Some of those youths later carried out a series of attacks against the Israelis and their collaborators.

Blat was conveniently located for resistance groups that came from the north to attack the Israelis or the SLA militia. The guerrillas would reach the village through a valley where the Litani River ran. Norwegian UN soldiers often waited there to catch the infiltrators. Even though according to international law it was legal to attack the occupiers, UNIFIL considered it its obligation to prevent attacks. However, it was not the practice within UNIFIL to hand over resistance fighters to the Israelis or to the militias they ran. Instead they seized infiltrators; took their weapons, interrogated them and escorted them out of the NORBATT area to the so-called "blue line," beyond which the UN had no responsibility. There they were set free, even if this area lay within the Israeli occupation zone.

A Shia from the village of Khiam, Joudad Abdallah, worked for the Shin Bet. His job was to find out what was happening in the area around Blat. One day Abdallah asked for a meeting with the leader of the Norwegian troops in the village. He wanted to discuss "some security matters."

The request was passed on by one of NORBATT's interpreters, Salma Salame, who was from Blat. The Norwegian officer accepted gladly to meet the man from Shin Bet, but the meeting had to occur outside the UN camp in Blat. Salma agreed the meeting could be held at her home in the village.

She was actually surprised that the Norwegian lieutenant was willing to meet an Israeli henchman who did their dirty work for them. She knew well that it was not good practice for a troop leader to discuss problems with Shin Bet or the SLA. It was the task of the observers from UNTSO's own liaison team. During the meeting, Salma did not participate in the conversation; she only translated. Even when the Norwegian lieutenant revealed UN procedures used when stopping infiltrators, she did not remark that it was unwise to give such information.[14]

The Shin Bet officer thought the Norwegians should turn infiltrators over to them, and not just escort them north to the border of the Norwegian UN area.

"If you turn the terrorists over to us, there will be an end to the attacks, and you will be able to do the job you were meant to do, namely to assure calm and order," he said.

"It is not our job to turn over anyone to you at all," answered the Norwegian lieutenant.

After the meeting, Shin Bet's henchman thought he had proof that Salma was participating in the process of letting infiltrators slip into the "security zone." It was she who translated when they were interrogated by Norwegian officers. Joudad Abdallah accused her of collaborating with the resistance movement. He would not accept she was merely an interpreter, and that NORBATT was following orders from UNIFIL HQ.

A few days later, a group of Palestinians managed to reach Marjayoun, south of Blat without being observed by neither the Israelis, the SLA militia nor the Norwegian UN soldiers. In Marjayoun, however, the Palestinians were spotted and taken prisoner. During interrogations, it came out that they had snuck through Blat, where they had also received help. The Israelis subsequently arrested dozens of people there, among them Salma's brother Nazih, who was studying to be an electrical engineer in Beirut and was home on a weekend visit. The 19-year-old was accused of having been part of the planning for an attack. This was not true: he did not belong to any fighting group.

On July 11, Salma received a message the Shin Bet's leader in Khiam, Riyad Abdallah, for a meeting. He was not permitted to come to Blat, but Salma was invited to his office in Khiam. The office was in the village several hundred meters from the prison center where Salma's brother was being held.

"There is no pressure, it is up to you if you want to come and explain yourself," Salma was told. "Also, nothing has happened to your brother. He will be released; it is only a matter of some investigation," explained the messenger.[15]

Salma got into a civilian car and left Blat through the UNIFIL control post. The soldier at the post checked the car carefully to be sure that she was not being taken by force. Since Salma thought she was just on her way to a meeting, she gave no sign that anything was abnormal. She had never met Riyad Abdallah before, but knew the Abdallah family had cooperated with the Israelis for many years.

When Salma arrived at Riyad Abdallah's office, a guard told her to empty her purse, and wrote down the contents. Only then did she understand she was being arrested. Looking out the car window on her way to the prison, she thought, "This is perhaps the last time I will see this landscape."

In Khiam two female guards met her, put a black hood over her head and brought her to the toilet, where she had to undress. Then she was taken to a cell and told to sit still and wait. Salma recognized the faces of the guards; one was from Bourj el-Molouk, the other from Qleia.

She was interrogated and tortured. She experienced a living death. Afternoons were the worst: she could see the sun going down through a small window and could hear children playing outside the walls. Children, laughing and playing, symbolized life. She and the others in the prison, on the other hand, were forgotten. It was only a few meters between the children and the prisoners, between life and death. Regardless who the children were, rich or poor, happy or unhappy—so long as they were out there, they were alive.

Salma had nothing to do but think and prepare herself for new rounds of torture. She did not know what was happening at home. Her brother sat in a cell a few hundred meters away, and did not know his sister was undergoing the same nightmare as he. Salma's other close relatives were disappointed to find that neither the leadership in NORBATT nor at UNIFIL headquarters in Naqoura took any steps to free them.

In Beirut, the entire spring of 1989 saw heavy artillery duels between Brigadier General Michel Aoun's forces and the opposition supported by Syria. The general had gotten control over the Christian militia, Lebanese Forces, led by Samir Geagea, and now wanted to force the Syrians out of West Beirut. From his bunker under the Presidential Palace, the general, dressed in an American field uniform, proclaimed that Lebanon should become "like the USA, like France."

Aoun had Saddam Hussein backing him. Ammunition and weapons from Iraq, including ground-to-ground missiles, arrived through the Jordanian port of Aqaba.[16] Leaders in Washington were worried and wanted an end to the weapons deliveries. US Ambassador April Glaspie was instructed to put pressure on the regime in Baghdad. To emphasize their seriousness, the US sent a warship to the coast of Lebanon.

In Beirut, conditions for the civilian population were becoming so difficult that Sunni Muslim Prime Minister Salim el-Hoss, who headed the competing administration, suggested that both he and Aoun resign.

"I implore everyone who is carrying weapons to show mercy to the people and let the weapons rest immediately. Stop, stop this massacre," Hoss said in a radio appeal.

The appeal did not help. Aoun's forces fired artillery at Syrian positions in West Beirut and in the Bekaa Valley. Both sides used tanks in fighting not far from the airport. The residences of the American, French, Belgian and Brazilian ambassadors were hit.

Aoun sharpened his rhetoric against the Syrian president. "What is left is to crush Assad's head. Lebanon will become his and his regime's graveyard," said the general.[17]

On April 13, the Lebanese were reminded it had been exactly 14 years since the civil war broke out. Around 100,000 Lebanese and Palestinians had been killed thus far, and twice as many wounded. Additionally, about 17,000 people had been kidnapped by various militia groups never to be seen again. It was assumed they had been killed. A series of committees were set up to try to find those lost, without any results.[18]

Even if the Lebanese fought against each other, the civil war was also a regional war. It was a war of identity, of belonging, of who would dominate, but also a war of what position Israel would have in the Middle East. While ongoing, it was difficult to grasp the context. The war in many ways could be compared with a chemical process that only becomes active when one element comes in contact with another. The civil war could also not have raged for 14 years if it had not been supplied from the outside. And in that context the theory of Prussian General Karl von Clausewitz pops up, namely, that war is simply nothing but a continuation of politics by other means.

In a new attempt to put an end to the war, the Arab League called its members together for a crisis meeting in Tunis on April 29. A committee was formed—a six nation committee to support Lebanon. Everyone asked if the time was not ripe to put an end to the bloodbath. Or was the Arab League just as impotent as it had proven to be before?

Ayatollah Khomeini became ill in the middle of May 1989 and died two weeks later. He was 86 years old. Speculation began immediately if the Islamic revolution's leader had left behind a political testament, and what importance that would have for Lebanon. The ayatollah had a message that he wanted his son Ahmad to read. Ahmad refused, however, and it became the task of President Ali Khamenei to address the people by radio and television.

In his testament, he stated that the Iranian revolution was a gift of God, and that it was unique. The Iranian people and the Muslims of the world had to protect this divine guardianship against the Americans and the Russians. The US was labeled a "terrorist state" and the Soviet Union as a "Satanic force, hostile to Islam."[19]

Khomeini's glass coffin was placed in the square where Friday prayers were normally said in the northern section of Tehran. Thousands of people beat their hands against their breasts and heads in mourning as they filed past the body. By midday emotions took the upper hand, and in the chaos that followed, eight people were trampled to death and 500 were injured. The next day Khomeini was buried in the Behesht Zahra Cemetery in Tehran.

After the ayatollah's death, a suggestion was made for a triumvirate to lead the country, but the so-called council of experts disapproved, and President Ali Khamenei was chosen to be the Supreme Leader. Khamenei was the son of a cleric from the city of Mashhad in Eastern Iran. He had been chosen as the country's president in 1981, after a bomb killed the sitting president, Mohammed Ali Rajai. Khamenei was known as a mullah with an open mind. He had even felt Khomeini's anger when he asked if Iran should have only one leader at the top. Now he was at the top himself with sovereign power.

CHAPTER FIFTY ONE

Truths and Lies

In Lebanon, Hizbullah's leaders and members closely followed the power struggle developing in Iran after Khomeini's death. Sheikh Abdel Karim Obeid in the village of Jibsheet was no exception. He had taken over as the village imam after Ragheb Harb was killed in 1984 by the Israelis' henchmen, among them Hussein Abbas, whose code name within Shin Bet was "Khomeini."

When the Israeli government approved a military plan in July 1989 that increased the number of Lebanese hostages, it figured Sheikh Obeid could be a valuable prisoner. He could perhaps provide some insight into the kidnapping of the American Lieutenant Colonel William Higgins and what had happened to Ron Arad?

The officer tasked with kidnapping the sheikh wanted to have someone involved who was known locally. Hussein Abbas was chosen. He had carried out several kidnappings and killings on Israeli orders, and was dependable according to his superiors in Shin Bet. For a period he had stayed in an Israeli barracks in South Lebanon and carried out his activity together with selected agents.[20]

It was his long beard that led him to choose the code name Khomeini when speaking on the field radio—somewhat in jest, since he was in fact Shia. The beard was useful camouflage when he operated outside the occupation zone: he could easily be seen as one of Hizbullah's or Amal's bearded supporters. The Israeli officers also called Hussein "the American" because he had been in the US and spoke English well.

When Abbas returned from his stay in the US, he had visited the new religious leader in the village, Sheikh Abdel Karim Obeid, and wanted to know who had killed his father, Ali. The sheikh invited him to his home, but did not answer the question. Afterward Abbas remained convinced that Obeid's men were behind the killing. He left Jibsheet with the Israelis in 1985 when the IDF withdrew to the south.

One day in July 1989, Abbas was called to a meeting in the Israeli town of Kiryat Shmona and briefed on the operation. Israeli special forces were to be brought at night in two helicopters and land outside Jibsheet. From there they would go on foot into the village, but Abbas was not told whether the Israelis were going to kill or kidnap Sheikh Obeid.

During the briefing, a large aerial photo was displayed of the area in Jibsheet where the sheikh lived. Abbas pointed out the sheikh's house and described what it looked like inside. He was surprised when one of the helicopter pilots asked what the people of Jibsheet lived on. They grew tobacco, olives and other agricultural products, he said, astounded that a pilot could be interested in such everyday matters while planning a deadly and dangerous attack.

The night of July 29, Abbas was picked up and brought to one of the helicopters, which took off from the base in Kiryat Shmona. Barely an hour past midnight the Israelis flew into Lebanon and northward through the valley toward Beaufort. Then the helicopter turned sharply to the west and landed in a valley just outside Jibsheet.

Sheikh Obeid was sleeping heavily when he awoke around 2 am by the noise of the Israeli jets. When he later heard the sound of helicopters, he thought they must have been UNIFIL's and did not imagine that Israeli soldiers were on their way to Jibsheet.

The Israelis approached Obeid's house from two directions. When they arrived, the soldiers put up lightweight ladders and climbed up to the sheikh's veranda. There they forced open the door into his bedroom. Obeid barely glimpsed the armed men pointing weapons at him before they knocked him out with an injection and carried him out of the house. His wife and children were locked inside a room.

When one of the neighbors opened his door to see what was happening, he was killed on the spot. The family contacted one of Amal's leaders, and later a cry for help went out over the loudspeakers in the minaret. By then the helicopters were long gone.

When the injection wore off and Obeid awoke, he asked, "What time is it?"[21] He was told it was 12:30. At first the sheikh thought he had been dreaming. Then he noticed the people around him were Israelis, but he did not understand where he was. He had not thought that he would be a target for them. He was only Jibsheet's religious leader, and he was mediating conflicts between Hizbullah and Amal. True, he urged Shias to use all their power in the fight against the occupation and not to kill each other. But that could not have been the reason for his kidnapping?

The Israelis had quite another idea about this man: they thought Obeid belonged to Hizbullah's leadership. In order not to give Obeid time to collect himself, the interrogation began immediately. The first questions concerned the Israeli air force navigator, Ron Arad, and the two Israeli soldiers who had been captured by Hizbullah in 1986.

Obeid pretended he was in a daze and that he did not understand what they were talking about. In order to gain time, and seek God's help, he said, "I cannot speak before I have prayed."

The officer refused: "There will be no prayers before you have talked." But then he changed his mind and said, "You may pray."

"I have to wash myself first," Obeid continued. "I can say nothing until I have washed myself and prayed." They took him to a cell where he showered and prayed. Then the interrogation began again. The sheikh felt better. He had won the first round by getting what he wanted.

The Israeli military powers waited 14 hours before they sent out an announcement saying that the Sheikh was responsible for Hizbullah activities in South Lebanon. He had been arrested because he was a *provocateur*, and had planned attacks against Israel. The Israelis insisted Obeid had also been involved in the kidnapping of William Higgins in February 1988. Obeid denied that he was a member of Hizbullah, but did admit that he had said in a sermon that Higgins had spied for the US while working as a peace observer.

Many condemned the kidnapping of the sheikh. The Iranian foreign ministry announced, "the kidnapping was a clear example of state terrorism." Even the new US President George Bush was critical, saying at a press conference that "I do not think kidnapping and violence help to bring peace." He added, "I think a lot about getting Colonel Higgins and the other hostages set free, but I am uncertain if the kidnapping of Obeid will be an advantage or not for an exchange of prisoners."[22]

In Lebanon the Organization of the World's Oppressed sent a typewritten statement in Arabic to western news bureaus on July 30, threatening to hang the kidnapped Lieutenant Colonel William Higgins if Obeid was not released before 3 pm the next day. The Israeli government said it would not release the Shia cleric even if this meant several western hostages would be killed. Instead, it repeated that Obeid would be released as part of a comprehensive series of hostage releases. At this point, there were 17 western hostages in Lebanon.

The next day news bureaus in Beirut received a typed announcement that Higgins had been executed. A videocassette was included with the announcement.

A few hours later in the *NRK* offices in Oslo, I also was able to see the 30-second recording, which was divided in two parts. The first 15 seconds showed a barefoot man dressed in a gymsuit with his ankles bound together. The camera was tilted up and revealed his body slowly swinging from a rope around his neck in a primitive gallows. Just half his face was visible, and his eyes were covered with a white blindfold. In the second part of the recording, the blindfold had been removed, and the face was clearly visible with two swollen eyes. There was no question it was William Higgins.

The videocassette and the typed message had been delivered around 4 pm. Beirut time. The note said that Higgins had been hanged one hour earlier, and that "since the criminal America and the Zionist enemy did not take seriously our decision to execute the American spy Higgins, and since Sheikh Abdel Karim Obeid [...] had not been set free within the deadline, we executed Higgins by hanging precisely at 3 pm."

Only a few minutes after the deadline had expired, Defense Minister Yitzhak Rabin announced that Israel was willing to release Lebanese Shias if all Israelis in Lebanese captivity and the western hostages were similarly set free. Rabin had intentionally waited until the deadline had passed, but said at his press conference that he did not know if Higgins was dead or alive.

In the US, the video of Higgins was studied carefully. Experts were unsure if he had actually been hanged. Earlier messages indicated that a guard had killed him in anger after the American warship USS Vincennes shot down an Iranian passenger plane and all onboard lost their lives. I spent some time investigating this drama, which had occurred in the Persian Gulf the year before. Even though the matter had nothing to do with Lebanon, I read everything I could find about it. The story was fascinating, and said something about the Americans' method of waging war.

Captain Will Rogers of the Vincennes was shaving when his telephone rang on July 3, 1988. The captain took the phone and heard the watch officer say, "Skipper, it is best you come down. It sounds like the Montgomery has stuck its nose into an anthill."[23] That July morning the Americans had observed several Iranian gunboats some 50 nautical miles northeast of where the frigate USS Elmer Montgomery was sailing through the western inlet to the Strait of Hormuz.

Every day giant oil tankers went through the strait, which was just 54 kilometers at its narrowest point. Gunboats belonging to the Iranian Revolutionary Guards would occasionally attack ship traffic going to and from Kuwait from bases on the islands of Hengam and Abu Musa. The US wanted to keep Kuwait's oil production going and escorted tankers that had been re-registered under the US flag.

A Seahawk helicopter flew from the Vincennes for a closer inspection. After 20 minutes the helicopter was over the Iranians. The pilots said the gunboats were circling a German cargo ship, while firing across its bow in harassment. On-board the Vincennes, Captain Rogers gave orders for battle stations, and sent the crew to ship side to be ready if they were attacked with light weapons. Previously the ship had held a dubious reputation in the US navy; it had been given the nickname "Robocruiser," and Captain Rogers was referred to as "trigger-happy."

A little before 9 AM, the Omani coast guard gave the Iranian Revolutionary Guards orders to pull back to Iran. The Omanis also insisted the Americans leave the area, and sent out the message, "American Naval Vessel, maneuvers at speeds up to 30 knots do not constitute normal passage. Please leave Omani territorial waters." The American officers on-board the Vincennes just laughed scornfully and did not even bother to answer while they maneuvered the ship into Iranian waters.

Around 55 nautical miles northwest of the American ship, Captain Mohsen Rezaian was at the controls of an Iran Air Airbus that was ready to take off from the strip at Bandar Abbas airport. The captain was set to start on the second leg of his route from Tehran to Bandar Abbas to Dubai. On-board were 290 passengers from six countries, among them 66 children. The plane left Bandar Abbas at 10:17, some 27 minutes behind schedule. The flying time was set for 28 minutes.

At the same moment Captain Rogers was in his windowless control room midship on the Vincennes, directing the mini-sea battle against the Iranian gunboats. Neither he nor Rezaian realized the passenger plane's route would take it right over the American missile cruiser.

The Vincennes' powerful radar registered a distant blip as the Iran Air plane took off from Bandar Abbas. And even though Flight 655 made the run from Tehran to Dubai twice weekly, the blip registered automatically as a "presumed hostile" because Bandar Abbas was both a civilian and a military airport. Somewhat later the alarm went off on-board. The plane was on course for the Vincennes and could be an Iranian F-14 fighter jet.

Captain Rogers was completely absorbed by the battle with the gunboats. He shouted that those firing should reload faster, and gave orders for a sharp turn to starboard. The ship had gone in a circle, and Captain Rogers was able to aim a cannon at the Iranian boats. They had fired five shots when the cannon froze. The skipper gave the order, "hard to Port!" The ship swung so sharply that books and papers fell from the console table.

On the control screen to his left, Captain Rogers saw that the plane was approaching. Rogers had previously decided the ship's radar should make note of all planes that came within a 30-mile radius; at 20 miles, the plane would be shot down. However, Rogers was now uncertain whether there was an air attack taking place. The plane was too high—over 7,000 feet. The officers looking at the radar screen thought for sure this was a fighter jet coming toward them. They sent out three warnings over the radio before Captain Rogers gave orders to fire two SM-2ER missiles at the plane.

On-board the passenger plane, which was now 10 nautical miles away, Captain Rezaian radioed to the control tower at Bandar Abbas that he had reached his first reporting point in the Persian Gulf. He had not heard any of the American warnings because they were sent over the wrong frequency to a nonexistent Iranian F-14. The captain of the plane only heard the voice from the control tower, which said, "Have a nice day."

He responded, "Thanks, the same to you."

A few seconds later the missiles struck. The passenger plane was hit at a height of 13,500 feet, eight nautical miles away from the ship, and it fell in flames into the sea. From the lookout posts on-board the Vincennes, everyone could see the plane was not an F-14, and some miles away the crew of the Montgomery saw the wing of a civilian aircraft fall into the sea.

There was silence aboard the Vincennes. The crew stopped firing at the gunboats of the Revolutionary Guards, which now were more than five kilometers away. Captain Rogers gave orders to go south, out of Iranian waters.

A few hours later Admiral William Crowe, Chairman of the Joint Chiefs of Staff, was behind the podium in the Pentagon press room, stating that a terrible accident had occurred. The admiral, dressed in his summer whites, emphasized that he did not have all the information, but said that the Iranian passenger plane had not responded to repeated warnings. Further, he said the Iranian aircraft was four nautical miles outside the civilian air corridor. This last piece was not true.[24]

He went on to say the plane was descending and had increased its speed when it approached the Vincennes. This was also not true. On a large map he pointed out the position of the Vincennes when the missiles were fired. It was also not the true position. In the Persian Gulf, Iranian helicopters and boats searched in vain for survivors amid the wreckage. They found only corpses in terrible condition. The following day thousands of people marched through Tehran's streets. Some carried flag-draped coffins over their heads while the people shouted, "Death to America!" "Death to Reagan!" "Revenge! Revenge!" Iranian and foreign journalists following the march reported seeing faces twisted with rage and sorrow. Similar funeral processions took place in other Iranian cities.

President Ali Khamenei said "the presence of Americans in the Persian Gulf was equivalent to war," and shooting down a passenger plane was one of war's "worst crimes." Ayatollah Khomeini challenged his people to fight against America and her lackeys. At the UN, Iran's envoy compared the event to the tragedy when the Soviet air force shot down Korean Air Lines 007 over the Sea of Japan in 1983.[25]

At the White House, Vice President George Bush was chosen to defend the United States before the Security Council. During the preparations for his remarks, however, it was nearly impossible to get hard facts out of the Pentagon. Bush's chief of staff was warned against letting the vice president express himself too precisely in front of the Security Council. At his appearance, Bush spoke mostly of the need to put an end to the war between Iran and Iraq. When he got to the plane incident, he repeated the lies from Crowe's press conference and put forward new ones: the vice president maintained the Vincennes had sailed off to protect a merchant vessel that was being attacked by Iran.

The Pentagon had all the facts on July 14, 1988, when Bush spoke to the Security Council. Recordings of the conversations on-board the Vincennes and all of its navigational data had been sent to the US on July 5 and reported to the Pentagon five days later. The Vincennes had been in Iranian waters. The Iranian passenger plane was well inside the civilian corridor and was climbing, not descending.

While fact-checking the story, I took note of a quotation from Nietzsche that hung over my desk: "The State does not tend toward the truth, but only toward useful truth—more precisely, whatever is useful to the State, be it truth, half-truth or lies." One hundred and fourteen years after Nietzsche wrote these words, they remained valid.

CHAPTER FIFTY TWO
Diplomacy and Presidential Murder

One year later, at the beginning of July, 1989, Lebanese newspapers reported that a shipment of Frog-7 ground-to-ground missiles was on its way to General Aoun in East Beirut. These missiles had a range that could reach Damascus. The Syrian navy had been alerted and had boarded the freighter on its way to Beirut and Jounieh.[26]

They ramped up their bombardment of East Beirut and sent reinforcements to the area around the Christian enclave. In the middle of August, the forces went on attack. The Syrians mainly wanted to capture the strategic village of Souk el-Gharb in the mountains above West Beirut and the airport, which was in Aoun's hands. The Druze militia and the PLO guerrillas fought on the Syrian side.

Brigadier General Aoun sought help from the Israelis, the real counter force to Syria in Lebanon. But Israeli officials were not impressed by the rebel officers's "war of liberation." One senior Israeli characterized Aoun's performance as "obtuse." Aoun, without prior consultation, was trying to change the regional strategic environment and had no realistic prospects for success. The US also advised Israel not to get involved in Aoun's affairs.[27]

Aoun complained that the US had "sold Lebanon to Syria." His supporters surrounded the embassy, where the diplomats felt their lives were in danger. Aoun said the Americans needed "a dose of Christian terrorism." In an interview with the French newspaper Le Figaro, the general implied his soldiers might take "20 Americans as hostages."[28] The Americans answered by closing the embassy in East Beirut and moving the staff to Damascus. A few days later, Aoun accused the American State Department of putting out "rumors" and "half-truths."[29]

Artillery shells were exploding at the same time over large parts of Beirut. The center of West Beirut was nearly unrecognizable. Nearly 40 percent of the population there had fled the area. The Commodore Hotel was no longer a hotel, but a concrete shell that smelled of urine and garbage. What for a generation of correspondents had been "the temple of truth," had suffered the same fate as so many other buildings in Beirut.

But still, the brass plate from Cairo-based correspondents thanking the hotel staff for their work during the Israeli bombardment in 1982 was still fastened to the wall in the lobby. The big, round bar with its red, vinyl-clad stools was still there as well. Otherwise, most everything else was gone. Syrian soldiers had set up a post in the building and guarded the street outside. In some of the West Beirut restaurants and bars that stayed open during the bombardments, guests recognized napkins, tablecloths, chairs and other things from the Commodore.

Defense Minister Johan Jørgen Holst left Oslo for New York in the fall of 1989 to discuss UNIFIL and Lebanon with the UN leadership. Holst used the occasion also to meet the US National Security Advisor, Lieutenant General Brent Scowcroft, on September 21. The general had just come from a meeting between President Bush and Soviet Foreign Minister Eduard Shevardnadze.

Scowcroft said the US had now gained confidence that Arab diplomacy could succeed in Lebanon. The US and Israel no longer demanded that Syria withdraw its forces from the country. He was able to say that President Bush had called the Pope to get him to put pressure on the Christian leaders in Lebanon. According to Scowcroft there were now possibilities for a long-lasting ceasefire in the country.[30]

The Saudis had been the drivers of Arab efforts, and about one week later, elected representatives from Lebanon arrived in the Saudi Arabian mountain town of Taif. Of the 99 representatives of the National Assembly elected in 1972, only 73 were still alive. Of these, 62 came to Taif. Eight did not show up for political reasons, but for personal ones, and three Shia deputies boycotted the Sunni Muslim Kingdom because Hizbullah's radio station had asked all the Shia representatives to stay away. A few months earlier the Saudis had executed several Shias following a bomb attack in Mecca. However, only three representatives complied.

In Taif, the Saudis and the Americans began to work in concert on the Christian representatives. After two weeks of intense discussions, they reached general agreement on a document that could end the civil war in the country.

The document of national reconciliation was a final version of an earlier, stillborn proposal to improve on the unwritten national pact of 1943 and the original constitution of 1926. The goal was to establish a fairer balance of power between the various Lebanese groups—in short, to reduce the prominence of the Maronites over the others.

At the heart of the negotiations in 1943 was the Christians' fear of being overwhelmed by the Muslim communities in Lebanon and the surrounding Arab countries, and the Muslims' fear of Western hegemony. In return for the Christian promise not to seek foreign, i.e., French, protection and to accept Lebanon's "Arab face," the Muslim side agreed to recognize the independence and legitimacy of the Lebanese state in its 1920 boundaries and to renounce aspirations for union with Syria.

In the new document, Lebanon's identity was more strongly tied to the country's Arab environment. The formulation "belong to the Arabs," replaced the phrase "Arab face" in the National Pact. At the same time it was emphasized that Lebanon belonged to all the citizens of the country—an assurance to the Maronites that Lebanon would never be drawn into a larger Arab entity.

The final goal was to put an end to the political division by religious group. The president would continue to be Maronite, the prime minister a Sunni, and the National Assembly president Shia. But the president's power was reduced in favor of the prime minister and National Assembly, which now would have 128 representatives, with just as many Muslims as Christians. Previously, there were six elected Christians for every five Muslims in the legislative branch.

The agreement in Taif also established the dissolution of all militia. At the same time, Syrian forces were permitted to remain in the country for a limited time. The Americans supported the Syrians "assisting" the Lebanese in the effort to enhance sovereignty over the entire country. It did not mean the US would permit Syrian forces to fight against the Israelis in South Lebanon. The Syrians could only "assist" in areas that were under Aoun's control.

The brigadier general, who continued to occupy the Presidential Palace, was thereby more isolated than ever before. But he still had supporters in East Beirut, and in the days following the signing of the Taif agreement, Christian sympathizers gathered nearly every day outside the palace. Toward the end of October 1989, the crowd had grown to 10,000. They applauded when Aoun said the Taif agreement took away Lebanon's sovereignty, and only "repaired a rotten regime."[31]

Fearing the agreement would disintegrate like so many others had before, the Americans and Saudis gathered the elected representatives for a meeting in Lebanon. The representatives assembled at an airstrip in the Syrian-controlled North Lebanon, where they could elect a new president on a formal basis. On November 5, 1989, they voted in a Maronite, René Muawwad from Zgharta, who had a seat in the National Assembly. Muawwad had been one of three possible candidates whom the Syrians found acceptable during discussion with the Saudis. He was also the preferred candidate of the US.

Parallel with efforts to finally end the civil war, the US looked to the UN for a solution to the unfortunate hostage affair. President George Bush asked the UN Secretary-General to contact Iran's newly elected president, Ali Akbar Hashemi Rafsanjani. Bush said he had some thoughts he wanted to convey to the Iranian president. Rafsanjani had taken over the presidency after Ali Khamenei had been named Iran's new religious leader.

It fell to an Italian UN diplomat to make contact with the Iranians. Giandomenico Picco had been the political advisor in 1976 to the UN peacekeeping force in Cyprus. The force's mission was to prevent fighting between Greek and Turkish Cypriots. The secretary-general had also used him for difficult missions in Afghanistan and the Middle East, and in an attempt to end the war between Iran and Iraq. Picco went immediately to the White House to find out more from Brent Scowcroft.[32]

Fourteen days later, he flew to Tehran in secret, carrying a message from the UN secretary-general. In the message, the UN leader said he knew that the Bush administration wanted a better relationship with Iran. If the hostages were set free, the US would release all Iranian deposits in American banks—billions of dollars that had been frozen after the occupation of the US Embassy in Tehran in 1979.

When Rafsanjani met Picco on August 25, 1989, the diplomat felt the president was not particularly interested in helping him. Rafsanjani said, "We have had no relations for some time with those who are holding the hostages. They are Hizbullah. When we were asked by Mr McFarlane, we did try to contact them. After the promises were not carried out, those groups became alienated. We cannot establish one-way relations. Those people are not easy to find. They do not have an address." [33]

For Picco, this was a surprise. The UN diplomat knew Rafsanjani had told Pakistan's foreign minister that he was ready to help the US. The condition was that Washington to demonstrate that it was no longer hostile toward the Islamic Republic. Now Rafsanjani said Iran was not ready to help the US until the kidnapped Sheikh Obeid from Jibsheet was set free. Iran, like the US, had its own interests to take care of.

"For us to help the US, we need signals," said Rafsanjani. "Bush can unfreeze the assets," he continued, "And if they cannot do that, they should also know that we too have Iranian hostages in Lebanon. Bush could help us by pressing the Maronite community, which is holding our hostages." The leader in Tehran had not forgotten the kidnapping of four Iranians with diplomatic passports who were on their way to the Iranian Embassy in West Beirut the summer of 1982. "The release of our hostages would be seen as an incentive for us," Rafsanjani added, and made a point to say he had accepted this message from the Americans because he had respect for the UN secretary-general, not for the Americans.

Rafsanjani was a true trader and this was his opening bid. He had to step carefully, because his opponents inside the Iranian regime were strong. During an extended period while he was president of the National Assembly, and now the president of the country as a whole, he had tried to limit the power of the Iranian Revolutionary Guards.

In Norway there was an election campaign. A new system of proportional representation had been established that increased the number of seats in the National Assembly. And when the vote was in, the supporters of the non-socialist, center-right parties were jubilant. Prime Minister Gro Harlem Brundtland yielded her position to Conservative Party member Jan Peder Syse. Together with the Christian People's Party and the Left, the Conservatives formed a government. In the Foreign Office, Kjell Magne Bondevik took over from Thorvald Stoltenberg. The friendly transfer took place October 16, 1989.

Some five weeks later, on the National Holiday of November 22, Lebanon's President René Muawwad was set to give his first speech as president. On his 16th day in office, Muawwad declared from the podium, "There is no dignity in a country without unity. There can be no unity without an agreement. Without reconciliation there can be no agreement. There can be no reconciliation without forgiveness and compromise."

Muawwad's enemies were not inclined to compromise, or even to let the president live, and assassins were ready. When Muawwad's bulletproof car arrived in the Sanayeh district of West

Beirut, a 200–300 kilo bomb exploded where it had been hid in a small building nearby. René Muawwad and 23 others were killed in the explosion.

The CIA thought that Michel Aoun was behind the killing because he was against any national reconciliation. By eliminating the pro-Syrian president, Aoun might have thought he could weaken Syria's prestige, as well as the prestige of those Lebanese Christians who wanted compromise with the Muslims. In a secret report, the CIA said that Aoun had previously talked about using "unconventional tactics" to promote his interests. The Americans thought he was behind a wave of car bombings in the Christian enclave. Some of the bombs exploded outside the homes of Christian parliamentarians who had gone to Taif.[34]

Others pointed the finger at Syria. The president had been killed in the Syrian-controlled area of West Beirut. Muawwad had refused to order an attack on Aoun in the Presidential Palace.

Two days after the assassination, Elias Hraoui from Zahle was elected the new president. A CIA situation report noted that Damascus viewed Hraoui as a defender of the Taif agreement. The Americans thought the Syrians would go to great lengths to prevent a new tragedy.

One of the first things President Hraoui did was to formally dissolve Aoun's government. He also ordered the general to move from the Presidential Palace. Aoun refused. He felt safe, ruling Baabda and the rest of the enclave that encompassed East Beirut, and he was intent on fighting.

Hraoui was in no hurry. First, the new government proclaimed a partial economic boycott of the area under Aoun's control. Supplies of gasoline, heating oil, weapons, ammunition and spare parts were halted. The head of the army, Lieutenant General Emile Lahoud, appealed to the ranks and officers who continued to support Aoun that they should come over to President Hraoui. This had little effect.

CHAPTER FIFTY THREE

In the Shadow of Khiam

In October 1989, the prisoners in the Khiam torture center had enough of the terrible treatment they were subjected to. Some began to bang on their cell doors and shout "*Allahu Akbar! Allahu Akbar!*" The unrest spread from cell to cell and to the women's section as well.

The prison chief with the wolf's gaze known as Abu Nabil stormed into the women's section and grabbed Kifah Afifi, the Palestinian guerrilla soldier who had been taken captive the previous year not far from the border with Israel. Afifi, who was now 18 years old, was dragged from her cell to the guardroom and thrown into the lit fireplace. He then pulled her out again, more frightened than injured, and ordered her to tell all the other women to end their protest. She refused and was beaten nearly unconscious by the guards.[35]

In the male section, things were worse. The guards shot teargas into the cells. Informants placed in with the prisoners shouted and begged to be let out. The teargas was choking, and two of the prisoners did not survive. After the disturbance had been put down, its suspected leaders were tortured in the worst way. Among them was Suleiman Ramadan, whom the Israelis had captured in 1985 and mistreated badly.

When the Israelis arrived and heard what had happened, conditions improved to a certain degree for the women. They were given old Israeli sleeping bags and proper, covered toilet buckets. The men, however, still used the old buckets and were only allowed to empty them once a week.

Within the Norwegian UN battalion, leadership was upset that the Lebanese in the Israeli services were harassing Norwegian soldiers on guard duty. Without provocation, Lebanese in Shin Bet had threatened the Norwegians with their pistols.[36] In November 1989, a confrontation arose near a control post by Ebl el-Saqi, where an exchange of fire killed one Lebanese tied to the SLA. His relatives swore revenge.

When five young Norwegian UN soldiers were getting ready to patrol a stretch of roadway between the villages of Kaukaba and Bourghoz on the afternoon of November 29, they had no reason to suspect an act of vengeance. There had been gunfire in the area earlier that day, so the soldiers were well prepared and took their task seriously. An Israeli base above Kaukaba had fired against the Hizbullah guerrillas further north. They had used artillery and had brought in new equipment through the NORBATT zone.[37]

A thunderstorm was underway when the five Norwegians drove their white armored vehicle from the base above Kaukaba at 4:30 PM. Their first task was to check for hidden bombs along the roadway, which wound over a gentle hill and past an Israeli artillery base before turning down toward the Litani valley and Bourghoz.

Twenty-three-year-old Rune Opland from Mosjøen was on the patrol. He had arrived in Lebanon one week before, and had just sent home his first letter, in which he wrote: "I am living on the top of a mountain, and below us there is a village which is called Kaukaba. We live in barracks, and they are quite nice. We get good food, but we buy a lot ourselves. Outside of where we live, traders come every day to sell us all sorts of things, from films on video to clothing and chocolate."[38]

The vehicle first went to the outermost Norwegian position in the UN area, a white stone house surrounded by barbed wire. The time was nearing 5 PM and it was dark when Corporal Torfinn Sollund from Fauske got out of the armored vehicle and went to the right side of the road. Rune Opland followed 15 meters behind on the opposite side. Both of them had powerful flashlights.[39]

The vehicle followed some 40 meters back, a searchlight fixed to the machine gun. Above the light fluttered the blue UN flag. Corporal Jo Inge Øverland sat at the machine gun, Lieutenant Ulf Larsen was further back in the hatch and Bjørn Stornes drove.

Half a kilometer away lay a curve in the road and the first house in Bourghoz. The village clung to the edge of the Litani gorge. The Lebanese resistance movement used the passage in the cliff below the village to place roadside bombs or to shoot missiles at the occupiers and their allies.

The Norwegians had nearly reached the curve when Sollund noticed something in the roadway. He gave a signal to stop. He then carefully approached and shone his flashlight on the object. It was an empty cardboard box, so Sollund gave the signal for the patrol to continue.

Shortly after came the explosion. Sollund saw a flash of light he thought was an antitank missile. Automatic weapons fire erupted, with bullets whistling past his ears and whipping up sand and stones from the gravel road. Sollund got down on one knee as he had been trained to do. In the light from the explosion he saw that Opland had also crouched down and was holding onto his helmet.

From the vehicle's steering hatch, Stornes saw flames from the muzzles of the attacker' guns and the hail of sparks from the projectiles that hit the road around Sollund and Opland. Several bullets struck the steel plating around the hatch where his head stuck out. Stornes grabbed the release to lower his seat, but it did not work.

After some seconds all went quiet—then the next missile hit. It detonated just beside the vehicle and the concussion was deafening. Stornes reacted instinctively, shifting into reverse and backing up blindly. Seconds later another missile exploded, followed by more machine gunfire. Bullets flew everywhere. There was another pause and then yet another missile went off.

Sollund thought it was safest to take cover in the vehicle. He looked around for Opland, but could not see him. He began to run after the armored vehicle as it backed off. He could hear the noise of the bullets hitting the armor plating. When he reached the vehicle, he banged his hand against his helmet to signal to the driver he wanted in. Seconds later he threw himself through the open back door.

At his machine gun, Øverland aimed toward the area of incoming fire. Lieutenant Larsen fired his weapon at the same time. Then all went quiet. After a quick discussion, they decided to turn off the lights of the vehicle and advance in search of Opland, who, Sollund thought, must have sought cover somewhere. Over the radio, Lieutenant Larsen called headquarters and asked permission to proceed. The answer from the officer on duty was negative; he ordered them to pull back and wait for reinforcements.

An hour later a larger UN force moved toward Bourghoz and found Rune Opland dead at the edge of the road. He had been hit by two shots to the head and chest. He had additional injuries from shrapnel in his arms and legs. By one of the attack positions they found a Soviet-made, PKM machine gun. A Hizbullah mark had been pasted on the magazine. That same evening, news bureaus in Beirut reported that guerrillas from Hizbullah claimed to have attacked an Israeli patrol near Bourghoz around 5:45 PM and killed or wounded nine Israeli soldiers. Meanwhile, several in NORBATT, suspected the attack was in revenge for the death of the SLA soldier a few weeks earlier. The relatives of the dead Lebanese indicated this.[40] The circumstances behind the killing of Rune Opland were never cleared up.

After the incident, the military's training program received some criticism. Colonel Sigurd Friis, who was the military advisor to the UN delegation in New York, could not understand how soldiers could be trained to crouch down and observe when attacked, instead of seeking cover immediately.[41]

At the beginning of 1990, preparations were underway at the Foreign Office in Oslo to receive an Iranian diplomat who knew a lot about what was happening in Lebanon. The Office hoped to use the occasion to learn about the situation regarding western hostages in Lebanon. It fell to Ane-Karine Arvesen in the Middle East section to write a memo for the meeting along with the envoy from the Islamic Republic, Director General Hossein Mousavian. She knew well that he was close to Iran's President Rafsanjani, and that he was in charge of the Iranian effort to free the 17 western hostages.

In her background memo, Ane-Karine described the internal conflicts in Iran over the past several months. After Ali Akbar Hashemi Rafsanjani had been elected president in August 1989, the power struggle increased. Rafsanjani, who had been head of the Iranian National Assembly, wanted a better relationship with the West. Part of the power struggle revolved around getting control over the western hostages in Lebanon. On the one hand there was Iran's government, and on the other, those behind Ali Akbar Mohtashemi, the former ambassador to Syria who had recently been the minister of interior.

Most of the hostages had been abducted while Mohtashemi had Khomeini's support in Tehran. At the time, Iran used hostage taking and bombings against the US and other countries' institutions as a tool to solve disputes. But since 1988, Iran ordered that no more hostages were to be taken in Lebanon. Ane-Karine wrote in her memo that, as Iran viewed it, "hostages were an entry ticket for a dialogue with the US, especially with regard to releasing the 8–10 billion dollars that the Americans had frozen."[42]

When the Iranian delegation arrived, they told the Norwegian diplomats that their country was making great efforts to find a solution to the hostage matter. At the same time, Mousavian reminded them that Iranians had been the first foreign victims of hostage taking in Lebanon after the Israeli invasion. Eight years had passed since the Lebanese Forces militia had kidnapped the four Iranian diplomats in Beirut. Iran was now hoping Norway could use its influence. Several witnesses had said the four had been killed and buried shortly after their capture, but the Iranians would not accept this.

A few weeks after the Iranian diplomat's visit, President Rafsanjani told the National Assembly that Iran had become more vulnerable following changes in Eastern Europe and the closer relationship between the US and the Soviet Union. To emphasize the president's point, the *Tehran Times* wrote in an editorial that all parties in Lebanon had to support efforts to free the hostages. Behind the scenes there were rumors that Rafsanjani himself had penned the article. When the president later held a press conference, he said that the hostage matter in Lebanon was now heading toward a solution.[43]

For the Lebanese prisoners in Khiam and Israel, little had changed. When the World Cup began in Italy in June 1990, the guards were mostly focused on the games. Even the resistance movement paused to follow the matches. From housetops throughout all of Lebanon, flags of various nations waved, symbolizing in part that the Lebanese had spread throughout the whole world.

There was silence over the whole country when West Germany played in the finals against Argentina on July 8. When the finals were over, shots could be heard celebrating the German victors. The finals were considered to be one of the most boring in the history of World Championship soccer, despite some dramatic moments. It made little difference to the prisoners in Khiam, where only the guards got to watch television.

Not much news came out of Khiam until the Israeli journalist Ron Ben-Yishai was given entry to the prison center. This happened as the soccer finals went toward their conclusion. The reporter had been Israel television's military correspondent, and later chief of the military radio station. Now he had become *Time Magazine*'s correspondent in Israel.

In his report from Khiam, he wrote that he had seen five men on their knees, motionless in a windowless cell as they waited to be inspected by the guards. The corridor outside the cell was lighted by a single electric bulb that hung from the ceiling. There was a strong smell of sweat in the cell, where the floor was partly covered by thin foam rubber mattresses and flimsy blankets. There was no furniture, only a small crock of water, a few cups and a large plastic bucket. The bucket was used both as a toilet and a wash basin.[44]

The journalist wrote that 304 men and women were crammed together in small cells, that most of the prisoners were Shias, many from Hizbullah and that none had been charged or convicted. Ben-Yishai also reported that the prisoners might be released if the interrogators thought they were innocent, but even then most remained until it was possible to have a prisoner exchange.

One of the prisoners, 27-year-old Ibrahim Bazzi, spoke to the Israeli journalist without emotion. Bazzi had hair clipped short and wore dark blue clothing. He said he belonged to Hizbullah. "I know I am a bargaining chip," he said, "My only hope is that all the western hostages are set free, and that I become part of the agreement." Another prisoner, Shia Hassan Mohammed Nasser, said that he had sometimes been beaten during his 19 months in Khiam, but had not been tortured or humiliated.

If Ben-Yishai had chosen to talk to other prisoners, he would very likely have received more testimony about torture—if the prisoners had dared to speak. And if the Israeli journalist had met four Lebanese in their 20s who later managed to break out of their little cell, he would have gotten some good stories. The youngest of the four was Daoud Faraj, the eldest was Massoud Abu Hadla, the smartest was Mohammed Assaf and the unluckiest was Mahmoud Ramadan. These were the four who would undertake the only successful escape in Khiam's history, but that was two years into the future.[45]

Daoud Faraj was a strong, powerfully built 19-year-old with a friendly smile and trusting eyes. He had been arrested just before he was to go to Beirut to study, when a man from Shin Bet found a reminder note in his pocket that he took to be a coded message. In reality, it was a list of medicines that Daoud was supposed to buy for his grandmother. The note was written by a 10-year-old girl and was full of grammatical errors. It was the errors which made the interrogators from Shin Bet suspicious.

They offered Daoud his freedom if he would become an agent for the SLA. "We will let you go to Beirut, but then you will have to report to us," the interrogator said. Daoud refused, and they let him go, only to arrest him again a few days later. This time he was blindfolded and taken to Khiam, where new interrogations began.

"Where am I?" asked Daoud

"You are in Tel Aviv."

The Lebanese interrogators insisted once more his note had been a coded message. Daoud was convinced that they wanted to impress their Israeli bosses—a coded message would have been a sign that they had found an important resistance member. Daoud sympathized with the resistance movement, particularly the Communists, but he himself had never been active.

When the interrogation was over, Daoud was put into a one-man cell and got the prisoner number 5520.

"This is your new name," the interrogator said, and then asked, "What is your name?"

"Daoud Faraj."

"No, your name is 5520," the interrogator emphasized, kicking him.

Daoud Faraj was a gifted youth who read a lot and had thought about studying psychology. Now his world was limited to cell number 10, and he realized that it was important to get used to his new environment.

The mattress on the floor was rotten. Like the other prisoners, he had a bucket for a toilet. He tried to sleep, but it was freezing so he covered himself with his jacket. Eventually he noticed that the prisoners in the next cell were trying to contact him, using a system of knocks to represent letters. Daoud quickly learned the letter codes and figured out the first question: "Who are you?"

"I am Daoud Faraj from Ainata."

"What is it like outside?"

"It is raining. There is war in East Beirut. General Aoun is fighting."

From another cell came:

"My name is Nasr Hussein. Did you play soccer for Aitaroun?"

"I played soccer, but I broke my wrist."

"I saw the game."

Somewhat later prisoner 5520 was moved to cell number 6. There were two other prisoners named Edinne and Ahmad. They also asked what had been happening.

"I don't know why I am here."

"You have to tell us the truth."

Daoud suspected them of being collaborators.

At the next interrogation, Daoud was whipped and had a bucket of cold water dumped over his head. This was just the beginning.

The Israeli journalist from *Time Magazine* did not get to hear Daoud's story. But Ben-Yishai interviewed several other prisoners who said their interrogations lasted usually between 20 and 35 days. For most, these were the worst days they had ever experienced in their lives. But like Hassan Mohammed Nasser, they said they had not been tortured or humiliated.[46]

When I read the article and the interviews, I took most of what was written there with a grain of salt. The prisoners had been interviewed while their guards listened. They did not dare tell of the torture chambers, about the batons or the wires attached to electrical apparatuses, or how the sweat eventually made their skin wrinkle as if they had spent hours in a bathtub. They also did not say anything about the smell of perspiration that nearly choked them, a smell that would not go away no matter how much they washed themselves.

When I read what John Homse,—identifiable although he was not named in the article—had to say to Ben-Yishai, I got confirmation that he knowingly covered up all the evil that occurred at Khiam. He acknowledged that "he could probably get the inmates to admit to almost anything," but he swore to using "the best methods," those which could obtain the information "through dialogue and cooperation." He continued, "We show them how meaningless it is, and how injurious it is for their families if they hold back information. Since I came here, there has been no torture or threats of torture. Beatings, yes, from time to time we beat them, but only with our hands, and never in a way which turns the prisoners into cripples or takes their lives."

It was not surprising that Ben-Yishai had been the journalist to get an exclusive visit to the prison. This former editor-in-chief of the Israeli military radio station was, as all Israel journalists were, subject to military censorship. He knew very well what was appropriate to write if one wanted to avoid falling out of favor. There were Israeli journalists who were more critical, but they were never given access to Khiam.

CHAPTER FIFTY FOUR

Correspondent in a New War

During the summer of 1990, I made preparations to move back to the Middle East for a new four-year stint. I had been appointed *NRK*'s Middle East correspondent in the region for the second time. The office and residence were no longer in Beirut, but in Amman. Johan Thorud, who had taken over from me the last time, chose to leave Lebanon. He thought it was too dangerous to live in Beirut and he was not the only one. Some correspondents chose Cyprus as their base of operations, others Jordan.

From the Foreign Office in Oslo, Ane-Karine requested a transfer to the Norwegian Embassy in Damascus, from which she could also cover Lebanon. The Norwegian Chancellery on Lue Bliss in West Beirut was still in use, but the day-to-day business was handled by locally hired Lebanese.

My new job in the Middle East started with a bang. On August 2, 1990, Iraq invaded neighboring Kuwait. It was impossible to get into the occupied oil sheikhdom, and the Iraqis would not give visas for Baghdad. I chose to go to Bahrain, where I reached contacts in Kuwait via telephone and interviewed refugees who had made their way out through Saudi Arabia.

The invasion of Kuwait would ironically contribute greatly to getting the western hostages in Lebanon set free. When the Iraqis invaded, they opened up the central prison in the capital. Among the freed prisoners were the 17 from the Dawa Party.

The UN secretary-general and the Americans worked intensively to make use of the new developments. On August 7, Secretary-General Javier Pérez de Cuéllar received the US National Security Advisor, Lieutenant General Brent Scowcroft, and advised him that the Iranians wanted the UN to mediate getting the hostages freed. Their condition was that the US had to pressure Israel to free captives in Khiam and hostages in other prisons.[47]

To show goodwill, Hizbullah promised to free the Irish teacher, Brian Keenan. After four and a half years of being chained to the wall in a small prison hole, he was told, "You may go home, Braham." The guards had never learned to say his name properly—it had become a blend of "Abraham" and "Brian."

The Irishman was turned over to the Syrian security service in West Beirut, per Syria's wishes. From there he went to Damascus so the world press and diplomatic service would be convinced that the Syrians were acting virtuously.

"What do you want?" Keenan was asked when he was free.[48]

"Give me Irish coffee, chocolate and ice cream."

Keenan thought it strange that he had answered like that: he did not actually like chocolate. When he was later given food, he could not eat anything. Back in Ireland, he received a thorough medical examination. To everyone's astonishment, it was discovered that he had significant amounts of arsenic in his body. The doctor said he must have ingested it with his food, in doses spread out over several months. The amounts were small at first, but just before his release the dosage had apparently increased, so much that it could have been deadly.

Keenan learned that arsenic leads to memory loss. He concluded that his kidnappers dosed him figuring that both the British and American intelligence services would debrief him, and that arsenic would make him a poor firsthand source. Traces of arsenic were also found in Frank Reed, but not in the other freed hostages.

Because of the blockade of East Beirut, most stores were closed. There were shortages of fuel, flour and fresh vegetables. But because certain members of President Hraoui's government thought the blockade was inhumane, a limited amount of smuggling was permitted through the front lines.

It proved no simple matter to get rid of Aoun. He tried to make the Americans happy by inviting them back to the embassy in East Beirut. Eight months had passed since the general's supporters had surrounded the embassy and forced the diplomats to flee. They had since worked from the embassy in the Syrian capital. The general said he understood the US had vital interests in the area, and was ready to adapt his policies accordingly. The Americans were not convinced.

I felt the time had come to visit Damascus. There, Ane-Karine briefed me on the latest developments as the Norwegian Embassy saw them. We also went to the Café Havana to hear what was happening outside the diplomatic circles. I had good contacts from my previous correspondent period; several Syrian colleagues were glad to speak to me, as long as it was off the record.

Café Havana was at the corner of al-Mutanabbi and Port Said streets. The latter was named after the entrance to the Suez Canal from the Mediterranean, and the former for Abu al-Tayyeb al-Mutanabbi, one of the great Arabic poets. I recalled his words about the king of the jungle: "When the lion shows his teeth, you must not think he is smiling at you." The Arabic word for "lion" is *assad*, and in Syria Assad was just as powerful as a king. Something said about the Syrian president was also not too dissimilar to al-Mutanabbi's characterization of the lion: the more he smiles, the harder he is negotiating.

Café Havana was a scene in itself, with gray marble floors in a square pattern, divided by strips of inlaid brass. The tables were also marble, and small speakers broadcast sorrowful old love songs that blended together with the gurgling of water pipes and the conversations of the guests. A brown half-wall was covered with a wooden board featuring cutouts of human forms stretching their hands toward heaven. In this place, one had the sense time was standing still.

Regular guests comprised journalists, academics, artists and politicians. There was nothing black and white about most Syrian politicians; they were just as gray as the marble. It was rare to learn anything from them that had not already been in the newspapers. To break the ice with a Syrian contact, I asked if it was true that the café had gotten its name, Havana, because it was right across the street from another café called Brazil. "No, the café was established by Syrians who had grown rich in Cuba in the 1940s," I was told, "Early in the 1980s the name was changed when the Syrian authorities began a campaign to make all names in town Arabic. Café Havana became Café Sulwan. That did not help much: to the guests it was always Havana." A decade later the original sign was back again.

My contact was afraid the waiters would inform one of Syria's many security services if they overheard anything that could be considered criticism of the president and his Alawite-dominated government. Only when the waiters were out of earshot did he tell me that Assad had decided to get rid of the rebellious Brigadier General Michel Aoun.

The US Secretary of State James Baker had given the green light for the Syrians to take action. The reasoning was simple: President Hafez al-Assad had gone along with the coalition formed to force Saddam Hussein out of Kuwait. The president had joined the coalition because he was deeply concerned Saddam Hussein would attack Saudi Arabia. Assad had learned of a letter that Saddam secretly sent to Iran's President Rafsanjani. In it he stated that he wanted peace with his neighbor along "our 840-kilometer long coastal strip." When Rafsanjani measured the coastline on a map of the Arabian Gulf, he understood that Saddam had great ambitions: An Iraqi coastline 840 kilometers long would stretch through Kuwait and Saudi Arabia to the United Arab Emirates.[49]

The information was a reminder to me that everything is connected with everything else in the Middle East. Hafez al-Assad received America's blessing to mount an attack in Lebanon because he had helped them in the Gulf.

From Damascus, I went to Lebanon. When I arrived in West Beirut on October 4, I could see that the economic boycott had not brought Aoun to his knees. Few believed he would give up willingly, and only the Syrians were strong enough to take him by force. For a Syrian intervention to be legal, however, the Lebanese government would have to ask for assistance. The lawful Lebanese authorities therefore wrote a letter to the government in Damascus requesting their help to put an end to "the rebellion and the abnormal situation" in Lebanon. This was in line with the agreement of Taif.[50] Syrian Vice President Abdul Halim Khaddam briefed the ambassadors from the US and France. The Americans urged the Israelis not to interfere, and France promised Aoun political asylum.

First, the Christian enclave and the Presidential Palace were surrounded by Syrian special forces, pro-Syrian militias, guerrillas from Hizbullah and 4,000 soldiers from the part of the army that did not support Aoun. Two Syrian planes then dropped a few bombs over the palace and the artillery fired a few rounds. This was enough to cause the general to flee to the French Embassy early on the morning of October 13, 1990.

At 8:30 a.m., Aoun allowed himself to be interviewed over the phone by a reporter from his own radio station. In the interview, he gave orders to his soldiers to surrender and report to the chief of the army, General Emile Lahoud. A bit later, however, he called one of his officers and said, "Don't bother with what I have said. Continue fighting, at least for four to five hours more." The soldiers followed the last orders. They fought, and after a few hours raised the white flag. It was a trap: when the Syrian soldiers came to take over the palace, they were met with heavy fire. Several were killed.

When the Syrians eventually took the palace, they showed no mercy. One after the other of Aoun's regular soldiers and officers were executed. Some were shot in the neck, others strangled. What little was left undamaged in the Presidential Palace was taken to Damascus as spoils of war. The Syrians also advanced into the headquarters of the government army in Yarze, and took with them all data equipment and the entire archive.

Afterwards, the Syrians and pro-Syrian militia groups moved into what had been Aoun's core area. One of the militia groups led by Elie Hobeika, the former chief of Lebanese Forces, went into East Beirut. Hobeika had left the Lebanese Forces and now supported the Syrians. Another group took over the mountain areas in Metn. At least 350 people were killed. Among the victims in the Lebanese vendetta was the son of former President Camille Chamoun. Dany Chamoun, his wife and two children were killed by five uniformed men who came to their apartment early in the morning of October 21, in the middle of the change of shift for the family's bodyguards. Chamoun lived in Baabda, and was among many of Aoun's political supporters who was shocked that the general had left the field of battle and sought refuge with the French.[51]

Brigadier General Aoun remained in the French Embassy in Beirut for several months before he was given safe passage out of the country to live in Paris. In the Lebanese capital, stories circulated about the French ambassador who did everything he could to avoid having dinner with the boring general.

CHAPTER FIFTY FIVE

A Fragile Peace

A dangerous peace dominated Beirut at the end of October 1990. For the second time in 15 years, the barricades along the Green Line were removed and the main roads between East and West Beirut were open for traffic. The first time had been when the Israelis moved in and took the entire city in September 1982. The American Embassy in East Beirut reopened, but the diplomats continued to feel insecure because Christian supporters of Brigadier General Aoun thought the Americans had "sold them to the Syrians."[52]

As a gesture of peace, the militias—Hizbullah excepted—sent some of their weapons out of the city. In this way the authorities had achieved the first part of the Taif agreement's program: a demilitarized Greater Beirut stretching 20 kilometers north to Nahr el-Kalb, and just as far south to Damour. After peace had come to Beirut, a ceasefire between Amal and Hizbullah took hold in the South, and resistance fighting against Israel became a higher priority. The old infiltration routes were reopened, and it was easier to transport weapons and explosives from the Bekaa Valley and Beirut to South Lebanon. Hizbullah and Amal additionally began to coordinate certain operations.

Hizbullah's relationship with Syria was not as warm as its relations with Iran. The American Professor Richard Norton gave me a good example of why this was. Norton, who previously had been an observer with UNTSO, met a friend in Beirut who was close to Hizbullah. When they began to discuss the party's relationships to Iran and Syria, the friend twisted his wedding ring and said, "I like my ring, but I like my finger better." The Lebanese Shia meant the ring, symbolizing Syria, could be taken off, while the connection with Iran, like the one with his finger, was organic.

He pointed to the fact that the oldest known Shia community in the Middle East originated in the mountain regions between Sidon and Tyre in South Lebanon. Later Shia clerics travelled from South Lebanon to Iran to share their learning with the priesthood of the Safavid Dynasty, which had at first been Sunni, but later went over to Shia Islam around the 1600s. At the end of the 1800s, many Iranians moved to Nabatiyeh and other South Lebanese towns. Some became merchants, others established coffee houses or grew tobacco. The Iranians had strong ties to the Lebanese Shia population that had grown over time. By 1990 it had lasted for about 500 years.[53]

Amal's pragmatic politicians put less emphasis on historical concerns than on geopolitical ones. For Nabih Berri, Syria was of vital importance. Without support from Damascus, he would easily lose the fight against Hizbullah. Berri said it this way: "Now and then you can look away from history, but you can never ignore geography."[54]

In November 1990, the Norwegian Labor Party was back in power. The center-right coalition government had been unable to govern for more than a year. Its three parties had split over disagreements about which positions Norway should take in the negotiations between the European Union and the European Free Trade Association.

Gro Harlem Brundtland became prime minister again, Thorvald Stoltenberg foreign minister, and Johan Jørgen Holst defense minister. The table was now set for a more active Norwegian Middle East diplomacy. After Saddam Hussein's invasion of Kuwait, the situation was extremely tense.

I was present in Saudi Arabia when President George Bush gave the order to attack Baghdad with cruise missiles, and the Iraqi occupation forces in Kuwait with air and ground forces. The date was January 17, 1991. It took only 48 hours to beat the Iraqis—with the help of Syrian forces, among others—I drove together with other journalists to Kuwait and on into Iraq.

Syria's contribution to the liberation of Kuwait gave President Assad even more freedom to act in Lebanon. With Syria at its back, the Lebanese government army now expanded its control southward into the country, where there had been fighting between Amal and Hizbullah.

When 2,500 government soldiers moved south on February 7, Ane-Karine Arvesen went with them. She learned that about 1,000 soldiers would takeover the area between the port cities of Sidon and Tyre. The rest of the force would be stationed in the so-called Apple Region, Iqlim el-Toffah. The area was strategically placed for infiltration into the Israeli-occupied zone in South Lebanon. Hizbullah had previously taken control over parts of the area thanks to help from Palestinian Islamists. The Palestinians were tied to the Islamic movement known as Attawheed, and they let the guerrillas from Hizbullah use their uniforms and emblems to sneak past the Amal militia that had surrounded their forces.[55]

Hizbullah's strong position in Iqlim el-Toffah led it to resist the government forces in their effort to control the area. At first, after the prominent Shia cleric Sayyed Mohammed Hussein Fadlallah had given the green light, the militia leaders accepted the army takeover. Amal was satisfied with this because their militia there was in retreat.

From Ane-Karine's report to the Foreign Office, the government army had been permitted to takeover some old T-54 tanks from the Syrians, and ordinary people were happy when a unit of the army arrived. It had been over 15 years since the Lebanese army had been able to move about the area freely.

In Jbaa, the biggest village in Iqlim el-Toffah, which lay some two kilometers from an SLA position, Ane-Karine learned that the Hizbullah guerrillas had taken off their militia uniforms and hidden their weapons. Hizbullah men continued, however, to patrol the roads in Volvo station wagons, their windows darkened with colored glass or curtains. The Norwegian diplomat drove through several empty villages on the way toward Jezzine. She observed some of the villages had been completely destroyed in the fighting between Hizbullah and Amal. In Tyre, she noticed the army had taken over the control posts that previously had been manned by Amal's militia. The same thing had happened on the main road south of the city, near the Palestinian refugee came of Rashidiya. Even further south, the UN flag and the blue-and-white Israeli flag dominated the landscape.

In Iran, leaders realized the time had now come to free the western hostages in Lebanon. In exchange, they demanded the release of the kidnapped Sheikh Obeid. For their part, the Israelis demanded freedom for air navigator Ron Arad, who, Mossad claimed, was being held captive in Iran. It was said Arad had been sold for several million dollars to the Revolutionary Guards in Lebanon, although the Israelis had no proof of this.[56]

At UN headquarters in New York, hostage negotiator Giandomenico Picco decided to go to Damascus and then on to Beirut in April 1991. At the border with Lebanon, he was picked up by the Danish UNTSO major, Jens Nielsen. Together they drove to the observer corps' office and encampment near the defense ministry in Yarze, east of Beirut.

Less than half an hour after their arrival, Picco received a telephone call. It was the Iranian chargé d'affaires, Amir Hossein Zamania, who advised that Fadlallah could receive the UN envoy that same afternoon. "Just wait for instructions," said the Iranian diplomat.[57]

Around 9 pm an armored Mercedes with darkened windows rolled up in front of the UNTSO villa. Picco got in among guards with automatic weapons and was driven to the Iranian Embassy. Half an hour later he was sitting in front of Fadlallah. Picco noticed the Shia religious leader wore a black turban like Ayatollah Khomeini. Picco sensed a strong aura about the cleric, who repeated that he was not Hizbullah's spiritual leader, but merely gave advice to Hizbullah leaders. Sometimes the advice was followed, others not.

Fadlallah went right to the matter at hand. He referred to the international atmosphere, which had become decidedly better, and said that the hostages should be released without financial payment of any kind. Fadlallah made a further point of saying that the UN channel was better suited for the purpose than a British or American channel, because only a UN diplomat could meet the kidnappers directly.

Picco had worked full-time for two years to solve the hostage crisis. He knew there were many detours to the goal. Now it was necessary to work on the Israelis. Release of the western hostages in Lebanon depended on the release of Lebanese hostages in Israeli custody. Picco hoped the Americans would help with this. One month later, in early May, Javier Pérez de Cuéllar told President Bush that the Iranians had promised to help and there was no talk of money.[58]

Several of the correspondents in Beirut, among them Juan Carlos Gumucio from *El Pais*, went on May 16th to the Bekaa Valley. They wanted to check if there was anything to the rumors the hostage matter was about to be solved. The Bolivian journalist found his way to the village of Nabi Sheet, and to Hussein Moussawi, who previously had been the unofficial spokesman for Islamic Jihad. The former school teacher, who had broken with Amal and formed Islamic Amal, now had gray streaks in his hair. He spoke like a member of Hizbullah. Moussawi said he agreed with the presidents of Iran and Syria who both said the US must convince Israel to release the 350 Arabs in Khiam.

"The chances for a solution are much better now than they have ever been," said Moussawi as he stirred the sugar in his glass of tea.[59]

For those held in Khiam the situation was unchanged. Their fate worried not only relatives and friends, but also certain Norwegian officers in NORBATT. The soldiers in Blat were particularly concerned about getting freedom for their interpreter, Salma Salame, before she rotted in captivity.

In the spring of 1991, the troop leader in Blat, John Egil Nilssen, was in his third tour of duty. He thought the battalion leadership had done too little to free Salma.[60] Lieutenant Nilssen had long tried to raise awareness of Salma's case, but without any particular success. The battalion's doctor, Vidar Lehmann, was also upset that more had not been done for her.

Finally, company chief Major Dag Heyerdahl, Lieutenant Nilssen and the battalion's information officer were given permission to contact Shin Bet in Khiam. They went to Hussein Abdallah, who was the supervisor for Blat, and were invited to have lunch with him. Besides being served a good Lebanese mezze with grilled food and red wine from the Bekaa Valley, nothing came out of the meeting. When Nilssen went back home at the end of the summer, 1991, Salma and her brother were still sitting in Khiam.

A few months later, another Norwegian company chief managed to get inside the walls of Khiam. He had built a good relationship with the Israelis and their Lebanese collaborators after he had led an attack on four infiltrators from the resistance movement.[61] The four guerrilla soldiers had tried to get through the Hasbani Valley during the night, but heavy fire from the Norwegian UN soldiers stopped them. An Israeli helicopter fired off illumination grenades to make the hunt easier. The Northern Command, General Yitzhak Mordechai, had personally thanked Heyerdahl when the two happened to meet at a crossroads near Ebl el-Saqi.

The Norwegian was let in to Khiam and shown about, but he was not allowed into any of the cells. He also did not get to contact Salma Salame, who was in the female section a few meters away. The company chief did not report the visit to his battalion leader since he had gone without permission from the highest level.

On August 5, Iran's UN ambassador confirmed to the secretary-general that the western hostages in Beirut would be released as a gesture toward the UN. The following day, Islamic Jihad sent out an announcement that the organization would send a representative to a meeting with the UN Secretary-General.

When the UN hostage negotiator next came to the Iranian Embassy in Damascus, he was told, "Go to Beirut at once. The Iranian Embassy will make contact when you get there."[62]

Early the next morning, Picco went to the Lebanese border, where UNTSO Major Nielsen from Denmark was waiting. A few hours later, he learned that the Englishman John McCarthy had been released. The British TV producer, who had been kidnapped on the way to the airport in April 1986, returned to London a free man—and at the same time came as a messenger for Islamic Jihad and for the Organization for the World's Oppressed. McCarthy had been instructed to ask the UN Secretary-General to help free Arab hostages in Khiam and in Israel.

In Beirut, Picco understood that Iran by no means had full control over the various groups holding the hostages in West Beirut. The joy over McCarthy's release and the belief that others would follow, came to an abrupt end when Jerome Leyraud, a Frenchman, was kidnapped off the street of Beirut the following day, August 9.

This was the first kidnapping in two years. Just a few hours before, Fadlallah emphasized in his Friday sermon that the kidnappings were over, and said even the most militant Iranians wanted that. Picco checked with the Iranian Embassy in Beirut, where chargé d'affaires Amir Hossein Zamania said he had no idea who could have taken the Frenchman. The Iranian diplomat was angry. The kidnapping put the leadership in Tehran in a bad light.

Chapter Fifty Six

Face to Mask

When the UN hostage negotiator sat at the Iranian Embassy in Beirut on August 10, he expressed his wish to meet the kidnappers face to face. The Iranian chargé d'affaires passed his message to Imad Mughniyeh, and Picco was asked to wait in the local headquarters of UNTSO's Observer Group Lebanon (OGL) in Yarze. A few hours later the message came: the kidnappers are ready.[63]

The Finnish Lieutenant Colonel Timo Holopainen, who was head of the OGL team in Beirut, was skeptical of the diplomat going alone. But Picco insisted that both the Finn and Danish Major Jens Nielsen stay behind, and added, "If I am not back early in the morning, you can first call the chargé d'affaires at the Iranian Embassy, then the Iranian UN ambassador privately and then Javad Zarif, who holds a high position in the foreign ministry in Tehran. Finally you can inform Pérez de Cuéllar."

A few minutes later Picco was on his way to the Iranian Embassy in a bulletproof diplomatic car. When he arrived at the embassy, the UN envoy asked his diplomatic contact if he wanted to come along to meet the kidnappers.

"Oh, no, Mr. Picco, I don't know these people. It is going to be between you and them," he said as he disappeared from the room.

A little later a younger man came in and said: "Finished here! Go! Go!"

It was 10 pm when Picco was locked out of the Iranian Embassy and started in a southerly direction toward the Shia part of the city. Not a person was to be seen in the streets until he noticed a man a short distance away in the light of a street lamp. Picco went toward the man, who began walking. Picco followed. They walked for about 10 minutes, then the figure disappeared. Picco stopped. At that same moment, he heard a car approaching at high speed. The car slammed on its brakes, and Picco turned away so not to provoke the men in the car by looking at them.

"Don't look! Don't look!" said the man who led Picco into the car and pushed his head down. Picco had in the meantime noticed there were two men in the front seat, and one in the back. He had also caught sight of some radio equipment. They drove in circles. From time to time Picco heard the driver say, "Down! Syrians! Down! Syrians!" He had the feeling the others in the car were just as nervous as he was, but for another reason: the Syrians were apparently hunting for the newly kidnapped Frenchman.

After 30 minutes, the driver parked the car in an alleyway. There another car was waiting. Both backdoors were opened, and Picco changed vehicles. For another half hour he was carted around without any idea where this was leading. When the car stopped, he had a hood placed over his head and was led up a flight of stairs into a room where several people were present, then into another room where a man removed his hood from behind.

Someone told him to take off his shoes and the double-breasted blazer he was wearing, and he was body-searched. He sat down in a corner sofa and remained there facing a wall that was covered by a white sheet. In front of him was a table with a bowl of fruit. About every five seconds, he heard beeping from a machine he could not see.

Two men came into the room. One of them sat down in front of Picco and the other at the far side of the table. The other men remained standing. Both wore knitted, black hoods with eyeholes.

The man at the table explained they were meeting with him because the Iranian government has assured them that the UN Secretary-General will talk with the Israelis and get them to agree to a prisoner exchange. The Secretary-General was a man of honor. He understood how difficult the situation was for people of the third world. The man spoke understandable English and made it clear he was Lebanese, not Iranian.

"You have to understand that for my brothers, Israel and the West are the same. Israel gets weapons and funding from the US and the West. We accept you as emissary, because you have proven in the past to our people that you understand us and also because of what you have done."[64]

The diplomat wrote down every word. But he put a question mark because he did not fully understand what the man was referring to. Perhaps he spoke of Picco's effort to put an end to the Iran–Iraq war in 1988. At that time he had also been an envoy of the Secretary-General, and had introduced the UN's ceasefire proposal.

Picco thought the man in front of him had to be Imad Mughniyeh, also known as Hajj Imad. The other could be his brother-in-law, Mustafa Badreddine, who had been in on the attacks against the American and French Embassies in Kuwait in 1983. Now he was back in Lebanon.

The kidnapping of the Frenchman the previous day threw a dark shadow over the meeting. The Lebanese man made clear none of his people was behind it. "To the contrary. Our people are now looking all over the city [for him]," he said.

The Syrians were furious because of the new kidnapping. An ultimatum came from Damascus: If Leyraud was not set free within 48 hours, the Syrians would go from house to house to find him.

For the UN diplomat, the Frenchman's kidnapping could be a dangerous development. There was apparently opposition to the political decision to release the hostages, something which could lead to delays and complications in freeing the other hostages. The Lebanese man explained to Picco that both the Syrians and the Iranians were pressuring his group to release all the hostages they were holding, but that such pressure could have the opposite effect.

Picco replied that if the release of the other hostages was delayed because of Leyraud's abduction, it would mean Islamic Jihad was allowing itself to be manipulated by two or three freelancers. The man across the table got the point and said, "I am speaking with the full authority on behalf of all the groups who are holding the American, British and German hostages." He added, "You have to prove the Secretary-General will make sure that countries involved reciprocate."

From the Germans, the kidnappers wanted to know the prison conditions of the Hammadi brothers. One of the brothers was serving a sentence for his participation in the hijacking of the TWA plane in 1985, and the other for having smuggled explosives into Germany.

"We have heard the prisoners are being mistreated. If this mistreatment continues, the German hostages will suffer just as much as the two brothers," said the man at the table. Picco also was told to make it clear to the British that they had to put pressure on Israel if they wanted freedom for the remaining three British hostages.

In the middle of the conversation, the masked man said, "You may call me Abdallah. We will now get one of the hostages."

"I have no interest in meeting him unless I can take him with me when I leave," answered Picco.

"You may not. First, security has to be taken care of."

"If I am to meet the man, I must be able to tell him he will be set free tonight or tomorrow."

"Abdallah" got up and stood behind Picco. Several other men had come, and Picco was able to determine that they had weapons. A few minutes later the chief kidnapper sat back down and said, "We have agreed to turn over one hostage to the UN. When do you want to receive him?"

"Immediately, but I want the release to occur without Syria being cheated out of some consideration," answered Picco. "It would not be very smart to ignore the Syrians."

The man behind him laughed, and Abdallah told Picco about Islamic Jihad's relationship to Syria and Iran: "The two countries must be looked at separately. Even if we accept the Syrian force in Lebanon, we stand on our own feet. The Iranians can also not decide what we are to do or not do."

Then he got up, fetched a Coca Cola and gave it to Picco.

A few minutes later a man in a blue jumpsuit with a white stripe across the chest was led into the room. Picco recognized him from photographs: it was Edward Tracy. The American had come to Beirut during the civil war to sell Bibles, but had ended up selling pornography. Tracy, who also called himself a writer, had been kicked out of his family. No one wanted to have anything to do with him.

Picco got up, embraced the man and said, "Mr. Tracy, I am so glad to see you. You will soon be free."

The man hesitated and then answered with a loud voice, "I am not Mr. Tracy!"

The men with the masks were just as surprised as the UN diplomat. They shouted, "This is a trick! Picco tricked us!" Everyone was confused that the hostage denied being Tracy.

"Wait a moment," said Picco. "This man is Tracy. I have his picture to prove it."

"I am not Tracy," the man insisted.

Abdallah looked around and asked in Arabic, "Who is this man? What is his name?"

He was cut off by the hostage, who raised his head, smiled and said: "I am not Tracy, my name is..." He mumbled something unintelligible.

"Look, I have seen his picture. This is Mr Tracy," Picco repeated. He looked at the man and said, "You are going to be freed."

"You mean I have to leave this place?"

"Aren't you happy?" Picco inquired.

"Do you know what cordon bleu is?" asked Tracy.

"Of course," answered Picco.

"Well, I have three cordon bleu meals a day here, and I don't pay for them," said Tracy.

Only then did everyone in the room realize that the man had lost his mind.

Finally he admitted, "Yes, I am Mr. Tracy."

The next day, August 11, the 60-year-old from Burlington, Vermont, was released. A Syrian intelligence officer turned Tracy over to the American Embassy in Damascus. He had by then been held captive for 1,757 days.

A group calling itself the Organization for Islamic Justice sent out an announcement highlighting Picco's activity as a UN negotiator. It went on to say that a new American hostage would be released within 72 hours. "We have asked Picco to go to Damascus to assist in these negotiations and to make certain the UN plays an important role to solve this crisis, in the way we wish."

CHAPTER FIFTY SEVEN
Barter and the Torture Report

In September 1991, Giandomenico Picco was back in Beirut. Once more he sat across from the man he assumed to be Imad Mughniyeh, who still called himself Abdallah. Another man with a knitted face mask was also present.

It had been arranged in advance that one American would be set free that evening. Picco advised that Israel would release 15 Lebanese captives. His Lebanese negotiating partner said Picco could take the American, Jesse Turner, with him right away. This surprised the UN envoy: thus far all the released hostages had been turned over to the Syrians, who then drove them to their respective embassies in Damascus. In this way, the Syrians got full press and TV coverage. Why should they be excluded this time?

Picco got confirmation that the relationship between Hizbullah and Syria was not the best. Now the Lebanese kidnappers wanted to demonstrate they were not beholden to Syria. The UN diplomat, for his part, wished to avoid a bad relationship with Syria and did not want to take the hostage with him.

"OK, come back tomorrow evening, then we will discuss this," said Abdallah.

Around 10 pm the next day Picco was picked up from the Iranian Embassy. Again he walked through the dark to be met by the kidnappers, and when a car stopped behind him a few minutes later, the Italian heard a familiar voice. It was Abdallah, who seemed nervous.

"What has happened?" asked Picco.

"They are searching for you."

"Who?"

"The Syrian intelligence service. They are also hunting for me. They know I will hand over Turner. The entire Syrian apparatus in the area has been activated. We must act quickly" said Abdallah, who grabbed hold of Picco and led him to the car. Picco could feel Abdallah's hand was wet with perspiration. He now understood better; both *CNN* and the Iranian news bureau *IRNA* had reported another hostage was going to be set free.

"What shall I do after I have gotten Turner?" Picco was unsure.

"You should go to the hotel where the Syrian intelligence service is located."

Picco understood that the message Islamic Jihad wanted to send to the Syrians was twofold. On the one hand, the organization wanted to emphasize that it would decide on its own who got the honor of receiving the freed hostages. On the other, Islamic Jihad did not dare ignore the Syrians completely.

Picco noticed the car had slowed down and stopped. Another came up alongside. The diplomat was more or less torn from the car and pushed into the other one. There sat a man with his head bowed. It was Jesse Turner.

"Professor Turner, I am Giandomenico Picco from the UN."

"I am so thankful," answered the American.

The driver drove a short distance and stopped at a dark spot. There he ordered both to get out from Picco's side. Outside, Turner took his rescuer by the hand. It was shaking as he said, "I am glad you know where we are, because I do not."

But Picco did not know exactly where they were either. The time was about 1 am, and it was dark. Where could they find the Syrians before that formidable party's frustration turned to anger?

"We have to walk a bit," said Picco. He figured Abdallah must have chosen a place to drop them that was at least somewhat familiar. They walked on, and suddenly Picco saw "UN" sign. He understood they had arrived at the UNIFIL House, close to the Kuwaiti Embassy.

Picco rang the bell and a sleepy Norwegian showed up. He was Lieutenant Colonel Tor Eid. Picco recognized him from his many helicopter trips between Beirut and Naqoura.

"May we come in?" asked Picco.[65]

"Of course," answered Eid, wondering who the other man was.

Picco turned to Turner and said: "This is a Norwegian officer. He is a fantastic man. Wait with him! You will surely get coffee or tea. You are among friends." Eid made tea, and only after Picco gave him instructions to hide Turner in one of the bedrooms did he understand the man was a freed hostage.

Picco got into contact with the Iranian Embassy and asked one of the diplomats to call Syrian intelligence. "Tell them they can find me on an open square near Bir Hassan," said Picco, who then went to the square to wait. A few minutes later a Syrian officer arrived and was brought to UNIFIL House, where he took custody of Turner. From Beirut, the freed American was driven to Damascus and turned over to the American Embassy there.

On September 11, 1991, 73 prisoners were released from Khiam. There was no doubt they had been bargaining chips—in other words, hostages. They were driven out in buses and turned over to the Red Cross.[66] The group included NORBATT's interpreter, Salma Salame, and her brother Nazih. Before Salma left her cell, she told one of the guards that she wanted to give Soha Bechara what she had left of her clothing. They had not been in the same cell, but had spoken together through cracks in the cell doors. Salma admired Soha: she did not complain like other prisoners, and when Salma was depressed and could not eat her food, Soha had tried to cheer her up. Now Salma wanted to give something back.[67]

Salma's brother, Nazih, could not avoid thinking about the prisoner who had been in Khiam the longest, Suleiman Ramadan, who was still in his cell. Nazih had gotten to know Suleiman during the short time they were allowed in the "sun yard" every other week. He had personally seen the scars on Suleiman's chest where torturers had burned the Star of David. Later, Suleiman had tried to eradicate the star himself by burning in the Communist hammer and sickle in its place.[68]

When Defense Minister Johan Jørgen Holst once more made an official visit to the Middle East at the end of September 1991, he thought Beirut gave a "sinister and hopeful impression"— sinister because of the great amount of destruction, hopeful because the city was reunited.

In South Lebanon, Holst was told the relationship between NORBATT and the Israeli army was "quite good." The Israelis "buttered up" the Norwegian officers and soldiers to give the Lebanese the impression Norway was on their side. Holst thought the Norwegians should exercise "a certain degree of caution" in their contacts with the Israelis, because Israel was an unlawful occupying power.[69]

When Holst was told Salma Salame had been freed from Khiam, he seemed relieved. He was surprised, though, that she had not received pay for her time in captivity. When Holst learned that she had not gotten her job back, either, "because her contract had expired," he became furious. Holst asked the head of the Norwegian contingent to take the matter up immediately with the UNIFIL leadership in Naqoura; he would follow up personally from Oslo. "This is a question both of humanity and decency," said Holst.[70]

Once more Holst was briefed on the torture in Khiam. The battalion's doctor, Vidar Lehmann, had treated several of the released prisoners, and he was able to tell hair-raising stories. Earlier in the year, he had seen a man in his late 20s whose face was disfigured from eczema, deep scars and infected boils. He was informed the patient was a Shia who had joined the SLA, but was brought to Khiam on suspicion of having cooperated with Hizbullah.

"What he had to tell would make a stone cry," Lehmann said later. The young man had been tortured in the worst way. For example, he had been hung with his arms bound behind his back for 11 hours. The story was so awful that the Lebanese interpreter translating for Lehmann began to cry.[71]

Dr. Lehmann had sent the man to the UNIFIL hospital in Naqoura. He asked to speak with the Force Commander. Lieutenant General Lars-Eric Wahlgren who could not find the time, instead Lehmann met with UNIFIL's second in command. The doctor told what he knew, and asked if UNIFIL's mandate included protecting the population from abuse. The answer was yes, but Khiam lay outside the UNIFIL area. Lehmann suggested that since most of the prisoners came from the area for which the peace force was responsible, UNIFIL could perhaps take action. The answer was no: Wahlgren's deputy said it would cause difficulties for the force. If UNIFIL got involved in such matters, the force's days would likely be numbered.

The deputy promised, however, to take the matter up at the next staff meeting. He also advised that he had heard rumors of torture in Khiam from one of the UN observers at the post nearby. The observer had heard female screaming from Khiam for a whole hour, and noted this in the logbook. The deputy told Lehmann the date of the entry. When later he drove to the observation post with a Swedish and a Canadian observer, he saw that the page in question had been torn out.

After Holst heard what Lehmann had to say, he asked for a report about torture in Khiam. He would make certain that Norwegian authorities raised the issue of torture with Israel, which was guilty of apparent breaches of human rights behind the walls of the old French barracks. Doctor Lehmann went systematically to work. He had personally examined 16 released captives between the ages of 16 and 36, among them two women. In his report he wrote there was "consistency between the individual descriptions."[72] The interrogation methods used were "effective since they had been used over many years." The prisoners had been "interrogated with methods that are generally defined as torture," wrote Lehmann. "They are held captive without trial for an unlimited period of time" under conditions which are unlawful. "The question of who has the final responsibility is more complicated," wrote the doctor, but said Israel in the final instance must be held "responsible for the Khiam center, and for everything that happens with the inmates."

The report, written in English and stamped "Confidential" out of consideration for the freed hostages' safety, was turned over to the battalion leadership, who had to make certain it reached Holst's hands. Major Kåre Morten Haugen, the head of the company staff, was given the job of bringing the report to Norway. He was going home anyway to brief a new NORBATT contingent in training. To avoid the Israelis getting hold of the report, Major Haugen taped the sealed envelope to his stomach before he left Ebl el-Saqi. He knew his baggage would be thoroughly checked, and that a report about torture in Khiam would be confiscated.[73]

Everything went well: the security personnel at Ben-Gurion Airport outside of Tel Aviv checked the baggage, but not the major. When he landed at Oslo's Fornebu Airport, Holst's chauffeur was waiting, as planned, and took the report to the minister. Holst read the report and decided he would take the matter up with the Israeli leaders the next time they met.

CHAPTER FIFTY EIGHT
Killing of a Friend

In October 1991, Imad Mughniyeh was again in Tehran. His immediate family lived there, and he travelled back and forth from Beirut with his Iranian passport. Western intelligence had long since discovered that Mughniyeh was the key man behind the bombings of the American and French targets in Beirut. Everyone was hunting intensively for the short man whose appearance eluded them, because he had reportedly undergone plastic surgery.

By chance, correspondents Lara Marlow and Robert Fisk were in Tehran at the same time he was. Both of them had long known the identity of the man behind the kidnapping of Terry Anderson and several others. Through their contacts in Iranian intelligence, the two journalists were able to meet Mughniyeh on the top floor of one of Tehran's downtown hotels.[74]

Mughniyeh presented himself as a representative of Islamic Jihad. Fisk, the Middle East correspondent for *The Independent*, was greeted with a strong handshake. Marlow, from *Time Magazine*, got a friendly nod; as a practicing Muslim, Mughniyeh did not shake women's hands.

After they sat down at a table, Fisk jumped right in: "To take innocent people hostage is wrong."

Without taking his eyes off Fisk, Mughniyeh answered, "It is a bad thing, but it is a conscious choice. There are no alternatives, and it is a reaction to a situation that is forced upon us."

The Lebanese wore a short beard and spoke Arabic. A young Iranian woman translated.

Fisk and Marlow took notes as Mughniyeh continued, "If you ask me why our people take innocent victims as hostages, then you should ask the same question of others. The Israelis kidnapped more than 5,000 Lebanese civilians in 1982, and kept them locked up in the Ansar Camp. Most of them were innocent."[75]

"Have you no compassion for Terry Anderson?" Fisk asked, referring to what his friend and colleague must have gone through all these years.

"Of course. My feelings for the mental anguish Anderson has been through is the same as my feelings for the Lebanese hostages in Khiam. But in addition they have been through both mental and physical torture." Mughniyeh picked an apple from a bowl on the table and cut it up while he spoke about CIA station chief William Buckley. Fisk and Marlow noticed he showed clear signs of anger when he mentioned the American's name. He said that Buckley's briefcase held revealing documents, among them a list of Lebanese who had been arrested and brutally tortured by Lebanese intelligence. Seven and a half years had passed since Buckley had influenced President Amine Gemayel's government, during a period when thousands of Muslims—both militia soldiers and civilians—had been taken by the government army.

"William Buckley was *de facto* president of Lebanon, not Amine Gemayel," said Mughniyeh. "We also have documents which show this. One of the important missions for the CIA station chief, let us say the most important, was to ensure President Gemayel's personal safety," he added.

Before Fisk and Marlow left the hotel room, Mughniyeh gave a clear warning: new western hostages could be taken if the Israelis did not stop kidnapping people in South Lebanon. After that, Mughniyeh took the Englishman's hand and held it in an iron grip for half a minute as he said goodbye.

A few days later on October 30, a large peace conference between the Israelis and the Arabs commenced at the Palace of the Orient in Madrid. King Juan Carlos shook the hand of all the participants before they went in to the opening session, which was being transmitted live by many of the world's TV stations. The envoys of Egypt, Israel, Lebanon, Syria and Jordan, along with the Palestinians from the West Bank and Gaza Strip, had gathered around the T-shaped table.

Officially, the conference was being run jointly by Washington and Moscow, but in fact the US was playing solo. The Cold War was over and the Soviet Union was on its deathbed, but Moscow had recognized its lack of power in the Middle East long before. Before the Israeli invasion of Lebanon in 1982, Soviet envoy Yevgeny Primakov had briefed the PLO leadership that the Soviets would not support Palestinian or Syrian forces in Lebanon if they were attacked. The US and Israel, in other words, had the land all to themselves.[76]

Now it was another situation. After six wars and a Palestinian revolt that had given the world a new word—Intifada, which in Arabic literally means "shaking off"—there was hope that peace was in the air. This hope grew throughout the 1990s, but then died. Neither the Bush nor Clinton administrations were willing to use their power to stop Israeli activities in the occupied areas.

The Madrid conference could have been a first step toward a comprehensive and lasting solution to the conflict. However, a controversial and completely pro-Israeli advisor, Dennis Ross, steered the "peace process" under both US presidents, and this, among other things, gave Israel full latitude to build Jewish settlements on the occupied West Bank and in East Jerusalem. Middle East correspondents followed the process with eagle eyes. This led many of us to neglect developments in South Lebanon. We were only given bits and pieces about what was happening on the field of battle there and in Khiam.

None of us realized what the Lebanese Shin Bet agent Hussein Abbas was doing. The young Shia who had shot Sheikh Harb in 1984 and later participated in the kidnapping of Sheikh Obeid now snuck north of the occupation zone and placed bombs along the roadways. He also took part in kidnapping several Lebanese whom the Israelis wanted to have in their "hostage bank" and hunted for Hizbullah agents inside the SLA.[77]

One day, Hussein received orders to take the life of a man he considered a friend. The man to be killed was Abdel Hadi Atwi. He, like Hussein, was a Shia and lived in the village of Markaba, not far from the Israeli border. Their mutual boss, Mohammed Gharamti, known as Abu Arida, had given the order. He, in turn, had gotten his orders from his Israeli boss. Abu Arida travelled back and forth between Lebanon and Israel. Prior to the Israeli invasion in 1982, he had been with the PLO in the Sidon area; now he had an Israeli citizenship.

"Pick up Abdel Hadi without anyone seeing it, interrogate him and kill him. He is working for the resistance movement," Abu Arida told Hussein. Another collaborator, Elias Darakhani, went along. They got into Hussein's BMW and found Abdel Hadi standing by himself near a gas station in Markaba, with a Kalashnikov hanging over his shoulder and a pistol in his belt.

Hussein stopped the car, got out, gave him a friendly greeting by kissing Hadi on both cheeks, and said, "I have to talk to you. We have taken a person from your village. He was preparing an ambush, and the Israelis are interrogating him right now. But they need your help. Maybe you know him."

"OK," answered Abdel Hadi and got into the car.

Hussein headed west toward the small, nearly empty village of Adshit al-Qusayr. They stopped in front of a large house and turned into the courtyard. Hussein said the Israelis were inside the house interrogating the prisoner. "You cannot go in with weapons," he added.

At this point Abdel Hadi looked suspiciously at the two others. He understood something was wrong, but it was too late. In an instant, Hussein took his rifle and pistol.

"Why are you doing that?" Abdel Hadi shouted.

"You cannot take weapons in with you," Hussein repeated and put the rifle and pistol into the car. Then he said, "There are no Israelis here. I have brought you here because I want to talk with you. I know you are working for the Israelis, but you are also working for someone else. Who are they?" He went on, "Why have you told the Israelis three times about upcoming attacks by Hizbullah, and each time the Israelis have been caught in an ambush? I want you to tell me what has happened. Who gave you the information?"

"I am only working for the Israelis, and for no one else," said Abdel Hadi.

Hussein responded by shooting him in the legs.

"Please, don't kill me," begged the wounded man, writhing in pain.

"OK, tell me everything, then I will let you live," said Hussein.

In exchange for this promise, Abdel Hadi admitted he had been a double agent. Elias Darakhani wrote down his words. When the double agent had told his story, he said, "You promised not to kill me." Hussein responded by putting his weapon on automatic and riddling Abdel Hadi's body full of holes.

"Stop! You will kill us!" shouted Darakhani. Some of the bullets ricocheted off the wall behind Abdel Hadi. Hussein stopped firing and realized he was lucky not to have been hit.

The killers retrieved two sheets from the car, wrapped Abdel Hadi's corpse in them and put him in the trunk. They returned to Markaba, where Hussein let Elias out before driving a few kilometers northeast to the little village of Bani Hayyan. There he placed the corpse by the roadside. He left the Kalashnikov in the dead man's hands in an effort to make it appear that he had been killed at that spot.

The body was found the next day, and by the time the Israelis and the SLA arrived, it had swollen up. They immediately assumed the man had been killed where they found him. The Israelis arrested 35 persons in the area, among them five women. The real killer got away.

Hussein began thinking more about his own future. He had a feeling that the SLA was beginning to fall apart. The militia had been infiltrated, and there was a brutal power struggle among the leaders. There had been a number of personally motivated killings.

After speaking with his Israeli boss in Shin Bet, Major Uri Oren, Hussein moved to Israel. One of his predecessors in Shin Bet had suggested Hussein undergo plastic surgery to travel freely without being recognized. Hussein refused, having had enough of the dangerous life. He followed the advice of the Persian poet Firdausi, who had written in his book *Shahnama (Book of Kings)*, "When you encounter great danger, be part wolf, part lamb."

Hussein felt the time had come for him to shed his skin. Before he went to Israel, he arranged for his wife and children to go to Denmark, where they would stay as political refugees. After that he divorced his wife and married a Palestinian woman with Israeli citizenship. He made his living helping militia soldiers from the SLA get away from Lebanon. Through contacts at the Argentinian and Thai embassies, he arranged for his clients to get tourist visas against a large honorarium. Then the defectors went on to other countries to get political asylum. Sweden and Canada were among the most popular countries.

When Hussein got into trouble with one of his superiors in Shin Bet, he obtained a false Lebanese passport. He used it to travel with his new wife to Argentina and then on to Denmark. When he arrived there on January 24, 1992, he applied for political asylum. His wife, with her Israeli passport, had no problem with the Danish authorities. Hussein himself had to stay many months at an asylum reception center before he was given permission to remain in Denmark. He started a youth club for immigrants and from then on called himself Danny Abdalla.[78]

CHAPTER FIFTY NINE
Last Hostage Out

In Beirut, a positive development had occurred in the negotiations to free the western hostages. When Giandomenico Picco was driven to the UNTSO headquarters in the capital on November 17, 1991, he hoped he could achieve a concrete result. In the course of the evening Picco was picked up by a diplomatic car and taken to the Iranian Embassy. There he was met by a young diplomat who said, "I have nothing to tell you. God be with you."[79]

When Picco left and went out to the road by himself, he was more apprehensive than usual. This was his first visit to Beirut since he had received Turner and delivered him to a Syrian intelligence officer. Now he had no promises from Israel that Lebanese hostages would be set free.

After half an hour, a car showed up; it stopped and Picco got into the back seat. He sat with his head between his knees while the car drove out of the city to a new meeting with Abdallah.

The meeting went better than expected, and a few hours later Picco was back at the local UNTSO headquarters with the promise from Islamic Jihad that two new hostages, Terry Waite and Thomas Sutherland, would be set free. The only thing Abdallah demanded was a guarantee that the UN Secretary-General would continue his work to get the Lebanese hostages in Israel set free.

"Tell the Iranians that if pressure from them continues, there will be an explosion," one of the masked men at the meeting said before Picco left. This seemed to indicate that if Islamic Jihad was pushed too far, they would take new hostages instead of releasing those they already had.

When Sutherland was freed after 2,347 days, he talked calmly about his depressions and about his neighbor, Terry Waite, who snored loudly. Waite was eight years younger at 52; he had spent 1,763 days as hostage. He said he trusted Hizbullah would free the remaining American hostages, Joseph Cicippio, Allan Steen and Terry Anderson. Just afterwards, Islamic Jihad announced that the fate of the western hostages would no longer be tied to freedom for the prisoners in Khiam. The hostages in West Beirut had become too great a burden for the organization.

When Picco met the Israeli-Lebanon coordinator, this time in Cyprus, he was promised the remaining American hostages would be exchanged for 24 Lebanese hostages in Israel. This time the Lebanese would be set free first. Picco also received an audiotape in which Sheikh Obeid sent greetings to his family.

Two nights later Picco, was once more outside an Iranian Embassy, but this time in Damascus. A car picked him up and drove him 40 minutes away to a remote stretch of road. After a while a car showed up as usual, and a masked man asked Picco to remove his jacket and tie. He was given a windbreaker and a pair of glasses with black paint on the inside of the lenses.

"Sit, don't lie, and close your eyes!" said the masked man before they drove off. A few minutes later they passed an unofficial border crossing into Lebanon, where Picco was presented as a VIP and did not have to get out of the car. Then he was driven to a house and brought to a room with the usual white sheets hanging about the walls.

When the masked Abdallah arrived, Picco thanked him for freeing Sutherland and Waite. Together they went over a list of hostages who had not yet been set free: three Americans, two Germans, three Israeli soldiers who probably were dead. In addition, there were the missing corpses of William Higgins and William Buckley. Abdallah again brought up the hostages the Israelis were holding in Khiam and other Israeli prisons.

Once they went through their lists, Abdallah took Picco's hand and held it with both of his own. The UN diplomat tried to read the eyes behind the mask. He thought to himself, this man will have to spend the rest of his life on the run.

Five days later on December 2, a guard told Joseph Cicippio, "Get dressed, Joseph, you are going home."[80]

Cicippio did not believe him; he had heard these words many times before. But when he was asked to crawl into a large carton, he did as he was told. He felt himself being lifted, carried down a few steps and placed in a vehicle. Breathing holes had been cut into the carton's sides. Later, he was transferred to another vehicle, and told to get into the back seat with the message, "I am going to remove your blindfold. Keep your eyes tightly shut. We are going to be very close nearby, and if you do something foolish we will take you back with us, or we will kill you."[81]

Cicippio remained in the car. A few minutes later he heard a car stop close by. Then he heard steps and a voice say, "Are you Joseph Cicippio?... You can open your eyes now. You are on your way back to freedom."

When Cicippio opened his eyes he saw four men in front of him, none of them masked. Cicippio could hardly believe his eyes. Shortly thereafter he was on his way to Damascus.

When he arrived, a man in uniform said to him, "No, those clothes will not do. Today is Syria's national holiday, and you must be dressed for the occasion." He made a call, and soon another man arrived with a suit, shirt, tie and socks. When Cicippio looked at himself in the mirror, he hardly recognized himself. He had become much thinner, and he had a grey cast to his face.

The next evening it was Allan Steen's turn. He had been kidnapped in January 1987, but had been held captive entirely separate from the other Americans. Then on December 4, Terry Anderson was brought from his cell, blindfolded, and put into a car. The trip was a short one. When he got out, he heard a voice say, "You are a free man."

Anderson removed his blindfold and threw it into the road. He looked around and recognized that he was in Baalbek. A little later he was on his way to Chtaura. Seven years earlier the road had been narrow, and the walls of the houses full of bullet holes. There had been much new construction and the roads were now better and wider. After a short stay at the headquarters of Syrian intelligence in the village of Anjar, he was driven to the foreign ministry in Damascus. Picco met him there.

"I have wanted to meet you for many years," Anderson whispered. The Italian smiled and pressed Anderson's hand, saying, "I have also."[82]

A bit later reporters and photographers from the *AP* arrived. Terry Anderson saw his old friend Bill Foley smile and cry as he took pictures. Anderson remained calm and read a message from his captors, expressly stating that these were not his own views. The organization wanted to stress what they had "achieved after all these years and all these efforts," namely that the West had been forced to take notice of the Organization of the World's Oppressed (one of the many names the kidnappers used for themselves). It showed that "there is a point to a small group of the faithful standing up to a superpower."

After he thanked the UN, Syria and Iran, and answered a few questions, Anderson asked to be permitted to leave. "I have an appointment with two beautiful women, and I am already late," he said. Everyone understood that he was referring to the daughter he had never seen, and to his wife Madeleine. Then Anderson was driven to the residence of the American ambassador.

"Do you want to meet Madeleine?" asked the female American diplomat accompanying him. "Yes, indeed."

Everyone left the room, and Anderson remained standing alone. Then Madeleine came in. She did not see him right away because the room was large and she was looking in a different direction. They met and fell into each others' arms. Madeleine cried. Terry stroked her hair and said, "It's all right. It's over. It's okay."

Terry could feel the tears coming on. He recognized the smell he had tried to recreate in his mind those 2,454 days which had passed since they last saw each other. Now it seemed only a few hours had passed since he had left her to play tennis. She was then in her sixth month of pregnancy.

At the Norwegian Embassy in Damascus, Ane-Karine Arvesen followed the developments closely. The day after Anderson's release, she wrote in a report to the Foreign Office that the political-economic hostage feud between Iran and the West was over. In the report she recalled that just one week earlier, Washington and Tehran had reached agreement on the repayment of 278 million dollars for weapons that the Shah's regime had bought before 1979, but had never been delivered. Now there would be further negotiations about the frozen Iranian funds in American banks. She wrote also that, "By getting the hostages and prisoners in Khiam and Israel released, Hizbullah could show its own clientele, the Shias in Lebanon, that they had gotten something in return for holding hostages for all these years. Iran had promised more economic aid to the Shia community in Lebanon."

The remains of William Buckley and William Higgins were still missing. Late in the evening of December 20, Higgins' body was left on a pile of garbage in West Beirut. A police station soon received a tip where to find it. Aid workers from the Red Cross picked up the body, which was partially decayed, and brought it to the American University Hospital. The pathologists took hair samples, measured the arms and legs and obtained x-rays of the mouth and teeth, so they could be sure of the corpse's identity. Then they turned the body over to the American Embassy.

Two officers from UNTSO stood at full attention as honor guard when Higgins' coffin was placed in an ambulance and driven away. Later, a criminologist in the US military, Richard C. Froede, discovered that Higgins had not died from hanging, but a stab to the neck.[83]

Seven days later the police found a new body in Beirut's southern section. "I think we have Buckley's remains," noted the police officer leading the patrol. He said they had received a phone call from a man who told them, "We have a new body for you. It is lying by the road to the airport, in a narrow street that leads to Haret Hreik." The police found the remains packed in a sheet and delivered them to the American University Hospital mortuary. "It's Buckley, the skeleton of Buckley," a pathologist established after running tests.

Buckley and Higgins were given a joint funeral at Andrews Air Force Base outside of Washington, DC, on the last day of 1991. Lieutenant Colonel Higgins was later buried at the Marine base in Quantico, VA, while a gravestone had already been set up for Colonel Buckley at Arlington National Cemetery, where many of America's heroes lie buried.

Six months later, June 17, 1992, the UN hostage negotiator was able to escort the final western hostages home. These were the German aid workers Heinrich Struebig and Thomas Kemptner.

CHAPTER SIXTY
Hizbullah's Two Tracks

The conflict in Lebanon was not just being fought in the Middle East. It had spread over to Latin America. On March 17, 1992, Israel's embassy in Buenos Aires was blown up by a van full of explosives, killing the driver and 29 innocent people. In addition, a Catholic church and school nearby were damaged. A total of 242 were injured.

Islamic Jihad issued an announcement that the bombing was revenge for the killing of Hizbullah's secretary-general, Sayyed Abbas Moussawi and his family. They were all killed by rockets from an Israeli military helicopter one month before. Islamic Jihad named an Argentine convert to Islam, called Abu Yasser, as the perpetrator.

A few weeks later the analysis section of the CIA maintained Iran was involved, and that Islamic Jihad was just a cover name for Hizbullah and the Iranians. The CIA had no doubt Hizbullah was the extended arm of Iran, and that Tehran was willing to let others carry out large-scale attacks all over the world in its interests.[84]

The Argentinian authorities later expelled several Iranian diplomats. Researchers said they had found conclusive proof that Iran had participated in the attack. The Argentinians also issued an arrest warrant for the Hizbullah operative, Imad Mughniyeh, who, they believed, was collaborating with Iran.[85]

Israeli leaders in the meantime did not hide the fact that the Israeli air force was behind the killings of Moussawi and his family on Monday February 16, 1992. That day marked the eighth anniversary of Sheikh Harb's assassination, and an air of unease had rippled through the crowd in Jibsheet that had gathered to commemorate the event. The whine of a pilotless Israeli drone and the rumble of jets had been heard in the area for several hours, and by the afternoon Israeli gunships were also evident. Lebanese villagers were accustomed to these sounds and sights—Jibsheet was less than eight kilometers from the closest Israeli fortified position on a hill overlooking Nabatiyeh—but the unusual high amount of air activity that day seemed fishy.

In the village of Tuffahta, on the road between Jibsheet and the coast, people heard helicopters before they saw two of them hanging in the air, the heavy beat of their rotor blades reverberating through the deep blue, late afternoon sky. Then they could see a dart of light that streaked toward the ground at a sharp angle. One of the American-built Apache AH-64 helicopters had unleashed a missile that struck a black Mercedes as it passed down the narrow road toward the village. The car exploded in a ball of fire. Two more laser-guided missiles homed in on the Range Rovers following just behind.

Moussawi had prayed at Sheikh Harb's tomb before leading the crowd of mourners up the hill to the mosque in the center of Jibsheet. Some of Moussawi's friends urged him not to drive back to Beirut that same afternoon, saying it was too dangerous. But the secretary-general of Hizbullah replied, "What's the matter? Do you think I am afraid of dying?"[86]

His bodyguards suggested Moussawi should at least switch cars, but he refused and climbed into the back seat of his Mercedes along with his wife Siham and their six-year-old son Hussein. The Israeli drone followed Moussawi's cortege as it left Jibsheet, transmitting pictures to the IDF operations center in Tel Aviv.

Originally, the Israelis had considered kidnapping Moussawi for use as a bargaining chip in an eventual prisoner exchange. When it was clear he was surrounded by too many bodyguards to be taken alive, Lieutenant General Ehud Barak said, "If he is already in sight, let's take him."[87]

A Lebanese working for the Israelis had also followed Moussawi's movements that day, and had given a clear message that Moussawi was accompanied by his family. Barak did not care. The decision to kill the Hizbullah leader was approved by Prime Minister Yitzhak Shamir and Defense Minister Moshe Arens. If the Israeli leaders had known what the consequences would be, they would have preferred Moussawi to his successor.

There was no doubt who would takeover when Moussawi was killed. Sheikh Hassan Nasrallah was chosen on instructions from Iran's Supreme Leader, Ayatollah Khamenei. The new secretary-general would become far more dangerous for Israel than Moussawi had ever been.[88]

Thirty-two-year-old Hassan Nasrallah had grown up in conditions of poverty as the oldest of nine children. His father was a greengrocer in Maslakh-Karantina, a Shia-dominated slum district in East Beirut. When the Christian militia captured Karantina and massacred a large number of Muslims during the civil war, the Nasrallah family had already left for the father's home town of Bazouriyeh. Hassan was later sent to Tyre for further education. There, as a 15-year-old, he joined Amal.

The following year, he travelled to Najaf in Iraq to study, where he met Abbas Moussawi. They were both taught by Ayatollah Baqir Sadr, one of Iraq's foremost Shia clerics. It did not take long for Hassan Nasrallah to also become taken with the teachings of Ayatollah Khomeini. When Saddam Hussein started his violent hunt for Shia Muslims in 1978, Ayatollah Sadr was hanged. Dozens of Lebanese students had to leave Iraq, among them Hassan Nasrallah.

During Israel's invasion of Lebanon in 1982, Nasrallah left Amal and joined the groups allied with Iran that would eventually form Hizbullah. Ten years later Hassan Nasrallah was not just the leader of Hizbullah, the most influential party in Lebanon; he was also the commander-in-chief for the world's most professional guerrilla organization.

Nasrallah and the rest of the leadership had decided the party should follow two tracks, one military, the other political. The military track would lead to a significant escalation of the fight against the Israeli occupation. The political track would lead to representation in Lebanon's new National Assembly, the first in 20 years.

Initially, Hizbullah had thought that the Taif agreement of 1989 was not in the party's interests. Lebanon's religious division of power ran contrary to Hizbullah's wishes, which were for a democratically elected, Islamic government. At the same time, party leaders understood it was impossible for such a government to be created in a short period of time, so they accepted the Taif agreement.[89]

The agreement had also said that Syria should help the Lebanese authorities to get control over the country. Since Syria was now supporting the current regime, there was little Hizbullah could do without coming into conflict with Damascus. Besides, the guerillas were completely dependent on Syria's help to get weapons from Iran for the resistance fight in South Lebanon.

Ayatollah Khamenei supported this pragmatic approach to Lebanon's internal political power struggle, but there had been much discussion within Hizbullah itself. The Party's first secretary-general, Sobhi Tufayli, wanted to fight anyone who opposed the vision of an Islamic state. However, he ultimately lost out to the two young leaders Abbas Moussawi and Hassan Nasrallah.[90]

In May 1992, there was an election scheduled in Israel. The Labor Party was on the offensive that spring with the motto, "Israel is Waiting for Rabin." Strategists in the party knew that the fight would be for the voters in the center, and therefore had sidelined the most radical members. Among these was Yossi Beilin, a former party spokesman.

In the middle of the election campaign a 44-year-old sociologist named Terje Rød-Larsen traveled from Norway to Israel. On April 29, 1992 he had lunch with Beilin. In Norway, Rød-Larsen was both the founder and leader of what was to become Fafo Research Foundation, an institution funded by the Norwegian Confederation of Trade Unions. Fafo had investigated the living conditions of Palestinians in the Occupied Territories, and the report was to be presented to a large international meeting in Oslo in May. Rød-Larsen was now in Israel to sell the idea of establishing a "secret channel" between Israel and the PLO, which would negotiate in parallel with the public effort taking place in Washington, DC.

After a three-hour lunch at an Indian restaurant in Tel Aviv, the two men were on first name basis. They agreed the fall of the Berlin Wall and the liberation of Kuwait had created an historic possibility for peace between Israel and the Arab states. Rød-Larsen left the restaurant so excited that he took his paper place mat with him; on it was a horoscope saying people born in 1947 (like Rød-Larsen) would throw themselves into a special mission with all their strength, and that one could be confident they would fulfil their mission. Back in Norway, he enthusiastically briefed the newly appointed undersecretary in the Foreign Office, Jan Egeland. Egeland, who was from Stavanger, was just as excited about the idea as Rød-Larsen.

About the same time, a young, trim, dark-haired Israeli lawyer was travelling around to several Israeli prisons. Zvi Rish, before he studied law, had been part of Shin Bet. Now he was working for an Israeli organization called The Association for Citizens' Rights. His job was to interview Israeli, Palestinian and Lebanese prisoners and find out how they were being treated.

With his background in the secret service, Rish could in theory get access anywhere. But when he came to the Bersheeva Prison, he was stopped at the entrance to one of the prison wings. "But I have permission from the minister of police in Israel to go where I want. The authority was signed by the minister," Rish argued.[91]

"The prisoners in this wing have nothing to do with the police or the minister," answered the prison guard who followed him.

"I am not leaving until I have seen the prisoners in this section," Rish insisted stubbornly.

"OK, wait. We will speak with the head of the prison."

The lawyer waited. Hours passed with no response, but he sat there patiently. Finally a guard came over to him. From his appearance, Rish thought the guard must have been an Israeli Arab. "The prisoners in this wing are from Lebanon. No one knows they are in Israel. I cannot say more. Call me," the guard said, who later would prove to be from one of the Bedouin tribes of the Negev Desert. He put a note into the lawyer's hand.

After continuing to wait for some time, Rish understood the effort was futile. He drove back to his home in Tel Aviv and called the prison guard at his private number. Only then did he find out there were 19 secret prisoners in the closed wing of the prison, all Lebanese Shias, and that most of them had been there for seven years.

"Find out if one of them is willing to talk with me, but he has to speak English since I do not speak Arabic. In such case, I can come to the prison as his lawyer. In this way we can get the Lebanese prisoners' case out into the open," Rish told the prison guard.

A few days later the guard called and said one of the prisoners was willing to meet him. But when Rish showed up at the prison director's office, he was again greeted with a cold shoulder and questions: "Do you have a legal power of attorney? How do you know the prisoner's name?"

"I am his lawyer, and I want to talk to my client. How I got hold of his name is irrelevant. I want in," answered Rish.

It did not work. Again, the lawyer went home without success. He would not give up, however and after several weeks of exchanging letters and confirmations that Rish was on the list of Israeli lawyers with security clearance, the prison authorities could no longer deny him access.

Rish learned the 19 Shias had all been kidnapped in 1985. Some of them were just children when they were brought to Israel. Several had been taken by the militia groups and "sold" to the Israelis. Ten had been tried and convicted of belonging to an enemy organization, namely Hizbullah. None had received long sentences—they varied from 10 to 20 months—and all had long ago completed their time, but were still held in captivity and had no form of contact with the outside world. The prisoners' families did not know where they were, or even if they were still alive. The Red Cross was also not aware of their existence.

Rish decided to take on the cases of all 19 prisoners. In the court documents the lawyer finally received, the prisoners were referred to as "Mar Plony," the Hebrew version of "John Doe." Israeli censors prevented any information from slipping out. It was obvious the authorities wanted to keep them for use in prisoner exchanges.

Court meetings for the 19 were held in Tel Aviv every three months, and usually took no more than five minutes. The prisoners, in theory, had lawyers, but had never been allowed to speak with them until Rish came into the picture. He thought it odd at first that the prisoners were driven from Bersheeva to Tel Aviv each time, since there were also judges in Bersheeva. Eventually he understood the reason: the municipal judge in Tel Aviv was Eliyahu Winograd. "He was not particularly independent, to put it mildly," Rish told me later.[92]

Every third month Rish tried to get the judge to let his clients out, and every third month he would also appeal to the Israeli Supreme Court. But neither Winograd nor the justices in the high court would listen to the his arguments. In 1992, the court ruled it was lawful to keep the Lebanese as hostages for use in prisoner exchanges, in the interest of Israel's security.

Rish did not accept the decision and had no intention to let the court system off the hook. He continued his work and appealed anew. He was convinced some of the judges would recognize it was unworthy of Israel, as a state ruled by law, to keep the Lebanese imprisoned even after they had served their sentences.

In Khiam, there were never any lawyer visits. The prisoners lived under even worse conditions than their counterparts in Israel. There was little public notice whenever someone was released after many years behind the walls, and few western journalists were interested to hear what they had endured.

One day, Dr. Vidar Lehmann received a list of the many young and innocent people who had been incarcerated. They were subjected to the prison's horror as a warning to others. Lehmann copied the list and sewed it inside the leather band of his UN beret. He had decided to turn it over to Amnesty International the next time he went to Norway. At Ben-Gurion Airport, his baggage was thoroughly checked, and he was personally interviewed about his contacts with civilian Lebanese. It was apparent the Israelis knew of Lehmann's work to help freed prisoners. He did not mention Khiam during the interviews, and no one discovered the list of names.[93] When he arrived in Norway, he gave the list to Amnesty International and they later included it as supporting documentation in their comprehensive report on abuses at Khiam.

After his service in Lebanon had ended, Lehmann continued to work to free tortured prisoners who lived in the Norwegian battalion's area, and try to get them to Norway. He managed to get just one man to Oslo. The man was Nazih Salame, the brother of Salma, who now had her job back as interpreter. Because of Lehmann's tireless work, NORBATT was given extra resources to finance follow-up treatments for former Khiam prisoners.

In Norway, Defense Minister Johan Jørgen Holst was no longer particularly focused on the torture of prisoners in Khiam. He had discussed Lehmann's report with the Israelis, but did little more after that. In the spring of 1992, he had been quietly asked to become a candidate for the position of Secretary-General in NATO. The German Manfred Wörner had held the position since 1988, and it was time to find a new leader. As a result Holst's priorities had changed.

As late as July 1992, Holst was the only candidate who had received his government's official support in the choice for the top position in NATO. Both the US and Great Britain were positively inclined toward Holst because he came from a country that was not a member of the European Union. Germany felt differently, however, and Chancellor Helmut Kohl was able to put an end to the Norwegian's ambitions. Ultimately Wörner was allowed to continue in the post for another two years.[94]

In Israel, Yitzhak Rabin's dream of becoming prime minister was fulfilled. He took over on July 13, presiding over the first Israeli government in 15 years to be led by the Labor Party. Rabin also took the position of defense minister in the new government, and Shimon Peres as foreign minister. Although he would have preferred to shut Peres out entirely, or to give him an insignificant ministerial position. He did manage to clip the wings of the "ingrown intriguer," as he referred to Peres in his memoirs:[95] He decided that he would personally take control of the peace negotiations with the Palestinians in Washington. These had formerly been the foreign ministry's responsibility.

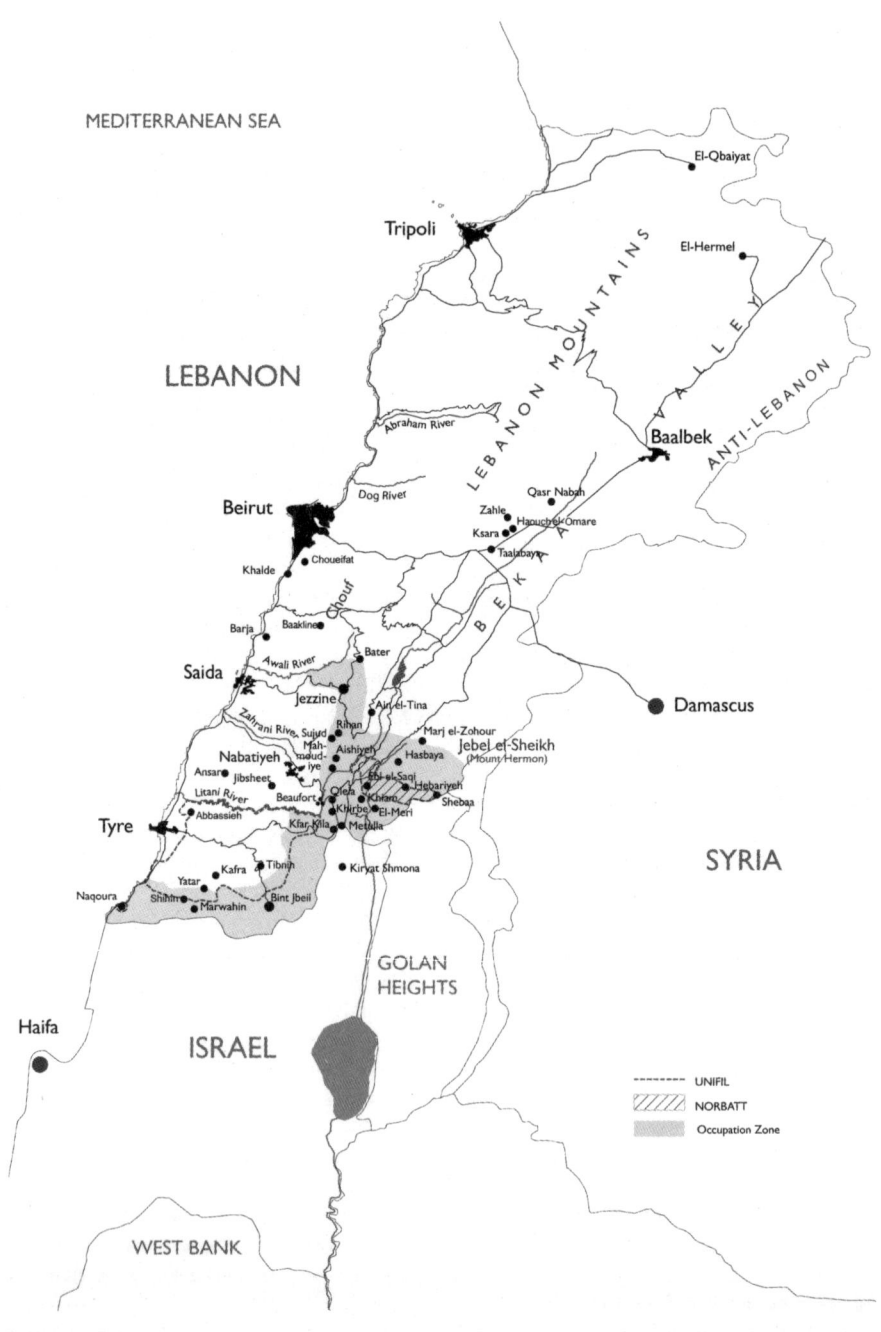

PART SIX

Hizbullah's Success

1992-1996

Four Lebanese prisoners in the infamous prison center in Khiam made a dramatic escape and got help from an unexpected source.

Israel launched a massive air and artillery attack on villages in Lebanon to get the civilian population to turn against Hizbullah, but the actions failed to change the public mood.

For the first time, the UN force had a Norwegian Force Commander, Major General Trond Furuhovde. The Israelis' military attack against Hizbullah was also directed at UNIFIL, but there were no real consequences since the US supported Israel in the United Nations.

The guerrilla attacks against the Israelis in South Lebanon were filmed by Hizbullah and used as a part of the fight for public opinion in Israel. The many attacks created a growing concern there.

MAIN CHARACTERS

Mohammed Assaf, Prisoner in Khiam
Mustafa Dirani, Leader of the Resistance Movement, The Faithful
Daoud Faraj, Prisoner in Khiam
Trond Furuhovde, Major General, Force Commander of UNIFIL
Saoud Abu Hadla, Prisoner in Khiam
Ahmed Hallaq, Lebanese Mossad Agent
Rafic Hariri, Prime Minister of Lebanon
Hagrup Haukland, Colonel, Chief of NORBATT
Mahmoud Ramadan, Prisoner in Khiam

CHAPTER SIXTY ONE
Four in Cell 8

In the summer of 1992, the young, slender-built Lebanese in cell number 8, Mohammed Assaf, was bent on escape. Assaf was Sunni and had come from the village of Hebariyeh in the Norwegian UN battalion zone. He had been taken captive by Israeli officers from Shin Bet four years earlier, on May 1, 1988. He was accused of being a member of the Lebanese Communist Party's resistance movement.

At first, he was driven to Hasbaya, where Shin Bet had an interrogation center. There guards tortured him and locked him in a small cell no larger than a cubic meter. After several days they sent him to Khiam, where the torture continued.

Like so many other prisoners, Assaf was hoisted up on a rope attached to the ceiling. He was beaten with batons, steel wire and guards' fists. His interrogators attached wires to his penis and fingers and shocked him until he passed out. After a while the interrogations ended, and his days became like those experienced by so many others in Khiam: he sat alone with his thoughts, talked with fellow prisoners, ate and slept, fearing all the time that the torture would resume.[1]

Thus far no one had managed to escape from Israel's infamous prison. When two prisoners had tried in July 1988, they were caught and beaten so badly that both had to be sent to hospital in Marjayoun. Four years later, Mohammed Assaf who was intent on escaping. "I have nothing to lose but my life," he said to himself and his three fellow prisoners in cell 8.

One of the three was Daoud Faraj, the young man who had been arrested when his shopping list was mistaken for a code. The two others were Mahmoud Ramadan and Saoud Abu Hadla. Saoud had been active in the resistance movement, and had been turned in by a neighbor in the village of Marwahin, close to the Israeli border. The fourth, Mahmoud Ramadan, did not know why he had been sent to Khiam, even though he had been accused of belonging to an enemy organization. In order to motivate his fellow prisoners, Assaf told them about *The Great Escape*, a film he had seen several times. It was based on a true story from the Second World War, where British, Australian, and American prisoners had managed to dig themselves out of a newly built German concentration camp, Stalag III. The camp had been specially built for war prisoners who had previously tried to escape from other concentration camps. The heroes in the movie also became Mohammed Assaf's heroes: Steve McQueen, James Garner, Richard Attenborough and Charles Bronson.

Mohammed told the story of *The Great Escape* as a serial, evening after evening, as his cellmates listened intently from the corners of the three-by-three-meter cell. He noted the expressions on the faces as he told the story. When he was finished, no one said a word. Assaf had not told the whole story, however because the Germans had discovered what was happening during the escape. Of 76 escapees, 73 were captured, and of these 50 were shot on direct orders from Hitler. Assaf mentioned nothing about this.

Assaf's cellmates seemed optimistic at first, but when they began to discuss how they themselves could get out, their mood dropped. The walls were brick, and the floors cement. They had only drinking mugs, a water container, a bucket and a few clothes. How could they possibly escape without suitable equipment?

The conditions in the German concentration camp were much better than the ones they faced. The prisoners in Stalag III had managed to get hold of equipment by bribing a German guard. In Khiam, such an attempt would likely have meant more torture and confinement in the "chicken cage," the 90-cubic-centimeter enclosure used for extra severe punishment.

Eventually, Mohammed Assaf convinced his cellmates they should at least try to escape, even if it was impossible to dig through the cement floor in the windowless room. Since the walls were made of a lighter concrete, perhaps they could hack their way into the little kitchen on the other side. Three days after Assaf suggested this method, Daoud was able to loosen a flat piece of iron from the frame of the door. At least now they had a working tool.

With the iron they began to pick away at the smooth wall that backed on the little kitchen. The prisoners worked in shifts. After each shift they replaced the piece of iron into the door frame and made certain the guards could not see it had been loosened. They covered the hole in the wall with soft soap, and placed the material they dug out into the toilet bucket, later dumping with the rest of the bucket's contents.[2] The four continued with their daily routines so no one would become suspicious. The guards would examine cells more carefully if they heard unusual noises, so the cellmates spoke loudly as they picked away during a shift.

After a few days, a prisoner across the corridor noticed Daoud replacing the piece of iron in the door.

"What are you doing?" he whispered.[3]

"We are hiding a small radio," Daoud answered. He was not sure the other man believed his explanation, and wondered if they would be turned in.

After eight days of hard work, they had only managed to dig eight centimeters into the wall, and when they hit a pipe on the ninth day, they abandoned the idea. They had to find another way. Perhaps they could dig a hole under the cell door? They worked on that for a few days, but it seemed so hopeless that Daoud, the youngest of the four, wanted to give up.

Mohammed Assaf stood his ground. Perhaps the rectangular lattice of iron bars could itself become their "tunnel"? If they managed to loosen at least five of the bars, they might be able to crawl through to the corridor. The bars were about 1.5 centimeters in diameter and ran vertically, placed about five centimeters apart. The flat iron "tool" might again prove useful.

The prisoners rolled together a sheet to serve as a rope, which they tied around one of the bars, lacing it past the next bar and then a third one. Then they inserted the piece of iron and twisted it like a propeller, squeezing the iron bars toward each other. They maintained the pressure for about 20 minutes while simultaneously shaking the bars. Then they removed the sheet, tied it in a different position, and repeated the procedure for another 20 minutes. Thus they managed to loosen the bars one at a time by weakening the welds at the upper end. They worked day after day, but only for short periods of time when the guards were taking their breaks or sleeping. They tried to hide their efforts from prisoners in adjacent cells, as well, knowing there were spies among them.

They made another strong rope out of woolen threads from their sweaters and socks. This would be used during the escape itself. Mohammed Assaf made a map of the area using threads to represent local roads, rivers and mountains, which the prisoners carefully studied. They also made a layout of the prison, and tried to calculate how much time they would need for each subsequent stage once they got through the door and out into the corridor.

There were two exits from their section of cells. One led to the 25-square-meter courtyard where they went for fresh air. Prisoners who were not in isolation or undergoing interrogation and torture were allocated 10 minutes in the sun. From there the escapees could reach the roof of the section by lifting each other up to the netting of steel wire and iron beams. Mohammed Assaf thought it would be possible to widen the openings in the netting.

Daoud Faraj, who emptied the trash each day, checked things out more carefully in the courtyard. Above a water tank he discovered a pipe and a small hole in the wall, which the last man could use as a foothold to get up to the roof. Daoud also noticed that the barbed wire strung along the edge of the courtyard roof was not properly attached.

If they could get to the roof, they would have to be careful. They did not know what things were like up there. Very likely there were guards patrolling, and possibly searchlights. Next they would have to climb down from the roof and safely navigate the minefield surrounding the center. They would have to get as far away from the center as possible, and stay hidden for at least half a day before they could be relatively sure of their escape. The plan was to go south toward Israel, because the Israelis, once the escape was discovered, would likely concentrate on the north side, which was the shortest route out of the occupation zone.

Finally, Saturday September 5, the four in cell number 8 were ready for the great escape. One month and 20 days had passed since they began their work. First, they removed the iron piece from the door frame and bent out the first of the bars. This made a bit of noise. They stopped to listen if anyone reacted, but everything was quiet. They removed the other bars, one after the other, and lined the bottom of the opening with some foam rubber to make it easier to wriggle out.

The opening in the cell door was 25 centimeters wide. Mohammed Assaf was supposed to be the first man out because he was the thinnest, but he got stuck. He started to panic, lost his temper and wanted to call the guards, but the others managed to calm him down and pull him back into the cell.

Quietly they went ahead to remove another bar. They had previously required four days for each one, but now they managed the last one in five minutes. Mohammed snaked his way through and out. The others followed. Out in the corridor they heard one of the prisoners in the neighboring cell whisper, "Good Luck." Another whispered, "You will be killed," and a third said, "Those of us who are left will get hell."[4]

CHAPTER SIXTY TWO

In the Minefield

At the Norwegian battalion headquarters a few kilometers from Khiam, Colonel Hagrup Haukland was ordered to increase patrol activity early on September 6, 1992. For the first time in 20 years, there was going to be an election for the National Assembly in Lebanon. Colonel Haukland was afraid the Lebanese resistance movement would use the election day to attack the Israelis or the SLA, and he did not want something to happen in the Norwegian battalion's area. The voting had already taken place in the Bekaa Valley and North Lebanon, then in Beirut and the Lebanese Mountains, and now it had finally reached South Lebanon, including the Israeli occupied areas.

Elections in Lebanon had never been completely free and democratic. Many of the former members of parliament had bought and paid for their seats. This time the Syrians were also in the mix. In the north, Syrian intelligence had disqualified some candidates and replaced them with ones they liked better. The weak Lebanese government that resulted had to operate on directives from Damascus. Both Muslim and Christian members shuttled between Beirut and the Syrian capital to stay close to the real center of power.

All Christian parties called for a boycott. The Christians' main complaint was that the election law, with its new election districts split geographically, appeared quite unfair toward the Christian communities. They also felt free and democratic voting could not be undertaken so long as Syrian troops were in the country. The Syrians were supposed to withdraw from the Beirut area and back to the Bekaa Valley by September 1992, according to the Taif agreement, even though the Lebanese government could request for them to stay longer. Assad rejected a suggestion to postpone the vote.

When the voters showed up in the Bekaa Valley on the first day of voting, a typical Lebanese performance took place. There were fist fights and there was shooting. "But there was no loss of life, and this was the first time in history," bragged the minister of the interior. This was not completely true: a policeman and two civilians were killed in a fight between supporters of competing candidates. The minister of the interior himself, was up for election, and excused the fact that he received a number of votes from long-dead Lebanese with the words, "it is not always easy to keep order in the registries." In South Lebanon, NORBATT's Post 4-27 reported wild shooting in Hasbaya late on Sunday evening. "It seems they are celebrating the election," wrote assistant R. Andersen in the battalion's logbook.[5]

Things were quiet in Khiam on Sunday evening. The four escapees—Mohammed, Mahmoud, Saoud and Daoud—wore dark clothes. They snuck quietly along the corridor out toward the courtyard. Prisoners' shoes were kept at the end of the corridor, and they retrieved their own. Out in the courtyard, they looked up at the sky. It was forbidden for prisoners to look up during their 10 minutes of sunshine. For the first time in four years, Mohammed Assaf felt freedom. He was lifted up by his friends and managed to make an opening in the wire netting with the help of two small pieces of rope. Then he crawled through and up onto the roof. A guard was patrolling slowly about 10–15 meters away. Mohammed lay flat.

When the guard had gone, the others came up the same way. Daoud was the last one. He grabbed hold of the water pipe, got one foot into the hole in the wall and raised himself up. His friends' helping hands then pulled him onto the roof. The four of them snaked their way forward along the roof—Mahmoud first, then Mohammed, Saoud and finally Daoud. They noticed two men up in one of the guard towers, heard female voices and realized they were on top of the women's section. They had given thought to going down and bringing Soha Bechara with them. She also belonged to the Communist Party, and everyone in Khiam knew that Soha had tried to kill General Lahd four years ago. He had survived his operation and had returned as chief of the SLA after a long hospital stay. But the escapees realized it would be too risky. The most important thing was to get away as quickly as possible.

A guard was shining a pocket flashlight across an area outside the camp. Mohammed pointed to the area of the roof which was least lighted, and crept further on over a 20-centimeter-wide wall that led to the westernmost part of the roof. When Mohammed got to the edge, he could see down to the ground, four or five meters below. He also observed two barbed wire barriers with five meters distance between them. Mohammed knew there were mines all over the area.

According to plan they were to descend in two groups—first Mohammed and Saoud. Each had brought along an iron bar from the cell door as a weapon in case a guard came too near. The escapees would also use the rods to poke into the ground and find a safe way through the minefield.

Mohammed and Saoud repelled down using the rope they had made from their socks and sweaters. They heard dogs barking and froze.

"Have we been discovered?" whispered Saoud. "No, it is only wild dogs. Take it easy. This will go well."

From the roof Daoud could just barely see the two on the ground. One of them carefully stuck a rod into the soil to check for mines. They snaked their way forward five–six meters to the first barbed wire barrier, which lay in a roll in front of them. With a piece of rope, Mohammed made an opening and crept through. Saoud followed. Mohammed got through the entire minefield and up to the next barbed wire barrier, a fence. He took off the clothes on his upper body so as not to get them stuck to the barbs. All went well; Mohammed made it through with Saoud right behind.

By now, Mahmoud and Daoud had easily gotten down from the roof and it was their turn. Daoud was so tense and excited he did not notice that the barbed wire had scraped his back. When the two had nearly reached the end of the minefield, Mahmoud looked back toward the guard tower. At that same moment he lost his balance, fell and put out his left hand to cushion his fall. He hit a mine and it exploded.

Mohammed saw the flash of light and heard the explosion. He crept back and saw Mahmoud lying in the minefield while Daoud stood next to him, rigid with fear.

"Leave me," whispered Mahmoud. "Save yourselves. Run!"

The three remaining prisoners sprinted off down an incline, saw a light in the distance, and ran toward it. It was a light by the road that passed a few hundred meters west of the prison. They followed the road toward the nearby UNTSO observation post and kept going south—in the direction of Israel.

The guards in the tower did not react when they heard the explosion. They thought it was a wild dog that had gotten into the minefield, something which had happened before. No one thought anyone would try to escape. Soha Bechara also heard the explosion. She thought it was the resistance movement attacking.[6]

After a while, the guards heard Mahmoud's cries for help. They fired off an illumination grenade and one got orders to go see what had happened. He refused, saying, "I do not want to die for the Israelis." The SLA man was afraid the resistance movement was starting an attack against the prison. Along with the other guards, he barricaded himself in a shelter and waited for reinforcements. The first to arrive was a special group from the SLA. It had the job of defending Khiam in case the prison was under attack. The group surrounded the facility and fired off more illumination grenades. Only then were the guards convinced the explosion was not part of an attack.[7]

Mahmoud lay bleeding in the minefield. He could not see out of one eye, and his right arm was badly injured. Half an hour later the Israelis arrived with jeeps and an armored vehicle. An officer shouted to the injured person in the minefield to find out who he was. When the Israelis were convinced it was an escapee lying there on the ground, they slowly pushed a metal plate out into the minefield. After two hours they had created a rescue path out to Mahmoud, who lay some 20 meters away. One of the Israeli soldiers snaked along it and grabbed hold of Mahmoud. Suddenly he heard Abu Nabil shout, "Be careful: he might be armed!" The Israeli soldier was scared and let go of the bleeding Mahmoud. Once they realized he had no weapon, the Israeli lifted him with the help of a crane, and he was sent by helicopter to the hospital in Marjayoun.[8]

In the meantime, the guards had discovered that cell number 8 was empty. All the prisoners were ordered to line up along the walls with their hands in the air. Israeli soldiers and SLA militia began the search for the escapees, but they headed in the wrong direction, just as the men had thought they would. As the three prisoners ran south, the Israeli hunters went north.

After running south for half an hour, Saoud was too tired to go further. Daoud and Mohammed took hold of him and dragged him on. Behind them they saw the illumination grenades like small suns over Khiam and the area to the north. They eventually reached a small valley and a path that they followed further south. With Saoud in tow, they made slow progress.

"You have to walk on your own," said Daoud. "If we don't get further away before the Israelis begin their search in earnest, we will be caught."

Daoud and Mohammed ran on. Saoud tried to keep up, but could not. He fell further and further behind. Finally, he could no longer see his friends.

A bit later, Daoud and Mohammed decided to change course. They ran toward the east, in the direction of the Hasbani River and the village of el-Meri. The Hasbani River ran southwards and became the Wazzani River when it flowed into Israel. The plan was to follow the Hasbani northward and walk along the riverbank so the Israelis' search dogs could not track them.

When they reached the river, they crossed at a shallow ford. Then they walked toward the north in the dark of night. When dawn came, they hid in the reeds near the river's edge; they wanted to wait again until dark. They heard nothing but the sounds of nature. Daoud sat quiet as a mouse on a rock, well hidden in the reeds. He was so still that a small bird landed on his shoulder and stayed there.

"Don't kill the bird," whispered Mohammed, "You have just gotten out of prison yourself, and can't deprive freedom to anyone any longer."

It had not even occurred to Daoud to do anything to the little bird. He just savored the moment. Only then did he notice he was bleeding from a sore he had gotten as he wound his way through the barbed wire. Both of them wondered what had happened to the other two. They were particularly concerned about Mahmoud. Did he die in the minefield? And what had become of Saoud? They figured he had taken the same route as them, but they had no idea that, around 4:30 P.M., he too had crossed the Hasbani River and now lay hidden in a vineyard not far from the village of el-Meri.

CHAPTER SIXTY THREE

No Promises

On the morning of September 7, 1992, Colonel Kjell Narve Ludvigsen at UNIFIL headquarters in Naqoura called Battalion Chief Hagrup Haukland at the Norwegian barracks on the so-called Falcon Heights above Ebl el-Saqi.[9] Ludvigsen had heard about the escape from Khiam on Lebanese Radio and wanted to know if Colonel Haukland knew anything. Ludvigsen, who was the chief of the Norwegian UNIFIL contingent, asked, "What is the worst thing that can happen?"[10] Haukland did not immediately respond.

Ludvigsen continued: "What would you do if the refugees came to your door? Be prepared for the worst."

That same morning, Rune Haugdal, NORBATT's operations officer, received reports there was heavy Israeli activity in the area around Khiam. From civilian Lebanese who worked there, the Norwegians had also heard about the escape attempt and the explosions in the camp. Some said all four escapees had been captured, others said one had been killed and three had gotten away. UNTSO observers near Khiam had also heard an explosion and seen the commotion that followed, but did not know much more than that.

Throughout the day, NORBATT positions reported seeing Israeli forces in the Hasbani Valley. At 4:04 p.m., Company A reported to the operations center on Falcon Heights that an Israeli colonel leading eight soldiers drove in to Post 4-2B and on toward Hasbaya: "They are continuing on to Post 4-2Bcp and are joining two cars which have been parked outside the Norwegian control post."[11]

At that time Daoud and Mohammed lay quietly in a reed clump near the river, expecting to see Israeli soldiers at any moment. Suddenly, a dog appeared. Perhaps he was one of the Israeli bloodhounds? It disappeared as quickly as it had come, and must have been a stray. They also saw a hunter, but he did not discover them either. As it began to get dark, they decided to walk on. The Hasbani River had become narrower, and it was easier to walk in the water. But Mohammed became more exhausted than Daoud. He felt his knee throbbing.

"I cannot go any further. Leave me here. I can manage on my own. You know I know this area." Mohammed's village, Hebarieh, was just five kilometers east of the river.

They found a hiding place from which Mohammed could see a UNIFIL post, but the watchtower was so far away he did not think the soldiers at the post would discover him. Daoud continued on alone. He decided to go west, and found a long stick to lean on as he walked.

Daoud did not exactly know where he was. He passed a few fields and climbed a high fence, finally coming to an olive grove. Suddenly, he saw a light and heard voices in a language he did not understand. He thought it was Yiddish. He tried to hide in the hollow of an olive tree. Many thoughts swirled through his mind: what should I say if they catch me? What will they do with me? Kill me?

Suddenly a light blinded Daoud. He could just make out soldiers pointing rifles at him, and heard a command in English that he should throw himself to the ground.

"Put your hands behind you!" said the voice. Daoud was not great at the language, but he understood. They searched him and tied his wrists together with plastic bands, then ordered him to get up and walk. The soldiers led him to a car. The plastic bands around his wrists tightened painfully. He also hurt from the sores on his back and arms. When Daoud asked for the bands to be loosened, the soldiers did the opposite, tightening them even more. Now Daoud was convinced he had been captured by the Israelis.

The car drove for just a few minutes before stopping in a village. There he saw a female soldier, the first woman he had seen in two years. He then realized the soldiers could not be Israelis, as their army did not use female soldiers in Lebanon. Daoud felt relieved, even though they put him into a small cage with iron bars.

Over the radio, a message had already been sent to Falcon Heights that a patrol from Company A had taken a captive, whom they believed to be a hunter. Now they locked him up in a military police cell in Ebl el-Saqi. The message was written into the logbook at 9:38 pm on September 7.

At the operations center, no one tied the message together with the escape from Khiam. It was not unusual for patrols to find hunters who were looking for wild boar. The usual procedure was to let them go at the edge of the NORBATT area after interrogation. That the "hunter" had no weapon, but only a walking stick, was not reported. The Israelis monitored the bandwidth with Norwegian speakers, but they did not give any importance to the message.

Since Daoud did not speak English, NORBATT's interpreter, Walid Eckhardt, was sent for.

"What is your name, where do you come from?" the interpreter asked the bearded, dirty and bloody man.

"I have escaped from Khiam."

"Together with whom?"

"Alone. What will you do with me? Hand me over to the Israelis?"

"I cannot promise anything," the officer questioning him answered through the interpreter.

When NORBATT's operations chief, Rune Haugdal, realized it was no hunter they were holding, but an escapee from the infamous Khiam, he contacted the battalion chief. Colonel Hagrup Haukland decided immediately not to use radio or telephone while discussing the prisoner.[12]

From Falcon Heights, Major Haugdal drove with Captain Erlend Sandal in the colonel's car down to the MP station in Ebl el-Saqi. Now the questioning of Daoud began in earnest.

"Are you alone?"

"We were four."

"Where are the others?"

"I will not tell you before you say what you will do with me. Will you turn me over to the Israelis?"

"I cannot promise anything," answered Haugdal. "If the Israelis know you are here, it will be difficult to avoid it."

Around the same time, Saoud Abu Hadla went east from his hiding place in the vineyard near the village of el-Meri. Eventually, he saw the lights of another village a bit further away; it had to be Kfar Shouba. He had remembered the map Mohammed Assaf had made while planning the escape.[13]

Suddenly, someone shot at Saoud. He tried to run back and hide behind some rocks, but felt one of the bullets enter his right upper arm. Then he heard some shouting in Arabic, "You are surrounded! Give up!"

Saoud did not answer.

"What is your name? Are you armed? Are you one of those who escaped from Khiam?"

Saoud felt blood running down his arm, which hung limp. He tried to lift it with his left hand.

"I give up!" he called out.

He heard soldiers coming closer, one of whom said, "Let's kill him."

Another answered, "No, we have to question him."

The man who had fired pushed Saoud brutally to the ground and put a foot on his injured arm.

"Where are the others?"

"I don't know! When the mine exploded, we each ran in separate directions."

"I will shoot you if you do not talk." Saoud listened as the militia soldier got ready to fire, but no bullet came. Instead, the soldier, whose first name was Bassam, pulled out a first-aid kit to bandage the wound.

Saoud was driven to an Israeli camp not far from the village of Abbasieh. When they got there, a number of Israeli soldiers stood waiting with men from the SLA. Saoud had to walk the gauntlet between two lines of soldiers, who, with a mixture of respect and contempt, talked about the man who had managed to escape from his cell in Khiam.

Saoud got new bandages, and was put on a stretcher. An SLA lieutenant asked loudly and clearly of the militia soldiers who had captured him, "Why did you not kill him?"

Shortly after, an Israeli lieutenant who spoke Arabic arrived. The Israeli turned toward Saoud in a friendly manner and asked, "Didn't you think your chances of being killed during the escape would be great?"

"For us it was better to try to escape and maybe die, than not to try," answered Saoud.

"Did you get help from the inside?"

"No, we did everything ourselves."

"And no one helped you later?"

"No."

A bit later, Saoud was driven to the hospital in Marjayoun, for more interrogations.

CHAPTER SIXTY FOUR

Smuggled Out

A few kilometers further north, in Ebl el-Saqi, Daoud Faraj was in the custody of the Norwegian military police. He gradually felt more confident the Norwegians would not betray him, and told them that one of the four escapees now lay exhausted in hiding with a ruined knee. Daoud offered to show them the way, but the Norwegians said that was out of the question and drove him to NORBATT headquarters on Falcon Heights above the village. There they locked him in an empty cubicle in an ammunitions bunker. The battalion's intelligence officer, Captain Erlend Sandal, began a lengthy questioning session with an interpreter. Meanwhile, a patrol was sent out to find Mohammed Assaf, who lay hidden in the valley southeast of Ebl el-Saqi.

In the meantime, the head of the company staff, Major Arve H. Lauritzen, called one of the battalion's two doctors, Carina Thielesen together with Nurse Solveig Ekem Enger to check out the patient. When Daoud saw the two women, he felt he had arrived in heaven. They washed the young Lebanese and tended his wounds. He got an injection in his arm, then fell asleep.[14]

Two hours later, they had found Mohammed Assaf and brought him in for treatment as well. He was in far worse condition than Daoud. After the doctor had examined him, he was also put in the ammunitions bunker, but separately from Daoud. The intelligence officer planned to question them both more closely, and he did not want them talking to each other.[15]

Colonel Haukland had already called Colonel Ludvigsen in Naqoura and said, "Now it has happened, what we talked about earlier." He did not say much more; both knew the Israelis were listening to their frequency. Haukland had decided ahead of time that he would not follow the usual procedure in this case. Normally, infiltrators would be driven out of the battalion's area and released. This time the colonel did not want to risk the prisoners being recaptured by the Israelis, then tortured and severely punished. There was also a danger they would be shot during an "escape attempt."

Doctor Thielesen reported to Colonel Haukland on the condition of the escapees. Mohammed was severely depressed, but had no physical injuries of importance. Daoud had his wounds cared for and seemed in good shape. The colonel heard the doctor say, "There is nothing serious affecting them." He understood that to mean everything was ready for them to follow their usual procedure.[16] Colonel Haukland, as mentioned, had another idea.

The battalion chief knew time was working against him. The longer the two Lebanese escapees remained in the camp, the greater the danger there was of raising the Israelis' suspicions. Imagine if Brigadier General Micha Tamir, who had fought in Lebanon since 1985, showed up at the entrance to the camp with a direct question: "Are you sheltering terrorists?"

"They have to get out, and quickly," Haukland said to his officers.

The escaped prisoners were questioned separately. Their stories coincided. Afterwards, the intelligence officer had allowed them to be in the same room with a hidden recorder. The interpreter confirmed to Captain Sandal the two really were escapees from Khiam and not provocateurs.

Colonel Haukland discussed alternatives with his staff. They could evacuate the men to Naqoura with one of UNIFIL's helicopters. They could ask UNIFIL's Force Mobile Reserve, which was stationed close to the city of Qana, for assistance. Both options were rejected. Too many would know about the matter, and the Israelis would probably sense something was going on.

Haukland decided his own men would smuggle the two escapees out of the Israeli occupation zone as quickly as possible. He realized this could result in a confrontation with the Israelis, and that if this operation was discovered, he would be sent home. It could even result in demands that Norway withdraw from UNIFIL, something the Israelis had wanted for a long time.

Haukland was scheduled to meet with the Israeli liaison officer in Metulla on September 8, at 8 a.m.. The battalion chief decided to go ahead with the meeting; cancelling it would give the Israelis an indication that something unusual was happening. When Haukland returned, he called Lieutenant Fred Eilers into his office. Eilers was the troop chief in the battalion's "muscle," the mobile reserve unit. The troop had three armored personnel carriers at its disposal. When Lieutenant Eilers sat in front of the battalion chief, the operations officer and NORBATT's intelligence officer, they explained to him that this was a very delicate matter and had to be handled with great discretion.

Lieutenant Eilers' troop was camped at the outer area of Falcon Heights. There was no through traffic since it was a dead end. Colonel Haukland wanted the fewest people possible to know about the two escapees they now had in custody. The battalion chief was afraid of leaks; he could not be sure that the civilian Lebanese who worked in the camp would keep quiet. The Israelis and the SLA probably had informants among them.

Around this same time, the colonel received a message that significant military activity had been noticed in the Hasbani Valley. Around 40 soldiers had been seen in the area around Hebarieh, the home village of one of the escaped prisoners. An Israeli officer was leading his own soldiers and the militia from the SLA. The Israeli identified himself to the Norwegian UN officer in the village as David. He said they were on the hunt for two SLA soldiers who had disappeared. The Norwegian officer made the Israeli aware of the "one-hour rule." There was an agreement between UNIFIL and the IDF that the SLA militia was not allowed to carry out operations in NORBATT's area lasting more than an hour.

Later in the afternoon on September 8, Daoud and Mohammed were placed in the fighting space of the personnel vehicle. Lieutenant Eilers was in command and Walid Eckhardt accompanied to interpret, since neither Eilers nor his men spoke Arabic. The soldiers had locked up the vehicles weapons and bound the two escaped prisoners to their seats with handcuffs; Lieutenant Eilers did not want them to get up and risk being seen. Each was provided with a Norwegian uniform jacket and a blue UN helmet for camouflage. Daoud and Mohammed were happy for the Norwegian UN force's help, and promised not to tell anyone about it. Both understood what consequences it would have for the battalion chief and for Norway's continued role in UNIFIL.

The transport from Falcon Heights first went via the Israeli crossing near Metulla. The armored vehicle escorted a bus of Norwegian soldiers who were off on leave. The Israelis did not suspect that inside the white UN-marked vehicle were two wanted Lebanese. The car then drove on through the occupation zone to Tibnin. The Israelis had not erected additional barriers on this stretch of road. They were searching for the escapees further to the east.

It had started to get dark when the vehicle drove into the Norwegian repair facility in the outskirts of Tibnin. They parked right inside the headquarters area, and Lieutenant Eilers walked into the staff building. There he politely interrupted a meeting in progress to request a one-on-one conversation with the chief, Lieutenant Colonel Egil Vindorum.[17]

He handed Vindorum a letter from Haukland, requesting that the lieutenant be given all possible support. The force from NORBATT and the two escapees needed to stay overnight at the camp, called Camp Scorpion, because they were not normally scheduled to patrol this area after dark. Colonel Haukland made it clear that the Israelis should be given no reason to suspect anything out of the ordinary was going on.

They were offered beautiful guest quarters, but chose a more remote shelter. Daoud and Mohammed would remain in the vehicle along with the interpreter. They were given combat rations and driven to an olive grove to relieve themselves before night came. No one in the repair company noticed anything abnormal.

Captain Sandal drove in a jeep from Tibnin to Naqoura where he briefed the head of the contingent, Colonel Kjell Narve Ludvigsen. Together they went to the political advisor for UNIFIL, Timur Göksel. The Turk, who had previously been the press spokesman for the force, was irritated when he heard what had happened: "Why do you Norwegians have to be so 'clever'? Couldn't you have found another way, and let the prisoners fend for themselves?"[18]

Göksel, of course, knew it was too late to let the prisoners go just like that. He sent one of his own Lebanese assistants to the Communist Party headquarters in Sidon. A plan was made for them to pick up the escapees the next day. The agreed-upon place lay inside the UNIFIL area, but outside the Israeli occupation zone.

The next morning, September 9, Sandal was given a landmark to look for on the road between Tibnin and Tyre: a Mercedes would be parked by the roadside with its hood open, as if the car had engine problems. The Norwegians embarked, and Eilers saw the Mercedes as expected. He ordered the vehicle to stop and asked the two men by the car if they needed help, which was the normal procedure in such cases.

While he spoke with the men, Daoud and Mohammed were let out. In the rush of the moment, they forgot to take off their uniform jackets, but then remembered just in time. One of the Norwegian soldiers made certain the jackets were returned before the Mercedes disappeared with the two happy Lebanese in the back seat.[19]

The Norwegians continued their patrol. Later in the afternoon, they were back at Falcon Heights. UNTSO's Team Sierra had come for a visit and said the SLA security service thought the escapees were still in the area. In the report from the observers it said "civilian sources say the escapees are in Beirut, something which Team Sierra doubts. If this were true, there would have been lots of publicity surrounding the escape."

The publicity came the next day. The Communist Party called a press conference in Beirut. While TV photographers filmed, Mohammed Assaf spoke first about the prison conditions in Khiam and how he and the others had escaped from the center. Daoud Faraj also related his background and how prisoners were treated in Khiam. Neither said a word about being helped to freedom by Norwegian UN forces right under the noses of the Israelis and the SLA. None of the journalists thought to ask if the escaped prisoners had received help from others.[20]

The next day, NORBATT's excellent local laundryman and man-of-all-trades, Louis Assi, brought in a newspaper article about the press conference. Assi translated that the two had managed to get to Sidon thanks to their military training. Lieutenant Eilers smiled to himself, but said nothing.[21] The same day NORBATT received a visit from Undersecretary Jan Egeland from the Foreign Office, and Elsa Eriksen from the Defense Department. Neither of the politicians was told anything about how the Norwegian soldiers had smuggled the prisoners out of the Israeli occupied area.

Colonel Haukland later said he had met Brigadier General Tamir in Metulla a few weeks after the escape.[22] The Israeli looked the Norwegian right in eye and said, "You managed this well, this thing with Khiam."

"What do you mean by that?" asked Haukland without a blink.

"It was you who helped those two who escaped."

"I know nothing about the matter," Haukland answered coldly.

The Israeli general said nothing more; Haukland understood he had been bluffing. Perhaps the infamous Israeli intelligence service is not so much to brag about after all, the Norwegian colonel thought to himself.

Saoud Abu Hadla was back in Khiam after 11 days in the hospital at Marjayoun. There he was placed in a two-square-meter, solitary cell without any of the other prisoners knowing he was back. The guards told them that all of the escapees had been shot and killed during their flight.

Mahmoud Ramadan had lost his right eye in the minefield, along with hearing in his right ear. His left arm was in poor condition and half his face was deformed. He remained in the hospital in Marjayoun for a month and a half, then returned to Khiam. More than two years and four months later, both got their freedom through a prisoner exchange between Israel and Hizbullah.

CHAPTER SIXTY FIVE

The Third Cup

The historic escape from Khiam was soon forgotten in Beirut as the election in the National Assembly took up most people's attention. Hizbullah was represented for the first time; the party and its allies won 12 seats.

There had been a tough internal struggle over whether Hizbullah would participate in the election or not. The party had 200,000 members and was therefore Lebanon's largest. It was to be a party for both the masses and the elite—an elite with a highly disciplined cadre.[23] Lebanon's most influential Shia cleric, Sayyed Mohammed Hussein Fadlallah, had argued in favor of Hizbullah putting up their own candidates. Fadlallah thought Lebanon could not become an Islamic state by revolution, only by a democratic process. The leaders of Hizbullah also agreed, but the political leadership did not want to tear down the party's ideological pillars: Destruction of the State of Israel, liberation of Jerusalem and an end to the codified division of power among Lebanon's religious groups.

After the election, President Elias Hraoui appointed the Sunni multimillionaire Rafic Hariri as prime minister. Hariri, who also had Saudi Arabian citizenship, now put his trust in the belief that the Soviet Union's break up would lead to the collapse of one-party states in the Middle East as well. He thought first of Syria; if it fell, Damascus' hegemony in Lebanon would come to an end. Hariri also thought the Palestinian-Israeli conflict could be resolved through negotiations taking place in Washington.

Later in October 1992, there was a lot of discussion about the upcoming election in the United States. At the Café de Paris on Rue Hamra, the regulars preferred George H.W. Bush to Bill Clinton, doubting a Democrat would be tough like the duo of Bush and Baker. The guests at the café pointed to Clinton's accusation that the Bush administration had a pro-Arab policy, which Clinton would reverse. "The issue is whether Israel can survive or not," Clinton maintained.[24]

People in Lebanon knew that President David Steiner in the American Israel Public Affairs Committee (AIPAC), the most powerful Jewish lobby group in the US, had bragged about how strong the group's influence was over American foreign policy. "…We have Bill Clinton's ear. I have talked to Bill Clinton. He's going to be very good for us… He said he's going to help us. He's got something in his heart for the Jews, he has Jewish friends… that will be the best we could do," Steiner said in a telephone conversation that was recorded and later found its way to the Middle East.[25]

Politics was not the only topic discussed at Beirut's Café de Paris. One of the guests told me about the many facets of drinking coffee: "If you want to achieve something but are afraid an offer of a bribe would be badly received, then offering of a cup of coffee before you deliver the actual message can open the way. In the same way—if you want to be rid of an enemy, you can just get someone else to serve him 'a cup of coffee.'"

Once I had finished two cups of coffee, and ordered a third, one of the men at the table said jokingly: "Don't drink that third cup of coffee, it means death. You are familiar with the expression *'Wahad la deif, wahad la keif, wahad la seif?'*" It meant, "the first is for the guest, the second is for enjoyment, the third is for the sword."

I asked for an explanation and was told the expression comes from the Bedouin tradition for mediating disagreements between two tribes or families. As a rule, a respected sheikh was given the task of finding a solution to a conflict, and he would of course serve coffee during the discussion. If, after two cups of coffee, the sheikh had not found a solution that both parties could accept, a third cup of coffee was served. This meant war.

Several weeks later, I found a different explanation for the meaning of the "third cup." I recall it was October 26, the day after the six Israeli soldiers had been killed by a roadside bomb in South Lebanon, and Israeli officials had called the attack a "threat to the peace process." The IDF's leadership asked the government for permission to carry out a powerful act of revenge. The defense minister approved the action, and Israeli bombers took to the air while artillery and gunboats fired wildly at a series of targets in Lebanon. The attacks were primarily directed at Palestinian refugee camps in South and North Lebanon. At least seven people were killed.[26]

This October day, I had been invited to the home of an old Armenian friend, Albert Aghazarian, in Jerusalem. Albert spent his days at Birzeit University north of Ramallah; he was a living legend and a bottomless source of stories. First he gave me a lecture about the political situation in Israel, then we spoke of my visit to the Café de Paris and the meaning of coffee in the Middle East.

Albert proceeded to expound how the Bedouins make coffee. The process is nearly religious: the raw coffee beans are roasted in a pan with utmost care, and it is very important not to roast too much. Then the beans are crushed in a mortar of stone, wood or brass. The crushing takes place in a steady rhythm—one long stroke and two short ones. "Daa-da-da, daa-da-da, daa-da-da," Albert illustrated.

Meanwhile the water kettle hangs over the fire or sits on the glowing coals. "The coffee needs to come to a boil three times," explained Albert as he demonstrated how the coffee maker holds a small stack of handleless cups in his left hand. With his right, he pours a squirt of coffee into the uppermost cup, and swishes the coffee around the bottom of it. This is then poured into the next cup, then the next, and the next. Every cup must be rinsed with the first squirt.

After the final cup has been rinsed, he throws the remainder onto the fire in honor of Sheikh Shadhilly from Yemen, the coffee drinkers' supreme protector. Only then can the coffee be enjoyed. Half a cup is offered to the oldest and most prestigious guest. Then the others each get half a cup in turn. A full cup is considered an insult. Just as great an insult would be to offer the guests a third cup.

"Why?" I asked.

Albert told the story of a Bedouin sheikh from Gaza who, during a drought in the 1800s, rode off with his men and camels to buy grain in Egypt. When evening came, he had crossed the border into Sinai. Around midnight, the sheikh saw a light far away. He had never been in this area before and thought the light must be from a village close by. He left his men and camels to check.

The light came from a house and he could smell the aroma of coffee and thought it must be an inn. He walked straight in, but the only ones in the lighted room were a woman without her veil, and her husband. The woman screamed and hid her face when she saw an unknown man in the doorway. The husband tried to hide his horror and asked the newcomer what he wanted. The sheikh explained he thought the house was an inn, but since he had been mistaken, he would leave immediately.

The man of the house insisted he stay, and offered the uninvited guest a cup of coffee. When the sheikh had finished, he was offered another cup, to which he said yes, with thanks. But when he was offered a third cup, he politely declined. The host insisted, but the sheikh refused. Then the host pulled out his sword. He was from a warrior clan—the Mamluks, descendants of the soldier–slaves who took power in Egypt and ran the country for nearly 300 years until 1517. Now the host was threatening to kill his guest if he did not take the third cup of coffee that he had been offered.

The sheikh again refused, and said that in such a case he preferred to be killed.

"Why?" asked the furious host.

"Because the first cup is for the guest, the second is for enjoyment, and the third is for the sword. Even though I am a warrior like you, I am weaponless because I came here to trade, not to make war."

"Your answers prove you are a true man," said the host. "I thought at first you were a robber, but I see I was mistaken. Stay here in my house as my guest."

The sheikh accepted the invitation, and when he later went on to do his errands, he learned that the host had grain to sell. It was a good trade, and in the years that followed, the sheikh and his tribe were provided with grain from the Mamluks.

"But the story does not end here," said Albert. "In 1811, Egypt's ruler Mohammed Ali gave orders for all Mamluks to be killed. The only one who was spared was the Gaza-sheikh's friend. He was allowed to hide in the Bedouin camp until it was safe to return home."

In Lebanon, it was not safe for anyone in the fall of 1992.

CHAPTER SIXTY SIX

Rabin's Revenge

After Israeli planes attacked positions near the village of Ain el-Tina in the Bekaa Valley on November 8, 1992, Hizbullah responded by shooting missiles at targets in Northern Israel. To the surprise of many, Prime Minister Yitzhak Rabin characterized Hizbullah's attack as a reaction to Israeli operations in South Lebanon.[27] Rabin went on to clarify that the missiles had not been directed at Israeli population centers. This was a departure from the usual Israeli line, which referred to Hizbullah as an organization dictated by senseless terrorism.

Israel's former intelligence chief, Major General Shlomo Gazit, also said that this time Israel had crossed the line. He stated, "Hizbullah did observe 'the rules of the game' for a long period. They refrained from shelling Israeli territory and from infiltrating. They limited their operations to the 'Security Zone.' It was our retaliation for their skilful strike at our soldiers inside the zone that made them escalate the fighting. We bombed and shelled many targets in Lebanon, including some far to the north. Only then did Hizbullah retaliate by shelling some Israeli localities—with no casualties."[28]

What did this mean? I asked myself. Had the Israelis realized that the occupation of South Lebanon was not serving their interests? Did they recognize that Hizbullah was not Iran's spearhead against Israel, but had become a national movement in Lebanon? The Americans did not display the same sense of nuance as Rabin and Gazit. The outgoing Bush administration was mainly concerned Hizbullah's attacks could destroy the peace process between Israel and the Palestinians. After the first Katyusha rockets had been fired against Israel, the American ambassador in Beirut, Ryan C. Crocker, woke up the Lebanese foreign minister at 3 AM.[29] The minister was asked to contact Hizbullah quickly to stop the attacks. In a press release a few hours later, Foreign Minister Fares Boueiz said the ambassador had threatened extraordinary actions. Boueiz said it was useless to justify Israeli attacks so long as Lebanese territory was occupied by Israel.

Ane-Karine Arvesen, who was still stationed at the Norwegian Embassy in Syria, reported what had happened. She continued to follow developments closely. The two of us no longer had the same close relationship as before; I now had another partner, but Ane-Karine and I still remained what she called "soulmates" in the years to come.

Hizbullah continued its attacks on Israeli forces in South Lebanon. On November 12, 1992, the guerrillas killed an Israeli soldier, and elsewhere attacked one of UNIFIL's Nepalese positions. The UN soldiers at the post had tried to get the guerrillas out of the village of Kafra, which lay near the Israeli occupation zone. A UN soldier was killed and three were wounded. In the exchange of fire, one from Hizbullah was also killed. A month and a half later, an Irish UNIFIL soldier was killed by a Hizbullah group.

In Israel, the leaders were more concerned with the Palestinians' largest Islamic liberation movement, Hamas, than Hizbullah. Hamas had as its objective to fight for a Palestine governed by Islamic principles. The most militant in the movement wanted war to achieve its goals. They thought the Jewish state would disappear just like the Crusader Kingdom had done in its time. Hamas had become a serious challenge for the Israelis in the West Bank and the Gaza Strip, even if the army largely managed to keep the Palestinians under control. Hizbullah had no ambitions to fight its liberation battle within the territory of the Jewish state.

Over the course of six weeks starting in December 1992, Hamas guerrillas killed two Israeli soldiers in the Gaza Strip, one of whom was a sergeant in the Israeli border police. Hamas viewed the sergeant as a legitimate target; he was in uniform and part of the Israeli military power. The Israelis thought the killing was a cowardly and brutal act.

Prime Minister Yitzhak Rabin decided to do something dramatic. After conferring with the Chief of the General Staff, Lieutenant General Ehud Barak, he ordered that hundreds of Palestinians from the West Bank and Gaza would be deported to Lebanon. At first, 1,200 Palestinians were arrested, of whom 415 were chosen for expulsion.[30] I reported to the *NRK* on the deportation and remembered what Israel's first president, Chaim Weizmann, had said: "The world will judge the Jewish state on the way it treats the Arabs."

The West had been immensely patient with Israel despite its brutal treatment of the Palestinians and Lebanese. This had apparently led to Israel's leaders not caring much about international law, breaches in which never led to consequences for the country. Of course, the Israeli leaders were concerned about world opinion, but so long as the US never weakened in its support, they felt secure that the international community would not impose sanctions against them.

Palestinians from the Gaza Strip and the West Bank were driven in buses to the border with Lebanon. Then they were taken further through Zumriya, an unofficial border crossing between the occupation zone and free Lebanon. NORBATT's chief, Colonel Hagrup Haukland, had tried to prevent the Israelis from driving the expelled Palestinians through the UN zone, but UNIFIL's top commander, Lieutenant General Lars-Eric Wahlgren, ordered him to let them pass. The Swede did not want to get into a conflict with the Israelis.

After the Palestinians had been off-loaded and left in a barren and wind-blown area, the chief of the Israeli Northern Command, Major General Yitzhak Mordechai, called Colonel Haukland to thank him for his goodwill. When Haukland hung up the phone, he said to the officers who were standing there, "That damned horse's cock has nothing to thank me for. If I had been able to decide, he would damned-well not have been given any permission."[31]

In Beirut, Prime Minister Rafic Hariri gave orders to deny the Palestinians entry to the Bekaa Valley north of Marj el-Zohour, which lay in the no man's land between the Israelis and the Lebanese government army. Hariri was afraid the deportations were the beginning of a new Israeli policy: This time 400, next time 4,000 and then 40,000. He of course knew what had happened in 1948, when the Zionists had driven about 750,000 Palestinians out of Israel. The 100,000 who came to Lebanon had now become 300,000, spread among 12 main camps and five smaller Palestinian gatherings.

Some of the deported Palestinians tried to march south, but were stopped by warning shots from the SLA. The militia had set mines and guarded the front lines with seven tanks. It would sporadically fire flares and illumination grenades into the area. The following day the Palestinians decided to turn back.

The Israelis refused to allow the Red Cross to bring supplies to the 415 Palestinians through the occupation zone. But the occupying power could not stop Colonel Haukland, who gave orders for large water tankers to be driven to the camp. Eventually, Hizbullah took on the task of helping the Palestinians. For a short period, the guerrillas stopped their attacks on the Israelis in South Lebanon as well. Hizbullah did not want to take international attention away from the deported Palestinians.

From Beirut, journalists and photographers went to Marj el-Zohour to report from the Palestinian's tent encampment in the wind-blown and snow-covered mountain landscape. The camp was made up of men from 16 to 67, among them 17 university teachers, 11 individuals with doctorates, 14 engineers, 36 businessmen and five journalists. There were also more than 100 university students and some 200 bearded clerics.

NRK's hired photographer filmed one of the deported Palestinians from the Gaza Strip as he read a letter to his family. Then we brought the videocassette to Gaza and recorded the family while they assembled around their TV and watched it. The report was shown in the *Daily News Hour* the following evening.

The UN Security Council adopted a resolution condemning the deportation as a breach of international law. The newly-elected President Clinton understood there could be no progress in the peace negotiations with 415 Palestinians exposed to the winter cold in Lebanon. Therefore, the newly appointed American Secretary of State Warren Christopher began to work carefully on Prime Minister Rabin.

The first conversation was both "formal and gruff." Yet Christopher was impressed by Rabin's candor when he "stated plainly what he was willing to do and what he would not do." Rabin promised to bring back 100 of the 400 expelled men immediately. The rest would be able to go home throughout the course of 1993.[32] In exchange, the US promised to block proposed sanctions against Israel in the Security Council. Rabin called a press conference on February 1, 1993, where he said Israel would permit helicopters to deliver supplies to the remaining 300 Palestinians.

While correspondents were busy reporting on the Palestinians in Lebanon's ice-cold winterscape, hundreds of young Lebanese recruits came back from training exercises in Iran. At the same time, there were ongoing discussions among the Shias in Lebanon about Iran's motives in helping them fight against Israel. There were more than just Hizbullah's secretary-general, Hassan Nasrallah, who had seen the danger of becoming too dependent on Tehran. Nasrallah and his supporters wanted Hizbullah to be a national resistance movement, not a tool for Iran.

Lebanese outside of Hizbullah were just as concerned about Iran's ambitions in Lebanon. Therefore, in the last half of January 1993, a Shia delegation went to Iran for discussions, led by the finance minister and National Assembly president. The latter, Nabih Berri, was still leader of Amal.

When the delegation returned, there was full agreement between Iran and Lebanon that the fight against Israel was Lebanon's affair, but Iran offered to support the resistance movement to the tune of one million dollars.

CHAPTER SIXTY SEVEN
General's Baptism by Fire

As Hizbullah's guerrillas made ready for a new spring offensive, a Norwegian general was getting ready to head to Lebanon's killing fields. UNIFIL Force Commander Major General Lars-Eric Wahlgren went home to Sweden in February 1993. The Swede had been UNIFIL's top officer for four years. I had interviewed him when he arrived in Naqoura in 1988. He was arrogant and absolutely sure the Israelis would withdraw their forces from Lebanon within a short period of time. When I permitted myself to suggest my doubts, he said, "The leaders in Israel have personally promised me this. And I trust them." When I asked for a departure interview nearly five years later, Wahlgren "made like a Swede"—i.e., he disappeared without saying a word.

UNIFIL's new chief, Major General Trond Furuhovde, was no novice when he arrived in Lebanon. The tall, trim officer had been UNIFIL's chief of staff in 1988, and when he arrived in Naqoura on February 23, 1993, it was a return to a familiar headquarters. The evening before Furuhovde formally took over, a welcoming reception was held in Norway House. Around 10 pm a message arrived that the Israelis had fired on a Nepalese UN outpost in the Shia village of Yatar. The presiding officer came to Furuhovde and said, "The deputy commander thinks we may as well take you over right away."[33]

The major general went immediately to the operations center and found out that the Israelis had killed a UN corporal and wounded a private. The Israelis said "terrorists" had put up a mortar emplacement near one of UNIFIL's positions. Furuhovde studied the large wall map. He knew Post 5-12A from his time as operations chief. Another message arrived that a civilian Lebanese had been killed kneeling on the floor in prayer when an SLA mortar shell hit his house.

Automatically, Furuhovde began to think how he should deal with the IDF over this. As chief of staff, he had experienced many different types of Israeli officers. Some were emotional and difficult to work with, others professional. A bit later, he received a phone call from the Israeli Brigadier General Baruck Spiegel. The short, slender Israeli was chief of the unit that was responsible for contacts with UNIFIL. Spiegel had previously been in command of the Golani Brigade, a position which was viewed as a springboard to the top of the Israeli military power structure. But since then he had overseen an unsuccessful operation south of Beirut, and his career had more or less stalled.

The Israeli general's voice seemed meek as he expressed deep regret over what had happened. Spiegel added that it had not been the Israelis who fired, but the SLA. He was also sorry this should happen on Furuhovde's first day as chief of UNIFIL, but added that terrorists from Hizbullah had put up a position close to a UN post to get cover there. UNIFIL had to understand this was not acceptable, and would of course have to carry its share of responsibility for the incident.

Furuhovde did not accept this feeble attempt at an explanation, which was actually a bad excuse. "There are international rules for conduct of war," said the Norwegian. Additionally, he stressed that he was "concerned that those heading the operation from the Israeli side seem to be poorly trained for operating in an area with UN forces, or simply don't care about the consequences." He pointed out that it was beyond all reason to use mortars in a densely populated area. Finally, he said: "It is easy to blame the SLA for firing at UN positions and civilian targets deliberately. But it is Israel who has the responsibility."[34]

The day following the attack, I arrived with *NRK* photographer Elfinn Haug in Naqoura. Together with Furuhovde, we drove to a Shia village, where the UNIFIL chief entered a house the that had been bombarded. There sat the father of the deceased, crying. "*Shukran, shukran*"— "Thank you, thank you," said the man, as he took the general's hands and invoked God. Furuhovde turned to me and asked, "Is there anything more painful than parents who have lost their children?"

Afterwards he inspected the bombed-out UN position, where one soldier had been killed and another wounded and was followed by Lebanese journalists. In interviews he expressed that the attack on the UN position was completely unacceptable. The general promised to take the matter up with UN headquarters in New York, and directly with the IDF.

When Furuhovde met Spiegel a few hours later at the border near Rosh Hanikra, just south of Naqoura, the Israeli offered him new regrets and excuses, but insisted he could not take responsibility for the SLA's actions. Attacks by "terrorists" were of such a character it was difficult to avoid hitting UN positions, particularly when Hizbullah operated in the shadow of these positions and local settlements. General Spiegel suggested to establish a new liaison arrangement, which in the future would assure safety for the UN troops. Corresponding to direct contact between the IDF and UNIFIL, also direct contact should be established between the SLA and UNIFIL positions.

Furuhovde thought this bordered on audacity. If he were to go along with something like this, UNIFIL itself would share responsibility in future "accidents." He told Spiegel, "My confidence in you will be further weakened if you come with more suggestions like these. The SLA was established by Israel, the militia has been educated and trained by Israel, it is under Israeli command, and it will be Israel's responsibility what it does, operationally and legally, as long as it exists."

Spiegel did not give in: "Technical errors are difficult to avoid so long as Hizbullah operates so close to UN positions. Only direct contact between the SLA and UNIFIL positions can help to reduce the possibilities for future losses."

Furuhovde repeated, "Israel is the occupying power in South Lebanon and must take responsibility for what the SLA does." He avoided any comparisons to the conditions in Norway during the German occupation, remembering well what the Norwegian battalion chief had gone through four years earlier.[35]

Toward the end of the meeting, Spiegel said that, in the wake of Secretary of State Christopher's visit to the region, it had been decided Israel would continue the peace negotiations with the Palestinians. "For that reason it is of vital importance that the hostilities in South Lebanon are kept at a low level," he said.

General Furuhovde reported back to the UN headquarters in New York, and unofficially to Johan Jørgen Holst, who had become foreign minister in the spring of 1993. Furuhovde spoke to Holst often by telephone, even though the foreign minister had lately been absorbed by the secret negotiations going on between Israel and the PLO in Norway. Holst thought the developments in Lebanon could affect the situation in the entire Middle East, and asked for detailed reports.

When Hizbullah attacked Israeli positions in the corridor north of the Christian city of Jezzine on July 24, 1993, Holst got yet another call from Furuhovde. The guerrillas had also attacked Israeli positions in the Finnish and Irish battalion areas, as well as a position a mere kilometer away from Beaufort. Furthermore, Hizbullah had fired Katyusha rockets toward Israel from positions north of the Litani River.

During the fighting, which took place over four days, the Israelis lost eight soldiers. Seven more were wounded. However, no Israeli civilians were killed. The Israelis used heavy artillery and mortars against UNIFIL's area, and new Israeli artillery was brought forward. The fuse had been lit. It was only a question of time before the explosion came.

CHAPTER SIXTY EIGHT
A Pre-planned Attack

Major General Furuhovde had long been considering a trip to Baalbek and the Bekaa Valley. The valley was important because many of Hizbullah's activities in South Lebanon were planned and prepared there. It was also an entry point to Syria and an important agricultural region for Lebanon.

In a routine meeting with his closest associates, Furuhovde asked, "Is it irresponsible of me to take a trip out of Naqoura now?"[36]

"Of course that is difficult to say," answered Nicolae Ion, the force's political advisor. Then he added: "If you have not received any signals from Israel, I doubt anything is about to happen immediately."

"The situation is tense, but it has been so for a long time. The rest of us are of course here; there is no shortage of manpower should something occur," said the chief of staff.

"Then I will go," said Furuhovde.

The general had been reading up on Baalbek's history. He had also read that Noah's ark had been built of Lebanon's cedar trees. After the flood, Noah is said to have remained in the Bekaa Valley, and to have been buried in the city of Zahle, south of Baalbek. As if that were not enough: The great conqueror Timur the Lame (also Tamerlane), a descendant of Ghenghis Khan—is said to have visited Zahle in hopes of seeing Noah's 31-meter-wide grave.

When Furuhovde, in an entourage of three cars, drove north from Naqoura along the coast, he did not have Noah's grave in mind. He sat quietly and stared out the window, wondering if it was right to leave headquarters in this situation. He was anxious as they continued on to Beirut and then over the mountains and down toward the Bekaa Valley.

Halfway down, Furuhovde asked his driver to stop: he wanted to test the connection with headquarters in Naqoura. Not a sound. It did not work.

"Let's try the Norwegian battalion," Furuhovde said to his driver, Second lieutenant Kåre From, a policeman from Sandefjord in Norway, "it is right down at the end of the valley there."

They made contact with the battalion and asked for a situation report. "All quiet in NORBATT, but there is firing in the distance," was the message from the officer on duty.[37]

When the general and his group drove on through Zahle and north towards Baalbek, they saw a Syrian anti-aircraft battery, Israeli fighter planes and enormous clouds of dust.

"Damn, there is an aerial attack against targets in the mountains southeast of Baalbek," the general said and grabbed the radiotelephone to order the other two cars to observe the air attack in the east.

"So they started today," he said to another in the car. Now there was nothing more to wait for. The Israelis were under way, and it was best to turn back to Naqoura immediately.

When Furuhovde reached Beirut, a staff member was there waiting with a hand-written message from the IDF, signed Lieutenant Colonel Yerushalmi, acting chief of the IDF liaison unit. The UNIFIL chief was surprised that it came from Spiegel's deputy, since the message was IDF's operations and war declaration. Furuhovde noticed the message contained the usual phrases about Israel's need for security and its legitimate right to self-defense. Further, the UN general was requested to stay calm and not be concerned. This made the Norwegian general mad.

By the time Furuhovde had read the letter, his car was a good distance south of Beirut. There was heavy traffic on the coastal road, particularly northbound. Further south, he could see people along the roadside looking toward the sky. Furuhovde asked his driver to stop, and they saw huge clouds of smoke rising up the mountainside east of the road.

"Let's drive," said Furuhovde. It was important to get to Naqoura as quickly as possible.

Near Zahrani, where the road comes in from Nabatiyeh and Jezzine, there was a traffic jam. Cars filled the northbound lane, four or five abreast. Southward the traffic proceeded single file, but the driver maneuvered the car safely through to the UNIFIL headquarters.

Furuhovde went immediately to the operations center. The first message about the Israeli offensive had arrived at 5:10 in the morning on July 25, after Hizbullah had attacked an SLA position on the Akiye Bridge over the Litani River.

The Israeli attack had been planned weeks before. Israeli radio and television had been given signals to set up a studio in Northern Israel, where the Israeli military correspondents were given exclusive access to pilots preparing for their missions.

Prime Minister Rabin informed his ministers about the details of the plan at a government meeting that same day, and its first phase was approved. Rabin also informed the opposition leaders to ensure their support, and he fully briefed the country's newspaper editors as well.

The Israeli foreign ministry sent out instructions to the country's ambassadors to put PR campaigns into motion. Foreign Minister Shimon Peres called in foreign ambassadors to hammer in the message: Israel has long shown restraint. Now you must ask the governments in your home countries to put pressure on Lebanon and demand the disarming of Hizbullah. There was absolutely no talk of the fact that Israel was an occupying power, and that Hizbullah was a legitimate resistance movement according to international law.[38]

After this, the Israelis attacked villages all over South Lebanon, and also north of the occupation zone. Villages in the Nepalese, Irish, and Finnish battalion sectors were attacked in addition to those in the Norwegian area. Hizbullah, for its part, fired Katyusha rockets toward northern Israel.

That same evening, the Israeli government approved an escalation of the attacks. A full-scale ground offensive was launched north of the occupation zone. Only four ministers, all from the left-leaning coalition party Meretz, voted against. Two ministers from the Labor Party abstained.

While the Chief of the General Staff, Lieutenant General Ehud Barak, briefed Israeli journalists on the results of the war effort the first day, a message arrived that a Katyusha rocket had killed two Israeli civilians and wounded 10 in Kiryat Shmona. From UNIFIL's headquarters, General Furuhovde sent a report to the UN in New York saying that the Israelis had put into motion the largest and most comprehensive attack against Lebanon since the 1982 invasion. The IDF called the offensive Operation Accountability.[39]

Yitzhak Rabin, who was both prime and defense minister, denied he had gone to war against Lebanon. Rabin wanted only to "put pressure on" the inhabitants in South Lebanon, and force the Shia Muslims to turn against Hizbullah. He likewise hoped the Shias in South Lebanon would "expel" the Hizbullah guerrillas from their villages.[40]

CHAPTER SIXTY NINE
The Seven Day War

The Middle East's strongest military power put into action its heaviest artillery and the world's most modern fighter planes. The Israelis fired on and bombed civilian targets and UN positions in the Finnish and Irish battalion sectors. Five villages in the Irish area were hit by artillery shells containing phosphorous. The battalion's intelligence officer, Captain Mark O'Brian, found 12 undetonated shells, all produced in the United States before 1977, and marked M110, the international technical designation for shells containing the chemical.[41] White Phosphorous causes deadly burns and emits a poisonous white smoke. UNIFIL's Force Commander Furuhovde said these weapons were banned in densely populated areas.[42]

The Israelis denied having used these banned shell types. Again the country lied, knowing full well that they would not be subject to punishment with the US behind them. Each suggested resolution in that direction was met by an American veto in the Security Council.

Yitzhak Rabin was running the war against South Lebanon as if he were still the Chief of the General Staff, as he had been in 1967, when Israel attacked Egypt. The Chief of the General Staff in 1993, Lieutenant General Ehud Barak, could only quietly accept that Rabin had been briefed directly by Military Intelligence instead of passing through him.

Every day Rabin flew from Tel Aviv to Northern Israel to talk with the ordinary soldiers and officers at the front. He demonstrated his own capabilities, and modified orders to the military as he saw fit. Foreign Minister Shimon Peres also flew to Northern Israel. In Kiryat Shmona he promised the population that Hizbullah's attacks would soon end, but toned down the possibility of a ground invasion north of the occupation zone.

On July 26, 1993, Rabin announced he would make South Lebanon uninhabitable unless Hizbullah's attacks against Israel stopped. In the course of the day, 54 Lebanese towns and villages north of the occupation zone were bombarded. Around 200,000 Lebanese fled. However, this was not enough for Rabin. Two days later he said he would make sure Beirut was inundated by refugees from South Lebanon.

In Northern Israel, 150,000 people went into bomb shelters every night. As the days progressed, several Israeli politicians began to doubt whether the government had clearly defined military objectives beyond destroying towns and villages and creating a new refugee problem. "This operation seems unclear," said Naomi Hazan from Meretz. "To drive the entire population from their homes will only increase instability in the Lebanese government, which is already weak. It has to be our task to strengthen this government."[43] The Israeli right also questioned Rabin's wisdom. Rafael Eitan, who had been Chief of the General Staff when Israel invaded Lebanon in 1982, thought it "unwise to set fire to the villages in South Lebanon. The inhabitants there have no influence over Hizbullah. Now the whole world will be against us because of these refugees."[44]

Because of the Israelis' huge attack, General Furuhovde had to reduce UNIFIL's activities in the operations area. IDF bombed without consideration for the white UN vehicles that brought food and equipment around to the battalions.

On the morning of July 28, the Israelis reduced firing in the UNIFIL area, but later in the afternoon the IDF demanded UNIFIL's vehicles keep off the roads. Furuhovde immediately sent a telegram to New York where he stressed it was unacceptable for Israel to limit the freedom of movement of the peace force.

At the same time the Israelis began bombing areas north of the Litani River. It was obvious they wanted the stream of refugees to continue towards Beirut. The unmerciful attacks on villages in South Lebanon's UN zone continued the following day. These villages were no longer habitable.

The unavoidable occurred: an Irish and Finnish UN position was directly hit. It was completely destroyed, but no one was injured because the crews had sought refuge in shelters just minutes before the shells impacted.

On July 29, General Furuhovde decided to challenge the Israelis. He said he would fly to the Norwegian repair company in Tibnin, and then to parts of the Irish battalion area. He warned the IDF, but received an answer that he could not take-off by helicopter or plane.

"I am the one who decides when a UN helicopter flies," responded Furuhovde.

He asked the helicopter pilot on duty if he was willing to fly under the existing conditions. If not, Furuhovde said he would ask someone else. The pilot did not hesitate, nor did the rest of the helicopter crew. The helicopter took off and proceeded through the air corridors as normal. In front and on the sides Furuhovde could see shells impacting. But the helicopter landed safely in Tibnin, and the general was able to see there were civilian refugees at both the Norwegian repair facility and at the Irish battalion headquarters.

When back in Naqoura, he called Brigadier General Spiegel and described in detail the results of the IDF bombings. He again asked the Israelis to stop their offensive. It was necessary for two reasons: lack of water would quickly lead to intolerable hygienic conditions and serious medical problems. Continued destruction would also have the completely opposite effect for Israel than the one they sought.

He was upset, and one could hear it in his voice when he said, "It is difficult to have confidence in Israel. On the one hand you say the goal is to stop Hizbullah, but on the other you do everything to prevent the UN from carrying out the simplest tasks. It is an unreasonable demonstration from the Israeli side. Finally, we will all be sitting back with a 'What now? Massive destruction, suffering, hate, continued fear and the feeling of being subjected to bloody injustice?'"

There was silence at the other end of the line.

"We will try to find a solution," Furuhovde continued, "but then you must stop firing on all of us."

That afternoon around 300,000 South Lebanese were refugees in their own country. Only then did US Ambassador Ryan C. Crocker feel the time was ripe to visit Lebanon's president, Elias Hraoui. The US wanted to help the refugees and would donate $400,000. It would not take the president long to calculate how much the Americans valued each homeless man, woman and child: a little more than a dollar. The Americans were generous toward the Israelis, however, as was highly visible in South Lebanon. The UN figured Israel had used 40 million dollars in the course of the first four days of fighting. It was just a small part of the annual military aid Israel received from the US.

One of the villages hardest hit was Jibsheet. Many of the inhabitants there had died in earlier resistance fights. Now they lay in the martyrs' graveyard. But even there they would not lie in peace. An Israeli Cobra helicopter fired a missile into the graveyard, and hit the grave of Sheikh Ragheb Harb. He had been buried there nine years ago. The house of his successor, the kidnapped Sheikh Abdel Karim Obeid, had also been hit by a missile. The family was not home, having fled to Beirut.

At 3 pm, the IDF again sent a message to UNIFIL that it was forbidden for the UN to drive on the roads or fly in their operating area. Furuhovde refused to accept the restriction. The IDF responded by saying that from now on, UNIFIL's movements would be considered "hostile."

Furuhovde refused to budge. He sent a telegram to New York, which left no doubt of his position. At the same time he emphasized his point by continuing to send supplies to his own troops and to the civilian population still remaining in the areas under attack. That same evening after dark, an Israeli patrol boat swept the beach outside the UN headquarters in Naqoura with its searchlights, and the crew opened fire on the beach with their heavy machine guns—just 10 meters from Furuhovde's encampment.

On July 30, things calmed down somewhat, even though Hizbullah and the IDF exchanged fire the whole day. Major General Yitzhak Mordechai, chief of the Israeli Northern Command, sent out a message to UNIFIL. In it, he demanded the UN force had to "help to get Hizbullah to stop firing Katyusha rockets at Israel." The general also threatened UNIFIL. He wrote, "If the peace force does not stop Hizbullah, the IDF will fire on UN positions that lie near Hizbullah mortar launch sites." Finally, the message repeated that it was forbidden for UNIFIL vehicles to drive on the roads. Once more, Furuhovde refused to follow the Israeli demand.[45]

On July 31 at 2 am, Hizbullah fired eight rockets toward Israel. Four of them were fired from launch ramps put up in the Fijian sector, and four in the Nepalese sector. The IDF fired from its side toward villages throughout the UNIFIL area of operations. The powerful assault lasted until noon. Then the Israelis backed off, and at 3 pm Furuhovde received a message that Israel would initiate a complete ceasefire. Suddenly an eerie silence fell across all of South Lebanon.

The decision to stop came from pressure within the Israeli coalition government, particularly from the Meretz Party, which had been established just prior to the 1992 election. Representatives of the party had threatened to support a no-confidence vote in the Knesset. The action proved conclusive in getting the government to ask the IDF to stop firing, where international protests had little effect.

"None of us has any problem with the IDF hitting hard at Hizbullah," said Meretz representative Dedi Zucker. "But we who know the outcome of the invasion of 1982 realize it does not lead to any solution to our problems in Lebanon. The harder you try, the deeper you dig yourself in."[46]

With the help of the US, an "understanding" was reached between Israel and Hizbullah. The IDF promised not to attack civilian targets in Lebanon. In exchange, Hizbullah would refrain from firing rockets into Israel. The agreement was an oral one, and never written down.

At exactly 6 pm the ceasefire and the so-called understanding took effect. For Hizbullah, this was a gift from God. Not only did the US, who had previously accused the party of having started the spiral of violence, had to polish its language; the superpower also had to ask nicely for Syria's help to put an agreement together. In this way, the US and Israel officially had to accept Hizbullah's right to attack Israeli soldiers within the so-called "security zone." When Lebanon's prime minister, Rafic Hariri, summed up what Israel had gained from the seven day offensive, he used one word: "Zero."[47]

The same day the ceasefire agreement became known, Foreign Minister Johan Jørgen Holst called Furuhovde and asked to be briefed. Furuhovde was furious and said, "It was so incomprehensible, and almost unreal that anyone could plan such destruction and at the same time call the operation 'Accountability.'" Both the general and the foreign minister agreed it was a known practice to give misleading names to IDF operations.[48]

Following the conversation, Holst wrote a memo to Prime Minister Gro Harlem Brundtland. He emphasized that the Israelis had systematically destroyed a series of Lebanese villages. He also reported on Israel's attempt to stop UNIFIL's activity and that Furuhovde had not yielded to the pressure. Neither the Norwegian prime minister nor foreign minister made anything more of the matter. Neither one wanted to complicate the relationship with Israel. For the government, the most important thing was to keep the secret Oslo channel open.

CHAPTER SEVENTY

Aftermath

At three in the morning on August 2, 1993, General Furuhovde received a phone call from the UN chief for peacekeeping operations, Kofi Annan from Ghana. Furuhovde thought Annan seemed tense when he said that Prime Minister Rafic Hariri wanted to send the Lebanese army into UNIFIL's operating area "to prevent Lebanese groups from fighting each other." Annan thought Hariri's motive was just an excuse. "The actual objective is to prevent Hizbullah from shooting rockets toward Israel," he said.[49]

"Has any agreement been reached? What about the size of the force? From what point in time? What will be the operational relationship between the Lebanese army and UNIFIL?" Furuhovde wanted to know. Annan said he did not know anything about it.

Early the next morning, Furuhovde flew to Beirut. He had gotten an appointment with Foreign Minister Fares Boueiz and Chief of the General Staff Lieutenant General Emile Lahoud. The foreign minister advised that Lebanon had not established any time frame for the operation in UNIFIL's area, but it would have to be put into action "as soon as possible."

"When refugees return home and see the extent of the damage, it will be easy for Hizbullah to stir things up, and let loose new violence in the region," said Boueiz, who hoped Hizbullah would not be resupplied with missiles.

"Are the Israelis informed of the plan?" asked Furuhovde.

He got no other answer than that all parties involved apparently had been consulted before the UN Secretary-General had given his agreement. The foreign minister said that if Furuhovde noticed any negative attitudes from the Israelis, he would like to know it as soon as possible.

In the military's supreme command in Yarze, Furuhovde learned one battalion would be inserted into UNIFIL's area. General Lahoud said he had not received orders to stop Hizbullah's fight with the Israelis. And if the army were to get this mission, a much greater number of forces would be needed, as well as "clear written orders" from the government. Furuhovde had a sense of the solid, well-trained general, who seemed calm and reflective. He understood what problems the general had to deal with in Lebanon, and Lahoud for his part knew a good deal about the UN bureaucracy.

When Nicolae Ion, UNIFIL's political advisor, came to Beirut the following day to inform the ambassadors of the permanent members of the Security Council, he learned that the US ambassador, was surprised by Lahoud's reservations concerning the mission. Crocker had hoped the politicians and Lahoud would be in agreement, and that the mission would encompass control over Hizbullah's activity.

Crocker thought the Lebanese army's mission in South Lebanon would have a positive effect on the peace negotiations in Washington. And when Ion asked whether the Israeli authorities knew about the Beirut government's plans for South Lebanon, Crocker confirmed the Israelis had been briefed.

"It is now important that UNIFIL be willing to take a calculated risk to contribute to movement in the peace process," the American ambassador said.[50]

In Damascus, President Assad was satisfied with the "understanding" between Hizbullah and Israel. He was also satisfied that only 300 Lebanese soldiers were to be sent into four villages that lay close up to the Israeli occupation zone. These were far fewer than had originally been planned, and than what the Israelis wanted. Therefore, there was only a small chance that the Lebanese army would get involved in Hizbullah's resistance fight.

On August 6, the Israelis asked once more for a meeting with Furuhovde at the border. Israel's liaison officer, Brigadier General Baruck Spiegel, had wanted to give the UNIFIL chief a briefing about Secretary of State Warren Christopher's visit to Israel. Spiegel advised that positive developments would occur in the Syrian-Israeli negotiations for a peace agreement between the two countries. Christopher had been in Syria, where President Assad had been very business-like, according to Spiegel. Spiegel also thought Prime Minister Rabin firmly believed the Syrians took the negotiations seriously.

The meetings in Jerusalem and Damascus signaled that "something positive was about to happen," Spiegel added. The Americans' negotiations coordinator, Dennis Ross, wanted to help work out the details on the basis of the results which Christopher had achieved. According to the Israeli general, a strengthening of the Lebanese government army was "quite positive." All actions that contributed to improving the government army's ability to control the situation would at the same time contribute to general security in the region.

Spiegel further advised important work was being undertaken to arrange direct communications between the IDF and the Lebanese government army. Several channels were being utilized, among them an American one. In the meantime, it was Israel's understanding that UNIFIL, with its experience in liaison work and knowledge of regional conditions, would be best suited for such a task. According to the IDF view, UNIFIL's task would not just be limited to establishing a connection between the IDF and the Lebanese army. UNIFIL would also be able to play a very important stabilizing role in the area. The IDF recognized that UNIFIL should become "a part of the process which should have as its objective to create a more optimistic future in the region" until a more lasting political solution was found.

Furuhovde carefully watched Spiegel as he spoke. So many new issues were raised that the conversation had to be characterized as startling. The Norwegian thought the Israeli's proposals would first have to be presented to the UN Secretary-General, Boutros Boutros-Ghali. The Israelis were making a useless calculation in an attempt to keep their grip on South Lebanon. It was apparent that they wanted to weave the Lebanese army and UNIFIL together to protect the IDF and the SLA in the occupation zone.

Both IDF and UNIFIL analysts had determined important changes were taking place in Hizbullah's pattern of operations as well. What happened on August 19, near the village of Shihin, not far from Naqoura, would increase the frustration among many Israelis who had to serve in South Lebanon.

It was around 5 in the morning when an Israeli patrol moved into an area after receiving a message that three bombs had been placed there. The bombs looked like rocks and were hard to differentiate from the real ones along the roadside. Six soldiers walked in two lines in front of a tank with another six men on-board. The foot soldiers were to check the road to verify if the message was true. Just as the patrol passed the "rocks" they were looking for, they exploded. Hizbullah's guerrillas were lying hidden nearby, and followed up by shooting at the soldiers who survived the explosion. In all, nine Israelis were killed. This was one more casualty than had occurred in the incident that caused Israel to go berserk in South Lebanon one month earlier.

In the *Daily News Hour's* morning broadcast that day, I reported from Jerusalem that the attack came just three weeks after Israel had carried out its massive, one-week bombardment of South Lebanon. Fifty villages were partially destroyed, 147 people had lost their lives and 450 had been wounded. The attack against the Israeli military column in South Lebanon was the deadliest the Israelis had experienced in nearly five years. And this was in line with the "understanding" which had been negotiated by the United States that attacks on the Israeli occupation force in South Lebanon was legitimate.

CHAPTER SEVENTY ONE

UNIFIL and Hizbullah

When Foreign Minister Shimon Peres landed at Oslo's Fornebu Airport a few hours after Hizbullah guerrillas had killed nine Israeli soldiers, he was met by Johan Jørgen Holst along with a group of journalists and photographers. Peres explained that Israel had made "a great effort to calm the situation in South Lebanon and Northern Israel to the benefit of all." He did not wish to say anything about whether Israel would seek revenge for the dead: "I only know about the matter from the mass media and need more information."[51]

Israeli planes had already taken off to attack targets in Lebanon. But this time they only fired at empty training camps in the Bekaa Valley near the Syrian border. Israel realized Hizbullah had not broken the "understanding" from June, and apparently did not want to escalate the conflict.

Some hours earlier in Stockholm, Holst and Peres had finalized the secret negotiations by telephone with Yasser Arafat in Tunis for a mutual recognition between Israel and the PLO. The agreement in principle was to be signed secretly at the Norwegian government's guest house that same evening with the Israeli foreign minister present. This was the draft of what later would be called the Oslo I Accord, an agreement that surprised the whole world. It was received with great enthusiasm, including the majority of Palestinians and Israelis.

Later, many would realize that the Israelis had fooled both the Norwegian facilitators and the Palestinian negotiators. Shimon Peres himself would outright say, "We fooled the Palestinians."[52] But in Oslo on August 19, 1993, Peres spoke neither about the still secret agreement with the PLO nor about the Palestinians in general. When asked if Hizbullah's attack on Israeli soldiers was justified Lebanese self-defense, he said, "Hizbullah is bombarding Galilee, which is not their land. The party gets its orders from Iran, which is not their land. It is serving a foreign agent with the purpose of creating provocations and to destroy the peace."[53] This was an apparent attempt to veil the truth about Israel's occupation of South Lebanon, and Hizbullah's right to fight against the occupation.

The United States condemned Hizbullah's attack on the soldiers, but not Israel's attack on Lebanon. An announcement from the State Department said the attack on Israeli soldiers in South Lebanon was executed to derail the peace negotiations that were resuming in Washington. Not one word was said that Israeli soldiers were lawful targets for the resistance movement, or that Hizbullah had not broken the "understanding" from June.[54]

In Israel, Vice-Foreign Minister Mordechai Gur said that most Israelis had exaggerated expectations for the understanding that had been reached. Many Israelis mistakenly believed that Hizbullah would stop its attacks against the Israeli army in South Lebanon. They were not informed that the oral agreement only stipulated that Hizbullah would not shoot missiles toward Israel so long as the IDF did not attack civilian targets in Lebanon. Chief of the General Staff Ehud Barak complained that the Lebanese army, which had sent several hundred soldiers to the UNIFIL zone following the ceasefire, had not done enough to stop Hizbullah's attacks.

Minister of Housing Benjamin Ben-Eliezer, another general with a background of operations in Lebanon, thought Israel could not stay passive against the "murderous behavior" that the attack on the soldiers represented. The minister got others' support when he pointed out that nothing in the ceasefire agreement said Israeli forces should be sitting ducks waiting to be killed. This was intolerable; Israel had to protect its soldiers.

Things had not gone as Rabin had planned. The Israeli army in South Lebanon was even more hampered than before. The agreement not to fire on civilian targets restricted IDF operations. Hizbullah on the other hand, could continue to attack in the occupation zone.

Before the Israelis had completed Operation Accountability, UNIFIL had started plans for what General Furuhovde called Operation Reconstruction. He meant it was important to get the civilian society operating again as quickly as possible. Hundreds of families had their homes destroyed. Schools and other important buildings lay in ruins. In Furuhovde's view, the international media had not shown particularly great interest in covering the Israeli conduct of war in South Lebanon. He thought the reason was the correspondents were awaiting an invasion similar to what had happened in 1982. When the ground invasion did not occur, the media lost interest. At the same time Furuhovde knew UNIFIL had not done very much to attract the world's attention.

In order to get reconstruction underway quickly, Furuhovde used $50,000 to hire an engineering company to repair roads and buildings. Swedish, Irish and Norwegian mine experts removed unexploded shells, bombs and mines. At the same time, Furuhovde intensified UNIFIL's cooperation with the United Nations Development Program to get the Lebanese authorities and companies going as quickly as possible.

Hizbullah had its own engineering company. It was repairing roads, building houses and removing unexploded shells and bombs, just as UNIFIL was doing. "Hizbullah was a party which apparently cared about helping ordinary people," Furuhovde told me later.

Not long after the Israelis' summer operations of 1993 had ended, General Furuhovde met with Nabih Berri, the leader of Amal, and president of the National Assembly. Furuhovde liked Berri. He was always cordial and well briefed, but each time Berri proposed that the Lebanese government army should operate together with UNIFIL, Furuhovde said that would not be acceptable. Berri also learned that UNIFIL had lost people because Hizbullah and Amal were firing from positions close to UN positions, and that there had been several confrontations between the militias and UNIFIL soldiers.

"Such discussions always ended when we agreed we had to find a method to serve the interests of both parties," Furuhovde told me, and added, "I know Berri is called 'the fox' by his enemies."

This reminded me of a Jewish legend which my Armenian friend in Jerusalem, Albert Aghazarian, had told me, and which I shared with Furuhovde.

In early times only one creature lived in the ocean, a combination snake and dragon by the name of Leviathan. The monster eventually felt quite lonely, so he convinced the Angel of Death to send one of every type of creature from the land into the ocean. There Leviathan could change them into fish, and he would have as many subjects as there were creatures on land.

One by one, the Angel of Death threw the various animals into the sea. The fox realized that he was next, but like the fox that he was, he decided to fool the Angel of Death and cheat Leviathan. He went down to the ocean on his own and sat at the edge of the beach. After a while, the fox noticed the shadow of the Angel of Death reflected in the water. That same second, he began to cry and complain.

"Why are you crying, dear fox?" asked the Angel, impatient to get his job done for Leviathan.

"I am sad for my brother who threw himself into the sea when he felt the Angel of Death approaching. It was as if he was in a hurry to become one of Leviathan's legionnaires. There he is now," sobbed the fox, waving sadly with his paw, which waved back from the surface of the water.

"Good," said the Angel, and flew off.

The fox went back to the forest, satisfied he had fooled both the Angel of Death and Leviathan. But eventually Leviathan discovered that there was no foxfish among his subjects. Dissatisfied, he lashed the water with his tail and asked his subjects if they knew why this was so. The long brown ratfish then told him how the fox had fooled the Angel of Death. Leviathan was furious and said, "Bring the fox to me alive. I will eat his heart and become just as sly as he. But do not tell him. Just tell the fox that I am dying, and that I wish to make him king of all the fish in my stead."

The ratfish found the fox and gave him Leviathan's message. As vain as the fox was, he went with the ratfish to the sea. But after he had thought about it some more, his doubts began to rise. What had he got himself into? Perhaps he was about to be fooled himself?

"Oh, my good ratfish," said the fox, "now that I cannot get away, tell me exactly what Leviathan said?" The ratfish told him then what Leviathan had said and that he would eat the fox's heart to become as sly as he was.

"My heart! Leviathan wants to eat my heart? Now you are in trouble," shouted the fox, and continued: "Why did you not say so when there was still time? I did not bring my heart with me. Did you not know we foxes never carry our precious hearts with us? They stay at home, in our dens."

The ratfish was worried, but the fox calmed her down with the words: "You won't have any problems if you bring me back to land so I can get my heart."

The ratfish did as the fox said, but as they neared the coast, the fox jumped ashore and was gone, chuckling over how dumb the ratfish could be. The fox never went back to the coast. That is the reason that to this very day there are no foxfish in the sea, according to the Jewish legend.

"The fox was fooled nonetheless: there is a fish called a foxshark, at least in Norway.[55] But it is possible that Nabih Berri is even more clever than his nickname suggests," said Furuhovde.

Later we talked about the relationship between Amal and Hizbullah. They were no longer using weapons in their struggle for power in South Lebanon. As a result, Hizbullah's relationship with Iran had deteriorated. It had begun to falter when Ali Akbar Hashemi Rafsanjani was elected president of Iran in 1989. In the years that followed, Rafsanjani tried to extend a hand to the United States to such a degree that it irritated Hizbullah's hard core.

In the days prior to the signing ceremony for the Oslo I agreement and the mutual recognition between Israel and the PLO, scheduled for Washington DC on September 13, 1993, Hizbullah and Palestinian factions, planned a protest march in Beirut's southern sections. President Elias Hraoui ordered the interior and defense minister to make sure the protest was cancelled.

Hizbullah insisted there had to be a public demonstration. Party leaders thought the agreement was a trap for the Palestinians, and they were supported by a number of Lebanese parties in West Beirut. A compromise was reached. In cooperation with the interior and defense ministries, the march was postponed, and the route was changed and shortened.

When the demonstrators marched into the main road leading to the airport, they were surprised by Lebanese soldiers who used live fire against them. Nine of the demonstrators were killed and dozens wounded. The leaders of Hizbullah gave orders not to use their weapons in retaliation. They understood the attack had been planned to draw the party into a confrontation with the government. The defense ministry explained there had been a breakdown in communications and a misunderstanding lay behind the attack on the unarmed demonstrators.[56] The conflict between the government and Hizbullah did not end there, but there were no armed confrontations. The party's secretary-general, Hassan Nasrallah, gave priority to the fight against Israel in South Lebanon, instead.

On the evening of October 22, a dinner was arranged in Nabih Berri's huge villa near Zahrani. Trond Furuhovde was one of the guests. After the meal, Berri proudly showed off his garden to the Norwegian general. When the two were back amongst the guests, it did not take long for a Lebanese intelligence officer to come over to Furuhovde. The UNIFIL general had known the officer and knew he was close to Chief of the General Staff Lahoud.

"Would you consider having a conversation with two representatives from Hizbullah? They both represent the party in the National Assembly," the officer asked.

After giving it some thought, Furuhovde agreed. It could be useful to meet the political leader class in Hizbullah. When he was introduced to the two representatives a few days later, he assumed they were both in their late 30s, or at most in their early 40s. They were immaculately dressed and gave the impression of being highly educated. Neither of them was pushy or arrogant, Furuhovde noticed with satisfaction.

He had carefully thought about what he would say. He had even discussed different possibilities with his closest associates. On this occasion there was no long conversation. The two wanted mainly to brief Furuhovde on Hizbullah's democratic ambitions, and emphasized it would be very unfortunate if he were to criticize the party in the media.

"I will continue my criticism until Hizbullah changes its pattern of operations. You are not shielding the civilian population," answered the general, "I cannot accept that the guerrillas for their own protection establish positions in densely populated areas and near my positions, and thereby expose both the civilian population and the UN to counterattack."

Despite the disagreement, the tone was pleasant and the atmosphere friendly and the meeting was useful for both parties. Furuhovde also pointed out that UNIFIL and Hizbullah had worked in a friendly "competition" to rebuild a war-torn South Lebanon.

"This, together with my positive comments about Hizbullah's civil activities, formed the basis for further contact between Hizbullah and UNIFIL," Major General Trond Furuhovde told me later.[57]

Hizbullah was not alone in taking on the tasks a normal state would have done. Other parties and their militias made sure people who lived within their domains got help, although none were as effective as Hizbullah. Its leaders were also not as corrupt as their counterparts in other parties. But then, Hizbullah also had advantages others did not have: they received around 140 million dollars per year from Iran, a significant sum in the Lebanese context, particularly because the dollar exchange rate was high compared with the value of the Lebanese Pound.

In order to organize help, Hizbullah established the Jihad Foundation for Construction (Mu'assasat Jihad al-Bina), following the pattern from Iran. Together with other organizations, such as the Martyrs' Foundation, projects were started that did not only benefit Shias. Christian and Sunni Lebanese also enjoyed the fruits of the Iranian funding. They got schools, low-price shops, pharmacies, cheap apartments, harvesting of land, water distribution facilities and Lebanon's first employment service.[58]

General Furuhovde could not help but be impressed with what Hizbullah had managed. In West Beirut's southern suburb, Dahiyeh, where the Lebanese state was invisible, Jihad al-Bina took on the job of supplying water and electricity, as well as garbage collection. Even after the civil war had ended, the state did not take these tasks back, and Hizbullah's initiatives allowed that part of the city to avoid a social catastrophe.

Instead of trying to create an Islamic revolution, Hizbullah continued to operate within the Lebanese system, even if it was a rotten one. This did not mean the radical Shias had embraced a western democratic system. The party recognized, however, that it could not immediately achieve the Islamic state's "absolute justice." Instead it directed the spotlight toward what was practically possible within the system—and outside of it, as well, when the leaders found it to their benefit.

CHAPTER SEVENTY TWO
Peace Process Gone Astray

It was quite normal for a Middle East correspondent to be on the job in Bethlehem and Jerusalem during Christmas, and when the holidays began in 1993, I was there. There was optimism among many Israelis and Palestinians for the prospects of peace, and I looked forward to a peaceful Christmas without drama. But it did not happen that way.

On the night of December 27, 1993, Israeli forces in South Lebanon attacked a UN patrol from the Norwegian battalion and killed Gorm Bjørnar Hagen. Hagen, together with four other soldiers and a dog, were out on a routine patrol, looking for possible infiltrators into NORBATT's area close to the village of Blat. It was dark and the soldiers were using flashlights. They knew the way and walked in a line, four meters apart. The last man had the blue UN flag sticking out of his rucksack.

An hour past midnight, the Israelis fired off a signal flare. This was a sign the area would be fired upon with artillery. The targeted impact area was not far from UN Post 4-23 north of Blat, and a radio message was therefore sent out to the patrol about this.[59]

From UNIFIL headquarters in Naqoura, the Israelis received a message that there were no other armed men in the area except NORBATT's patrol. The IDF immediately withdrew the warning about the shelling. But the communications man in the patrol, Lars Oddvar Solberg, had just barely finished responding to the message that the Israelis would not be firing when he saw a flash of light from a hill further north, near the village of Aishiyeh. It was an Israeli Merkava tank that was shooting at them.

The shell landed behind the Norwegian patrol. Shortly after, a new shell hit that was filled with five-centimeter-long steel projectiles resembling darts. Lieutenant Øyvind Berg heard a terrific bang as the darts hit the rocks. Berg was along as an observer in the patrol, which normally had only four men.[60] Berg and the others ran toward some boulders where they threw themselves down. A new shell exploded close by. The patrol leader, Corporal Helge Eliassen, ordered everyone to run toward a house at the edge of Blat. Suddenly, Berg felt blood streaming down his arm. He called to Eliassen that he was wounded and noticed that his left leg began to fail. Berg lay down on the ground while his comrades gave him first aid.

Suddenly, they discovered Gorm Bjørnar Hagen was nowhere to be seen. They fired off a light flare for better vision, then two men ran down toward the big rocks where they had taken cover. Just 10 meters away they found Hagen, who was seriously injured. One steel arrow had hit the 21-year-old in the head, one in his right eye and another in his neck. Hagen had great difficulty breathing.

Over the radio, a message was sent that he had to be evacuated by helicopter. By the time the UN helicopter landed, Hagen had lost consciousness. At the field hospital in Naqoura, just before 4 in the morning, Hagen was declared dead. Lieutenant Berg was sent to Rambam Hospital in Haifa.

Later in the morning, I got hold of Major General Furuhovde by telephone. He told me what had happened, and together with a hired photographer, I immediately left Jerusalem for the hospital in Haifa, where I interviewed the wounded lieutenant. Using my mobile phone, Berg was able to talk to his immediate family in Norway, while the photographer recorded the conversation. A bit later I met Furuhovde at the border with Lebanon. He was furious that the Israelis disregarded their agreements and established routines.

Foreign Minister Shimon Peres called Undersecretary Jan Egeland and expressed his regrets at what had happened. Foreign Minister Johan Jørgen Holst was in the hospital in Oslo after suffering a serious stroke. Egeland responded by saying the Norwegian authorities expected that those responsible would be made to answer for their actions. A few hours later the Foreign Office received a letter from Peres, where he again regretted the action and promised that "a full investigation will be undertaken from the Israeli side, and everything will be done to ensure that this will not happen again."[61]

There had been a long series of episodes between the UN and Israel. The Israelis had always insisted that every confrontation was a matter which only affected the UN and Israel, not particular countries within UNIFIL. But for Israel, the relationship with Norway was more important than ever. It was vital to maintain the friendship, so that Israel, through Norway's intermediary in the Oslo Channel, could continue negotiations with a weak PLO. Undersecretary Jan Egeland recognized the difficult situation that had developed, and said it would be a tragedy if "this event were to have an effect on the current peace negotiations."[62] The Israeli tank commander responsible for the attack was given two weeks' arrest, and a 21-day suspended sentence. An Israeli second lieutenant was sentenced to one week's arrest and a 28-day suspended sentence. In the Foreign Office, the matter was considered closed.

Israel's occupation of South Lebanon was not high on Norway's daily agenda. Nearly everyone working on the Middle East in the Foreign Office was focused on maintaining close relations with the US superpower. One of the most experienced Norwegian diplomats thought Norway was not so much occupied with creating peace in the Middle East, as it was with sipping Champagne with the powers that be in Washington.

This meant Norway was also not particularly concerned with the screams that its UN observation post near Khiam could still hear coming from the prison. Torture victims there knew little or nothing of what was happening outside their own cells. The inmates tried to make the best of the monotonous daily existence, which would be interrupted at irregular intervals by interrogation and torture.

Soha Bechara was serving her time in solitary confinement. Through the years she had been given a number of offers that could have reduced her sentence. Among these were a request to sign a plea to Hizbullah to release the war prisoner Ron Arad. She refused. Abu Nabil had then asked her to appeal for help from the Communist Party in Lebanon to work for Arad's freedom. Soha refused once more.

She agreed, however, to meet with Roger Auque, a French journalist who had been a Hizbullah hostage six or seven years ago. He interviewed Soha for 20 minutes in a courtyard surrounded by barbed wire. Auque was most interested in the assassination attempt against Lahd, but she also managed to say that she was against the taking of hostages.[63]

One morning she dressed for her allotted time in the shower when she felt something stuck in the sponge she used to wash herself. Without the guards noticing, she took out a thin little square of cardboard and put it into her shoe. She then showered as her heart beat wildly.[64]

When she finished and dressed again, she was anxious to be back in her cell to find out the contents of the secret message. Instead she was sent to Abu Nabil. He was not alone; an Israeli who called himself Tommy was also there.

"What is wrong with you? You seem upset," Abu Nabil said.

"I am always upset when I meet an Israeli," Soha answered.

That morning neither Abu Nabil nor Tommy had any new offer for her. Once they had finished interrogating her, Soha was brought back to her cell. She was shaking as she took the piece of cardboard from her shoe, but to her surprise she could not find any message on it. She turned it in different directions, but found nothing. That could not be possible. There had to be a message!

Time and again she turned the bit of cardboard. Only when she held it up to the light, could she see a short text in Arabic had been scratched onto it, apparently with a bit of wire.

The message was a greeting from Kifah, the Palestinian guerrilla soldier who had been captured during an attempt to sneak into Israel just a few weeks before Soha herself had made her attempt against General Lahd's life. Soha had barely seen Kifah in Khiam. She heard from other inmates how Kifah had been tortured, and how she had resisted.

From then on the two women sent messages to each other twice a week. Everything depended on whether they managed to get writing materials. They used the same method the American hostages had used when they were in captivity. The foil from the French soft cheese became a pen; rolled to a point, it could be used to scratch messages onto cardboard or paper. Their mailbox was the trash bucket in the washroom.

Neither Kifah nor Soha had any idea that Hizbullah had over 500 guerrilla soldiers in the UNIFIL operating area. In the course of a few hours, several thousand reinforcements could be brought in from the Bekaa Valley and West Beirut. Increasingly, the guerrillas dared to undertake frontal attacks against the Israelis, supported by good intelligence. They were able to mount several simultaneous operations using infantry, mortars and rockets. The attacks had all the characteristics of a sophisticated offensive operation. At times the firing was so intense that the Israelis could barely hold their ground with the help of air support and artillery. Hizbullah would often attack in difficult terrain, and after the attacks the guerrillas would hide in camouflaged caves. The Israeli Northern Command had never experienced anything like this.

In addition to Hizbullah, the Israelis were also being attacked by resistance groups from Amal and other Palestinian groups. But these operations were more sporadic and were of little military significance. On a number of occasions, Palestinians tried to get across the border to infiltrate Israel. When two Palestinians tried to get through the Norwegian battalion's area near Shebaa on March 12, 1994, they were discovered. One was taken prisoner by the Norwegians and sent to UNIFIL headquarters in Naqoura to be interrogated. The other had hidden in a cemetery in Shebaa. He was found by civilian Lebanese who reported him to the SLA. The Palestinian chose to surrender without a fight. He threw his weapon away, got up and stood completely still with his hands over his head. Nonetheless, the SLA men mowed him down. The Norwegian soldiers stood there paralyzed and watched the execution before the corpse was thrown into the trunk of a militia vehicle and driven away.[65]

As *NRK*'s Middle East correspondent, it was impossible for me to stay up to date with everything taking place in Lebanon when my eyes, to a large extent, were on the so-called Oslo Process. Like other correspondents, I followed the peace negotiations between Israel and the PLO closely. Finally, Norway had been given a big role in the Middle East, and we did not want to miss out on this.

When the follow up to the Oslo I Accord was to be signed in Cairo in May 1994, Yasser Arafat was flown to Egypt in a Norwegian plane, accompanied by Foreign Minister Bjørn Tore Godal and a large press corps. In the Egyptian capital, the Norwegians, who had expected to receive a prominent position, were shunted off to the side. Foreign Minister Godal was not given a place on the podium, but had to be satisfied with a front-row seat in the hall. The facilitators of the Oslo Channel, Terje Rød-Larsen and Mona Juul, where relegated to the guest gallery along with the press.

When the so-called Cairo Agreement became public, it showed Arafat had yielded to the Israelis on all important points. He was so accommodating that certain Israeli ministers were concerned they had gone too far. "When you twist Arafat's arm in the name of security, you have to be careful you don't break it. Arafat will not be able to control the West Bank and Gaza with a broken arm," warned Environmental Minister Yossi Sarid.[66]

Neither Prime Minister Rabin nor Foreign Minister Peres cared. They had dictated the terms of the agreement that gave the Palestinians self-governing authority over 65 percent of the Gaza Strip, along with a small enclave in Jericho. The Israelis had ensured for themselves the right to keep control over water, electricity and the roads to and from the Jewish settlements.[67]

In theory, the Palestinian areas would be widened in three phases to include the rest of the West Bank. In the first phase, the Palestinians would get responsibility for tourism, education, culture, health and social welfare. They would also take over collection of direct taxes. In the second phase, the Israeli forces would be "redeployed" so that they were no longer in "Palestinian population centers." In the third phase, free elections were to be held on the West Bank and in Gaza. In practice, the table was set for increased colonization of the West Bank. Prime Minister Rabin threw salt in the Palestinian wound by advising he did not intend to let them have their own state.

In Norway, there were a few or none in the political leadership who raised their voices when it turned out that the "peace process" was going in an entirely different direction than the facilitators had hoped. Norwegian politicians only wanted to bask in the international sunshine that the Oslo Process had afforded. At the same time, they did not give up the hope of a future Palestinian state.

In Jerusalem and Tel Aviv, Israeli politicians were struggling with an aching sore point—namely, air navigator Ron Arad, who had been missing for eight years. Relatives and friends constantly complained that Israeli officials had done little to repatriate the war prisoner. The criticism would not stop, despite the fact Mossad had employed all of their methods to get Arad free.

Nothing helped. The Israelis were not even sure who was holding Arad prisoner. For that reason the government in Jerusalem decided Mustafa Dirani—Amal's former security chief, now head of the Resistance Movement of the Faithful—had to be kidnapped. He was the one who was responsible for Arad during the first years of his captivity.[68]

The 41-year-old Dirani lived in the village of Qasr Nabah in the Bekaa Valley. The village was beautifully situated north of Zahle, where it surrounded the remains of a Roman temple. It was also known for its wild rosebushes and fragrant rose water.

While the Israelis were forging their plans, Mustafa Dirani received a visitor from Norway. His younger brother, Sobhi, who spoke good Norwegian after six years in the country, came to his birthplace to celebrate the end of the Muslim annual pilgrimage to Mecca, Eid al-Adha.[69] Of course, neither brother knew the Israelis had been gathering information about the village for many months. It lay in the heart of Hizbullah's core region. There were diverse opinions as to whether Dirani could provide any new information about Ron Arad's fate, but finally Chief of the General Staff Ehud Barak found support for his theory that this was the man who could fill in the information gaps necessary to get Arad back.[70]

On the evening of May 21, 1994, the commando group that trained to kidnap Dirani was ready at a helicopter base near the border with Lebanon. Dirani's family in Qasr Nabah was gathered at home. Half an hour before the helicopters were to take off, the chief of Israel's military intelligence, Uri Saguy, was asked to come to Prime Minister Yitzhak Rabin's apartment in Tel Aviv. There sat Ehud Barak, the chief of Mossad, Major General Shabtai Shavit, and Rabin's military advisor, Major General Danny Yatom.

Rabin seemed unsure. "Will the operation succeed?" he asked.

"I have given you all the intelligence information we have, but I cannot guarantee anything with regard to the future," said Saguy.

After much back and forth, Rabin was convinced.

In Mustafa Dirani's two-story house, the atmosphere was festive. It was the evening before the holiday, and the family only went to bed after midnight. Two hours later, Sobhi was awakened by a strange noise. His brother, who was sleeping beside his wife and baby daughter, awoke as well from the sounds and heard someone speaking Arabic with a Palestinian accent. He saw the door to the bedroom open, and five men came into the room. Then he was torn from his bed and pushed onto the floor.

One of the soldiers asked Mustafa in Arabic, "Where is Ron Arad?"[71]

"I don't know."

"We will kill you."

"I don't know."

"We will kill Ali, your son, if you don't talk."

The soldiers rummaged through the bedroom before they carried Mustafa out of the house and put him on a stretcher. Sobhi saw one of the soldiers standing with the barrel of his rifle against his brother's head. Then Mustafa was loaded into a jeep and driven to the waiting helicopter.

Back in the village, Dirani's family was in shock, and soon the whole village was on its feet. Some said they had seen a jeep from the Lebanese army and soldiers with Lebanese uniforms. Others had seen a familiar face among the kidnappers, a distant relative of Dirani. It was apparent he had been recruited by the Israelis and now was working as their agent.

Among the correspondents it was known that both Israel and Hizbullah spent a lot of time and resources recruiting agents from the other side. The methods varied. In some cases classic honey traps were set with women in the lead role. In other cases the recruiters took the long way around to get their prize into the trap.

CHAPTER SEVENTY THREE
Recruited by Mossad

My correspondent period in the Middle East ended August 1, 1994, and I immediately began to plan a new book that would be called *All for Israel: Oslo–Jerusalem 1948–1978*. The title is a play on words of the Norwegian King Haakon VII's motto, "All for Norway."

I wanted to tell the story of how Norwegian politicians, scientists, officers and UN envoys had allowed themselves to be used by Israel ever since the state was established. These key Norwegians put Israel's interests before Norway's and did everything Israel asked, without asking questions themselves. The police in Oslo gave Mossad's representatives Norwegian passports in order to smuggle Jews out of the Soviet Union. Norwegian officers agreed to spy for Israel. Norway also sold heavy water to Israel, knowing full well it would not be used for peaceful purposes. After a Norwegian inspection of the Israeli atomic reactor, a faked report was prepared.

In order to document the information, I travelled between Norway and the Middle East on unpaid leave from the *NRK*. I spoke with Norwegian politicians who had participated in relevant operations, dug into Norwegian and Israeli archives and met retired Mossad officers who had operated in various countries in the 1950s and 60s.

It was only later, as so often happens by chance, that I came across the story of Ahmed Hallaq. It did not happen often that correspondents got the smell of agent-recruiting and other actions taking place in the shadows. But when it happened, we were given good illustrations of how the war in South Lebanon took on many facets. The unique story of Ahmed Hallaq is no exception.

In the summer of 1994, two years had already passed since Hallaq had received his first telephone call. It came from a Moroccan he vaguely knew, who asked Hallaq to help him check out a matter in return for a sizeable payment.[72]

Hallaq was 40 years old, a Lebanese Sunni from the little village of Barja near Sidon. Twelve years earlier he had joined a Palestinian organization called al-Saiqa. The guerrilla group had been formed by Syria's Socialist Baath Party, but was run by the country's secret services. Ahmed Hallaq had not joined because he supported the Palestinian cause, but for the money. His salary was higher than what he got as a sergeant in the Lebanese army.

The Moroccan who had called Hallaq in 1992, said the Americans were looking for a print shop in the Sidon area that could make counterfeit dollar bills. Would he come to Cyprus to talk about the matter? Hallaq said yes, but because he was afraid of flying, he went to Limassol by boat from Jounieh north of Beirut. In Cyprus, he spoke with a Lebanese man who gave him a fat advance and said it was the CIA that was looking for the printer.

Back in Beirut, Hallaq began to search. At the same time he continued to cash his pay from al-Saiqa. But when he was wounded in a firefight, and had to go to hospital, the mission for the Americans was put on hold. When he had recovered, he was again called by the brother of the Lebanese man he had met in Cyprus. Now he learned he could forget about the print shop and the counterfeit dollars. The Americans would pay a lot of money for information on the remains of Israeli soldiers who had disappeared during the invasion in 1982.

He was surprised and asked, "Why would the US help the Israelis with this? And why have you chosen me?"

"The CIA has a video that shows you sitting on an Israeli tank that had been captured in Khalde during the invasion in 1982. The Americans think there was a dead Israeli soldier in the tank," the Lebanese man said.

Hallaq agreed to take the job. He needed the money. However, he insisted on meeting his American employer.

"My brother has only had telephone contact with them in Cyprus," answered the Lebanese, whose first name was Soheil. He asked if it was okay to make a tape recording of Hallaq's voice, and said that he also needed a photo to prove to the Americans that they had actually met. Hallaq got $200 for showing up.

Twenty days later Hallaq again heard from Soheil: "The CIA is satisfied, but you have to get new identification documents with a false name. The Americans will pay."

Fifteen days later Hallaq was asked to come to Marjayoun in the Israeli occupation zone in order to meet his American employer. He received a false ID card with the name Michel Daboul. Immediately, Ahmed Hallaq the Sunni became a Christian. As he got ready for the trip, Soheil said, "It is not the Americans I am going to meet, but the Israelis." Hallaq was surprised. But when he heard the Israelis would pay any amount to get information about the missing Israeli soldiers, it was okay. "I will help the Israelis even if I have fought against them," he said, thinking about his pay.

Hallaq, as planned, went first to the village of Baakline in Chouf north of the occupation zone, and from there was driven by a certain taxi driver in a yellow Mercedes to the "border crossing" near Bater, north of Jezzine. Then they proceeded further south to the border town of Kfar Kila, and instead of Marjayoun, it was Metulla in Israel. Here he was introduced to a man from Mossad who called himself Danny.

Danny was a short, rather fat fellow about 45 years old, bald on top, with long, reddish-blonde hair hanging over his ears and down his neck. The Mossad man was dressed in a dark blue jacket and blue pants, and spoke perfect Arabic with a Palestinian accent. From Metulla he was driven to Haifa, where he met several officers from Mossad. They were called Mike, Tommy and other American-sounding names. Hallaq did not remember them all.

For 11 days he stayed in Haifa. He was questioned in detail about his service with the Syrians and the Palestinians. He also had to undergo a lie detector test. In the evenings, they went out to restaurants. Mossad's men did not want their newest conquest to be alone or bored. They did want, of course, to have control over what he did. When Hallaq was driven back to Lebanon, he had $5,000 in his pocket. He had never had so much money.

The search began for people who could help him find the dead Israeli soldiers. Hallaq sought out the brothers Tawfiq and Wafiq Nasser from Bekaa, who were old friends of his. Both were willing to help, if paid, and began the search for someone who knew more about the matter. After a while it seemed clear the Syrians had taken the bodies of the Israelis they were looking for. But they did not get much further.

Again Hallaq was driven to South Lebanon and on to Israel. He told about the two brothers whom he had recruited, and reported on the progress of the hunt for the remains of the soldiers. Hallaq brought along photographs of his two cohorts, and got fake ID papers for them both.

In the fall of 1994, Hallaq was again asked to go to Cyprus to meet his Mossad handler. Again he took the boat from Jounieh to Limassol. There, he called the Israeli Embassy in Nicosia and gave the agreed-upon name. When he met Danny a few hours later, he was told to drop the hunt for the missing remains. His new mission was to find Fuad Mughniyeh, brother of Hizbullah's important military leader, Imad Mughniyeh. Hallaq knew both Fuad and Imad from the time they had worked for the Palestinians—He for al-Saiqa, and the brothers for Fatah.

"First you are to observe and become friends with Fuad, and then we will see if he can be recruited," said Danny, and gave his agent another $3,000.

Back in Beirut, Hallaq briefed his compatriots, Tawfiq and Wafiq: "We have a new target—Fuad Mughniyeh. But we are just supposed to find him, not kill him, so relax."

In South Lebanon, Hizbullah continued its resistance against the Israelis. On August 6, the guerrillas succeeded in killing two Israeli soldiers. Ten days later three men from the SLA lay buried in the village of Khirbe, where there was a separate graveyard for militia soldiers and collaborators who had been killed. The names of the "martyrs" had been chiseled into stone markers decorated either with a cross or a crescent moon.

One morning two months later, about 20 men from Hizbullah sneaked toward an Israeli position on a hilltop called Dabshe, just above Nabatiyeh. Dawn had come when the guerrillas attacked. The post was manned by soldiers from the Givati Regiment. Three of the four Israeli soldiers on watch on the west side hid. The rest of the 70 locked themselves inside the bunker. Only one Israeli soldier was killed in the attack. The guerrillas withdrew without any losses after they had planted and filmed the green-and-yellow Hizbullah flag flying from the top of the Israeli outpost.

One of the Israeli soldiers later said it had been a strange experience: "We had all said 'let them come,' but never thought they would dare. But there was the flag." Hizbullah had its own version of the attack: "Our men saw dozens of Israeli soldiers fleeing into the forest, and we destroyed one Merkava tank."[73] The video recording of the attack shocked Israel. The *Jerusalem Post* wrote that it was the most impressive recruiting film anyone in Hizbullah could dream of.

In Beirut all was peaceful, and when the Lebanese songstress Fairuz walked onto the stage at the Square of the Martyrs in the center of the city on September 17, 1994, over 40,000 people were waiting excitedly for her first concert in Lebanon since the civil war began in 1975. At that time, she had said she would not sing again until there was peace in the land. When Fairuz began to sing "*Bahibbuk ya Lubnan, ya Watani*," or (I love you, Lebanon, my homeland), many thought she stood as a symbol for the new Lebanon, even if there was no peace yet in the far south of the country.

The Square of the Martyrs, the pulsating heart of the old Beirut that had been the front line for two decades, was scheduled to be rebuilt. The warlords who started the war on that day 19 years ago would hardly have recognized the area which now lay open to the sea. Four days after the concert, President Hraoui lay the foundation stone that symbolized the beginning of the reconstruction of Beirut's Downtown.[74]

Mossad's new agent, Ahmed Hallaq, had more important things to think about than a concert. He decided to draw his wife, Hanan Yassin, into the secret work he was involved in. His Mossad handler had asked Hallaq to get close to Fuad Mughniyeh carefully, through common friends. But this became more difficult than Hallaq had thought. When he made his first attempt, he realized Fuad did not want anything to do with Sunni Muslims who did not follow the Koran's prohibition against alcohol.

After a new meeting in Cyprus, Hallaq was ordered to sketch a map of the area where Fuad had his workplace, a small shop in the Sfeir area in Dahiyeh, the Shia-dominated southern section of Beirut. In November 1994, the sketch was finished, and Hallaq again got a message to come to Cyprus. The weather was bad and the boat was cancelled, so he asked his wife to fly to Larnaka since he was still afraid of flying. He gave her precise descriptions and explanations for how to proceed: Check into a hotel, call the Israeli Embassy, present yourself, and ask for a meeting.

When Hanan, with the map in her handbag, met the plumpish Mossad agent, Danny, who always was dressed in the same blue clothes, received the money and a new false ID card for her husband. Hallaq would have to come to Israel. About a week later, Hallaq was there. The calendar showed December 7, 1994. "Forget the sketch you made of Fuad Mughniyeh's shop," said Danny. "Now I will show you a video."

The video showed Fuad Mughniyeh's shop and the area around it. Hallaq had to study the video four times. He was not told who had taken it, but the recording looked like it had been taken by a hidden camera. What Hallaq found out was that they intended to kill Fuad. Thus Mossad might lure his brother Imad to the funeral, where they would have people ready to assassinate him.

A Mossad agent who called himself Mike explained how a bomb would be used to kill Fuad Mughniyeh. Hallaq's mission was to detonate the bomb with the help of a walkie-talkie-like device, hidden in a secret compartment at the bottom of a black shoulder bag. Another agent—Hallaq did not know who—would plant the explosive. No one told him where the bomb would be hidden, but he had to be sure that Fuad was sitting behind his writing desk in his shop at the right moment. He was to drive to about 50 meters from Fuad's shop, get out of his car, push the button and leave the area.

During his stay in Israel, not far from Tel Aviv, the Mossad agents took him for sightseeing in Jerusalem. They went to restaurants and cafés, and when the training period was finished on December 19, Hallaq got $7,000, a black leather shoulder bag and orders to get to Beirut. The bomb had already been placed and was ready to be detonated. When the operation was over, he should immediately leave town and go to South Lebanon. A yellow Mercedes would pick him up at 1 pm from Baakline, in Chouf.

If the operation had to be postponed, the same car would pick him up the next day at the same time. He was given a telephone number in Switzerland to call when the operation was over. If Fuad Mughniyeh was not there, and the operation had to be put off, he should say the code word "Ford." If all went according to plan, the code word was "BMW."

Hallaq called his wife, Hanan, through a switchboard in France, and told her to wait for him the next day by the clinic in Baakline. She should bring with her one of the other cohorts, Wafiq Nasser. His brother Tawfiq was out of the country. On December 20, Ahmed Hallaq's wife and his friend waited in Baakline, a village built of yellow stone atop a hill covered in olive trees. Druze men walked by, dressed in typical, black baggy pants and white caps. The women wore white veils that covered their mouths. No one noticed the car parked by the little clinic. It was lunchtime when Hallaq showed up, and they drove to a restaurant nearby, where, during the meal, Hallaq bragged about how easy it would be to push the button that would set off the bomb.[75]

After lunch they drove to the couple's home in Barja to fill the black shoulder bag with children's clothes and diapers. Then went on in the direction of Fuad Mughniyeh's shop. They parked the car on the low rise that Hallaq had seen on the video. From there they could see Fuad sitting together with someone else in a black car outside the shop.

"What should we do?" asked Wafiq.

"Nothing now. He has to be inside the shop and in his office," answered Hallaq before they drove away and agreed to meet again the next day at 9 am.. Hallaq and Hanan went to West Beirut where Hallaq called the number in Switzerland. No answer, but he spoke the word "Ford" when he heard the answering machine turn on.

The next morning, Hallaq felt lousy. He had slept badly and had the shivers despite the December day being warm. He packed some clothes in the black bag, and together with Hanan and their one-and-a-half-year-old daughter, and drove to get Wafiq. Despite their agreement, Wafiq was not at home. The couple ate lunch at a restaurant in the Raouche district of West Beirut. He was nervous and had some *arak*. Then they drove slowly toward Fuad's shop in the southern section.

At 4 pm he parked his car again on the low rise with its view of Fuad's shop. While his wife and baby were in the car, he walked down toward the shop and Mughniyeh came out to greet him. Hallaq was asked to come in, but said no: "I have drunk *arak*, and I know that you in Hizbullah do not like those who drink." They exchanged a few words before Hallaq left and Mughniyeh went inside.

Hallaq pulled out the black bag, placed it under his left armpit, and walked away. While he watched Fuad sit down behind his desk, he pulled out the trigger mechanism, followed the instructions he had been given, and pushed the button. A huge explosion came from Mughniyeh's shop. Hallaq did not wait any longer, but put the bag into his car, got behind the wheel and drove off, first toward Choueifat and Khalde, south of town. He stopped at a supermarket and bought a bottle of J&B whiskey and a cigar to celebrate the day. He put the trigger mechanism for the bomb into a black plastic bag and drove to the coast to dispose of it. Then the family drove home to Barja, where Hallaq drank several glasses of the J&B.

Time passed slowly. Hallaq could not sit still, and took his wife with him to visit some friends in a neighboring village. The news reported the bomb attack. When the announcer mentioned the dead and wounded, no one noticed any expression on Hallaq's face to indicate his guilt.

The following day, Hallaq drove to Baakline with his wife and daughter to wait for the yellow Mercedes. They ate together before he left. Hanan drove home to their two other children while her husband was driven to Israel, where he would be received by his Mossad handler. Hallaq became uneasy when Danny just said hi, neither kissing him on the cheek as he had done at previous meetings, nor taking him by the hand to congratulate him on a job well done.

They drove to a place near Tel Aviv where he would be living for a while. Here he met agents Mike and Tommy, who were extremely happy, and said he had done an outstanding job. The agreed upon reward, $200,000, would have to wait. The money would be paid over a longer period of time, but as agreed, Hallaq's wife, Hanan would fly from Beirut to Cyprus to pick up the first payment. When Hanan went to meet Danny in Limassol, there was no money, only excuses and the message that she would have to wait a bit longer. When she came back to Beirut, she was arrested.

It did not take long for Ahmed Hallaq's name and picture to appear on Hizbullah's television station *Al-Manar*, (The Lighthouse), which broadcast from a small basement in Beirut's southern section. When Hallaq learned his wife had been arrested and that he was also being sought "dead or alive," he asked the Israelis for help. Danny tried to calm him down. "We have to wait for a political solution, and that the peace process gives results and a prisoner exchange comes along."

He decided to wait and do as the Israelis requested. In Beirut, however, Hizbullah began their hunt for the man who had killed Imad Mughniyeh's brother. The Syrians were also eager to get hold of the man who had deceived them. And they wanted Ahmed Hallaq alive.

CHAPTER SEVENTY FOUR
Israeli Censors and Lebanese Unity

In Khiam, Soha Bechara, who for a while had been together with other women prisoners, was again put into a solitary cell—not into the smallest one, as before, but one that was somewhat larger with a small window. From her cell she could hear when the telephone rang in the guardroom. A few months earlier, on August 3, 1994, Soha had heard the announcement in the women's section that someone would be set free.[76]

She looked out of the little window that let light into her cell. One of the guards went to a particular cell and called: "Farida!" When the iron door was opened, a woman came out beaming with joy. The guard went to another cell, where a woman named Mona was being released. Then she stopped in front of a third door and called out, "Kifah!"

From the window, Soha could see that Kifah was being led out and that she was holding a little package in her hands. It belonged to Soha; Kifah had taken care of some of her things when she had been put into solitary confinement. Soha coughed to get attention, but now Kifah was too excited to hear the discreet signal. Calming herself down, Soha consoled herself that at least her belongings would now be free.

Part of the reason Kifah was being released owed to the efforts of Israeli human rights lawyers. One of them, Lea Tsemel, who had taken on her case. The 49-year-old Tsemel was from Haifa, and was widely known to be one of the first Israeli lawyers to defend Palestinian rights in the courts. Now she had been authorized by Soha's parents to bring her case before the Supreme Court. Like so many other news-hungry Israelis, Lea Tsemel listened to the news broadcasts that showed new footage from Lebanon. Some reports came from Hizbullah's TV-station, *Al-Manar*, and were taken up by Israeli television.

With 18 correspondents and video journalists in South Lebanon, Hizbullah's channel produced many new reports on the conflict with the Israelis. The pictures showed, among other things, the guerrillas planting the Hizbullah flag on SLA positions, and how they placed roadside bombs to target Israeli tanks and military columns. Viewers occasionally saw and heard screaming Israeli soldiers who lay wounded by the roadside. These images made an incredibly strong impression on public opinion in Israel.

The IDF Northern Command had introduced strict censorship on Israeli journalists. The press could scarcely publish anything other than communiqués from the army. The censorship was far stricter in Lebanon than what was practiced in the occupied Palestinian areas. By denying Israeli journalists access to South Lebanon, and also refusing to allow them to interview ordinary soldiers and officers in active service, the authorities made it difficult for the press to get hold of the most interesting stories.

Criticism of the Northern Command eventually grew so strong that something had to be done. The head of the Command gave two Israeli journalists access to a military unit in South Lebanon. The two were former *Time Magazine* correspondent Ron Ben-Yishai, who now worked for the largest Israeli newspaper, *Yedioth Ahronoth*, and his colleague Yossi Walter, from the newspaper *Maariv*. Together they were allowed to stay at a base at the edge of the occupation zone for 24 hours. There they spoke with both regular soldiers and officers.[77] Much of what they heard accorded well with what I myself had seen and heard during my reporting trips in South Lebanon.

The Israeli soldiers spoke about having been attacked by Hizbullah and forced to seek cover. For 45 minutes they lay hidden, not daring to lift their heads. They had been ordered not to respond to the attack, but to run into the "rabbit cage"—a name they used for their shelter.

"We are shaken," one of the soldiers said, without wanting to admit he had been outright frightened. He did not hide his admiration for the Hizbullah elite forces, both as individual soldiers and as organized units.

The head of the Israeli unit in South Lebanon also spoke well of the enemy's fighting prowess: "Hizbullah is like a mini-Israeli army, and can do everything just as well as we. They are good at attacking because they use the same methods that our officers, in their time, had taught the Iranian soldiers under the Shah, and that today's Iranian officers under Khomeini are teaching Hizbullah." That was, of course, pure nonsense.

The Hizbullah guerrilla's goal was classic: the enemy should bleed slowly. And bleed the Israelis did. The number of Hizbullah attacks against the IDF had grown by a factor of 10 within four short years, from 19 in 1990 to 187 in 1994. The guerrillas claimed their fight was more "moral" than the Israelis' or the SLA's. Hizbullah's secretary-general, Hassan Nasrallah, had made it quite clear: the guerrillas should only fire on civilian targets in Israel if Israel hit civilian targets in Lebanon.

In order to improve the Israeli soldiers' morale, Prime Minister Yitzhak Rabin went to South Lebanon on January 11, 1995. Once more, Rabin insisted Syria was pressuring Hizbullah to attack the Israelis so as to get the Israelis to compromise. He repeated that if Hizbullah was forced out of South Lebanon, the border between the two countries would be peaceful. This was the classic Israeli claim that had been countered with identical logic before: If Israel withdrew, there would be no need for Hizbullah to fight. The Lebanese army could then take care of peace and order.

Everyone who came to Beirut at the beginning of 1995 noticed that living conditions had improved for many. People felt safer now the civil war was over. Even if the streetlights in the city did not work, there was still electricity 12 hours a day and 18 hours a day on weekends. Inflation had been reduced from 131% in 1992 to 15–20% three years later. The stores were filled with goods, all priced in dollars.

One reason political calm had spread over Beirut was that the Israelis had managed what the Lebanese government had failed to achieve: they had given the Lebanese national pride. The majority in Lebanon demanded for the Israelis to withdraw from South Lebanon, and in March 1995, on the 17th anniversary of Israel's first invasion, the Lebanese went on general strike. Many tied yellow ribbons labeled "425" onto their dresses, jackets and cars. The number symbolized the Security Council resolution 425 from 1978, which demanded full Israeli withdrawal. There was a noticeable increase in support for the prisoners in Khiam. The National Assembly met for a special session over the Israeli occupation in Nabatiyeh, just a few kilometers from the Israeli front line.

The Israelis had done their part to unite the Lebanese more than ever. Almost every day, they attacked more "terrorist targets"—that is, homes and villages. On top of that, they forbade 1,800 Lebanese fishermen to sail in Lebanese waters at night. During the day it was forbidden to fish further out than one kilometer from shore. Initially the Israelis introduced these bans for fishermen from Tyre, on February 25, 1995. Two weeks later, the Israeli navy expanded the blockade north to Damour. The ban then encompassed two-fifths of Lebanon's coast. It had little to do with Israel's security. What the Israelis really wanted was to put pressure on the Lebanese to break with Syria.

Hizbullah increased the intensity of attacks against the occupiers. Some 80 attacks took place between January and February. The Lebanese government's unyielding tone toward Israel caused increasing counter pressures. On the one hand, there was pressure from the SLA to cooperate with the Israelis; on the other, many who were allowed to leave the occupation zone found themselves harassed by the Lebanese army. According to Lahd, the army had "a list of 4,000 names of those accused of cooperating with Israel." He said that "if this harassment [of them] continues, people will ask Israel to annex the zone, even if they want to belong to a free and united Lebanon."[78] In order to assure people in the border zone that they would not be abandoned, 13 members of the Israeli government went to Lahd's "capital," Marjayoun. They invited the general for an official visit to the Knesset, where they yet again reassured him that South Lebanon would forever be tied to Israel.[79]

CHAPTER SEVENTY FIVE

When the Bowl is Full

On April 1, 1995, Major General Trond Furuhovde completed his term in UNIFIL. He was unable to renew his contract because he had irritated key people at the UN in New York. Many Lebanese would have liked to have the Norwegian remain, unsuccessfully. The bureaucrats at headquarters had decided that a Polish Major General, Stanislaw Wozniak, would takeover.[80]

Over the course of that spring and summer, the battle for who would become the new president in Lebanon had begun. Elias Hraoui had been elected for six years, and his term would be over in November. Hraoui personally would have liked an additional three years, but he was barred from seeking them by paragraph 49 of the constitution.

President Hraoui came from the village of Haouch el-Omara in the Bekaa Valley, not far from Lebanon's oldest wine-making estate, Ksara. Besides being elected to the National Assembly, he had been a successful exporter of fruits and vegetables. When the civil war destroyed his business, Hraoui got by by importing fuel oil.

Ksara, with a history dating back to 1857, had done well throughout the civil war. Not a single grape harvest was lost. Even during the Israeli invasion, Ksara had produced wine. Later some rich Lebanese and Syrians took over, and the fortress estate became a significant tourist attraction. Even I was tempted, and drove one spring day to Ksara. There I ran into a little group of Lebanese priests who were also interested in a tour.

We were led into the catacombs dating from Roman times. The underground passages were several hundred feet long. The guide told us the catacombs had been discovered by chance. One of the monks had seen a fox carrying a chicken in its mouth. The monk followed it, and the fox darted down into a hole in the ground. He checked more closely and discovered the hole led to an underground network of passages.

At that time, there was not much talk about the catacombs, which during the First World War had become the hiding place for Christian families when the Ottomans forced youths into their army. Later the catacombs became an underground storage area for tens of thousands of wine barrels and bottles.

After the tour, we were brought to a bodega where we were able to sample selected wines. There was a lot of talk about the upcoming presidential election, about Lebanese politics, and about what was true and what was not.

One of the Lebanese priests, with a jovial moon face, red cheeks and wild dishevelled black hair, found time to tell a story. It was about two priests, an older and experienced one, and a young and newly ordained one. The young one had invited the older priest for a good meal. During the first course, which was lentil soup, the young priest asked:

"Must I always tell the truth?"

"Yes, of course. You know the eighth commandment."

When the guest had emptied his plate, the host offered him more, as was the tradition.

"Shbe'et"—I have had enough, answered the older priest.

It was useless for the host to pressure him.

The next course was rice and okra stew with salad. The guest served himself well. When the host politely asked him to serve himself more.

Each time he answered: "Shbe'et."

When the two went out onto the terrace after the meal to enjoy coffee and cognac, the young priest said:

"I have been thinking about telling the truth. I do not think it is always necessary."

"What do you mean by that?" "Each time I tried to get you to help yourself to more of the various courses, I was told your stomach was full. But then you ate just as well when new dishes were put on the table," said the young priest.

The older priest looked over at a table where there was a half-full bowl of pomegranates, and said:

"Can you fill the bowl completely up?"

The host got some more pomegranates, and soon the bowl was full to the brim with the round, dark red fruit. The older priest asked the host to fetch a bag of large dried peas and poured the peas into the bowl with the pomegranates. Then he shook the bowl, so that the peas fell down and filled the empty spaces.

"Is it now full?" asked the guest.

The host nodded.

Then the guest asked for a bag of uncooked rice. He asked the host to pour the rice into the bowl, which he then shook. The small grains of rice found their way into the bowl and the spaces between the peas and the pomegranates.

The older priest asked: "Is the bowl full now?"

The host nodded. The guest then took a bottle of wine and poured it into the bowl. The liquid filled the spaces between the pomegranates, peas and grains of rice.

"Now you understand that the bowl and I are alike," said the older priest. The bowl was full of pomegranates, but could still take the peas, grains of rice, and the wine. I served myself with the one dish after the other. But there was room for new dishes. I spoke the truth."

The young priest nodded, and the older one continued:

"Young man, in the future you can fill your life with yourself and your occupation, just as the pomegranates filled the bowl. But you can get more out of life by also having other interests, such as literature and music—just like the peas and grains of rice in the bowl."

The older priest paused a moment. The younger one asked, impatiently: "What about the wine?"

"Now here you are at the core of the matter," answered the wise priest. "No one can live a full life if he does not take the time to share a bottle of wine or two with his friends."

Those of us who were sitting about the tasting table at the Ksara fortress, smiled, nodded, and eventually went each our way.

I was particularly satisfied to have added yet another story to my collection.

About this same time, Nabih Berri was in meetings with Lebanese bishops, imams and a series of political leaders. Berri wanted their opinion on the possibility of calling the National Assembly into a special session. A proposal had been made to change paragraph 49 of the constitution and open the way for an extension of the presidential term.

After consultations, Berri went to Syria to brief President Hafez al-Assad about his investigations. He was able to tell the Syrian president that there was no parliamentary majority in favor of extending President Hraoui's mandate. This surprised both Assad and Vice President Abdul Halim Khaddam, who both wanted Hraoui to remain in his post. Since there was disagreement on the question, Berri was "advised" not to call a special session, but to wait until October, when the fall session would normally open.

In Berri's wake, Prime Minister Rafic Hariri came to Damascus. He emphasized it was important to get stability in the Lebanese economy. The political uncertainty which followed as a result of the fight over the presidential election, had a negative economic effect, Hariri said. The National Bank had to inject 40 million dollars per day to defend the value of the country's currency. Hariri, therefore, wanted a new strengthened team of ministers to hold the line until October, when the presidential election would take place. President Assad gave the green light for a new government. Then Hariri resigned as prime minister, only to be renominated by President Hraoui and asked to form a new government. Several of Hariri's new ministers were his personal associates.

Assad had given his approval because Hariri supported an extension of the presidential term by three years. Hariri was afraid a new president might disturb the work he himself was leading to restore the economy. If Emile Lahoud became the new president, this might easily happen. According to paragraph 49 of the constitution, officials and high-ranking officers could not stand for election as president unless they had withdrawn from their positions at least two years prior. Several wanted to change this and thereby permit a Chief of the General Staff in active service to also be elected president.

Prime Minister Hariri was against this, mainly because he could not stand the general. But even those who respected Lahoud questioned if it would be smart to open the door for a military leader to become president, especially since Lebanon, seen through western eyes, was the only country in the Arab world with something approaching a democratic government. Lahoud's supporters maintained, on the other hand, that a general would not necessarily bring the entire army into the Presidential Palace with him. They pointed to General Dwight D. Eisenhower in the United States, and General Charles de Gaulle in France which had led democratic states. Lahoud could do the same.

It was no secret that the relationship between Hariri and Lahoud was poor. Hariri thought Lahoud tied Lebanon's security and defense too strongly to Syria, a police state which represented something quite different from the open and free market system that Hariri supported. But he did not air this view loudly.

After Lahoud had been named Chief of the General Staff in November 1989, with the support of Syria, the general had taken over control of all military matters as far as he could. Lahoud thought that the Chief of the General Staff did not have to report to the government, and had let the army grow from 20,000 to 60,000 men five years later. The newcomers were demobilized militia soldiers from various parties, in addition to conscripts, which in Lebanon lasted one year.

Within political circles it eventually became clear that the Syrian leaders wanted to have Lahoud as president, but only after Hraoui was allowed another three years. Hafez al-Assad's son Bashar, who had been called home to Syria from his medical studies in England, was one of Lahoud's supporters. Bashar returned back to Damascus a year after his older brother, Basil, had been killed in a car accident. At first, the Syrian president had thought Basil would "inherit" the presidency in Syria, where the Baath Party and the president ruled with an iron hand. But when Basil died, the situation changed. Bashar had to be taught how to rule, and with this education came the job of running Lebanon by proxy from Damascus.

Since 1982, Syria's spearhead in Lebanon had been General Ghazi Kanaan, who belonged to Syria's ruling Alawite minority. As chief of Syrian intelligence in Lebanon, Kanaan was the most dangerous and powerful man north of the Israeli occupation zone. It was he who ran Syria's day-to-day policies in Lebanon. In Damascus, he was constantly being watched by Vice President Khaddam and the president.

Kanaan's philosophy was simple: the Lebanese were smart, creative and successful business people, and they should stick to what they did well. The Syrian elite would take care of the politics. He also wanted to leave the Lebanese media alone, so long as they did not write or speak of matters that damaged Syria's interests in Lebanon.[81]

Early in October 1995, General Kanaan stated publicly for the first time that President Hraoui's term should be extended. He dropped the political bombshell at a party with Lebanese parliamentarians. There was no one who dared oppose the 53-year-old general when he told the shocked politicians that the vote this time would be carried out by a show of hands. Normally, a vote to change the constitution occurred by a secret ballot.[82]

Later it was said that Assad had only sent out a trial balloon to see the reaction in the United States. The silence in Washington assured the Syrians that Hraoui could continue. Assad was personally not sure that the time was ripe for General Lahoud to take over the Presidential Palace. Speculation about the extension ended when Assad was interviewed by the Egyptian newspaper, *Al-Ahram*. In its October 11 edition, he said the Lebanese leadership was positively inclined toward an extension of the presidential term.

The next day, 22 parliamentarians went to the Presidential Palace to congratulate Hraoui. Later still, 110 of the 128 representatives voted in favor of the change in the constitution, while 11 voted against, and seven were absent.

The Syrian president was thinking long-term. Hraoui now had good support, and Assad made sure that General Lahoud had his position as Chief of the General Staff extended by three years as well. For Assad, Lahoud was a valuable asset who could be useful later—as president.

CHAPTER SEVENTY SIX
Finally, The Red Cross

For Soha Bechara October 9, 1995, began as most other days. But later in the day, when her cell door was opened, she suddenly saw a woman with brown eyes and long hair. She wore an armband from the International Committee of the Red Cross. The woman said in French, "You must be Soha."[83]

The 43-year-old Claire Bellmann from Switzerland was excited when she entered the cell. She knew Soha had been in isolation for long periods during her stay at Khiam, but she quickly realized this was not just any ordinary woman she was meeting; Soha was a stunning creature who stood upright in her cell with a big smile and shining hair. Clair said she was happy finally to be in the prison center after many years of unsuccessful attempts. Now the Red Cross would try to make conditions better for the prisoners. "We will get you books and other things that can make life easier for all of you," Soha heard.

The day was an historic one for the Red Cross Committee as well. It had taken many years to negotiate an agreement to meet each and every one of the 191 prisoners in Khiam, among them a dozen women. The breakthrough came after increasing international pressure following several reports of torture and mistreatment had been made public.

One year before, the inmates in Khiam had been allowed to receive letters from their families. Until then, the prisoners, whom several human rights organizations called hostages, had been cut off from the outside world. Some had been in Khiam for over 10 years. Among them were guerrilla soldiers who had fought the Israelis and their allies, but also people who had done nothing more than refuse to pay taxes to occupiers' collaborators, or refuse to allow their sons to join the SLA or simply people who had relatives in the resistance movement. And also people who had been jailed out of personal revenge. The prisoners did not have enough clothing, and the food was bad. They had no access to books or writing materials. They passed their time by telling each other about films and tv-series they had seen, or just watching what the guards were doing, and guessing what was happening as they went cell to cell.

Claire Bellmann spoke Arabic in addition to French and English, and knew a lot about the Israeli prisoners in Lebanon. Thirteen years before, she had been the Red Cross envoy to the concentration camp at Ansar. Now, along with three other Arab-speaking representatives, a doctor and a translator, she was taken around the prison. The Red Cross Committee had a permanent representative in Marjayoun, Balthazar Staehelin, but he had not been to the prison before.

After their first meeting, Claire learned more about Soha's situation. She was told in detail about the interrogations and about her years in isolation where she practiced Yoga to keep her spirits up. Soha told her that when the prisoners had first received letters from their families earlier that year, it gave them a feeling of hope. Soha had to read the first letter she got out loud in front of a guard. The letter was written in a standard form developed by the Red Cross, and contained only a short message. Soha recognized her father's handwriting, but when she tried to read, the words stuck in her throat. The female guard gave her a pen and left her alone. She was given only 15 minutes to scribble down a reply—it was the first time in her life she had written a letter to her family. She quickly put down some words on the paper. Then she reread the letter from her father.

When the first visit from the Red Cross was over, the guards went after the prisoners to find out what they had said, and many of the inmates were afraid that more visits would not be allowed. But visits continued, as did more letters, and the food gradually improved.

Lieutenant Dror Barashi of the Golan Brigade did not care what was happening in Khiam. He did not even know that representatives of the Red Cross had interviewed prisoners there, as he got ready to drive into South Lebanon on October 12. His intention was to remain in the occupation zone for only a few days. Dror's father Shlomo had come from Kurdistan to Israel as a four-year-old. I knew Shlomo from before, and he put me in contact with other soldiers who had fought side by side with Dror.[84]

It was dark when the four civilian vehicles filled with Israeli soldiers drove north toward the Golani Brigade's base by the Shia village of Aishiyeh. They used civilian vehicles in order to confuse the resistance movement. Nonetheless the atmosphere among the soldiers was tense and they sat on full alert in the dark as they drove along the road which wound its way northward below the Crusader fortress, Beaufort.

When they were two kilometers away from the camp, the atmosphere in the vehicles improved. They were past the most critical points, and the soldiers relaxed. But then it happened: just near a little cluster of houses on the left side of the road, a roadside bomb exploded and struck the second vehicle. Seconds later the third vehicle was struck by a missile. In the fourth vehicle, which was a minibus, sat six men. Private Itay Koren was sitting in the seat next to Lieutenant Barashi. The lieutenant first jumped out through the sliding door of the minibus and ran toward a cluster of trees on the right side of the road. Itay ran around the vehicle trying to find shelter on the left side. A little later Itay was ready to attack. But it was too late, the woods were empty, and the guerrillas had evaporated. Two soldiers were dead.

A few minutes later reinforcements arrived from the base in Aishiyeh. Only then did Itay notice the pain in his foot. When his fingers felt the spot, they found a bullet hole. He also saw Lieutenant Dror Barashi lying on the ground with open eyes. There was no blood to be seen, and he had pearls of sweat on his face, but his gaze was empty. Itay realized that his superior and close friend was dead. The sight of him lying there would haunt the young Israeli's dreams for years.

Four days later, six Israeli soldiers were killed and a seventh was wounded. The casualty list had reached 22 in the first 10 months of the year, versus 21 for the entire previous year. The six soldiers were killed by a bomb that shredded their armored vehicle, close to the same spot where Dror and two of his soldiers were killed. Hizbullah announced that they were behind both attacks.

Foreign Minister Shimon Peres said in a radio interview on October 13, that the escalation in South Lebanon was dangerous for all parties. As Israeli gunboats bombarded Lebanon from the sea and military helicopters fired missiles at the ground Peres was saying, "There is no doubt Syria must cooperate to prevent an explosion, and that the Lebanese government must also help."

That same day, Prime Minister Yitzhak Rabin had flown to the place where the nine Israelis had been killed within four days. He chose to travel on the Jewish holy day of Simchat Torah to demonstrate how seriously he, as both prime minister and defense minister, viewed the situation. Just a few hours after his visit, one of the SLA positions nearby was attacked.

The next day, the Rabin government assembled for a crisis meeting. The Israelis were worried Hizbullah had significant forces north of Israeli positions and that they were trying to take SLA positions so that footage of them planting the Hizbullah flag could be broadcast throughout Lebanon and the entire Middle East. The Israelis in South Lebanon were put on highest alert. The soldiers used what they had of advanced equipment to check the terrain during the night. If they noticed suspicious movements, tanks would fire shells that scattered thousands of small steel arrows in all directions.

CHAPTER SEVENTY SEVEN

An Agent Returns

The war waged against the enemy's intelligence services rarely made the headlines. The agents lived and died in the shadows. When the stories now and then reached the surface, they could be almost unbelievable. Ahmed Hallaq, the man who had killed Imad Mughniyeh's brother, was bored in Israel, but he could not go back to his home. He had been sentenced to death in absentia. His wife sat in prison. His children were being cared for by others. Finally, he could take no more of Israel. He sought out his contact in Mossad and said, "I have to leave."[85]

His Mossad handler asked, "What about Costa Rica?"

Hallaq said no.

"What about the Philippines?"

That he accepted. He was given a passport under the name Ahmed Hassan al-Fouani, and left Tel Aviv. He carried $5,000 and the telephone number of a Mossad agent in Manila named Roy.

He checked into the Hotel Travel One, and could now enjoy life on his $2,000-a-month salary from Mossad, but he knew he would have to be on his guard. He was sought, after all, by both Hizbullah and Syrian intelligence.

After 135 days in Manila, Hallaq could not stand life bar hopping any longer. He missed the Middle East. The Mossad agent Roy got him a return ticket, and on October 5, 1995, Hallaq was back in Israel. But he still felt unsettled there. He wanted to return to Lebanon even if it was risky. The least amount of risk would be to settle down in the Israeli "security zone."

Mossad found a house for Hallaq in the Christian village of Qleia, and paid his rent, but reduced his monthly salary to $900 since it was a lot cheaper to live in South Lebanon than in Manila. He got two ID cards from the Israeli defense ministry. One showed he was an agent for Shin Bet, and noted that the bearer of the card did not speak Hebrew. The other indicated that the bearer Michel Kheir Amin, connected with the intelligence service of the SLA, and that he was allowed to carry a gun.

From Qleia, Ahmed Hallaq could follow along with what was happening in Lebanon and in Israel. When Prime Minister Yitzhak Rabin was killed on December 4, 1995, he was just as surprised as most that the murderer was a 26-year-old Jewish student. I was collecting material for my new book in Amman, Jordan, when I heard news of the killing. I thought of what Rabin had said to me when I sat at his home in Tel Aviv the year before: "I began as a warrior for a Jewish state. I hope I can end up as a statesman who created peace between Israel and the Arabs." I had understood it was the Palestinians that Rabin was referring to. His policies toward Lebanon were uncompromising.

In South Lebanon, Ahmed Hallaq tried to live as normal a life as possible. But the occupation zone was small and transparent, and it did not take long for rumors to reach Syrian intelligence that Hallaq had been seen there.

One of Syria's contact men in the zone was the Christian Lebanese, Moufid Nohra, a short man with dark hair, a big nose, and a pronounced chin. He lived in Ebl el-Saqi and had previously worked in Beirut for the secret services. One day early in 1996, Moufid Nohra got a call from Beirut. The question came: "Can you check if Hallaq is in the zone?"[86]

Nohra found nothing until one day in January, he met a friend of his younger brother, Ramzi. Both Ramzi and his friend Salim Salameh worked with the Israelis.[87] Salim told him he had rented out a house in Qleia to a foreign Lebanese. It was the Israelis who had asked him to rent the house to the unknown man. Salim described the renter as tall, strong and with an accent from the Sidon area.

Nohra drove to Qleia and parked his car a short distance from the house. After waiting a while, he saw the man. He recognized Hallaq from the time they had both worked for the Syrians in Beirut. Then he called his contact in intelligence and said, "Our friend had come back from Israel." The contact wanted to be sure it was the right man: "We want confirmation on video."

He spoke with Ramzi about his mission. Ramzi, who thought the Israelis' days in Lebanon were numbered, agreed to help. He wanted to be prepared for the day when new bosses came to the area. Ramzi had bet on horses for years, and thought he had mastered the game. He had become rich smuggling drugs, and had flaunted his wealth by building an impressive house of natural stone in the middle of the village. Norwegian UN soldiers who drove through Ebl el-Saqi could see the large villa surrounded by a beautiful garden and a wall with cast iron lanterns, with two large lions in marble decorating the end of the driveway.

He was smart, had a good sense of humor, and was a master at juggling lies and people. He had perhaps inherited this from his grandfather. At the outbreak of the Second World War, his grandfather had spied for the British in South Lebanon, but had been exposed by the Vichy French forces in the country, and was executed in an open square in front of one of the village's churches. Ramzi had no plans to step into his grandfather's trap by choosing the wrong side.

When the Israelis invaded Lebanon in 1982, Ramzi had allowed himself to be recruited by two competing intelligence services. In exchange, the Israeli agents closed their eyes to his activities smuggling drugs out of Lebanon via Israel. He was, however, arrested by the police in Israel—but after a quick sentence, which he partially served outside of jail, he went back to Lebanon and resumed his life.

Moufid and Ramzi were quite different. The 37-year-old Ramzi was sharp, cunning and careful, while the somewhat older Moufid was careless and boasting. He did not hide his admiration for Hizbullah's resistance fight, which was unusual for a Christian in the occupied zone.

Ramzi had a good network. He had earlier been acquainted with the infamous Mohammed Gharamti, better known as Abu Arida, who was the local security chief in the area. Everyone knew Abu Arida's background as leader of the Israeli-controlled National Guard in Sidon, until the Israelis and he left the city in 1985. Now Abu Arida's responsibilities included, among other things, Ahmed Hallaq's security.

Abu Arida had been a guest in Ramzi's impressive house on several occasions. He had seen Ramzi's four black Mercedes Benzes, all the same type and the newest model, and his silver-white Mercedes as well. All were kept in a garage underneath the villa. A complete security system had been installed inside and out, including hidden video cameras.

When Abu Arida brought Hallaq with him to Ramzi's house for the first time, the hidden camera in the living room was on. Ramzi served his guests Scotch whiskey of the best brand, Royal Salute. Hallaq, who presented himself as Michel Kheir Amin, apparently appreciated the exclusive whiskey. He knew it had first been produced in 1953 in honor of Queen Elizabeth II, for her coronation. He knew also the whiskey was guaranteed to be at least 21 years old, and that it cost about $900 per bottle. Only Ramzi's most prominent guests were served this brand. Others had to be satisfied with Johnny Walker, Black Label, or Chivas Regal.

Moufid made sure the tape was sent to Syrian intelligence in Beirut. But when the agents studied the video, they were uncertain of the man's identity. He had been wearing a cap that hid the upper part of his face. New pictures were asked for. Again Abu Arida and Hallaq were invited to visit Ramzi, and again Hallaq sat in front of the hidden video camera.

CHAPTER SEVENTY EIGHT
Whiskey with Valium

Moufid sent the new video to Beirut, but the Lebanese and Syrian intelligence agents still could not say for sure that this was Ahmed Hallaq, since the man on the tape wore the same cap. However, when Syrian intelligence chief Major General Ghazi Kanaan saw the tape he noticed that the man was having his hand in his pocket the entire time. "This is Hallaq," said the general. He recognized the man's habits from the time he was in al-Saiqa. Kanaan gave orders for the man in the video to be kidnapped and brought to Beirut.

When Moufid got the order, he grew skeptical. It would be easier to kill Hallaq than to kidnap him. But the orders were clear: the traitor should be taken alive and brought before the court in Beirut. Moufid received further orders to ally himself with two men from Qleia. The one, Bassam al-Hasbani, was Ramzi's brother-in-law and a secret agent for Lebanese and Syrian intelligence. The other was Salim Salameh, the man who had rented the house to Hallaq. Salim was offered $50,000 for the job, along with the promise that his sentence for treason would be revoked.

Moufid invited Salim to his home and they both sat in the living room and faced a picture of the Virgin Mary hanging on the wall. Moufid briefed him on the plan and the offer from the intelligence service. Salim quickly agreed.

When Moufid got up an hour later to find a pack of cigarettes, he could see out of the corner of his eye that Salim had reached into an inner pocket and seemed to be fumbling with something. Immediately, Moufid understood Salim had taped the conversation on a small recorder. After he left the house, Salim drove back to Qleia, where he went to see Bassam and told him what had happened, including how he had taped his conversation with Moufid. He did not know Bassam worked for Lebanese and Syrian intelligence as well, and told him that he wanted to give the recording to the Israelis when the time was ripe.

Bassam raised the alarm with his contact in the intelligence service, and a few days later Moufid got a phone call with orders from Kanaan to cancel the operation; the Israelis would very likely learn about the plan. Moufid called Salim and Bassam in Qleia and asked them to come to Ebl el-Saqi and told them that the operation had been called off.

Once both of them had left, Moufid began to think about what he could do to kidnap Hallaq without their involvement. He knew it was just a matter of time before the Israelis would discover the plot and arrest him. He first spoke with his brother, Ramzi; then they briefed Ramzi's loyal guard and jack-of-all-trades, Fadi Kusail. The three agreed to go ahead with the kidnapping anyway, but it had to happen quickly!

The two brothers and Fadi thought they would need a fourth person along on the operation, since Hallaq was strong. They chose Maher Touma, a friend of theirs from Ebl el-Saqi who tolerated a lot of whiskey. Besides, he had a brother who was the chief of an SLA "border crossing" near Bater north of Jezzine, and this might prove useful.

The plan was to invite Hallaq to enjoy more Royal Salute, but this time they would mix it with Valium. They would get him drunk, inject him with a sedative, tie him up, drive him to the control post near Bater and turn him over to the Syrians. But how would they lure Hallaq into the trap without his protector, Abu Arida?

On the evening of February 19, 1996, the four conspirators sat in Moufid's home to put the final touches on their plan. They crushed Valium tablets and mixed the powder into a bottle of Royal Salute. They had also procured a syringe, sedative capsules and ether. In order to fool Hallaq to believe Abu Arida was coming along, they got hold of a yellow Mercedes E230, just like Abu Aridas'. The car was on loan from Maher's brother-in-law. The four of them sat talking late into the night about possible alternatives if something went wrong.

Around noon the next day, Maher and Ramzi drove the yellow Mercedes to Hallaq's house. Maher parked the car outside the house so Hallaq would not see the plates. Ramzi went in and invited Hallaq to lunch. He gave the impression that Abu Arida was also invited, but was running late and would come later in another car. Hallaq was obviously bored. He knew well that Ramzi would serve him Royal Salute, a whiskey he would never get to taste otherwise. So he agreed.

In order to drive into Ebl el-Saqi, they had to go through the UN control post manned by the Norwegian UN soldiers. Ramzi showed a Lebanese ID card to his guest and said: "The Norwegian soldiers do not check ID cards closely. They only look to see if the card is real and basically cannot tell the difference between those of us with dark skin and dark hair." At the previous crossings on their way to Ramzi's house, it was Abu Arida who had arranged for the fake IDs.

On the way to the village, Ramzi said, "This is a Norwegian military area. The Norwegians take care of security here, and they do this thoroughly. You have nothing to fear."

Hallaq answered with the Arabic saying, "Places where you feel safe, you should fear."

They were inside the house, when Fadi arrived with nuts and the whiskey. Ramzi called to Moufid via the Ebl el-Saqi telephone operator and said, "Come and eat lunch with us." This was the code phrase. Moufid put an automatic rifle into a big sack and went the few hundred meters from his house to his brother's, where he sat down in the kitchen so that Hallaq would not be suspicious. Fadi made sure Hallaq got his Royal Salute. Ramzi drank only beer, while Maher got Black Label.

From the kitchen, Moufid called his contact in the intelligence service and said: "Our friend is here. But I don't know what will happen." In the meantime, Ramzi showed Hallaq around the huge palace he had built with some of his millions earned from drug smuggling.

Moufid looked at the clock. He knew the "border crossing" north of Jezzine would close at 5 pm. He could not wait too long, even if Hallaq had not become very drunk despite all the whiskey he drank, and the Valium it contained. In the living room the blinds were down, and Moufid asked Fadi to turn off the power, and the moment it went dark he stormed in, pointed an automatic weapon at Hallaq and said, "Don't move, Hallaq. We are from Hizbullah and have surrounded the house".

When Hallaq tried to get up, Maher hit him on the head with a pistol. With blood pouring down from the back of his head, Hallaq cried out, "Let me go! If not I will fuck your sisters."

"If you say one word, I will kill you," answered Moufid.

Ramzi shouted, "Don't kill him, you'll spill blood all over the living room."

Hallaq appealed to Ramzi, "You have a pistol, shoot him!"

"No," answered Ramzi.

They dragged Hallaq over into another room, and got him to his knees. Maher loosened Hallaq's belt, opened the buttons on his pants, and pulled them down. Hallaq thought he was going to be raped, while Fadi understood Maher was going to inject the sedative into his backside.

Hallaq screamed: "Kill me! I will tell you everything, just shoot me afterwards. Don't hand me over to Hizbullah. They will cut me up into little bits. Or just send me to the Syrians! I will manage to fix everything with General Kanaan."

Instead they taped Hallaq's eyes and mouth, and gave him several shots of Valium. Fadi fetched the bottle of ether, and held a cloth in front of Hallaq's face, saying, "Smell this you son of whore!"

Hallaq still would not lose consciousness. In his excitement, Fadi had forgotten to open the ether bottle. Eventually they bound Hallaq's hands and feet as well, whereupon they rolled him into a sheet and carried him to Ramzi's silver-white Mercedes, which was in the garage underneath the house. They drove out the back way—Ramzi and Fadi in a BMW, with Moufid and Maher taking the Mercedes.

Near Aishiyeh, where the Israelis had a base, the road was blocked by two Israeli tanks. Out came the ID cards that indicated the kidnappers worked with the Israelis. Ramzi shouted "shalom" to the soldiers and said some words in Hebrew. They passed them through without checking the vehicle. Further north they stopped to check that Hallaq had not choked where he lay in the trunk. Then they drove through Jezzine and on toward the final SLA post. Maher, Moufid and Ramzi were now leading in the BMW, while Fadi followed in the Mercedes with Hallaq still in the trunk. He was to drive on alone, while the other three turned back to Ebl el-Saqi.

At the control post in Bater was an SLA guard whom Moufid knew. They were both bodybuilders, and Moufid got out of the car and started up a conversation with him about which proteins worked best for strength training. At the same time he told Maher to open the gate. When the Mercedes was through the barrier, Moufid whistled so Fadi himself would close the gate behind him, as was the practice. He stopped just before the next control post, which was manned by soldiers from the Lebanese army. The Syrians also had an intelligence office there.

Moufid had called his intelligence contact in advance, and described the Mercedes in which he would arrive. After some waiting, a Syrian colonel arrived. Fadi turned over Hallaq to the Syrians, and left for Beirut. The two others went back to Ramzi's house to wash away the blood and get rid of Hallaq's sunglasses, shoes, pistol and other belongings which might have remained in the house. Then they drove home to Moufid's house and had dinner.

The following day, Fadi came back. By then the alarm had already spread throughout the occupation zone that Hallaq had disappeared. Ramzi, Moufid and Maher were asked to come to Metulla to report what they knew. They asserted their innocence over the phone, but the Israelis wanted to look them in the eyes.

Moufid refused to go, but Ramzi and Maher drove to Israel, where Mossad questioned them the whole night. Since no one had seen them pick up Hallaq in Qleia, they stuck with their story. They repeated it to a Mossad chief who had come from Tel Aviv. The Israelis were at a loss as to what had happened. Perhaps Hallaq had been kidnapped, but he could also have been a double agent who now had chosen to join the Syrians.

Mossad's man said, "If Hallaq is still in the zone, it is okay, but if he is out, we need to know right away." He knew Hallaq had recruited three Syrians who were now in Israeli service. If they were exposed, it would mean death for all three.

Ramzi and Maher were arrested, while Moufid and Fadi had gone into hiding in Ebl el-Saqi. At first they considered turning themselves over to the Norwegian battalion to keep the Israelis from taking them by force, but chose three days later to flee to the Bekaa Valley and then to Beirut.[88]

In Beirut, Ahmed Hallaq was condemned to death for the murder of Fuad Mughniyeh. On September 21, 1996, he was led before 10 men who were ready with their rifles. There was no 21-gun salute for him; the doctors who examined his body after the execution counted nine bullets.

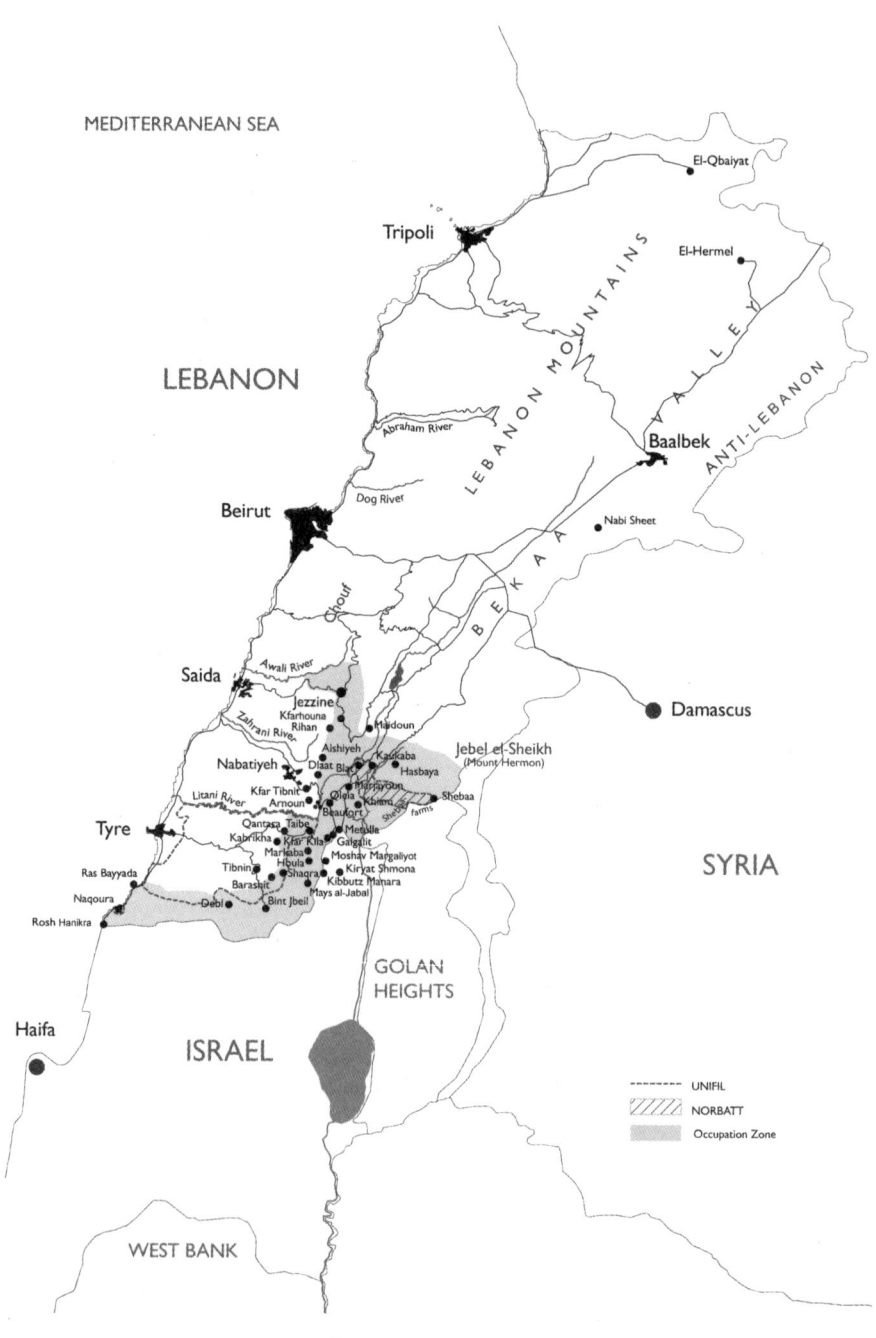

MEDITERRANEAN SEA

El-Qbaiyat

Tripoli

El-Hermel

L
E
B
A
N
O
N

M
O
U
N
T
A
I
N
S

LEBANON

V
A
L
L
E
Y

Abraham River

Baalbek

A
N
T
I
-
L
E
B
A
N
O
N

Dog River

Beirut

Nabi Sheet

B
E
K
A
A

Chouf

Awali River

Saida

Jezzine

Kfarhouna
Rihan

Maidoun

Jebel el-Sheikh
(Mount Hermon)

Zahrani River

Aishiyeh
Kaoukaba

Nabatiyeh

Diaat Bla

Hasbaya

Kfar Tibnit

Qlaia

Marjayoun

Litani River

Arnoun

Khiam

Shebaa

Damascus

Beaufort

Sheeba farms

Qantara

Taibe

Metulla

Tyre

Kabrikha

Kfar Kila

Galgalit

Marbaba

Moshav Margaliyot

Tibnin

Hbula

Shaqra

Kiryat Shmona

Ras Bayyada

Barashit

Kibbutz Manara

Naqoura

Debl

Bint Jbeil

Mays al-Jabal

Rosh Hanikra

GOLAN
HEIGHTS

SYRIA

Haifa

ISRAEL

-------- UNIFIL

/////// NORBATT

Occupation Zone

WEST BANK

PART SEVEN

Lebanese Quicksand 1996-1998

Israel's conduct of war in Lebanon became more brutal with Prime/Defense Minister Shimon Peres as the driver. An example of this is that the Israelis killed over 100 civilian Lebanese who sought refuge in a UN camp in the town of Qana, all in the course of a few minutes. This brought no consequences for the perpetrators.

UN Secretary-General Boutros Boutros-Ghali's mandate was not renewed following pressure from the United States, which was unhappy with his handling of the situation in the Middle East.

Resistance to the occupation of South Lebanon grew in Israel, led by the Four Mothers, an organization founded by four women with sons who were soldiers in Lebanon. The organization also got support from leftist politicians and officers.

Hizbullah continued its advancement. The guerrilla's military capability increased and inflicted a number of humiliating defeats on Israel.

MAIN CHARACTERS

Boutros Boutros-Ghali, UN Secretary-General
Dan Harel, Brigadier General, Head of the IDF's artillery
Franklin van Kappen, Major General, Military Advisor to the UN Secretary General
Amnon Lipkin-Shahak, Lieutenant General, Israel's Chief of the General Staff,
Benjamin Netanyahu, Israeli Opposition Leader, later Prime Minister
Shimon Peres, Israel's Prime Minister and Defense Minister

CHAPTER SEVENTY NINE
Operation Grapes of Wrath

In the spring of 1996, Israel had new elections. Prime Minister Shimon Peres was certain of victory. The Labor Party's leader had led in the opinion polls by around 20 percent over the opposition leader, Benjamin Netanyahu. In the election campaign, Peres spoke a lot about his desire for peace with the Palestinians and the Lebanese. There were many who favored the well-spoken politician with his vision for a new Middle East.

However, not everyone believed what Peres had said. Now and then when I saw him put on his proper face and speak warmly about his ideas, it brought to mind an old children's story. It was about the hunter who had shot a bird on a cold and rainy morning. A little boy, seeing the hunter bent over the dead bird, thought the raindrops on the man's face were tears. The boy turned to his mother and said, "Mamma, look at that big man crying because the bird is dead."

The mother answered curtly, "Don't worry about the tears, but look at what he does with his hands." This is the way it was with Peres. He said one thing, but did another.

Benjamin Netanyahu wanted the election postponed, and the Likud leader put forth a number of proposals for ways to achieve this. Some of them were so ridiculous that "Bibi" showed up in a newspaper cartoon saying that the elections should be on the 35th of May. After much back and forth, the elections' date was set for May 17, the same date, 13 years earlier, Israel and Lebanon had signed their short-lived agreement for the invaders' withdrawal. Hizbullah, for its part, had no plans to interfere with the election campaign or to move its war of liberation over onto Israeli soil. The guerrillas wanted to get the Israelis out of South Lebanon. The difficult terrain in that part of the country gave them big advantages. The valleys were deep, the ridges of the hills were high and the mountains were covered with brush and trees for excellent cover. For Israel, South Lebanon became like a pool of quicksand. The death of an Israeli colonel and three soldiers killed by a land mine in South Lebanon on March 4, 1996, renewed debate over how the war was being fought, and if it was right to have Israeli soldiers in the country. The Israelis' Christian allies felt the zone guaranteed Galilee's security. They intensified their lobbying both in Israel and in the United States, and maintained that pulling out of South Lebanon would expose Northern Israel to a million radical Shias backed by Iran.

On March 10, an Israeli soldier was killed and four more were wounded by a roadside bomb, and 10 days later a car bomb killed an Israeli officer. Now the officer corps wanted revenge! But retaliation only led to the wounding of eight additional Israeli soldiers.

The officer corps' call for revenge did not stop here, but grew stronger. Military leaders no longer wanted to be bound by the 1993 "understanding" that forbade them attacking civilian targets. The officers did not care that Hizbullah had kept its side of the agreement and refrained from firing missiles at Israeli towns.

Prime Minister Peres agreed with the officer corps, and renewed the promise Rabin had made earlier to crush the Palestinian Islamists and Hizbullah. Netanyahu tried from his side to assure voters that only Likud had the key to peace in the region. This change of roles confused many Israelis, who associated Labor as the party of peace and Likud as a party full of hawks.

On March 30, when the Israelis killed two civilian Lebanese who were in the process of repairing a water tower in the village of Yatar at the edge of the UN zone, it was the "straw that broke the camel's back" for Hizbullah. Israel had breached the agreement that civilian lives were to be spared. The guerrillas then fired 28 Katyusha rockets into Israel, aimed at unpopulated areas. It was clear that Hizbullah did not desire a repeat of the seven-day war of 1993.

Israel, it seems, picked up this signal from Hizbullah and said the attack against civilians in Yatar had been a "mistake." Israeli soldiers had seen several people up on a rooftop and thought they were "terrorists." Shimon Peres immediately contacted the US Secretary of State, and France's president to inform them Hizbullah would get an official apology and an assurance the Israeli attack had been a mistake.

Many higher-level Israeli officers did not like the prime minister's apology. They thought Israel's restraint was a sign of weakness and feared the country was about to lose its credibility. Even more humiliating was that Hizbullah's leader, Sheikh Hassan Nasrallah, said the rocket attack against Israel was only a partial retaliation for civilian deaths, and that the population in Northern Israel would be wise to stay in their shelters a few more days.

The IDF once again put their hired hands to work in South Lebanon. Early in the evening of April 9, 1996, 16-year-old Mazen Farhat walked up the narrow lane behind his parents' house in Barashit, in the UNIFIL zone, and behind him trudged his cousin, Mohammed, and his 8-year-old brother, Ibrahim. From the village, they could see an SLA outpost on a steep hill further south, dominating the village.

As the three children passed along a stone wall, Mazen noticed a gray rock lying beside the road that had not been there before. Like all the villagers in the area, Mazen was well aware of the "rock bombs" often used by Hizbullah, the SLA and the Israelis.

The bomb suddenly exploded and killed Mazen instantly. Ibrahim, who had been a few meters behind his elder brother, was knocked unconscious, but survived with serious shrapnel wounds, together with his cousin, Mohammed.

The villagers had no doubt who was behind the bombing, but the Israelis, at first, denied any knowledge of the incident, and maintained the bombs had to be from an earlier time. UN investigators, however, determined that the traps consisted of four bombs, not one. The serially linked explosive charges were packed with steel ball bearings and fitted with anti-tampering mechanisms, then hidden beneath the "rocks." The next day, a bomb expert from Hizbullah appeared on an *Al-Manar* television news, displaying fragments of the four bombs. He said that the wiring, the Israeli-manufactured battery, and parts of an antenna proved the bomb was produced by the IDF.

These facts, and Israel's repeated breaches of the 1993 "understanding" not to attack civilian targets, led Hizbullah to fire new rockets at Northern Israel the next morning. No one was killed, but 13 civilians were injured. Hours later, an Israeli soldier was killed and three more were wounded when Hizbullah pounded an IDF post with mortar.

The Israeli government answered by ordering a massive attack against Lebanon. Israeli planes took to the air loaded with missiles and bombs, and the IDF artillery joined in. The offensive, code-named Operation Grapes of Wrath, would become the most massive attack on Lebanon since the invasion of 1982. Foreign Minister Ehud Barak threatened that no one in South Lebanon should feel safe, and warned civilians to flee to the north.

The name of the operation was not randomly chosen. In the Hebrew Bible, Moses describes the revenge God would send upon the enemies of the Israelites.

On April 12, Hizbullah repeated its rocket attacks against Northern Israel. The evening before, many Israeli civilians had been ordered to bomb shelters or advised to leave their towns.

In South Lebanon, around 5,000 people sought refuge in the UNIFIL camps, while tens of thousands of civilians fled northward. Among them were Ibtisam Youssef and her five children, who lived in the village of Sohmor, far south in the Bekaa Valley. The IDF had given the residents of Sohmor a deadline of 6 pm to leave the village, after which they would bombard it. Ibtisam's husband, who worked in Beirut, called his wife and asked her and the children to come to Beirut. At first she refused, but finally she was convinced to go.[1]

She telephoned an uncle who promised to pick her and the children up. At exactly 2 pm the uncle arrived along with his wife, their daughter and his sister. They drove a Volkswagen minibus. On the way out of the village, an Israeli helicopter showed up and fired a missile that exploded right in front of them.

A little later, the minibus broke down, and Ibtisam, fearing for the lives of her children, decided to split the family up. It was not unusual in Lebanon for families to do this when fleeing: if anyone was killed, the others at least might survive. Ibtisam's sister, who was with her, took the two eldest children, and went toward Qaraoun, a village further north where they agreed to meet up again. Ibtisam remained with her three younger children and the uncle's family. They wanted to wait until the bombardments had stopped before moving on. They took refuge in a garage.

They never got any further. The garage was struck by a rocket. Ibtisam, the three children, the uncle, his wife and their daughter were all killed. Only the uncle's sister survived.

The next day, an ambulance full of women and children was hit by a missile from an Israeli military helicopter just after it had passed through a UN control post. When the world saw pictures of a little girl who lay dead in the ambulance, the Israelis said the ambulance was carrying people from Hizbullah. The guerrillas would have to bear the blame themselves that two women and four children had been killed. From the Israeli perspective, anyone who had not already fled South Lebanon was a terrorist.

A meeting of the UN Security Council was called for April 15 at 6 p.m., New York time. Lebanon requested the meeting but it did not take long for US Ambassador Madeleine Albright to suggest to her Lebanese colleague to postpone it. The reason was that the US envoys, Warren Christopher and Dennis Ross, needed more time to discuss the matter with Syria, Lebanon and Israel.

The Lebanese were convinced the Americans only wanted to give Israel more time to carry out their operations. Lebanon therefore refused a postponement. Then Albright asked for a briefing on the Lebanese UN ambassador's complaints, and what he would say to the Security Council. She made it clear the US would use its veto against any resolution directed at Israel.

Parallel with the fight over South Lebanon, the "peace process" between the Israelis and the Palestinians had moved into a critical phase during the spring of 1996. Palestinians with bombs strapped to their bodies, hidden in bags or loaded into cars were carrying out a series of attacks that took the lives of dozens of innocent Israelis.

It had been a Jewish immigrant, Baruch Goldstein from Brooklyn, who had begun the violent developments two years earlier. On Friday morning February 25, 1994, Goldstein had entered the Ibrahimi Mosque in Hebron with an automatic weapon hanging over his shoulder. It was the fifth day of Ramadan. Seven hundred Palestinians were gathered for prayers in the mosque.

Without warning, Goldstein raised his weapon and began methodically firing at the Palestinians who were praying. A few minutes later, the dead and the wounded lay atop one another on the floor. Blood was sprayed on the walls and ran over the carpets and floor. Once Goldstein's first magazine was empty, he reloaded and continued firing. He put the weapon on half-automatic: he didn't want to waste ammunition. He had seven magazines with him.

As he fired, hundreds of Palestinians tried to find a place to hide, and many managed to take shelter behind a wall. Here they remained for around 10 minutes, as Goldstein squeezed the trigger 110 times until his weapon froze. Before the attacker could load yet another magazine, some of the Palestinians stormed him. They beat him to death with a fire extinguisher before his body was virtually torn to shreds.

The shrieks and shots had alarmed the Israeli forces outside the mosque, and when the soldiers at the observation post saw Palestinians fleeing the mosque, they opened fire. Several were injured. Behind them lay 29 dead, among them the mutilated perpetrator. Many more wounded were evacuated, or received first aid on the spot.

Hamas promised revenge. "We will hit back, but we will choose the right moment, place and target," said the Palestinian doctor, Mahmoud Zahar.

The Palestinian revenge was gruesome. Israel's response was just as merciless. The spiral of violence increased and continued after Yitzhak Rabin had been killed and Shimon Peres became prime minister.

The Palestinian attacks weakened Peres politically, and turned to President Clinton for help. The upcoming elections in Israel were also important for the United States. Clinton conferred with Egypt's President Hosni Mubarak, and together they arranged a so-called peace conference in Sharm el-Sheikh. Leaders from 27 countries, among them Prime Minister Gro Harlem Brundtland from Norway, showed up in solidarity with Israel's "war against terror."

Peres realized he could not hit the Palestinians too hard in the Gaza Strip and West Bank. This could lead to the collapse of the "peace process" with the Palestinian self-governing authority, who now was primarily serving Israel. But the same restrictions did not cover Hizbullah. The solidarity conference gave a green light for a large-scale offensive against the Lebanese guerrillas, which in reality was mainly directed at the civilian population. An official in the Clinton administration told *Newsweek* that the US had given Israel the go-ahead, but also warned, "If something goes wrong, then don't come running to us."[2]

The loss of six more Israeli soldiers' lives in Lebanon and Katyusha rockets toward Northern Israel were the excuses for putting in heavy weaponry. April 1996 had arrived, and one month was left before the election in Israel.

On Monday, April 15, four Norwegian officers were given the task of driving supplies to the civilians in South Lebanon. Second Lieutenant Atle Paulsen was one of the officers. He and the others were first sent to Tyre, where UNIFIL had its supply base. There they picked up food, blankets and medicines intended for isolated villages. They were also to evacuate civilians in the western and southern areas of the UNIFIL zone.

Four trucks with Polish crews also went. In addition there were two armored personnel carriers with a French escort and four cars with room for journalists and photographers. Israeli aerial and artillery bombardment became increasingly more intense that UNIFIL had problems delivering supplies, even for their own battalions. The white-painted UN vehicles came under direct Israeli fire. Taking cover underneath the vehicles when the artillery shells landed 10–15 meters away they could hardly believe the Israelis were ready to go to war against the UN.

In UNIFIL's logbook 4,200 artillery shells were tallied, along with 52 helicopter attacks and close to 300 air raids over the western section of the UNIFIL operating area—all in the course of one day. That same day, Hizbullah fired just over 100 rockets into Northern Israel. In the town of Qana, where Fiji's battalion had its headquarters, Hizbullah guerrillas tried to mount a rocket launcher near one of the UN positions. The Fijians wanted them out of there and this led to an exchange of fire, and one of the Fijian officers was shot in the chest and was taken to the field hospital in Naqoura.

On Tuesday April 16 the Security Council met, and after four hours of discussion, a four-line announcement came that the fighting in Lebanon should cease. On Wednesday morning, the US proposed a ceasefire. The proposal was built upon the understanding from 1993 that the parties were not to attack civilian targets. The new proposal further stated that Hizbullah should guarantee the safety of Israeli soldiers in South Lebanon. But Hizbullah rejected the proposal. Both the Lebanese government and Hizbullah referred to the UN resolution 425 from 1978, which demanded that Israel withdraws from Lebanese territory.

Even more Lebanese now fled their homes and villages. Around 60 civilians from the village of Majdal Zoun were given protection on April 17 in a UNIFIL camp near their village. The camp was manned by soldiers from Nepal. Majdal Zoun had been bombarded for several days. In addition the main road to the village had been bombed one kilometer northwest of the UN base.

That same Wednesday morning, a unit of the UNIFIL Polish engineers' corps came to repair the road. Israeli planes came in over the area at 11 a.m., and dropped a bomb just 150 meters from the UN repair crew. The soldiers continued their work, but when the Israelis fired again half an hour later using tanks, the peace soldiers chose to pull back.

Ten minutes later, Israeli artillery put the UN base itself under direct fire. Eight shells landed in the middle of the camp. The shells were of two types: Half of them were to explode in the air above the target to maximize the splinter effect against personnel; the other half to explode on the ground to maximize damage to buildings. The 60 civilians in the camp were in the shelters and came out unscathed from the attack.

The chief of the UN camp, Lieutenant Colonel Rana Dhoj Limbu, reported the attack by radio. He said there were no Hizbullah guerrillas in the camp or nearby. The guerrillas were around the village of Yatar, 10 kilometers further east. The colonel stated that the Israelis had also failed to give any warning that the UN camp would be fired upon, as was the practice when an area in the UN zone was put under fire.[3]

"The firing did not occur by mistake," maintained Limbu. "The base has been there for 12 years. The Israelis know it well. It lies near one of the Israelis' positions. Perhaps the Israelis fired because they did not like that we gave protection to the civilians," he said further.

Early on the morning of April 18, Israeli planes attacked the town of Nabatiyeh. According to eyewitnesses, Hizbullah had fired off a rocket from a hill nearby a few hours earlier. The Abid family was still sleeping when the Israeli bombs exploded in their house. Out of 11 family members only the 18-year-old son, Ibrahim, survived, in addition to his father, who was away on pilgrimage to Mecca. His mother Fawziya had given birth to a son just three days earlier, and died together with eight of her children.

Eight days had passed since Peres had given approval for the massive air and artillery attack against Lebanon. The villages of South Lebanon were nearly empty of people. Around 400,000 South Lebanese had fled north. Only the eldest and poorest remained. Those who saw that UN columns had managed to get through to their villages, crept cautiously out of their cellars and houses. But most seldom got help. Between 60 and 70 percent of all the UN vehicles that tried to get to the civilian population were prevented by Israeli rockets and fighter planes.

To scare away the greatest number of people, Israeli fighters also dive-bombed over Tyre and dropped concussion grenades. The ear-deafening explosions caused the entire town to shake. At the same time the jets regularly crossed the sound barrier right over the UNIFIL supply base in Tyre.

CHAPTER EIGHTY

Massacre in Qana

Early in the morning of April 18, 1996, Hizbullah's intelligence service received a message that a patrol of Israeli soldiers was on its way to an unpopulated area south of the village of Qana. The Israelis were so-called "spotters" whose job was to direct artillery fire toward a target further north.[4]

The Israelis had been localized, and Hizbullah ordered its team in Qana to fire. A launch ramp for Katyusha rockets was 200 meters southwest of the Fijian UN camp in the village, and a ramp for mortars was in a graveyard just 350 meters southeast of the camp, where hundreds of civilian Lebanese, mostly women and children, had sought refuge.

While three young men were putting up the mortar ramp, a Fijian column drove by. In one of the vehicles sat Sergeant Eroni Matanikoroca. He looked at his watch; it was 1:35 p.m. "We have to drive into the camp and take shelter. The Israelis will shoot back," he shouted.[5] The column drove straight into the camp. At the gate they were ordered to park as usual.

It was not the first time Hizbullah had fired against the Israeli forces from positions close to the Fijian headquarters in Qana. Earlier in the year the guerrillas had on several occasions put up their launch ramps near the camp. A Fijian sergeant had objected to this and had decided to inform the Israelis. When the Hizbullah guerrillas mounted their launch ramps nearby the next time, he called via the NORBATT switchboard to the IDF liaison office in Metulla, and told them about the Hizbullah activity. He gave the Israelis precise coordinates.

What the sergeant did not know was that the Norwegian soldiers, who worked at the switchboard, were given orders to listen to all conversations going into Israel. It was not because of any suspicion of a breach of neutrality that the Norwegian battalion leader had given this order. The reason was primarily because there were only a certain number of civilian phone lines available, and the Norwegians did not want unnecessary civilian traffic on an overloaded network. When the operator on duty, Jørn Inge Hestnes, heard the Fijian giving coordinates to the Israelis, he alerted NORBATT's chief of operations, Major Harald Vaadal. The major advised the battalion chief, Colonel Leif Arne Ljøkjell. With the help of a Fijian officer, the Israelis' spy at the UN camp in Qana was exposed and sent home.[6]

On April 18, there was no Fijian to report to the IDF, but the Israelis' own radar network showed where the rockets and mortar shells were coming from. The data report was read at the Israeli Northern Command and in an artillery unit near the Lebanese village of Yarin, about 12 kilometers from the Mediterranean coast. In the meantime, the leader of the Israeli commando group that had been fired upon sent out a message that they were in grave danger and needed artillery support.[7]

The chief of the artillery unit asked the Northern Command for instructions. The targets were less than 350 meters from the UN camp in Qana. In the headquarters of the Northern Command one of the Israeli intelligence officers warned the chief, Brigadier General Amiram Levine, "The targets are too close to the UN camp."

The answer came back: "Fire!"

Just a few minutes later the first artillery shells hit outside the camp. Eroni Matanikoroca, who had seen the Hizbullah's firing preparations at the graveyard, tried to get into one of the secure rooms in the bomb shelter in the camp. But it was impossible to find space. The rooms were filled with refugees and soldiers.

Eroni ran toward an armored personnel carrier and jumped in to join the others already there. He heard two shells hit nearby, but could not see anything but black smoke. The third shell landed in the barracks where the Fijians usually had their traditional dance evenings. The so-called Vanua house, named for one of the Fijian islands, was just 10 meters from the armored vehicle. And that building was also full of civilian Lebanese. After the shell had exploded, Eroni could hear a chorus of shrieks. Then all was quiet.

The shell impacts were concentrated on two areas. One lay around 100 meters south of the UN camp, where there was a small cluster of houses about 75 meters from the spot where the mortar ramp had been. In all, 17 shells exploded. Sixteen of them did so as they hit the ground; these were the type that was effective for destroying equipment and ammunition.

The other impact area was in the middle of the camp. There several shells exploded just above the ground in order to have the maximum effect against people. It was meant for enemy forces, but in the Qana camp it was used against civilians and UN soldiers.

The driver of the armored vehicle in which Eroni was hiding started it up and drove away. A shell that hit just 10 meters away lifted the vehicle into the air and it bounced out to the edge of the road. The driver managed to maneuver it back onto the road. When they got to the main gate, several shells landed. The driver turned and drove back. He wanted to try to get out the eastern gate. But more shells hit there, and he decided to return and park the vehicle.

Some of the soldiers inside began to cry. They thought it was over for them, and prayed to God to be saved. Each time a shell hit, the vehicle shook. Between impacts the soldiers looked out the small windows and could see corpses and body parts lying about.

When the explosions stopped, Eroni jumped out. He took some first aid equipment and ran toward Vanua house. Inside he saw two heaps of dead bodies, one in the south end of the building and the other at the north end. The artillery shells had exploded in the middle of the house and had thrown its victims to both sides.

The dead were everywhere. Eroni went outside and sat down to collect himself. Then he went back into the bombed out building. There he found a woman who was still alive. She called, "Fiji! Fiji!" Several more soldiers arrived. They managed to pull the screaming woman out of the heap of bodies, and Eroni saw she was trying to contain her innards within her stomach with her right hand. Then she collapsed and died. Eroni could not control himself anymore. He ran back outside and fainted.

The UNIFIL supply column headed by Second Lieutenant Atle Paulsen was out on mission in the UN zone when the Israeli artillery barrage against Qana began. He heard the shells pass over them, and suddenly heard a Fijian officer shouting on the radio: "I have looked death in the face. It is everywhere." Then the radio was silent.

Paulsen and his men drove toward Tyre. The radio silence was constantly broken by new messages. The losses were growing. In Tyre, Paulsen learned that the UNIFIL reserve forces had been sent to the Fiji headquarters in Qana, and that his team also had to go there. The entire sanitation unit of UNIFIL was being mobilized.[8] The reserve forces had their camp 800 meters from the Fijian headquarters. Among the soldiers in the so-called Force Mobile Reserve was Gunnar Brandsdal, along with 27 other Norwegians. At first Brandsdal had not reacted to the sounds of the bombardment. The impacts were not dangerously close. Israel's bombing and artillery fire were a part of daily life, and Brandsdal stayed in bed, tired as he was after having been out on mission the whole night. When the thuds became more powerful, he got up and went out to see what was happening. He could not see the artillery shells landing in the Fijian headquarters, but since he had brought his video camera with him, he directed it toward Qana and recorded the black smoke rising from the camp.[9]

Some of Brandsdal's colleagues had heard the engine sounds of a pilotless drone since the first impact thuds were heard. But the sky was cloudy and they could not see where the drone was. After a while it became visible, and Brandsdal aimed the camera toward the drone without thinking much about it. Later, he recorded two helicopters of the Cobra type over the village of Kafra, two or three kilometers away. When he heard on the radio that people had been killed in the UN camp, he understood the drone and the helicopters had to have been flying observation posts for the artillery.

Brandsdal went back in and put on his uniform. The others did the same. They knew that when the attack was over, they would be sent to assist. The attack lasted seventeen minutes, and 15 minutes later 12 Norwegian and five Fijian soldiers were asked to drive to Qana in two of the force's vehicles.

Upon their arrival, they could see dead and dying people all over. Heads, arms and feet had been ripped off. Women lay on the ground with their insides spilling out. Children had been thrown about. One dead woman was hanging from a tree, another from one of the flat rooftops. The worst were not the dead, but all the dying people who struggled to stay alive.

Fijian soldiers had begun to gather the dead and body parts. They could not count the number of dead. One corporal was in shock. "I cannot find a whole person, only pieces!" he shouted. The odor of blood, burned flesh, urine and gunpowder, along with the screams of the injured and panicked turned the UN base into a hell on earth. There were no men from Hizbullah there; it was only civilian Lebanese who screamed.

One soldier from Fiji was standing in a sea of dead bodies. He could not utter a single word as he stood holding a headless child in his arms. There were body parts everywhere. A head, the soldiers were trying to match with a body. It was impossible there were many who were missing their heads. Dead children lay in their dead parents' arms and stared blankly into the air. Mutilated corpses that were unrecognizable were placed to one side so someone might later be able to identify them by their teeth. Eventually a swarm of people from neighboring villages came into the UN camp. Many of them began to tear the blankets off the corpses of their mothers, sisters or other close relatives, as they shouted "Allahu Akbar!"

Brandsdal's team got orders to escort an ambulance of the wounded to the helicopter pad. Others gave first aid. People came streaming in—so many that one soldier was assigned to keep them at a distance. Others were told to count corpses. Bodies put in body bags were placed in one of the barracks. When there were no more body bags, transparent plastic sacks were used. After a while the entire floor was covered with dead men, women and children.

In the open area outside, relatives and friends called and shouted, "Crush Israel! Israel is killing us! Death to the Jews!" A mass of people pushed against the barricades the UN soldiers had erected. Some were afraid when a Lebanese suddenly pulled out a pistol and aimed it at the UN soldiers. Beside himself with sorrow and anger, he attacked a CNN camera woman. He tore her camera away and threw it to the ground.

Second Lieutenant Paulsen and his team continued with the clean-up. Under a floor in one of the bombed barracks, he found three additional bodies. Two of them were completely charred and impossible to identify, the third was a girl of perhaps 10 years of age. When all had been packed in bags and carried off in vehicles, Paulsen felt he could barely hang on any longer. But he pulled himself together, and said to himself it was the least he could do for these innocent victims. He noticed that a number of the soldiers could not take the pressure, and were about to fall apart.

When they were nearly finished with the clean-up, the air raid alarm went off. Paulsen said a little prayer: "Please, not again." Everyone headed for the shelters. The impacts followed a few minutes later; but this time they were 300–400 meters away.

After the vehicles carrying the dead had left, the horde of civilians left too. With blood-soaked uniforms, Paulsen and his men sat down in the armored vehicles. No one said a word on the way to Tyre. At the hospitals they encountered weeping men, women and children as the dead and dying were brought in. Personnel from the Red Cross put the big orange body bags on the floor. They undid the zippers of every bag and felt for a pulse on each and every body. When they were sure there was no sign of life, they pulled the zippers up again. In all, 109 men, women and children were killed in Qana that day.

CHAPTER EIGHTY ONE

Israel's Lies

When the first report of the Qana massacre arrived at UN headquarters in New York from UNIFIL, the alarm bells went off. Secretary-General Boutros Boutros-Ghali immediately decided to send his military advisor, Dutch Major General Franklin van Kappen, to Lebanon. The general was instructed to go that very evening and take with him any experts he would need. He chose Lieutenant Colonel Geoffrey Dodds, an artillery expert from Great Britain.[10]

In Israel, Chief of the General Staff Amnon Lipkin-Shahak had drawn up talking points for the IDF: "Israel was fighting against Hizbullah in Qana. When the guerrillas fire on us, we return fire in self-defense. I know of no other rules in this game, either for the army or for civilians."[11]

The UN Security Council convened and the Arab countries, with Egypt in the lead, demanded a resolution condemning Israel and an immediate halt to the attacks against Lebanon, as well as an Israeli withdrawal from occupied areas. But as usual, the resolution lacked the support it needed to pass. The Security Council resolution number 1052 only managed "to regret" the Israeli attack and demand an immediate ceasefire.

General van Kappen and Colonel Dodds landed in Beirut, and had permission from the Israelis to drive unhindered along the coastal road to Naqoura. They received a French UNIFIL escort as they drove southward early the next day, April 20. When the column of UN vehicles had come several miles south of Beirut, they were fired upon by Israeli gunboats. These were not warning shots; the shell impacts were so close that the column had to seek shelter further inland.

UNIFIL's headquarters contacted the Israelis again, and were once more given the clear signal. That did not help much: after a few more kilometers, General van Kappen and his entourage were again fired upon and had to seek shelter. UNIFIL contacted the Israelis yet again, but astoundingly the UN envoys were shot at again after being cleared. The general and his group spent most of the day trying to get to Naqoura, where finally they were briefed by the UNIFIL Force Commander, Major General Stanislaw Wozniak.

On April 21, van Kappen and his men went to Qana. The Dutch general and the British colonel still believed the Israeli explanation that the incident had been an unfortunate mistake. In Qana, the envoys discovered Hizbullah had fired one Katyusha rocket and one 120 mm mortar shell. The two firing locations had already been found and marked. The wire to the Katyusha was still lying on the ground. There were also marks in the soil from the mortar.

When van Kappen and Dodds stood on the roof of the highest building in the UN camp, they both understood Israel's explanation of a firing error was false. It was not that only a single shell had hit the camp, but 13. It was also obvious the Israelis had undertaken a "clear change in target": the first shells had landed outside the camp, while the next set fell inside the camp's perimeter. The UN artillery expert was able to confirm the Israelis had used different types of artillery shells. Eight of the 13 shells were the anti-personnel sort that exploded while they were in the air, the other five were meant for buildings and material and exploded when they hit the ground.

The fact the Israelis had changed targets during the firing, was "difficult" to explain without having had "some form of visual control," the UN experts determined. In other words, the Israelis had to have had observers who could see the camp while the attack was underway. From the UN logbooks, the investigators could see the firing had begun at 2:08 p.m. and lasted until 2:25 p.m.

In all, 40 eyewitnesses were interviewed by the general's associates—civilian Lebanese, Fijian soldiers, soldiers from the Lebanese army and several from UNIFIL's Mobile Reserve unit. The Fijian battalion chief, Lieutenant Colonel Warne Waqanivavalagi, said that he and his men had done all they could to stop the artillery attack. Their UN posts near the Fijian headquarters had fired off red emergency flares, but the Israelis continued to shoot for at least 10 minutes after UNIFIL had repeated that the UN camp was full of civilian Lebanese.

From Lebanon, Major General van Kappen was flown to Israel in a UN helicopter to meet with high-level officers, among them the Deputy Chief of the General Staff, Major General Matan Vilnai, who immediately took the offensive: "You at the UN are hiding Hizbullah terrorists in the camps. You let them fire with mortars toward our positions at a visible distance from the UN camps. They do this because they know it is difficult for us to fire back at them there. We are fed up with this. You let them take advantage by giving refuge to terrorists in your camps. You let Hizbullah use you as shields."[12]

The Dutch general stayed calm and answered, "For the UN, only the human rights law is valid, whether the people are soldiers or civilians. We cannot stand at the gates of the UN camps and ask the women who come if they are married to a member of Hizbullah, or if they have a son in Hizbullah. When people are exposed to danger, or there is a war going on, and they try to find protection in the UN camps, then we help. We realize Hizbullah is misusing the UN. Therefore Hizbullah also must be blamed. But can you, a civilized nation, for that reason fire on a UN camp full of civilians? In my book, that is a war crime."

The head of the Israeli artillery forces, Brigadier General Dan Harel, explained the background for what had happened. Early in the afternoon on April 18, an Israeli patrol had come under fire from mortars fired from Qana. The general would not give a precise account of where the Israeli patrol had been—if, for example, it had crossed "the red line" marking the border between the Israeli occupation zone and the rest of Lebanon. It was well-known Israeli incursions north of "the red line" would be considered an aggressive act that normally would have led to Hizbullah retaliation. But Brigadier General Harel said the patrol had been "near the red line." A shell had landed just 40 meters from the patrol, which immediately asked for help. The artillery base then began the procedure for "cover fire."

It did not take long for Major General van Kappen to understand that the Israeli officers continued to mislead the UN. Instead of correcting them, he asked for more detail. The chief of the IDF artillery, Brigadier General Harel, showed lots of goodwill. He said that one of the two separate targets in Qana lay 200 meters southwest, the other 350 southeast of the UN camp. He also advised the artillery battalion on the Israeli-Lebanese border had checked with the Northern Command before it fired, exactly because the targets were so near the UN camp. Only when the artillery commander had his orders confirmed were 38 shells fired against the first target, according to Harel.

The battalion consisted of three batteries, each with four 155 mm cannons. Harel explained further that the two types of shells had been fired in random order. Some of the shells exploded in the air over the target, others exploded when they hit the ground. "It is certainly regrettable that some few shells passed their mark and hit the UN camp," Harel added.

Major General van Kappen did not believe the different types of shells were fired by chance, but he did not say this out loud. He just asked if the Israelis had changed targets during the firing.

"No. The firing only took place for three to five minutes, from 2:07 to 2:12, and there was no time to change target data."

"What about the other target?"

"The other target was fired by another battery at the same location. The four cannon fired 40 shells from 2:11 until 2:17."

As for the impact area among the civilians in the camp, Brigadier General Harel explained that the impact pattern could be explained by the fact the cannons had fired so much that the "barrel speed could no longer be synchronized." This would cause shells firing on the same target to land in different places. The UN artillery expert flatly rejected this theory, but said nothing at that time.

"Were Israeli helicopters and drones in the air during or after the firing?" asked van Kappen.

"No." This time it was Major General Vilnai who answered.

"Can you check this once more to be sure?" asked van Kappen. He was going to meet the Chief of the General Staff, Lieutenant General Amnon Lipkin-Shahak, later.

The Israeli officers admitted that during the firing, they had not realized a large number of Lebanese refugees had taken shelter in the camp. They placed great emphasis on the fact it was not Israeli policy to fire on civilians or the UN. To the contrary, the Israeli forces did all they could to avoid loss of civilian life. The event in Qana was therefore deeply regrettable.

Major General van Kappen just replied, "A UN camp is nevertheless not a lawful target, whether there are civilians in the camp or not." In addition, van Kappen knew UNIFIL had informed the Israelis that they were bombarding a UN camp full of civilians. This was written in the FIJIBATT logbook. Van Kappen could therefore not understand how the Israeli officers could deny this.

He said he would like to inspect the artillery battery that had fired. He wanted to check if it was old and worn, and to gauge the discipline among the ordinary soldiers and officers. To his surprise, this request was granted, and together with his other investigators, he found a battery in tip-top shape, with professional firing crews and well qualified officers.

He became more convinced that the Israelis had not made any mistake. He felt they had consciously fired on the UN camp. The Dutch general based his belief mainly on facts on the ground. That the Israelis were lying about the helicopters and the airborne drone near Qana.

CHAPTER EIGHTY TWO

More Lies

While the UN experts were collecting data on the ground, the Israeli government issued an announcement on April 21, 1996 that "Operation Grapes of Wrath" began after Hizbullah attacked Israel in cooperation with Iran, Hamas and Islamic Jihad. It claimed these entities were working together to destroy the peace process and to attack peaceful civilians, either in the northern areas, Jerusalem, Tel Aviv or other places. The government communiqué further stated that the military actions began after a long period of restraint and constant efforts at diplomatic dialogue. Peres called the operation a war without alternatives that had the support of the entire government.[13]

The following day, Peres took to the podium in the Knesset and thanked everyone who had taken part. He thought "Grapes of Wrath" was not a departure from the road to peace. To the contrary, the operation was necessary to save the peace. This was not a chosen operation, said Peres, but the fulfillment of a national obligation: self-defense on the one side, eliminating threats to the peace process on the other.[14]

In Lebanon, few believed Peres, and did not turn against Hizbullah, as the Israeli war planners had hoped. More than ever, the population supported the resistance movement. Even the Christians joined the Muslims in contacting the many TV shows that ran 24 hours a day. They wanted to know where they could find a Hizbullah recruiting center, how many Katyusha rockets had been fired toward Israel in the past day or where they could send money to buy more rockets.

A rich Christian woman donated $15,000. She was interviewed live on a radio station and said the only condition she put on the gift was that Katyushas be bought and fired at Israel's settlements in her name. She said: "Our people in the South have as much right as the Israelis to live a safe and secure life, and if Israel insists on carrying out its policy of displacing us, then we too will apply the same policy and displace their northern settlers. We, as a people, regardless of our religion and sects, are 100 percent behind the Resistance..."[15]

Among the witnesses van Kappen and his associates interviewed in Qana was Corporal Gunnar Brandsdal in the UNIFIL Mobile Reserve. In the days since the attack, he had not thought much about the videotape he had made. But when he was asked if he had seen drones or helicopters in the air during or after the bombardment, he was able to confirm it. Only later did it occur to him that the drone and the helicopter might have been visible on the tape he had recorded, including the exact time of the recording. Brandsdal sent a message to his troop chief, who drove to Naqoura with the tape. Brandsdal himself and several others in his troop had made sure to keep copies of their own.

When van Kappen received the cassette, he gave orders that no one say a word about it. At the same time, Brandsdal was told to make a tape of the two positions Hizbullah had fired from and to send it on to van Kappen.[16]

When he met with Israel's Chief of the General Staff, Lipkin-Shahak, he said, "General, I have only one question. Were there any Israeli helicopters or drones in the air, before, during or after the bombardment of Qana?"

"No," answered the Chief of the General Staff—the same answer the other generals, Levine and Harel had given before.

Major General van Kappen asked then to meet with the Israeli Chief of the General Staff. When they were alone, the UN officer said: "I know that you as general receive a large amount of information. Could you not personally check the matter one more time?" The Israeli seemed credible when he promised he would.

After the meeting, van Kappen called the leader of the UN peacekeeping operations, Kofi Annan, and said he would have to remain in the Middle East another day: "I am waiting for an answer from the Israelis."

"OK," answered Annan from New York.

The next day van Kappen again went to see Lieutenant General Lipkin-Shahak. "I have checked the matter," said the Chief of the General Staff, "There were no drones or helicopters in the air, before, during or after the bombardment."[17]

In addition to the oral response from the Chief of the General Staff, van Kappen received a written answer from the head of the Israeli liaison office for foreign forces, Brigadier General David Tzur. "There were no helicopters or mini-RPVs that flew over the Qana area on April 18, before or during the event," it said in black and white.[18]

Major General van Kappen was angry. He was tempted to play the video for the Israeli, but he did not. The film contained a recording of Israeli helicopters and one drone, and was clear proof that the Israelis were lying. But it was the facts on the ground in Qana, the pattern of the impacts, which provided the most important proof.

The UN envoy was surprised the Israeli military forces were continuing their attacks at the same time talks were going on with the defense leadership. Even for UNIFIL it was so dangerous to drive on the roads that 60 to 70 percent of all UN supply columns had to abandon because of rocket attacks and bombings from fighter aircraft.

The big toll of civilian losses in Qana put South Lebanon and Israel's occupation of the country firmly on the international agenda. Once more the US got the Israelis out of a bind. President Clinton asked for a ceasefire and sent Secretary of State Warren Christopher to the Middle East. He made it clear that a ceasefire had to be based on Israel's and America's conditions: Hizbullah was to be disarmed, and if the guerrillas stopped attacking Israeli soldiers in the course of the next six to nine months, Israel would be willing to enter "discussions" about a complete withdrawal from Lebanon.

Hizbullah rejected the ceasefire proposal once more, and Christopher had no other choice but to ask for Syria's help. In Damascus he met with Hafez al-Assad, who endorsed a French proposal, which would reaffirm the July 1993 understanding, safeguarding civilians on both sides of the border, but permitting Hizbullah to continue resisting the Israeli occupation.

The Israelis insisted they wanted the US, not France, to broker a deal, but after several days of shuttle diplomacy between capitals in the Middle East, Christopher capitulated. Assad had even refused to meet the hapless American Secretary of State on April 23, on his third visit to Damascus in four days.

On April 26, it was announced that an understanding had been reached to end the fighting. Hizbullah was prohibited from carrying out attacks against Israel, as Israel could not attack civilians in Lebanon and both sides agreed not to launch attacks from populated areas or other civilian sites. The understanding came into effect at 4 in the morning on April 27, 1996. The "April Understanding" additionally established a monitoring group consisting of delegates from Lebanon, Israel, Syria, France and the US to watch for any breaches. On April 30, 12 days after the massacre in Qana, the ceasefire between Israel and Hizbullah came into effect. It was obvious to everyone the agreement was not made in the USA, but in Paris, Tehran and Damascus.

The same day, 90 victims of Qana were to be interred. Thousands of people had come to participate in the burial. The weather was hot, and hoses were used to cool off the mass of people. The crowds shouted in rhythm, "*Allahu Akbar*," before music from loudspeakers mounted on cars drowned out the shouts. The coffins were carried through the town's small main road. On the way to the open place near the UN camp where the dead were to be buried, young men walked between the caskets and beat their hands against their chests while shouting slogans, according to the Shia funeral tradition. Soldiers, men from the civil defense and mourners participated in taking the linen-clad bodies out of the coffins and laying them side by side in the mass grave.

During the ceremony, my colleague Robert Fisk was standing on a rooftop in the camp, together with a Fijian officer who cried as the victims were put into the ground. The officer said that many of the dead children had been the same age as his own. Fisk heard there was a tape recording of the bombardment and of Israeli helicopters, but the Fijian did not have a copy himself. The British journalist gave him his visiting card and said he could call him whenever he had any new information. The approach would pay off later.

In Tyre, church bells echoed and verses from the Koran resonated as Muslims and Christians united during the government-organized mass funeral there. Turbaned Muslim clergymen and black-robed Christian bishops led the funeral procession. The coffins were transported in a convoy of Red Cross ambulances to a Roman-built arena on the outskirts of the city, where the service was led by Sheikh Mohammed Shamseddine, Lebanon's top Shia Muslim cleric. Prime Minister RaficHariri and Parliament Speaker Nabih Berri stood at his side.

"The Jews have committed a holocaust in Lebanon," said Shamseddine, "Oh, Lord, forgive them their trespasses as we wed those martyrs to your mercy."[19] Lebanon declared April 18 a national day of mourning to be observed every year.

In the "April Understanding" between Israel and Hizbullah, the ban on Israeli attacks against "civilian and civil targets" in Lebanon was made even stronger than in the "Understanding" of 1993. "The rules of the game" had changed in Hizbullah's favor. In 1995, the Clinton administration had determined Hizbullah was an enemy of the peace process. One year later it accepted that the guerrillas had the right to fight the Israelis in Lebanon. For Hizbullah's secretary-general, Hassan Nasrallah, this new "understanding" was nothing more than "a fantastic victory."[20]

Before van Kappen left Lebanon, he told the UNIFIL force commander that the investigation into the bombardment at the Qana camp should continue. His own report did not state who in Israel was ultimately responsible. He was convinced the bombardment was not an unfortunate miscalculation, or a technical or procedural mistake. The camp was bombed with full consideration, on orders from officers at a high level.[21]

When Secretary-General Boutros-Ghali read the conclusion of van Kappen's preliminary report and saw Corporal Brandsdal's videotape, he decided to make the report public.

"I will take full responsibility," said the Secretary-General.[22]

UN diplomats realized that the report was explosive regarding Israel. At UN headquarters, there were bets among the staff as to whether the Secretary-General would dare to cross Israel and the United States. Those who thought he had the will to put forth a critical report about Israel recalled that his chances to be re-elected as Secretary-General were virtually nil. The best-informed people knew the race was already over for the Egyptian. That January, the secretary of state discussed with Bill Clinton the issue and agreed: the US did not want to support Boutros-Ghali's re-election.[23]

The Secretary-General found himself in a difficult position, and announced that he had sent his military advisor to Lebanon to investigate the issue. Everyone knew van Kappen was back, and the media were looking for the report. Around 5,000 UNIFIL soldiers were also waiting for the release of the report. Furthermore, the entire Arab world was watching him, and there were other situations he had to take into consideration, as well. There would soon be another presidential election in the US, and Bill Clinton wanted a second term. Shimon Peres would soon be up for re-election as well.

The Secretary-General thought he had taken all precautions so the UN report would be as objective and fair as possible. When Israel's foreign minister, Ehud Barak, called and asked for more time to look into what had happened Boutros-Ghali was quick to agree. He also wanted the Israelis to have the opportunity to see Corporal Brandsdal's video, and to answer further questions.[24]

Israel's UN ambassador met with Kofi Annan, since he was responsible for the UN peacekeeping operations, and General van Kappen was present too and asked, "Why do you deny there were two helicopters and one drone over the Qana area before, during and after the bombardment?"[25]

"Because there were none," answered Ambassador David Peleg.

The 54-year-old diplomat, whose parents were from Lithuania, was both arrogant and self-assured.

"Then you will see a drone and two helicopters," replied the Dutch general, who then played the video. The ambassador was shocked. "This film is a fabrication," he said, "This we have to check."

"Fine, go ahead," answered van Kappen.

When the Israeli ambassador met van Kappen later there was no longer any talk of the film being fabricated. Ambassador Peleg had with him the chief of the Israeli artillery, Brigadier General Dan Harel. He maintained that, in its eagerness to cooperate with the UN, Israel had given van Kappen information that was wrong. That is why the Israelis had not managed to complete their own investigations.

The brigadier general talked on without showing the least sign of shame at replacing old lies with new ones. He explained a mistake had taken place when the officer from the Northern Command checked the distance from the bomb targets to the UN camp. One error was that the push-pin which marked the UN camp on the map indicated it was 100 meters north of its actual position. The second mistake was that the artillery man had measured the distance between the camp and the target at 350 meters, when in reality it was only 180 meters. Harel went on to say that he had also been given incorrect information about the shell types that had been fired.

He additionally had to admit that there had been a drone in the air over South Lebanon, but it was only over Qana around 2:18 p.m., he claimed, and the pilotless aircraft only had a narrow viewfinder. It was so narrow that it was unable to sight Qana until 2:21, and only nine minutes later, at 2:30, it registered the village clearly, it was six minutes after the UN forces had registered in the logbook that the bombardment was over. In order to demonstrate how little the drone had observed Harel played a few minutes of the recording from the air. It did not show any pictures from Qana. He continued to insist that the two helicopters visible on Corporal Brandsdal's video, had been sent north of the "red line" after the Israeli patrol had come under attack. The helicopters were supposed to localize and attack the source of the fire; but the pilots had not found the target, and thus left the area.

"What route did the helicopters take?" asked van Kappen.

"I don't know. I would have to look further into this," Harel gave as an excuse.

Van Kappen knew that the Israeli was lying. What made him even more upset was the subsequent Israeli campaign to impugn him personally. When van Kappen heard that he was supposedly part of an anti-Jewish vendetta, he said, "My wife is Jewish. I am not anti-Israeli." This was the only argument by which the general could defend himself.[26]

CHAPTER EIGHTY THREE

United States Pressures the UN

Prime and Defense Minister Shimon Peres had not achieved anything militarily in Lebanon, but the deaths of more than 100 civilian Lebanese who had sought refuge with the UN sat like a scar on the Israelis. The war against Hizbullah had become a nightmare for Peres. Now he exerted all his energy into getting control over the impending political catastrophe. Peres had to save Israel's face by whatever means possible.

He again sought help from President Clinton, who once more became Israel's premier defense advocate. The president simultaneously took on the task as the international campaign leader for Peres. On April 28, 1996, Clinton showed up at the annual meeting of AIPAC. He was the first sitting president ever to address the meeting, and now he promised to always maintain the relationship between Israel and the US regardless of what Israel did. "No one will drive a wedge between us," said Clinton, who shared the podium with Peres. To huge applause from the audience, the president acquitted Israel of the mass killings of civilians under "Operation Grapes of Wrath".[27]

During dinner at the White House in honor of Peres, Clinton said the US "stands side by side with Israel in good times and bad because our countries share the same ideals: freedom, tolerance and democracy." Clinton added that Peres, who had created a vision for a new Middle East, was America's partner for peace.[28]

While discussions were going on at the UN headquarters about whether van Kappen's report should be made public or not, Robert Fisk received a phone call in Beirut from the Fijian officer he had met in Qana on the day of the mass funeral. Fisk was given a map coordinate, and a few minutes later he was on his way south toward Qana together with his regular driver. The meeting place was an intersection, where the driver stopped and waited. A bit later a white UN jeep showed up. Fisk got out, and the Fijian officer threw a videocassette into the front seat as he said, "This is for the children of Qana."

On May 6, Fisk published the story of the secret video in *The Independent*. From New York, he wrote that the Qana report would most likely be a watered down version of van Kappen's draft, thanks to enormous pressure from the US.[29] Fisk made sure *CNN* got a copy of the tape. It was then just a question of minutes before all the TV stations in the world could show that the Israelis were lying when they said there were neither drones nor helicopters over the area when the bombardment of Qana took place. Both the date and times were visible on the pictures.

That same afternoon, Secretary-General Boutros-Ghali was scheduled to brief the Security Council members on the main conclusions of the van Kappen report. Once again he chose to postpone the briefing. His excuse was he was expecting further explanations from Israel on a number of questions. The Israelis had previously answered why they had fired on one of the targets near the UN camp, but had not said why two different fields of impact were 140 meters apart. They had not explained why they initially targeted the first impacts outside the camp and then fired right into it. Further, they had not said why they used two different shell types, or offered details surrounding the helicopter and drone over flights, as van Kappen had requested on April 21.

The general in a supplemental explanation had written it was "unlikely a significant technical mistake and/or procedural mistake had led to the bombardment of the UN camp. However, this cannot be completely ruled out." General Manfred Eisele, the second in command of the UN peacekeeping operations, had checked the technical part of the report line by line. The German had 40 years experience in artillery. Kofi Annan had also gone through the report word by word. He proposed a number of changes that made it more readable for general readership. The conclusion, however, was clear: "The pattern of the shell impacts in the Qana area showed it was unlikely the bombardment of the UN camp was the result of any technical-procedural error."[30]

At his home in Zeist, Netherlands, the general told me later what the bases for his conclusions were: "What was conclusive for us was that the artillery battery had changed from one target to another. First it fired at one target outside the camp. Then it fired toward the camp itself. Between these targets there were no impacts. If one were talking about an unreliable or poor artillery battery, we would have found an impact here or there. The bombardment of the camp was precise, and that was only possible by having a 'spotter,' an observer, on the spot, either on the ground or in the air. A drone sends information directly to the artillery battery; a man on board a helicopter can do the same. Therefore it was so important to determine if there had been helicopters and at least a drone with a view of the attack target as the bombardment was taking place."

The general went on to say the combination of artillery shells had changed with the target: "The mix of shells which explode as they hit the ground and shells which explode in the air over the target [inside the camp] was not the same mix as during the firing on the area outside the camp. A change in the combination of shells fired is a conscious act. This proves also, the Israelis were not truthful when they insisted that the mass killing was the result of a firing error. I do not doubt the bombardment of the UN camp was on orders from a high level. This does not mean the camp was fired upon by order of Peres or Lipkin-Shahak."

When I was at van Kappen's home, thoughts came to me what the chief of the Israeli artillery base had said to his men five minutes after the last shell fired at the UN camp had exploded: "This is war. You must continue to fight like the good soldiers you are. Those sonovabitches are firing at you, and what can you do? You have fired well, and you must continue to do so—there are millions of Arabs."[31]

One hundred Arabs more or less, what did that mean? Neither ordinary soldiers nor officers talked about the victims as Lebanese. They used the word *arabushim*, a Hebrew word created to insult Arabs—the final five letters in the Hebrew word for rats, *akhbarushim*, inserted after the word for Arabs.[32]

On May 8, the UN Secretary-General put van Kappen's report before the Security Council in a closed meeting. Boutros-Ghali had in advance said that he was "aware of the implications the conclusions in the report could have for the peace process in the Middle East." But pointed out he used great care, and that "the report was objective and fair."[33]

The report hit the Security Council like a political bombshell. The Israelis were furious, as expected, and the US stood at their side. Ambassador Madeleine Albright said she was "very upset by the unfair conclusions in the report."[34]

This time the US stood alone. None of the other members of the Council supported the Americans' verbal attack on the UN. The Egyptians regretted the report did not contain a clear condemnation of Israel. The Russians were ready to go along with any form of reaction from the Security Council, but suggested also that a resolution or statement would have to consider the ceasefire, and focus on the peace process.

Shimon Peres attacked the UN directly. In interviews, he put the entire blame for the massacre on UNIFIL and repeated his claims that Israel had not received word there were hundreds of civilians in the camp at Qana. "We had no idea of this. It was a scandal that UNIFIL allowed civilians into the camps without Israel being informed of this," Peres said to CNN. UNIFIL's spokesperson Timur Göksel immediately rebutted the Israeli prime minister. He had personally reported to the Israelis about the 6,000 civilian Lebanese who had sought shelter in the various UNIFIL camps.

The United States did not want the report made public because the Clinton administration was afraid any criticism of Israel would ruin Shimon Peres' chances in the elections. When the report came to the Security Council, the US naturally would not accept a resolution that condemned Israel. During the debate in the Council, the US still had to listen to harsh words about Israel's attack on Qana. Great Britain, France and Germany all criticized Israel, but no one would take on the burden of going against the wishes of the US. The strong pressure from Israel and the United States caused the UN leadership to drop any further investigations of Israel's actions.

Amnesty International completed its own investigation conducted by high-level military experts. The human rights organization concluded Israel had attacked the UN camp "with intent." Not even this investigation had any consequences for Israel.

CHAPTER EIGHTY FOUR

Four Mothers

In Israel, Prime Minister Shimon Peres felt he had to get the Jewish settlers on the West Bank and Gaza Strip over onto his side if he wanted to win re-election in May 1996. Yossi Beilin, the man Rabin had called "Peres' puddle," arranged for a meeting with Rabbi Yoel Bin-Nun. He was the leader of the Ofra settlement on the West Bank, founded by the extremist Jewish movement called Gush Emunim.

Through Beilin, Peres promised that, "Any final agreement [with the Palestinians] would guarantee Israeli sovereignty over the western parts of Judea and Samaria." No removal of existing settlements, and the government would provide security for the settlers and allow "natural growth"—a vague expression that could involve massive expansion. The agreement with the rabbi concluded that a future line of separation with the Palestinians would not coincide with the "Green Line." The "Green Line" described the border between Israel and Jordan as it was before 1967. Peres, therefore, went much further in support of the settlers than any right-wing government had previously done.[35]

When I asked Yossi Beilin about the agreement, he confirmed that the document contained the government's true positions. "Since the Oslo Accord was made, we have accepted the principle of natural growth in the settlements. We have never forbidden Jews to build kindergartens," Beilin said.[36]

The Israeli weekly *Nekuda* figured out that the Likud government had given the settlers in the illegal colonies 500 million shekels (about $200 million) through 1992. After this the Labor government tripled the subsidies. But in the 1996 election campaign, Benjamin Netanyahu outbid the Labor Party by promising a Likud government that would be open to another half a million Jews moving into the West Bank.

In opinion polls, Peres was leading his challenger between four and six percentage points, but up to 16 percent of the voters had not made up their minds yet. One poll showed that 80 percent of those undecided would vote for Netanyahu if there were new suicide attacks in Israel.

On May 29, 1996, the Israelis went to the polls. Benjamin Netanyahu beat Shimon Peres by a narrow margin because the sitting prime minister had driven away his natural allies: the Palestinian citizens of Israel. Peres had taken them for granted, Christians as well as Muslims. Over 30,000 voters put blank ballots into the urns. This was their way of showing disapproval for Peres and the massacre in Qana.[37]

UN Secretary-General Boutros Boutros-Ghali was a second loser. After he had refused to bend to the pressure from the US and Israel to stamp the van Kappen report as secret, the US was more intent than ever on getting rid of him. The superpower accomplished its aim, and when Robert Fisk saw the Secretary-General one day, he said, "You became the latest victim of the Qana massacre."[38]

"No. The American's hunt for me began last year," answered Boutros-Ghali.

He knew the American secretary of state, Madeleine Albright, had been working for over a year to prevent the renewal of his contract after the initial five-year term. One of the arguments was that Boutros-Ghali had not been willing to undertake reforms in the UN administration. At the same time, the Americans tried to make him the scapegoat for the US's unsuccessful policies in Iraq and Somalia.

Even though the American soldiers killed in Somalia were not under UN command, Albright's press spokesman, James Rubin, put the blame on Boutros-Ghali. Rubin was also the mouthpiece when the US tore into Boutros-Ghali for offering Prime Minister Yitzhak Rabin to send UN observers to Hebron. The offer came after Baruch Goldstein had killed the 29 Palestinians in the Ibrahimi mosque. After that massacre, the Palestinians wanted UN protection. Israel refused supported by the US.

In keeping with US wishes, Kofi Annan became the new UN Secretary-General. He had previously led the peacekeeping operations. Albright knew well that open support of the 59-year-old from Ghana would be "the kiss of death." For that reason, she ran her campaign in the shadows.

The Israelis liked Kofi Annan because he had helped to soften van Kappen's report on Qana, and had not pushed to start an investigation that could have exposed the Israeli side, before, during and after the bombardment of the UN camp.

In the fall of 1996, my period of leave from the *NRK* ended. What I had dug up created a certain amount of attention both in Norway and in Israel. I found some of my information in boxes in a previously unexamined Israeli archive. I found more in Norwegian archives. The material included a letter from Haakon Lie and other Norwegians who were helping Israel obtain heavy water in order to produce atomic weapons. In the book I also revealed that the first Secretary-General of the UN, the Norwegian Trygve Lie, had secretly helped the Zionists before the State of Israel came onto the map. Also exposed was Lie's military advisor, the Norwegian colonel Alfred Roscher Lund, as a secret agent of the Zionists at the UN, he had been recruited by Chaim Herzog, who later became president of Israel.

I also made television documentaries for the *NRK* on the book's stories, and later I began once more to make television reports of current events in the Middle East. In South Lebanon, I interviewed the political advisor in UNIFIL, Timur Göksel, who said the Israelis had strengthened their positions in the occupation zone. They had also changed tactics in order to oppose a steadily strengthening Hizbullah.

Fresh Israeli soldiers kept coming to Lebanon. One of them was an officer, Noam Nizmaho. He was not afraid of Hizbullah. To the contrary, Noam *wanted* to go to war against Hizbullah like the tough Israeli soldier he wanted to be. The 23-year-old Israeli lieutenant loved rock music and had Gabriel Garcia Márquez' novel *One Hundred Years of Solitude* among his belongings. He headed up a troop with orders to ambush the guerrillas before they could mount an attack. Noam thought he could manage to get himself some "ears"—the expression soldiers used when they had killed someone from the Lebanese resistance.[39]

It was raining when Noam and his men went into Lebanon one day in January 1997. It was cold as well. He felt like an officer he had seen in an American film about Vietnam. He was the hero in the film—trained to kill, not to take prisoners. Everything depended on crushing the "terrorists," the word used for Lebanese who fought to free their country. Noam's dream was to meet a "terrorist" and be the quickest on the draw. Then he could come home and say he had gotten himself an "ear."

With his night vision goggles ready, Noam lay in waiting for the guerrillas to sneak into the occupation zone. When one of the soldiers saw something suspicious move, he began to shoot. The others followed and started shooting wildly. After a few minutes, Noam gave the order to stop. It was apparently nothing. When dawn came, they left the area and drove back to their camp in Israel. Noam called his commander to report. The first question he got was, "Do you have any ears with you?" Crestfallen, had to answer no.

A few nights later, a group from Hizbullah snuck into the occupation zone and planted a bomb that exploded and injured three Israeli soldiers on patrol in the morning hours. The Israelis responded with artillery fire against Iqlim el-Toffah, the rugged Apple Region, where Hizbullah had forward bases. Some 60 shells landed in the area on January 8, 1997, but did little damage. Hizbullah continued its infiltrations, and on January 30, they succeeded once more. Three Israeli soldiers were killed.

Hizbullah guerrilla attacks on patrols and vehicles caused the Israelis to bring greater numbers of soldiers to and from bases in South Lebanon with American-built Sikorsky helicopters. The largest type, CH-53, had the official Israeli name Yasur, but were called "Mack Trucks" by the pilots. The CH-53 could carry 65 passengers, a mechanic and two pilots.

When two helicopters took off in bad weather from a base in Galilee on the night of February 4, they had on-board soldiers headed for bases in South Lebanon, including Beaufort. However, the soldiers never got there. The two helicopters collided as they circled near the base, waiting for the all-clear signal to fly into dangerous South Lebanon. It was rainy and foggy, and the pilots had poor visibility when the two made contact and fell to the ground near a *moshav* (a cooperative). Not one of the 73 on-board survived.

There was a period of national mourning in Israel. Prime Minister Benjamin Netanyahu said it was the worst accident that had ever "happened in Israel in peacetime." He added that it was out of the question to pull Israeli forces from Lebanon. Defense Minister Yitzhak Mordechai said the same thing.

One of my journalist friends in Beirut, Juan Carlos Gumucio, who was the correspondent for the Spanish newspaper *El Pais* went to see Hizbullah's military leader in South Lebanon, Sheikh Nabil Qaouk. The sheikh maintained the helicopter accident was nothing more than "God's curse on Israel."[40]

In the northern Israeli town of Rosh Pinah, Rachel Ben-Dor decided to do something more than mourn the loss of the soldiers. Rachel and three other mothers of soldiers, got together to form a group they called Four Mothers. Rachel told the others what they wanted to hear: "From the moment our children were born, we knew what would happen. War would come. People are killed. Something is rotten here. Something must change."[41]

Hundreds of others joined the four mothers. They made stickers with the words "Freedom from Lebanon—97," which were handed out all over the country. They arranged acts of protest near the border with Lebanon, and every time a soldier was killed, the women demonstrated outside the defense ministry in Tel Aviv.

A Jewish immigrant from the US, Linda Ben-Zvi, ran the Four Mother's campaign with the foreign media. She had participated in the American anti-Vietnam war demonstrations in the 1960s. Now she was able to say 20,000 Israelis had signed a petition demanding retreat from Lebanon. She also accused politicians and military planners of not changing their Lebanon policies because it would mean a loss of prestige. Linda's husband, Shmuel Ben-Zvi, who had earlier been an officer in the elite Sayeret Matkal, came to meet the Israeli defense minister. When Ben-Zvi mentioned Vietnam, Defense Minister Yitzhak Mordechai exploded. Like many other politicians, he had previously been a general. Both Mordechai and Ben-Zvi knew the Americans had lost over 50,000 soldiers in an unsuccessful war over some 20 years, in an effort to prevent the Communists from North Vietnam from taking over the whole country. To Ben-Zvi's thinking, it was obvious that Hizbullah would achieve the same thing in Lebanon.

After the meeting with the minister, Ben-Zvi repeated what he had said to him: "When you write your memoirs, you should not use the same excuse US Secretary of Defense Robert McNamara used."[42] Mordechai was offended by the comparison. "It hit a nerve," Ben-Zvi said. He admitted there was a difference between the American conduct of war in Vietnam and the Israelis' in Lebanon, but felt the war in Lebanon was also a guerrilla war that could not be won. "The topographic conditions favor the opposition," Ben-Zvi said, also pointing out that Hizbullah had the support of the local population and had open borders with Syria. He understood the government in Israel would not change its policies in Lebanon. It would be tantamount to admit that its politicians had made mistakes over many years, during which there were far too many unnecessary deaths. "They are prisoners of a concept, and it is difficult for them to change," thought Ben-Zvi.

CHAPTER EIGHTY FIVE

Humiliation

In Lebanon, Hizbullah's leaders realized if the war against the occupiers was to succeed, they had to win over public opinion in Israel. The propaganda war was at least as important as the war of weapons. Since 1985, Hizbullah had broadcast its radio messages with the help of old radio transmitters that were gifts from Iran. As of 1992, the party had its own TV station, *Al-Manar*. Now the time had come to use the Internet.

Young Shias who supported Hizbullah looked for training at the American University of Beirut (AUB). A 41-year-old professor, Børre Ludvigsen, invited in 1997 to the university to build up a new digital document center, was now on the faculty. Ludvigsen had grown up in Sidon, where his father was a Norwegian who had worked for the Trans-Arabian Pipeline Company, which transported oil from Saudi Arabia to Lebanon.

Before he was hired by the university, he had built an Internet server he called Al-Mashriq, where he placed a huge amount of material about Lebanon: thousands of texts, old manuscripts, photographs and sound recordings, including songs by Fairuz, who still brought tears to the eyes of the Lebanese whenever she sang. Ludvigsen also had contact with Lebanon's political parties. Everyone was favorable to the idea of placing information out onto the Internet, but the only one who was willing to contribute written material was Hizbullah. The party's media people had seen Ludvigsen's website and contacted him via email.[43]

Hizbullah's TV station invited Ludvigsen to a meeting to discuss the dissemination of information on the Internet. Before any meeting could be set up, people from Hizbullah arrived at his home, including several of the party's political leaders. They had brought with them photographs of the war in 1996, and asked if he could give a seminar for TV and radio journalists, and for those in charge of the movement's website. Ludvigsen agreed.

The seminar was to be held in Hizbullah's core area, in the southern part of Beirut. It was dark when Ludvigsen was picked up. When the chauffeur drove through the small backstreets, he said with a smile, "This will go fine, we don't kidnap people anymore." Ludvigsen was not afraid of Hizbullah; he was more afraid of Israeli bombers. But everything did go fine, and the professor conducted his seminar in a well-equipped locale for the many interested and bright Lebanese. He taught them about organizing, building and creating web servers, and how they should safeguard themselves against hackers.

When I later met *Al-Manar's* director, Abdallah Qassir, he briefed me on how Hizbullah media people had developed their strategy. On the TV side, some of the most important things were to film guerrilla attacks and send in the footage as quickly as possible. "Now and then we will wait for the Israelis' media version of the attacks, before we show they were not telling the truth."

Hizbullah's leaders had also begun a systematic effort to get the officers in the SLA militia to switch sides. They were tempted and threatened: if they were unwilling to become double agents or deserters, they risked being killed. Abu Arida, one of the SLA officers began to realize the Israelis' time in South Lebanon was nearing an end. He had personally been sentenced to death in absentia by a Lebanese court, and when Ahmed Hallaq was convicted and executed, Abu Arida decided to switch sides. After Hallaq's kidnapping, Shin Bet had begun to suspect that Abu Arida was not completely reliable. When the Israelis determined he was working for the enemy, following several months of investigation, they arrested him then sent him to an Israeli prison. Later Abu Arida's wife and children were deported from the home they had in Qleia, and dropped off without money or possessions at the crossing between the occupation zone and "free Lebanon," where they were.[44]

A few miles further south, Hizbullah guerrillas planted a roadside bomb on August 18, 1997, near the village of Kfar Houna. The bomb detonated at the same moment a military vehicle from the SLA was passing, but instead of killing the two in the vehicle, the fragments from the bomb killed two young sisters passing by. The teenagers were 14 and 16 years old, the daughters of an officer in the SLA who previously was on the same stretch of road.

In mourning and anger, the family demanded revenge. A few hours later, an artillery battery near Jezzine aimed at Sidon. Four 155 mm artillery shells landed in the center of the city. The shells were the anti-personnel type. Nine civilians were killed, among them three boys aged 6, 12 and 13. More than 30 others were injured.

Not many minutes passed before Hizbullah answered by firing Katyusha rockets toward the SLA base in Jezzine. The Lebanese government army received orders to fire at the militia; as the generals did not tolerate the SLA waging war on the civilian population in Sidon. Over 100 artillery shells landed in the occupation zone. The Lebanese army did not differentiate between civilians and military targets, either. Killing a 60-year-old man and injuring two women.

The Israelis got involved and fired from an artillery battery at the village of Kfar Melki. They hit houses, but no one was killed. The houses were unoccupied and partially ruined from an earlier bombardment. The firing had been a demonstration by the Israelis: they did not want any further escalation.

The IDF's spokesman, Oded Ben-Ami, tried to explain the attack against Sidon. Ben-Ami had previously been a TV reporter, and now a brigadier general. He said as follows: "It was not Israel which fired. I repeat: We did not fire on Sidon today. We coordinate with the SLA in the security zone, but Jezzine is outside this zone. General Lahd has his forces in the city. They are not our responsibility. They are outside our control."[45] Defense Minister Yitzhak Mordechai maintained as well that the SLA had attacked without Israel's knowledge or desire. "We will request General Lahd to stay within the understanding of 1996," the minister said.

The chief of the Northern Command, Major General Amiram Levine, insisted he was doing his best not to injure civilians. He threatened Hizbullah, "Do not make the mistake of firing at civilian targets in Israel in response." This did not help. "Antoine Lahd is a tool of Israel," answered Hizbullah's secretary-general, Sheikh Hassan Nasrallah. "For what Lahd does, Israel has total responsibility. We asked the enemy to read our message of this morning very carefully."[46]

The following morning, August 19, 63 Katyusha rockets landed in Israel. Many fell in the Mediterranean sea outside the city of Nahariya. Others exploded in an open area further north. Some fell in the densely populated areas along the border with Lebanon, and in the Israeli occupation zone.

Israeli fighter planes took to the air. First they bombed Hizbullah positions in the Bekaa Valley, then a civilian vehicle was fired upon south of Sidon, and thereafter the planes destroyed a power station 25 kilometers south of Beirut. A number of high-tension towers were also destroyed near Sidon. In addition, the Israelis bombed the Lebanese army's artillery installations that had fired at Jezzine.

Hizbullah did not yield. One bomb took the life of a man who dared to drive on the dangerous road south of Jezzine, and an SLA driver was killed by a roadside bomb near the village of Ain Ebl. Later, Hizbullah carried out a coordinated attack against militia positions in the occupation zone.

This continued for several days. Hizbullah attacked with machine guns and mortars. The Israelis used artillery. Nasrallah's message to Israel was crystal clear, and the Israeli papers quoted army officers who had been "impressed" by what they had seen in the course of one weekend. It was obvious Hizbullah had learned from the Israeli army's *modus operandi*. The guerrillas improved from operation to operation.[47]

The Israeli Northern Command thought Hizbullah had to be crushed on its home turf. Israeli soldiers in South Lebanon could not just sit and wait to be attacked. On August 28, an elite unit was ready to thrust into the Shia areas just north of the Israeli occupation zone. The target was Wadi Hujuar, a valley with heavy vegetation west of the village of Qantara in the Finnish UNIFIL battalion operating area.

The Israelis first encountered a guerrilla group from Amal. The fighting lasted for several hours. They were the superior force, and killed four militia soldiers without any difficulty—but then came reinforcements from Hizbullah. The Israelis were under such pressure that they had to withdraw to one side of Wadi Hujuar. Hizbullah's men were on the other side. In order to get to safety, the Israeli patrol asked for artillery support.

One battery fired 155 mm shells toward the Hizbullah forces, but instead of driving the guerrillas away, the explosions ignited a fire that moved in the direction of the Israeli soldiers along the valley's dense growth. In panic, the soldiers left their heaviest equipment and ammunition behind as they ran up the side of the valley to escape the flames. The ammunition left behind exploded and created a red fireball that rose several tens of meters into the air. Corporal Ronen Laloush ran as he held his hands in front of his face to protect it from the flames. His hands felt numb as he climbed up the hillside to escape. Not all the Israeli soldiers managed to get away. When the underbrush in the valley had burned itself out, the corporal realized that three of the soldiers under his command had become charred corpses.

Major General Amiram Levine regretted that "friendly fire" killed three of his soldiers. He of course understood that the accident would give political ammunition to the growing number of Israelis who demanded a withdrawal from Lebanon. When Defense Minister Mordechai heard the news during a ceremony at the Israeli Command and Staff College, he said, "We have a mission to defend those who are under our command; to my great sorrow we have not succeeded this year."[48] Both Israeli officers were doubtful that Israel should have forces in South Lebanon. Still, neither of them voiced their inner thoughts.

This was not the last of the bad news for the Israelis. Hizbullah had eventually built up an advanced intelligence apparatus in South Lebanon. The guerrilla's local commandant, Sheikh Nabil Qaouk, could say with satisfaction that he had penetrated the Israelis' secret services. Hizbullah had been able to receive information from the Israelis' unmanned drones that repeatedly flew over a specific area north of the occupation zone. The resistance movement's analysts believed the Israelis were mapping an infiltration route.[49]

Ghalib Farhat, a citrus farmer in Insariyeh, a small village on a headland overlooking the Mediterranean sea midway between Tyre and Sidon, had no idea what Hizbullah's intelligence apparatus knew, but every other day, at the end of August 1997, he heard the sounds of Israeli reconnaissance drones circling over his village. He could not see the small, pilotless planes over his citrus groves, but the farmer realized the Israelis were up to something in the area, even if his village was far from the front line.[50]

Adding to Ghalib Farhat's unease was the strange Hizbullah activities that had begun at the same time the drones appeared. Late each evening, a car drove past his house in the outskirts of Insariyeh with its headlights switched off. At the end of a narrow lane lined with pine trees, a handful of men would climb out of the car, and slip into the orange groves on either side of the dirt road. The farmer assumed they stayed there all night, but he did not see them at daybreak.

At around 10 p.m. on September 4, the men in the car entered the groves, as usual, while Farhat and his wife, Kholoud, watched television and their four children slept in the next room. Some hours later, 16 elite Israeli soldiers silently landed on the beach some two kilometer west of Insariyeh, near an abandoned house.

The Israeli marines, all dressed in matte-black clothing with soft rubber boots, were from the elite Sayeret Matkal unit 13, led by Lieutenant Colonel Yossi Kurakin. They crossed the main road and began the hard uphill slog east toward the north of Insariyeh, through banana plantations, olive and citrus groves.[51]

At the same time, a slender, hollow-cheeked 19-year-old fighter from the Amal movement was crouched among bushes just north of the village. Three of his comrades hid near him, all armed with Kalashnikov rifles and RPGs .

Insariyeh and the surrounding villages were traditional Amal strongholds, where Hizbullah had only a light presence, and now the Amal fighters were part of a backup unit deployed there to support an ambush squad from Hizbullah, hidden among the orange trees a few hundred meters to the north. The local Amal commanders some days earlier had been informed that resistance fighters from Hizbullah were on operational duty each night, but for security reasons were only told that if they should hear shooting and explosions, they would know what was happening. "Be careful that you don't shoot us in the confusion. Our men will be out there, too."[52] The Hizbullah fighters were split into three units—two with six combatants and one with eight. Their commander, who was from the village, was Abu Shamran.

The Israeli elite soldiers walked quietly through the dense undergrowth on the steep climb leading to the northern end of the village. As they reached the crest of the hill, they moved onto a dirt track between an orange grove and a line of scrawny pine trees.

Abu Shamran and his men from Hizbullah were hiding among the orange trees less than five meters away. They could hear the soldiers whispering to each other in Hebrew. When the naval commandos bunched up on reaching an iron gate beside the lane, Abu Shamran silently gave the order to explode a roadside bomb knocking the Israelis to the ground. Before they recovered from the shock of the blast, another bomb exploded in a large burst of orange flame. The Hizbullah guerrillas then opened fire with machine guns and RPGs. One bullet struck Lieutenant Colonel Yossi Kurakin in the head, killing him instantly. A third blast caused by a bullet detonating explosives carried by Sergeant Itmar Ilya, the unit's sapper. The blast tore the Israeli to bits, killing and wounding more members of the team. Eleven of the 16 commandos were now dead.

The surviving Israelis tried to withdraw while evacuating their dead and wounded, but Hizbullah guerrillas immediately attacked them. They returned the fire, and hand to hand fighting ensued. The Israelis asked for support while the fighting continued in the dark. One Israeli evacuation unit was flown in. A Cobra helicopter gunship unleashed TOW anti-tank missiles into the orange trees and blasted the area with 20 mm chain guns, creating a perimeter of fire to allow the rescue helicopters to land.

The Hizbullah fighters pulled out of the ambush site and slipped away, while the Amal fighters opened fire with their weapons, before pulling back themselves. Twenty minutes had passed since the first explosion.

Under cover of fire from the Cobras, two CH-53 rescue helicopters touched down in open fields, letting reinforcements disgorge about a hundred meter from the ambush site. The Israelis split into two groups and formed a defensive ring, while the medics began ferrying dead and wounded into the helicopters. While the Cobra combat helicopters peppered the ground with fire, the evacuation unit took off. After just a few minutes in the air, they discovered two bodies were missing. One of the choppers turned around and landed. The soldiers on-board jumped out to look for the missing soldiers, but despite scouring the darkness with their night vision goggles, they found no trace of them. They failed to realize at the time that one of the missing commandos was already on-board. The body parts of Sergeant Ilya were lying scattered over the battlefield, some even hanging from the trees.

Hizbullah's machine gun fire had stopped, but they pounded the Israeli rescuers with mortar, killing a doctor. The unit was ordered to leave the area, while nearby Lebanese army aircraft units blindly pumped rounds into the night sky and fired illumination shells to light up the ambush site. An Israeli F-16 jet fired a missile at one of the anti-aircraft positions, while Israeli missile boats fired a few rounds toward Insariyeh to silence the mortars.

When the news of the Israeli disaster reached the government, urgent contacts were made to the Americans to pass a warning: Israel would respond with massive force if Hizbullah prevented the rescue mission from proceeding. Hizbullah pulled back, and the Lebanese army began moving into the area. Shortly before dawn, more than four hours after the first explosion, the last rescue helicopter lifted off and headed towards Israel. Back on the battlefield, mingled with the smell of burning wood was the stench of fresh blood. Pieces of human flesh were scattered among the debris—a jawbone with a set of teeth, white blobs of brain matter, an elbow and two fingers joined at the knuckle.[53]

The elite forces were once again been humiliated by the Lebanese militias and 12 elite troops were dead. For the Israelis, it was the worst single-day casualty toll in South Lebanon since 1985.[54]

In October 1997, an Israeli commission of inquiry concluded that the naval commandos had fallen by chance into the Hizbullah ambush. The investigation claimed there had been no breach of intelligence that could have forewarned the guerrillas. Over the next 18 months two more army inquiries were held, as well as a separate investigation by the Knesset. All produced inconclusive results. No one in Israel could dream of Hizbullah's ability to intercept video-transmissions from Israeli drones and watch them in Beirut.

Minister of Infrastructure Ariel Sharon had come to think of South Lebanon as a burden for Israel. The general and former minister of defense had not been present when the government approved the Insariyeh, but he had previously opposed Defense Minister Mordechai's plans to increase commando operations against Hizbullah. Sharon thought it would be better to pull the army out of South Lebanon and employ deterrent methods against both the guerrillas and the civilian population. The Sayeret Matkal fiasco had created a fight within Benjamin Netanyahu's government that yielded serious consequences.

CHAPTER EIGHTY SIX
Internal Strife in Israel

On July 9, 1997, Amnesty International published its report, "Israel's Forgotten Hostages. The Lebanese prisoners in Israel and in the Khiam Prison." The report stated that around 130 Lebanese were in Khiam without trial or justice. In addition, at least 21 Lebanese were sitting in Israeli jails after they had completed their sentences, or without even a trial. Amnesty concluded that the prisoners were hostages, and that they should be either put on trial or released.

After the Israeli mass media released parts of the report, an Israeli soldier contacted the newspaper *Haaretz* and turned over pictures from inside Khiam with the note, "a picture is worth a thousand words."[55] One picture showed men who were standing with their faces to a brick wall, black hoods pulled over their heads; they were being interrogated. In the right corner of the picture was a cell of three square meters, where several prisoners could be pressed in. The Israeli soldier said he had often escorted officers from Shin Bet and Mossad to and from Khiam. Another Israeli soldier had previously contacted an Israeli weekly publication and said the intelligence agents' Lebanese chauffeurs were given the opportunity to torture prisoners as an outlet for their anger and frustration.[56]

These reports did not lead to any change in Israeli policies. The authorities stuck by their old refrain: they had nothing to do with Khiam. The Israeli mass media did not follow up either. They had enough to cover Hizbullah's fight against Israeli soldiers in South Lebanon.

In September 1997, two months after the release of the Amnesty report, orders were given that the International Red Cross Committee would no longer be given access to prisoners in Khiam. Officially, it was SLA General Lahd behind the order, and the Israelis could not interfere. The Jewish state was not officially an occupying power in South Lebanon, but was only assisting the SLA in its work to control the "security zone."[57]

In Lebanon, the IDF continued its operations, independent of the debate in Israel. One week after the failed Israeli action in Insariyeh on September 5, 1997, Brigadier General Moshe Tamir received the green light to begin a major operation code-named "Wild View."

The objective was to reverse opinions following the operation that had cost so many Israeli lives. One group from the elite unit, Egoz, was to carry out the operation on the heights south of the Shia village of Sujud, between the Litani and Zahrani Rivers. The goal was to find guerrilla soldiers and kill them.

For two days, three teams of Israelis searched for Hizbullah guerrillas in an area just north of the occupation zone, without running into any. Then on the third day, September 13, just before the unit was set to return to its base in Rihan, one of the teams discovered three armed men. The Israelis did not immediately open fire, but sent a dog out to follow their trail. When the dog began to howl, the soldiers went forward and shot into the bush-covered area. Later they found ammunition in the bush, but no one injured or dead.

The other Israeli team found no guerrillas, but the third team noticed men in uniform fleeing. Some were apparently injured. The Israelis saw the men seeking shelter behind some boulders, and an exchange of fire ensued. The Israelis were fired on from a higher elevation nearby. It was clear they had also split into several teams.

One of the three Israeli teams got into position and covered the other two, which advanced toward the Hizbullah "cover" unit. The Hizbullah team above was between the three Israeli teams; besides, there was also one more guerrilla team in the area. The Israelis feared they might shoot their own soldiers and asked for outside support.

The leader of the Israeli Special Forces unit, Brigadier General Moshe Tamir, was in radio contact with the teams from the northern Israel operations center. He ordered helicopter support, but when the helicopters approached, they came under fire from the Lebanese army, which also had a post in the area. The Israelis then sent attack helicopters against two armored vehicles that the government army had parked at its post. Six Lebanese soldiers were killed, along with a woman who warned the soldiers about the approaching helicopters.

It began to get dark. The Israeli commando soldiers were ordered to withdraw. During their retreat, they discovered the bodies of two uniformed guerrillas. This was reported by radio to General Tamir, who told them to bring the bodies with them. The general thought Hizbullah's guerrilla group was so large it had to be led by a high-ranking officer.[58] Many in Israel raised their eyebrows over this decision—Hizbullah might attack. But Tamir remained resolved; the bodies could be used in exchange for the dead Israeli who was missing after the Insariyeh misery.

All the discussions came by radio, and there were many who were listening to what was being said. The chief of the Northern Command, Major General Amiram Levine, left the final decision as usual to the chief of the unit. Tamir thought of his own grandfather, who had been killed in 1948, but had never been found. He remembered how much his grandmother had grieved over not being able to bury her husband's remains, and did not want the family of the Israeli soldier lost in Insariyeh to suffer like that. Tamir got his way, and after the bodies of the two Hizbullah soldiers were brought to Israel, it was quickly discovered that one was the 18-year-old Hadi Nasrallah, the son of Hizbullah's secretary-general. Israeli radio did not wait long to broadcast the news.

In Beirut, Sheikh Nasrallah announced there was no question of negotiating with the Israelis to get his dead son back. The sheikh offered no compromise in his rhetoric and said, "Hadi chose this way himself. I thank God for having chosen a martyr from my family."[59]

Nothing would get Hizbullah to give up its fight against Israel's occupation. And on October 8, before dawn broke, one of the guerrilla elite units snuck up to an Israeli position just 150 meters from the border. The guerrillas silently killed two Israeli soldiers and disappeared before they were discovered.

The Hizbullah action became a vitamin injection for the Lebanese. In order to join other than just Shias to the fight against Israel, the party created special groups open to anyone, regardless of religion. If someone was killed in the fight, Hizbullah made certain his immediate family received free housing, free medical treatment, free education for the young and a monthly pension of $350 dollars. These were the same grievance benefits that were provided to the families of the regular Islamic resistance movement.[60]

In the Israeli officer corps, many quietly began to talk about the usefulness of being permanently stationed in Lebanon. The resistance movement was becoming more dangerous. Hizbullah's intelligence capability was so good, the guerrillas knew when the chief of the Northern Command or another high-ranking officer came to inspect the force in South Lebanon, at which point they would open fire with mortars. The head of the army's liaison section in Lebanon, Brigdier General Eli Amitai, had been wounded in such a mortar attack. Later he was wounded again by a roadside bomb.[61]

Chief of the General Staff Amnon Lipkin-Shahak was forced to admit it was difficult to get good intelligence about Hizbullah's activities and plans in Lebanon. The sly old Uri Lubrani, who was the architect of Israel's policies in the country, tried to dampen the pessimists: "There are ups and downs in Lebanon all the time. This is a battle which will be won on points, not on a knockout. We will not give up."[62]

Labor Party politician Ephraim Sneh, who in his time had been chief of the Northern Command, believed "the main objective of our presence in the zone has been achieved. It is now calm in Northern Israel. With a retreat it will not be so. Hizbullah has openly declared the party will help to liberate Palestine."[63]

In order to sweep away the comparison between Lebanon and Vietnam, Sneh said, "The Vietcong did not want to liberate America. The Vietcong did not engrave the Washington Monument into their symbol, as Hizbullah does with Jerusalem." Sneh knew Hizbullah often used pictures of the Dome of the Rock Mosque in Jerusalem on its placards.

The debate about withdrawal crossed political lines. Some on the left defended continuing occupation, while many on the right thought withdrawal would be best. Opinion polls in the fall of 1997 showed that 60 percent of Israelis were against withdrawal from South Lebanon. They remained rather passive, while the 40 percent who wanted the soldiers home were activists.

When Likud held its party conference on November 9, 1997, a group of 20 women gathered outside the entrance to Jerusalem's International Conference Center to protest. The women shouted, "We are not political. This is not directed at Bibi." The demonstrators used the prime minister's nickname. The police did not want to listen to their arguments, and the women were driven back to a parking area. The protesters erected banners. One read, "Every victim has a name," and featured the names of soldiers who had been killed in Lebanon.

Most of the delegates to the party conference were hostile toward the activists. "You want the Shias on the border. You want the army on its knees. You are showing the enemy we are cowards," the demonstrators heard one of them say.

"Go to Hell!" another shouted.

"Go home and let us have our conference in peace!" came from a third.

"It is okay that you go home in the evening, but what about our soldiers?" asked one of the women in the crowd.

The organization Four Mothers gained increasing support from the grassroots. Labor Party's Yossi Beilin, who had formed the Movement for Peaceful Retreat from Lebanon, also noticed increased support. Beilin was no stranger to the idea Hizbullah could attack Israel, but he thought it was easier to fight on one's own soil than in Lebanon. Actually, he had little belief Hizbullah would come into Israel. He pointed to the operation in October when the guerrillas were only a few meters from the border and they killed Israeli soldiers, but made no attempt to move into Israel. According to Beilin, this showed that the violence was directed at Israel in Lebanon, not against the state in and of itself.[64]

On November 5, 1997, *Haaretz* revealed that a high-ranking but unnamed Israeli officer had proposed Israeli withdrawal from Lebanon. The officer had told his colleagues in a speech that his view was shared by others who were fighting in South Lebanon. The increasing losses of their own soldiers could no longer be justified.[65]

Two days later, an Israeli TV reporter revealed that the high-ranking officer was no other than the chief of the Northern Command, Major General Amiram Levine. The general had been expected to become the next chief of Mossad. The present chief, Danny Yatom, was on his way out. He had been responsible for the fiasco in Amman, Jordan, two months earlier, when agents had made a failed attempt to kill the political leader of Hamas, Khaled Mashal, who was living in exile. Not only had Mossad failed in the assassination attempt, but the agents had been arrested by the Jordanian police. To get them released, the Israelis had to agree to release the founder of Hamas, Sheikh Ahmed Yassin, who was imprisoned in Israel. Not since the fiasco in Lillehammer, Norway, in 1973, when Mossad agents mistakenly took the life of an innocent Moroccan, Ahmed Bouchikhi, had the intelligence agency made such a big blunder.

Although it was unusual for an Israeli general in active service to go against the government's official policy, Levine allowed himself to be interviewed by Israel's largest newspaper. "The present situation where Hizbullah gets us to bleed, cannot continue," he said. "If you give me the means and freedom to take the initiative, and put in motion a long series of offensive actions, I would be in a position to put Amal and Hizbullah on the defensive."[66] The general went on to say, "If we decided to pull ourselves back, I would suggest it be done in stages so that it would not seem to be a retreat. But before we begin a withdrawal process, we must give them a shock they won't soon forget. We should do as we did during Operation Grapes of Wrath, but we should make it even more painful for them. If not, Amal, Hizbullah and the Palestinians will drive us back to the border fence."

The criticism caused Levine to be called a charlatan, but it did not stop other critics of Israel's occupation policies in Lebanon.[67] At the end of November 1997, the foreign ministry yielded to the demands of the critics to analyze the situation anew. The conclusion was unambiguous: the army would have to remain in Lebanon.

The architects behind the concept of the "security zone" were unmovable. They thought the war in Lebanon was directed against the most anti-Semitic ideology the world had known since the Second World War. This was a war against Khomeinism, against Tehran, not against Nabatiyeh. A nation that cannot stand sacrifices cannot exist in the Middle East.

The leader of Four Mothers could not hide her disappointment when she commented, "We send our children to Lebanon so they can commit suicide. This is madness. They have no chance."[68]

One of the many Israelis who also did not buy the arguments from the IDF leadership, was Arik Ben-Zvi. A few years earlier, he had been what one might call "gung ho"—enthusiastic, unafraid and unstoppable, an Israeli elite soldier who had enlisted willingly for a reconnaissance unit in South Lebanon. The goal then had been to hunt and kill Hizbullah guerrillas. Three of Arik's soldier-colleagues did not survive the mission. He left the service himself, after eight months, and told everyone he met that morale among the soldiers was at "the bottom of the barrel." He quickly discovered that public opinion in Israel was changing. "Israel is running a stupid and not well thought-through policy in Lebanon," said the 22-year-old veteran.[69]

Most people had previously tolerated that Israel lost a few dozen soldiers in South Lebanon each year. This was a cheap price to pay for peace in Galilee, one thought. But the losses were increasing. Arik felt the same frustration that he thought many American soldiers in Vietnam must have felt. In the course of a few months he had become a student activist who argued in favor of Israeli withdrawal from South Lebanon, the Golan Heights, West Bank and the Gaza Strip. "The Israelis are bottled up with the belief the army can solve everything, but we must look reality in the eyes: the war is lost!"

CHAPTER EIGHTY SEVEN
Trial Balloon

The first month of 1998 was just a few days old when Israel's Defense Minister Yitzhak Mordechai released a trial balloon. In an interview with a Lebanese weekly magazine published in Paris, he indicated Israel was willing to withdraw completely out of South Lebanon. The Israeli general-turned-politician wanted a new interpretation of the UN Security Council's resolution 425. Mordechai wanted to put less emphasis on the demand for full Israeli withdrawal without conditions, and more on Israel's demand for international support in terms of maintaining peace and security. This meant Hizbullah had to be disarmed.

Mordechai had Ariel Sharon behind him. The architect of the invasion of 1982 thought Israel should combine withdrawal with a clear warning to Syria: Damascus had to guarantee calm along Israel's northern border. If not, there were would be consequences for Syria.[70]

The Israeli leaders were not speaking from a position of power and strength. In 1997, Israel's losses in South Lebanon had been higher than any year since 1985. Over 100 soldiers had been killed in just the past 12 months. Comparing the death tolls of guerrilla soldiers and Israeli soldiers went in Israel's disfavor. Previously, the Israelis had taken the lives of three guerrillas for every soldier they lost. Now the ratio was two to one. At the end of 1997, it was approaching one to one.[71]

After the Israelis had discovered that their British Centurion tanks were vulnerable to Hizbullah's Sagger rockets, they replaced them with the Israelis' own Merkava. However, Hizbullah received updated Sagger rockets, and the guerrillas' experts eventually discovered a weak spot in the Merkava armor. This meant Hizbullah fighters were able to take Israel's most modern tank out of the game.

For correspondents in Lebanon, it became clear that Hizbullah's security service was becoming more effective. Over a one-year period, more than 100 Lebanese had been arrested, among them several women, who were suspected of working for the Israelis. Hizbullah's spy hunters had also exposed the deputy leader of Amal's security service in the village of Ain Baal as an Israeli agent. He had hidden a two-way radio and a paint box with maps behind the television set in his living room. The maps showed Hizbullah's infiltration routes into the occupation zone.[72]

When another three Israeli soldiers were killed by a mortar shell not far from an outpost near Blat on February 26, 1998, the debate about an Israeli withdrawal from Lebanon reached the surface again. Just one week later, I travelled to South Lebanon to report from the occupation zone, where about 100,000 Lebanese were now living. About 60 percent of the population in the area was Shia, about 30 percent were Christians. The third largest group was the Druze. In addition there were Sunnis and a few Alawites.

I learned that the Lebanese generally thought the Israelis' days in Lebanon were numbered. SLA's fear that Hizbullah would infiltrate the zone caused the security service, which numbered some 400 men, to use a lot of its time interrogating people. After rough interrogations, those still suspected of being Hizbullah agents were turned over to the Israelis.

I went to the village of Hasbaya, where Shin Bet had an office. There I met Nidal Jamal, a feared Druze who worked for the secret service. The rather slope-shouldered, short and slightly built Lebanese had at times created problems for the Norwegian UNIFIL soldiers. Some of these confrontations featured threats and even live fire.

I got into a conversation with Nidal, who was dressed in a short-sleeved Lacoste shirt and matching Levis, and, in good English, he told me that the Israelis paid monthly salaries of up to $600 for higher-ranked officers in Shin Bet. The militia soldiers received up to $480 per month at the most remote outposts, and soldiers only got to about $300. Nidal said the Israelis had previously given a bonus of $250 for each enemy killed, but that had ended now. The SLA was no longer going on the offensive. The most important thing now was to defend oneself and survive.

Through Nidal, I tried to get into the prison at Khiam. But, no. And it had been the Israelis who decided, even though I knew from before that they deferred to the SLA.

In Israel, I learned that Lea Tsemel, the lawyer, was continuing her work with the most famous inmate in Khiam, Soha Bechara. An international campaign had been started for her release, led by a group of French lawyers, but they got nowhere.[73]

Another lawyer, Zvi Rish, continued his work on behalf of Lebanese clients in Israeli prisons. Rish had gone to the Supreme Court with his case, but it took a lot of time to get the ruling made public. Only on March 5, 1998, did the Supreme Court make their old ruling public, after a three month delay. The ruling was written by Supreme Court Justice Aharon Barak, who admitted Israel had held a number of Lebanese men as hostage for up to 10 years. The ruling also determined the hostages presented no threat to Israel. Through the years I had reported that Israel was taking hostages just like Hizbullah, but this was the first time the Jewish state admitted that Lebanese had been kidnapped in order to use them as "bargaining chips."

The Israeli kidnapping of Lebanese had been intensified following the capture of the air navigator Ron Arad in South Lebanon in October 1986. At first, they had taken some dozen hostages in an attempt to use them for trade. Several of these were sentenced for belonging to an enemy organization, but were not released even after their sentences had been served.

CHAPTER EIGHTY EIGHT

Last Night with the Gang

In Norway, the military supreme command had for years been trying to end Norway's participation in UNIFIL, but the Foreign Office fought against this, and had won every battle. In the summer of 1998, the Foreign Office made an about face, since it was now under the leadership of Knut Vollebæk of the Christian People's Party. Both Prime Minister Kjell Magne Bondevik and the foreign minister at first were skeptical of the proposal to pull Norway out of South Lebanon. Both were positively inclined to a Norwegian UNIFIL engagement, but because it was difficult to get volunteers for service, and because Norway had been in Lebanon for 20 years, the matter came up for re-evaluation in December 1997.

At a government conference, Development Minister Hilde Frafjord Johnson, also from the Christian People's Party, was the only one to point out the government could be suspected of giving in to Israel. It had been no secret that the Israelis were dissatisfied with the Norwegians who refused to yield to pressure from the Israeli occupation forces and the militia of the South Lebanon Army.[74]

When it was clear Norway was serious about its plans to pull out of UNIFIL, a number of negative foreign policy reactions developed. UN Secretary-General Kofi Annan asked Norway in a letter to continue its mission. Washington reacted negatively, as well. A Norwegian withdrawal would, according to the Americans, harm the peace process between the Israelis and the Palestinians.

Norway had other priorities. Foreign Minister Knut Vollebæk was being considered for the presidency of the Organization for Security and Cooperation in Europe—starting January 1, 1999. For Vollebæk, it was more important for Norway to show its muscle by sending significant forces to the Balkans than to remain in South Lebanon. The Foreign Office then gave up its multi-year fight against the defense department for the mission. Vollebæk had also gotten Prime Minister Bondevik on his side.[75]

The government informed the UN Security Council, and India agreed to takeover the Norwegian area. The Israelis were happy: the Indians were easier to deal with than the Norwegians.

In Khiam, no one cared whether there were Norwegians or Indians patrolling the area further to the north. A few prisoners were set free, but others took their places.

On the morning of September 3, 1998, at 7:50, a female guard came to Soha Bechara's cell and said, "You can gather your things together! What have you done to make Abu Nabil punish you and put you in cell number one?"[76]

"Nothing," answered Soha.

She pulled her few things together, showered, brushed her hair and waited. Soha had the feeling the time had come for her to be set free. She had a visit from her mother one month before, and learned that the campaign for her freedom now had taken off. French public opinion once more had played an important role with General Lahd, and in Israel, Lea Tsemel had worked tirelessly on Soha's case before the Supreme Court.

One of the doctors from Marjayoun whom the SLA used asked Soha a number of general questions, then wrote a report as she watched. He turned to her and said, "Congratulations!" He gave her a couple of pills with the words, "Take these before you leave. You have not been in a car for a long time."

At 8:30, the guards brought Soha to Abu Nabil's office. The man with the wolf's gaze, her greatest enemy in Khiam, was sitting behind his desk.

"You are going to be released," Abu Nabil said. "This is your bag which you came with." He pointed, and Soha looked behind the desk. She got her bag, put her one hand into it and found a tube of cream and some perfume bottles.

"Nothing missing?" Abu Nabil asked as he looked at her.

Soha searched around in the bag, but did not find the watch or cassette with pop-music from 1988. She avoided saying anything. When she was driven through the gate a few minutes later, it was only the third time in 10 years that she had been outside the walls. The two other times she was driven to the hospital in Marjayoun. Then she had worn handcuffs and a black hood over her head. Now she could see and move freely.

The news of her release came as a surprise to most Lebanese. The *Voice of the South*, the SLA radio station, first reported the news she was out of Khiam and was on her way to Beirut. In Lebanon, all radio and TV stations interrupted their programming and said the very symbol of Lebanese resistance was now a free woman. Three hours later, a pale and tired woman got out of a car marked IRCR—The International Red Cross Committee. The car stopped outside the prime minister's office, where Rafic Hariri waited together with a large group of the media.

In Tel Aviv, General Lahd told me he had personally decided to free Soha. In Jerusalem, Lea Tsemel scoffed at the claim. "It was international pressure which led him. This is proof that Israel can be pressured," she said.[77]

Three months later, around midnight on November 29, 1998, the Lebanese in the village of Ebl el-Saqi bade their final farewell to the Norwegian UN soldiers. After 20 years in South Lebanon, it was over. When the soldiers left the village, it was like a funeral and a wedding at the same time. There was dancing, singing and sorrow.

"For us it was also sad to say farewell," said the battalion chief, Roy C. Grøttheim, who did not hide his surprise at the order for withdrawal. The battalion leadership had the impression up to the last moment that Norway would continue to be represented in UNIFIL, even if it was with a smaller force.[78]

Defense Minister Dag Jostein Fjærvoll, the figurehead during the retreat, had tears in his eyes. During the press conference in NORBATT's headquarters, the emotional minister said this had weighed heavily on him. He understood the local population was also sad the Norwegians were disappearing after 20 years. But Fjærvoll did not regret the government's decision that it was now time for Norway to end its stay in South Lebanon.[79]

The handover ceremony took place at the parade grounds at Falcon Heights, with its majestic view of Mount Hermon. With bagpipes and drill demonstrations, the Indians took over command from the Norwegians.

In his speech during the ceremony, UNIFIL's Force Commander, Major General Jioji Konousi Konrote, had difficulty pronouncing Defense Minister Fjærvoll's name. But he got the Norwegians present to smile when he thanked "Mr. Farewell" and Norway for its efforts.

When the Norwegians left Lebanon, I was in Jerusalem writing my new book, *Annas Hus*, or *Anna's House*, about the conflict between the Zionists and the Palestinians from the 1880s up to 1948. I lived near the office of Lea Tsemel, and knew she was working to get additional prisoners released from Khiam. The release of Kifah Afifi and Soha Bechara was encouraging. Together with other lawyers, she filed an appeal with the Supreme Court arguing against the IDF claim that Israel had no control over the infamous prison at Khiam.

The lawyers concentrated on getting two minors released, along with Suleiman Ramadan, who had been in Khiam for 13 years—longer than anyone else. In an effort to show that the SLA was taking good care of the inmates, even Prime Minister Netanyahu's office wrote a letter to the lawyers in December 1998, saying that Suleiman Ramadan had received a prosthesis to replace his amputated right leg. He was under constant observation by doctors tied to the SLA, it was said.

A doctor from the Red Cross had also examined the prisoner and determined he had no health problems. When an Israeli human rights organization member investigated the matter more closely, another picture emerged. One of the released prisoners had said Ramadan's cell was so crowded he could not make use of his prosthetic leg. And the leg itself had still not healed.

The appeal by the lawyers contained facts which the Israelis did not want to admit publicly. First, Israel had military bases near three villages in South Lebanon. Second, the Israelis sent prisoners to Khiam. Additionally, prisoners were brought to Israel to be tested with lie detectors. The Israeli human rights lawyers believed these facts showed Israel had full control over South Lebanon. The prison in Khiam, for example, was supplied with food and equipment from Israel. In addition, a point was made of the fact the Red Cross was denied access to the prison until Hizbullah returned the corpse of the dead Israeli sergeant Itamar Ilya. This could be taken as proof that Israel was behind the decision.

No, answered the Israeli authorities: "As a part of the cooperation between Israel and the SLA, the SLA stopped the visits of the Red Cross and the prisoners' families until Hizbullah delivered the remains of Ilya. This did not show the IDF had control, but that there was cooperation between the SLA and the IDF."

When the Israeli Supreme Court accepted the appeal, the judges discussed who had responsibility for what happened in Khiam. The human rights lawyers maintained Israel had the responsibility. The Israeli military authorities maintained it was the SLA. Previously, this had been upheld without discussion. This time three of the judges wanted more information. They gave the IDF two months more to present their case anew.

Suleiman Ramadan remained incarcerated in Khiam with half a throbbing leg.

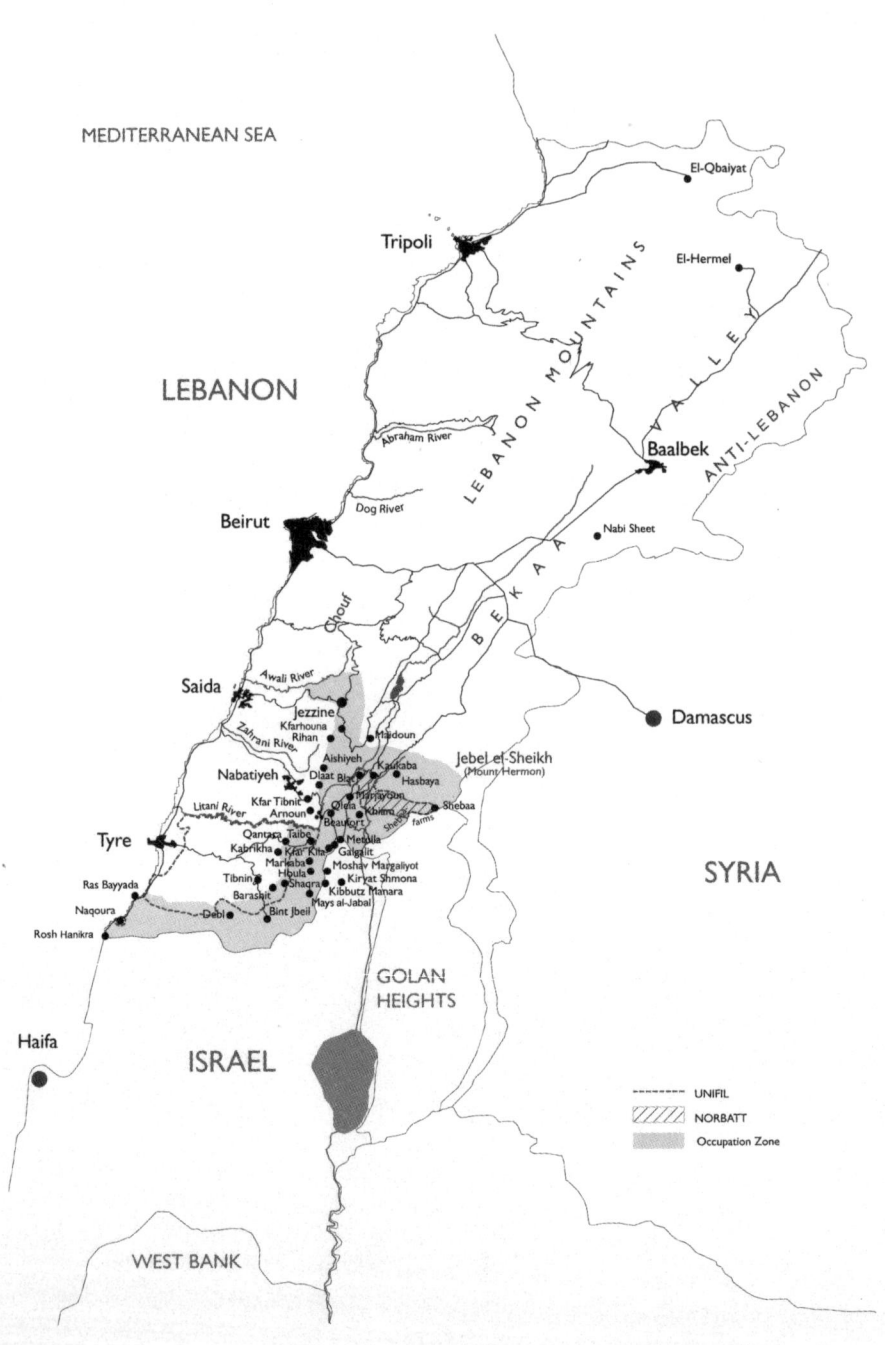

PART EIGHT

Israel's Defeat 1999-2000

After a new election in Israel, Benjamin Netanyahu was voted out as prime minister. The country's new prime minister, Ehud Barak, promised a complete military retreat from Lebanon within a year. The promises resulted partly from Hizbullah's increased fight prowess and partly from domestic opposition, which continued to grow.

Even if Israel's plan for retreat seemed solid on paper, it did not proceed as expected. Neither Hizbullah nor Israel stopped fighting as discussions about the procedures for retreat went on.

The Israelis were forced to advance their withdrawal, and in May 2000, Israel's longest war was over, and the country's first military defeat was a fact.

Main Characters

Kofi Annan, UN Secretary-General
Ehud Barak, Israel's Prime Minister and Defense Minister
Antoine Lahd, General, Chief of the South Lebanese Army (SLA)
Benjamin Netanyahu, Israel's Prime Minister
Terje Rød-Larsen, UN Special Coordinator for the Peace Process in the Middle East
Danny Yatom, Prime Minister's Military Secretary

CHAPTER EIGHTY NINE

Fired on the Air

On October 15, 1998, Lebanon's National Assembly elected the country's Chief of the General Staff, Lieutenant General Emile Lahoud, as the new president. The election was finished in 20 minutes. For the first time since 1949, one candidate got all the votes. President Lahoud had the support of the US, but it was no secret he was Syria's man. It had been leadership in Damascus who made certain Lahoud became president, even though he was not a politician with a natural base among the population.

In Lebanon, the new president was regarded as a strong man. Many thought Lahoud could provide balance between the Sunnis' Rafic Hariri, Walid Jumblatt of the Druze, Nabih Berri from the Shias and Hizbullah's Hassan Nasrallah. But it did not take long for him to demonstrate that there was one man above him in Lebanon, namely, the Syrian intelligence chief. General Ghazi Kanaan had now been President Assad's extended arm in Lebanon for 16 years. He decided to put the newcomer in his place.

Just before Lahoud's predecessor, Elias Hraoui, left the Presidential Palace, he had asked President Assad for three favors, among them that Hraoui's friend would become Lebanon's ambassador to Tunisia . The Syrian president left the matter to Major General Kanaan, who turned down two of the favors, but agreed to the third: Hraoui's friend would become ambassador. But when he went to visit Lahoud, the new president refused to appoint him. Hraoui complained to Kanaan, who said, "Did Lahoud say that? This is one size too big for him! Tomorrow your man will go to bed as ambassador."[1] And so he did. Lahoud gave in the next day.

The man who had organized the new president's long election campaign was also one of Syria's men. Colonel Jamil Sayyed, a Sunni from the Bekaa Valley who, since 1990, had worked in the headquarters of the intelligence service in Beirut. When Lahoud became president, the colonel became chief of the service with the Syrians' blessing—in practice, he was Syrian intelligence's eyes and ears in Lebanon.[2]

President Hafez al-Assad had initially wanted Rafic Hariri to continue as prime minister. But Assad recognized the animosity between Hariri and Lahoud could complicate Syrian control over Lebanon. The election therefore was won by an economist, Selim el-Hoss, who had been prime minister three years earlier.

Hoss was a complete opposite of Hariri. He was reserved where Hariri was outgoing, careful where Hariri was daring, closed where Hariri was open, incorruptible where Hariri was known to let himself be bribed. But most importantly, Hoss would not make problems for Lahoud.

Outwardly, Syria's choice of Lahoud as president was popular. He seemed different from other politicians. People said he even drove his own car. Sharp analysts believed the new president would be able to clean up the corruption in Lebanon and show that the state was boss. These hopes proved illusory, but Lahoud was still very different from his predecessors. The newspaper editors, for example, discovered this when they received orders not to print caricatures of the president.[3]

For Hizbullah's resistance fight in South Lebanon, a change of presidents and a new government did not mean much. Hizbullah was ascendant. Guerrilla attacks became more and more daring, and live pictures of the attacks found their way to the media by way of Hizbullah's own TV station.

On November 16, 1998, seven Israeli soldiers from the Golani Brigade left their fortified compound on Sheikh Abbad Hill, east of Houla village, close to the Israeli border. The outpost on the hill was established in 1978, when Israel occupied the southernmost part of Lebanon.

The seven soldiers walked casually down the road toward a firings range to test their weapons. The area was deemed relatively safe, and the soldiers were not expecting an attack, as they walked in a bunch down the road. Less than 40 meters from the gate, they were hit by a large roadside bomb. Three were killed instantly, and the other four were wounded. For the IDF, this was the highest casualty toll in a single incident since the Insariyeh disaster more than a year before.

The attack was videotaped by a Hizbullah cameraman. The tape was whisked out of the occupation zone and aired on *Al-Manar's* TV station a few hours later, even before the Israelis had been able to notify the families of the dead soldiers.

Eight days later, UN observers along the border with Israel witnessed another attack. One of the observers, Canadian Captain Philip Balden, was on duty at the UNTSO's observation post near the village of Markaba, southwest of Metulla, on November 22. An Israeli military outpost had been erected close to the white UN building. The two posts were so close to each other that two yellow cats meandered back and forth between them to get fed at both places.

When the bomb went off at 11:37 pm near the Israeli post, the explosion blew in the door of the UN post. The observers were not injured and stayed calm as Israeli forces came running. They could see that Israeli soldiers at the post had been killed. Captain Balden was able to watch the Hizbullah broadcast during the news at 1 AM.[4]

The Canadian captain was impressed by Hizbullah's attack. The guerrillas had to have crossed several kilometers of enemy territory, placed the bomb, filmed the explosion and then delivered the video to the TV station in a very short time. The next morning, Hizbullah's guerrillas followed up by attacking five posts of the SLA using mortars. The Israelis responded with aerial bombardment of areas where Hizbullah had strong support.

In a briefing before the Knesset's foreign and defense committee, one of Israel's senior intelligence officers said that Syria had given Hizbullah the orders for the offensive. This was not true. Hizbullah was in charge of the guerrilla offensive, and on November 25, another large hidden bomb was detonated on the road outside Sheikh Abbad Hill, in almost exactly the same location as the ambush nine days earlier. This time two Israeli soldiers were killed. More soldiers died the very next day from a double roadside bomb just 400 meters from the border fence. The attack was a Hizbullah classic. The first bomb disabled two armed personnel carriers without killing the soldiers inside. But the second bomb targeted the rescue force, killing two soldiers. Nothing could stop the Lebanese resistance any longer.

The Israeli officer who briefed the Knesset members in November 1998, said that Hizbullah's first priority was now to take Israeli soldiers captive: "This is a strategic decision they took in order to get Lebanese freed from Israeli captivity."[5] The briefing also revealed the Israeli Military intelligence did not agree with Defense Minister Mordechai's view that it was now about time to pull the army out of South Lebanon.

The many Israeli losses in one month caused Prime Minister Benjamin Netanyahu to look for a scapegoat. A tough election campaign lay ahead, and disagreement between the defense minister and the defense leadership made it easy to let the ax fall on Yitzhak Mordechai. Fully in the open, he was given the boot on January 24, 1999. The prime minister read the dismissal letter live during the evening TV news on the Israeli state channel. According to the prime minister, Mordechai had acted fraudulently because he had sought a promise from Netanyahu to become the defense minister in a new government if Likud won the election, while at the same time working behind the scenes to form a new political party. The prime minister gave the defense minister 48 hours to clean out his office.

Earlier that Sunday, Mordechai had shown up at the weekly meeting of the government wearing a prayer shawl and carrying a Bible in his hand. For the entire government, the defense minister, who apparently realized his career in the government was at an end, read aloud from the *Book of Psalms*: "For far too long have I lived among those who hate peace. I want peace, but if I say a word, then they are ready to fight."[6] Then Mordechai left the meeting.

Following Netanyahu's TV appearance, Mordechai was given a chance to respond live as well. A television camera was put up outside the dismissed minister's house, and the solid little man, who originally came from Iraq, looked straight into the TV-camera and said, "Mr Netanyahu has sent me a letter full of half-truths, lies and insults which suit a petty politician. I am sorry to have to say that the head of the government is a man whom I do not trust, and is not worthy of the confidence of the Israeli people. Look me in the eyes and tell me who do you think speaks the truth."[7]

Mordechai went on to say Netanyahu was a poor leader, and he spoke of all the "peace haters" in the right-wing government coalition. "Many a time I have left the room in order to avoid listening to all the lies which are being served up in the government," he managed to add.

The Labor Party leader, Ehud Barak, was pleased with all the fuss. He said simply, "Mordechai joins a long line of honorable Likud politicians who are sick and tired of Netanyahu." Barak felt confident that he and the Labor Party would win the election on May 17, 1999, even if Generals Yitzhak Mordechai and Amnon Lipkin-Shahak were about to form a new middle-of-the-road party that could siphon votes from both Barak and Netanyahu.[8]

CHAPTER NINETY
The General's Last Car Trip

For ordinary Israeli soldiers and officers in South Lebanon, the situation was becoming critical. They were being held captive by a war where the primary goal was to stay alive. The newspapers used phrases like "Israel's Vietnam," "That Cursed Place," and "Moloch"—the last referring to the heathen god to whom the Israelites had prayed, and who demanded human sacrifice.

The debate among the politicians became more heated, and the morale of the soldiers in South Lebanon dropped. Television pictures of wounded or dead Israeli soldiers created waves of protest. In addition, the Israeli security service discovered that the grassroots among the SLA militia, which was dominated by Shias, was rotting. Ever more young men secretly went over to Hizbullah. Some of them were discovered and killed by their own, while others were sent to Khiam.

At the end of February, 1999, I read a headline in *Haaretz*, "Three officers killed in Lebanon." The three had been killed when a commando group led by Major Eitan Balasha was ambushed north of the occupation zone. Hizbullah's intelligence service had been informed of the incursion ahead of time.

Israeli newspaper commentators wrote that nothing had changed in 30 years, except that the Israelis previously were fighting Palestinians while now they were fighting for their lives against Hizbullah. In the course of the past 30 years Israel had tried everything—small wars and large ones, commando operations, tank and artillery attacks. Nothing had worked. There was no peace with its neighbor to the north or peace for the Israelis who lived along the border. The only thing that had changed was that the enemy was far more sophisticated than before.[9]

The Knesset member Yossi Beilin, who led the movement to pull troops from Lebanon, asked the new defense minister, Moshe Arens, to re-evaluate the occupation. "Everyone was convinced it had to be possible to protect northern Israel from the international border at a much lower price in blood," wrote Beilin in a letter to the minister, the most hawkish of all Israeli hawks. "I am asking you to make a brave, responsible and necessary effort. You will be remembered as the one who put a stop to the march of foolishness, and the one who with decisiveness gave life to those soldiers who perhaps would have had to sacrifice it on the altar of the Lebanese Moloch."[10]

Defense Minister Arens replied the time was not right to undertake anything at all. "In my opinion, a unilateral withdrawal would be gambling with the security of the population in northern Israel, and that is a gamble which must be forbidden. This was my opinion before and it is my opinion today," Arens stated.[11]

Across the border, Hizbullah invited a group of 70 journalists to a press conference in South Lebanon. The journalists were served croissants and Turkish coffee. They heard about the fighting power of the Islamic resistance movement, were shown Sagger rockets and 120 mm mortars and were allowed to interview widows of fallen resistance men. During the press conference, a sheet was handed out which said an Israeli soldier had been killed half an hour earlier. This news had not yet been confirmed in Israel, but it would be later.[12]

Israel's highest ranking officer in South Lebanon, Brigadier General Erez Gerstein, was worried about developments. Officially, though, Gerstein said Hizbullah was being beaten. The general also said that every demand for an Israeli withdrawal from South Lebanon would put lives at risk because Hizbullah would then carry out "terror attacks" against Israel.[13] It was generally recognized that the 38-year-old general, who was from a kibbutz, was going to reach the highest levels in the IDF. Gerstein was adored by his soldiers, and he showed no fear. Nearly every day he drove around the occupation zone in an armored Mercedes, one of many civilian vehicles that rolled along the roads in South Lebanon.

Late on Sunday morning, February 28, 1999 the general drove with a column of four vehicles north past Ebl el-Saqi, and then east to Shebaa. His Arab-speaking driver, Imad Abu-Rish, had a radio operator by his side, Staff-Sergeant Omer Alkabetz. Gerstein was in the back seat together with Israeli radio reporter, Ilan Roeh. They were going to Shebaa to give their condolences to the family of a local SLA intelligence chief murdered two months earlier in a dispute over sharing of proceeds in the lucrative cross-border smuggling operation into and out of Syria. Shebaa lay a few hours' donkey ride over the mountain passes of Mount Hermon, northeast of the village.

Shortly before midday Gerstein and his company left Shebaa. The Israeli column had to drive back the same way. Everything went fine until the vehicles drove into an open stretch of road between Kaukaba and Ebl el-Saqi, in the Indian UNIFIL sector. There the Mercedes carrying Gerstein broke an infrared beam and detonated a roadside bomb. Gerstein and Roeh were captive in the back seat of the burning car, which rolled down a ravine. All four lost their lives. Not since the Israeli invasion in 1982 had an Israeli general been killed in Lebanon. A few hours later, the explosion was shown on Hizbullah's news broadcast and then on Israeli TV.

The killer bomb and three others had been planted a month earlier by a Hizbullah Special Forces team that infiltrated the occupation zone through the rugged hills above Kaukaba. A second Hizbullah unit slipped back into the zone after a couple of weeks to change the battery of the main bomb, but the batteries on the others had not been replaced, which spared the Israelis further casualties.[14]

At a press conference in Tel Aviv that same evening the Israeli Chief of the General Staff Lieutenant General Shaul Mofaz said the attack would be avenged. The use of the word was an echo of what was said in the days before Operation Grapes of Wrath three years earlier. But the assassination of Israelis in South Lebanon was not contrary to the agreement entered into between Israel and Hizbullah in 1996. Attacks against military targets in South Lebanon were permitted.

The Lebanese prepared for the worst. Hospitals were put on emergency footing and schools were closed. People in South Lebanon still were not frightened. "This is our country, we stand firm," said an inhabitant in the village of Barashit to a journalist who showed up. No one would get them to flee.

UNIFIL and UNTSO noticed the Israelis brought new artillery to the border area. It felt like a show of muscle to intimidate a man who was feeling secure in his own strength. "This is just show. There will be no major action. The Israelis are tired of war. This is a campaign. The government does not want a repeat of what happened before the election in 1996, when Peres lost," said Timur Göksel when I called him.

In Israel, more and more people thought the occupation could not continue. The officers who supported it replied that Israel should be able to tolerate 30 dead soldiers a year. They pointed out there were 4.8 million people in the country, and that earlier wars had been far costlier. During the war leading up to the formation of the state of Israel, their forces lost 30 soldiers a day. The officers complained the politicians lacked the will to pay the price, and were hindering a military victory. Those who screamed for retreat, made Israel weaker, thought the supporters of continued occupation.

Prime Minister Netanyahu placed all the blame on the former Labor Party government, arguing that Israel's loss in Lebanon could be traced back to the agreement Peres had made in 1996. If that agreement to avoid attacks against civilian targets had not existed, Israel could have attacked wherever it wanted in Lebanon. Labor Party leader Ehud Barak announced that he would pull Israeli forces back from Lebanon in the course of one year if he came to power. A bit later the same promise came from Netanyahu, like a weak echo.

A few weeks after General Gerstein had been killed, *The Guardian's* man in the Middle East, David Hirst, travelled south to test the morale in the occupation zone. Journalists were seldom welcome in occupied South Lebanon. If they came from Israel, they had to be escorted by an Israeli officer and wear bulletproof vests and helmets. If they came from Beirut, they were required in advance to sign a document where they promised not to call on General Lahd, his men or the Israeli military.[15]

David Hirst first drove to Nabatiyeh, then to the village of Kfar Tibnit then on to the most southerly post which was manned by soldiers from the Lebanese army. At that post, he got out of his taxi and walked half a kilometer further south. The car was not allowed to go any further.

"It was spooky ," Hirst said when he told me about the line of burned out car wrecks, barbed wire and earthen berms he had passed. "It was like going through a war front between two states. One of the first things I noticed was a sign on which was written that you risked your life if you drove further by car." All Lebanese and journalists, who were familiar with the area, knew Israeli soldiers would open fire on every vehicle, for fear it was full of explosives. But the strange thing was that Hirst did not see any Israeli soldiers on the roads.

The British journalist, who had reported from Lebanon since the 1960s, wrote there were now only 75,000 Lebanese left in the occupation zone, which had previously numbered some 400,000 inhabitants. Many had emigrated, but emigration was not something very new. South Lebanese during the centuries were always known to emigrate. In the villages there was often a pattern: The Shias had often gone to West Africa or the US, the Christians to the US and Canada, and the Druze to South America. The Sunni Muslims went to the oil-rich Gulf states.

For those who remained, living conditions varied from village to village, depending on local tradition, religion and circumstances. In Qleia, just south of Marjayoun, most people managed well. The majority of the population was Maronite, and many had higher-level positions in the SLA. In the Shia town of Bint Jbeil, many were helped by the approximately 10,000 emigres who had gone to the United States, and particularly to Dearborn, Michigan. They sent money to the 2,000 Shias who were still in the village, which previously had been famous for its shoe production. In Shebaa, farther to the east, the inhabitants lived off fruit production, and by smuggling cigarettes to Syria on donkeys, which could find their way by themselves. The animals would carry back cans full of subsidized Syrian heating oil. The inhabitants of the occupation zone were closely following developments in Israel. Ehud Barak's promise to withdraw within a year after being elected, raised both expectations and concerns.

In an election year, it was especially important for the government to reduce the number of Israeli losses. Defense Minister Moshe Arens decided for that reason to reduce the number of soldiers in South Lebanon. When Arens was interviewed on television on April 9, 1999, he said that 80 percent of the permanent military positions in South Lebanon were now manned by soldiers from the SLA. The change of personnel had begun quietly in January, after four Israeli soldiers were killed by a Hizbullah attack. The soldiers who survived the attack gathered all the equipment at the post, blocked the entrance, and disappeared. The army leadership said it was up to General Lahd to do what he wanted with the post.

Israel wanted to negotiate an agreement with Lebanon for an orderly retreat. In addition, the Israelis wanted to get an arrangement for the future relationship between the two countries. In Beirut, Prime Minister Selim el-Hoss said it was not realistic to negotiate with Israel about anything at all without Israel negotiating in parallel with Syria about the future of the Golan Heights. Hoss made reference to the May 17 agreement from 1983, which had only led to domestic strife, and that any new agreement with the Jewish state would lead to civil war. "We stick to the Security Council resolution 425 from 1978. It demands immediate and unconditional withdrawal from Lebanese soil," said Hoss.[16]

CHAPTER NINETY ONE

Power Shift in Israel

In Israel, a direct election of the prime minister was set to take place. There were four candidates but only three of them were serious contenders: Benjamin Netanyahu, Ehud Barak and Yitzhak Mordechai, who had been appointed leader of the newly formed centrist party.

Outwardly, the fight among the leaders of the three parties was framed as a dispute over the peace process with the Palestinians. The Labor Party embraced the Oslo Process, but had no intention of permitting the Palestinians to form their own state. Likud wanted to withdraw from the negotiations with the Palestinians, and also did not want them to have their own state. Even the new centrist party did not want a Palestinian state side by side with Israel.

On April 12, 1999, right in the middle of the campaign, reports came that yet another Hizbullah bomb had taken the life of a soldier in Lebanon. Prime Minister Netanyahu knew he had to portray himself as a politician of action, and that same evening he called together the so-called kitchen cabinet—some of the central members of the government—along with the top military leaders, to discuss what should be done.

The defense leadership told the ministers that Noam Barnea was supposed to have disarmed a roadside bomb near the village of Arnoun close to Beaufort, when he was killed. Hizbullah's bomb was a more advanced type than the Israelis had foreseen, and it blew up as the soldier was standing over it. It had been the third one to explode in the same area. The Israeli politicians now claimed that Hizbullah had breached the agreement of 1996, because bombs and ammunition were being hidden in private homes in Arnoun.[17]

The government decided to undertake a major action in the nearly deserted Shia village. There were no battles, since Hizbullah's guerrillas had disappeared before the Israelis arrived. But house after house was checked in the hunt for weapons and guerrilla cells. Then the village was fenced in with barbed wire. Students from Nabatiyeh came and removed the barbed wire barriers in an action that received widespread media coverage in Lebanon.

When the Israelis again were out of Arnoun, Prime Minister Netanyahu declared the government would introduce a new policy in South Lebanon. Nobody really was clear just what this meant, except that it served as raw meat for election purposes. Since the campaign was going badly for him, many believed Netanyahu would lose. When election day came, Bibi was so desperate he let himself be interviewed by a radio station that operated without a license. The pirate station belonged to the oriental party, Shas. After the interview, Netanyahu went to a second station that was operating unlawfully. He was fully aware the two stations were transmitting without licenses, and even if they had them, that it was against the law in Israel to electioneer on the same day people placed their ballots in the voting urns. The prime minister's last-minute, feverish attempt to gather votes was a modern version of the cry Shakespeare imagined for King Richard III's at Bosworth Field: "A horse! A horse! My kingdom for a horse!"

Netanyahu's words fell on deaf ears. Only half an hour after the polls had closed, the results were clear. Netanyahu conceded defeat on receipt of the initial returns.

The Labor Party's promise of peace and Ehud Barak's assurance he would pull Israeli soldiers out of the Lebanese muck had hit home with most Israelis. They were sick of Lebanon and Netanyahu. Now they shouted their acclamations for the brave general, Israel's most highly decorated officer. Barak had a long list of accomplishments. In 1973, dressed as a woman, he had taken part in killing three Palestinian leaders in Beirut. He had been the key officer during a glamorous rescue action in 1976, following the kidnapping of an Air France plane with 248 passengers on-board, that was forced to land at Entebbe in Uganda. Barak had also led the operation in 1988 that took the life of the PLO deputy Abu Jihad in Tunisia. He was said to have been a brilliant staff officer, chief of military intelligence, and had been Chief of the General Staff as well as foreign minister. He had studied mathematics, and his hobby was to take apart and reassemble clocks. On top of it all, he played the piano.

The power shift in Israel led to a renewed focus on the occupation in South Lebanon. Iran was also given a more prominent role in the Israeli agenda, even though Barak did not view Iran as the country's biggest threat. For him that was Iraq's Saddam Hussein.

Not even Barak did anything to improve conditions for the 130 prisoners in Khiam. The prisoners in Khiam were not being interrogated by the Israelis, but Mossad's officers were still present as before. The Israelis also still held 42 Lebanese in domestic prisons. It was business as usual.

Khiam's oldest prisoner, 70-year-old Hassan Seayad, was set free, and the press and human rights organizations were provided with yet another witness. At first Hassan did not say anything about torture, since his wife was still being held captive. Only when she was released and both were out of the occupation zone did Hassan Seayad dare to speak. However, torture in Khiam was no longer news to the big, international newspapers. The Israelis' claim not to be responsible for what happened at the prison was also old news. It was as if the leading American and European politicians approved of the Israeli lies. Not even in Norway were there many who took up the issue, despite the fact that reports of torture were well known.

In June 1999, around 300 SLA militia soldiers left their posts around Jezzine in the northern part of the occupation zone; the Israelis had pulled out of the city earlier. The withdrawal was given little coverage in the international news media, even though this was the first withdrawal since Israel had set up the so-called "security zone" in 1983, in which Jezzine was included.

"Gone with the Wind," said one woman from Kfarhouna, one of the villages south of Jezzine, as she stood next to the wreck of a car which had been smashed by an Israeli tank. What amused the woman was that the car belonged to one of the SLA militia soldiers. But then she turned more serious: "We never know what will happen. We are living in war, not in peace."[18]

In Beirut, Hassan Nasrallah said he could not guarantee the safety of people who had been associated with the SLA militia in Jezzine. "Turn yourselves over to the police and be tried by the court," was Nasrallah's advice.

Jezzine had once had 30,000 inhabitants, but the number had shrunk to 5,000 under Israeli and SLA domination. Some of those who remained went out into the streets with Lebanese flags, but otherwise, mainly police were to be seen. Things became livelier when a press conference was called and a number of the 203 from the SLA, who had turned themselves in, appeared.

Around 100 of the SLA forces in Jezzine had chosen to move southward, but even there they and other militia members feared for the future. Some of the officers had written a letter to Ehud Barak before he took over as prime minister. In it, the Lebanese asked for political asylum for them and their families if they should get into difficulty. The answer from Barak's spokeswoman was simple: Israel will show responsibility toward the SLA. The problem will be discussed and solved. Some SLA soldiers, however, were not appeased. Three of them contacted Israeli journalists in Metulla. The young Lebanese were dressed in uniforms with Hebrew script over their right chest pockets, and were in a serious frame of mind. None of them wanted their names to be known, but they wanted the message sent to the Israeli government and to the greatest number of people. "If Israel does not take care of me, I have no other choice. I will have to join Hizbullah or a similar organization and will be forced to fight against Israel," said one of the youths.[19]

The three men pleaded mainly for themselves and their families. The mood was similar to the one in Saigon during the months leading up to the American retreat. Everyone was afraid of being killed, and thought first about themselves.

"If Israel and Lebanon make an agreement where you get a full guarantee of protection, would you rather stay in Lebanon?" the journalist from *Yedioth Ahronoth*, Israel's largest newspaper, asked.

"No, that is out of the question," the three answered in unison.

"Not even if Syria gives you its guarantee?"

"No. In Lebanon, everything is based on personal revenge. This is not a conflict which can be solved through a formal agreement between governments. It is the revenge which scares us; promises are of little help."

The three soldiers explained that Hizbullah and the Lebanese government divided the SLA into four parts: Torturers and higher officers in the SLA and Shin Bet were the most hated and in mortal danger every day. Collaborators, such as they were, would be severely punished. Those who had joined the SLA to survive were less hated. Then there were those who had been forced to join the SLA, who would be forgiven.

"Do you have regrets?"

"From the age of seven, we played with rifles that our parents had hidden. We joined the SLA when we were 16–17. There was no doubt that we would do the same thing as everyone else in our family. We were SLA yes-men."

"Do you have any regrets of conscience for what you have done?"

"Every one of us has a job to do. We have peace in our souls. In certain villages we are heroes, in others we are traitors. In Lebanon, the opinions vary from man to man, from family to family."

"Are your lives threatened?"

"The authorities in Lebanon have passed death sentences on two of us. We have been sentenced in absentia for high treason. We have fought for Israel and defended the country's border. To the authorities in Beirut this is a blood alliance which goes deeper than military cooperation. Some in the SLA, particularly the Christians, feel a stronger bond with Israeli culture than the Islamic one, which has made advances in Lebanon after Hizbullah became stronger."

The three young men who formally had sought asylum in Israel, were waiting for their case to be put before the Supreme Court. And they feared for their lives if Israel gave up South Lebanon. Zvi Rish, the lawyer, who earlier had discovered that Israel was holding Lebanese in secret captivity, was handling their case. In a written submission to the Supreme Court, he had explained that the militia soldiers would be "butchered by Hizbullah" if they remained behind when the Israelis pulled out of Lebanon. Rish was supported by Brigadier General Yossi Peled, who had previously been the chief of the Israeli army in South Lebanon. Peled told Israeli radio that the wives and children of the militia soldiers would also be murdered unless they got away. Israel's Supreme Court took the case, but did not issue any ruling.

CHAPTER NINETY TWO
Rød-Larsen's Return

At the end of June 1999, the fight for South Lebanon spread once more to northern Israel. The SLA militia had wounded civilian Lebanese, this time in an attack against Kabrikha, a village north of the occupation zone. Hizbullah fired rockets toward Kiryat Shmona and northern Galilee, killing two Israelis. Israeli planes bombed Beirut and Bekaa. Large portions of the Lebanese capital were left in darkness. Planes also bombed three bridges, a football field and a telephone switching station. Eight Lebanese were killed.

Ehud Barak was furious because he had only been briefed about the attacks after they had been carried out. The decision to execute them had been made in a telephone conversation between the outgoing prime minister and the defense minister. It had not been necessary to have a government decision, however, because the principle of resuming bombing of civilian targets had been approved by the government in advance.

When Barak formally took over as prime minister on July 6, one of his first acts was symbolic. The retired lieutenant general bowed his head before the granite block and flame that marked the grave of Yitzhak Rabin. Barak sought to show respect for his brave and respected officer–colleague, but later said it was Rabin's reputation as a peacemaker he most wanted to inherit.

Barak was Israel's fourth prime minister in seven years. He decided to put the Wye River Memorandum between Israel and the Palestinian Authority on ice. This was an agreement for further Israeli withdrawal from the West Bank that had been negotiated by President Clinton and signed by Benjamin Netanyahu and Yasser Arafat in October 1998. Instead, Barak wanted a separate agreement with Syria. The goal was to isolate Iran and the radical Palestinian organizations that had their headquarters in Damascus, including Hamas.

In order to achieve this, Barak wanted a secret channel to Syria. He appointed General Danny Yatom, the prime minister's chief of staff, to find a way to open one. The general had been head of Mossad under Prime Minister Netanyahu, until he was fired for the bungled operation in Amman. Yatom wanted to use the UN's newly appointed coordinator for the Middle East, Terje Rød-Larsen, as the contact man with Damascus. The Norwegian had been the Secretary-General's regional coordinator for the Middle East until 1996, but had left the position to become minister for planning in Norway. After just 35 days Rød-Larsen decided to pull out of the government. He became later a roving ambassador in The Middle East. . In the fall of 1998 Kofi Annan asked him to become the Secretary-General's representative in the Middle East, headquartered in Gaza City.

In November 1999 Rød-Larsen was invited to the Israeli prime minister's office to meet Major General Danny Yatom. Prime Minister Barak's chief of staff wanted to brief the UN diplomat on the status of the negotiations between Israel and Syria that were being held in Shepherdstown, West Virginia.

At Yatom's office, Rød-Larsen learned that Syria's foreign minister, Farouk al-Sharaa, and the other negotiator from the Syrian side, former ambassador to the US, Walid Muallem, had both returned to Syria for consultations in Damascus. Rød-Larsen knew from before that President Hafez al-Assad wanted a peace agreement if Israel returned the occupied the Golan Heights. The Norwegian realized Israel was not ready to give back the entire area, which was rich in water resources and was a strategic location, but knew Barak was intent on getting some agreement with Damascus, coordinated with Israel's announced withdrawal from Lebanon.

To Rød-Larsen's surprise, Yatom asked: "Do you have a plane at your disposal?"[20]

"What do you mean?"

"We want you to go to Damascus and bring a message. But before you leave, we want to have a detailed conversation. And another thing: Is it possible for me to go with you secretly to Damascus in the UN plane?"

"When would that be?"

"Probably in January. But you must not tell this to anyone."

"I have to have the agreement of the Secretary-General," answered Rød-Larsen, "and I would have to go personally to New York if this becomes a reality."

"Do not talk with other Israelis about this," emphasized Yatom.

The general went on to say the government was preparing itself politically for a retreat from Lebanon. The prime minister had set July 2000, as the deadline, but the retreat could begin in March if there were no further negotiations with Syria. Regardless, Israelis thought Syria was not interested in creating problems during their retreat. Yatom added that Iran, however, could cause trouble. He thought Iran had a greater influence over Hizbullah than before. It was apparent the Israeli general wanted to keep the myth alive that Hizbullah was a tool of Iran, and not a national resistance movement in its own right.

That same day, Rød-Larsen reported to Kofi Annan about the conversation. The Norwegian suggested Annan speak with the Americans about it. "Since the Oslo Process began, I have often experienced that the PLO and Israel ask me to create the conditions for secret discussions, but also to involve the US. My experience is that the Americans will accept a third party if they themselves believe they cannot otherwise achieve anything. But this has to be done in such a way that it does not put them in an embarrassing position," he wrote in his report to the UN Secretary-General.[21]

In December 1998 and January 1999, negotiations continued between Syria and Israel. An American proposal was put forth during the negotiations in Shepherdstown on January 8, showing that the Syrians were flexible and sympathetic to some of the Israeli demands. In the proposal the US developed, the Syrians had agreed the front line from June 4, 1967—the day before the outbreak of the Six Day War—did not necessarily have to become the final border between Israel and Syria. This was a military line that could be adjusted. The Syrians also recognized that an Israeli listening post at an elevation of 2,814 meters on Mount Hermon could remain where it was, but that the station in the future would have to be manned by experts from the US or France, and not Israelis.

But then everything came to a halt: Israel was not willing to give up the occupied Golan Heights. Barak insisted on retaining the entire Sea of Galilee, as well as the eastern and northeastern shores of the Sea. President Assad ordered his negotiators to go home. Nothing ever happened with Danny Yatom's secret visit to Damascus, either.

In South Lebanon, General Antoine Lahd told his closest associates he might withdraw as head of the SLA. But outwardly he said something else: "We can hold out for 200 years against Hizbullah. I just need three things: Money from Israel so I can pay my soldiers, weapons and ammunition from Israel, as well as open borders, so our soldiers can be treated in Israeli hospitals and the civilian population in South Lebanon can work in Israel."[22]

Internally, a quiet power struggle was taking place for who would succeed the 72-year-old general, who for the most part stayed in Paris, where his wife and children lived. A colonel, 25 years his junior, Akl Hashem, from Debl, who was chief of the western sector, was viewed as a possible heir. He had fought side by side with the Israelis for 23 years. Colonel Hashem spoke fluent Hebrew, knew a lot of the political intrigues in Israel, and was well-known by the maître-d's at Tel Aviv's best restaurants.

For Hizbullah, the 47-year-old colonel became the perfect target. He was both the SLA's new strongman, and a collaborator who had obtained Israeli citizenship. Hashem had sent innumerable people to be tortured in Khiam, and he was, according to Hizbullah's intelligence service, personally responsible for a series of killings. If they could get hold of Hashem, it would shake the entire foundation of the SLA.

On January 30, 2000, a hit-team waited near Hashem's vacation house outside of Debl where he had been born. Over time, Hizbullah had gained so many helpers within the Israeli-controlled militia that it had been even easier to take action than Hizbullah had thought. Rain and strong wind had allowed the guerrillas to get close to the house without being seen. They placed a powerful bomb by the entry gate.

As so many times before, there was a Hizbullah photographer on hand when the bomb exploded. Hashem was killed, and the recording was shown on the *Al-Manar* news broadcast a few hours later. In Tyre and Nabatiyeh, people came streaming out onto the streets and passed out candy to children. The Israelis swore revenge.

Israeli intelligence learned that a prominent Hizbullah member would be driving along a certain road not far from Nabatiyeh on February 5. An Apache helicopter lifted off from its base in northern Israel, spotted the car and fired a rocket. But the rocket missed, and before they could fire a second one , the man had gotten out of the car and taken cover. Six Lebanese in another car, among them a mother and her two children, were injured.[23] Hizbullah immediately released an announcement. The attack was an obvious breach of the 1996 understanding not to attack civilian targets. Furthermore, the statement said the attack would be avenged and that the resistance movement would "choose the time and place."

The day after, three Israeli soldiers were killed in the occupation zone; a fourth was severely wounded. The recording of the attack again appeared on the news, and in Israel, the pictures of the wounded soldier were particularly strong stuff. "They brought once more the valley of death into the living rooms of the ordinary Israeli," wrote an Israeli newspaper commentator.[24]

The top levels of the IDF suggested Israel should now break the agreement of 1996, about not attacking civilian targets. Barak followed their advice, despite the fact Hizbullah had abided by both the agreement and international law. On February 8, the Israeli air force bombed three power stations—one near Beirut, the other two in the Bekaa Valley and Tripoli. Once more Israel answered with collective punishment against the civilian population. Outwardly, Prime Minister Barak said something quite different. "Our goal is not to strike against civilians," he told reporters in Kiryat Shmona while the air force was bombarding new civilian targets in Lebanon, "Our goal is not to close the door for possible peace negotiations, but our main responsibility is to defend Israel's inhabitants, the army and all who are working for it."

The reason the Israeli generals wanted to ignore the agreement from 1996 was, they maintained, that Hizbullah to an increasing degree was breaking the agreement by establishing command posts in villages and using these when they sent their deadly rockets against Israeli soldiers. The generals wanted revenge and were supported by the majority of people. For many Israelis, it was humiliating to bear witness to their own proud army not being able to stand up to an Arab guerrilla force.

But not all Israelis wanted revenge. David Grossman, one of Israel's leading authors, repeated the demand for an Israeli retreat in a newspaper article: "Evacuate the outposts, bring the soldiers home and regroup them along the border. Leave! Learn to live with scorn, swallow the empty pride, stop giving sustenance to the pitiful fire of our arrogance which continues to burn while more and more soldiers die. We went into this war as losers, and if Barak gets us out now, it will be his first victory as prime minister. But to do that he has to realize we have lost this war. We have lost. It is okay to say it out loud. No one will die saying it. That is not what people die of."[25]

When Barak was asked how long the fighting would continue, he answered, "I am not a prophet. I am only the prime minister in Israel."

Two days later, on February 10, life seemed normal in South Lebanon and northern Israel. In Kiryat Shmona people left their bomb shelters after Israel had promised not to bomb Lebanon if Hizbullah stopped firing rockets at Israel. The next morning the radio station *Kol Israel* reported that things were generally quiet in the border area.

CHAPTER NINETY THREE
Mannequins at Beaufort

It had been a long time since Israeli soldiers at Beaufort had been on the offensive. It was also a long time since anyone had used his free time to go on a pleasure trip to the Crusader fortress. Everyone had heard the legends that the fortress had tunnels below it which went down to the Litani River. The Crusaders had used them to get water during the siege. When Beaufort was conquered in 1982, the fortress had only been partially cleared of mines. In the coming years Israeli soldiers only ventured into the first two sub floors. There they had looked for tunnels and fantasized about kings and knights who had walked over the same stones. But the soldiers dared not go further down, for fear of mines from the days when the Palestinians held Beaufort.

Now the officers did all they could to avoid losing a single soldier and took no chances. Previously they had attacked possible opponents in different ways. One type of attack was "to warn and attack." Then the soldiers were divided into two teams, one with scouts and sharpshooters, and one with an attack force. Another type was the "thermometer ambush." Then they would used anti-tank rockets. When there was a tank involved, the action was called an "artichoke ambush."

Most exciting was the "become-one-with-nature ambush." The soldiers would camouflage themselves as trees or bushes one day, another day they might hide in a rock. The last required careful preparation: first scouts were sent out to the place where the ambush would later take place. The scouts photographed the terrain from many angles and brought samples of rock back to the camp. Along with the photographs and drawings, the samples were sent to Israel so that artificial, hollowed-out versions could be fabricated. The artificial rocks were then brought to the ambush location. Soldiers might stay hidden in such a blind for three days while they waited for guerrilla soldiers to show up.

This epoch was now over. The myth that Israel won every battle—because they had first class soldiers, first class weapons and fought a third class enemy—was over. Now the enemy was of the highest caliber. And the soldiers the Israelis fought were willing to die. The Israelis were not. For the Israeli soldiers at Beaufort, daily life had become much more dangerous. Those who were not on guard duty stayed for the most part in their protected rooms underground, and behind strong walls of concrete. Every time the soldiers stuck their heads out, it was as if they were flirting with death.

On February 11, 2000, yet another Israeli soldier was killed and another wounded by a missile. Hizbullah had replaced their old Russian ones with new American versions. The so-called TOW rockets had come to South Lebanon hidden in vehicles carrying vegetables or cement. The rockets were fired from tubes the guerrilla soldiers balanced on their shoulders. The shooter used the sight to follow the rocket during its entire flight and guide it to its target. The nose of the rocket could penetrate concrete walls up to a meter thick. The Israeli officers who remembered that the US had sold TOW missiles to Iran through Israel in the 1980s, commented that they were now getting their deadly offerings returned.

Why did the Israeli army and air force not react in the wake of the attacks at Beaufort? It was a military correspondent at Israel's biggest newspaper who asked the question. He also gave the answer: Barak thinks the negotiations with Syria will resume. He does not want any military action that can ruin the political track. In addition, it is impossible to send the inhabitants of northern Israel into their bomb shelters every other day.[26] The correspondent knew just as well as the politicians and the military that Hizbullah would shoot rockets toward Israel if they resumed the bombing of civilian targets in Lebanon.

On February 12, the Israelis' radar station on the Bayyada Heights, south of Tyre, was attacked with the same American-made rockets. Once more Israel said Hizbullah was destroying the chance for peace between Israel and Syria. The Israelis demanded Syria put a leash on the guerrillas, but Damascus responded that Hizbullah was a legitimate resistance movement.[27]

On February 13, the Israelis could again watch footage of wounded soldiers evacuating from an outpost; this one was called Karkum. The wounded soldiers' screams, and the fear in their eyes as they fled Hizbullah mortars, traumatized many. Israeli newspapers printed interviews with officers who were finding it difficult to explain to their soldiers why they had to do service in Lebanon.

A 20-year-old lieutenant told the newspaper *Yedioth Ahronoth*, "We constantly hear the prime minister talk about retreat within four months, but see what is happening to my friends, see how many have been killed in just the last days. I am afraid it will be our outpost which will be hit the next time. We are all afraid, everyone fears the rockets." The officer continued, "I know of desperate soldiers with parents who are trying to convince them to report sick, I know of soldiers who think they are going to die. This is a very difficult situation."

One day the soldiers at Beaufort received reinforcements. These were 25 mannequins, which they decked out with uniforms, shoes, helmets and had weapons. They placed them at the guard posts in the Beaufort camp, and gave each one a name, which they wrote on its helmet and jacket. From a distance the figures looked like regular soldiers, and every other hour, the arms would he moved so the enemy would not discover the trick. Living soldiers also manned the posts, but they were much better protected than the mannequins.

The soldiers at Beaufort did not talk much about the upcoming withdrawal, but everyone knew Ehud Barak had promised Israel would be out of Lebanon in the course of the summer. At times they glanced over at a sign on which was written, "If you do not stick together, you will be hanged together."

Over February and March Israeli public opinion was demanding ever more strongly that the withdrawal advance, but Barak said Israel would not flee from Lebanon. Neither the pressure from Hizbullah nor public opinion mattered. Not even the wish of six ministers for immediate withdrawal seemed to have any effect on the head of the government. The former Chief of the General Staff, Lieutenant General Amnon Lipkin-Shahak, who was now minister of tourism, said he would prefer the removal of forces from Lebanon only after an agreement with Syria—but because a date had already been set for withdrawal, one might just as well do it right away.

The UN special coordinator for the peace process in the Middle East, Terje Rød-Larsen, met with three men he had known previously: Minister for Regional Economic Cooperation Shimon Peres, Justice Minister Yossi Beilin, and the prime minister's chief of staff, General Danny Yatom. America's ambassador, Martin Indyk, was also on the list for a meeting.

Following these appointments, Rød-Larsen reported to Kofi Annan: "Hizbullah is in the process of developing a strategy where the guerrillas focus only on Israeli military outposts and on the SLA. The Israelis do not expect Hizbullah to attack Israel. Hizbullah has new and more sophisticated weapons from Iran. Neither the Israelis nor the Americans are counting on new negotiations with Syria. There will, therefore, be a unilateral Israeli withdrawal from Lebanon."[28]

In Hizbullah, the strategy was clear: After Israel's retreat, which was expected in June–July, collaborators would not be killed or punished without public trials and valid sentences. Hizbullah's secretary-general, Hassan Nasrallah, said the same thing, loudly and clearly. Most observers believed the promises. But the assurances helped little: higher-level officers in the SLA said they counted on being killed if they stayed in Lebanon when the Israelis disappeared. The militia soldiers, Israel's supporters through nearly 25 years, were delivered a slap in the face when Israel's highest court threw out Zvi Rish's case on behalf of three men from the SLA. The court found no grounds to offer them asylum after the authorities had earlier rejected their request.

When the SLA chief, Antoine Lahd, heard the government in Israel had also formally decided to remove all forces from Lebanon by July 2000, he permitted an interview with *Yedioth Ahronoth*: "No one bothered to show me the wording of the government decision before it was made public. It was as if I had nothing to do with this matter."[29]

The Israelis did not let foreign journalists come near their forces in South Lebanon. Only select Israeli mass media got access. When a photographer from *Maariv* took pictures of SLA militia soldiers in early March 2000, they tried to hide their faces. Somewhat later an Israeli officer arrived and asked the photographer not to make the pictures public. "It could be life-threatening for them," the officer explained, "they will simply be killed."[30]

Militia soldiers from the SLA had many questions: How will you help us? May we come to Israel later? Will you send us abroad? Will you give us compensation? What will happen to those who work in Israel? Will the border be closed? Will the hospitals and clinics in Israel accept us? They got no answers.

The Arab-language weekly *Kul al-Arab* in Nazareth interviewed a former intelligence officer, Lieutenant Colonel Danny Reshef, about the situation. He admitted there were many officers and soldiers in the SLA who had made contact with Lebanese and Syrian intelligence for rehabilitation. The Israeli officer thought that higher-level SLA officers could be sent to Australia, Canada, Denmark or France. He went on to say, "There are in all 2,400 men in the SLA, of whom 60 percent are Muslims. It is not unnatural that they remain with us. But more than half of these have relatives in Hizbullah, and they would now be considered suspicious persons. A large number of them have become our enemies." In the SLA ranks, the mood worsened with every passing day.

CHAPTER NINETY FOUR
One Step Forward and Two Back

On March 22, 2000, at 3:15 pm the phone rang at Kofi Annan's home in New York. Israel's Prime Minister Ehud Barak was on the line. Barak first said Pope John Paul II was in Israel, and the government in Jerusalem had resumed negotiations with the Palestinians. Then he repeated that all Israeli troops would be out of Lebanon by July. The withdrawal could best be carried out after an agreement with Syria and Lebanon, he said. If that was not possible, it could be coordinated either with European nations or with the UN Secretary-General's special envoy.

"What do you think of this proposal?" Barak asked.

"The ideal thing would of course be an Israeli withdrawal after an agreement, but if that is not possible with Syria and Lebanon, various scenarios might be possible. I have quietly spoken about this during my visits to England and France, and in the UN we are planning on a discreet withdrawal. The response depends upon Lebanon and Syria. I hope you will give me an indication of Israel's further plans," answered Annan.

"The distance is small, but it does not necessarily mean we are near to an agreement. What remains has huge symbolic importance, something which makes it difficult," said Barak.

Prime Minister Ehud Barak continued to hope to arrange an agreement with the Lebanese government for an orderly retreat, along with an arrangement for a future relationship between the two countries. In order to get this, he had to make a supplemental agreement with Beirut's leader behind the scenes—Hafez al-Assad—regarding an Israeli withdrawal from the Golan Heights. However, a conclusive meeting on the matter between Presidents Clinton and Assad in Geneva on March 26, 2000, made no progress. That meant there would be a unilateral Israeli withdrawal from Lebanon. President Clinton was irritated that Prime Minister Barak had lured him and Assad to Geneva under the pretext that Israel had important news to relate. It became clear to Clinton that the Israelis had come with nothing new, but when President Assad asked his American colleague not to blame Syria for the fiasco, Clinton just said, "The world will judge."[31]

On the evening of March 31, Rød-Larsen was at Barak's private home. Barak's chief of staff, Danny Yatom, was also present.[32] Rød-Larsen was told the Israelis had not expected President Assad would change his position. The only question the Syrian had posed to President Clinton was, "Will I get my land back?"

Assad had demanded that the future border between Syria and Israel mirror the one from before the 1967 war. This meant Syrian sovereignty over the Golan Heights and the Syrian portion of the Sea of Galilee, not just the eastern shoreline. However, Assad was still flexible with regard to future border details and practical arrangements between Israel and Syria, if an agreement were reached. There was even talk that Israelis would be given free access to parts of the Golan Heights if they abandoned their formal occupation.

Barak went on to say that Israel was willing to give concessions regarding the eastern shoreline of the Sea of Galilee. Barak could accept a line of demarcation where all the Arab villages near the Sea would fall under Syrian sovereignty. But Israel demanded a 200–300 meter wide zone along the eastern shore for "security purposes."

Israel, in the meantime, could be willing to make "swap deals" that would compensate for adjustments along the eastern shoreline. But this was not good enough for Assad, who wanted to have all the land back, just as Egypt had gotten.

"No Israeli government will accept this," said Barak.

The prime minister continued that he now had no other choice but to withdraw the Israeli forces out of Lebanon without any agreement. Rød-Larsen was not given a specific date, only that it could happen over the course of four to six weeks. Barak had not decided. There was disagreement inside the government.

What Rød-Larsen did learn was that Israel would attack Syrian targets in Lebanon if their soldiers were attacked during the retreat. Beyond this, Barak did not want to involve himself in internal Arab issues. He would not even insist on a Syrian retreat from North Lebanon. It would be up to the international community to get the Syrians out of Lebanon.

Early on the morning of April 2, *Kol Israel's* news program related that Israel would not accept Syrian forces south of the Litani River. The reaction came after Lebanon's defense minister, Ghazi Zaiter, had said Lebanon might ask for Syrian help to install missiles with a range to reach Tel Aviv. After the Syrians had corrected the Lebanese on this, the minister apologized for the statement, saying it was taken out of context.[33]

Each passing week, the Israelis' language regarding Lebanon became more war-like. In the Knesset, Foreign Minister David Levy said "that crazy organization" Hizbullah's "declared goal" was "to kill Jews." The Lebanese should know, he implied, that if Kiryat Shmona burns, Lebanon will burn: "One action will lead to another. Blood for blood, soul for soul, child for child."[34]

The Israeli leaders were on a road they had never travelled before. For the first time in Israel's history, they would be leaving occupied Arab land without getting anything in return.

In order to prepare himself for the Israeli withdrawal, and the UN's job to confirm the retreat, Terje Rød-Larsen began to research the history of the border between Lebanon and Palestine. The first real attempt to establish a border was made by the British diplomat, Sir Mark Sykes, and his French colleague, François George-Picot. On behalf of Great Britain and France, the two had secretly tried to divide the Middle East among themselves in 1916. When the First World War was over, a new attempt was made to draw a border, but it did not receive international recognition. A borderline was drawn in 1923, as well, but it was rather porous and of little practicality. The Mandate powers, Great Britain and France, were satisfied by entering into a tax and customs agreement for the area.

So it was until 1936. That was when the Palestinian Arabs began to revolt against the British and the Zionists. This led to a guerrilla war from Lebanon that crossed the uncertain border in attacks on Jewish settlements in Northern Palestine. The British responded by setting up a double fence which was called Tegart's Wall, after Sir Charles Tegart, who was in charge of the construction work. The fence split private farm areas and grazing grounds, and did not function as intended. It was torn down in 1939, by which point the Palestinian revolt had ebbed away.

When the war between the Zionists and Palestinian Arabs broke out again in 1947, the Lebanese government army attacked Jewish settlements in Palestine. In June 1948, two Jewish settlements near the border were occupied. When the Israeli government army went on the offensive in October, Lebanese forces were driven back, and the Israelis occupied 15 villages in South Lebanon, only then to pull out. Additionally, Israelis annexed seven Shia villages in Palestine, deported the inhabitants, stole their valuables and destroyed their houses. At that time the Shias were referred to as *metawalis*, from the word *wali*, which in Arabic means "to be loyal and holy,"— that is, loyal to Imam Ali.

When the ceasefire negotiations began in 1949, the British–French border from 1923 was made the basis for the line of demarcation, even if no one accepted it as the final border. But after the Israelis invaded South Lebanon in 1978, the government no longer cared where the border went. The Israelis had removed many of the original border markers. They moved fences and stone markers, eating their way into Lebanon.

The UN observer corps, UNTSO, which had patrolled the border since 1948, stopped making note of the stones, because many of them lay in the middle of mine fields. And many of the local experts who should have known where the former demarcation line was, no longer had anything but a general knowledge of the situation. Therefore, the UN made it clear to Prime Minister Ehud Barak that the organization would be unable to confirm that the Israelis were out of Lebanon if the border between the two countries was not absolutely clear.

On April 3, General Antoine Lahd held a chaotic press conference in Metulla, The general, who still had some 2,400 men under arms, said that if his men were given amnesty, he would be willing to accept Lebanese control over the border district after the Israelis were out. "If not, we prefer death. No one wants to become a refugee. My men prefer the Massada-method." Lahd was referring to the legend of the Jewish zealots who, in the year 74, committed collective suicide instead of coming under Roman dominion. Few journalists believed him.[35]

Israeli Brigadier General Benny Gantz, who was sitting at Lahd's side, said Israel would take care of the SLA militia and their families if they wished. Israel had an obligation toward the SLA and the population in the security zone. "We are ready. Whether they come or not, it is up to them," said the general, who had been named chief of the occupation zone the year before, after his predecessor, Erez Gerstein, was killed by Hizbullah.

A little later in the day, Terje Rød-Larsen briefed Secretary-General Annan by telephone. He had learned behind the scenes that the Israeli retreat would occur in May, not July, as had been announced earlier. Annan was informed the Israeli leadership was split in its view of how the withdrawal should take place. Within the army and among certain politicians there was still opposition to a full retreat. The opponents thought Israel was not prepared, and had told Rød-Larsen that the retreat would occur in two phases. In the first phase, the Israelis would leave 90 percent of the occupied area, and in the second, the remaining 10 percent. The whole action would take place with cooperation from the UN. Israel would accept the UN's later designation of the line of demarcation, Barak had promised.[36]

On Tuesday, April 4, Foreign Minister David Levy, Secretary-General Kofi Annan, and Terje Rød-Larsen met at the Palais des Nations in Geneva at 2:10 pm. Levy's main message was: By July, Israel will be out of Lebanon; not a single outpost would remain. But a verbal promise was not good enough for the UN. Israel therefore made up a written agreement, pledging a full retreat. Both the Secretary-General and Levy signed the agreement. Levy did not expect Lebanon or Syria to create any problems, but he did not disregard that other "elements" would try to interfere in the process. In such a case, Israel would retaliate strongly.

Kofi Annan answered that the UN should be informed as soon as the withdrawal was going to begin. The Secretary-General did not say anything about what Rød-Larsen had heard in his private briefing, that this would occur as soon as May. The next day in Rome, the Secretary-General banned any discussion of the Israeli withdrawal until he had flown back to New York to inform the Security Council of what Foreign Minister Levy and Prime Minister Ehud Barak had told him—that a full Israeli withdrawal from Lebanon would occur on or before July 6, 2000.

Annan reported further that Rød-Larsen had met Lebanon's President Emile Lahoud, and received a letter saying that Lebanon would put conditions on the UN's confirmation that Israel was out of Lebanon. In 1985, Israel had also announced a full retreat; that time it had been a show for the media. The Lebanese did not want a re-run. The president also wanted financial compensation for the Israeli destruction that had occurred since 1978.

In Metulla, just south of the border with Lebanon, General Antoine Lahd sat in front of the press corps. He seemed resigned, nearly beaten. His jacket hung loose from his shoulders, his voice was barely audible. "I have weighed if I should leave, but have decided to remain, regardless how difficult it might become," Lahd told the journalists, who all knew he had secured his own retreat in Paris. Once more the general talked about the Jewish myth of Massada, in an attempt to relate to his Israeli hosts.[37]

Others hoped things would go just as well as in Dunkirk in May–June 1940, when the British and French forces were evacuated under intense German attack. One of my Israeli colleagues took the story back further: "In the worst case the retreat could lead to a defeat like the one in 1812, when Napoleon had to retreat from Moscow. But," he added, "it will probably be like Saigon in 1975. We Israelis will likely save our lives, but this time it will be with our tail between our legs."

In April, the ministers in the Israeli government were given new analyses of what would happen on the military and political level when Lebanon and the Lebanese in the southern area of the country were left to themselves. The picture sketched in the reports, was largely the same: following the withdrawal, there will be fighting on the Israeli side of the border. One of the most highly classified documents said, "Israel needs to employ the country's deterrent forces in order to retaliate with a far more potent dose, a dose which is not proportional with the force of the attacks against us."[38] This was a re-work of the Hebrew Bible's saying: Hundreds of eyes for one eye, hundreds of teeth for one tooth.

CHAPTER NINETY FIVE

Rape on Orders

On April 12, 2000, Israeli Minister of Justice Yossi Beilin read the judicial opinion penned by Supreme Court Justice Aharon Barak. It concluded that Israel had to set free the 13 Lebanese who had been taken hostage for use as bargaining chips. It had been mainly Ron Arad, the captured air navigator, whose freedom Israel had hoped to buy.

The Israeli Supreme Court was split six to three in its ruling. The decision overturned a previous ruling: in 1997, the court had determined that such deprivation of freedom was legal. But now, after eight years of work, there was finally a breakthrough for the lawyer Zvi Rish's view, thanks to Justice Aharon Barak (who, incidentally, was not related to the prime minister). "Barak has changed his view since the ruling of 1997. Since the decision at that time he has been unable to get the thought out of his mind, and now he has the courage to say he was mistaken," Rish told me when we were together in his office in Tel Aviv.[39]

When Rish took on this case in 1992, he had exposed the fact 19 hostages were originally being held in a closed-off wing of the Bersheeva Prison. One had been set free earlier for reasons of health, and five others had been sent to Lebanon in December 1999 as a gesture toward Syria. The Israelis maintained they wanted this to be a sign of goodwill in advance of negotiations for an agreement between the two countries.

The court's ruling in April 2000, however, had no impact on the Israelis' two most prominent hostages in Israel, Sheikh Abdel Karim Obeid and Mustafa Dirani. These two were also Rish's clients, and were being held prisoner in Israel without indictment or trial. To legalize their status, the government planned to propose a new law.

At first, Mustafa Dirani had not wanted any help from the Israeli lawyer. "But when he learned that I had defended many Palestinians, he changed his mind," said Rish.

"I wish you knew what had happened during my interrogations," Dirani said at their first meeting. "If you knew that, your black hair would turn white."

"What had happened?"

Dirani told him he had been raped by a soldier from the military police on orders from the lead interrogator, an officer who called himself "Major George." Later Dirani had a wooden baton shoved into his lower colon. Despite ugly sores and bleeding, he received no medical for several days. The doctor then only gave him a soothing salve, and did not question him about the reason for the bleeding.[40]

He had also been beaten, denied sleep and chained in a fetal position until his arms and legs grew numb. To humiliate the religious Shia further, Dirani was stripped naked during interrogations and photographed. He had also been forced to drink large quantities of paraffin oil and got diarrhea. The interrogator put a diaper on Dirani which stayed on him for several days while he was not allowed to clean himself. When the interrogators could not stand the stench any longer, his diaper was removed.

Mustafa Dirani had been the security chief of Amal when Ron Arad was kidnapped in 1986, and was responsible for him. Rish came to understand that Dirani had been taken prisoner because

Israeli intelligence wanted to find out what had happened to Arad while he was in Dirani's custody. But six years had passed since Dirani's capture, and there were no arguments in favor of his torture except the one that the prisoner was a so-called "ticking time bomb" who could save Israeli lives if he revealed what he knew.

Dirani maintained that he had brought Arad with him to the village of Nabi Sheet in the Bekaa Valley when he broke with Amal and formed The Resistance Movement of the Faithful. Arad had been held captive in an apartment, guarded by Dirani's guerrilla group. Dirani said that Arad had been moved to Maidoun in Bekaa, and was there when the Israelis attacked and bombed the village in May 1988. When the guards left Arad to check on their families, the Israeli managed to flee. Had he died in the Israeli aerial attack? Was he killed while fleeing? Did he get lost? Dirani said he had no idea what had happened to Ron Arad.[41]

Early in 1989, Israeli intelligence had picked up information indicating that Dirani had sold Arad to the commandant of Iran's Revolutionary Guards in Lebanon, Ali Reza Askari. After that, all traces of Arad had gone cold. When Yitzhak Rabin was prime minister in 1992, he ordered Mossad to investigate further, in parallel with Israeli military intelligence. The following year, Rabin held a press conference where he insisted Arad was in Iranian hands, although he offered no proof of this.[42]

After Zvi Rish sued the state of Israel on his client's behalf and demanded millions in compensation for the rape, among other things, Dirani was examined on March 26, 2000, by an Israeli criminal pathologist, Lieutenant Colonel Chen Kugel. After he had interviewed the prisoner and examined him, Kugel wrote in his report that Dirani's rectum featured "a linear scar," probably "as a result of forced entry into the anus of a long object (for example a baton or an erect penis)."[43]

The Israeli military police responsible for the interrogation were opposed by the guards in the secret prison where Dirani was held. They said Dirani was lying and had made up the story of the rape. Dirani maintained that the soldier who had raped him had a tattoo on his left arm and was nicknamed "Kojak." If the investigators were interested, they could certainly find him. And they did— Kojak was interviewed and said he had acted under orders from "Major George."

Sheikh Obeid had not been subjected to the same abuses as Dirani, but both continued as prisoners in Israel. The government's proposed new special law, the so-called Obeid–Dirani Law, passed the Knesset, making it technically legal to hold the two kidnapped Lebanese prisoner without trial. In 2004, the case of Dirani's rape and abuse came before the court in Israel. That same year, before the case ended, both he and Obeid were set free in a prisoner exchange.

CHAPTER NINETY SIX
Complicated Border

Even though the rape of Mustafa Dirani caused big headlines in Israel, it was the upcoming retreat from Lebanon that captured the interest of the United Nations. UNIFIL's force commander, Major General Seth Kofi Obeng, was asked to come to New York for a meeting with the UN's chief cartographer, Miklos Pinther. Then the UN team went to Washington, DC, to meet experts at the State Department. The Americans gave Terje Rød-Larsen and his team nine detailed satellite maps with a scale of 1:15,000.

The maps showed the border from Rosh Hanikra in the west to the Hasbani River in the east. The borderline was drawn from measurements dating to 1924 and 1949, and it had been analyzed and interpreted according to the most modern methods. In addition, the UN delegation received two maps showing the border in the extreme southeast between Syria and Lebanon. Miklos Pinther was able to determine in the meantime that there were inaccuracies in the existing maps and documents. Instead of trying to draw the border more precisely, he proposed trying to find "a practical borderline that was as close as possible to the international border, and that could be used to verify Israel's withdrawal from Lebanon."[44]

Kofi Annan accepted this view, and on April 29, Pinther was on the Israeli side of the border fence with Lebanon, escorted by three others from the UN, including "the intelligence officer" in UNTSO's Lebanon team, Major Jon Veel. Besides observing the situation along the border, there was little new to learn from the cartographer. In the UNTSO archives in Jerusalem, there were no maps prior to 1949, nor were there any geographical coordinates for the border to be found. The Israelis had looted the UN headquarters in Jerusalem in 1967, when the IDF took East Jerusalem and the West Bank. The Norwegian general Odd Bull, who at the time was heading UNTSO, told me later the Israelis stole everything they came across, including many of his private belongings like his family silver.[45]

Not until April 17 did the Israelis officially inform the UN Secretary-General that all forces would be withdrawn from Lebanon in accordance with Security Council resolution 425. Once more Terje Rød-Larsen flew to Beirut together with the UN map experts. To Rød-Larsen's surprise, he was confronted by a new Lebanese demand.[46] The Lebanese government informed him that, in addition to the area the Israelis had occupied in 1978, they had seized another area of some 25 square kilometers in 1967. There were now 14 farms on the land, most owned by people who lived in the village of Shebaa.

Rød-Larsen was skeptical of the demand. In the first place, Lebanon had not taken part in the Six Day War of 1967. Secondly, UN mapping experts pointed out that the area, according to the 1923 border agreed upon by France and England, in fact belonged to Syria. The 1949 ceasefire agreement between Israel and its neighboring states also indicated that the Shebaa Farms were in Syria.

The Lebanese advised that the Syrians had officially given the area to Lebanon in 1951, and that there were no international markers for the border between Syria and Lebanon. The exchange had occurred through "an oral agreement between the two countries and was not documented."[47] Lebanese spokesmen pointed out further that the inhabitants of Shebaa and the villages nearby had property transfer documents stamped by official authorities. The UN experts were unmoved. The handwritten, signed documents dated to the 1940s, before the alleged transfer agreement between Syria and Lebanon, and did not prove the properties were Lebanese. Both military and civilian Lebanese maps made after 1951 also showed that the Shebaa Farms lay on the Syrian side of the border.[48]

Behind the scenes, Rød-Larsen worked to make certain the UN would be prepared when the Israelis withdrew from Lebanon. On April 26, he wrote a memo to Secretary-General Annan regarding his meeting with Prime Minister Barak two evenings earlier. Barak had informed him that the withdrawal from Lebanon would begin at the end of June or beginning of July, and that it would take a maximum of two weeks. Furthermore, Barak wanted UNIFIL to fill the vacuum left by the Israeli forces.[49] He also insisted that Rød-Larsen draw up an unofficial border between Israel and Lebanon, promising that Israel would respect it. The so-called "Larsen Line" would only be valid between Lebanon and Israel. The border between Lebanon and the so-called Israeli-occupied part of Syria should be excluded.

Rød-Larsen wanted to know what would happen with the SLA. He referred to the Israeli UN ambassador, who had said in New York that 3,000–4,000 members of the SLA and their families would move to Israel. Barak thought the number would be smaller. "An offer will be made to the militia soldiers and their families, but we expect most will say no thanks," said Barak, indicating that the UN and the international community should put pressure on the authorities in Lebanon to give amnesty for the SLA.

One of those who did not say no thanks was a 41-year-old Shia, Yussef Siblini, from Naqoura. Every Sunday he took his wife and six children with him to Nahariya so they could get used to a permanent life in Israel.[50] Siblini realized he would have to be separated from his parents, relatives and his four-story house. In reality, however, Israel was the only life insurance policy he had: a Lebanese court had condemned him in absentia to 50 years in prison.

Siblini had joined Major Saad Haddad's forces in 1978 and received military training in Israel. He spoke fluent Hebrew, having first learned the basics in a course offered by the Israeli army. His two older daughters, who were 19 and 20 years old, respectively, were both born at the hospital in Nahariya. "It is difficult for us to imagine that we have to move to Israel. I know Israel will not abandon us and that we will get help, but it will be exile, and I will become a refugee," he determined.

Others in the SLA chose to desert. Early in May, 200 militia soldiers left their posts and went north, well aware they might be punished for having worked with the enemy. Among the deserters was Major Emile Nasser, who had commanded the SLA forces in Jezzine before the retreat of 1999.

Many of those who remained in the SLA, expected they would get economic assistance from the Israelis. One officer from Shin Bet said to Israeli journalists, "There are rumors among the Lebanese that every soldier will get $15,000 before Israel retreats. That is a lot of money, enough for us to buy a house. This is the most important reason they continue to go to work and do not run off. For most of the Shias in the SLA, loyalty to Israel will disappear the very moment they get their money. They will also not be punished by Hizbullah. Only the Shias with senior positions have anything to fear, and they will certainly run off."[51]

Neither Hizbullah nor Israel had stopped fighting while discussions about the withdrawal operations were taking place. On May 4, an 80-year-old Lebanese woman and her daughter were killed in an Israeli artillery attack. Hizbullah responded by firing 20 Katyusha rockets toward northern Israel. The attacks that day followed a well-known pattern: First Hizbullah had attacked military targets in the occupation zone. Then Israel responded by firing artillery at civilian targets north of the occupation zone. Hizbullah retaliated with rocket attacks against northern Israel. In this attack an Israeli soldier was killed, while several thousand people in the border area went into their shelters.

In Jerusalem, the government's security cabinet met to discuss the response. Once more the decision was to send in planes and artillery against civilian targets, on the recommendations of military leaders. That same evening, the air force bombed civilian targets near Tripoli in North Lebanon, a power plant near Beirut, the highway from Beirut to Damascus and the Bekaa Valley.

The following morning, the planes returned. Tripoli and large areas around Beirut lost power. The Lebanese civilian population was being punished.

Prime Minister Selim el-Hoss thought these actions again revealed the Israelis to be barbaric and arrogant, and he stated so clearly when he received Terje Rød-Larsen on May 6.

"No one can accept attacks against civilians," Rød-Larsen said to the press which waited outside after the meetings, adding that "Such actions are of particularly little help in these times."

Hizbullah's guerrillas did not sit with their hands in their laps while the Israelis bombed Lebanon from north to south. A dozen Katyusha rockets landed in northern Israel, although no one was killed or wounded. The Lebanese did not want any escalation, and Hizbullah was satisfied with frightening tens of thousands of Israelis.

Of the roughly 24,000 inhabitants of Kiryat Shmona, many newcomers from the former Soviet Union were displeased that they had to bear the heaviest burden amongst the Israelis. When soldiers showed up around dinner time on May 5, bringing milk, they were asked, "What about bread, and toys for the children, telephones and television sets?" The soldiers shouted back and asked the people to get to their shelters.

"Hizbullah is trying to convince the Lebanese they have won the war, and that the Israeli army is withdrawing with its tail between its legs," Hanan Rubinski, secretary in one of the kibbutzes along the border, told the journalists who arrived.

Early in the morning on May 7, everyone with a radio could hear Chief of the General Staff Lieutenant General Shaul Mofaz say that Hizbullah would try to attack forcefully, before, during and after the withdrawal. Mofaz was interviewed as he sat with General Antoine Lahd, at one of the army's outposts near Marjayoun. The SLA leader assured the outside world his forces would retain the border strip from the Mt Hermon to Naqoura after the Star of David had stopped flying in Lebanon. Lahd knew that this was not true, and so did Hizbullah.

A UN delegation came from New York to meet Prime Minister Barak and his associates. On behalf of the Secretary-General, Rød-Larsen announced three important decisions. The UN forces would not fill the vacuum in South Lebanon left by the Israelis. The peace force would also not take up positions by the border to protect Israel. Only a full Israeli retreat would be accepted by the Security Council.

Prime Minister Barak had kept a lot hidden from the UN. One secret at that point was that Israel's military intelligence had Imad Mughniyeh in their sights. Mughniyeh used a mobile telephone; the Israelis could use triangulation to locate him and were ready to take out the top of their list of assassination targets. But Barak said no—not because he had anything against the action, but because he feared its consequences.

Barak well remembered what had happened following the assassination of Hizbullah's Secretary-General Abbas Moussawi and his family in 1992. As Chief of the General Staff, it was he who had given the order then. Now he did not want a repeat of Hizbullah's revenge. After Moussawi's killing, 29 people had lost their lives in the explosion at the Israeli Embassy in Buenos Aires. The objective of achieving an orderly retreat from Lebanon now had higher priority. The Israelis figured they would have opportunities to get Mughniyeh later.[52]

CHAPTER NINETY SEVEN
Collapse

On paper, the Israeli withdrawal plan had seemed convincing. The ground forces would pull back gradually, first from the least important outposts, which the SLA militia would takeover. The first two such outposts were near Kfar Kila and Ras Bayyada. One was right up against the Israeli border, the other north of Naqoura. The Israeli officers thought that the SLA would hold them to defend their homes—the outposts were close to the villages where the militia soldiers lived—at least until the Israelis were completely out of the country. Chief of the General Staff Lieutenant General Shaul Mofaz had clearly said, "The IDF will not run off. When we leave, we will do it from a position of strength."

On May 15, 2000, the Israelis left their post near Taibe while the SLA militia remained. The Israelis emphasized that the retreat from Taibe did not mean any change in the schedule. "We will be in Lebanon until July 7. Everything is proceeding according to plan," said the military spokesmen.[53]

But not everyone in the SLA was convinced. Some feared Hizbullah would start an offensive against the posts that the Israelis were gradually evacuating. They also noticed that Kol Israel's military correspondent said, "The more outposts the Israeli defense force gives up, and the more equipment the army moves out of Lebanon, the more Hizbullah escalates its attacks."[54] The reporter pointed out there was disagreement among the Israeli generals. Some of them wanted things to speed up in the course of the coming two weeks, but Ehud Barak stood firm. He wanted the retreat to take place at a slower tempo.

The UN had selected May 15 as the deadline for Israel and Lebanon to deliver data about the borderline between the two countries. That evening, the UN cartographer had just received a single map and a few documents related to the Shebaa Farms. Despite constant reminders, the UN had not received enough information from Lebanon about the 1923 borders or maps and coordinates from the 1950s. The Israelis had also not been particularly helpful with map coordinates. Their bureaucrats had informed Terje Rød-Larsen that they had coordinates, but later said they could not find the relevant documents in the archives. However, they did provide documents with their own description of the border with Lebanon.[55]

The SLA militia soldiers were afraid for their lives, and on May 18, militiamen from two small posts decided to lay down their weapons. The Lebanese had watched the Israeli forces on their way out of the country and saw that they would have to fight against Hizbullah on their own. Then on Saturday, May 20, the collapse began in earnest—from Hasbaya in the east to the Mediterranean in the west. That day the Druze battalion in the eastern sector fell apart.

Early on Sunday morning, the IDF left its post in Bint Jbeil in the central part of the border strip. The Israeli officers told their Lebanese allies that they and their families had to flee to Israel. The battalion commandant and his two remaining regiment chiefs understood what was happening, but not all of the ordinary soldiers did, although there had been rumors that selected Lebanese were being urged to go. Some of the men drove off to Israel with their families, but others remained behind in Lebanon.

That afternoon, a high-level Israeli officer briefed the mayor of Kiryat Shmona. "There is much to indicate the central part of the security zone has collapsed. This can lead to our pulling out sooner than planned," he said, adding "It does not make the situation any easier that General Lahd is out of the country."[56]

That same day, a small crowd of mourners gathered in Ghandourieh, a front line village, to mark the seventh day since the death of an old woman. The mourners and the dead woman were exiled residents of Qantara, a town four kilometers to the east, just inside the occupation zone. The SLA had pulled out of Qantara a few days before, and two exiles who had sneaked into the village and passed messages back that there were no Israelis around. Now the only obstacle to return was a Finnish UNIFIL post at a swing gate on the road.

The unarmed group approached the UN post from the north. The Finnish soldiers had orders not to let civilians into the Israeli-occupied area through their post, but Nazih Mansour, an MP with Hizbullah in the crowd, insisted on proceeding. The UN soldiers checked with headquarters in Naqoura, and were told, "Let them through, but warn them." The Finns then opened the gate and watched the Lebanese surge down the narrow, pothole-riddled lane into Wadi Hojeir, before climbing the steep eastern slopes of the valley into Qantara.[57]

A little later they approached another Finnish UN post. One man in the crowd now waved a yellow-and-green Hizbullah flag, and when they arrived at the post, another said, "We are going to Taibe. We have our homes there."[58]

When the SLA men at the fortified post on a hill above the village saw the crowd approaching, they fired a few warning shots, but they were unable to quell the triumphant advance. Using a bullhorn, the Hizbullah MP called on the militiamen to surrender. Around 16 of them did. Others ran off south towards Addayseh, close to the Israeli border. The large crowd then continued on south toward the border, their procession coming close to dividing the eastern and western parts of the occupation zone.

Hizbullah's leaders were totally surprised by the developments. They had plans for the Israeli withdrawal, but rather than mount a final offensive against the departing Israelis, they decided to take advantage of the momentum created by the civilian marches. "The popular movements changed all our programs," said the Hizbullah MP, Nazih Mansour.[59]

Early on the morning of May 22, more Lebanese drove south in a densely packed convoy of cars, minibuses, pickup trucks and motorbikes. They knew that the front line was on the move. The convoy drove down the steep western slope of Wadi Saluki towards Shaqra. Hizbullah had urged former residents of Houla to assemble beside the Irish UNIFIL post on the eastern outskirts of the village, ready for the march. From there they would go towards Houla, three kilometers west of the Israeli border kibbutz of Manara.[60]

The exiled Lebanese from Houla needed little encouragement. They or their parents and relatives had been through a lot since October 1948, when the Israeli soldiers had crossed the border and massacred many of the town's inhabitants. Nearly 38 years later, in 1985, I had met an older Israeli officer who knew of the massacre. Colonel Dov Yeremiayh told me there were about 100 Lebanese in Houla at the time, and that the invaders had met no resistance. There also had not been any hostile activity toward the Israelis in the area. Women and children under 15 were exiled, and most of the men between 15 and 60 were killed. One of the officers responsible for the atrocity was tried and sent to prison, but got amnesty and later became the director of the Jewish Agency. Now, 52 years later, the survivors of the Houla massacre and their descendants were ready to go back to their village.

The Irish soldiers at the checkpoint tried in vain to dissuade the crowd of several hundred from proceeding on the road where no civilian had driven since 1985, when the Israelis had established their latest front line. But again the Lebanese would not listen, even when Israeli artillery guns shelled the slopes of Wadi Saluki, starting a bush fire. In a final attempt to stop the crowd from reaching Houla, an Israeli jet bombed the road a few hundred meters from the village. But the crater was not big enough to close the road, and the Israelis decided to give in.

From Kibbutz Manara, which lay right at the border with Lebanon, Israelis could watch what was happening through. "Vietnam close to home," mumbled one of the observers. The only thing missing were American helicopters trying to evacuate soldiers as they had in Saigon.

The Lebanese crowd, buoyed by their success at entering Houla, now turned their attention to Markaba, northwest of the kibbutz. When the crowd approached, SLA soldiers in Markaba tried to block the road. Two Israeli Apache helicopters buzzed the crowd, which was being led by a pair of youths on bicycles. The helicopters continued to circle over them but did not fire.

Part of the group approached the village of Mays al-Jebel further south, and had to pull back somewhat when a tank shell exploded nearby. The clattering sound of machine guns could be heard, but the unarmed Lebanese on the road to their former homes did not run. They continued on towards Markaba as they shouted and screamed slogans against the Israelis. Enthusiastic Hizbullah supporters carrying party flags surged up the road just a few meters from the border fence, in full view of Israeli soldiers.

The occupation zone was now split in two. The marchers had established a narrow bridgehead between Markaba and Houla. The Israeli military leaders knew that this was the end, and their only concern became to withdraw their own soldiers as fast as possible.

Late in the evening on May 22, UNIFIL's political advisor Timor Göksel received a phone call at his home in Haifa. It was from Sheikh Nabil Qaouk, chief of Hizbullah in South Lebanon. He said, "The Israelis are bombarding Tibnin. We will not fire. But if the bombardment does not stop within one hour, we will fire toward Israel. You've got one hour."

Göksel immediately called the IDF liaison office and after 15 minutes finally got an officer on the line.

"I am just the messenger," Göksel said. "You know that. You have tapped my telephone and know that this is serious. You now have 40 minutes."

"What do you think?"

"Hizbullah is going to fire toward Israel. You are bombarding Tibnin just to keep the SLA alive. I have done my job," Göksel said and hung up.

After 20 minutes he got another call, this time from the IDF.

"We have stopped firing," said the voice on the phone.

Göksel checked. It was true. And he then got another call from Sheikh Qaouk: "Brother, thank you. You have stopped the war."

In New York, the calendar still showed May 22 when Kofi Annan briefed the Security Council about the dramatic developments in South Lebanon. He said that if the Israeli retreat continued at its current pace, it would be difficult for the UN to confirm a full withdrawal, as the world organization had promised to do. The reason was that they still lacked fully acceptable maps. The UN cartographer had obtained the English and French texts to the agreement from 1923, as well as two sets of maps, but there was not a single set with the signatures of both parties. Nor did the maps share a common set of coordinates.[61]

In Paris, General Antoine Lahd had urged French authorities to call for UNIFIL soldiers to protect the Christian villages while the Israelis evacuated. According to the general, the Israelis had promised to remain in Lebanon until the school year was over—that is, until the end of June.[62] Since the SLA had collapsed, however, General Lahd returned to Israel on May 23. At the airport outside Tel Aviv, he was met by an Israeli colonel who told him he could not drive into Lebanon. Lahd also learned that his meeting with Ehud Barak had been cancelled. He could do nothing else but drive to Metulla.

UNIFIL's Timor Göksel had arrived at the border station near Rosh Hanikra on May 23, around 7 am. He too learned from the Israeli officers that he could not drive into Lebanon. But unlike General Lahd, Göksel said, "I must go in, I am going in."[63]

"Yes, we will let you in, but you cannot drive," said the Israeli officer in command, "There are 3,000 Lebanese on the roads—frightened men surrounded by their families, neighbors and friends. Many are sitting there waiting to come into Israel. It is not possible to get through the mass of people by car." When Brigadier General Benny Gantz, the IDF security coordinator in South Lebanon, showed up, he said the Israeli officers assigned to Marjayoun had locked the doors to their offices and left for Israel.

"Yes, I know that," said Göksel. "You are out. But you need me in Lebanon. UNIFIL is there."

"Okay," the general said, and sent a couple of soldiers with Göksel to help get through the large crowds on their way to Naqoura. At UNIFIL headquarters there was total confusion. The officers did not exactly know what had happened in the course of the last several hours, and no one was curious enough to drive out and look until Göksel did so with his own car.

A few kilometers north of Naqoura, at a small port that the SLA had used, the gates were locked. There was an unmanned tank inside, with its mounted machine gun and ammunition belts hanging out. Göksel decided not to go in, afraid of possible mines there. Suddenly, a pair of young men from Hizbullah showed up. They had heard from people in the neighboring village that the militia had disappeared. Göksel called the Lebanese army office in Tyre and said the Israelis were gone. Then he drove on north. At the SLA's first control post, the boom was lowered across the road, and cars were waiting on the other side. None of the drivers dared to lift the boom, thinking the SLA post was manned as usual.

Göksel called once more to the Lebanese army, and a bit later some civilian-clad sergeants from the intelligence service appeared. They were from the area and well-known. About the same time, 10 men from Hizbullah arrived by car, and then more drove into the area that had been under Israeli control since 1978. Militia soldiers mingled with the people and kissed them, saying, "Welcome back to Lebanon."

The Israeli air force continued to bomb South Lebanon, but did not direct their fire at civilian targets or Hizbullah bases. The planes bombed the abandoned defense positions previously held by the IDF and SLA; the Israelis did not want their weapons and equipment to go to Hizbullah. The Lebanese who had entered the 12 villages in the "security zone" did not care if the Israeli positions went up in flames. They were more focused on celebrating their own victory.

On May 23 at around 11:30 am, the *BBC*'s driver, Abed Takkoush, parked his Mercedes on the road between Mays al-Jebel and Houla, near the border with Israel. The 53-year-old had with him the experienced Middle East correspondent Jeremy Bowen, and the Lebanese photographer Malek Kenaan. The three had started off from Beirut early in the morning and driven the coast road south into the villages of the former occupation zone. On the way, they had heard over the radio that the Israeli occupation was crumbling a lot faster than anyone had thought. Not long after the car arrived in the occupation zone, the *BBC* team stopped near an abandoned Israeli post to take pictures of discarded newspapers and juice bottles with Hebrew writing. The photographer also took some great pictures of women ululating—a traditional cry executed with a roll of the tongue—out of joy at being rid of the Israelis and their Lebanese allies.[64]

In every village they passed, the driver stopped and asked people when they last had seen the Israelis, and if the road ahead was safe. The team also listened to local radio stations and kept their windows open to listen for explosions or gunfire, but everything was quiet. They parked their car by the border so the *BBC* correspondent could do a so-called "standup"—that is, stand looking directly into the camera lens while talking about the local situation—with the border fence and Kibbutz Manara in the background. He got out of the car with the photographer while the driver, Abed, remained behind to telephone his oldest son. Bowen, dressed in a light red shirt, waved with his arms at the Israelis across the border to signal that the two of them were civilians. Kenaan, the photographer, was busy setting up his camera tripod.

While Bowen concentrated on finding some suitable words, he heard a sudden bang like a thunderclap. He turned and saw Abed's car in flames, black smoke rising to the sky. They had been fired on by the Israelis, despite being clearly visible and dressed in civilian clothes.

As the photographer kept his camera running, Bowen saw Abed's kicking feet in the car window. His clothes were on fire as he managed to extract himself and fall down face first onto the ground. Bowen's first thought was to run the 100 meters over to his friend to see if there was anything he could do, but he reconsidered. Abed was almost certainly dead, and Bowen knew the first rule in war was not to make yourself a victim. After 10 minutes without any gunfire, Bowen moved forward from the building he and Kenaan had sought refuge in. They soon had to seek shelter again, however, when the Israelis resumed firing at them. It took several hours for an ambulance to reach the scene and collect Abed Takkoush's charred body.[65]

In Northern Israel, the dramatic developments in South Lebanon elicited widespread fear. Late in the afternoon of May 23, the inhabitants of the border towns and kibbutzim were warned to go into their shelters. It was known that another two civilian Lebanese had been killed in Israeli aerial attacks. In Kiryat Shmona, thousands chose to head south.

"The central part of the security zone has fallen. Hizbullah is near us. What we feared has become reality," said the chairman of the council for Moshav Marglaiyot, Eitan Davidi.[66]

CHAPTER NINETY EIGHT

Exit Lebanon

In Khiam, a huge crowd gathered outside the prison on May 23, 2000. Behind the walls, the guards began to worry. Would there be an attack? There were no Israelis to be seen. On the roads outside, frightened men from the SLA were fleeing to Israel with their wives and children.

In one of the cells sat 35-year-old Suleiman Ramadan, who had been held captive in Khiam since 1985. His cellmates had only been incarcerated for a few months.[67]

Suddenly, screams were heard. Was there a prison uprising underway? No one in the cell knew the SLA had collapsed, and that the Israelis were on their way out of Lebanon. Then shots were heard, and one of Suleiman's cellmates began shouting, "We will be killed! The guards are executing the prisoners!"

"Relax, it has to be something else," said Suleiman. But after a while he too began to fear this could be dangerous. He went over to the door and tried to look out through the hatch. Perhaps it was Lahd's men who were going berserk? He shouted through the door, "Guards! Don't do anything rash. Think about your families. Think. The Israelis only want to get us to fight each other."

It was the only thing he could think to say. He heard a number of screams from outside, and then again in the corridor. Then he suddenly heard a voice asking, "Where is Suleiman?" A few seconds later another: "Where is Suleiman?" In the corridor, he saw a face he had known before. It was a former prisoner. Suleiman felt relieved, and asked, "What is happening?"

"The Israelis have pulled out."

Suleiman reached his hand out through the hatch and bellowed, "Break down the door!"

These had been some unbelievable moments: first terror of possible execution, then elation. The corridor filled with screaming men. They broke open the locks with crowbars and sledgehammers to free the prisoners. Suleiman learned that the mayor of Khiam had made an agreement to let the guards leave the prison in their own cars without being attacked by the crowd. Once the guards had gone, the prisoners could be set free.

Suleiman's cellmates stormed out. He just sat on his bed and thought about the time that had passed. At first Khiam had been a hell on earth. Later the conditions had improved, and now he was a free man. He could not comprehend all of this. Suleiman put on the gymsuit he had received from his mother, gathered the few things he owned, and put them in a plastic bag. Then he took out a cigarette and lit it. He finished smoking, then lit another. For the first time, everything was quiet around him.

Suleiman limped on one leg from cell to cell to see if there was anyone left. All the cells in his section were empty. Then he limped out, where he saw a seemingly lifeless prisoner lying on the ground. Suleiman bent over and rubbed the man's wrist, then massaged his neck. As he was doing this, an ambulance came into the courtyard. They took the man, and Suleiman rode along, continued to massage the man who eventually regained consciousness.

Soon journalists arrived. Some were given a tour by former prisoners. The torturers had disappeared, but the horror, disgust and loathing hung in the air. The stench from the toilets ripped into the noses of the newcomers. The men's isolation cells were holes in the ground with openings cast from concrete. Here was the window frame where prisoners were tied up, naked, and held for several days. There were the electric wires that had been connected to a dynamo, there the handcuffs, batons and whips.

They also found hundreds of letters from families that the inmates had never been allowed to read. Only after the Red Cross gained access were the prisoners allowed to read letters and books. Now the books lay there visible, spread about. On one bed was *Les Misérables* by Victor Hugo, Sayyed Mohammed Hussein Fadlallah's teachings and a collection of plays by the Syrian author, Saadallah Wannous.[68]

In the women's section there were names and drawings on the walls: "Zeina Koutash, born 3/9/79, arrested 7/5/99, freed 3/1/2000." Ismahan Ali Khalir, who was 19 when she was sent to Khiam, had written, "How many drops of blood have been spilled on our land and have not bloomed." Then followed the words, "Remember me."[69]

A few hours earlier in the day, Salma Salame, the interpreter from Blat who first worked for NORBATT and later for the Indian UN battalion, had met 15 terrified SLA men from the village. They were standing outside the gate to the little Indian UNIFIL camp in Blat. Some had their wives and children with them, and they were begging for protection. The Indian soldiers had orders not to let anyone into the camp. The frightened SLA people then went to Blat's *husseinieh*, the Shia religious community house.

At around 5 pm Salma's older brother, Salam Salame, arrived together with other joyous members of the resistance. Salam had for many years been in the Communist Party guerrilla group and had participated in a number of actions against the Israelis in the occupation zone. Now they rode cars into the village, waving the Communist red-and-white flag, decorated with a green cedar tree and a yellow hammer and sickle. Others waved Amal's green black and red flag—but most held up the Hizbullah yellow and green.

Eventually the 15 men from the SLA gathered at Salma's home. When men from Hizbullah showed up, they surrendered their weapons. Hizbullah assured the families no one would be killed or hurt. Everyone would be turned over to the Lebanese government army. Many in the SLA, particularly the Christians, had feared the Hizbullah guerrillas would take revenge and kill them all.

On the evening of May 23, the IDF evacuated its last outposts: Karkum in the western sector, Rihan, Aishiyeh, Dlaat, Galgalit, Shreifa, Shani and Beaufort further east. Also these posts were bombed by Israeli aircraft so Hizbullah could not enjoy use of the equipment that had been left behind. Earlier in the day, the Israeli forces at Beaufort had received orders to destroy the encampment. One of the soldiers crawled up onto a bulldozer and started to dig up the asphalt. The bulldozer smashed sheds and storage bins, and crushed trash containers; Hizbullah would get nothing for free. The encampment on the north side of the fortress castle was already mined and ready to be blown up.

One of the Israeli officers went to the company's recreation room to cast a final look at the wall on which was written, "In memory of our friends in the Alon Company—the best and the smartest—who fell in the helicopter tragedy, February 1997." These were the two helicopters which collided, killing 73 soldiers, 33 of whom were headed to Beaufort. The accident made a strong impression on Israeli public opinion and was an important reason for the foundation of the movement, Four Mothers.

On another wall was written, "Beaufort was conquered by soldiers of the Golani Brigade's reconnaissance unit...Where can you find men like this?" Now it was all over. Israel had not won anything at all, but had confirmed once more that military power is not enough to achieve victory.

Later in the evening the orders came to destroy the encampment and return to Israel. The force left the camp and drove south in the dark. The camp was blown up and fired upon by helicopters during the night.

Prime Minister Barak had come to northern Israel some hours before to meet the commanders in the area. He allowed an interview with the Israeli government channel, but he denied that the hasty retreat was humiliating for Israel, despite the fact it had been planned for July. Barak said he was proud to bring the boys home, so that they could defend Israel on its own soil.

Early on the morning of May 24, as the first rays of sunshine turned South Lebanon's killing fields to gold, the last Merkava tanks drove through the gate at Metulla and into Israel. The Israeli soldiers clapped and shouted when the last tank released a cloud of black exhaust and the soldiers unfolded the Israeli flag.

At 6:42 am Major Kobil Dostkam snapped shut the lock on the gate with the words, "It feels good. I hope the good feeling lasts." The retreat from Israel's Vietnam was over—after 22 years, two months and ten days.

A little before the last tank passed the border, 40-year-old Brigadier General Benny Gantz sat in an old, armored Mercedes. He wanted to personally see the last man out. As a young soldier, the general had been part of the invasion of 1978. Now he said calmly, "I came to Lebanon as a young man, and leave Lebanon as an old one."[70]

With night vision binoculars hanging from his chest, Gantz said the IDF had misjudged the lasting power of the SLA. He had not expected a total collapse. When he was asked if Israel had suffered a humiliating defeat, the general shrugged his shoulders before he said, "Hizbullah is a well trained guerrilla. When it comes to waging war with a regular army, I doubt soldiers from any other country would have managed as well as ours."

Antoine Lahd had spent the night at the Cedars Hotel in Metulla. The SLA chief no longer wore his uniform when, a few hours later, he sat at the lunch table in a newly ironed lilac shirt and sports coat, his bodyguards holding journalists back from the table. Lahd was in no mood to talk. As he ate, his villa in Marjayoun was being ransacked by guerrilla soldiers from Hizbullah who had planted the party flag in his yard.

Just 30 miles further south, in the cooperative Korazim, just northwest of the Sea of Galilee, Lahd's countrymen were not sitting around the lunch table. In a parking area constructed for the Pope's visit to Israel a few months earlier, two large tent camps had been put up. This was where many of the roughly 7,000 Lebanese who had fled their homes had been placed. They were furious. One of them said, "How can Israel dare to put us in camps like this? We are not Palestinians!" The Lebanese were referring to how Palestinian refugees were treated in 1948.

In the village of Kfar Kila, not far from Metulla, Hizbullah's guerrillas were parading on the road along the border. The soldiers waved flags, honked horns, shouted and fired into the air with their automatic weapons. In Beirut, Prime Minister Selim el-Hoss congratulated the resistance movement and said the Israeli army left Lebanon "frightened and beaten, with the tail of its defeat wagging between its legs."

Everyone from the SLA militia who had been taken by Hizbullah, was turned over to the Lebanese authorities. Many who had previously looked at Hizbullah as a gang of fanatics had to admit the takeover of South Lebanon had been exemplary. UN Secretary-General Kofi Annan called Hassan Nasrallah and praised the orderliness Hizbullah had shown.

***

Israel's retreat from Lebanon was the end of a long chapter in the history of the Jewish state. It began with a dream that the neighboring state could be partly occupied, and the rest controlled through an allied Christian government in Beirut. The dream ended with the recognition the Israelis had not understood the Lebanese willingness to mount a resistance.

The Israelis' recognition was like an echo of the words of the Palestinian poet, Mahmoud Darwish, from 1982. When the PLO leadership and guerrillas left Beirut in August of that year, he wrote,

"We did not understand Lebanon.

We never understood Lebanon.

We will not understand Lebanon.

We will never understand Lebanon."[71]
THANKS

The road from the first sentence in *Goodbye Lebanon* has been a long and crooked one. Some of those pointing the way, have been with me from the beginning, others came later. Professionals and insightful friends have carried me on their strong shoulders.

Toufoul Abou-Hodeib, Halvor Elvik, Edvard Hambro, Kari Karamé, Arve H. Lauritzen, Børre Ludvigsen, Jens Mjaugedal, Henry Notaker and Peter Scott-Hansen read all or parts of various drafts of the Norwegian manuscript. They all came with ideas for improvement and pointed out inaccuracies and mistakes. They have my many thanks. Børre Ludvigsen additionally has my appreciation for all the time he spent making the maps in the book.

Harald Engelstad has been the editor of the Norwegian version of the book and Ivar Larssen-Aas the editor of the original manuscript. Both of them had a great impact on the final book. Thanks also to the grant committee of the Norwegian Professional Authors and Translators Association and the board of Fritt Ord, who made it possible for me to take time off from the *NRK* for nearly three years to work on the book.

I also owe thanks to the many who helped with the translations from Arabic and Hebrew: Mohammed Alayoubi, Maisoon Assadi, Nathalie Bkai, Adir Olshanetski, Ibrahim Srour and Lea Tsemel. I also owe a special thanks to Peter Scott-Hansen, who translated my manuscript from Norwegian to English even before knowing that the book might be published outside Norway.

In the first part of the work on *Goodbye Lebanon*, I was greatly helped by old notes, diaries and footage from reporting trips. In addition I have been given help and goodwill from the Norwegian Foreign Office archives, the Defense Department, The National Archives, *NRK*'s Library, the library of the Defense Museum, from the Institute for Palestine Studies in Beirut, and the American University of Beirut.

Not least I want to thank all who have helped me: Mohammed al-Abd, Ghad Abdallah, Danny Abdalla (formerly Hussein Abbas), Marwan Abdallah, Albert Aghazarian, David Ignatius, Pierre Altounian, Mohammed Alayoubi, Torleiv Anda, Terry Anderson, Mohammed Assaf, Robert Baer, Ehud Barak, Shalom Barashi, Ramzi Bekai, Ron Ben-Yishai, Kjell Magne Bondevik, Nora Boustany, Ragnar Bratland, Shlomo Brom, Gro Harlem Brundtland, Jacob Børresen, John Carolan, Gaiz Demirdjian, Mustafa Dirani, Sobhi Dirani, Thor Eid, Walid Eckhardt, Fred Eilers, Esber Esber, Mohammed Fadlallah, Daoud Faraj, Rabih Farhat, Sheharezade Faramarzi, Ali Fawaz, Robert Fisk, Tony French, Micha Friedman, Meir Gilboa, Arne Gjermundsen, Steve Gotowicki, Roy C. Grøttheim, Geries Haddad, Saoud Abou Hadla, Per Olof Hallqvist, Atallah Hamoud, Kåre Morten Haugen, Rune Gaugdal, Hagrup Haukland, Jørn INge Hestnes, David Hirst, David Hyman, Odd Iversen, Mahmoud Jalloul, Nidal Jamal, Walid Jumblatt, Ola Kaldager, Amnon Kapeliouk, Franklin van Kappen, Elie Karame, Jan Erik Karlsen, Brian Keenan, Ibrahim Khalaf, Talal Khalil, Wassim Khalil, Hussein Kubeysi, GG La Belle, Antoine Lahd, Imad Lalousse, Paul Lalousse, Amnon Lipkin-Shahak, Leif Arne Ljøljell, Kjell Narve Ludvigsen, Eroni Matanikoroca, Mohammed Matouk, Diana Mahfouz, Sami Megido, Tom Mehager, Don Mell, Rueven Merhav, Robert Mood, Mathias Mossberg, Ibrahim Moussawi, Moufid Nahra, Shlomo Nakdimon, Noam Nizmaho, Abdel Karim Obeid, Amir Oren, Ori Orr, Bernard Pascal, Atle Paulsen, Suleiman Ramadan, Agneta Ramberg, Zvi Rish, James Ron, Peter Ræder, Terje Rød-Larsen, Per Sabbasen, Mohammed Salah, Salah Salah, Nazih Salame, Salma Salame, Erlend Sandal, Daniel Seaman, Erik Schjenken, Pierre Schori, Itmar Shapira, Ola Solvang, Torfinn Sollund, Hassan Srour, Ingemar Stjernberg, Thorvald Stoltenberg, Wegger Strømmen, Trond Synnestvedt, Eliezer Tsafrir, Lea Tsemel, Thomas Twetten, Jan Vidar Utheim, Egil Vindorum, Knut Vollebæk, Harald Vaadal, Elie Wardini, Odd Wibe, David Zonsheine, Younes Younes, Martin Yttervik.

Any mistakes or deficiencies are of course entirely my responsibility.

Odd Karsten Tveit

Notes

Chapter One: The Letter at Beaufort Castle

1 *Davar*, 3 June 1983.

2 Letter from Yehoshua Zamir to Prime minister Menachem Begin, 28 June 1982. http://www.mideastweb.org/survivalzamir.htm.

3 Schiff and Ya'ari, p. 126.

4 The 12th, a Christian sect, arrived in the middle of the 1990s when 4,000 Coptic Christians were given citizenship.

5 Mackey, p. 161.

6 3rd Canto, "inferno", *The Divine Comedy*, Dante Alighieri.

7 The estimate of the dead varies. Israel Defence Forces (IDF) maintained that 700–800 were killed. Bayan Nuwayhed al-Hout listed 1,300 by name in her book *Sabra and Shatila: September 1982*. The Red Cross delegates found 328 bodies in Sabra and Shatila in the days following the massacre.

Chapter Two: Attack on the United Status

8 Information from Professor Børre Ludvigsen, November, 2008.

9 Interview with Robert Baer, former CIA agent in the Middle East, Tel Aviv March 12, 1998. Baer 2002, pp. 98, 181.

10 *AFP*, 18. April 1983, http://www.wlcu.com.au/war.htm.

11 *AFP* 18 April 1983.

12 Interview with Saleh Deek, Beirut 1983.

13 Dean, p. 132.

14 Op . cit. pp. 133-134.

15 Weiner, p. 389.

Chapter Three: Hotel Commodore and The Smuggler's Inn

16 The opposition in Lebanon was also strongly critical that Lebanon had not broken diplomatic relations with France and England when they together with Israel, attacked Egypt in 1956. Eveland, pp. 180-182.

17 In 1969, the crisis about armed Palestinian presence in Lebanon was solved in Cairo. In 1990, the second civil war ended which had begun in 1975, with the help of Saudia Arabia, and in 2008, Lebanon was given help by Qatar and The Arab League to solve a serious government crisis.

18 Interview with David Hyman, Jerusalem, May, 2009.

19 Interview with Itamar Shapira, Jerusalem, April 7, 2009.

CHAPTER FOUR: LITTLE TEHRAN

20 Baer, 2002, p. 101.

21 Agha & Khalidi, p. 13.

22 Information from Børre Ludvigsen, January 7, 2010, Toufoul Abdallah, January 9, 2010.

CHAPTER FIVE: ESCAPE FROM ANSAR

23 Text of the agreement: http://almashriq.hiof.no/lebanon/300/320/327/israel-lebanon.txt.

24 Boykin, p. 305.

25 Kennedy & Brunetta, p. 46. This was not the first time the CIA had been kept out. The content of the Reagan Plan for the West Bank, September 1982, was also supposedly unknown to the CIA until it had been made public by *The New York Times*. This was because the CIA is not to be a policy body, and the White House (under both Republican and Democrat administrations) cuts the CIA out when it comes to policy decisions.

26 Cockburn, pp. 194-195.

27 Geraghty, p. 33.

28 West, p. 69, fn. 219.

29 Interview with Raouf, Tripoli, September 1983.

CHAPTER SIX: SQUEEZE OUT THE PAST

30 Hitti, p. 244.

31 Eisenberg, pp. 41-48.

32 Eisenberg, p. 39; Weizmann, p. 313.

33 Dayan, p. 228.

34 Rokach, pp. 291-292.

35 Other rabbis cited *the Book of Joshua* 1: 3/5: "I have given you every place where the sole of your foot treads, just as I promised Moses. Your territory will be from the wilderness and Lebanon to the great Euphrates River—all the land of the Hittites—and west to the Mediterranean Sea. No one will be able to stand against you as long as you live. I will be with you, just as I was with Moses. I will not leave you or forsake you." *Yedioth Ahronnoth*, April 15, 1978.

36 Soldiers came from Canada, France, Fiji, Ghana, Ireland, Iran, Nepal, Nigeria, Sweden, Senegal and Norway.

37 *Washington Post*, September 27, 1982; *Toronto Star*, March 17, 1983.

CHAPTER SEVEN: THE FROG AND THE SCORPION

38 In the same way the name of the Palestinians largest guerrilla group, Harakat al-Tahrir al-Watani al-Filastini, became the acronym Fatah.

39 In exchange, the Shah's envoys in Lebanon were informed. In this way, the CIA's station chief in Beirut gained as well from Sadr's impression of what the Soviet and East German envoys did in Syria and Lebanon. Bergman, pp. 51-52.

40 Quietly, Israel supported Moussa Sadr's fight for the Shia power in South Lebanon. They did not realize Sadr practiced *taqiah* a tactic which involves disguising oneself to others, and which was a part of Shiite tradition. Sadr got the Israelis to believe Amal would become an ally of the Jewish state during an invasion to crush the PLO in Lebanon. Taheri, 1988, pp. 160–165.

41 To many Shiites in Lebanon, Sadr was the vanished Imam, the hidden Imam who lived among them, and who one day would return and lead the reconquered world.

42 Only many years later did Assad admit it had been a mistake to kill Kamal Jumblatt. Interview with Walid Jumblatt, Beirut, February 2010.

43 Clancy, Stiner and Koltz, p. 246.

44 Salem, p. 117.

45 McFarlane and Smardz, p. 251.

46 In another exchange of words with McFarlane, Geraghty said: "Sir, I can't do that. It will cost us our neutrality...We are sitting ducks!" Geraghty, p. 65.

47 Clancey, Stiner and Koltz, pp. 242–243; Salem, pp. 116–117.

48 Brinkley, p. 176.

49 Geraghty, pp. 61–62.

50 Mackey, p. 209.

51 Interview with Yitzhak Shamir, Tel Aviv, 1996.

52 *Yedioth Ahronoth*, April 13, 1983, *The New York Times*, April 14, 1983. Menachem Begin used the expression "two-legged beast" in a speech in the Knesset. *Amnon Kapeliouk*: "Begin and the Beast", *New Statesman*, June 25, 1982.

CHAPTER EIGHT: FATEFUL DAY

53 Today there is an impressive Shiite sanctuary in Najaf over the grave of the man respected by all Muslims.

54 Jafri, pp. 174–221.

55 Interview with Salma Salame, Beirut, January 31, 2010.

56 Interview with Hussein Kubaysi, Nabatiyeh, January 24, 2007.

CHAPTER NINE: OCTOBER SURPRISE

57 Bergman, p. 68.

58 Interview with Robert Baer, Tel Aviv, March 12, 2008; Baer 2008, p. 63.

59 Anderson, pp. 58–59.

60 Pollack, p. 209.

61 Interview with Robert Baer, Tel Aviv, March 12, 2008.

62 Interview with Ane-Karine Arvesen, Beirut, 1983.

63 Clancey, Stiner and Koltz, p. 251.

64 The expression BLT could also be another play on words: The two runways resemble da sandwich, like the American standard containing Bacon, Lettuce and Tomato.

65 Hammel, pp. 293–295.

66 *The Inquirer*, Philadelphia, October 17, 1993, Magazine Section.

67 Hammel, pp. 331–382.

68 Nir Rosen: "Lesson Unlearned," *Foreign Policy*, 20.10.2009.

69 Clancey, Stiner and Koltz, p. 253 and p. 260.

70 Blanford, p. 59.

CHAPTER TEN: CADMUS AND THE SERPENT

1 Clancey, Stiner and Koltz, p. 239.

2 Interview with R.W. Apple Jr., Beirut, 1983.

3 *The Middle East Reporter*, December 3, 1983.

CHAPTER ELEVEN: FROM FLOWERS TO BOMBS

4 Aerial photographs from 1935 show clearly how the sand had built up on both sides of the break-water, which only partly had been built by the Romans, and which disappeared in the sand until it was "rediscovered" during excavations. See: http://almashriq.hiof.no/general/900/930/933/tyr-poidebard/tyr-1934.jpg.

5 The Israelis themselves called the secret organization which worked side by side with Mossad and the IDF's intelligence organization Aman, as *Shabak* – an acronym for *Sherut Bitahon Klali*, General Security Service.

6 Blanford, p. 53.

7 *Jerusalem Post*, November 22, 1983.

8 Interview with Mohammed Hussein Fadlallah, Bir Abed, 2008.

CHAPTER TWELVE: GROWING SHIA ACTIVISM

9 Interview with the war prisoners, October 9, 1983.

10 Interview with Embassy Councellor Gunnar Flakstad, Oslo, 1985.

11 Source in The International Red Cross Committee.

12 Telephone interview with Diana Mahfouz, Beirut, February, 2010.

13 Anderson, p. 62.

14 Hussein Moussawi, August 21, 1997, quoted by Saad-Ghorayeb, p. 113.

CHAPTER THIRTEEN: THE FIGHT FOR WEST BEIRUT

15 Other members of the SSNP were braver. It was in fact a member of the SSNP who had placed the bomb which killed the newly elected president, Bashir Gemayel September, 1982. Another member of the SSNP carried out the first assassination in West Beirut against Israelis: an officer and two soldiers who sat at Wimpy's Café in Hamra. Bazzi, p. 28. Interview with Yussef Bazzi, Beirut, May 2008.

16 Copy of telex in author's archive.

17 UNTSO was established in May 1948, to supervise the ceasefire in Palestine. The headquarters were in Jerusalem. The following year their scope was widened to supervise the ceasefire between Israel and the neighboring states. Offices were set up in Beirut, Damascus, Amman and Cairo.

18 Traboulsi, p. 234.

CHAPTER FOURTEEN: DEFEAT

19 Interviews with Ane-Karine Arvesen and the bartender, Younes Younes, Beirut, 1984.

20 *Wall Street Journal*, February 3, 1984.

21 Ball, p. 76.

22 Wright, p. 112.

23 The expression "the green line" was also used for the ceasefire line between Israel and Jordan in 1948. It derived from a line drawn on the map with a green pen.

CHAPTER FIFTEEN: A DROP OF HONEY

24 A formal agreement was first signed in August, 1975. The year before, Israel and Egypt agreed on an Israeli withdrawal from the east side of the canal.

25 The Soviet Union at this point was practically frozen out of the peace efforts in the Middle East. Rashid Khalidi, pp. 142–143.

26 Seale, pp. 277–280.

CHAPTER SIXTEEN: ASSASSINATION IN JIBSHEET

27 Hamzeh, p. 24.

28 *Al-Hayat*, July 25, 2003; Qassem, p. 94.

29 Interviews with Danny Abdalla (formerly Hussein Abbas), Copenhagen, July 2, 3 and 4, 2009, August 21 and 23, 2009.

30 *Al-Hayat*, July 25, 2003.

CHAPTER SEVENTEEN: THE JOURNALIST AND THE SPY

31 Foerstel, p. 55.

32 Sis Levin, p. 48.

33 Sis Levin, p. 59.

34 Bergman, p. 97.

35 *Canada Free Press*, October 25, 2006.

36 Thomas, p. 344.

37 Thomas, p. 346.

38 Anderson, p. 63.

39 Sis Levin, p. 67.

40 Sis Levin, p. 80.

CHAPTER EIGHTEEN: "I WANT YOU!"

41 Blanford, p. 75.

42 CIA, Directorate for Operations, Apr. 4, 1984: "Islamic Jihad Claims Responsibility for Buckley Kidnapping. DO0122, DECL, OADR DRV, HUM 4-82, NORTH, ALL PORTIONS SECRET.7.

43 Thomas, p. 352.

44 Weir, p. 13.

45 Ibid.

46 Wright, pp. 101–102.

47 Martin & Walcott, p. 205.

48 Undated memo, CIA Directorate of Operations,"Buckley Kidnapping Talking Points."

49 Gendzier, p. 365.

50 Thomas, p. 354.

CHAPTER NINETEEN: FROM CORRESPONDENT TO OFFICER

1 http://almashriq.hiof.no/lebanon/300/380/385/railways/resources/middleeast/

2 Taveit 1985, pp. 258–260.

3 Interview with Antoine Lahd, Tel Aviv, March 13,2008; interview with Eliezer Tsafrir, HaSharon, March 12, 2008.

CHAPTER TWENTY: BROTHER AGAINST BROTHER

4 Herr 1980, p. 7.

5 *The Daily Star*, February 5, 2010. According to a study 17,400 civilian Lebanese "disappeared" in the period 1975-1990 without later having been accounted for.

6 Tveit 1985, pp. 35–38.

CHAPTER TWENTY ONE: A GAME THEY CANNOT MASTER

7 Sis Levin, pp. 121–122.

8 Op.cit., p. 91.

9 Martin & Walcott, pp. 207–208.

10 Interview with Robert, Tel Aviv, March 12, 2008. CIA Directorate of Operations, June 25, 1984, "Buckley Kidnapping Update". DO 1846.

11 Interview with Robert Baer, Tel Aviv, March 12,2008.

12 Risen, pp. 72–73.

13 Woodward, p. 379.

CHAPTER TWENTY TWO: "MERRY CHRISTMAS"

14 In West Beirut, another group kidnapped Peter Kilbern, a librarian at the American University of Beirut, the same day, but according to the CIA, freelancers were behind this. They wanted

to sell Kilburn to the highest bidder, but got no offers, and so killed him. Kilburn's body was found April 17, 1986, together with the bodies of two other hostages, British Leigh Douglas and Philip Padfield who were also employed at the AUB. The revolutionary organizations of Socialists and Muslims maintained they had been executed as revenge for the US bombing of Libya on April 15, 1986.

15 *The New York Times*, December 23, 1984.

16 Sis Levin, pp. 139–140, 158.

17 Jerry Levin, p. xi.

18 *NTB*, December 27, 1984.

19 Monthly UNIFIL analysis January, 1985. Copy in author's archive.

CHAPTER TWENTY THREE: "I AM BUCKLEY"

20 Dawahare, p. 18.

21 Interview with former Amal leader, Beirut, February 8, 2010.

22 Interview with Augustus Richard Norton, Beirut, 2006.

23 Woodward, p. 396.

24 Jerry Levin, pp. 175–176.

25 *The Washington Post*, February 16, 1985.

26 Martin & Walcott, p. 215.

CHAPTER TWENTY FOUR: RETREAT AND REJOICING

27 Interview with Ori Orr, Israel, 2008.

28 Dawahare, p. 126.

CHAPTER TWENTY FIVE: ISRAEL'S REVENGE

29 The Americans lost 59,000 soldiers in Vietnam. Wright, p. 217.

30 Dawahare, pp. 65–66.

31 Blanaford, p. 70.

32 Tveit, 1985, pp. 270–277.

CHAPTER TWENTY SIX: A GRUESOME MONTH

33 Fadlallah, p. 142 and p. 154. Interview with Fadlallah, Beirut, 2008. *Ash-Shiraa* Magazine, March 18,1985.

34 Interview with Robert Baer, Tel Aviv, March 12, 2008.

35 Interview with Don Mell, Beirut, 1985, and Washington, D.C., 2008; interview with Sheherezade Faramarzi, Beirut, 1985 and 2008.

36 Martin & Walcott, pp. 219–220.

37 Bergman, p. 73.

38 *Al-Ahd*, special edition, March 1986. Qassem, pp. 99–100.

39 The Israelis had determined the attacks against them were not led by a professional higher command. Hizbullah carried out its actions, and the Amal militia had its agenda. Just like the secular groups, Amal had its own cells. The militia carried on its own fight as well, even if in theory it had joined in a national resistance movement.

40 Interview with Riad al-Assad, Beirut, September 3, 2008.

41 *The Daily Star*, March 13, 1985.

42 Report to UNIFIL, March 1985; *Newsweek*, March 25, 1985.

43 *An-Nahar, As-Safir*, March 12, 1985.

44 Interview with Mohammed Salah, Saida, 2008, *AP, Reuters, AFP* (Agence France-Presse).

45 Interview Riad al-Assad, Beirut, September 3, 2008.

46 *AP*, March 12, 1985,*Yedioth Ahronoth*, March 15, 1985.

CHAPTER TWENTY SEVEN: "DON'T TAKE IT PERSONALLY"

47 Interview with Gerry LaBelle, Beirut, 1985.

48 Interview with Don Mell, Beirut, 1985, and Washington, D.C., 2008.

49 Telephone interview with James Ron, Cyprus, January 1, 2008. *Washington Report on Middle East Affairs*, August/September 2000, p. 22.

50 Telephone interview and e-mail from James Ron, January 15, 2008.

CHAPTER TWENTY EIGHT: BUCKLEY'S LAST DAY

51 *Newsweek*, April 22, 1982.

52 *L'Orient Le Jour*, May 21,1985.

53 Jacobsen, pp. 40-41.

54 Op . cit., pp. 52–53.

CHAPTER TWENTY NINE: HIJACKING IN ATHENS

55 *Middle East International*, 14.6.1985.

56 Zimmermann, p. 23.

57 Bergman, p. 101.

58 Zimmermann, pp. 67–68.

CHAPTER THIRTY: TRIANGULAR GAME

59 Interview with Odd Wibe, Beirut, 1985.

60 *Los Angeles Times*, June 20, 1985.

61 Parsi, p. 115.

62 Byrne, p. 98.

63 Ledeen, p. 102.

64 Martin & Walcott, p. 228.

CHAPTER THIRTY ONE: MISSILES FOR HOSTAGES

65 Bar-Zohar, 2007, p. 380.

66 McFarlane and Smardz, p. 19.

67 Martin & Walcott, pp. 228–229.

68 Interview with Robert Baer, Tel Aviv, March 12, 2008.

69 Taheri, 1988, p. 170.

70 McFarlaane and Smardz, p. 23.

71 Martin & Walcott, pp. 227–230.

72 The Tower Commission Report, *The New York Times Special*, New York, 1987, p. 27.

73 Op. cit., pp. 229–230.

74 McFarlane and Smardz, p. 27.

75 Op. cit., pp. 31–32.

76 Weiner, p. 601.

77 The Tower Commission Report, *The New York Times Special*, New York 1987, p. 29.

78 Weir, p. 166.

79 Stiner, Clancey and Koltz, pp. 262–263.

80 Weir, p. 176.

81 Op. cit.

CHAPTER THIRTY TWO: ADVANCED CARPET TRADE

82 Thomas, p.368.

83 *The Washington Post*, March 11, 1987; Taheri, 1988, p. 174.

84 Oliver North himself received an analysis from Manucher Ghorbanifar of the internal power struggle in Iran. In it, it seems that Ghorba's most important contact was Iran's vice-prime minister. During the time of the Shah, he had worked for Ghorbanifar and was now a powerful man who could play an important role in an Iran after Khomeini. The truth was something different. Ghorbanifar's contact was only one of several vice-prime ministers. His main job was to protect Prime Minister Mir-Hossein Mousavi, who previously had been foreign minister for a few months. Mousavi became prime minister when the Islamic Republic's first president, Abolhassan Banisadr had to flee to France after a failed attempt to reduce the power of the clergy. It was said Mousavi first and foremost got the prime minister job because he was strongly anti-American.

85 Interviews with Odd Wibe, 1985–2010.

86 Regan, pp. 319, 325.

87 Copeland, p. 267.

88 McFarlane and Smardz, p. 330.

CHAPTER THIRTY THREE: FREE TICKETS TO DISNEYLAND

89 Martin & Walcott, p. 334.

90 Bergman, p. 117.

91 Martin & Walcott, pp. 336–338.

92 Powell, p. 300.

93 Twetten's great grandfather had had his family name Americanized because the immigration officer thought Tveiten was impossible to pronounce.

94 Since the Americans were on Saddam Hussein's side in the war between Iraq and Iran, they could not give valid intelligence material to the Iranians. To North, however, this false material would be an extra bargaining chip.

95 Martin & Walcott, pp. 342–343.

CHAPTER THIRTY FOUR: A HORRIBLE PRISON CAMP

1 Follow-up Committee for support of Lebanese Detainees in Israeli Prisons, "Freedom for the Lebanese hostages in Khiam and Israeli prisons," Issue 2, p. 2. Bechara, pp. 90–91.

2 Interview with Suleiman Ramadan, Baalbek, 9.2.2010.

3 T.S. Eliot: www.eliotswasteland.tripod.com section I.

4 McCarthy and Morrell, p. 24.

5 Interview with Arne Gjermundsen, Beirut 1986.

CHAPTER THIRTY FIVE: WITH CAKE TO TEHRAN

6 Fisk 2005, p. 300.

7 Taheri, 1988, p. 197.

8 Op. cit.

9 McFarlane and Smardz, pp. 57–58.

10 Op. cit., p. 63.

11 Taheri, 1988, p. 201.

12 McFarlane and Smardz, p. 65.

13 Martin & Walcott, p. 350.

14 Interview with Robert Baer, Tel Aviv, March 12, 2008.

15 The Chronology, p. 433.

16 *The Washington Post*, August 6, 1986.

CHAPTER THIRTY SIX: SCREAMS FROM KHIAM

17 *Haaretz*, September 21, 2007.

18 Interview with Salma Salame, Blat, 2008. Bechara, p. 81.

19 Amnesty International report 1997: Israel's Forgotten Hostages: Lebanese Detainees in Israel and Khiam Detention Centre.

20 Cicippio & Hope, pp. 5–10.

21 Mieh Mieh was near the village of the same name. There are different interpretations of the name. One is that it derives from the Arabic word for water—*mayeh*—a lot of which is found in the area. The camp was originally built during the Second World War. Lebanese who had

cooperated with the pro-Nazi Vichy regime, were interned there when the Allied forces invaded Lebanon and Syria during the summer of 1941.

CHAPTER THIRTY SEVEN: EXPOSÉ

22 The Chronology, p. 507.

23 Op.cit., p. 534.

24 Jacobsen, pp. 219 - 221.

25 Seale, p. 490.

26 Mouro, p. 78.

27 Coughlin, p. 296.

28 Bar-Zohar 2007, p. 383.

29 Takeyh 2009, pp. 52–53. The cancelled unsuccessful operation also had an ugly epilogue. Amiram Nir disappeared as the anti-terrorist expert when Yitzhak Shamir took over as prime minister after Peres, and became a businessman in South America. In December, 1988, Nir was killed when his small plane crashed in Mexico. Many reports claimed that the crash was not an accident. The most astonishing thing that later turned up was that Nir left behind an archive, which the Israeli journalist Ronen Bergman made public in the book, *The Secret War with Iran*. It relates that Vice President George H.W. Bush, during a visit to Israel, was briefed by Nir about the illegal activities taking place. One of the issues during the 1988 US presidential campaign was how much Bush knew about the Iran–Contra affair. Nir did not reveal what he had said to Bush. Bergman, p. 112.

CHAPTER THIRTY EIGHT: DAMASCUS IN BEIRUT

30 *Newsweek*, December 2, 1991.

31 Interview with Walid Jumblatt, Beirut, February 10, 2010.

32 Waite, pp. 3–5.

33 Jaber, p. 135.

34 Cicippio & Hope, p. 31.

35 Op.cit., p. 31.

36 Interview with the Palestinian, Beirut, 2008 and 2010.

37 *An-Nahar*, February 26, 1987.

CHAPTER THIRTY NINE: A FURIOUS NORWEGIAN

38 Blanford, p. 85.

39 Interview with Ali Fawaz, Beirut, March 6, 2008.

40 Minutes from meeting June, 11, 1987. Interview with the note-taker.

41 Testimony of Ali Ahmad Khashish, who was arrested November 1, 1985 and released July 21, 1996.

42 Interview with Jacob Børresen, Oslo, December 11, 2000; interview with Torleiv Anda, Mandal, December 13, 2000. Minutes from the conversation, dated June 16, 1987.Tveit, 2005, pp. 212–213.

43　Op. cit.

44　Interview with Ali Fawaz, Beirut, March 6, 2008.

Chapter Forty: The Art of Diplomacy

45　Interviews with Ola Kaldager, 1987–2010.

46　Interview with Robert Baer, Tel Aviv, March 12, 2008. Baer 2002, p.148.

47　Interview with Ane-Karine Arvesen, Tehran, August 1987.

48　Pedahzur, p. 83. Bergman, pp. 149–151.

49　See http://www.mia.org.il/letter.html.

50　Interview with Peter Ræder, Oslo, 2010.

Chapter Forty One: The Secrets of the Rose

51　The fight was between the two royal houses, Lancaster and York. The name, War of the Roses, comes from the fact the Lancasters had a red rose and the Yorks a white one in their respective coat of arms. The wars led to the Tudor family—a branch of the House of Lancaster—coming to the throne.

52　Interviews with senior UNTSO servicemen in Jerusalem 1988–2008.

53　Copy of telex in author's archive.

54　Notes from Per Olof Hallqvist in author's archive.

55　Interview with Odd Wibe, Oslo, 2009. Wibe's report in author's archive.

Chapter Forty Three: An Arrogant UN Colonel

56　UNRWA's debriefing of Stening and Jørgensen, Vienna March 4, 1988. Interview with Ane-Karine Arvesen, March 9, 1988.

57　Jørgensen, p. 24.

58　Besides there had been members of Abu Nidal's organization who, on orders of the Iraqi intelligence service, had tried to assassinate Israel's ambassador to London in June, 1982. It was this attempt which resulted in Israel's expanded invasion of Lebanon north to Beirut.

59　Jørgensen, p. 65.

60　Op. cit., p. 72.

61　Interviews with Odd Wibe, 1988–2009.

62　Interview with Per Olof Hallqvist, Lund, 2009; interview with Salah Salah, Beirut, October 21, 2009.

63　Interview with Tor Planting, Helsinki, June 2008.

64　Telephone interview with Tor Planting, March 27, 2008.

Chapter Forty Four: Into the Trap

65　Blanford, p. 89.

66　*AP*, February 20, 1988, Blanford, p. 89.

67 Interview with retired Lieutenant Colonel Steve Gotowicki, Pentagon, 2008 together with UN officers in Lebanon, 1987–88.

68 Interview with Mustafa Dirani, Beirut, 2008; interview with Ola Kaldager, Oslo, 2008; interview with Tor Planting, Helsinki, 2008; interview with Timur Göksel, Beirut, 2008.

69 *The New York Times*, February 18, 1988.

70 Interview with Robert Baer, Tel Aviv, March 12, 2008.

71 *The New York Times*, February 27, 1988.

72 *CIA's Terrorism Review*, Secret, March 10, 1988, CIA's website.

73 Interview with Tor Planting, Helsinki, 2008.

CHAPTER FORTY FIVE: SPY ALARM IN THE FOREIGN OFFICE

74 Interview with Ane-Karine Arvesen, 1988.

75 Copy of report in author's archive.

76 Telephone interview with Torleiv Anda, Mandal, 2009.

77 Copy of report in author's archive.

78 Interviews with Ola Kaldager and Wegger Strømmen, 1988–2009.

79 Interviews with Ola Kaldager, 1988–2009.

80 Secret: Läget för de kidnappade UNRWA-tjenestemännen, 1988-02-24. (The state of the kidnapped UNRWA service men). Copy in author's archive.

81 Debriefing of Stening and Jørgensen, March 3 and 4, 1988. Copies in author's archive.

82 Jørgensen, p. 139.

CHAPTER FORTY SIX: SWEDISH RANSOM

83 Interviews with Per Olof Hallqvist, 1988–2009; interview with Ingemar Stjernberg, Stockholm, September 24, 2009.

84 Interview with Salah Salah, Beirut, October 21, 2009.

85 Interview with Pierre Schori, September 24, 2009, along with interviews with a first-hand source, 2008–2010.

86 Op. cit.

87 Telephone interview with Gro Harlem Brundtland, September 16, 2009; interview with Thorvald Stoltenberg, May, 2009; interview with Bjørn Kristvik, Nakholmen, June 6, 2010.

88 Interviews with Johan Jørgen Holst and Marianne Heiberg, 1988–1990.

89 Interviews with Ingemar Stjernberg, Stockholm, September 24, 2009; interview with Ane-Karine Arvesen, Oslo, 1988.

90 Interview with Geries Haddad, Beirut, 2008; telephone interview with John Carolan, July 23, 2009.

91 Stening in his debriefing to UNRWA's coordinator, Gallagher, and security chief, John Carolan, March 4, 1988.

92 Op. cit.

93 Secret report to the Swedish foreign ministry by Rolf Gauffin, dated 1988-03-04. Copy in author's archive.

94 Op. cit.; interview with Ane-Karine Arvesen, 1988.

95 Interview with Odd Wibe, 2009.

96 Letter dated April 2, 1988. Copy in author's archive.

97 *Reuters*, March 12, 1988.

98 Interview with Salah Salah, Beirut, October 21, 2009.

CHAPTER FORTY SEVEN: SHIA AGAINST SHIA

99 Interviews with Tor Planting, Naqoura and Helsinki, 1988–2008.

100 *Time Magazine*, May 30, 1988.

101 Anderson, p. 279.

102 Top Secret CIA-report to Robert B. Oakley, Special assistant to the President for National Security Affairs, August , 1988.

103 *Maariv*, July 28, 2006.

104 *The Washington Post*, May 5, 1988.

105 *Kol Israel*, May 5, 1988.

CHAPTER FORTY EIGHT: LEBANON'S "PROTECTOR"

1 Bechara, p. 57–58.

2 Copy of notes in author's archive.

3 Glass, p. 266.

4 Interview with Marianne Heiberg, Oslo, 1988.

5 *Human Rights Watch Report* 1999, p. 45.

6 *Hadashot*, December 14, 1988.

CHAPTER FORTY NINE: ISRAEL VERSUS NORBATT

7 Written report to UNIFIL's Force Commander from Colonel Jan Erik Karlsen, dated February 2, 1989. Copy in author's archive.

8 Interview with Jan Erik Karlsen, Oslo, 2009. *AFP*, February 3, 1989.

9 Written report from Major General Jan Erik Karlsen, June 28, 2009.

10 *Arbeiderbladet*, February 6, 1989.

11 *Aftenposten*, February 10, 1989.

12 The Storting's (Parliament) Question Period, Wednesday, February 14, 1989.

13 *Dagbladet*, February 6, 1989.

CHAPTER FIFTY: SALMA'S FATE

14 Interviews with Salma Salame, Blat, 2008 and 2010.

15 According to the report from NORBATT's doctor, Lieutenant Colonel Vidar Lehmann, in a letter to Norwegian Popular Assistance, October 2, 1991.

16 Wilson, pp. 88–89.

17 *Voice of Lebanon*, April 18, 1989.

18 *Middle East Reporter*, May 17, 2008. Later the Lebanese government proposed a law giving amnesty to Lebanese who had committed war crimes during the civil war.

19 Keesing's Record of World Events 1989, p. 36724.

CHAPTER FIFTY ONE: TRUTHS AND LIES

20 Interview with Danny Abdalla (formerly Hussein Abbas), Copenhagen, April 3 and July 5, 2009.

21 Interview with Abdel Karim Obeid, Beirut, May 15, 2008.

22 *Reuters*, July 3, 1989.

23 *Newsweek*, July 13, 1992.

24 *BBC*, July 3, 1988.

25 The Korean passenger plane was shot down September 1, 1983. All 269 on-board were killed. *Newsweek*, July 13, 1992.

CHAPTER FIFTY TWO: DIPLOMACY AND PRESIDENTIAL MURDER

26 *An-Nahar*, July 6, 1989. The information about the Frog missiles later proved to be a part of General Aoun's propaganda war.

27 Harris, p. 257.

28 *An-Nahar*, September 2–4, 1989.

29 *The New York Times*, September 8, 1989.

30 Notes from the meeting. Copy in author's archive.

31 *An-Nahar*, October 25–26, 1989.

32 Pérez de Cuéllar, pp. 103–105.

33 Picco, pp. 113-114.

34 CIA's National Intelligence Daily, Top Secret, March 19, 1989, p. 31.

CHAPTER FIFTY THREE: IN THE SHADOW OF KHIAM

35 Bechara, p. 84.

36 Interview with Robert Mood, Jerusalem, May 30, 2010; announcement from Ola Solvang, May 31, 2010.

37 Telephone interview with Torfinn Sollund, June 3, 2010.

38 Text of letter released by Ola Solvang, May 31, 2010.

39 Based on unedited manuscript by Ola Solvang for an article in *Nordlys* together with a telephone interview with Torfinn Sollund, June 3, 2010.

40 Interview with Robert Mood, Jerusalem, May 30, 2010; telephone interview with Torfinn Sollund, June 3, 2010.

41 The experiences from Bourghoz became a guideline for NORBATT's chief of operations, Major Robert Mood. "If you are fired upon, there is only one valid thing to do. That is to get your nose to the ground, get into a position to fire, and shoot back. In such a situation you will react auto-

matically. You will do what you were trained to do," said Mood in an interview with journalist Ola Solvang in *Nordlys*. E-mail from Ola Solvang, May 31, 2010.

42 Interview with Ane-Karine Arvesen, Damascus, 1990.

43 *The Washington Post*, January 19, 1992.

44 *Time Magazine*, July 16, 1990. Telephone interview with Ron Ben-Yishai, Tel Aviv, November 9, 2009.

45 Interviews with Daoud Faraj, Beirut, 2008 and 2009.

46 *Time Magazine,* July 16, 1990.

CHAPTER FIFTY FOUR: CORRESPONDENT IN A NEW WAR

47 de Cuéllar, p. 112.

48 Interview with Brian Keenan, Beirut, September 18, 2008.

49 Baker, p. 300.

50 *An-Nahar*, October 11, 1990.

51 Dany Chamoun had previously been the leader of the Tiger Militia, which was crushed by Bashir Gemayel's Lebanese Forces in 1980. Chamoun was one of the Lebanese politicians who had close contact with the Israelis.

CHAPTER FIFTY FIVE: A FRAGILE PEACE

52 CIA's Terrorism Review, Secret, January 10, 1991, p. 11.

53 Chehabi, pp. 10, 51.

54 *Journal of Palestine Studies*, No. 141, pp. 50–61.

55 Interview with Kassem Sabbah, Beirut, May 13, .2010.

56 CIA's Terrorism Review, Secret, March 21, 1991, p. 1; Bergman, p. 153.

57 Picco, pp. 139–141.

58 Op. cit., p. 144.

59 *El Pais*, May 17, 1991.

60 Written announcement from John Egil Nilssen, April 7, 2010.

61 Telephone interview with the former company commander, April 20, 2010.

62 Picco, p. 153.

CHAPTER FIFTY SIX: FACE TO MASK

63 Picco, pp. 157–168.

64 Picco, op. cit.

CHAPTER FIFTY SEVEN: BARTER AND THE TORTURE REPORT

65 Telephone interview with Tor Eid, 30.6.2008.

66 Interview with Wassim Khalil, Rashaya al-Foukhar, 26.11.2009; interview with Nazih Salame 27.11.2009.

67 Interview with Salma Salame, Beirut, 31.1.2010.

68 Interview with Nazih Salame, Blat, 2009 and Oslo, 2010.

69 Confidential report by Johan Jørgen Holst, 29.9.1991.

70 Salma Salame had her contract renewed. When I met her in Blat later, she was once more in UNIFIL service. She had also received compensation for her time in captivity, paid by Norway. The UN denied all responsibility.

71 Lehmann, pp. 76–77.

72 Report from Lehmann to the Defense Ministry, September, 1991.

73 Telephone interview with Kåre Morten Haugen, 21.4.2010.

CHAPTER FIFTY EIGHT: KILLING OF A FRIEND

74 Interviews with Robert Fisk, Beirut, 1991–2010.

75 Fisk 1989, pp. 655–656.

76 Rashid Khalidi, p. 146.

77 Interviews with Danny Abdalla (formerly Hussein Abbas), Copenhagen, August, 21 and 23, 2009.

78 Interview with Danny Abdalla, Copenhagen, January 16, 2010.

CHAPTER FIFTY NINE: LAST HOSTAGE OUT

79 Picco, p. 238.

80 Cicippio & Hope, p. 139.

81 Cicippio & Hope, p. 147.

82 Anderson, p. 3.

83 *Reuters*, 23.12.1991. Report of Richard C Froede to the American Academy of Forensic Science.

CHAPTER SIXTY: HIZBULLAH'S TWO TRACKS

84 CIA memo, April 1992: "Iran: Enhanced Terrorist Capabilities and Expanding Target Selection." CIA memo, July 1992: "Lebanon's Hizballah: Testing Political Waters, Keeping Military Agenda."

85 Norton 2007, p. 79.

86 Blanford, p. 97.

87 Bergman, p. 169.

88 *Ash-Shiraa*, April 10, 2000, p. 24.

89 Elie Salem: "The Taif Agreement", Lebanese Center for Policy Studies, 1992. Augustus Richard Norton: "Lebanon after Taif: Is the Civil War over?", *Middle East Journal*, Summer 1991, pp. 471– 473.

90 Hamzeh, p. 110.

91 Interview with Zvi Rish, Tel Aviv, 2008.

92 Justice Winograd became internationally known in 2006, when he became the leader of the so-called Winograd Commission which was appointed by the government to investigate Israel's

conduct of war against Lebanon in the summer of 2006.

93 Lehmann, p. 79.

94 *Dagens Næringsliv*, July 25,1992, and November 7, 1992.

95 Slater, p. 415.

CHAPTER SIXTY ONE: FOUR IN CELL 8

1 Interview with Mohammed Assaf, Beirut, October 27, 2009.

2 Interview with Saoud Abu Hadla, Beirut, November 2, 2009.

3 Interview with Daoud Faraj, Beirut, 2008–09.

4 Interview with Daoud Faraj and Saoud Abou Hadla, Sidon, February 6, 2010.

CHAPTER SIXTY TWO: IN THE MINEFIELD

5 NORBATT/UNIFIL, War Logbook 1992, National Archives RAFA521, box 138.

6 Bechara, p. 85.

7 Interview with a former SLA militia soldier, Haifa, February 20, 2010.

8 Ibid; Bechara, p. 85.

CHAPTER SIXTY THREE: NO PROMISES

9 The name of the barracks which were built before the Norwegians arrived, was dubbed *Falke-høyden* (Falcon Heights) by the Norwegian contingent. The Arabic name for the heights is Jabal Qalaat Jabbour which means Fortress Mountain.

10 Telephone interview with Kjell Narve Ludvigsen, June, 14, 2009.

11 NORBATT's daily war logbook, September 7, 1992.

12 Interviews with Hagrup Haukland, Walid Eckhardt, Erlend Sandal, Rune Haugdal and Daoud Faraj 2008–2009.

13 Interview with Saoud Abu Hadla, Khalde, February 2, 2010.

CHAPTER SIXTY FOUR: SMUGGLED OUT

14 Interview with Carina Thielesen, 2009; interview with Daoud Faraj, Beirut, 2008-2009.

15 Interview with Erlend Sandal, September 6, 2009.

16 Interview with Hagrup Haukland, Ullensaker, April 7, 2009; telephone interview with Carina Thielesen, June 14, 2009.

17 Telephone interview with Egil Vindorum, June 17, 2009; Written statement from Fred Eilers.

18 Written commentary from Erlend Sandal. Copy in author's archive.

19 Interview with Daoud Faraj, Beirut, 2008–2009.

20 Recording of the press conference in Beirut. DVD in author's archive.

21 Telephone interview with Fred Eilers, June 16, 2009.

22 Interview with Hagrup Haukland, 2008–2009.

Chapter Sixty Five: The Third Cup

23 Hamzeh, p. 74.

24 *Middle East International*, No. 438, November 20, 1992.

25 The conversation between Steiner and Haim (Harry) Katz on October 22, 1992 was recorded on tape and led to Steiner's resignation as president of AIPAC.

26 *AP*, October 27, 1992.

Chapter Sixty Six: Rabin's Revenge

27 *Middle East International*, No. 348, November 20, 1992.

28 Palmer Harik, p. 167; *Middle East International*, December 18, 1992; *Yedioth Ahronoth*, November 12, 1992.

29 Katyusha (also known as 'Stalin's organ') was a Soviet missile system which was taken into use toward the end of World War Two. The system was usually placed on trucks, but in the course of the war it was also mounted on tanks, armored trains, naval vessels and boats. Compared with the cannon, the system is relatively cheap and easy to produce. It is mobile and can also be quickly moved from the place it fired from– before it comes under fire from enemy's artillery.

30 Tveit, 2005, p. 368.

31 Interview with Arve H. Lauritzen, Oslo, April 9, 2010.

32 Christopher, pp. 195–196.

Chapter Sixty Seven: General's Baptism by Fire

33 Interviews with Trond Furuhovde, 1993–2005 and unpublished manuscript in author's archive. The second in command, was the Nepalese Brigadier General Shiva Ram Khatri.

34 Trond Furuhovde, unpublished manuscript. Copy in author's archive.

35 Op. cit.

Chapter Sixty Eight: A Preplanned Attack

36 Op. cit.

37 Op. cit.

38 *The Jerusalem Report*, August 12, 1993.

39 Trond Furuhovde, unpublished manuscript. Interviews with Trond Furuhovde, 1993–2005.

40 Hirst, p. 250.

Chapter Sixty Nine: The Seven Day War

41 *The Irish Times*, August 29, 1993.

42 Trond Furuhovde, unpublished manuscript.

43 *The New York Times*, July 28, 1993.

44 Op. cit.

45 Trond Furuhovde, unpublished manuscript. Interviews with Trond Furuhovde, 1993–2005

46 *The Sunday Times*, August 1, 1993.

47 *The Independent*, August 2, 1993.

48 Trond Furuhovde, unpublished manuscript. Interviews with Trond Furuhovde, 1993–2005.

Chapter Seventy: Aftermath

49 Ibid.

50 Conversation between the US Ambassador Ryan C. Crocker, and the UNIFIL political advisor, Nicolae Ion, Beirut, August 4, 1992. Trond Furuhovde, unpublished manuscript.

Chapter Seventy One: UNIFIL and Hizbullah

51 Tveit, 2005, p. 442.

52 *Maariv*, October 25, 1995.

53 *NRK's Daily News Hour*, August 19, 1993.

54 *Reuters*, August 19, 1993.

55 Also called foxshark in Sweden, Denmark and Germany. In English the fish is called a Tresher shark.

56 Qassem, pp. 112–113.

57 Interviews with Trond Furuhovde, 1993–2005.

58 Jaber, p. 149.

Chapter Seventy Two: The Peace Process Gone Astray

59 Announcement from Erlend Larsen, April 25, 2010.

60 Interview with Øyvind Berg, Haifa, December 27, 1993.

61 *NTB*, December 27, 1993.

62 *Aftenposten*, December 28, 1993. From the defense department's side, it was said the killing of the Norwegian UN soldier would not have consequences for Norway's engagement in the area. Since the establishment of UNIFIL in 1978, in all 20 Norwegians had lost their lives; four of them were killed in military operations.

63 Roger Auque had been kidnapped in Beirut in January 1987, after he had interviewed Terry Waite. In 2008, Auque was named French Ambassador to Eritrea.

64 Bechara, p. 97.

65 Telephone interview with former battalion chief, Colonel Ragnar Bratland, December 11, 2009.

66 *Jerusalem Report*, March 10, 1994.

67 *Middle East International*, February 18, 1994.

68 Bergman, p. 150.

69 Interview with Sobhi Dirani, Qasr Nabah, September 6, 2008.

70 Bergman, p. 160.

71 Interviews with Mustafa Dirani, Beirut, 2008 and Qasr Nabah, 2009.

CHAPTER SEVENTY THREE: RECRUITED BY MOSSAD

72 Information taken from the court case against Ahmed Hallaq, Beirut, 1995.

73 *The Guardian*, November 10, 1994.

74 The demolition and reconstruction which was being done by Prime Minister Rafic Hariri's company, Solidere, was controversial. And there were many who regarded the concert as a sign that Fairuz supported the controversial rebuilding of the city center. Fairuz' own son, the composer, Ziyad Rahbani, was among those who had signed a petition that she should not perform. It did not help.

75 Based on the testimony of Ahmed Hallaq and Hannan Yassin during the trial against them in Beirut in 1995.

CHAPTER SEVENTY FOUR: ISRAELI CENSORS AND LEBANESE UNITY

76 Bechara, p. 102.

77 *Middle East International*, February 3, 1995, pp. 18–19.

78 *Middle East International*, March 17, 1995, p. 3.

79 Interview with Antoine , Tel Aviv, March 13, 2008.

CHAPTER SEVENTY FIVE: WHEN THE BOWL IS FULL

80 Interviews with Trond Furuhovde, 1993–2005.

81 Traboulsi, p. 246.

82 *Al-Hayat*, October 1995.

CHAPTER SEVENTY SIX: FINALLY THE RED CROSS

83 Telephone interview with Claire Bellmann, Geneva, November 9, 2009.

84 Interview with Itay Koren, Jerusalem, April 28, 2009.

CHAPTER SEVENTY SEVEN: AN AGENT RETURNS

85 Based on testimony during the trial in Beirut in 1995.

86 Hallaq had also been thought to have taken part in the assassination in Malta, where Palestinian Fathi Shaqaqi had been killed October 25, 1995. He was the leader of the Palestinian organization, Islamic Jihad which had its headquarters in Damascus. Interview with Moufid Nohra, Ebl el-Saqi, November 28, 2009.

87 A few years before, the Ramzi brothers and Moufid belonged to the pro-Iraqi part of the Baath Party. Both had been in Iraq for military training. They had also been at the front in the war with Iran for a short period. When Ramzi came back to Beirut, he became an informant for Iraqi intelligence, which competed with the Syrians. He was exposed and arrested, however, but was set free when he promised the Syrians he would work as a double agent.

Chapter Seventy Eight: Whiskey with Valium

88 Ramzi was sentenced to four years in prison, not for kidnapping, but because he had been in contact with enemy organizations. In July, 1998, he and 49 other Lebanese in Israeli captivity were exchanged for the remains of an Israeli commando who had been killed in a failed operation in Insariyeh in Lebanon. When the Israelis pulled out of Lebanon in 2000, Ramzi and Moufid came back to Ebl el-Saqi to continue their smuggling activity. Two years later, on June 12, 2002, Ramzi and his cousin, Elie Issa, were killed by a roadside bomb near Kaukaba.

Chapter Seventy Nine: Operation Grapes of Wrath

1 Jaber, pp. 185–186.

2 *Newsweek*, May 6, 1996.

3 Tveit, 2005, p. 647.

Chapter Eighty: Massacre in Qana

4 Interview with Franklin van Kappen, Zeist, March 20, 2002.

5 Interview with Eroni Matanikoroca, Naqoura, September 11, 2008.

6 Interviews with Harald Vaadal, Oslo, April 2, 2008, Leif Arne Løkjell, Oslo, April 3, 2008. Løkjell decided not to brief the Force Commander, Polish Major General Stanislaw Wozniak. Instead, he briefed the Fijian battalion chief, who sent the sergeant home without reporting the matter to UNIFIL headquarters.

7 Interview with *Haaretz* military correspondent, Amir Oren, Tel Aviv, March 18, 2008.

8 Written report from Atle Paulsen, 2005.

9 Interview with Gunnar Brandsdal, Bergen, October 11, 2001.

Chapter Eighty One: Israel's Lies

10 Interview with Franklin van Kappen, Zeist, March 20, 2002. Tveit, 2005, pp. 656–662.

11 Interview with Amnon Lipkin-Shahak, Tel Aviv, April 14, 2002.

12 Interview with Franklin van Kappen, Zeist, March 20, 2002.

Chapter Eighty Two: More Lies

13 Official Israeli Government Communique, April 21, 1996.

14 Shimon Peres in the Knesset April 22, 1996.

15 Jaber, p. 197.

16 Interview with Gunnar Brandsdal, Bergen, October 11, 2001; telephone interviews with Frank Stølan, Bardu, 2001; interview with van Kappen, Zeist, March 20, 2002.

17 UN Report, May 1, 1996, p. 2. In an interview with Amnon Lipkin-Shahak, Tel Aviv, April 15, 2002, the general denied he had lied to van Kappen, and added: "I checked with an officer who gave me an answer, and that answer I passed on. Only later did I find out that there were helicopters near Qana."

18 RPV (Remotely Piloted Vehicle).

19 *AP*, April 30, 1996.

20 And Hizbullah did not waste any time. Up until the end of June 1996, two months after the ceasefire had been agreed upon, Hizbullah had killed nine Israeli soldiers. The attacks were in line with the new rules of warfare in the battle for South Lebanon. Jaber, pp. 146, 167.

21 Interview with General Franklin van Kappen, Zeist, March 20, 2002.

22 Boutros-Ghali, p. 263.

23 Albright, p. 208.

24 Boutros-Ghali, p. 262. Interview with Franklin van Kappen, Zeist, March 20, 2002.

25 Interview with Franklin van Kappen, Zeist, March 20, 2002.

26 *Time Magazine*, May 20, 1996.

CHAPTER EIGHTY THREE: UNITED STATES PRESSURES THE UN

27 *Middle East International*, May 10, 1996, p. 3.

28 Op. cit.

29 *The Independent*, May 6, 1996.

30 Interview with Franklin van Kappen, Zeist, March 20, 2002.

31 *Kol Ha'ir*, May 10,1996. The Hebrew weekly magazine based the story on interviews with five soldiers and officers from the artillery base.

32 Op. cit.

33 Boutros-Ghali, p. 262.

34 *Reuters*, May 8, 1996.

CHAPTER EIGHTY FOUR: FOUR MOTHERS

35 *Middle East International*, No. 525, May 24, 1996.

36 Interview with Yossi Beilin, 1996.

37 If Peres had received these votes, he would have won the election by some 15,000 votes more than Netanyahu.

38 Interviews with Robert Fisk, 1996–2010. Boutros-Ghali, p. 264.

39 Interview with Noam Nizmaho, Tel Aviv, April 5, 2009.

40 *El Pais*, February 19, 1997.

41 *Jerusalem Report*, March, 1997.

42 *Jerusalem Report*, December 11, 1997.

CHAPTER EIGHTY FIVE: HUMILIATION

43 Interview with Børre Ludvigsen, 2008.

44 *The Independent*, August 27, 1997.

45 UNIFIL Daily News Report, August 19, 1997.

46 *Jerusalem Report*, December 11, 1997.

47 *Haaretz*, August 24, 1997.

48 *Jerusalem Post*, August 29, 1997.

49 Hassan Narsallah, TV address, August 9, 2010.

50 *Al-Ahad Weekly*, September 6, 1997.

51 *An-Nahar*, September 5, 1997; *Haaretz*, September 9, 1997.

52 *Al-Ahad Weekly*, September 6, 1997; Blanford, p. 188.

53 Blanford, p. 192.

54 *Kol Israel*, April 15, 1997.

CHAPTER EIGHTY SIX: INTERNAL STRIFE IN ISRAEL

55 *Haaretz*, July 25, 1997.

56 *Kol Ha'ir*, January 17, 1997.

57 Interviews with Lea Tsemel, Jerusalem, 2009–2010.

58 Tamir, pp. 164–170.

59 *Al-Manar*, September 14, 1997.

60 *Xinhua News Agency*, December 9, 1997.

61 *Jane's Intelligence Review*, October 1997, p. 460.

62 *Jerusalem Report*, December 11, 1997.

63 Op. cit.

64 Op. cit.

65 *Haaretz*, November 5, 1997.

66 *Yedioth Ahronoth*, November 27, 1997.

67 *Haaretz*, November 30, 1997.

68 *Jerusalem Report*, December 11, 1997.

69 Interview with Arik Ben-Zvi, Tel Aviv, 2009.

CHAPTER EIGHTY SEVEN: TRIAL BALLOON

70 *Haaretz*, March 18, 1998.

71 *Jerusalem Report*, December 11, 1997.

72 *The Independent*, January 13, 1998.

73 Copy of power of attorney dated January 29, 1998. The family had 10 years earlier given a power of attorney to the French lawyers.

CHAPTER EIGHTY EIGHT: LAST NIGHT WITH THE GANG

74 Notes from the government conference, December 11, 1997.

75 Interview with Kjell Magne Bondevik, Oslo, February 19, 2008; interview with Knut Vollebæk, The Hague, April 16, 2008.

76 Bechara, pp. 132–133.

77 Interview with General Antoine Lahd, Tel Aviv, March 13, 2008; interview with Lea Tsemel, Jerusalem, November 2009.

78 Interview with Roy C. Grøttheim, Jerusalem, 2009.

79 *Dagbladet*, November 29, 1998.

CHAPTER EIGHTY NINE: FIRED ON IN THE AIR

1 Young, p. 73.

2 Harris, p. 288.

3 Young, p. 61.

4 *The Guardian*, March 13, 1999.

5 *Maariv*, November 25, 1998.

6 *Book of Psalms*, 120: 6,7.

7 *Haaretz*, January 24, 1999.

8 Op. cit.

CHAPTER NINETY: THE GENERAL'S LAST RIDE

9 *Maariv*, February 24, 1999.

10 *Haaretz*, February 24, 1999.

11 Op. cit.

12 *Haaretz*, February 19, 1999.

13 Matthew, p. 5.

14 Blanford, p. 224

15 *The Guardian*, March 13, 1999.

16 *Al-Ahram Weekely*, May 6–12, 1999.

CHAPTER NINETY ONE: POWER SHIFT IN ISRAEL

17 *Yedioth Ahronoth*, April 13, 1999.

18 *The Washington Report*, July-August, 1999.

19 *Yedioth Ahronoth*, June 11, 1999.

CHAPTER NINETY TWO: RØD-LARSEN'S RETURN

20 Interview with Terje Rød-Larsen, New York, 2007.

21 Interview with Terje Rød-Larsen, New York, 2007.

22 Interview with Antoine Lahd, Tel Aviv, March 13, 2008.

23 *AFP*, February 5, 2000.

24 *Mid East Mirror*, February 7, 2000.

25 *Yedioth Ahronoth*, February 8, 2000.

CHAPTER NINETY THREE: MANNEQUINS AT BEAUFORT

26 *Yedioth Ahronoth*, February 13, 2000.

27 *AP* and *Reuters*, January 12, 2000.

28 Interview with Terje Rød-Larsen, New York, 2007.

29 Interview with Antoine Lahd, Tel Aviv, March 13, 2008.

30 *Maariv*, March 7, 2000.

CHAPTER NINETY FOUR: ONE STEP FORWARD, TWO BACK

31 Bregan, p. 55, p. 58 and p. 62.

32 Interview with Terje Rød-Larsen, New York, 2007.

33 *Kol Israel* Evening news at 7 A.M., 2.4.2000. *BBC News*, 3.4.2000.

34 *The Independent*, March 25, 2000.

35 *Los Angeles Times*, April 4, 2000.

36 Interview with Terje-Rød Larsen, New York, 2007.

37 *Reuters*, April 5, 2000.

38 *Yedioth Ahronoth*, April 7, 2000.

CHAPTER NINETY FIVE: RAPE ON ORDERS

39 Interview with Zvi Rish, Tel Aviv, 2008.

40 Interviews with Mustafa Dirani, Beirut, 2008 and Zvi Rish, Tel Aviv, 2008. Bergman, pp. 165–166.

41 *Haaretz*, January 8, 2008.

42 Bergman, p. 153.

43 Op. cit., pp. 166–167.

CHAPTER NINETY SIX: COMPLICATED BORDER

44 The Identification of the Line of Withdrawal of Israeli Forces from Lebanon – Cartographic Section Dep. of Public Information, United Nations, New York (UNNY) (2000), p. 3.

45 Tveit, 1996, p. 359.

46 United Nations Security Council, Report of the Secretary-General on the Implementation of Security Council Resolutions 425 (1978) and 426 (1978), Document S/2000/460, 22 May 2000.

47 *The Daily Star*, Beirut, May 9, 2000.

48 Interview with Terje Rød-Larsen, New York, 2007, and with Timur Göksel, Beirut, 2008.

49 Interview with Terje Rød-Larsen, New York, 2007.

50 *Yedioth Ahronoth*, April 28, 2000.

51 *Haaretz*, May 11, 2000.

52 Imad Mughniyeh was killed in Damascus, February 12, 2008.

CHAPTER NINETY SEVEN: COLLAPSE

53 *The New York Times*, May 18, 2000.

54 *The Observer*, May 21, 2000.

55 Interview with Terje Rød-Larsen, New York, 2007.

56 *Haaretz*, May 23, 2000.

57 Blanford, p. 263.

58 Interviews with Timur Göksel, Beirut, 2008–2009.

59 Blanford, p. 264.

60 Interview with Ibrahim Khalaf, Beirut, February 1, 2010.

61 In addition, the cartographers had an unsigned English text from 1950, called "Report of the Mixed Armistic Sub-Commission for Demarcation." But both the geographic coordinates and the maps themselves belonging to this text were missing. The UN experts also had a map in a scale of 1:50,000 which the Lebanese had given them, dated 1967. In it the Shebaa Farms were shown as part of Lebanon. But when the UN checked the ink, they discovered that the lines which were drawn in came from a later date. The map was then filed away because the borderline was forged. Interview with Terje Rød-Larsen, Oslo, 2000.

62 Interview with Antoine Lahd, Tel Aviv, March 13, 2008.

63 Interviews with Timor Göksel, Beirut, 2008–2009.

64 Bowen, p. vx.

65 In an announcement from the IDF June 16, 2000, it said the attack had been a "tragic mistake." According to the Israelis the crew of a tank had "observed a suspicious vehicle with persons dressed in civilian clothes, and they were suspected of being members of the Lebanese terrorist group which was attacking IDF tanks and vehicles with anti-tank weapons." The Israeli investigation concluded by saying that under operating conditions and in the light of the data known at the moment, "the tank crew was acting in line with relevant procedures under such circumstances." IDF's report was at odds with eyewitnesses who told Amnesty International that there were no signs Israeli forces were threatened. There were no "hostile military activities near the Israeli border, either in this or other areas." *BBC* stated in a statement that the Israeli report did not take into consideration the overwhelming material which showed that the IDF carelessly fired on civilians who were on the road near Kibbutz Manara.

66 *Haaretz*, May 23, 2000.

CHAPTER NINETY EIGHT: EXIT LEBANON

67 Interview with Suleiman Ramadan, Baalbek, February 9, 2010.

68 *Al-Ahram Weekly*, June, 1-7, 2000.

69 *The Independent*, May 25, 2000.

70 Op. cit.

71 Darwish, p. 45.

BIBLIOGRAPHY

Agha, Hussayn and Ahmad S. Khalidi: *Syria and Iran: Rivalry and Cooperation*, London 1995

Ajami, Fouad: *The Vanished Imam: Musa al Sadr and the Shia of Lebanon*, London 1986

Albright, Madeleine: *Madam Secretary: A Memoir*, New York 2003

Anderson, Terry: *Den of Lions*, New York 1994

Baer, Robert: *See No Evil: The True Story of a Ground Soldier in the CIA's War on Terrorism*, New York 2002

Baer, Robert: *The Devil We Know: Dealing with the New Iranian Superpower*, New York 2009

Baker III, James A.: *The Politics of Diplomacy: Revolution, War and Peace, 1989–1992*, New York 1995

Ball, George W.: *Error and Betrayal in Lebanon: An Analysis of Israel's Invasion of Lebanon and its Implications for U.S.-Israeli Relations*, Washington 1984

Bar-Zohar, Michael: *Ben-Gurion: A Biography*, London 1978

Bar-Zohar, Michael: *Shimon Peres: The Biography*, New York 2007

Barak, Oren: *The Lebanese Army: A National Institution in a Divided Society*, New York 2009

Bazzi, Yussef: *Yasser Arafat Looked at Me and Smiled: Diary of a Fighter*, Beirut 2005

Benziman, Uzi: *Sharon: An Israeli Caesar*, London 1987

Bergman, Ronen: *The Secret War with Iran*, New York 2007

Bechara, Soha: *Resistance: My Life for Lebanon*, New York 2003

Bkassini, Georges: *The Road to Independence: Five Years with Rafic Hariri*, Beirut 2009

Blanford, Nicholas: *Warriors of God: Inside Hezbollah's Thirty-Year Struggle Against Israel*, New York 2011

Blumenthal, Sidney: *The Clinton Wars: An Insider's Account of the White House Years*, London 2003

Boutros-Ghali, Boutros: *Unvanquished: A U.S.-U.N. Saga*, New York 1999

Bowen, Jeremy: *War Stories*, London 2006

Boykin, John: *Cursed is the Peacemaker: The American Diplomat versus the Israeli General, Beirut 1982*, Belmont 2002

Bregman, Ahron: *Elusive Peace: How the Holy Land Defeated America*, London 2005

Brenner, Lenni: *Zionism in the Age of Dictators: A Reappraisal*, Chicago 1983

Brinkley, Douglas (ed.): *The Reagan Diaries*, New York 2007

Bulloch, John: *Death of a Country: The Civil War in Lebanon*, London 1977

Byrne, Malcolm: *The Chronology*, New York 1987

Cannon, Lou: *President Reagan: The Role of a Lifetime*, New York 1991

Carmel, Shaul and Ileana Cudalb: *Yitzhak Rabin: Peace Killed Its Soldiers*, Bucharest 1997

Charara,Walid and Frédéric Domont: *Le Hezbollah, un mouvement Islamo-Nationaliste*, Fayard 2004

Chehabi, H.E.: *Distant Relations: Iran and Lebanon in the Last 500 Years*, London 2006

Cicippio, Joseph with Richard W.: *Hope: Chains to Roses: The Joseph Cicippio Story*, Waco 1993

Clancy, Tom with Carl Stiner and Tony Koltz: *Shadow Warriors: Inside the Special Forces*, New York 1991

Clinton, Bill: *My Life*, London 2004

Cockburn, Leslie: *Out of Control*, New York 1987

Copeland, Miles: *The Game Player: Confessions of the CIA's Original Political Operative*, London 1989

Coughlin, Con: *Hostage: The Complete Story of the Lebanon Captives*, London 1992

Pérez de Cuéllar, Javier: *Pilgrimage for Peace*, London 1997

Christopher, Warren: *Chances of a Lifetime*, New York 2001

Daalder, Ivo H. and I.M. Destler: *In the Shadow of the Oval Office: Profiles of the National Security Advisers and the Presidents they served – from JFK to George W. Bush*, New York 2009

Dante Alighieri: *The Divine Comedy*

Darwish, Mahmoud: *Memory for Forgetfulness*, Beirut 1982

Dawahare, Michael: *No Country but War: A reporter's Sketches of Lebanon*, Rockville 2008

Dayan, Moshe: *Story of My Life*, London 1977

Dean, John Gunther: *Danger Zones: A Diplomat's Fight for America's Interests*, Washington 2009

Deeb, Lara: *An Enchanted Modern: Gender and Public Piety in Shi'i Lebanon*, Princeton 2006

Dobbs, Michael: *Madeleine Albright: A Twentieth-Century Odyssey*, New York 1999

Eisenberg, Laura Zittrain: *My Enemy's Enemy: Lebanon in the Early Zionist Imagination, 1900–1948*, Wayne 1994

Elazar, Daniel J. and M. Benjamin Mollov: *Israel at the Polls 1999*, London 2001

Erlich, Reese: *The Iran Agenda: The Real Story of U.S. Policy and the Middle East Crisis*, Sausalito 2007

Eveland, Wilbur Crane: *Ropes of Sand: America's Failure in the Middle East*, New York 1980

Fadlallah, Mohammed Hussein: *For Islams skyld (arabisk) (For Islam's Sake—Arabic)*, Beirut 1989

Fisk, Robert: *Pity the Nation*, London 1989

Fisk, Robert: *The Great War for Civilisation*, London 2005

Foerstel, Herbert N.: *Killing the Messenger: Journalists at Risk in Modern Warfare*, Westport, Connecticut 2006

Follow-up Committee for the Support of Lebanese Detainees in Israeli Prisons: *Lebanese Hostages in Israeli Prisons, Al-Khiam, the Concentration Camp of Death*, Beirut 1996

Gendzier, Irene L.: *Notes from the Minefield: United States Intervention in Lebanon and the Middle East, 1945–1958*, New York 1997

Geraghty, Timothy J.: *Peacekeepers at War: Beirut 1983—The Marine Commander tells his Story*, Dulles 2009

Glass, Charles: *Tribes With Flags: A Journey Curtailed*, London 1990

Golan, Matti: *Road to Peace: A Biography*, London 1982

Gordon, David C.: *Lebanon: The Fragmented Nation*, London 1980

Gordon, David C.: *The Republic of Lebanon: Nation in Jeopardy*, London 1983

Gup, Ted: *The Book of Honor: The Secret Lives and Deaths of CIA Operatives*, New York 2001

Haber, Eitan: *Menachem Begin: The Legend and the Man*, New York 1978

Hagi, Einav: *Tamir's Last Battle*, (in Hebrew)

Halberstam, David: *War in a Time of Peace: Bush, Clinton and the Generals*, London 2002

Haley, P. Edward and Lewis W. Snider (ed.): *Lebanon in Crisis: Participants and Issues*, Syracuse 1979

Hammel, Eric: *The Root: The Marines in Beirut, August 1982 –February 1984*, Orlando 1985

Hamzeh, Ahmad Nizar: *In the Path of Hezbollah*, New York 2004

Harik, Judith Palmer: *Hezbollah: The Changing Face of Terrorism*, London 2004

Harris, William: *Faces of Lebanon: Sects, Wars and Global Extension*, Princeton 1999

Harvey, Dan: *Peacekeepers: Irish Soldiers in Lebanon*, Dublin 2001

Hazleton, Lesley: *After the Prophet: The Epic Story of the Shia-Sunni Split in Islam*, New York 2009

Herr, Michael: *Rapporter*, Oslo 1980

Higgins, Robin: *Patriot Dreams: The Murder of Colonel Rich Higgins*, Quantico 1999

Hirst, David: *Beware of Small States: Lebanon, Battleground of the Middle East*, London 2010

Hitti, Philip: *Lebanon in History: From the Earliest Times until the Present*, London 1957

Hobbes, Thomas: *Leviathan*, London 1651

Horovitz, David (ed.): *Yitzhak Rabin: Soldier of Peace*, London 1996

Hovsepian, Nubar (ed.): *The War on Lebanon: A Reader*, Northampton 2008

Human Right Watch: *Persona Non Grata: The Expulsion of Civilians from Israeli-Occupied Lebanon*, New York 1999

Hurwitz, Harry Z.: *Begin: A Portrait*, Washington 1994

Inbar, Efraim: *Rabin and Israel's National Security*, Washington 1999

Iskandar, Marwan: *Rafiq Hariri and the Fate of Lebanon*, London 2006

Jaber, Hala: *Hezbollah: Born with a Vengeance*, New York 1997

Jacobsen, David: *My Life as a Hostage: The Nightmare in Beirut*, New York 1993

Jafri, S.H.M: *The Origins and Early Development of Shi'a Islam*, Beirut 1979

Jørgensen, William: *Gissel i Libanon (Hostage in Lebanon)*, Oslo 1988

Kanaan, Claude Boueiz: *Lebanon 1860–1960: A Century of Myth and Politics*, London 2005

Khalaf, Samir: *Civil and Uncivil Violence in Lebanon*, New York 2002

Keenan, Brian: *An Evil Cradling*, London 1993

Kennedy, David and Leslie Brunetta: *Lebanon and the Intelligence Community*, Harvard 1988

Khalidi, Rashid: *Sowing Crisis: The Cold War and American Dominance in the Middle East*, Boston 2009

Khalidi, Walid: *Conflict and Violence in Lebanon: Confrontation in the Middle East*, London 1979

Korbani, Agnes G.: *U.S. Intervention in Lebanon, 1958 and 1982: Presidential Decisionmaking*, New York 1991

Kurzman, Dan: *Soldier of Peace: The Life of Yitzhak Rabin*, New York 1998

Ledeen, Michael: *Perilous Statecraft: An Insider's Account of the Iran-Contra Affair*, New York 1988

Lehmann, Vidar: *Blå beret, raud jord: Feltlege i FN-tjeneste,(Blue Beret, Red Earth: A Field Doctor in UN Service)*, Oslo 2010

Levin, Jerry: *West Bank Diary: Middle East Violence as Reported by a Former American Hostage*, Pasadena 2005

Levin, Sis: *Beirut Diary: A Husband held Hostage and a Wife Determined to set him Free*, Illinois 1989

Litvinoff, Barnet (ed.): *The Essential Chaim Weizmann*, New York 1982

Mackey, Sandra: *Lebanon: Death of a Nation*, New York 1989

Majd, Hooman: *The Ayatollah Begs to Differ: The Paradox of Modern Iran*, New York 2008

Martin, David C. and John Walcott: *Best Laid Plans: The Inside Story of America's War against Terrorism*, New York 1988

Matthews, Matt. M.: *We Were Caught Unprepared: The 2006 Hezbollah-Israeli War*, Fort Leavenworth 2009

McCarthy, John and Jill Morrell: *Some Other Rainbow*, London 1993

McDermott, Anthony and Kjell Skjelsbæk (ed.): *The Multinational Force in Beirut 1982–1984*, Gainesville 1991

McDonald, Henry: *Irishbatt: The Story of Ireland's Blue Berets in the Lebanon*, Dublin 1993

McFarlane, Robert C. and Zofia Smardz: *Special Trust*, New York 1994

Meisler, Stanley: *Kofi Annan: A Man of Peace in a World of War*, New Jersey 2007

Miller, Judith: *God Has Ninety-Nine Names: Reporting from a Militant Middle East*, New York 1996

Moin, Baqer: *Khomeini: Life of The Ayatollah*, New York 1999

Mouro, Gladys: *An American Nurse Amidst Chaos*, American University Beirut Press 2001

Munro, John M.: *A Mutual Concern: The Story of the American University of Beirut*, Delmar 1977

Noe, Nicholas (ed.): *Voice of Hezbollah: The Statements of Sayyed Hassan Nasrallah*, London 2007

Norton, Augustus Richard: *Amal and the Shi'a: Struggle for the Soul of Lebanon*, Austin 1987

Norton, Augustus Richard: *Hezbollah: A short history*, Princeton 2007

Parker, John W.: *Persian Dreams: Moscow and Tehran Since the Fall of the Shah*, Washington 2009

Parmet, Herbert S.: *George Bush: The Life of a Lone Star Yankee*, New York 1997

Parsi, Trita: *Treacherous Alliance: The Secret Dealings of Israel, Iran, and the U.S*, Yale 2007

Pedahzur, Ami: *The Israeli Secret Services and the Struggle Against Terrorism*, New York 2009

Petran, Tabitha: *The Struggle Over Lebanon*, New York 1987

Picard, Elizabeth: *Lebanon: A Shattered Country*, New York 1988

Picco, Giandomenico: *Man Without a Gun: One Diplomat's Secret Struggle to Free the Hostages, Fight Terrorism, and End a War*, New York 1999

Pintak, Larry: *Beirut Outtakes: A TV Correspondent's Portrait of America's Encounter with Terror*, Lexington 1988

Polk, William R.: *The Opening of South Lebanon, 1788–1840*, Harvard 1963

Pollack, Kenneth M.: *The Persian Puzzle: The Conflict Between Iran and America*, New York 2005

Powell, Colin: *My American Journey*, New York 1996

Primakov, Yevgeny: *Russia and the Arabs: Behind the Scenes in The Middle East from the Cold War to the Present*, New York 2009

Qassem, Naim: *Hizbullah: The Story from Within*, London 2005

Rabad, Ahiyah: *Lebanon Lexicon*, Beirut 2005

Rabil, Robert G.: *Syria, the United States and the War on Terror in The Middle East*, London 2006

Rabinovich, Itamar: *The War for Lebanon 1970–1983*, London 1984

Ramazani, R.K.: *Revolutionary Iran: Challenge and Response in The Middle East*, Baltimore 1988

Randal, Jonathan C.: *Going All the Way: Christian Warlords, Israeli Adventurers and the War in Lebanon*, New York 1984

Randstorp, Magnus: *Hizb'allah in Lebanon: The Politics of the Western Hostage Crisis*, New York 1997

Reinharz, Jehuda: *Chaim Weizmann: The Making of a Zionist Leader*, New York 1985

Reeves, Richard: *President Reagan: The Triumph of Imagination*, New York 2005

Regan, Donald: *For the Record: From Wall Street to Washington*, London 1988

Risen, James: *State of War: The Secret History of the CIA and the Bush Administration*, New York 2006

Rokach, Livia: *Israel's Sacred Terrorism*, Belmont 1980

Saad-Ghorayeb, Amal: *Hizbu'llah: Politics and Religion*, London, 2002

Sabbagh, Suha (ed.): *Arab Women: Between Defiance and Restraint*, London 1996

Sacher, Howard M.: *A History of Israel: From the Rise of Zionism to Our Time*, Oxford 1977

Salem, Elie A.: *Violence and Diplomacy in Lebanon: The Troubled Years, 1982–1988*, London 1995

Salibi, Kamal: *Crossroads to Civil War: Lebanon 1958-1976*, Delmar 1976

Salibi, Kamal: *The Modern History of Lebanon*, Delmar 1977

Salibi, Kamal: *A House of Many Mansions: The History of Lebanon Reconsidered*, Berkeley 1988

Sankari, Jamal: *Fadlallah: The Making of a Radical Shi'ite Leader*, London 2005

Sayigh, Rosemary: *Too Many Enemies: The Palestinian Experience in Lebanon*, London 2004

Schiff, Ze'ev and Ehud Ya'ari: *Israel's Lebanon War*, New York 1984

Schulze, Kirsten: *Israel's Covert Diplomacy in Lebanon*, New York 1998

Schulze, Kirsten: *The Jews of Lebanon: Between Coexistence and Conflict*, Brighton 2001

Shultz, George P.: *Turmoil and Triumph: Diplomacy, Power, and the Victory of the American Ideal*, New York 1993

Seale, Patrick: *Asad: The Struggle for The Middle East*, London 1988

Segev, Samuel: *The Iranian Triangle: The Untold Story of Israel's Role in The Iran-Contra Affair*, New York 1988

Shackley, Ted: *Spymaster: My Life in the CIA*, Dulles 2006

Sharett, Moshe: *Personlig dagbok (hebraisk), (Personal Diary—Hebrew)*, Tel Aviv 1979

Sharon, Ariel with David Chanoff: *Warrior: An Autobiography*, Bnei Brak 1989

Shlaim, Avi: *The Iron Wall: Israel and the Arab World*, London 2000

Silver, Eric: *Begin: A Biography*, London 1984

Slater, Robert: *Rabin of Israel*, Cornwall 1993

Smit, Ferdinand: *The Battle for South Lebanon: The Radicalisation of Lebanon's Shi'ites 1982–1985*, Amsterdam 2000

Sullivan, Joseph G. (ed.): *Embassies under Siege: Personal Accounts by Diplomats on the Front Line*, Washington 1995

Taheri, Amir: *Nest of Spies*, New York 1988

Taheri, Amir: *The Cauldron: The Middle East Behind the Headlines*, London 1988

Taheri, Amir: *The Persian Night: Iran under the Khomeinist Revolution*, New York 2009

Tamir, Moshe "Chicko": *Uerklært krig, (hebraisk) (Undeclared War—Hebrew)*, Tel Aviv 2005

Takeyh, Ray: *Hidden Iran: Paradox and Power in the Islamic Republic*, New York 2006

Takeyh, Ray: *Guardians of the Revolution: Iran and the World in the Age of the Ayatollahs*, Oxford 2009

The Chronology: The Documented Day-by-Day Account of the Secret Military Assistance to Iran and the Contras, The National Security Archive 1987

Thomas, Gordon: *Secrets and Lies: A History of CIA Mind Control and Germ Warfare*, Connecticut 2007

Thubron, Colin: *The Hills of Adonis: A Quest in Lebanon*, Boston 1968

Traboulsi, Fawwaz: *A History of Modern Lebanon*, London 2007

Traub, James: *The Best Intentions: Kofi Annan and the UN in the Era of American World Power*, London 2007

Tveit, Odd Karsten: *Nederlag: Israels krig i Libanon, (Defeat: Israel's War in Lebanon)*, Oslo 1985

Tveit, Odd Karsten: *Alt for Israel: Oslo-Jerusalem 1948–1978, (All for Israel: Oslo-Jerusalem 1948-1978)*, Oslo 1996

Tveit, Odd Karsten: *Annas hus: En beretning fra Stavanger til Jerusalem, (Anna's House: An account from Stavanger to Jerusalem)*, Oslo 2000

Tveit, Odd Karsten: *Krig og Diplomati, (War and Diplomacy)*, Oslo 2005

Vance, Cyrus: *Hard Choices: Critical Years in America's Foreign Policy*, New York 1983

Van de Ven, Susan Kerr: *One Family's Response to Terrorism: A Daughter's Memoir*, New York 2008

Verrier, Anthony: *International Peacekeeping: United Nation Forces in a Troubled World*, London 1981

Vocke, Harald: *The Lebanese War: Its Origins and Political Dimensions*, London 1978

Waite, Terry: *Taken on Trust*, London 1994

Ward, Steven R.: *Immortal: A Military History of Iran and its Armed Forces*, Washington, 2009

Weinberger, Caspar W. with Gretchen Roberts: *In the Arena: A Memoir of the 20th Century*, Washington 2001

Weiner, Tim: *Legacy of Ashes: The History of the CIA*, New York 2007

Weir, Ben and Carol with Dennis Benson: *Hostage Bound, Hostage Free*, Philadelphia 1987

Weinberger, Naomi Joy: *Syrian Intervention in Lebanon*, Oxford 1986

Weizmann, Chaim: *Trial and Error: The Autobiography of Chaim Weizmann, First President of Israel*, London 1949

West, Nigel: *Seven Spies Who Changed the World*, London 1991

Wilson, Joseph: *The Politics of Truth*, New York 2004

Wooodward, Bob: *Veil: The Secret Wars of the CIA 1981–1987*, New York 1987

Wright, Robin: *Sacred Rage: The Wrath of Militant Islam*, New York 1986

Young, Michael: *The Ghosts of Martyrs Square: An Eyewitness Account of Lebanon's Life Struggle*, London 2010

Zamir, Yehoshua: *Survival is not Enough*, Tel Aviv 1992

Zimmermann, B. Christian: *Hostage in a Hostage World: Hope Aboard Hijacked TWA 847*, St. Louis 1985

INDEX